Lecture Notes in Computer Science

Lecture Notes in Artificial Intelligence 15662

Founding Editor

Jörg Siekmann

AF802174

Series Editors

Randy Goebel, *University of Alberta, Edmonton, Canada*
Wolfgang Wahlster, *DFKI, Berlin, Germany*
Zhi-Hua Zhou, *Nanjing University, Nanjing, China*

The series Lecture Notes in Artificial Intelligence (LNAI) was established in 1988 as a topical subseries of LNCS devoted to artificial intelligence.

The series publishes state-of-the-art research results at a high level. As with the LNCS mother series, the mission of the series is to serve the international R & D community by providing an invaluable service, mainly focused on the publication of conference and workshop proceedings and postproceedings.

Isabelle Bichindaritz · Beatriz López
Editors

Case-Based Reasoning Research and Development

33rd International Conference, ICCBR 2025
Biarritz, France, June 30 – July 3, 2025
Proceedings

Springer

Editors
Isabelle Bichindaritz
State University of New York
Oswego, NY, USA

Beatriz López
University of Girona
Girona, Spain

ISSN 0302-9743 ISSN 1611-3349 (electronic)
Lecture Notes in Artificial Intelligence
ISBN 978-3-031-96558-6 ISBN 978-3-031-96559-3 (eBook)
https://doi.org/10.1007/978-3-031-96559-3

LNCS Sublibrary: SL7 – Artificial Intelligence

© The Editor(s) (if applicable) and The Author(s), under exclusive license
to Springer Nature Switzerland AG 2025

This work is subject to copyright. All rights are solely and exclusively licensed by the Publisher, whether the whole or part of the material is concerned, specifically the rights of translation, reprinting, reuse of illustrations, recitation, broadcasting, reproduction on microfilms or in any other physical way, and transmission or information storage and retrieval, electronic adaptation, computer software, or by similar or dissimilar methodology now known or hereafter developed.
The use of general descriptive names, registered names, trademarks, service marks, etc. in this publication does not imply, even in the absence of a specific statement, that such names are exempt from the relevant protective laws and regulations and therefore free for general use.
The publisher, the authors and the editors are safe to assume that the advice and information in this book are believed to be true and accurate at the date of publication. Neither the publisher nor the authors or the editors give a warranty, expressed or implied, with respect to the material contained herein or for any errors or omissions that may have been made. The publisher remains neutral with regard to jurisdictional claims in published maps and institutional affiliations.

This Springer imprint is published by the registered company Springer Nature Switzerland AG
The registered company address is: Gewerbestrasse 11, 6330 Cham, Switzerland

If disposing of this product, please recycle the paper.

Preface

The International Conference on Case-Based Reasoning (ICCBR) is the preeminent international meeting on case-based reasoning (CBR). Through 2009, ICCBR (http://www.iccbr.org) had been a biennial conference, held in alternation with its sister conference, the European Conference on Case-Based Reasoning (ECCBR), which was located in Europe. These international conferences were launched at the European level by the first ECCBR conference, organized in Kaiserslautern, Germany in 1993. From 2010, ICCBR and ECCBR were merged in a single conference series, called ICCBR. ICCBR 2025 (http://2025.iccbr.org/) was the thirty-third in this series of international conferences highlighting the most significant contributions to the field of CBR. The conference took place from 30 June to 3rd July 2025 in the city of Biarritz, France, on the beautiful campus of the Université de Pau et des Pays de l'Adour (UPPA), in the Institute of Technology of Bayonne, Montaury Campus.

Previous ICCBR conferences were held in Sesimbra, Portugal (1995), Providence, Rhode Island, USA (1997), Seeon Monastery, Germany (1999), Vancouver, BC, Canada (2001), Trondheim, Norway (2003), Chicago, Illinois, USA (2005), Belfast, UK (2007), Seattle, Washington, USA (2009), Alessandria, Italy (2010), London, UK (2011), Lyon, France (2012), Saratoga Springs, NY, USA (2013), Cork, Ireland (2014), Frankfurt am Main, Germany (2015), Atlanta, Georgia, USA (2016), Trondheim, Norway (2017), Stockholm, Sweden (2018), Otzenhausen, Germany (2019), Salamanca, Spain (2020 & 2021), Nancy, France (2022), Aberdeen, UK (2023), and Mérida, Mexico (2024).

Day 1 of the conference hosted the seventeenth Doctoral Consortium and three workshops. The seventeenth Doctoral Consortium allowed doctoral students to connect with senior research mentors from the CBR community. The three workshops were dedicated to *"Case-Based Reasoning and Large Language Model Synergies (CBR-LLM)"* (2nd Workshop), *"Beyond Attribute-Value Case Representation (BEAR)"* (3rd Workshop), and *"Building Collaborations for Case-Based Reasoning Research and Funding"* (CBR-ResFund) (1st Workshop).

Days 2, 3, and 4 comprised scientific paper presentations on theoretical and applied CBR research. The presentations and posters covered a wide range of CBR topics including Large Language Models, foundation models, adaptation, explainability, case mining, case retrieval, similarity, agents, recommender systems, knowledge management, knowledge representation, planning, image classification, temporal reasoning, textual CBR, bioinformatics, and medical applications. In addition, a poster session allowed for interactive and in-depth discussions of research advances.

The conference was proud to present three distinguished invited speakers: Claire Gardent (CNRS/LORIA, France) introduced the audience to the parallels between Case-Based Reasoning and Retrieval Augmented Generation (RAG) approaches; Ralph Bergmann (University of Trier and DFKI, Germany) proposed a new unified experience-grounded architecture for reasoning conceived as a collaborative process orchestrated among specialized agents; and David Leake (Indiana University Bloomington, USA) presented a vision for the future of CBR in the age of Generative AI. We are grateful for their innovative ideas.

This volume includes 21 papers from oral presentations and 9 from posters, for a total of 30 papers. These were chosen from a total of 81 submissions. In addition, the volume contains one paper and two abstracts from invited speakers. The accepted papers were chosen based on a thorough and highly selective review process. Each paper was single-blindly reviewed and discussed by four reviewers and revised according to their comments. Reviewers were encouraged to reach a consensus when they did not agree, which they generally managed to accomplish through lively discussions. The papers in this volume provide a representative snapshot of current CBR research, ranging from *Theoretical/Methodological Research* to *Applied Research*.

Many people participated in making ICCBR possible. Isabelle Bichindaritz (SUNY Oswego, USA) and Beatriz Lòpez (University of Girona, Spain) served as Scientific Chairs this year. They also took the initiative to propose ICCBR 2025, thus inviting us all to beautiful Southern France. Philippe Roose (Université de Pau et des Pays de l'Adour, France) helped with the local organization as Conference Chair. The organization team was very diverse, having Kyle Martin (Robert Gordon University, UK) and Xiaomeng Ye (Berry College, USA) as Workshop Program Chairs; and David Leake (Indiana University Bloomington, USA) and Mirjam Minor (Goethe University Frankfurt, Germany) as organizers of the Doctoral Consortium. This diverse team together with the authors, the invited speakers, the Program Committee, and additional reviewers were the stars of the CBR community in 2025. They made the conference happen and we want to thank them for their brilliant performances that are recorded in this volume. We gratefully acknowledge the generous support of the sponsors of ICCBR 2025.

Additional help was provided by students from UPPA in France. In support of local arrangements, thanks to the Local Arrangements Committee from the Université de Pau et des Pays de l'Adour. The submission and reviewing process was supported by the use of EasyChair. Finally, we thank Springer for its continuing support in publishing this series of conference proceedings.

May 2025

Isabelle Bichindaritz
Beatriz López

Organization

Program Committee Chairs

Isabelle Bichindaritz	SUNY Oswego, USA
Beatriz Lòpez	University of Girona, Spain

Steering Committee

David W. Aha	Naval Research Laboratory, USA
Belén Díaz-Agudo	Complutense University of Madrid, Spain
David Leake	Indiana University Bloomington, USA
Mirjam Minor	University of Trier, Germany
Barry Smyth	Trinity College, Ireland
Rosina Weber	Drexel University, USA

Program Committee

Kerstin Bach	Norwegian University of Science and Technology, Norway
Shahina Begum	Mälardalen University, Sweden
Ralph Bergmann	University of Trier, Germany
Florian Brand	University of Trier, Germany
Derek Bridge	University College Cork, Ireland
Marta Caro-Martínez	Universidad Complutense de Madrid, Spain
Sutanu Chakraborti	Indian Institute of Technology Madras, India
David Corsar	Robert Gordon University, UK
Sarah Jane Delany	Technological University Dublin, Ireland
Belén Díaz-Agudo	Universidad Complutense de Madrid, Spain
Viktor Eisenstadt	University of Hildesheim, Germany
Jonah Fernandez	University of Girona, Spain
Michael Floyd	Knexus Research, USA
Béatrice Fuchs	LIRIS, Université Jean Moulin Lyon III, France

Ashok Goel	Georgia Institute of Technology, USA
Mehmet H. Goker	SurveyMonkey, USA
Lisa Grumbach	DFKI, Germany
Julien Henriet	Université Bourgogne Franche-Comté, FEMTO-ST Institute, CNRS UMR 6174, France
Maximilian Hoffmann	University of Trier, Germany
Vahid Jalali	Indiana University Bloomington, USA
Stelios Kapetanakis	University of Brighton, UK
Mark Keane	University College Dublin, Ireland
Joseph Kendall-Morwick	Washburn University, USA
Luc Lamontagne	Laval University, Canada
David Leake	Indiana University Bloomington, USA
Jean Lieber	LORIA - Inria Lorraine, France
Anne Liret	British Telecommunications plc, France
Lukas Malburg	University of Trier/German Research Center for Artificial Intelligence (DFKI), Germany
Kyle Martin	Robert Gordon University, UK
Mirjam Minor	Goethe University Frankfurt, Germany
Stefania Montani	University of Piemonte Orientale, Italy
David Ménager	Parallax Advanced Research, USA
Emmanuel Nauer	LORIA, France
Ikechukwu Nkisi-Orji	Robert Gordon University, UK
Deepak P.	Queen's University Belfast, UK
Enric Plaza	IIIA-CSIC, Spain
Luigi Portinale	Università del Piemonte Orientale "A. Avogadro", Italy
Juan A. Recio-Garcia	Universidad Complutense de Madrid, Spain
Pascal Reuss	Universität Hildesheim, Germany
Francesco Ricci	Free University of Bozen-Bolzano, Italy
Brian Schack	Indiana University Bloomington, USA
Jakob Michael Schoenborn	DGC AG, Germany
Alexander Schultheis	DFKI, Germany
Barry Smyth	University College Dublin, Ireland
Manuel Striani	University of Piemonte Orientale, Italy
Jerzy Surma	Warsaw School of Economics, Poland
Antonio A. Sánchez-Ruiz	Universidad Complutense de Madrid, Spain
Deepika Verma	NTNU, Norway
Ian Watson	University of Auckland, New Zealand
Rosina Weber	Drexel University, USA
Stefan Wess	Empolis, Germany
Kaitlynne Wilkerson	Indiana University Bloomington, USA

David Wilson	University of North Carolina at Charlotte, USA
Nirmalie Wiratunga	Robert Gordon University, UK
Xiaomeng Ye	Indiana University Bloomington, USA
Christian Zeyen	DFKI, Germany

Additional Reviewers

Brand, Florian
Islam, Mir Riyanul
Jayawardena, Lasal
Pirie, Craig
Rauch, Christopher
Tel, Tolga

Sponsoring Institutions

Artificial Intelligence Journal, USA
LIUPPA-T2I, France
Springer-Verlag, Germany
State University of New York at Oswego, USA
University of Girona, Spain

Invited Abstracts

Case-Based Reasoning and Retrieval Augmented Generation

Claire Gardent

CNRS/LORIA, Nancy, France

Abstract. In Natural Language Processing (NLP), Retrieval Augmented Generation (RAG) has been gaining traction as a way to complement the parametric knowledge encoded in Large Language Models (LLMs) with explicit information collected on the fly to expand the input query with relevant knowledge.

This talk started by briefly summarizing the impact of neural approaches on natural language processing (NLP), explaining how these methods have revolutionized the field by addressing some of the key challenges raised by natural language. The presentation went on to discuss the parallel between RAG approaches, which retrieve and generate, and Case-Based Reasoning, which retrieves, reuses, revises and retains. This latter part of the talk was based on NLP examples Dr. Gardent has been working on with her students: retrieval-based question answering and summarizing, generating Wikipedia biographies and verbalizing knowledge graphs.

CBR Tomorrow: Cases in the Age of Generative AI

David Leake

Luddy School of Informatics, Computing, and Engineering, Indiana University, Bloomington, IN, 47408 USA

Abstract. Case-based reasoning (CBR) research has a long history, starting more than four decades ago, inspired by insights on human memory, reasoning, and learning. Since that time, CBR research has elucidated the principles, methods, and practice of CBR and illuminated rich opportunities for synergies with other AI approaches. In 2022 artificial intelligence had a watershed moment: With the release of ChatGPT and subsequent models, generative AI took the world by storm, capturing public attention, transforming AI practice, challenging beliefs about the nature of intelligence, and recasting expectations for future society. What does generative AI mean for the future of case-based reasoning? To answer, I first touch on CBR history, revisiting the meaning of CBR through foundational motivations, tenets, and past insights. I then highlight why cases remain vital: what CBR can do that large language models cannot, the roles of CBR separately and in concert with generative AI, and why CBR-inspired memory matters. From this analysis I propose opportunities for tomorrow's CBR.

Keywords: Case-Based Reasoning · Cognitive Science · Episodic Memory · Foundations · Large Language Models · AI Safety

Contents

Invited Talk

EXAR: A Unified Experience-Grounded Agentic Reasoning Architecture

Ralph Bergmann[1,2(✉)], Florian Brand[1,2], Mirko Lenz[1,2], and Lukas Malburg[1,2]

[1] Artificial Intelligence and Intelligent Information Systems, Trier University, 54296 Trier, Germany
{bergmann,brand,lenz,malburgl}@uni-trier.de
[2] German Research Center for Artificial Intelligence (DFKI), Behringstraße 21, 54296 Trier, Germany
{ralph.bergmann,florian.brand,mirko.lenz,lukas.malburg}@dfki.de
https://www.wi2.uni-trier.de

Abstract. Current AI reasoning often relies on static pipelines (like the 4R cycle from Case-Based Reasoning (CBR) or standard Retrieval-Augmented Generation (RAG)) that limit adaptability. We argue it is time for a shift towards dynamic, experience-grounded agentic reasoning. This paper proposes *EXAR*, a new unified, experience-grounded architecture, conceptualizing reasoning not as a fixed sequence, but as a collaborative process orchestrated among specialized agents. *EXAR* integrates data and knowledge sources into a persistent Long-Term Memory utilized by diverse reasoning agents, which coordinate themselves via a Short-Term Memory. Governed by an Orchestrator and Meta Learner, *EXAR* enables flexible, context-aware reasoning strategies that adapt and improve over time, offering a blueprint for next-generation AI.

Keywords: Case-Based Reasoning · Retrieval Augmented Generation · Large Language Models · Agents · Reasoning

1 Introduction

Case-Based Reasoning (CBR) has long provided a well-founded methodology for solving problems through the reuse of experience in the form of cases. Since the seminal work by Aamodt and Plaza [1], the CBR community has developed robust methods for implementing the 4R cycle–retrieve, reuse, revise, and retain–and has demonstrated their effectiveness in a wide range of applications. However, CBR has typically been applied in well-defined, bounded problem spaces, where case structures, similarity measures, and adaptation knowledge can be explicitly engineered and maintained, causing considerable knowledge engineering efforts [4].

In contrast, recent advances in large language models (LLMs) [39], retrieval-augmented generation (RAG) [11], and agentic hybrid reasoning systems (e.g.,

© The Author(s), under exclusive license to Springer Nature Switzerland AG 2025
I. Bichindaritz and B. López (Eds.): ICCBR 2025, LNAI 15662, pp. 3–17, 2025.
https://doi.org/10.1007/978-3-031-96559-3_1

[13,30,38]) have shifted the focus of AI research towards open-ended, dynamic, and incompletely modeled environments. These systems rely on external information retrieval, tool usage, and generative reasoning to solve problems that cannot be exhaustively predefined. However, they still suffer from hallucination, are constrained by limited context windows, typically lack persistent and structured memory, do not support experience-based analogical reasoning, and offer only rudimentary mechanisms for reflection and continuous learning from their own problem-solving behavior.

Recent research has begun to explore the integration of CBR with LLM-based approaches, for example, by using LLMs to support retrieval and adaptation in CBR, or by embedding structured case memory in LLM-centric architectures. A recent research manifesto by Bach et al. [3] articulates this emerging convergence and proposes a systematic integration of CBR into neuro-symbolic and agentic AI paradigms.

In this paper, we propose *EXAR*, a unified architecture for Experience-Grounded Agentic Reasoning that generalizes both traditional CBR and modern RAG systems. We argue that it is time to break the CBR cycle, originally conceived as "cycle of sequential steps" [1] and to overcome the rigidity of static RAG pipelines, in favor of plan-based, goal-directed orchestration of reasoning processes. In this agentic perspective, reasoning steps such as retrieval, adaptation, prompt construction, symbolic inference, LLM-based generation, evaluation, and reflection are dynamically selected and composed based on the problem, context, memory state, and task goals. We envision that this orchestration process is itself experience-grounded: it can learn from problem-solving traces over time and adapt its internal control flow accordingly. The resulting architecture enables the integration of symbolic and sub-symbolic reasoning services under the control of a persistent, structured memory of heterogeneous knowledge units. This positions CBR not only as a technique, but as the conceptual backbone for building explainable, adaptive, and modular reasoning agents and presents a renewed view of CBR as a central enabler of explainable, adaptive, and modular AI agents.

The remainder of this paper is structured as follows: Sect. 2 presents the state-of-the-art in CBR, LLMs, and their integration, as well as recent multi-agent architectures in agentic hybrid reasoning. Section 3 introduces our proposed experience-grounded agentic reasoning architecture, *EXAR*. Section 4 discusses interpreting existing CBR-LLM approaches within the *EXAR* architecture. Section 5 outlines challenges related to employing *EXAR*, and Sect. 6 describes initial implementation steps. The paper is summarized, and an outlook is provided in Sect. 7.

2 State-of-the-Art

Recent research has begun to explore the interplay between Case-Based Reasoning (CBR) and large language models (LLMs) [3], as well as their integration into more complex, agentic reasoning architectures.

2.1 Using LLMs for CBR Tasks

A growing number of approaches have explored the use of large language models to support individual components of the CBR cycle. Most prominently, LLMs have been applied to case adaptation [20], which is traditionally one of the most knowledge-intensive steps. Prompt-based adaptation strategies allow LLMs to transform retrieved solutions to fit new problems, either through zero-shot instruction prompting or in-context few-shot prompting using similar past cases. In addition, LLMs have been explored as similarity assessors [21,34], for example, by generating structured feature comparisons between cases and queries or by paraphrasing case descriptions to normalize semantic variations. More recently, LLMs have also been employed to generate new cases from existing ones from unstructured text corpora, such as manuals or web data, reducing the burden of manual case authoring [7,29], or to aid in the creation of the vocabulary of the cases [7]. A first study has shown that LLMs can be effectively embedded into CBR pipelines to improve flexibility and expressiveness, although challenges remain with regard to consistency, control, and explainability [32].

2.2 Using CBR to Overcome LLM Weaknesses

Although LLMs demonstrate impressive fluency and generalization, they suffer from several well-documented limitations, including hallucinations, lack of long-term memory, poor control over reasoning behavior, and static knowledge based on the training data cutoff. In this context, CBR has been proposed as a means to ground LLM outputs in a structured, verifiable experience. Case-based memory structures can serve as an external memory layer for LLMs [33], enabling more context-aware and traceable reasoning. When integrated into RAG pipelines, case bases provide targeted, high-quality prompt context, outperforming unstructured retrieval from generic corpora [36]. Moreover, the reuse of past cases as exemplars for few-shot prompting allows for context-sensitive generalization, with better alignment to task-specific constraints [9]. CBR also contributes to explainability and traceability in LLM-based systems. Since each generated output can be linked back to specific retrieved cases, the reasoning trace becomes more interpretable and auditable [12]. Additionally, CBR structures enable reflection mechanisms, such as evaluating past outcomes, detecting failure patterns, and adapting future behavior accordingly, thus addressing key deficits in LLM autonomy.

2.3 Agentic Hybrid Reasoning

Beyond isolated interactions between CBR and LLMs, recent work has shifted toward agentic architectures that embed reasoning processes within autonomous, tool-using agents [13,30,38]. In such systems, reasoning is modeled not as a fixed pipeline, but as a dynamic sequence of actions selected to achieve a goal, possibly involving multiple modalities and memory structures. Multi-Agent architectures such as CAMEL [23], and MetaGPT [15] exemplify this trend. These systems operationalize reasoning through combinations of LLM-based generation, retrieval, tool use, subgoal formation, and reflection. However, most of them lack persistent, structured long-term memory and cannot effectively reuse prior problem-solving experience in a structured way. To address this, emerging proposals suggest augmenting agentic reasoning with case-based memory systems that serve both as episodic storage and strategic reasoning guidance [33]. This hybridization opens the door to plan-based orchestration of reasoning steps, such as retrieval, reuse, adaptation, generation, and validation, selected dynamically based on the current goal, task context, and memory state. In this view, CBR evolves from a standalone reasoning paradigm into a core memory and control structure within agentic, neuro-symbolic reasoning systems, supporting explainability, modularity, and continuous learning.

3 The *EXAR* Architecture

We introduce *EXAR*, a unified architecture for Experience-Grounded Agentic Reasoning, designed to integrate the core concepts of CBR, RAG, and other reasoning paradigms within a dynamic agentic control architecture. *EXAR* aims to overcome the limitations of static reasoning pipelines, such as in CBR and, thus, to overcome the "cycle of sequential steps" [1]. In the following, we present an architectural overview of *EXAR*. Afterwards, we discuss the individual layers of the architecture and their specific tasks and relationships to other layers in the architecture.

3.1 Architecture Overview

Figure 1 provides an overview of the proposed *EXAR* architecture, which is structured into four conceptual layers. The *Data & Knowledge Layer* encompasses all domain-relevant information sources within a given application context such as databases, documents, logs, or distributed information silos, but also implicit expert knowledge of humans. This layer represents what is sometimes referred to as the organizational memory in enterprise settings. In a preprocessing step, this information is extracted, analyzed, and partially formalized into (semi-)structured entities, which we refer to as *Knowledge Units (KUs)*. These KUs are persistently stored in the *Long-Term Memory (LTM)* and serve as the primary knowledge base for reasoning. The core reasoning processes take place in the *Neuro-Symbolic Reasoning Layer*, which consists of a set of interacting reasoning agents. These include the classical CBR and RAG processing steps as well as potentially other reasoning methods, including the usage of tools by the agents. The agents exchange reasoning artifacts and intermediate results via a shared *Short-Term Memory (STM)* that reflects the dynamic reasoning state, functionally similar to nodes in a search or inference graph. The overall reasoning flow is governed by the *Orchestrator* (sometimes also called Controller in the literature [30]), which selects, configures, and activates agents based on the current task, context, and internal reasoning state. This enables flexible,

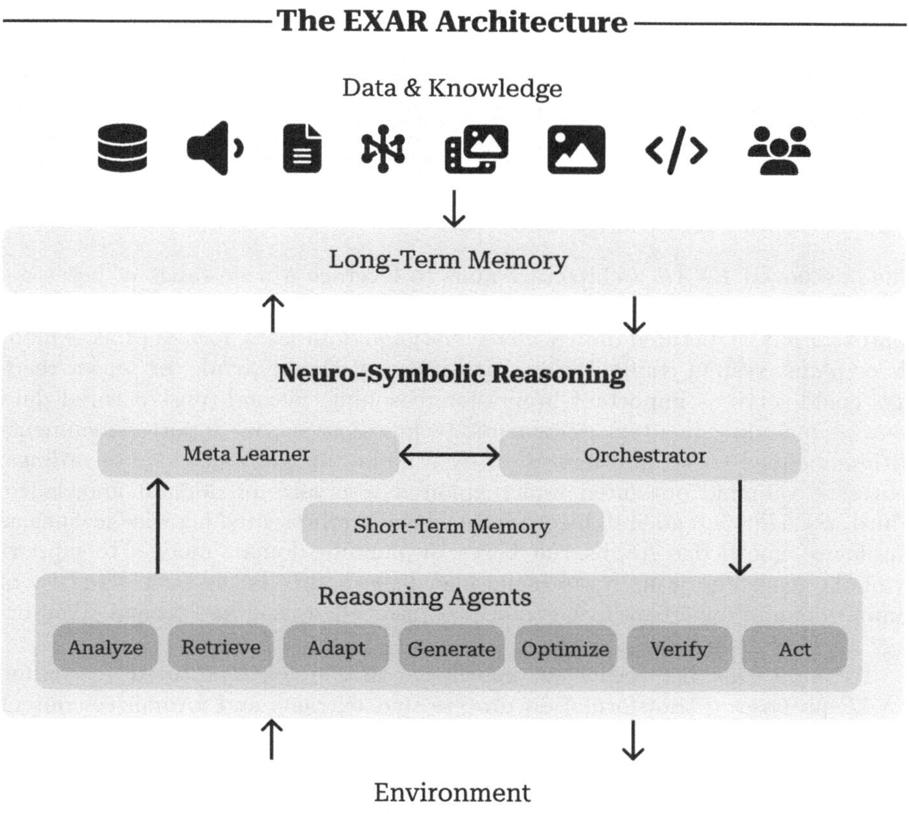

Fig. 1. Architecture Overview of *EXAR*.

plan-based reasoning strategies that go beyond static pipelines, breaking the sequential structure of the traditional CBR cycle, and overcome the rigidity of static RAG pipelines in favor of dynamic, goal-directed orchestration of reasoning processes. A dedicated *Meta Learner* observes the ongoing reasoning process in an introspective manner. It captures reasoning experience, detects patterns, and supports the continuous improvement of orchestration strategies by feeding learned meta-knowledge back into the Orchestrator. Finally, the *Environment Layer* represents the external environment in which the problem solver operates. It provides interfaces for interacting with users (e.g., via GUI, chat, or XR interfaces), external systems (e.g., cyber-physical systems, web applications, or even humans), and input/output modalities (e.g., problem definitions, solution delivery, explanations). Problem instances are supplied by the environment and solutions are communicated back upon completion. In the following, we provide a detailed description of each component of the *EXAR* architecture.

While *EXAR* adopts an agent-oriented architecture, it differs from classical multi-agent systems (MASs). In *EXAR*, reasoning agents do not represent autonomous entities with individual goals, but instead form a coordinated, goal-aligned cognitive agency whose internal collaboration is centrally orchestrated to solve a single problem instance.

3.2 Data and Knowledge Sources

The envisioned *EXAR* architecture aims to leverage a wide range of heterogeneous knowledge sources, depending on the specific domain and problem-solving context. First, structured data such as relational databases, formal process models or plans, system configurations, architectural layouts, code, or sensor readings could serve as important inputs for reasoning. Second, unstructured data sources, including free-text documents, technical or service reports, documents with embedded tables and figures, or even audio, images and video recordings, represent valuable but often underexploited reservoirs of domain knowledge. Third, *EXAR* is intended to incorporate formally represented knowledge, such as ontologies, knowledge graphs, rule bases, or planning domain models, to support symbolic reasoning. Finally, a crucial knowledge source is the tacit expertise of human domain experts, which requires explicit elicitation and formal structuring.

To make this heterogeneous knowledge usable for structured reasoning, *EXAR* proposes a transformation process that extracts and formalizes content into a persistent, queryable representation in the LTM. This transformation involves data connectors, parsers tailored to specific formats and structures, and information extraction techniques, including those based on fine-tuned LLMs. Additionally, interactive knowledge engineering approaches, potentially LLM-supported, are foreseen to capture and formalize implicit expert knowledge. The outcome of this process is a set of KUs, designed to encapsulate diverse knowledge representations in a form that reasoning agents can effectively access and process within the *EXAR* architecture.

3.3 Long-Term Memory

The LTM in *EXAR* serves as a persistent and structured memory layer for storing all relevant forms of knowledge and experience in the form of KUs. It extends the classical notion of knowledge containers from CBR [28] by supporting a broader range of representation formats, abstraction levels, and storage technologies. KUs typically result from pre-processing external sources, but may also emerge dynamically during neuro-symbolic or meta-reasoning processes.

Each KU comprises (a) a *content component*, which may include text fragments (chunks), prompt templates, time series, RDF/OWL graphs, logical rules, planning models, similarity functions, structured cases, or reasoning traces; (b) an *index component* supporting access and retrieval, which may consist of keywords, embeddings, or semantic annotations; (c) a *confidence score* estimating its trustworthiness; and (d) *provenance information*, such as the original source, transformation history, or generation context.

The LTM supports *index construction* and persistent storage using index-specific technologies such as vector databases, triple stores, graph databases, relational databases, or case bases. It enables various *retrieval strategies*, including keyword search, lexical search, SQL, SPARQL, and similarity-based retrieval using embeddings or explicitly modeled similarity measures. *Validation* is supported through consistency checking, external fact sources, or LLM-based judging, which may contribute to generating or updating confidence scores. Additionally, *reflection* on stored content, e.g., for summarization, generalization, abstraction, or improvement of retrieval performance through similarity learning or reorganization of KUs, is envisioned. In this way, the LTM constitutes a continuously evolving knowledge base that supports all reasoning activities within the *EXAR* architecture.

3.4 Reasoning Agents

According to the introduced neuro-symbolic reasoning layer, *EXAR* conceptualizes reasoning not as a monolithic process, but as the interaction of specialized agents that operate over a shared STM. This agent-based structure enables modular, compositional, and dynamically orchestrated reasoning strategies that go beyond classical pipelines such as the CBR 4R cycle or standard RAG flows. Agents are activated by the Orchestrator and exchange reasoning artifacts via the STM, allowing for both parallel and sequential execution of reasoning steps under a unified control model. The Orchestrator is also responsible for the management of the STM, e.g., for the deletion of entries after a (sub)task is completed successfully. Each agent is intended to perform a specific reasoning function such as retrieving knowledge, transforming representations, constructing plans, generating content, or evaluating outcomes while contributing to a larger, goal-oriented reasoning plan. This modular decomposition allows for fine-grained control, reuse of reasoning capabilities across tasks, and introspection through the Meta Learner. To achieve their goals, the agents may use tools to interact with other systems, such as running inference of neural networks, invoking APIs, running symbolic planners, or using the Python interpreter.

A first group of agents, the *Analyze agents*, supports the *analysis and transformation of high-level queries or problem descriptions*. These agents decompose tasks, interpret user intent, and translate input into internal representations for downstream reasoning. They may generate subgoals, planning templates, or structured queries. *Retrieve* agents perform retrieval in the sense of CBR and RAG, using symbolic conditions, semantic similarity, embeddings, or hybrid techniques to access relevant knowledge units from the LTM. They may exploit learned similarity models, ontological constraints, LLM supported query expansion, or decomposition.

Adapt agents are responsible for transforming retrieved knowledge units into usable solutions. They realize the reuse phase in CBR and may rely on handcrafted rules, learned operators, or LLM-based adaptation patterns. These agents can operate with explicit knowledge or learn their behavior from prior traces and reflective feedback. They implement structured problem-solving methods such as automated planning, rule-based inference, or constraint propagation. They operate on formal representations like logical rules, RDF graphs, or planning domains and may complement or refine outputs from other agents. Closely related are *generate agents*, which invoke LLMs or other generative models to produce problem solutions, content fragments, summaries, or completions. Such agents may be general purpose or tailored to domain-specific tasks.

Another group of agents (the *Optimize Agents*) focuses on *prompt construction and optimization*. These agents generate or refine prompts for generative models based on task context, user input, and current STM content, possibly optimizing for efficiency, coherence, or robustness.

To ensure output quality, *EXAR* includes *verification agents*, sometimes called judge agents. They verify results using consistency checks, symbolic systems, confidence estimation, or LLM-based grading, and feed their assessments into the STM, enabling downstream validation, feedback loops, and reflection—similar to the *revise* phase of the 4R cycle. Furthermore, these traces can be used to fine-tune agents using Reinforcement Learning with Verifiable Rewards (RLVR) [19]. Finally, *act agents* manage interaction and communication with the environment. They include user-facing interfaces such as chat or GUI agents.

This agent structure enables *EXAR* to integrate diverse reasoning paradigms such as retrieval based, rule based, model driven, and generative methods into a unified architecture, guided by dynamic orchestration and continuously improved through meta-level learning.

3.5 Orchestrator and Meta Learner

The orchestration component in *EXAR* governs the reasoning process by selecting, configuring, and sequencing reasoning agents according to the task, context, and internal system state. Rather than relying on a fixed reasoning cycle, *EXAR* envisions a spectrum of orchestration strategies, ranging from static pipelines to dynamically generated reasoning plans.

At the more static end of this spectrum, the Orchestrator may follow predefined reasoning procedures, such as the classical CBR 4R cycle or standard forms of RAG, where the sequence of retrieval followed by generation is fixed. Advanced variants of RAG such as iterative, recursive, or adaptive RAG extend this principle with limited feedback or multi-step reasoning but still rely on relatively rigid control flows. Such configurations are suitable for well-understood domains and recurring problem types with minimal variance in reasoning demands.

Toward the dynamic end of the spectrum, *EXAR* anticipates more flexible orchestration based on plan generation or search. This includes reasoning workflows that are dynamically constructed depending on the current problem state, retrieved knowledge, and prior experience. Approaches such as Process-Oriented CBR (POCBR) can be employed to represent and adapt reasoning strategies explicitly, treating reasoning steps as composable process fragments. In more complex cases, the Orchestrator may apply planning techniques or utilize learned reasoning graphs to construct agent execution sequences on demand.

The *Meta Learner* supports the Orchestrator by observing and analyzing executed reasoning processes over time. Its function is to reflect on the effectiveness, efficiency, and quality of reasoning strategies and to improve future orchestration decisions accordingly. This reflection process may rely on techniques developed in POCBR to adapt process structures or may employ Reinforcement Learning (RL) to optimize agent selection and sequencing based on task outcomes and performance signals. The results of meta-level reasoning are represented as new knowledge and stored persistently in the LTM in the form of knowledge units, enabling continuous learning and improvement of reasoning control. This corresponds to the *retain* phase in CBR, enabling reflective control learning.

Together, the Orchestrator and Meta Learner enable *EXAR* to shift from static reasoning pipelines toward context-sensitive, adaptive, and experience-grounded orchestration of diverse reasoning capabilities.

3.6 Environment

The environment layer in *EXAR* provides the interface between the reasoning system and its external world. It serves as the entry and exit point for problem-solving activities by enabling interaction with users, application systems, or physical environments. The environment component is essential for embedding *EXAR* into real-world scenarios, as it supports the acquisition of problem information, the delivery of solutions, and the communication of intermediate reasoning steps.

This interface may take different forms depending on the deployment context. It can be realized as a standalone user interface for entering queries, interacting via chat, or managing reasoning sessions. It may also be integrated into existing application software, acting as a reasoning backend that receives tasks from the host system and returns results or suggestions. In more immersive or sensor-based environments, the interface could include XR-based components for visual reasoning support or a direct connection to a cyber-physical system that provides sensor data and receives control actions.

The primary function of the environment interface is to obtain all relevant information required to define a problem instance. This includes user goals, constraints, preferences, and contextual events from technical systems. The second core function is to deliver solutions, recommendations, or action plans back to the user or connected systems in a structured and actionable way.

To foster transparency and user trust, the interface should also support visualization and simulation of reasoning processes and allow explanation of proposed solutions. This enables users and systems to assess the plausibility, applicability, and consequences of alternative outcomes, thus supporting informed decision-making in complex environments.

4 Existing Work in Light of *EXAR*

Table 1 provides an overview of current work in the intersection of CBR and LLMs, interpreted in the context of our proposed *EXAR* architecture. This overview is divided into more general methodologies consisting of CBR/POCBR, RAG, and agentic reasoning (see Sect. 2) and concrete hybrid approaches combining several of these general methods. For this purpose, we conducted a literature review of papers published by the CBR research community, with a focus on the proceedings of the *International Conference on Case-Based Reasoning (ICCBR)*. In this process, we selected six papers that propose a hybrid approach that combines CBR and LLMs. These papers are interpreted in the context of the *EXAR* architecture in the accompanying table, illustrating the generality of the proposed architecture.

Table 1. Applying *EXAR* Components to Existing Approaches.

Approach	Data & Knowledge	Long-Term Memory	Neuro-Symbolic Reasoning	Environment
CBR/POCBR [1,25]	Mostly structural data	Cases	Retrieve Adapt Verify	Domain-generic
RAG [11]	Mostly unstructured text and/or images	Text chunks with Embeddings	Retrieve Generate Optimize Verify	Domain-generic
Agentic Reasoning [15,23]	Structured or unstructured data	N/A	Analyze Retrieve Adapt Generate Optimize Verify Act	Domain-generic
CBR-RAG [36]	Unstructured legal documents	Textual cases consisting of QA pairs	Retrieve Generate	Domain experts asking legal questions
CBR-Ren [10]	Unstructured financial documents with text, numbers, and tables	Textual cases with explanations	Retrieve Generate	Domain experts doing financial analysis
RAG for Explaining Business Process Models [26]	Structured data in form of business processes	Procedural and textual cases with process model explanations	Retrieve Generate	Domain experts needing BPM explanations
On Implementing CBR with LLMs [34]	Structured medical-triage dataset	Attribute-value case for each patient with triage decision	Retrieve Adapt Generate	Domain experts making triage decisions
Adapting Graphs with WordNet and LLMs [20]	Structured argument graphs, lexical data	Graph cases, vector features, adaptation rules	Adapt Verify	Domain experts searching for arguments
LLsiM [21]	Structured data	Preference relations, similarity configs	Retrieve Generate	Domain-generic

5 Research Challenges

Based on the analysis of existing work and our own experience in building CBR systems integrating neuro-symbolic aspects, we propose a set of open research challenges. Although by no means exhaustive, this first version touches on the most important aspects of the proposed architecture. For a more general overview of challenges related to CBR and LLMs, we refer the interested reader to Bach et al. [3].

Data and Knowledge
C1 (Multimodality). How to represent and process multimodal knowledge sources (text, images, video, etc.) in a unified way?
C2 (Vectorization). When to use vector representation and when to use symbolic representation? How to combine both?
C3 (Expert Knowledge). How to elicit and formalize expert knowledge in a way that is usable for reasoning?

Short-Term and Long-Term Memory
C4 (Reflection). How to reflect on the stored knowledge to keep it relevant and maintainable?
C5 (Conflicts). How to resolve potential conflicts from different knowledge sources? Should they be merged or kept separate?
C6 (Merging). How to update the LTM with new external information or learned knowledge from the STM?

Reasoning Agents
C7 (Design). How to design agents that are specialized enough to be effective, but general enough to be reusable across different tasks?
C8 (Prompting). How to migrate away from manual prompt engineering to programmatic prompt generation?
C9 (Cost). How to balance the cost of LLM generations and agent executions with the need for high-quality results?

Orchestrator and Meta Learner
C10 (Safety). How to safely execute agents in a sandboxed environment while allowing interaction with required resources?
C11 (Determinism). How to deal with non-deterministic results obtained from the reasoning agents?
C12 (Coupling). How strong should the agents be coupled? Should they be allowed to communicate directly or only through the STM?
C13 (Planning). How to select reasoning agents and generate, store, and re-use execution plans for them in a cost-effective manner?

Environment
C14 (Interaction). How to design appropriate interaction types that allow for

deep integration of the environment?
C15 (Personalization). How to incorporate potential needs for personalization for different users?
C16 (Explainability). How to provide introspection into the reasoning process to increase user trust?

6 First Steps Towards Implementation

While *EXAR* is presented as a conceptual architecture, its realization can build upon a variety of existing frameworks and libraries that address key components of the system. This section outlines suitable technologies that provide starting points for implementing each layer of the *EXAR* architecture. As the field is expanding rapidly, the selection of libraries and tools should be understood as a starting point, not a complete overview.

The diverse data sources from the *Data and Knowledge Layer* can be parsed and structured by popular libraries such as LangChain [8] or LlamaIndex [24], which support document ingestion, text chunking, metadata extraction, and embedding-based indexing, which are essential for transforming heterogeneous data into structured knowledge units (KUs). Transformer-based neural networks are increasingly used for various pre-processing steps such as the text extraction from documents like PDFs. HuggingFace offers a variety of models accessible through the transformers library [37].

The *Long-Term Memory* in *EXAR* requires persistent and queryable storage of KUs across multiple knowledge representations. Triple stores such as Apache Jena [2] support RDF and OWL-based KUs, while relational databases such as PostgreSQL offer scalable indexing[1]. Case-based reasoning components of the long-term memory can be implemented using the CBRkit [22], which provides reusable similarity functions, case models, and retrieval mechanisms, or ProCAKE [5], which additionally supports process-oriented CBR and structural reasoning on complex case representations.

In the *Reasoning Layer*, a wide variety of reasoning agents can be realized using existing tools and libraries. Adaptation agents can rely on symbolic tools, such as AI planning systems like FastDownward [14]. Libraries like Outlines [35] can help to generate well-formatted inputs for the symbolic tools. For generative agents, the transformers library [37] or dedicated inference libraries like vLLM [18] or SGLang [40] offer a wide support of models. Prompt engineering and optimization agents can be supported by frameworks like DSPy [17], which enable prompt programming and evaluation in structured workflows. Verification agents can use tools such as VAL [16], which can verify the validity of PDDL files.

The *Orchestrator* in *EXAR* may initially rely on fixed execution templates using standard orchestration libraries such as LangChain [8], LlamaIndex [24]

[1] PostgreSQL also support vectors through extensions such as pgvector (https://github.com/pgvector/pgvector).

or CBRkit [22]. More advanced agent-based orchestration can draw from emerging multi-agent frameworks like CAMEL [23] or PydanticAI [27] which allow dynamic, goal-driven interaction between agents. Process-oriented reasoning strategies can be modeled using ProCAKEs [5] process adaptation mechanisms. For the Meta Learner, machine learning libraries such as TorchRL [6] or verl [31] can be used to learn orchestration policies based on reasoning traces, performance signals, or feedback loops. Experience and strategy knowledge resulting from meta-reasoning can be represented and stored in the LTM as KUs.

The interaction with the *Environment Layer* can be realized using a variety of interface frameworks, for example by providing humans with a chat interface or a GUI or by interacting with the world through APIs.

These existing tools offer a solid foundation for implementing the components of *EXAR*. While no single framework covers all architectural elements, their combination enables flexible and modular prototyping of experience-grounded agentic reasoning systems.

7 Summary and Outlook

In this paper, we propose *EXAR*, a unified architecture for hybrid agentic reasoning. The aim of *EXAR* is to provide the basis for a more flexible orchestration of reasoning pipelines. This is not only relevant in the context of RAG approaches, but also in CBR, where the rather static "cycle of sequential steps" [1] should be broken up for a more flexible use of the CBR methodology. *EXAR* consists of four individual layers (i.e., *Data & Knowledge*, *Long-Term Memory*, *Neuro-Symoblic Reasoning* and *Environment*) that describe how knowledge can be transferred into a long-term memory, which is in turn used by agents to perform reasoning tasks in an environment. The main module of *EXAR* is the *Neuro-Symbolic Reasoning* layer, which enables the flexible orchestrator of individual reasoning agents to solve a faced problem by using a shared short-term memory. The *Meta Learner* component enables the self-incremental learning of the agents for future problem-solving situations.

In the future, we want to provide a reference implementation for the *EXAR* architecture, which can be used by the CBR-LLM research community. As a starting point, we extended our CBRkit library [22] with a *synthesis* module consisting of built-in LLM providers and prompting functions for straightforward integration of retrieval and adaptation results with the capabilities offered by generative AI models. Our vision is to provide an integrated framework for building experience-grounded applications that is both easy-to-use and customizable enough to support a wide range of use cases. In addition, we plan an extended literature review to demonstrate that existing approaches by the CBR research community can be interpreted in the *EXAR* architecture. Finally, we aim to evolve our own CBR approaches in alignment with the *EXAR* architecture, thereby creating a foundation for integrated implementations and joint research initiatives.

Acknowledgments. The authors would like to thank all members of the research group at Trier University and the German Research Center for Artificial Intelligence for their valuable discussions and contributions to the development of the ideas presented in this paper.

References

1. Aamodt, A., Plaza, E.: Case-based reasoning: foundational issues, methodological variations, and system approaches. AI Commun. **7**(1), 39–59 (1994)
2. Apache Software Foundation: Apache Jena (2021). https://jena.apache.org/
3. Bach, K., et al.: Case-based reasoning meets large language models: a research manifesto for open challenges and research directions. HAL Sci. **hal-05006761v1** (2025). https://hal.science/hal-05006761. Working paper or preprint
4. Bergmann, R., Althoff, K.-D.: Methodology for building CBR applications. In: Lenz, M., Burkhard, H.-D., Bartsch-Spörl, B., Wess, S. (eds.) Case-Based Reasoning Technology. LNCS (LNAI), vol. 1400, pp. 299–326. Springer, Heidelberg (1998). https://doi.org/10.1007/3-540-69351-3_12
5. Bergmann, R., et al.: ProCAKE: a process-oriented case-based reasoning framework. In: 27th ICCBR Workshops. CEUR Workshop Proceedings, vol. 2567, pp. 156–161. CEUR-WS.org (2019)
6. Bou, A., et al.: TorchRL: a data-driven decision-making library for PyTorch. In: ICLR 2024 (2024). OpenReview.net
7. Brand, F., Malburg, L., Bergmann, R.: Large language models as knowledge engineers. In: 32nd ICCBR Workshops. CEUR Workshop Proceedings, vol. 3708, pp. 3–18. CEUR-WS.org (2024)
8. Chase, H.: LangChain (2022). https://github.com/langchain-ai/langchain
9. Dannenhauer, D., et al.: A case-based reasoning approach to dynamic few-shot prompting for code generation. In: ICML Workshop on LLMs and Cognition (2024)
10. Feng, B., et al.: CBR-Ren: a case-based reasoning driven retriever-generator model for hybrid long-form numerical reasoning. In: 32nd ICCBR. LNCS, vol. 14775, pp. 111–126. Springer (2024)
11. Gao, Y., et al.: Retrieval-augmented generation for large language models: a survey. CoRR abs/2312.10997 (2023)
12. Gates, L., Leake, D., Wilkerson, K.: Cases are king: a user study of case presentation to explain CBR decisions. In: 31st ICCBR. LNCS, vol. 14141, pp. 153–168. Springer (2023)
13. Hatalis, K., Christou, D., Kondapalli, V.: Review of case-based reasoning for LLM agents: theoretical foundations, architectural components, and cognitive integration. CoRR abs/2504.06943 (2025)
14. Helmert, M.: The fast downward planning system. J. Artif. Intell. Res. **26**, 191–246 (2006)
15. Hong, S., et al.: MetaGPT: meta programming for a multi-agent collaborative framework. In: ICLR 2024 (2024). OpenReview.net
16. Howey, R., Long, D., Fox, M.: VAL: automatic plan validation, continuous effects and mixed initiative planning using PDDL. In: ICTAI 2004, pp. 294–301. IEEE Computer Society (2004)
17. Khattab, O., et al.: DSPy: compiling declarative language model calls into self-improving pipelines. CoRR abs/2310.03714 (2023)

18. Kwon, W., et al.: Efficient memory management for large language model serving with PagedAttention. In: SOSP 2023, pp. 611–626. ACM (2023)
19. Lambert, N., et al.: TULU 3: pushing frontiers in open language model post-training. CoRR abs/2411.15124 (2024)
20. Lenz, M., Bergmann, R.: Case-based adaptation of argument graphs with word-net and large language models. In: 31st ICCBR. LNCS, vol. 14141, pp. 263–278. Springer (2023)
21. Lenz, M., Hoffmann, M., Bergmann, R.: LLsiM: large language models for similarity assessment in case-based reasoning. In: 33rd ICCBR. LNCS, Springer (2025)
22. Lenz, M., Malburg, L., Bergmann, R.: CBRkit: an intuitive case-based reasoning toolkit for python. In: 32nd ICCBR. LNCS, vol. 14775, pp. 289–304. Springer (2024)
23. Li, G., et al.: CAMEL: communicative agents for "mind" exploration of large language model society. In: NeurIPS 2023 (2023)
24. Liu, J.: LlamaIndex (2022). https://github.com/run-llama/llama_index
25. Minor, M., Bergmann, R., Görg, S.: Case-based adaptation of workflows. Inf. Syst. **40**, 142–152 (2014)
26. Minor, M., Kaucher, E.: Retrieval augmented generation with LLMs for explaining business process models. In: 32nd ICCBR. LNCS, vol. 14775, pp. 175–190. Springer (2024)
27. Pydantic: PydanticAI (2024). https://github.com/pydantic/pydantic-ai
28. Richter, M.M.: Knowledge containers. In: Readings in Case-Based Reasoning. Morgan Kaufmann Publishers (2003)
29. Sen, A., et al.: Counterfactual-based synthetic case generation. In: 32nd ICCBR. LNCS, vol. 14775, pp. 388–403. Springer (2024)
30. Shen, Y., et al.: HuggingGPT: solving AI tasks with ChatGPT and its friends in hugging face. In: NeurIPS 2023 (2023)
31. Sheng, G., et al.: HybridFlow: a flexible and efficient RLHF framework. In: EuroSys 2025, pp. 1279–1297. ACM (2025)
32. Sourati, Z., Ilievski, F., Sandlin, H., et al.: Case-based reasoning with language models for classification of logical fallacies. In: IJCAI 2023, pp. 5188–5196. ijcai.org (2023)
33. Watson, I.: A case-based persistent memory for a large language model. In: 32nd ICCBR Workshops. CEUR Workshop Proceedings, vol. 3708, pp. 19–25. CEUR-WS.org (2024)
34. Wilkerson, K., Leake, D.: On implementing case-based reasoning with large language models. In: 32nd ICCBR. LNCS, vol. 14775, pp. 404–417. Springer (2024)
35. Willard, B.T., Louf, R.: Efficient guided generation for large language models. CoRR abs/2307.09702 (2023)
36. Wiratunga, N., et al.: CBR-RAG: case-based reasoning for retrieval augmented generation in LLMs for legal question answering. In: 32nd ICCBR. LNCS, vol. 14775, pp. 445–460. Springer (2024)
37. Wolf, T., et al.: Transformers: state-of-the-art natural language processing. In: EMNLP 2020 - Demos, pp. 38–45. ACL (2020)
38. Yang, J., et al.: SWE-agent: agent-computer interfaces enable automated software engineering. In: NeurIPS 2024 (2024)
39. Zhao, W.X., et al.: A survey of large language models. CoRR abs/2303.18223 (2023)
40. Zheng, L., et al.: SGLang: efficient execution of structured language model programs. In: NeurIPS 2024 (2024)

CBR and Generative AI Synergies

AlignLLM: Alignment-Based Evaluation Using Ensemble of LLMs-as-Judges for Q&A

Ramitha Abeyratne(✉), Nirmalie Wiratunga, Kyle Martin, Ikechukwu Nkisi-Orji, and Lasal Jayawardena

Robert Gordon University, Aberdeen, Scotland
{r.abeyratne,n.wiratunga,k.martin3,i.nkisi-orji,l.jayawardena}@rgu.ac.uk

Abstract. Evaluating responses generated by large language models (LLMs) is challenging in the absence of ground-truth knowledge, particularly in specialised domains such as law. Increasingly, LLMs themselves are used to evaluate the responses they generate; however, this approach is prone to bias and inherent errors. To address these issues, we propose an unsupervised ensemble method that employs multiple general-purpose LLMs as a 'collective judge', rather than relying on a single model. Here we introduce a novel application of case alignment as an aggregation mechanism, achieving higher correlation with supervised metrics than unsupervised LLM-as-a-judge baselines. Specifically, we construct two spaces for the ensemble: one for reconstructed questions by the ensemble given the model's original responses ('problem-space'), and another for the set of answers generated in response to those reconstructed questions ('solution-space'). By applying similarity-based alignment metrics across these two spaces, we gauge how closely our ensemble-based evaluation metric correlates with accuracy-based metrics that rely on ground-truth data. Our results on two legal Q&A datasets show significant correlations using this alignment strategy, suggesting that it can effectively evaluate LLM-generated responses even when ground truth is unavailable.

Keywords: LLMs-as-Judges · Case-alignment · Legal Q&A

1 Introduction

Large Language Models (LLMs) have made significant strides in natural language understanding and generation, enabling applications in domains such as conversational AI, code generation, and reasoning tasks [18]. However, evaluating their responses in specialised fields like law remains a critical challenge [26]. The absence of reliable, cost-effective evaluation methods complicates the assessment of LLM-generated responses particularly when ground-truth references are unavailable [25]. This challenge pertains not only to factual accuracy

Code available at https://github.com/RAbeyratne/aligned-ensemble-judge.

© The Author(s), under exclusive license to Springer Nature Switzerland AG 2025
I. Bichindaritz and B. López (Eds.): ICCBR 2025, LNAI 15662, pp. 21–36, 2025.
https://doi.org/10.1007/978-3-031-96559-3_2

but also to the overall quality of their outputs. Typically, evaluation relies on human-annotated gold standards which are both time-consuming and expensive [4]. In response to these challenges, recent studies have explored the use of LLMs as self-evaluators [28]. However, this approach can still be influenced by individual model biases, raising concerns about the reliability of LLM-based judgments [25]. While some efforts have explored using ensembles of LLMs to improve evaluation robustness and reduce biases [13], the challenge of effectively aggregating their judgments remains an open question.

In this paper, we introduce an unsupervised ensemble evaluation method that employs multiple general-purpose LLMs as an "ensemble judge," rather than relying on a single model. Our key contribution is the novel use of case alignment as an aggregation mechanism by repurposing a technique that is traditionally employed in casebase maintenance [5,21]. This method constructs two evaluative spaces: a "problem-space", derived from reconstructed queries (or legal questions, in our application) generated by model responses, and a "solution-space", comprising the corresponding solutions (or answers) to those queries. By aligning these spaces through similarity-based metrics, we estimate response quality even in the absence of gold-standard answers. Our framework equally builds upon reverse generation [7], where LLMs generate questions from provided answers which facilitates the assessment of coherence and contextual alignment. These reconstructed texts are then converted to vector representations to enable alignment analysis between the two spaces. Accordingly we make the following two contributions:

- Unsupervised ensemble LLM evaluation methods inspired by case alignment. We propose an ensemble method that employs multiple general-purpose LLMs as a collective judge to reduce bias and improve evaluation reliability which employs a novel CBR mechanism. By applying semantic similarity-based alignment metrics across the case base, we estimate response quality without requiring ground-truth data.
- Comparative study on two legal datasets: Australian Legal QA and Sri Lankan Supreme court law datasets. We perform reverse generation on the dataset followed by evaluation metrics to compare and analyse results with the gold standard.

In the remainder of the paper, Sect. 2 covers related work; followed by the ensemble aggregation methods in Sect. 3. Evaluation on two legal datasets and results appear in Sect. 4 followed by conclusions in Sect. 5.

2 Related Work

The increasing use of LLMs as evaluators, conceptualised as "LLMs-as-Judges" [28], marks a transformative shift in AI evaluation methodologies. Unlike traditional lexical metrics such as BLEU [20] and ROUGE [16], LLMs provide a means to exploit their contextual representations. This allows evaluators to dynamically adjust and refine their criteria based on specific tasks, offering flexibility and precision beyond what conventional metrics can achieve [13]. However, this paradigm is not without challenges: prompt design heavily influences LLM-based evaluations, introducing potential biases and inconsistencies [3]. Our work addresses this issue by exploring effective aggregation methods within LLM ensembles, reducing reliance on any single prompt's design.

2.1 Evaluation Types of LLM Judges

Broadly, LLM-based approaches for evaluating responses can be categorised into pairwise evaluation, single-answer scoring, and retrieval-augmented approaches. Each comes with distinct advantages and limitations that impact its suitability for our work.

Pairwise evaluation is a commonly used strategy for assessing relative differences between two candidate responses, where two candidate answers are presented to the model alongside the task, and the preferred response is selected based on predefined criteria [28]. While effective in comparative assessment, this method is prone to position bias where a candidate is consistently preferred based on its placement. This issue can be mitigated by conducting multiple rounds of evaluation with swapped positions. Despite its advantages, pairwise evaluation is unsuitable for our problem of evaluating generated responses in a question-answer task, as there are no multiple candidate answers to compare.

When only a single response needs to be evaluated, single-answer scoring is typically used. In this approach, the LLM assigns a score within a predefined range, which is then used to grade the response [10]. However, this method often fails to adequately capture nuances or subtle attributes of the response, limiting its ability to fully assess the answer quality [28]. Additionally, the assigned score can vary significantly across different evaluating LLMs, introducing inconsistency in assessment. Another drawback is verbosity bias, where longer responses are systematically favoured over shorter ones, making it unsuitable for scenarios requiring length-independent evaluation [28].

A simpler alternative and effective approach involves having the judge LLM generate its own reference answer using the same process as the evaluated response [27]. Although it does not address the challenge of incomplete or unreliable internal knowledge of LLMs, the generated outputs can then be assessed using embeddings to measure the semantic alignment between the model's response and answer to be evaluated.

Given the limitations of LLMs' knowledge, Retrieval-Augmented Generation (RAG) techniques incorporate external knowledge into the model's contextual input [12]. This allows general-purpose LLMs to act as domain-specific experts. For example, RAGChecker employs this strategy in a similar manner to [27], but evaluate responses solely based retrieved RAG context [22]. However, this RAG method is unsuitable for our use case, as we aim to assess the correctness of generated answers without access to ground-truth responses for retrieval. Moreover, retrieved contexts may include irrelevant information, introducing potential noise in evaluation. A related approach, RAGA, evaluates answer relevance by reverse-generating multiple potential questions from a response and comparing them against the original question [7]. However, this method does not incorporate RAG context, making it susceptible to hallucinations when necessary knowledge is absent from the model's training data. In addition, using one LLM for similarity assessment weakens evaluation reliability. To address these challenges, we integrate RAG context into the reverse-generation step and introduce improved alignment metrics with an ensemble of LLM judges, enhancing evaluation robustness.

2.2 Architectures of LLM Judges

A typical LLM judge uses a single model for evaluation. This approach depends heavily on in-context learning [6], where the model evaluates responses based on contextual information in the input without requiring parameter updates. However, the evaluation prompt plays a critical role, potentially introducing biases [8] and limiting objectivity. Additionally, LLM biases and knowledge constraints affect reliability. These biases include the previously mentioned position bias, verbosity bias (preferring longer answers), sentiment bias (leaning towards overly positive or negative tones), and token bias (favouring responses with certain token patterns). Avoiding pairwise or grading-based evaluations can help mitigate these issues [28]. The use of multiple-judge models enhances robustness and fairness while minimising hallucination. In addition, self-enhancement bias, where an LLM favours its own outputs, can be reduced by using different models for generation and judgment [14].

Hybrid human-LLM judge systems integrate human oversight to improve accuracy, with LLM judges acting as supporting agents. Some systems refine evaluation criteria for automated judges [24], addressing criteria drift. Others position a human reviewer at the final stage for thorough review [19], commonly used in critical fields like healthcare. While highly accurate, hybrid systems are time-intensive, which limits scalability.

Multiple LLM judges improve the accuracy and robustness of evaluation by mitigating biases and leveraging the strengths of several models [13]. These models can be structured sequentially or independently. Sequential models require coordination, where one LLM's output influences another [15]. Competitive models refine outputs iteratively to improve evaluation quality [2]. An approach which deploys independent LLM judges should be more scalable as it ensures diverse assessments without requiring complex coordination.

3 Inter LLM Ensemble

Our approach follows a RAG-based ensemble approach, which is illustrated in Fig. 1. Specifically, we use a snippet S to provide domain-specific "augmented" context that informs the question-answering process. This snippet context can be either retrieved from a knowledge source or constructed from a given document.

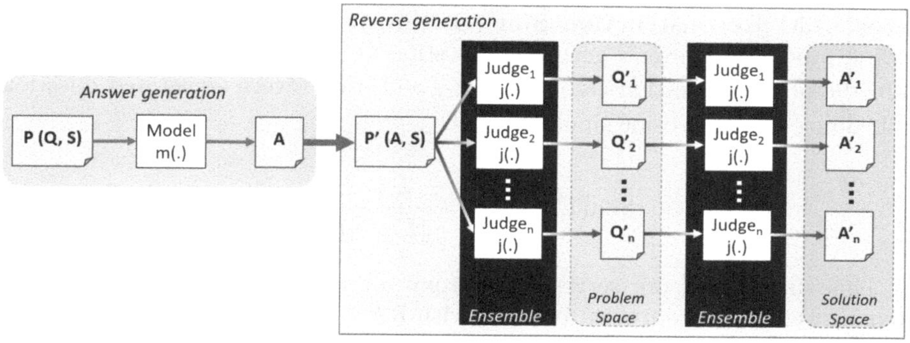

Fig. 1. Reverse generation workflow with LLM judges

Let $m(\cdot)$ be the *generating function*, implemented by a LLM, and let $j_i(\cdot)$ for $i = 1, 2, \ldots, n$, denote the *judge functions*, each also an LLM but potentially distinct from $m(\cdot)$. We denote by Q the original question, S the snippet providing domain-relevant context, and P a prompt guiding generation. The generative step proceeds as follows:

$$A = m(Q, S, P),$$

where A is the answer generated by the model $m(\cdot)$. Next, we use a specialised prompt P' to *reverse-generate* a question for which A is presumably the correct answer:

$$Q'_i = j_i(A, S, P'),$$

where Q'_i is the reverse-generated question produced by the i-th judge model $j_i(\cdot)$. To obtain contextual representations, we feed the original question Q, the answer A, and each reverse-generated question Q'_i back into the generating model. Given $m(\cdot)$, which represents a multi-layer LLM, we use $m_l(\cdot)$ to denote the subnetwork up to layer l, from which we extract our embeddings as follows:

$$\vec{E}_Q = m_l(Q), \quad \vec{E}_A = m_l(A), \quad \vec{E}_{Q'_i} = m_l(Q'_i).$$

We use these *contextual* embeddings (rather than simpler ones) to capture the full semantic relationships encoded by the model.

3.1 Basic Similarity-Based Measures

Since our goal is to approximate the accuracy of the generated answer by assessing inter-model agreement in the judge ensemble, we treat the semantic similarity among these embeddings as a proxy for correctness (unsupervised). Next, we describe two fundamental similarity-based metrics that operate on these embeddings.

Inter LLM Reconstruction Sim (ILRSim). Given n judge models, each having produced a reverse-generated question Q'_i from the answer A. We compare the original question embedding $\vec{E}_Q$ and each reverse-generated question embedding $\vec{E}_{Q'_i}$ via cosine similarity [11]:

$$\mathrm{Sim}(\vec{E}_Q, \vec{E}_{Q'_i}) = \frac{\vec{E}_Q \cdot \vec{E}_{Q'_i}}{\|\vec{E}_Q\| \, \|\vec{E}_{Q'_i}\|}$$

This similarity score serves as a proxy for the correctness of the generated answer A. Conceptually, it aligns with RAGAs' "answer relevance" framework [7], but we employ multiple judge models to mitigate biases from any single LLM and have also utilised RAG to augment the prompts with S to address hallucination. Higher scores suggest better semantic alignment between Q and Q'_i. We aggregate by averaging over all judge-model similarities:

$$\mathrm{Sim}_{\mathrm{avg}} = \frac{1}{n} \sum_{i=1}^{n} \mathrm{Sim}(\vec{E}_Q, \vec{E}_{Q'_i}) \tag{1}$$

where $\mathrm{Sim}_{\mathrm{avg}}$ represents the combined correctness of A. In this manner, *ILRSim* yields a single value (ranging from 0 to 1) that captures the overall semantic coherence of the system's output.

Inter LLM Reconstruction Error (ILRError). In this approach, we measure *reconstruction error* between the original and reverse-generated question embeddings. For each judge model, we compute the squared difference between $\vec{E}_Q$ and $\vec{E}_{Q'_i}$ using mean squared error (MSE) [9]. We then aggregate these errors across all judge models:

$$\mathrm{MSE}_{\mathrm{avg}} = \frac{1}{n} \sum_{i=1}^{n} \left\| \vec{E}_Q - \vec{E}_{Q'_i} \right\|^2. \tag{2}$$

In contrast to *ILRSim*, this metric is *inversely* related to accuracy: a lower $\mathrm{MSE}_{\mathrm{avg}}$ indicates that the reverse-generated question embeddings are closer to the original question embeddings, implying a more accurate answer A. While MSE values are always non-negative, they may exceed 1 depending on the embedding space; normalisation (if applied) can keep this metric in the range $[0, 1]$.

3.2 Alignment-Based Measures

Inter LLM Reconstruction Alignment (ILRAlign). Alignment between the problem space and solution space offers direct insights into the accuracy of generated answers. This concept is heavily inspired by the case alignment literature in Case-Based Reasoning. The core idea with this methodology is that similar problems have similar solutions [17]. To adopt such a metric in the context of LLM evaluation we form the problem space with question representations

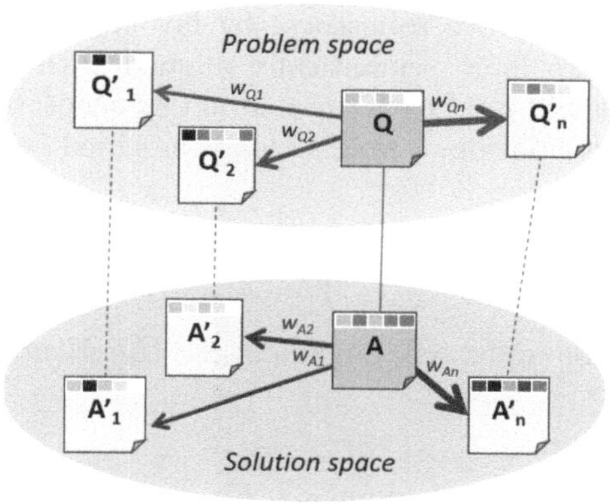

Fig. 2. Neighbourhood analysis in reverse generated embedding spaces.

while the solution space contains answer representations. Figure 2 depicts this visually, with embeddings used in both spaces derived from model m_l.

An additional generation step is required to compute alignment. The reverse-generated question Q_i' from each judge LLM is combined with the snippet S and prompt P to produce a new answer A_i'. This process is repeated for all judges:

$$A_i' = j_i(Q_i', S, P)$$

The resulting pairs, (Q_i', A_i'), are then mapped into problem and solution spaces by converting them into embeddings via the original model $m(.)$. Specifically,

$$\vec{E}_{A_i'} = m_l(A_i').$$

The alignment is then computed using these vector representations. Each pair's alignment score is based on both problem and solution similarity. Let $\vec{E}_{Q_i'}$ and $\vec{E}_{A_i'}$ represent the embeddings of the reverse-generated question and the new answer, respectively. The alignment score ILRAlign is calculated as:

$$\text{ILRAlign} = \frac{1}{N}\Big(\alpha \sum_{i=1}^{N} \text{Sim}\big(\vec{E}_Q, \vec{E}_{Q_i'}\big) + \beta \sum_{i=1}^{N} \text{Sim}\big(\vec{E}_A, \vec{E}_{A_i'}\big)\Big), \quad (3)$$

where α and β can be used to tune the relative importance of each similarity component and are typically set to 0.5. This approach ensures that the evaluation incorporates the individual judges' knowledge, providing a robust measure of alignment for the newly generated response. A higher alignment score indicates that the generated response aligns more closely with the judges' outputs.

Weighted Inter LLM Reconstruction Alignment (WILRAlign). While all judge models contribute to ILRAlign, assigning uniform importance can allow outliers or less-reliable judges to skew the final result. We therefore introduce a weighted approach to improve robustness by favouring judges whose reverse-generated questions are more semantically aligned with the original, on the assumption that they will produce more relevant or accurate answers. To determine each judge's contribution, a weight, w_i, is assigned based on *problem* similarity:

$$w_i = \frac{\mathrm{Sim}(\vec{E}_Q, \vec{E}_{Q'_i})}{\sum_{j=1}^{N} \mathrm{Sim}(\vec{E}_Q, \vec{E}_{Q'_j})}$$

We then compute the weighted alignment, *WILRAlign*, by applying these weights:

$$\text{WILRAlign} = \sum_{i=1}^{N} w_i\Big(\alpha\,\mathrm{Sim}(\vec{E}_Q, \vec{E}_{Q'_i}) \;+\; \beta\,\mathrm{Sim}(\vec{E}_A, \vec{E}_{A'_i})\Big) \tag{4}$$

Weighting in this manner ensures that judges with stronger alignment to Q have greater influence in the evaluation judgements. Figure 2 demonstrates this visually. Here the denominator ensures that the weights sum to 1, normalising each judge's contribution; and that outliers or less-reliable judges exert reduced influence on the final alignment score. Similar to *ILRAlign*, a higher *WILRAlign* indicates stronger agreement with the original query and its associated solutions.

4 Evaluation

Our primary aim is to determine how well our proposed unsupervised metrics compare with traditional supervised metrics when assessing response quality. To achieve this, we created multiple dataset versions with progressively increasing

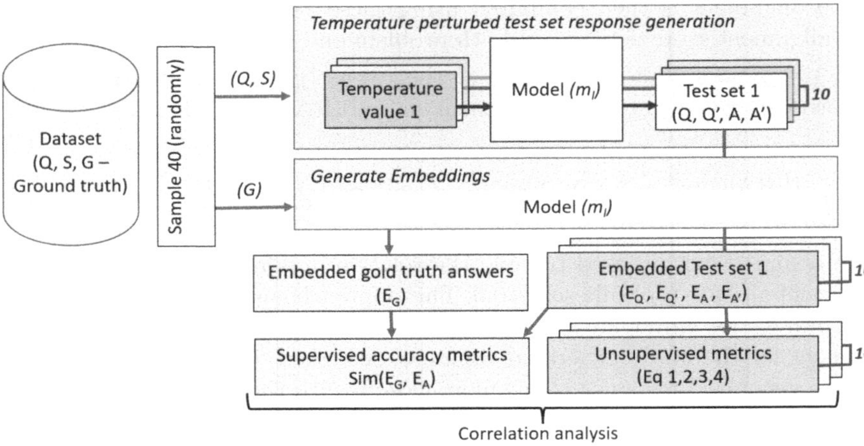

Fig. 3. Evaluation methodology

difficulty levels, controlled by the model's temperature parameter. These increasingly perturbed datasets enabled us to generate a range of responses, which we then evaluated using both supervised and unsupervised metrics to study their correlation. Figure 3 illustrates our evaluation methodology, showing how we create 10 test sets consisting of varying response quality by repeatedly generating answers for the same 40 randomly selected instances at increasingly higher temperature settings. Starting with a baseline temperature, we incrementally increase it for each subsequent round of generation. As the temperature rises, we expect the model's responses to degrade in quality. This range of responses allows us to calculate varying levels of response accuracy and, in turn, examine how well our unsupervised metrics correlate with supervised measures.

Each of the 40 randomly selected instances includes a question (Q), a snippet (S), and a ground-truth answer (G). The ground-truth answers, G, are used by supervised metrics to compare against the embedding (E_A) of the answer generated by the model m, with quality measured by $sim(E_G, E_A)$. In parallel, we compute unsupervised metrics that rely on reverse-generated embeddings (rather than E_A), as detailed in Sect. 3. As shown in the figure, all embeddings are produced by the model being evaluated, m. Given the 10 test sets, each containing 40 instances, we obtained a total of 400 results for our comparative study of supervised and unsupervised metrics. Specifically, we examined the extent to which the unsupervised metrics correlate with the supervised metric $sim(E_A, E'_A)$ using the Pearson correlation coefficient [23]. A strong correlation would indicate that our approach can serve as a reliable alternative when ground-truth data is unavailable.

We organised our correlation experiments under two main themes: (1) the LLM-as-a-judge scenario, in which we compare the accuracy of content generated by individual judges to the ground truth, and (2) the ensemble-of-judges approach introduced in this paper. The first theme explores how closely individual judges mimic the ground truth, while the second demonstrates the utility of our new unsupervised metrics relative to supervised ones. For the ensemble results, we compared various unsupervised metrics, including individual judges' answer similarity (Answer Sim, $sim(E_A, E_G)$), BM25, ROUGE-L, BLEU, ILR-Sim (Eq. 1), ILRError (Eq. 2), ILRAlign (Eq. 3), and WILRAlign (Eq. 4).

4.1 Datasets

We utilise two legal datasets to construct our test sets and evaluate our methodology: the Australian Legal Question Answering (ALQA) dataset [1] and the Sri Lankan Supreme Court (SLSC) dataset. While both datasets consist of question gold-truth answer pairs accompanied by a text snippet containing the necessary information to answer the question, they differ in their sources. ALQA dataset was created using the Open Australian Legal Corpus, the largest publicly available database of Australian law. In contrast, the SLSC dataset was compiled by creating question-answer pairs after scraping publicly available Sri Lankan Supreme Court cases from 1999 to 2017. Both datasets represent distinct legal frameworks and linguistic structures which enables a more robust evaluation.

We performed a parameter-tuning experiment to determine a suitable temperature range for the ALQA and SLSC models, generating answers for both test sets across a range of temperature values. Since each model has unique internal weighting, the temperature range and increments were model-specific. We then calculated the cosine similarity between each answer and the ground truth, visualised the results, and identified an elbow-curve to select 10 representative temperature values per model (Fig. 4). This elbow marks the region most sensitive to temperature change, allowing us to determine the range where variation has the greatest impact. This resulted in eight sets of model-specific test sets for four models - ALQA[1] and SLSC[2]—each containing 400 question-answer-snippet triplets (i.e., 40 unique question-snippet combinations, each with 10 answers generated at different temperatures), where increasing temperature correlates with decreasing similarity to the gold standard. The test sets generated by varying temperature ensure that we capture responses of differing quality, facilitating a meaningful comparison with the ground truth. These results reinforce the validity of our approach.

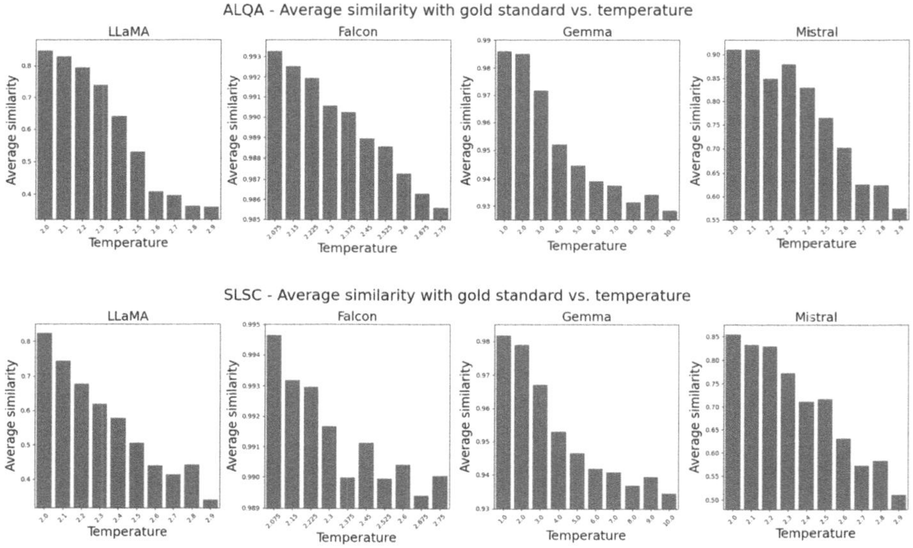

Fig. 4. ALQA and SLSC dataset average similarity correlation vs. temperature

4.2 LLM Models and Prompts Used

We selected four open-source LLMs, each capable of running locally for text generation. These include the 7-billion-parameter versions of Llama 2-chat, Falcon,

[1] https://huggingface.co/datasets/Ramitha/alqa-master-40.
[2] https://huggingface.co/datasets/Ramitha/sl-master-40.

Gemma, and Mistral v0.2. These models were used both as generators and as judges in turn using a leave-one-out strategy, where when one model generates responses the rest served as evaluators forming the ensemble of judges.

Table 1. Prompts used for generation

Scenario	Prompt
P - Answer generation	Generate an answer to the below question based on the provided snippet. Question: 'Q' Snippet: 'S'
P' - Question generation (except Gemma)	Your task is to generate a clear and concise question based on the provided snippet and answer. Ensure that the generated question directly corresponds to the snippet's content and leads to the given answer. Here is the input: Snippet: 'S' Answer: 'A' Generate the most appropriate question.
P' - Question generation (Gemma)	Generate the question that was asked regarding the below snippet and provided answer. Ensure that the generated question directly corresponds to the snippet's content and leads to the given answer. Snippet: 'S' Answer: 'A' The output should contain only the question (do not output the answer to the question).

Table 1 presents the prompts used for text generation (as shown in reverse generation process, Fig. 1). While all LLMs generated outputs using two uniform prompts across both phases, Gemma exhibited significant hallucinations and failed to regenerate questions with the standard prompt. To mitigate this issue, we employed a specialised prompt for Gemma. After running the selected language models, we extracted contextual embeddings from the last layer of the model (m_l). We then measured textual relatedness using cosine similarity.

4.3 Results

Table 2 presents the correlation results in the llm-as-a-judge scenario where individual judges are used as evaluators on the ALQA and SLSC datasets. There are two ways in which we can use an LLM as a judge: 1) compare how closely the model's generated answers align with each LLM judge's answers, $sim(E_A, E'_A)$, versus their similarity with the ground truth, G, i.e. $sim(E_A, E_G)$; and 2) compare the similarity between a reverse generated question from a judge to the original question $sim(E_Q, E'_Q)$ versus $sim(E_G, E_A)$. This analysis provides insight into how well LLM judges align not only with human-like answer preferences but also with how they interpret and reconstruct the question space. By comparing question and answer correlations, we assess whether consistency in problem formulation (question similarity) or alignment in solution space (answer similarity) is a better indicator of LLM evaluation reliability.

With both datasets, answer generation exhibited notably low correlation values when judged individually. Overall, the correlations range from slightly negative to positive but tend to be relatively small. We also noted that when Falcon

Table 2. Correlation analysis of LLM-as-a-judge on ALQA and SLSC using j_i generated answers & reverse generated questions.

Dataset	Model (m)	Answer-ground truth correlation (j_i)				Question-ground truth correlation (j_i)			
		Llama	Falcon	Gemma	Mistral	Llama	Falcon	Gemma	Mistral
ALQA	Llama	N/A	0.0617	0.0542	0.0032	N/A	0.3955	0.5193	0.3660
	Falcon	−0.1948	N/A	−0.0253	−0.1896	0.0623	N/A	0.1317	−0.0548
	Gemma	0.0172	0.1102	N/A	0.1356	0.4175	0.2874	N/A	0.3745
	Mistral	0.0298	−0.0152	0.0472	N/A	−0.0104	0.2465	0.1558	N/A
SLSC	Llama	N/A	−0.1052	0.1040	0.0477	N/A	0.3238	0.3072	0.2728
	Falcon	−0.1026	N/A	−0.1393	−0.1267	−0.0841	N/A	−0.0250	−0.1310
	Gemma	0.2546	0.0228	N/A	0.2054	0.3383	0.3425	N/A	0.3648
	Mistral	0.2792	0.1841	0.1403	N/A	−0.1034	0.0677	0.1448	N/A

is the model, several judges (e.g., Llama, Gemma, and Mistral) exhibit negative correlations. Such variations suggest that no single judge is consistently aligned with the model's output, highlighting the importance of using multiple judges or an ensemble approach. Another notable observation is that the similarity between reverse-generated question embeddings and the original question embeddings exhibits a strong positive correlation—on average, approximately 489% higher than the correlation observed for the similarity between ground truth and generated answers. This suggests that question-level alignment may additionally offer a more reliable signal for evaluation compared to answer-level alignment. This bodes well for case alignment-based metrics.

Table 3. Correlation analysis of ensemble-of-judges on ALQA and SLSC

Dataset	Model (m)	Sim ($E_A, E_{A'}$)	Unsupervised lexical			Unsupervised ensemble			
			BM25	ROUGE	BLEU	ILR Sim	ILR Error	ILR Align	WILR Align
ALQA	Llama	0.0629	-0.1709	0.5280	0.5519	0.4926	-0.4715	0.9304	**0.9354**
	Gemma	0.1260	-0.2210	0.4131	0.4564	0.4350	-0.4073	0.7397	**0.7540**
	Falcon	-0.2040	-0.2149	-0.1160	-0.1022	0.0824	-0.0792	0.8180	**0.8181**
	Mistral	0.0159	-0.1559	0.2152	0.2376	0.1924	-0.2007	0.8314	**0.8430**
	Avg.	0.0002	-0.1907	0.2601	0.2859	0.3006	-0.2897	0.8299	***0.8376***
SLSC	Llama	0.0318	0.0233	0.4167	0.4346	0.3824	-0.3468	0.8994	**0.9112**
	Gemma	0.1930	-0.0249	0.4801	0.4617	0.4441	-0.4085	0.6600	**0.6729**
	Falcon	-0.1435	-0.1778	-0.0475	-0.0100	-0.1080	0.0829	0.7846	**0.7847**
	Mistral	0.2429	-0.1519	0.0800	0.1414	0.0760	-0.1394	0.8658	**0.8717**
	Avg.	0.0811	-0.0828	0.2323	0.2569	0.1986	-0.2030	0.8025	***0.8101***

Table 3 presents the correlation results for ensemble-based unsupervised metrics. The results indicate that an ensemble-of-judges provides significantly stronger correlations than individual judges (125% higher than the mean of all results in Table 2). In both datasets, the average similarity among individual judges showed no meaningful correlation with the gold standard. Lexical-based methods such as BM25, ROUGE, and BLEU performed the weakest, reinforcing their limitations in capturing deeper semantic relationships. Since these methods formed the foundation of RagChecker [22], our findings suggest they are insufficient for question-answering evaluation.

Conversely, ensemble-based approaches consistently outperformed single-judge methods as seen in Table 2. ILRSim, inspired by RAGAs [7], improved upon lexical methods by using multiple judge LLMs, though it still demonstrated only moderate effectiveness. Its primary limitation lies in its reliance on problem space evaluation, lacking the deeper contextual understanding obtained when both problem and solution spaces are analysed for semantic alignment. Accordingly, our alignment-based measures, particularly WILRAlign, achieved the best results across all evaluations. Fisher's Z-test confirmed that these two methods significantly outperformed all baselines, demonstrating statistically significant correlations ($p < 0.05$).

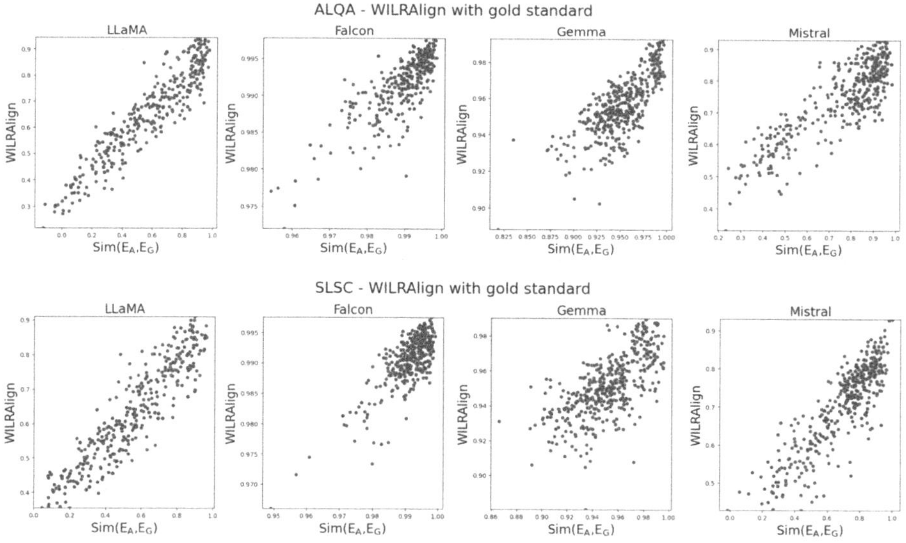

Fig. 5. WILRAlign correlation with gold standard

WILRAlign consistently outperformed ILRAlign due to its similarity-weighted approach, which prioritises semantically relevant alignments and mitigates spurious matches (Eq. 4). In contrast, ILRAlign applies a uniform alignment strategy without semantic prioritisation (Eq. 3). Figure 5 presents eight scatter plots, each showing the correlation between the gold truth-based similarity, $\text{sim}(E_G, E_A)$, values and the WILRAlign-based evaluation scores for the four different LLMs which were used as models on the two datasets. These plots provide a detailed view of how WILRAlign aligns with the gold standard across different model configurations, further reinforcing its effectiveness. These visualisations also confirm that the Llama model performed best as a generating model, likely due to its broader range of similarity variation in embeddings (as seen in Fig. 4). This suggests that WILRAlign's effectiveness is further enhanced when applied to models with richer and more nuanced embedding spaces, reinforcing its robustness in semantic evaluation.

5 Conclusion

In this paper, we introduced an unsupervised ensemble evaluation method for assessing responses generated by LLMs in legal question-answering tasks. Our approach uses multiple general-purpose models as a collective judge, employing a novel application of Case-Based Reasoning through case alignment to estimate response quality in the absence of ground truth. By constructing alignments in both the problem space and solution space, we demonstrated that our similarity-based evaluation metrics outperform traditional lexical metrics and existing unsupervised LLM-as-a-judge baselines. Our experiments using two legal Q&A datasets (Australian Legal QA and Sri Lankan Supreme Court decisions) demonstrated that the similarity-weighted alignment-based metrics, especially WILRAlign, showed the highest correlation with accuracy-based supervised metrics, proving to be an effective, scalable alternative for LLM evaluation. Future work will investigate improved weighting strategies for alignment and the broader application of embeddings in evaluation. We also plan to extend our comparative study to additional datasets and domains to further validate its effectiveness.

References

1. Butler, U.: Open Australian legal QA (2023). https://huggingface.co/datasets/umarbutler/open-australian-legal-qa
2. Chan, C.M., et al.: ChatEval: towards better LLM-based evaluators through multi-agent debate (2023)
3. Chen, B., Zhang, Z., Langrené, N., Zhu, S.: Unleashing the potential of prompt engineering in large language models: a comprehensive review (2024)
4. Choi, J., Yun, J., Jin, K., Kim, Y.: Multi-News+: cost-efficient dataset cleansing via LLM-based data annotation. In: Al-Onaizan, Y., Bansal, M., Chen, Y.N. (eds.) 2024 EMNLP, pp. 15–29. ACL, Miami (2024). https://aclanthology.org/2024.emnlp-main.2/
5. Craw, S., Massie, S., Wiratunga, N.: Informed case base maintenance: a complexity profiling approach. In: AAAI Conference on Artificial Intelligence (2007). https://api.semanticscholar.org/CorpusID:7886047
6. Dong, Q., et al.: A survey on in-context learning. In: Al-Onaizan, Y., Bansal, M., Chen, Y.N. (eds.) 2024 EMNLP, pp. 1107–1128. ACL, Miami (2024). https://aclanthology.org/2024.emnlp-main.64/

7. Es, S., James, J., Espinosa Anke, L., Schockaert, S.: RAGAs: automated evaluation of retrieval augmented generation. In: Aletras, N., De Clercq, O. (eds.) 18th EACL: System Demonstrations, pp. 150–158. ACL, St. Julians (2024). https://aclanthology.org/2024.eacl-demo.16/
8. Fei, Y., Hou, Y., Chen, Z., Bosselut, A.: Mitigating label biases for in-context learning. In: Rogers, A., Boyd-Graber, J., Okazaki, N. (eds.) 61st ACL (Volume 1: Long Papers), pp. 14014–14031. ACL, Toronto (2023). https://aclanthology.org/2023.acl-long.783/
9. Hodson, T., Over, T., Foks, S.: Mean squared error, deconstructed. J. Adv. Model. Earth Syst. **13** (2021)
10. Kim, S., et al.: Prometheus: inducing fine-grained evaluation capability in language models (2024)
11. Lahitani, A.R., Permanasari, A.E., Setiawan, N.A.: Cosine similarity to determine similarity measure: study case in online essay assessment. In: 4th CITSM (2016)
12. Lewis, P., et al.: Retrieval-augmented generation for knowledge-intensive NLP tasks. In: 34th NIPS, NIPS 2020. Curran Associates Inc., Red Hook, NY, USA (2020)
13. Li, H., et al.: LLMs-as-judges: a comprehensive survey on LLM-based evaluation methods (2024)
14. Li, R., Patel, T., Du, X.: PRD: peer rank and discussion improve large language model based evaluations. Trans. Mach. Learn. Res. 2024 (2023). https://api.semanticscholar.org/CorpusID:259360619
15. Liang, S., Zhang, B., Zhao, J., Liu, K.: ABSEval: an agent-based framework for script evaluation. In: Al-Onaizan, Y., Bansal, M., Chen, Y.N. (eds.) 2024 EMNLP, pp. 12418–12434. ACL, Miami (2024). https://aclanthology.org/2024.emnlp-main.691/
16. Lin, C.Y.: ROUGE: a package for automatic evaluation of summaries. In: Text Summarization Branches Out, pp. 74–81. ACL, Barcelona (2004)
17. Massie, S., Wiratunga, N., Craw, S., Donati, A., Vicari, E.: From anomaly reports to cases, pp. 359–373 (2007)
18. Naveed, H., et al.: A comprehensive overview of large language models (2023)
19. Pan, Q., et al.: Human-centered design recommendations for LLM-as-a-judge. In: Soni, N., Flek, L., Sharma, A., Yang, D., Hooker, S., Schwartz, H.A. (eds.) 1st HuCLLM, pp. 16–29. ACL, TBD (2024). https://aclanthology.org/2024.hucllm-1.2/
20. Papineni, K., Roukos, S., Ward, T., Zhu, W.J.: BLEU: a method for automatic evaluation of machine translation. In: 40th ACL, ACL 2002, pp. 311–318. ACL, USA (2002). https://doi.org/10.3115/1073083.1073135
21. Raghunandan, M.A., Wiratunga, N., Chakraborti, S., Massie, S., Khemani, D.: Evaluation measures for TCBR systems. In: Althoff, K.D., Bergmann, R., Minor, M., Hanft, A. (eds.) Advances in Case-Based Reasoning, pp. 444–458. Springer, Berlin (2008)
22. Ru, D., et al.: RAGChecker: a fine-grained framework for diagnosing retrieval-augmented generation (2024)
23. Sedgwick, P.: Pearson's correlation coefficient. BMJ **345**, e4483–e4483 (2012)
24. Shankar, S., Zamfirescu-Pereira, J., Hartmann, B., Parameswaran, A., Arawjo, I.: Who validates the validators? Aligning LLM-assisted evaluation of LLM outputs with human preferences. In: 37th ACM UIST, UIST 2024. ACM, New York (2024). https://doi.org/10.1145/3654777.3676450
25. Tan, S., et al.: JudgeBench: a benchmark for evaluating LLM-based judges (2024)

26. Wiratunga, N., et al.: CBR-RAG: case-based reasoning for retrieval augmented generation in LLMs for legal question answering (2024)
27. Zhao, R., Zhang, W., Chia, Y.K., Xu, W., Zhao, D., Bing, L.: Auto-arena: automating LLM evaluations with agent peer battles and committee discussions (2024)
28. Zheng, L., et al.: Judging LLM-as-a-judge with MT-bench and chatbot arena. In: 37th NIPS, NIPS 2023. Curran Associates Inc., Red Hook, NY, USA (2023)

Visual Question Answering to Generate Case-Based Explanations for Image Classification

Ángel Bastardo-Rojas and Marta Caro-Martínez(✉)

Department of Software Engineering and Artificial Intelligence,
Universidad Complutense de Madrid, Madrid, Spain
{abastard,martcaro}@ucm.es

Abstract. To clarify how artificial intelligence models for image classification obtain their predictions, instance-based explanations give examples of other predictions obtained by those models for similar images. XAI (eXplainable Artificial Intelligence) techniques find those examples by getting images similar to the query using similarity metrics that consider image features. In this work, we introduce a Case-Based Reasoning approach that obtains these types of explanations (explanations by examples and counterfactuals) using Visual Question Answering techniques that take advantage of the high performance achieved by Large Language Models. We have evaluated our approach through an offline evaluation, in a context where images to classify and explain may be low quality. We obtained promising results and confirmed the benefits of using multimodal models in XAI, combining knowledge focused on images and natural language.

1 Introduction

Nowadays, Artificial Intelligence (AI) has been applied in many daily and crucial tasks, such as disease diagnosis, movie recommendations, traffic prediction among others. The AI models used have become more complex in the last few years, with the development of deep learning techniques. The field which helps users understand these complex AI model behaviours is eXplainable Artificial Intelligence (XAI). Making the AI model's prediction more transparent for users also increases the user's trust, making AI techniques more useful too [2,3,9]. One of the most successful explanation types provided by XAI techniques is instance-based explanations [9], called case-based explanations if they are obtained through Case-Based Reasoning (CBR). These types of explanations provide examples of similar situations where the AI model has obtained the same prediction (called factual explanations or explanations by examples) or different predictions (called counterfactual explanations) [9]. To explain image classification, explanations by examples offer similar images that are the same class, while counterfactual explanations provide the user with similar images that are another class. To find the most similar images to a query (the image to explain), the most used similarity metrics are based on the image features [11].

© The Author(s), under exclusive license to Springer Nature Switzerland AG 2025
I. Bichindaritz and B. López (Eds.): ICCBR 2025, LNAI 15662, pp. 37–51, 2025.
https://doi.org/10.1007/978-3-031-96559-3_3

Multimodal models, which are deep learning neural networks that learn representations and make predictions where different data modalities are involved, for example, images and text, are widely used in the literature. Moreover, considering the high performance of new natural language processing algorithms, such as Large Language Models (LLMs) and transformers-based models, applying multimodal models in image processing could also improve the performance in image-related AI tasks [3,7]. Visual Question Answering (VQA) is the task in which AI multimodal models answer questions related to images [3,7] (see an example in Fig. 1). In this work, we propose the use of multimodal models, in particular VQA models, to obtain instance-based explanations, both explanations by examples and counterfactuals in image classification. We hypothesise that, using multimodal models, we can provide better examples for users, also including additional personalised natural language descriptions about the images. To do that, we have developed a case-based post-hoc and model-agnostic explanation method to explain single-class image classification. First, a VQA model is employed to generate the case base: the natural language descriptions of the images. After that, in the retrieval step, textual and semantic similarity metrics are used on the descriptions to find the most similar cases (the explanation cases) to the image to explain. Together with those explanation cases, the method will retrieve their textual descriptions. Finally, in the reuse step, we personalise the explanation by performing a filter that only obtains the textual descriptions that better fit the user's goals.

(a) **Q**: What is the background of the image?; **A**: The background of the image is a pink couch.

(b) **Q**: Is it rainy or sunny?; **A**: It is sunny in the image.

Fig. 1. Example of the LLaVA VQA model [10] answering questions.

To determine whether the method works as we expect and improves the performance of only image-based case-based explanations, we have evaluated it. We conducted an offline evaluation in which we compared the explanation cases obtained by our baseline (using an image-based similarity metric: pixel-to-pixel) and the cases obtained by our method. We measured the difference between the cases and the query: the more similar the explanation cases are to the query, the more useful they are to identify the query class. Moreover, we measured the regions of the images that contribute to understanding the image, so we make sure that we do not lose those regions even when we only use semantic and text-based knowledge to obtain the explanation cases. According to the results obtained, our CBR method improves the instance-based explanations that we can obtain if we use image-based similarity metrics. Furthermore, the personalised description provided with the explanation examples improves the understanding of the explanations, personalising the experience. Therefore, we can conclude that the use of multimodal models in XAI is a promising approach that we should deep dive into in future research.

This paper is organised as follows. In Sect. 2 we discuss some related work about VQA techniques, XAI and instance-based explanations. Section 3 describes our CBR method: the case base generation, the explanation cases retrieval, the similarity metrics that we can use within our method, and the personalised adaptation that the method includes to the explanation. In Sect. 4, we present the evaluation that we have performed and the results obtained. Finally, we end the paper with some conclusions in Sect. 5.

2 Related Work

Instance-based explanations show instances similar to the prediction and help us understand that prediction [16]. When they are implemented through CBR, they are also called case-based explanations. Instance-based explanations are classified into three main groups: factual, counterfactual, and semi-factual explanations [9]. Factual explanations show a similar instance whose prediction is the same as the prediction to be explained. These are often referred to as explanations by examples in the literature. In contrast, counterfactuals are a type of explanation where the similar instance offers a different prediction, so the target users can detect what is required to change the prediction. In contrast, semi-factual explanations offer an instance with the same prediction as the one to explain, but in this case, it includes an even-if statement to clarify that even if some instance's features are modified, the prediction will not change [9]. In general, instance-based explanations are very popular, and there are many works in the literature that dive into this area of research [9]. To explain image classification through instance-based explanations, when finding similar images, the most common approach is to use image-based similarity metrics, which compare image-based features [11]. For example, the work [4] introduces ProtoPNet, an interpretable approach that finds the prototypical parts within the image, and finds similar labelled-images that contain those parts to perform the classification.

There are works in the literature where the effectiveness of adding information to support case-based explanations is proven [6]. There are also works that use natural language modules with this purpose [8]. Visual Question Answering (VQA) is the AI task that answers questions about images [3]. The most recent approaches are based on multimodal models that use LLMs to take advantage of both visual and textual information. There are some works in the literature that used transformer-based models to enhance explainability, for example in the work [12], where an LLM module is used to personalise a natural language explanation provided with a visual explanation in hip fracture classification. In the work [7], the approach proposed introduced counterfactual explanations for VQA models, showing similar images to the query where the answer to the same question is different for both images. There is much future work to carry out personalising explanations through LLMs and CBR [1], where VQA can make an impact due to its huge potential when describing image classification. Previous works have focused on using LLMs to include additional information in the image-based explanations. However, in this paper, we explore the use of VQA techniques to directly generate instance-based explanations themselves for image classification, not only as a support for visual cases.

3 Case-Based Explanation Method

Instance-based explanations, also called case-based explanations when they are obtained using CBR, are considered one of the most successful explanations today, as they fit the user's mental model [9]. In image classification, they show a set of similar images to the query, so the user can see the differences between the images, comparing the class of the query and the classes of the rest of cases. In this work, we focus on factual explanations (explanations by examples), and counterfactual explanations, since they are the most popular in the literature. Factual explanations in image classification provide similar images to the query, considering that these images need to be the same class as the query class. In counterfactuals explanations for image classification, the similar images have to be a different class from the query class. To obtain the similar images, instance-based explanation methods use image-based similarity metrics, such as pixel-to-pixel, one of the most popular ones.

The case-based explanation method proposed in this work aims to take advantage of natural language processing approaches and their current high performance when obtaining case-based explanations in image classification. First, the method translates the images into a text that describes it. This task is the main one to carry out when building our method's case base. The success of our method lies in obtaining a complete and accurate description of the images. To perform this task, we employ VQA models. Then, our method uses text-based or semantic-based similarity metrics to find the explanation cases, i.e. the similar images to the query. This task is performed during the retrieval step. Our hypothesis is that the explanation cases should be more useful for the target users to understand the image classification because our method should find more accurate similarities between images when using textual descriptions. The method leverages both CBR and VQA, combining them to find relevant explanations and drive their quality. Finally, we carry out the reuse step. In this step, we personalise the explanation: we allow XAI practitioners to decide what their explanation main goal is. According to that, the case-based explanation method will support the explanation cases showing to the user the knowledge, obtained by the VQA model, related to this explanation goal. It is important to note that our explanation method is post-hoc and model-agnostic, since all the CBR process carried out is independent of the AI model process that generated the prediction. In Fig. 2, we show an overview of the process executed by the case-based explanation method.

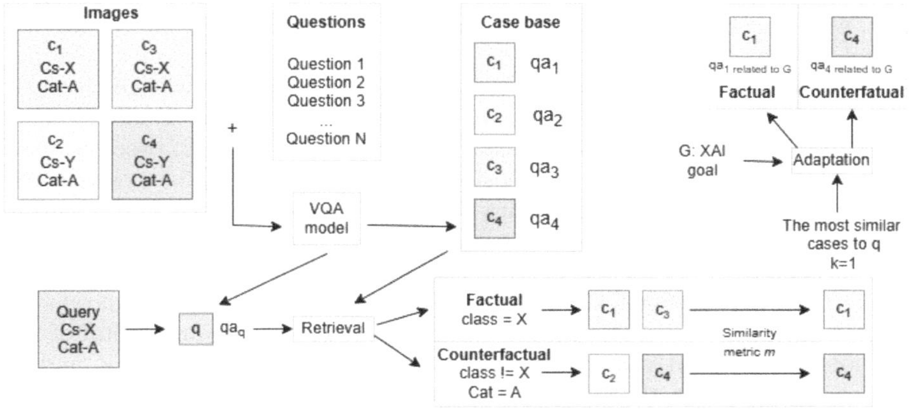

Fig. 2. Overview of the VQA case-based explanation method. *Cs* denotes class, *Cat*, category, and *qa*, descriptions that contain pairs of questions and answers.

In the following subsections, we detail the whole process: how we create the case base (Sect. 3.1), how we retrieve the explanation cases (Sect. 3.2), and how we adapt the explanation to personalise it (Sect. 3.3).

3.1 The VQA-Based Case Base

Our main goal when building the case base for our method was to obtain a complete description of the cases (images) in text format. We needed to take into account that the description has to be as detailed as possible. It has to include a description of the prediction, but also, the context, background, luminosity details, colours, descriptions of other less important elements in the picture, or the interactions between the elements. However, not all questions can be asked for all the images. We have to consider that there are different types of entities in images and that in single-class images there is one main entity. In general, we can find four different main entities: humans, animals, objects, and landscapes. Depending on these types of entities, we can ask specific questions about an image. For example, if there is a person in the image, we need to ask about the person who appears in the image's gender and age. If there are many people, we should ask whether they are interacting. If the main entity in the image is an object, we should not consider such questions. Therefore, we will have some general questions to ask on all the cases, but other questions that should be asked only when the type of the image requires it.

Moreover, we wanted to include knowledge about explanation features and goals discussed in the literature: debugging, effectiveness, efficiency, trust, persuasiveness, satisfaction, education, and transparency [2]. The reason behind the addition of this knowledge is to help users understand the prediction better. For example, to improve the XAI education goal we can ask "Can you give essential concepts that are relevant to the situation described?", and to improve users' trust, we can ask "Is there anything that might create doubt or uncertainty for you to say they are {class}?".

For these reasons, the questions' purpose is to obtain knowledge that: (1) describes what elements are shown in the image, for example, "Does the main entity in the image have any elements that characterise it?"; (2) describes how the image is shown (colours, luminosity, and image quality), for example, "Is the image bright?"; and (3) describes the image in terms of explanation goals-related knowledge, for example, "Do you focus on parts of the {class} to infer that the main entity in the image is a {class}?". The final set of questions used in our method are predefined and they were formulated through expert knowledge. The complete set of questions is available on GitHub[1]. There are a total of 220 questions to build our case base, however we only consider between 45 and 60 of those depending on the type of images that we need to explain.

Therefore, we used a VQA model to generate detailed descriptions of the cases within our case base. We asked the model the set of questions, obtaining a detailed textual description of every image. The structure of the cases in the case base C is as follows:

$$\forall c_i \in C \rightarrow c_i = \langle D_i, S_i \rangle$$

c_i represents a case in our case base. D_i (description) represents an image i and its class obtained with an AI model. S (solution) represents the explanation to show the target user to explain that classification.

The formalisation of the description for a case c_i in our case base is as follows:

$$D_i = \langle r_i, cs_i, cat_i, qa_i \rangle$$

where r_i is the visual representation of the case (i.e. the image itself); cs_i is the class predicted by the AI model for the image; $cat_i \in \{human, animal, object, landscape\}$ is the category of the class; and $qa_i = \{(qu_k, a_k), ..., (qu_j, a_j)\}$ is the set of question & answer tuples that describe the image in a text format. The questions $\{qu_k, ..., qu_j\}$ are those asked to the VQA model, which is going to generate the answers.

Alternatively, the formalisation of the solution is the following:

$$S_i = \langle ec_i, t_i \rangle$$

where ec_i is the set of explanation cases obtained in the retrieval step (Sect. 3.2), and t_i is the personalised textual explanation that supports the explanation cases, obtained in the reuse step (Sect. 3.3).

[1] https://github.com/angelldavidd/Trabajo/blob/main/Preguntas.md.

3.2 Retrieving Explanation Cases

To perform the retrieval step, we start from the case base C and our query q (the image to explain). Every case $c_i \in C$ is denoted as $c_i = \langle(r_i, cs_i, cat_i, qa_i), (ec_i, t_i)\rangle$. q has an image representation r_q classified as the class cs_q in the category cat_q. Its translation into a natural language representation using a VQA model is denoted as qa_q, i.e. the set of questions and their corresponding answers that describe the image q. In the retrieval step, we are going to perform a MAC/FAC (many-are-called, few-are-chosen) schema, well known in the literature about CBR [5]. The first step is the *filtering step* (MAC) where we are going to select the cases in the case base C that can be explanation cases. Depending on the type of explanation that we want to show, this condition will change. If we want to retrieve explanation by examples, in this filter, the method will select those cases where $cs_i = cs_q$: the class of the explanation cases have to be the same as the class of the query. On the contrary, if we need to obtain counterfactual explanations, the filtering step will perform the condition $cs_i! = cs_q \& cat_i = cat_q$. Therefore, the method is going to retrieve, as explanations, those images in the case base that do not share their class with the query, but do share their category with the query. This step is formalised as follows:

$$f_q = filter(q, C, expType) = \forall c_i \in C : \begin{cases} cs_i = cs_q, & \text{if } expType = factual \\ cs_i! = cs_q \& cat_i = cat_q, & \text{if } expType = cFactual \end{cases}$$

After the MAC step, we carry out the *sorting step* (FAC). In this step, we apply similarity metrics to obtain the k most similar cases to q from f_q.

$$ec_q = first(sorting(q, f_q), k)$$
$$sorting(q, f_q) = \{c_i, \ldots, c_j \in f_q \mid s_{qi} \geq s_{qj}, \forall c_k \in f_q : s_{qk} = sim_m(q, c_k, m)\}$$

where $first(set, k)$ is a function that returns the first k elements in the set, and $sim_m()$ is a function that returns the similarity score between q and the case c_k using the similarity metric m. Since our method describes the cases through textual knowledge, we have proposed both text-based and semantic similarity metrics as the metric m to be used in our approach. The **text-based similarity** metrics that our method uses are the following [15]:

Levenshtein distance. Measures the number of insertions, deletions, and substitutions needed to transform one text into another.

Cosine similarity. This metric transforms the text into vectors of words and gets a score computing the angle that is formed with those two vectors.

Overlap coefficient or Szymkiewicz–Simpson coefficient. Returns a score calculated as the number of common tokens that both texts contain divided by the number of tokens that the shortest text has.

Bag distance. Takes into account the number of appearances of different words in both texts without considering their order. As a result, it gives the biggest difference between the number of times that the words appear in both texts.

Jaccard. Defines the similarity between two sentences as the intersection of words divided by the union of the words. When the sentences are remarkably long, the similarity tends to be smaller.

Note that the values obtained with the distances need to be transformed to similarity values before obtaining the similar cases to the query. Regarding the **semantic similarity metrics**, we used two different implementations that use pre-trained BERT models:

Web similarity[2]. An interface that makes use of fine-tuned BERT models to find similarities between texts. It is specially focused on text that can be found on the web.

SBERT [13][3]. SBERT is a sentence transformers that uses transformers-based models like BERT, RoBERTa, or XLM-RoBERTa to compute dense vector representations for sentences, paragraphs, and images. Among other tasks, it allows to find similarities between texts.

As a result from the retrieval step, the method has found the explanation cases ec_q to show the target user as factual explanations or counterfactuals. In the next section, we define how the method supports these cases through a personalised text.

3.3 Personalisation Through the Reuse Step

Once we have our explanation examples ec_q, we can create explanations by examples or counterfactuals. However, we cannot always access good quality images: we might encounter situations when we need to classify images that are blurred, pixelated or have noise. For example, when capturing images through IoT (Internet of Things) sensors or cameras: when the camera resolution is low, the lightning is poor, the weather affects the image capturing, or there are limitations in bandwidth or storage. In these contexts, it is even more important to obtain enriched explanations that help users understand the classification and clarify what entities appear in the images, as well as the AI behaviours. The reuse step in our method aims to enhance the explanation cases ec_q with a text t_i. The method will show a textual explanation $te_i \in t_i$ for every explanation case $c_i \in ec_q$. The explanation te_i is a personalised portion of text from the description kept in the case base for the case c_i. This initial description contained the answers $a_i \in qa_i \in D_i$ that the VQA model generated in response to the questions $qu_i \in qa_i \in D_i$. To personalise this description, the XAI design user will indicate to the method what their purposes are regarding the explanation that they need to achieve. The method will filter the initial answers, choosing only the ones that answer the questions related to that XAI goal. The XAI goals defined in the reuse step are the well-known XAI goals in the literature, the same used to build the case base already discussed in Sect. 3.1. For example, if the XAI

[2] https://pypi.org/project/semantic-text-similarity/.

[3] https://pypi.org/project/sentence-transformers/.

design user needs to persuade the end users on the AI model's image classification decision, then the method will show the answers to the questions related to the persuasiveness goal. The XAI design user can also say to the method whether to show the questions related to the image features. The formalisation of this operation is as follows:

$$\begin{aligned} te_i &= adapt(G, iFeat, c_i) \\ adapt(G, iFeat, c_i) &= questionsG(G, c_i) \cup questionsIF(iFeat, c_i) \\ questionsG(G, c_i) &= \{a_{ij}, ..., a_{ik} \in qa_i \mid type(qa_i) = G\} \\ questionsIF(iFeat, c_i) &= \{a_{ij}, ..., a_{ik} \in qa_i \mid type(qa_i) = IF \text{ and } iFeat = True\} \end{aligned}$$

where G is the goal that the design user wants to achieve; $iFeat$ is a boolean value to indicate whether the design user wants the method to show the answers related to image features ($True$) or not ($False$); $c_i \in ec_q$ is an explanation case; and $type()$, a function that returns the question & answer qa_i type, which can be an XAI goal, or IF if qa_i is related to image features. An example of a resulting explanation obtained with our method within an IoT problem is shown in Fig. 3.

(a) Query classified as "cow".

(b) Explanation example.

The black and white pattern on the cow's body is a distinctive feature of cows and is not commonly seen in other animals. Additionally, the cow is standing in a grassy field, which is a typical environment for cows. The combination of these visual clues and the context of the image leads to the conclusion that the livestock are indeed cows.

Fig. 3. Example of a factual explanation obtained with our approach for a pixelated image. The image on the left is the one classified by a black-box model, while the image on the right is the factual explanation example obtained with our approach. The text below is the natural language explanation adapted to the efficiency goal (which helps users decide rapidly if the classification is correct). This text is shown with the explanation example in (b).

4 Evaluation

With the evaluation, we aimed to assess if the explanation cases obtained with our VQA and case-based method are useful for explaining image classification, and if using multimodal models can enhance the explainability of the cases retrieved. Our hypothesis was that the explanation cases obtained with our method would be more similar to the query than cases obtained with an approach that only takes image features into account. If they are more similar, users will understand better the classification predicted by an AI black-box model. Our evaluation consisted of two parts. First, we compared the similarity between a query and the explanation cases obtained with our method, and the cases obtained with a baseline: a case-based approach that uses the pixel-to-pixel similarity metric. Second, we compared the quality of the important parts of the image that help understand the classification of the cases retrieved by both approaches. For the cases obtained with our approach to be useful, we expected the quality of their important parts would not be lower than the quality of the image parts obtained with the baseline. Therefore, we can provide better explanation cases without losing the important parts in the image that help recognise the classification only using textual knowledge. The code and the results generated during the evaluation are available on GitHub[4]. In the following sections, we describe the dataset used (Sect. 4.1), the evaluation metrics employed (Sect. 4.2), the experimental setup (Sect. 4.3), and the results obtained (Sect. 4.4).

4.1 Dataset

The dataset chosen to perform the evaluation was the CIFAR-100 dataset[5]. The reason behind this choice is two fold: (1) the dataset contains a wide variety of images that can be classified using the entity categories human, animal, object, or landscape, which are required to ask the specific questions to build the case base; and (2) the images in the dataset are pixelated. Although our method can be used for all types of images, we wanted to use a dataset of low-quality ones to simulate the issues that could happen when IoT sensors capture such data. The CIFAR-100 dataset is a single-class dataset that contains 6K 32×32 colour images: 600 images for 100 classes each. These classes are varied and specific, such as dolphin, girl, clock, or forest, among others. Moreover, every image belongs to a superclass, which includes the previous classes. For example, dolphin is included in the "aquatic mammals" class, girl is in "people", clock in "household electrical devices", and forest in "large natural outdoor scenes". We used the superclass to assign the entity categories (human, object, animal, or landscape) required by our approach. This way, the method can ask and answer the questions defined in our method for each of these categories. We selected 250 images for each of these categories to create the dataset used in our evaluation.

4.2 Evaluation Metrics

As a result of the evaluation, for a given query, we obtain k explanation cases from every configuration of our method, and k explanation cases from the app-

[4] https://github.com/angelldavidd/Trabajo/tree/main.
[5] https://www.cs.toronto.edu/~kriz/cifar.html.

roach using the pixel-to-pixel similarity metric. We have used two different evaluation metrics: RMSE to assess the similarity between the cases and the query that they explain, and ROAD to assess the quality regions in the images that help recognise the image class:

Root Mean Square Error (RMSE). Returns a score that shows the difference between the query and the case in terms of their pixels: it calculates the difference between each pixel in both images. It is defined as follows:

$$RMSE = \sqrt{\frac{1}{N}\sum_{i=1}^{N}(Q_i - c_{j_i})^2}$$

where Q_i represents the value of the pixel i in the query Q image, c_{j_i} represents the value of the pixel i in the explanation case c_j, and N is the total number of pixels within the images.

Remove and Debias (ROAD) [14]. This metric retrieves a score that indicates how important some regions in an image are to understand the image class. The metric requires transforming the images into heatmaps, we performed this transformation using the XAI model Grad-CAM. From a heatmap, ROAD darkens the most important parts in the image, assessing the prediction obtained when hiding those important parts. The higher the ROAD score is, the more important the hidden zones are, i.e., the more helpful the regions in the image are to understand the image class.

4.3 Experimental Setup

We started the experiment from our dataset of 1,000 images, 250 for each category (human, animal, object, landscape). Furthermore, each of those images retained the specific class that they had in the original CIFAR dataset, for example dolphin, baby, or clock. The first step was to generate the case base. To create it, we applied LLaVA (Large Language-and-Vision Assistant) [10], an open-source conversational AI model that has been fine-tuned on GPT-generated data. LLaVA was designed to follow instructions in both text and images, using LLaMA/Vicuna as its foundation. For every image in our dataset, we asked LLaVA to answer the predefined questions that we described in Sect. 3.1, considering the image category. As a result, we saved all those images in the case base, along with their descriptions: the image itself, its class and category (both obtained from the CIFAR dataset), and the pairs of questions and answers, with the answers generated by LLaVA. The next step was to find the explanations by examples and counterfactuals for every image by performing a leave-one-evaluation. To find both types of explanations we used the similarity metrics described in Sect. 3.2, which use the pairs of questions and answers to find the similarity scores[6]. Moreover, we also calculated the similarity values obtained

[6] The implementation of the text-based metrics were carried out with the TextDistance library: https://pypi.org/project/textdistance/, while the semantic-based metrics were implemented with the libraries mentioned in Sect. 3.2.

with the baseline approach: the pixel-to-pixel similarity metric[7]. This metric only used the pixels in the image to obtain the explanation cases, without considering the question and answer pairs that describe the image. For every image in the case base, we obtained k explanations by examples and k counterfactuals, where $k \in [1, 2, 3]$. Once we had the explanatory cases, we calculated RMSE and ROAD. For $k \in [2, 3]$, the RMSE and ROAD values are the mean calculated from the individual values. Since the ROAD values can be negative, we normalised them to interpret them better. To make both RMSE and ROAD results more understandable, we calculated the percentages of improvement of our method compared to the baseline. The results are shown and discussed in the next section.

Table 1. Results obtained in the evaluation (the best results in bold). M denotes the metric used: Bag distance (B), cosine (C), Jaccard (J), Levenshtein (L), Overlap (O), SBERT (SB), Web similarity (WS), or pixel-to-pixel (P2P). ET denotes the explanation type: factual (F), or counterfactual (CF). The symbol % denotes the percentage of improvement of our approach compared to the baseline.

		RMSE						Normalised ROAD					
		K1		K2		K3		K1		K2		K3	
M	ET	Value	%	Value	%	Value	%	Value	%	Value	%	Value	%
B	F	93.00	28.63	92.01	27.47	91.53	26.02	0.86	5.57	0.86	1.70	0.86	0.02
C	F	85.88	34.35	85.95	32.43	86.21	30.40	0.87	6.93	**0.88**	**3.91**	**0.87**	**2.30**
J	F	85.29	34.76	85.38	32.85	**85.92**	**30.65**	0.87	7.31	0.88	3.88	0.87	2.15
L	F	85.94	34.36	86.39	32.13	86.64	30.12	**0.88**	**7.62**	0.88	3.73	0.87	2.11
O	F	85.58	34.48	86.77	31.78	86.97	29.76	0.87	6.49	0.87	3.08	0.87	1.50
SB	F	**84.46**	**35.35**	**85.36**	**32.96**	86.15	30.58	0.87	7.04	0.87	3.52	0.87	2.04
WS	F	84.37	35.33	85.49	32.79	86.11	30.58	0.87	6.76	0.87	3.49	0.87	1.87
P2P	F	131.75	-	128.05	-	124.74	-	0.84	-	0.85	-	0.86	-
B	CF	94.32	33.49	94.13	32.72	94.37	31.72	0.84	0.57	0.84	-1.62	0.84	-2.09
C	CF	92.45	34.70	92.77	33.51	92.95	32.63	0.88	5.51	0.88	2.65	0.88	1.89
J	CF	92.07	34.99	92.92	33.46	93.14	32.49	0.88	5.66	0.88	2.49	0.87	1.82
L	CF	92.99	34.39	93.26	33.33	93.31	32.54	0.88	6.13	**0.88**	**3.24**	**0.88**	**2.45**
O	CF	92.04	35.17	92.75	33.70	93.01	32.71	0.87	4.11	0.87	1.86	0.87	1.31
SB	CF	90.97	36.02	91.75	34.48	92.58	33.14	**0.88**	**6.18**	0.88	2.95	0.88	2.32
WS	CF	**90.49**	**36.31**	**91.12**	**34.92**	**92.34**	**33.29**	0.87	4.17	0.87	1.34	0.86	0.61
P2P	CF	142.54	-	140.58	-	138.90	-	0.85	-	0.86	-	0.86	-

[7] Implemented with the Pillow library: https://pillow.readthedocs.io/en/stable/reference/ImageChops.html.

4.4 Results

Table 1 shows the results obtained in the evaluation using RMSE and ROAD to compare the quality of the explanation cases retrieved by our approach and the baseline. Regarding the RMSE values, we can see that our approach improves the baseline for every configuration studied. Overall, the similarity metrics that obtain the best results are the semantic-based similarity metrics. SBERT achieves the best score for the factual explanations when we retrieve $k = [1, 2]$ cases, with the highest score being 84.46 (for $k = 1$, with a 35.35% improvement over the baseline). Web similarity achieves the best score for every k value when retrieving counterfactual explanations. In this case, the best score is obtained again when $k = 1$ (90.49 with 36.31% of improvement) outperforming the scores for $k \in [2, 3]$. These results support the utility of semantics when retrieving explanation cases. The meaning of the text that describes the images is crucial for obtaining the most similar cases to the query. The exception occurs when retrieving $k = 3$ factual explanation cases, when the best score is achieved using the Jaccard similarity metric (85.92 with a 30.65% of improvement). Nevertheless, SBERT and Web similarity follow closely, achieving very similar scores. In general, we can conclude that the improvement percentage is always above 30%, which indicates that our approach improves the baseline's performance by approximately one-third. For every configuration, the worst improvement is found when we obtain $k = 3$ explanation cases, which was the expected behaviour, since the more explanation cases we need, the more difficult is for the approach to find suitable similar cases. It is also noticeable that our approach offers better explanation cases when providing factual explanations than when providing counterfactuals. The RMSE values are lower when we obtain explanations by examples, although the difference with the RMSE obtained when getting counterfactuals is not very remarkable. However, our approach shows a greater improvement over the baseline when retrieving counterfactuals than when obtaining explanations by examples.

Regarding the normalised ROAD values, we can notice that all the values are very similar for any configuration. This might be due to the fact that all images in the dataset are pixelated, so it is more difficult for ROAD to find the most important regions in the images. Therefore, we can conclude that explanation cases retrieved by any approach when images are of low quality (for example, in the IoT domain) are going to be less effective than in other situations with higher quality images. Nevertheless, we can also conclude that our approach achieves retrieving explanation cases with slightly more important regions than the baseline. In most cases, the percentage of improvement of our approach over the baseline is positive, except obtaining counterfactuals using the bag distance when $k = [2, 3]$ (the percentages of improvement are -1.62% and -2.09%, respectively). This behaviour may be happening because features that bag distance does not consider like the order, meaning or frequency of the words or the size of the text in this context is essential. Moreover, when analysing the normalised values of ROAD, we can observe that the semantic-based similarity metrics are not the ones that achieve the best results as clearly as when we analysed the

RMSE values. To retrieve factual explanation cases, the Levenshtein distance is the best one when $k = 1$ (7.62% of improvement), and cosine when $k = [2, 3]$ (3.91% and 2.30%, respectively). To retrieve counterfactuals, the best similarity metric is SBERT when $k = 1$ (6.18% of improvement), but Levenshtein is again the best one when $k = [2, 3]$ (3.24% and 2.45%, respectively).

In summary, we can confirm that our approach obtains more accurate similar cases, both for factual and counterfactual explanations, compared to an image-based approach, thus improving the understanding of image classification. Those cases also include slightly more useful regions in the images, which improves the explanation quality over the baseline. Semantic-based similarity metrics have proven to be among the best approaches for retrieving explanation cases. Together with the fact that the text generated by the VQA model can be used to personalise the explanation cases regarding the users' goals, this work opens the door to achieve promising results when employing multimodal models in XAI for image-related AI tasks. In future work, our aim is to carry out a user study in which we will validate the usability of the complete explanations offered by our method.

5 Conclusions

In this work, we have proposed the use of VQA models as a technique to implement an XAI method for image classification. When implementing case-based explanations for image classification, the most common approach is to employ image-based similarity metrics to obtain the explanation cases. Our XAI method enriches this approach, leveraging LLM-based VQA multimodal models and CBR to offer explanations by examples and counterfactuals for single-class image classification. VQA is used to describe the cases, while text-based and semantic-based similarity metrics are used to retrieve the explanation cases. In the reuse step, the method filters the textual knowledge generated by the VQA model considering the XAI objective to achieve. By performing that adaptation, the method shows users a personalised textual explanation that supports the explanation cases. According to the results obtained in the evaluation, the method enhances the understanding of the AI model's behaviour in predicting the image class. It obtains better explanation cases than an image-based approach while maintaining the same quality of regions in the image to help understand the classification. The method achieves these results only using textual knowledge instead of visual information. Therefore, this work and its results encourage further research on the use of multimodal models in XAI for visual-related AI tasks.

Acknowledgements. Supported by the SHOW-X project funded by the Comunidad de Madrid through the UCM, the AUDITIA-X project PID2023-150566OB-I00 funded by MCIN/AEI/10.13039/501100011033, and the SI4/PJI/2024-00032 project funded by the Comunidad de Madrid through the UAM.

References

1. Bach, K., Bergmann, R., Brand, F., Caro-Martínez, M., et al.: Case-based reasoning meets large language models: a research manifesto for open challenges and research directions (2025)
2. Caro-Martínez, M., Jiménez-Díaz, G., Recio-García, J.A.: Conceptual modeling of explainable recommender systems: an ontological formalization to guide their design and development. J. Artif. Intell. Res. **71**, 557–589 (2021)
3. Caro-Martinez, M., Wijekoon, A., Diaz-Agudo, B., Recio-Garcia, J.A.: The current and future role of visual question answering in explainable artificial intelligence. In: CEUR Workshop Proceedings (2023)
4. Chen, C., Li, O., Tao, D., Barnett, A., Rudin, C., Su, J.K.: This looks like that: deep learning for interpretable image recognition. In: Advances in Neural Information Processing Systems, vol. 32 (2019)
5. De Mantaras, R.L., et al.: Retrieval, reuse, revision and retention in case-based reasoning. Knowl. Eng. Rev. **20**(3), 215–240 (2005)
6. Gates, L., Leake, D., Wilkerson, K.: Cases are king: a user study of case presentation to explain CBR decisions. In: International Conference on Case-Based Reasoning, pp. 153–168. Springer (2023)
7. Goyal, Y., Khot, T., Summers-Stay, D., Batra, D., Parikh, D.: Making the V in VQA matter: elevating the role of image understanding in visual question answering. In: Proceedings of the IEEE Conference on Computer Vision and Pattern Recognition, pp. 6904–6913 (2017)
8. Hendricks, L.A., Hu, R., Darrell, T., Akata, Z.: Generating counterfactual explanations with natural language. In: ICML Workshop on Human Interpretability in Machine Learning, pp. 95–98 (2018)
9. Kenny, E.M., Keane, M.T.: On generating plausible counterfactual and semi-factual explanations for deep learning. In: Proceedings of the AAAI Conference on Artificial Intelligence, vol. 35, pp. 11575–11585 (2021)
10. Liu, H., Li, C., Wu, Q., Lee, Y.J.: Visual instruction tuning. In: Advances in Neural Information Processing Systems, vol. 36 (2024)
11. Parejas-Llanovarced, H., Caro-Martínez, M., Orozco-del Castillo, M.G., Recio-García, J.A.: Case-based selection of explanation methods for neural network image classifiers. Knowl.-Based Syst. **288**, 111469 (2024)
12. Queipo-De-Llano, E., Ciurcau, M., Paz-Olalla, A., Díaz-Agudo, B., Recio-Garcia, J.: Explainable classification system for hip fractures: a hybrid CBR + LLM surrogate approach. In: CEUR Workshop Proceedings, vol. 3708, pp. 65–80 (2024)
13. Reimers, N., Gurevych, I.: Sentence-BERT: sentence embeddings using siamese BERT-network. In: Proceedings of the 2019 Conference on Empirical Methods in Natural Language Processing. Association for Computational Linguistics (2019)
14. Rong, Y., Leemann, T., Borisov, V., Kasneci, G., Kasneci, E.: A consistent and efficient evaluation strategy for attribution methods. arXiv preprint arXiv:2202.00449 (2022)
15. Wang, J., Dong, Y.: Measurement of text similarity: a survey. Information **11**(9), 421 (2020)
16. Yadav, C., Chaudhuri, K.: Behavior of k-NN as an instance-based explanation method. In: Joint European Conference on Machine Learning and Knowledge Discovery in Databases, pp. 90–96. Springer (2021)

Integrating Case-Based Reasoning with LLM for Expense Fraud Detection

Xiaoyu Ge[1,2(✉)] and Jiao Xu[1,3]

[1] CVTE Research, Guangzhou, China
xujiao@cvte.com
[2] The Australian National University, Canberra, Australia
xiaoyu.ge@anu.edu.au
[3] Xidian University, Xi'an, China

Abstract. Organizations face major challenges in detecting employee expense fraud because of scarce data, intricate fraud patterns, and the requirement for explainable results. This paper implements a novel application that integrates Case-Based Reasoning (CBR) with Large Language Models (LLMs) to address these challenges. Our system represents expense activities as spatiotemporal events, uses LLMs to generate fraud detection rules within a constrained function space, and applies CBR to retrieve similar cases, minimize hallucinations, and improve explainability. The system implements a complete CBR cycle—retrieve similar fraud patterns, reuse detection rules, revise rules through LLM interaction, and retain verified cases. We evaluated the system with more than 200,000 real-world expense events and the results show that the integration of CBR with LLMs effectively constrains hallucinations while generating high-quality, explainable fraud detection rules. This approach offers a practical solution for applying AI in high-stakes domains requiring reliability and explainability.

Keywords: Case-Based Reasoning · Large Language Models · Fraud Detection · Explainable AI · Generative AI

1 Introduction

Expense fraud causes substantial economic losses for organisations, with the Association of Certified Fraud Examiners estimating annual losses at approximately 5% of organisational revenue [5] which translates to an estimated $5 trillion in fraud losses annually. These financial impacts demand effective detection methods, yet several challenges complicate identification and prevention. The ACFE reports [4] that typical fraud schemes continue undetected for approximately 12–18 months before discovery, with expense reimbursement fraud being particularly persistent, underscoring the urgency of addressing this specific type of corporate fraud. In this paper, we focus on employee expense fraud, which involves false or inflated expense claims submitted by employees for reimbursement, rather than addressing all types of corporate fraud.

Expense fraud detection faces several key problems: First, true fraud cases are rare among all expenses which makes it hard for AI to learn patterns from

© The Author(s), under exclusive license to Springer Nature Switzerland AG 2025
I. Bichindaritz and B. López (Eds.): ICCBR 2025, LNAI 15662, pp. 52–66, 2025.
https://doi.org/10.1007/978-3-031-96559-3_4

limited examples. Second, unlike traditional financial transaction fraud which deals with discrete banking events, expense fraud occurs across different types, locations, and times of expenses with varying data precision and granularity, making simple rules ineffective. When a system finds possible fraud, it must give explanations that people can understand, backed by supporting evidence. Also, those committing fraud continuously change their tactics to avoid detection, which means fraud detection systems must constantly adapt and improve. Traditional methods have significant limitations: rule-based systems are explainable but struggle with new patterns, machine learning approaches prioritise accuracy over transparency, and LLMs show potential but face concerns about hallucination and reliability.

In this paper, we combine CBR with LLMs to address these challenges in expense fraud detection. CBR provides a structure for learning from past fraud cases while maintaining transparency, while LLMs contribute pattern recognition and rule-generation capabilities. The CBR component both provides domain knowledge and constrains LLM hallucinations through case-based verification, which addresses a key limitation in using Generative AI for high-stakes applications. Our system represents expense activities as spatiotemporal events with explicit uncertainty modeling. Each expense transaction (e.g., taxi rides, hotel stays) includes location information, time intervals with earliest/latest bounds, and domain-specific attributes. This representation helps identify impossible activity patterns (indicating fraud), such as being in two distant locations simultaneously or claiming expenses without the corresponding travel records.

Our implementation includes a complete CBR cycle with LLM integration at key points. In the retrieval phase, the system uses embeddings that capture relationships between events to find similar historical fraud cases. The reuse phase applies detection rules from similar cases to new expense events. When existing rules fail, such as missing suspicious patterns or incorrectly flagging legitimate expenses, the revision phase uses LLM to generate or modify rules based on observed events and domain knowledge. The retention phase adds verified cases with their detection rules to the knowledge base after validation.

Evaluation on more than 200,000 real-world expense events shows that our integrated approach effectively constrains LLM hallucinations while generating explainable fraud detection rules. By using both function-level constraints and case-based verification, the system harnesses LLMs' capabilities while maintaining the reliability needed for financial applications.

2 Related Work

Fraud detection typically employs supervised methods with labeled datasets and unsupervised anomaly detection [6]. Traditional approaches include rule-based systems and manual audits [8], but these struggle with class imbalance where only 0.1% of records are fraudulent, leading to costly false positives [6]. While supervised models like neural networks can capture complex patterns [2], they require labeled examples and face limitations with diverse expense data spanning multiple event types with spatiotemporal relations. Unlike financial transaction fraud which focuses on discrete banking events, expense fraud detection involves analyzing complex relationships across various activities with differing data formats and contextual significance, making many traditional fraud detection methods inadequate.

Case-Based Reasoning offers transparency and learning from historical cases, with its retrieve-reuse-revise-retain cycle aligning well with fraud detection workflows [7]. CBR provides explainable decisions through intuitive precedents while reducing the knowledge engineering effort [1], though it suffers from data scarcity and uncertainty [1]. Graph-based methods address hidden fraud [16], but require graph relationships not always available in expense systems.

Recently, Large Language Models have shown promise in financial fraud detection, providing reasoning in human-friendly terms [13]. However, they face challenges with hallucination in high-stakes domains like fraud auditing. Recent work proposes integrating LLMs with CBR, leveraging episodic knowledge from concrete past cases [10,12]. Studies show that LLMs with access to past cases significantly improve problem solving accuracy compared to standalone approaches [14]. Other combined approaches include Deep Symbolic Classification [11] and CBR-RAG [15].

Our work builds upon these foundations by integrating CBR with LLMs, using LLMs to generate and discover fraud detection rules that overcome CBR's limitations. This approach combines CBR's transparent reasoning with LLMs' generative capabilities, creating a robust system that adapts to evolving fraud techniques while maintaining explainability.

3 Problem Statement

Employee expense fraud is defined as physically impossible activities in expense reports or activities that violate company expense policy. In our domain, an employee will seek reimbursement for various activities: transportation such as flights, railway, taxi, and driving (fuelling a car), accommodation such as hotels. In addition, employees are required to perform daily check-ins for business activities where the location and the date of the business visit will be recorded.

We model each expense activity as a spatiotemporal event defined as a tuple: $E = e_1, e_2, \ldots, e_n$ where each $e_i = (type_i, l_i, t_i, u_i, id_i, amount_i, S_i)$ contains the event type $type_i$ (taxi, hotel, etc.), location information l_i with varying levels of precision (city and/or specific address), time interval t_i represented as a quadruple (earliest_start, latest_start, earliest_end, latest_end) to capture temporal uncertainty, user/employee ID u_i, unique event identifier id_i, expense amount $amount_i$ (when applicable), and additional event-specific attributes S_i.

The time interval representation allows us to model different levels of temporal precision. For example, we know exact start/end times for taxi rides, flights, and fueling events, but for other events we may only know the date, so the earliest start and latest start are defined as one minute after the beginning and one minute before the end of the day, respectively.

Similarly, we have varying levels of location certainty. We know the exact addresses for taxi pick-up/drop-off points and hotel locations, while for other events we may only know the city where the event occurs.

In our system, fraud cases are represented as 6-tuples: $C = \{c_1, c_2, \ldots, c_m\}$ where each $c_j = (v_j, E_j, r_j, V_j, A_j, s_j)$ includes a vector embedding representation v_j for similarity-based retrieval, a set of events E_j involved in the fraud pattern (primary events and context), a detection rule reference r_j that follows the naming convention FD-EventType-Pattern corresponding to the Python implementation that identifies this fraud pattern, violation details V_j with structured evidence about the specific company policies or logical constraints violated, recommended actions A_j or previously taken measures to address this type of fraud, and a case status s_j (new, verified, false positive).

Figure 1 presents an example case from our system, illustrating how these components are instantiated in practice for a multi-city taxi use pattern without any intercity transportation records. Multiple cases in our case base may be detected by the same rule (as in Fig. 1). Cases store references to rules rather than duplicating them, enabling efficient storage of numerous violation instances while maintaining a centralised rule repository.

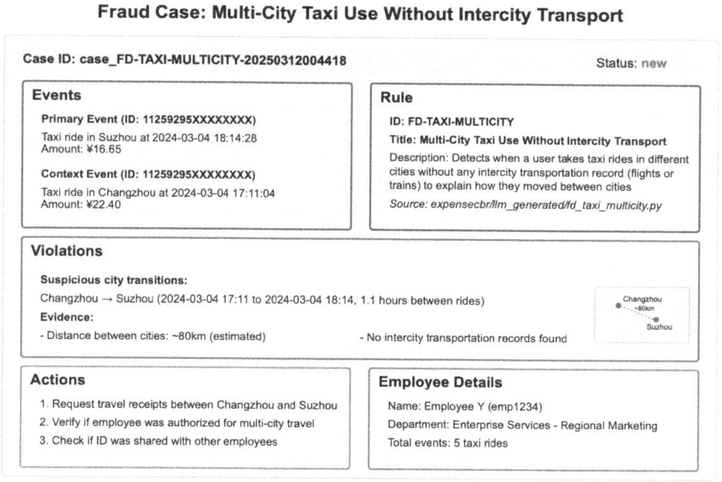

Fig. 1. Example case of a multi-city taxi use pattern without corresponding intercity transportation records.

When a new event is logged, the system searches the case library to find past fraud cases with similar patterns. Given a new event e_{new}, we define the following problem:

1. Find the set $C_{sim} \subset C$ of most similar cases to e_{new} based on the distance between their feature vectors

2. Apply the detection rules $\{r_j | c_j \in C_{sim}\}$ to e_{new} and its context events to determine if fraud is present
3. If fraud is detected, generate a report with the specific violations and recommended actions
4. If no rule detects fraud but the pattern is suspicious, or if an existing rule incorrectly flags legitimate activity, generate a new rule r_{new} using LLM
5. Verify r_{new} through test cases and historical data, then create a new case c_{new} if verified

Our employee expense fraud detection system detects two major types of violations:

1. Physical Impossibility Violations: These involve spatiotemporal contradictions, such as an employee claiming to be in two distant locations simultaneously. Formally, this can be expressed as: $\exists e_i, e_j \in E$ where $u_i = u_j$ (same employee), t_i overlaps with t_j, and the distance between l_i and l_j exceeds what is physically possible given the overlap in time.

2. Policy Violations: These involve semantic rules defined by company policies rather than physical constraints. For example, claiming taxi expenses for regular commuting between home and office. Formally, we can define a set of policy rules $P = \{p_1, p_2, ..., p_k\}$, where each policy p_i is a predicate function:

$$p_i : \mathcal{P}(E) \rightarrow \{true, false\} \tag{1}$$

Here, $\mathcal{P}(E)$ denotes the power set of E, allowing policies to be applied to either individual events or groups of events. A policy violation occurs when $p_i(e) = true$ for some event $e \in E$ or $p_i(G) = true$ for some subset $G \subset E$.

For example, a commuting policy violation could be defined as:

$$p_{commute}(e) = \begin{cases} true & \text{if } type(e) = \text{taxi} \wedge is\_commute\_route(e) \\ false & \text{otherwise} \end{cases} \tag{2}$$

where $is\_commute\_route(e)$ checks if the event represents travel between an employee's home and workplace during typical commuting hours.

Both types of violations can be encoded in our detection rules r_j, and our CBR framework handles them uniformly by representing them as cases with specific violation types and associated resolution actions.

4 Overview of the System Architecture

Our fraud detection system combines case-based reasoning with large-language models through a design that supports reliability, clear explanations, and adaptability. The system follows the complete CBR cycle while providing guardrails for the creation and testing of LLM rules. Figure 2 shows the system design that has the following main components:

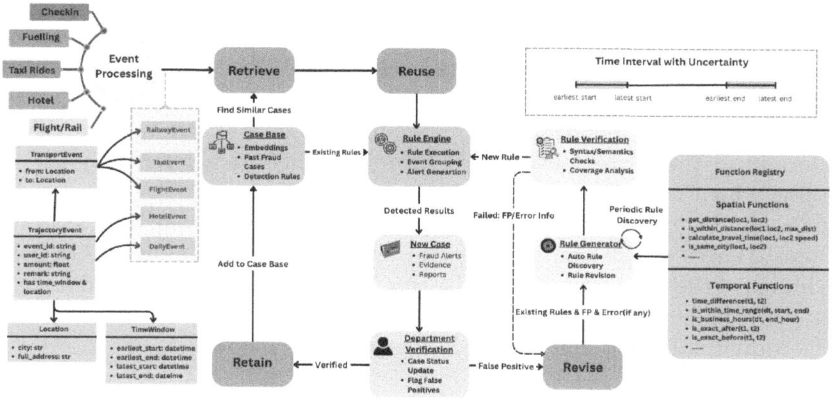

Fig. 2. Overview of the system design and data models

- **Event Processing Module:** Converts raw expense data into structured events with time and location information. Each event includes location details (with varying levels of detail), time ranges (earliest/latest start and end times), employee ID, and specific details like expense amounts.
- **Function Registry:** Contains verified building block functions for fraud detection rules (spatial, temporal, and business rule checking). Constrains LLM rule generation while allowing extensibility as new fraud patterns emerge.
- **Rule Engine:** Executes detection rules on event groups with various strategies (single events, grouped by date, or time windows) and generates standardised alerts. The rule engine is agnostic to the underlying rules through standardised interfaces, ensuring all rules follow consistent patterns regardless of their specific detection logic. It maintains statistics about system performance, including detection rates and false positive trends, to help evaluate and refine the rule base over time.
- **Case Base:** Stores fraud cases with their detection patterns, rules, violations, and resolving actions, using vector embeddings for similarity retrieval.
- **LLM Interface:** Manages interactions with LLMs, giving them the right context and templates to create and revise detection rules.
- **CBR Controller:** Orchestrates the complete CBR cycle, handling case retrieval, rule application, generation, and retention.

Our modular design integrates rule execution and creation. By limiting LLMs to work with a set of predefined functions, the system uses AI's pattern recognition and generative strengths while maintaining the reliability and clear explanations needed for fraud detection.

5 A CBR System for Fraud Detection

In this section, we will go through the Retrieve, Reuse, Revise, and Retain processes of the CBR system with adaptations to incorporate LLM capabilities.

5.1 Retrieve and Reuse

Given a new expense event, we create vector representations that capture key characteristics for similarity retrieval. When analyzing expense fraud, a single event often cannot be determined fraudulent in isolation. Our system therefore considers both the current event and its related historical events by the same employee, which we call "contextual events".

For each new event, we generate query embeddings at two time scales: day and week. These query embeddings are created by combining the individual embeddings of the current event and its recent historical events, with more recent events given higher weights to reflect their greater relevance.

The individual event embedding is computed as follows:

$$E(event)=w_1 \cdot f_{type}+w_2 \cdot f_{amount}+w_3 \cdot f_{time\_seq}+w_4 \cdot f_{loc}+w_5 \cdot f_{semantic}+w_6 \cdot f_{user}$$

where f_x represents feature vectors for different aspects of the event, and w_i are the corresponding weights for the type of event (w = 2.0), expense amount (1.8), temporal patterns (1.0), location details (1.6), event-specific attributes (1.2), and user information (0.8) were determined through empirical testing on the dataset used in our evaluation. The final vector is normalised to unit length for consistent similarity computation.

Regarding location, the system encodes both city information and specific addresses using hashing functions. The temporal embeddings capture time of day, duration, day of week, business hours indicators, and time uncertainty through earliest/latest timestamps. The amount embeddings use logarithmic scaling with threshold indicators set according to company's policy (e.g., maximum hotel price).

The system then retrieves the most similar cases from the case base using cosine similarity between the vectors through rejection sampling. In rejection sampling, we discard cases detected by the same rule and continue retrieving until we have k cases detected by distinct rules, or no more similar cases above a similarity threshold can be found.

5.2 Revise with LLM Rule Generation

The revision process in our CBR system is triggered in the following scenarios: (1) when domain experts identify suspicious patterns that no existing rule detects, (2) when existing rules incorrectly flag legitimate activity as fraudulent. In both cases, we leverage LLMs to generate or modify detection rules through a structured approach. Beyond these reactive scenarios, 3) we also use LLM proactively for automated rule discovery to find potential fraud patterns, with generated rules following the same routine of case revision and verification.

For rule discovery and revision, the system prompts the LLM with contextual information about the fraud detection domain, describing both physical impossibility violations and policy violations.[1] The LLM receives the event data model

[1] See prompt/rules/assessment details at: https://github.com/fantastdd/iccbr2025_submission.git.

with explanations of core data structures including `TrajectoryEvent`, `Location`, and `TimeWindow` classes with their properties and methods, along with a registry of available helper functions: 1) **Spatial functions** for distance calculation, proximity checking, travel time estimation, and location comparison. 2) **Temporal functions** for time difference calculation, interval checking under uncertainty, overlap detection, and business hours verification. 3) **Context** data structures providing configuration information and default values. Each fraud detection rule in our system follows a standardised interface with three key components:

1. **Grouping function:** Determines how events are organised before analysis. It accepts a rule object and a list of events, returning an iterable of event groups. The system provides predefined strategies such as `group_by_date`.
2. **Detection function:** The core logic that identifies suspicious patterns. It accepts a rule object, a list of events (from a single group), and a context dictionary. It returns `False` when no fraud is detected, or events detected as suspicious (triggering events).
3. **Alert formatting function:** Transforms detection results into human-readable alerts. It accepts a rule object, the triggering events, the evidence data, and the context data, returning an informative report (including generated narrative explanations) according to a predefined template.

We provide factory functions to simplify rule creation with different event grouping strategies: *create_single_rule(detect_fn, alert_fn)* processes each event in isolation; *create_multi_rule(event_types, detect_fn, alert_fn)* groups events by specified activity types, allowing detection of patterns across different event categories; and *create_win_rule(detect_fn, win_size, alert_fn)* creates groups by sliding a window of the specified size over events chronologically, enabling detection of temporal patterns within defined time frames.

This structured approach constrains the LLM to work within a defined function space while leveraging its common-sense knowledge to discover novel fraud scenarios. The generated Python code must use only verified functions from the registry, follow the standardised interfaces, produce structured output with explicit evidence fields, and include documentation.

The system improves rule quality through best-practice guidance that encourages the LLM to focus on physical impossibility patterns, implement appropriate thresholds to minimise false positives, follow code quality standards, and generate informative alerts with specific evidence and actionable information.

When performing rule revision (as opposed to discovery), the system provides the LLM with a narrative description of the suspicious pattern or incorrectly flagged legitimate activity. This expert-guided revision leverages domain knowledge that helps improve the quality of revised rules, while rule discovery enables the system to identify novel fraud patterns that might not be apparent to human experts.

During rule execution, the rule engine groups events according to the rule's strategy, applies the detection function to each group, formats alerts for positive detections, and returns structured results with all identified alerts. Figure 3 shows

```
def detect_suspicious_taxi(rule, events, context):
    ...
    sorted_es = sorted(events, lambda e: e.time_window.earliest_start)
    # Identify consecutive short-interval rides
    for i in range(1, len(sorted_es)):
        time_gap = rule.time_difference(
            sorted_events[i-1].time_interval.latest_end,
            sorted_events[i].time_interval.earliest_start, "hours")
        location_ok = rule.is_within_distance(
            sorted_events[i-1]...., sorted_events[i]...., 2)
    # Record if time gap is within the threshold and location ok
    # Flag sequences exceeding amount threshold
    # Return suspcious events or False
    ...
def format_suspicious_taxi(rule, events, extra_data, context):
    ...
rule_suspicious_taxi = create_daily_rule(
        "FD-TAXI-SEQUENTIAL",              # Rule ID
        "Sequential Taxi Rides",           # Title
        "Detect short-interval rides likely indicating expense splitting",
        ["TaxiEvent"],
        detect_suspicious_taxi,
        format_suspicious_taxi
)
```

Fig. 3. A simplified version of the rule for detecting sequential taxi rides that may indicate expense splitting.

an LLM-generated rule for detecting sequential taxi rides that may indicate expense splitting fraud (simplified due to the space limit (see Footnote 1)). This rule demonstrates our approach's key strengths through its use of verified spatial and temporal functions from the function registry, clear fraud pattern detection for short-interval rides with high total costs, structured evidence collection, and adherence to our daily rule template structure. The rule shows how LLMs can create effective detection logic while staying within our constrained and verifiable function space.

5.3 Retain with Rule Verification

Before incorporating new rules into the case base, our system subjects them to rigorous verification through a multi-stage process. First, we prompt the LLM to create synthetic events that should trigger the rule. The rule is then executed against these events to confirm it functions as expected. Second, we apply the CBR retrieval process to the synthetic events to determine if existing rules already cover these cases. If all synthetic events match existing rules, we flag the new rule as potentially redundant. Third, we execute the rule against historical data to ensure it does not flag an unrealistic percentage of events (below 5% based on [5]) and doesn't incorrectly flag previously confirmed legitimate events. Finally, all cases identified by rules start with a "new" status and are forwarded to the risk control department, which evaluates each case as either "verified" (suspicious activity) or "false positive" (legitimate activity).

If verification fails, the system initiates another revision cycle with specific feedback to the LLM about why the rule failed. In cases where multiple revision attempts fail, the system escalates to domain experts for manual rule creation or refinement. For redundancy issues, we identify existing rules that already cover the pattern. For excessive matches, we share threshold violation data, and for false positives, we present examples of legitimate events incorrectly flagged. New rules enter a probationary period where they generate alerts but with lower priority and do not participate in rule subsumption until the rules get verified. This approach ensures that our system evolves through continuous operational feedback while maintaining high-quality standards.

The retention mechanism evaluates rule performance, revising or removing those with high false positives. It consolidates rules when newer ones subsume older ones, and it flags challenging cases for expert review. For particularly challenging cases where rule verification repeatedly fails, we retain the case with an empty detection function, flagging it for human expert review. This ongoing revision-retention process balances LLM capabilities with practical considerations, resulting in a system that evolves through operational feedback.

6 Evaluation

We implemented our integrated CBR-LLM system within Guangzhou Shiyuan Electronic Technology (CVTE), a China-listed company with approximately 7,000 employees worldwide. The evaluation used a dataset of 206,123 expense events collected over a 393-day period from December 2023 to December 2024. This dataset covers activities from more than 2000 employees across 352 cities, providing a diverse sample for our analysis. The dataset includes six categories of expense events with different distribution patterns. The most common are daily check-ins (49.51%) and taxi rides (29.16%). Transportation-related events make up 20%, comprising railway trips (15.77%), fuel transactions (2.29%), and flights (0.70%). Hotel stays account for the remaining 2.57%. About 70% of the events include precise location data, whereas only 30% have an exact time window.

6.1 Rule Generation Quality

We used Claude 3.7 Sonnet [3], a state-of-the-art large language model renowned for its code generation capabilities, to generate 100 fraud detection rules from scratch, without human assistance in formulating the initial detection patterns. These rules were evaluated by a domain expert from the risk control department using a four-point scoring system (0–3), with higher scores indicating greater potential for fraud detection (the complete list can be found here (see Footnote 1)).

The results demonstrated that a significant portion of LLM-generated rules were of high quality with 40.6% of rules received ratings of 2 or 3, with an average

Table 1. LLM-Generated Rule Quality Assessment

Rating	Description	Count	Percentage
3	Highly valuable	14	13.9%
2	Valuable	27	26.7%
1	Potentially useful	42	41.6%
0	Less relevant	18	17.8%
Rules rated 2 or higher		41	40.6%
Average score across all rules		1.37	
Code quality evaluation (sample size: 20)			
- Rules passing verification without modification		17	85%
- Rules requiring revision (avg. 1.3 cycles)		3	15%

score of 1.37 across all rules (see Table 1). We list the top 10 highest-rated fraud detection rules in Table 2.

The ratings show that the most valuable rules are those focused on detecting spatiotemporal inconsistencies. Specifically, rules detecting physical impossibilities (such as being in two distant locations simultaneously) and documentation mismatches between different expense types (hotel/flight/taxi records) received the highest ratings. Conversely, rules focused on travel patterns that might have legitimate explanations (such as same-day returns or rides with colleagues) received lower ratings. The system's rule verification procedures automatically filtered out lower-quality rules during later stages, as detailed in our ablation studies.

To evaluate the LLM's ability to generate functional code without human intervention, we randomly selected 20 generated rules to check for both syntactic and semantic correctness. As shown in Table 1, 85% of these rules passed verification without any modification, while the remaining rules required minor revisions (such as adjusting thresholds to more realistic levels) before passing all verification checks. This demonstrates the effectiveness of our constrained generation approach in producing deployment-ready code.

6.2 Case Study: Real-World Fraud Detection Performance

The system so far has identified 5,758 cases as suspicious from the dataset and reported them to the company's risk-control department. At the time of writing, the department had verified 2,897 cases, confirming 97% (2,817 cases) as genuinely suspicious and classifying only 3% as false positives. The accuracy is high in part because the department may be prioritising cases that they already feel suspicious, creating potential selection bias. However, the result still indicates that our method effectively detects genuinely fraudulent activities.

Of the total reported cases, approximately 13.6% were related to physical impossibilities (such as check-in location conflicts with expense records and simultaneous expense records across different locations), while 86.4% involved

Table 2. Top 10 LLM-Generated Rules Ranked by Expert Evaluation

Rule ID	Description
FD-DAILY-UBIQUITOUS	Detects users with activity records in multiple distant cities on the same day, which is physically impossible
FD-HOTEL-FLIGHT	Identifies logical conflicts between hotel check-in dates and flight itinerary dates
FD-FLIGHT-CITY	Detects when a flight destination doesn't match hotel city, with no transportation records explaining the discrepancy
FD-TAXI-MULTICITY	Identifies taxi rides in different cities without intercity transportation records to explain the movement
FD-EXP-TIMETRAVEL	Detects contradictions where reimbursement submission dates precede actual expense dates
FD-HOTEL-MISSED-FLT	Identifies when hotel checkout date is later than scheduled flight departure on the same day
FD-FLIGHT-HOTEL-GAP	Detects logical conflicts between flight arrival dates and hotel check-in dates
FD-TRANSPORT-DUP	Identifies claims for multiple forms of transportation on the same route during the same timeframe
FD-TAXI-HOTEL	Detects discrepancies between taxi arrival dates and hotel check-in dates, or between taxi departures and checkouts
FD-TAXI-COMMUTE	Identifies employees using taxi services for regular commutes between home and office, violating company policy

policy violations. The direct financial impact of these cases amounted to ¥252,138. Further analysis of the total expenses made by the identified personnel revealed a upper bound of ¥5,500,000 in questionable transactions, as individuals caught committing fraud in one scenario often exhibit similar patterns across other expense categories. Due to confidentiality and ongoing investigations, we cannot provide details about all detected rules. However, we highlight two particularly effective detection rules created through our approach as examples:

Rule FD-TAXI-COMMUTE: An LLM-generated rule from a narrative description provided by risk-control department, this rule identifies employees using taxi services for commute trips, which violates company policy. This rule achieved high precision with few false positives. The false positives initially stemmed from using incorrectly inferred home locations, as the rule originally set the confidence value of inferred locations to a low threshold. Through our CBR refinement cycle, the rule has been revised to improve the setting of threshold values that have eliminated false positives without missing any actual violations.

Rule FD-TAXI-MULTICITY: This rule was generated by the LLM from scratch and identifies physically impossible city transitions that would be challenging for human experts to detect. By analyzing taxi rides across multiple cities without corresponding intercity transportation records, the rule successfully uncovered non-obvious fraud patterns that traditional rule-based systems would likely miss.

While some generated rules did not detect fraud instances during the evaluation, the risk-control department considered them valuable for their potential to identify emerging fraud patterns. These rules are kept active in the system background to continuously monitor incoming events (through rejection sampling in the retrieval phase). We also evaluated retrieval performance with $k = 5$ for each rule, using 60% of the detected cases for the case base and 40% for testing. This gave an average recall of 86% and precision of 49%. Precision is less critical as unmatched rules simply fail. However, the 14% of missed cases suggests that during cold-start phases, applying all rules to new events may be beneficial until enough cases are accumulated for effective retrieval.

6.3 Ablation Studies

We conducted two ablation studies examining: (1) constraint impact on rule generation quality and (2) CBR verification effectiveness.

Impact of Constraints on Rule Generation: We compared code produced by the LLM under two experimental conditions: R1 with both template and provided function constraints (full constraint), and R2 with template but without function and grouping constraints (partial constraint). We also considered a theoretical third condition, R3, without any constraints (lacking the model for temporal/location uncertainty). Human experts with programming backgrounds manually evaluated the code quality and logical correctness of the generated rules. They found that 85% of rules in R1 were free of logical errors, compared to only 40% in R2, demonstrating that our full constraint approach significantly improves rule quality.

For the R2 condition, we analysed 10 randomly selected rules and found 60% contained hallucinations, mainly related to spatiotemporal reasoning. We found temporal inconsistencies where the LLM used wrong time window boundaries when comparing event times and missed that negative time gaps between events represent serious logical impossibilities. Spatial reasoning errors included failing to account for realistic travel times between locations and applying the same time buffers regardless of actual distances. Combined spatiotemporal errors showed up as the LLM checking for connections between events only within narrow timeline windows, applying incorrect operation sequences when analyzing transportation combinations, and treating bidirectional time differences as equally suspicious when real-world temporal sequences are directional (detailed hallucinations are listed here (see Footnote 1)).

While we did not conduct a formal experiment for condition R3, we can reasonably expect that removing all constraints would lead to even more serious errors, particularly in temporal reasoning, as R3 lacks the fundamental time interval uncertainty model (earliest/latest start/end times) required for accurate fraud detection in our domain. These results support that without our constrained function registry approach, LLMs struggle particularly with accurately reasoning about time intervals with uncertainty and spatial relationships. The evaluation confirmed that the fully constrained approach (R1) effectively minimised hallucination compared to the partially constrained condition (R2), with a substantial reduction in spatiotemporal reasoning errors.

CBR Verification Effectiveness: We analysed how effectively our CBR verification procedure identified problematic rules created by LLM. For the generated rules, 25% were identified due to duplication or subsumption of existing rules, and 10% were rejected for exceeding reasonable fraud thresholds or incorrectly flagging known legitimate events. For example, the system identified through case-coverage testing that the "Hotel Duplicate Date Different Cities" rule (which detects when an employee books hotels in multiple cities for the same dates) completely subsumes both the "Hotel Multiday No Checkout" rule (which flags hotel stays without proper checkout records) and the "Hotel Stay No Arrival" rule (which identifies hotel bookings with no evidence of travel to that location) with 100% coverage of historical cases. This evaluation demonstrates the complementary nature of our approach: while function constraints prevent basic logical errors in rule generation, the case-based verification addresses rule relationships and real-world applicability, capturing issues that syntactic constraints alone would miss. These ablation studies show how our integrated approach successfully constrains LLM hallucinations while maintaining the benefits of generative AI for fraud detection rule creation.

This case-based approach to subsumption testing is more practical at this stage than formal logical verification, avoiding the complexity and computational cost of translating Python code into formal logic, which can be time-consuming or even undecidable for complex rules. One promising direction would be to investigate the possibility of adopting ASP as an intermediate language for formal verification of generated rules [9] which is not the scope of this paper.

7 Conclusion

We have developed an effective system for expense fraud detection by combining CBR and Generative AI to address common problems like data scarcity, complex patterns, and the need to explain decisions clearly. The system identified thousands of suspicious cases in the real world with a low false positive rate, which confirms its effectiveness while providing the transparency needed for investigations. The implementation of the full CBR cycle provides a framework for detecting both physical impossibility violations and policy violations in expense data. The CBR cycle enables adaptation to evolving fraud tactics through rule refinement and case retention.

We show how CBR constrains LLM hallucinations through verification mechanisms. By limiting LLMs to a predefined function registry and validating generated rules against historical cases, we maintain reliability while benefiting from the generative capabilities of LLMs. This research provides a blueprint for combining LLMs with CBR in high-stakes domains requiring reliability and explainability.

References

1. Adedoyin, A., Kapetanakis, S., Petridis, M., Panaousis, E.: Evaluating case-based reasoning knowledge discovery in fraud detection. In: ICCBR Workshops, pp. 182–191 (2016)
2. Ali, A., et al.: Financial fraud detection based on machine learning: a systematic literature review. Appl. Sci. **12**(19), 9637 (2022)
3. Anthropic: Claude 3.7 sonnet. Large Language Model (2025). https://www.anthropic.com/claude. Accessed Mar 2025
4. Association of Certified Fraud Examiners: Occupational fraud 2022: A report to the nations. Technical report, Association of Certified Fraud Examiners (2022)
5. Association of Certified Fraud Examiners: Occupational fraud 2024: A report to the nations. Technical report, Association of Certified Fraud Examiners (2024)
6. Bolton, R.J., Hand, D.J.: Statistical fraud detection: a review. Stat. Sci. **17**(3), 235–255 (2002)
7. Cho, J.S.: The process of internal corruption detection using the criminological approach based on case-based reasoning. Eur. J. Bus. Manag. Res. **9**(6), 170–176 (2024)
8. Kapetanakis, S., Samakovitis, G., Gunasekera, P.B.D., Miltos, P.: The use of case-based reasoning for the monitoring of financial fraud transactions (2017)
9. Kaur, N., McPheat, L., Russo, A., Cohn, A.G., Madhyastha, P.: An empirical study of conformal prediction in LLM with asp scaffolds for robust reasoning. arXiv preprint arXiv:2503.05439 (2025)
10. Tulving, E., et al.: Episodic and semantic memory. In: Organization of Memory, vol. 1, pp. 381–403 (1972)
11. Visbeek, S., Acar, E., den Hengst, F.: Explainable fraud detection with deep symbolic classification. In: World Conference on Explainable Artificial Intelligence, pp. 350–373. Springer (2024)
12. Watson, I.: A case-based persistent memory for a large language model. arXiv preprint arXiv:2310.08842 (2023)
13. Wilkerson, K.: LLM reliability and CBR: how case based reasoning can improve the performance of large language models. In: DC at ICCBR2024 (2024)
14. Wilkerson, K., Leake, D.: On implementing case-based reasoning with large language models. In: ICCBR, pp. 404–417. Springer (2024)
15. Wiratunga, N., et al.: CBR-RAG: case-based reasoning for retrieval augmented generation in LLMs for legal question answering. In: ICCBR, pp. 445–460. Springer (2024)
16. Yu, H., Liu, Z., Luo, X.: Barely supervised learning for graph-based fraud detection. In: Proceedings of the AAAI Conference on Artificial Intelligence, vol. 38, pp. 16,548–16,557 (2024)

LLM-Driven Case-Base Populating for Structuring and Integrating Restoration Experiences

Fethi Ghazouani(✉), Franco Giustozzi, and Florence Le Ber

Université de Strasbourg, Engees, INSA, CNRS, ICube UMR 7357, 67000 Strasbourg, France
fghazouani@unistra.fr, franco.giustozzi@insa-strasbourg.fr, florence.leber@engees.unistra.fr

Abstract. In Case-Based Reasoning (CBR), a case-base is a structured knowledge collection, often represented as an ontology with a TBox (conceptual structure) and ABox (concrete cases). This work emphasizes the need for a case-base to integrate knowledge from unstructured texts describing hydro-ecosystem restoration experiences, forming the foundation for a CBR framework to address new restoration challenges. However, populating the case-base from unstructured texts presents challenges due to fragmented, inconsistent, and implicit information. Therefore, we propose leveraging large language models (LLMs) to extract knowledge from unstructured texts, where the ontology population is approached as a generative knowledge extraction task. The results demonstrate that LLMs can effectively extract structured knowledge, facilitating the creation of a case-base for future projects.

Keywords: LLM · Case-Base · Case-Based Reasoning · Ontology · Unstructured Texts

1 Introduction

The restoration of hydro-ecosystems is a major challenge for the sustainable management of water resources. Consequently, legal requirements have driven stakeholders to undertake restoration operations on dams and hydroelectric power plants to enhance the ecological functioning of water bodies. These regulations mandate the re-naturalization of intervention areas, a process that cannot be effectively carried out without a comprehensive understanding of past restoration projects. However, despite efforts to collect feedback on these operations, the data often remains dispersed and difficult to utilize. This observation highlights the need for a structured approach to analyzing and integrating restoration experiences, leading to the consideration of a case-based reasoning framework, where experiences are formalized as reusable cases.

Case-based reasoning (CBR) is a problem-solving paradigm that leverages the specific knowledge derived from previously encountered, concrete problem

© The Author(s), under exclusive license to Springer Nature Switzerland AG 2025
I. Bichindaritz and B. López (Eds.): ICCBR 2025, LNAI 15662, pp. 67–80, 2025.
https://doi.org/10.1007/978-3-031-96559-3_5

situations (cases) to address new challenges [1]. A case represents a problem resolution, typically described as a pair (*problem*, *solution*), and is stored in a case-base, where each element is referred to as a source case. Such a base is a set of already solved problems associated with their solutions. The CBR process involves solving a new problem, called the target problem, by finding a similar past case in the case-base and reusing it to address the current situation. Thus, the case-base plays a crucial role in the CBR process, serving as the repository of accumulated knowledge and experiences that enable efficient problem-solving. A well-structured and comprehensive case-base enhances the effectiveness of CBR by providing a rich source of diverse, relevant cases that can be adapted to solve new, complex problems. However, constructing the case-base itself is a significant challenge, as it requires the collection, organization, and formalization of diverse real-world cases, often from unstructured data sources. Moreover, this base should be well-structured, and capable of integrating domain knowledge and perform reasoning over it to ensure that it can support effective problem-solving.

In this study, an ontology for hydro-ecosystem restoration is developed as a knowledge base to formally represent the concepts and relationships specific to restoration operations. This ontology facilitates the systematic analysis of feedback and serves as a structured reference framework to support decision-making and guide future restoration projects. However, instantiating this knowledge base from unstructured texts presents several challenges. Restoration reports and project descriptions often contain fragmented, inconsistently formatted, and implicit information, making it difficult to extract, standardize, and integrate into the ontology. In this paper, we focus specifically on the automatic population of an ontology using Large Language Models (LLMs) from unstructured texts. Here, ontology population is approached as a generative knowledge extraction task, aiming to identify entities and their relationships in the form of triples. The LLM is employed to extract these target triples from texts, while leveraging the domain ontology as a guiding framework to ensure the relevance and accuracy of the extracted knowledge.

The rest of this paper is organized as follows. Section 2 reviews the related work on knowledge extraction from unstructured documents. Section 3 presents the knowledge base and the strategy for populating it using LLMs. Section 4 describes the experimental setup and results. Finally, Sect. 5 concludes the paper and outlines future research directions.

2 Related Work

Extracting information from semi-structured or unstructured texts is a highly complex task due to the context-dependent nature of natural language. Unstructured texts often contain variability in expression, domain-specific terminology, and implicit relationships that are not machine-readable. Entities and relations in a natural language text need to be identified in order to be linked to a specific Knowledge Graph (KG) or Base (KB). This highlights the need for Knowledge Extraction (KE) over unstructured text in order to represent the data in a structured format. Representing the unstructured data in a structured format facilitates applying other tasks such as data integration, entity alignment and KG/KB population. Despite these challenges, KE plays a crucial role in transforming raw textual data into structured, machine-readable knowledge [2]. It involves extracting entities, identifying relationships, and capturing other relevant structured information from text [3].

In this section, we specifically focus on approaches aimed at extracting knowledge from unstructured documents to integrate information into KG or KB. According to [4], existing methods can be examined from two main perspectives: a semantic point of view and a generative Artificial Intelligence (AI) point of view. The first category focus to identify and structure concepts and relationships to match the knowledge domain. Methods in this category are generally based on natural language processing techniques, using machine/deep learning algorithms [5–7], or rule-based algorithms [8–10] to identify entities and relationships from text. However, these approaches require extensive human supervision or the development of specific rules for each application.

The second category has recently gained more attention leveraging the large language models to automatically generate instances and property assertions, enabling dynamic and scalable knowledge integration. The advent of large language models, such as GPT from OpenAI [11], LLaMA from Meta [12], Claude from Anthropic [13], PaLM from Google [14] and Qwen from Alibaba Cloud [15], has revolutionized natural language processing by offering remarkable capabilities in text comprehension and generation. Trained on large quantities of unlabeled data through large-scale self-supervised pre-training, these models can be adapted to a wide variety of specific tasks. LLMs have received significant attention from researchers exploring their potential across various KE tasks and applications. Xu *et al.* [3] summarizes existing state-of-the-art approaches that integrate LLMs for KE tasks based on a generative paradigm. Various studies have shown that LLMs can generalize effectively by learning from KE training data through fine-tuning [16–18], as well as extracting knowledge in few-shot and zero-shot scenarios using only in-context examples or instructions [19–21]. Additionally, LLMs can model generated knowledge in a universal format by capturing inter-task dependencies through instructive prompts. In [22], authors have investigated the impact of different prompting techniques to generate a case base for a CBR system. Their approach relies on existing structured knowledge rather than extracting it from unstructured input text.

Generally, generative KE enables the extraction of structured triplets in the ⟨*subject-predicate-object*⟩ format. Li *et al.* [23] illustrates the potential of LLMs to efficiently extract knowledge through the application of In-Context Learning (ICL) [24]. ICL is based on the concept of "learning by demonstration", where the model learns to perform tasks by observing provided examples [25]. This technique is particularly beneficial for LLMs, which, due to their large number of parameters, can perform KE tasks without requiring additional training or fine-tuning, simply by responding to carefully designed inputs, such as customized textual prompts. However, crafting effective prompts remains a major challenge, making prompt engineering essential for enhancing their efficiency. In [25], authors have used various prompts engineering techniques to extract knowledge from texts. The extracted triplets were then evaluated according to the guidelines of an ontology. Another work [19] explores the construction of knowledge graphs from unstructured text data, by evaluating the effectiveness of different approaches, including Zero-Shot Prompting (ZSP), Few-Shot Prompting (FSP) and Fine-Tuning (FT), applied to LLMs. In [21], LLMs were evaluated for their effectiveness in extracting knowledge from texts, specifically for constructing knowledge graphs. The authors emphasize the crucial role of domain ontology in guiding knowledge extraction and structuring knowledge graphs. Gillani *et al.* [20] have demonstrated how LLMs can effectively identify and extract relevant entities and relationships from unstructured textual data using prompt engineering. The performance of LLMs has been improved for knowledge extraction from unstructured Thai texts through advanced prompt techniques [26], where the extracted knowledge was used to enrich a financial products ontology. Similarly, Kouhoue et al. [27] leveraged an LLM to extract knowledge from real estate listings to populate a domain ontology. Their approach demonstrates how LLMs can facilitate the transformation of unstructured textual data into structured semantic representations, enhancing the usability and interoperability of domain-specific knowledge.

As shown in various studies, LLMs have demonstrated strong capabilities in knowledge extraction from unstructured texts, particularly for constructing and enriching KGs and KBs. In this study, we leverage LLMs to extract knowledge from experience feedback texts on restoration operations to enrich our case-base.

3 Methodology

This section presents the proposed methodology, which consists of two main stages. The first stage involves constructing the case-base, i.e. structuring and integrating concepts and relationships related to hydro-ecosystem restoration operations. The second stage focuses on populating this case-base using LLMs to automatically extract and integrate knowledge from unstructured texts.

In our framework a case is made of the two following parts: (problem) the description of a river site where the ecological functioning is altered, e.g. salmons can not jump over an existing dam that is too high, (solution) the operation conducted to improve the ecological functioning, e.g. building a fish ladder, and its effect. Several pieces of information describe the two parts (see Fig. 1, bottom). The aim of the system is to help stakeholders choose a relevant solution for a given situation and to avoid some errors or drawbacks. For example, suppose another site with a dam on a river, this dam being too high for trouts who live in this river. Then the solution of the previous case can be retrieved and adapted, e.g. with lower steps in the fish ladder or a different slope and direction, depending on the river flow.

3.1 Case-Base Construction: The TBox

The construction of the case-base adopts an ontological approach to provide a structured representation of domain knowledge while enabling effective reasoning and inference. The process of building this case-base is driven by the analysis of data from a variety of sources, such as restoration feedback, operation reports and interview files. These documents contain essential information about the restoration operations carried out (e.g., artificial river creation), the affected geographic areas (e.g., Bas-Rhin), the impacted species (e.g., anadromous), the concerned water bodies (e.g., river), and the existing structures (e.g., dams). This step is conducted in collaboration with experts in the field, to ensure an accurate and coherent representation of knowledge specific to the hydro-ecosystem restoration context.

Therefore, the constructed ontology integrates concepts such as the types of realized restoration measures (*restorationMeasure*), such as reconnection, pool creation (*poolCreation*) or bank restoration (*bankRestoration*); the types of water bodies (*waterBody*) such as *river* or *pool*; the involved structures or obstacles (*structure*), such as dams (*dam*) and weirs (*weir*); the geographical zones (*geographicZone*); the types of migratory species (*migratorySpecie*); and the main contractor of a restoration operation (*mainContractor*). It includes relationships between concepts, such as '*realizedIn*', linking a restoration measure to a geographical area, '*associatedTo*', which associates a restoration measure with a structure, or '*isLocatedOn*', which locates a structure in a watercourse. Finally, data properties such as '*hasCost*' (cost of a restoration measure), '*startsAt*' or '*hasHeight*' (height of a structure) document quantitative and temporal information on restoration operations. Figure 1 shows an extract of the main components of the hydrosystem restoration case-base.

3.2 Case-Base Enrichment (ABox): LLM-Based Approach

The second stage of the proposed methodology involves enriching the case-base from documents on feedback from restoration operations. In this stage, we consider case-base enrichment as a generative knowledge extraction task, aiming to identify and structure entities and their relationships in the form of triples, essential for populating the case-base. In this case, an LLM is used as a target triplet extractor from texts, while relying on the domain ontology to guide the identification and structuring of relevant entities and relations, ensuring that the extracted knowledge is semantically coherent and aligned with the conceptual framework of the case-base. Figure 2 illustrates the overall pipeline for triplet extraction from unstructured text. As depicted in the figure, the LLM processes an input prompt that includes a description of the knowledge extraction task (TD), the ontology (O), and the input text (IT). Additionally, an optional set of examples ([EX]) can be provided to demonstrate the extraction process across various input texts, enhancing the model's ability to generate accurate and contextually relevant triplets.

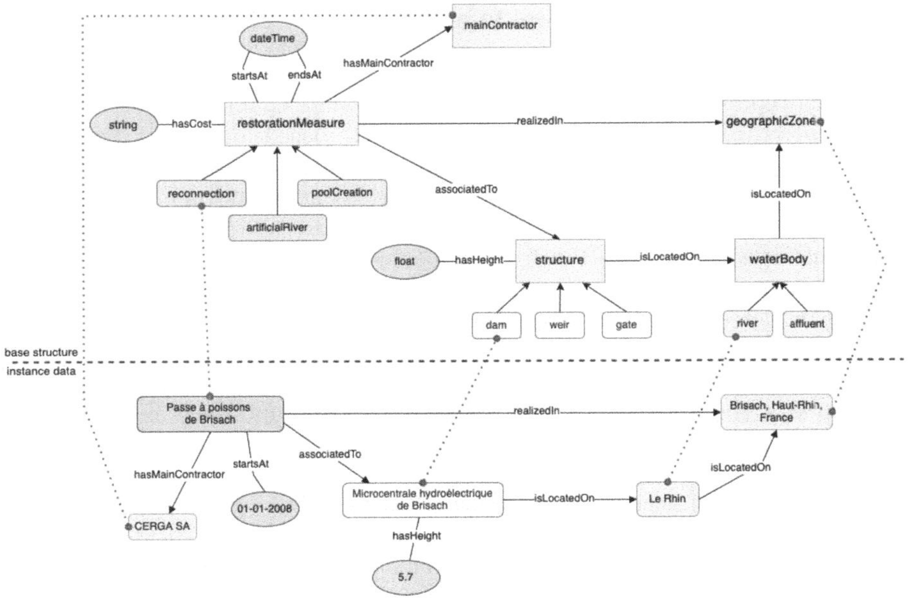

Fig. 1. An extract of the hydrosystem restoration case-base

The generative knowledge extraction process can be formulated as follows:

$$LLM(\texttt{Prompt}(TD, [\texttt{EX}], O, IT)) = [(h,r,t)_0, (h,r,t)_1, \ldots, (h,r,t)_i] \quad (1)$$

where $(h, r, t)_i$ represents an extracted triplet from the input text, and i denotes the total number of predicted triplets.

The LLM generates triplets based on the provided input prompt. Thus, a prompt engineering phase is conducted to determine the most suitable prompt for our task. This step is crucial in such approaches, as the quality and structure of the input prompt significantly impact the accuracy and relevance of the model's generated outputs. Prompt engineering relies on user-defined schemas, incorporating domain-specific knowledge to explicitly guide output generation. Three important paradigms are generally used when designing prompts: *Zero-*, *One-* and *Few-Shot*:

- Zero-shot prompting is the simplest form of prompting. It consists of providing the model with an instruction without any examples and asking it to generate a response.
- One-shot prompting includes exactly one example demonstrating how the task should be solved with different input data.
- Few-shots prompting essentially provides the model with a few examples of the desired outputs. By learning from these examples, the model adapts to a specific pattern, enabling it to perform similar tasks more effectively.

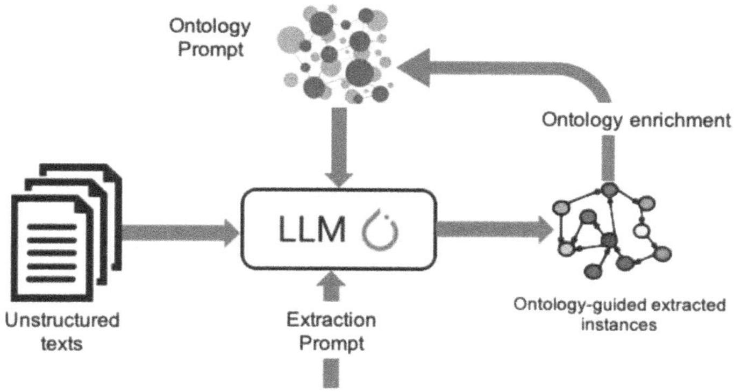

Fig. 2. LLM-driven Knowledge Extraction

The current work employs two main prompting approaches adapted to our context: Direct Prompting, which includes only the target description (TD) and the input text (IT) to be processed, and In-Context Learning, which enriches the prompt by incorporating a relevant example (EX) demonstrating the task on a different input. As a preliminary step, we tested several prompting formats, including basic zero-shot, template-based zero-shot, and one-shot variants, to determine the most effective strategy for our task. Performance was evaluated based on the completeness and structure of the extracted triplets. We observed that template-based prompts significantly reduced hallucinations by constraining the model within a predefined context, while one-shot prompts (i.e., In-Context Learning) improved precision by guiding the model through pattern recognition.

For the zero-shot test (Direct Prompt), the prompt includes a clear description of the task, with a detailed presentation of the case-base to be populated and the input text. This case-base specifies the concepts, relationships and properties associated with hydro-ecosystem restoration operations, providing a structured framework to guide triplet generation. In a second step, this prompt was further enhanced by integrating a structured template (in Turtle format) to better guide the generative extraction of triplets, ensuring consistency in the output format. Figure 3 illustrates the zero-shot prompt in both cases: without a template, where the model relies solely on the task description, and with a template, which provides a predefined structure to standardize the extracted triplets.

The "one-shot" prompt, shown in Fig. 4, adopts layered prompting structure to guide the model in generating triplets and converting them into turtle format. Indeed, given the complexity of the input required for knowledge extraction—comprising the input text, an ontology reference, a task description, and an illustrative example with a formatted output—we adopted a layered one-shot prompting strategy. This structure was chosen over a simpler single-block prompt format due to its enhanced clarity and effectiveness. Initial experiments with single-step one-shot prompt often produced inconsistent and structural incorrect outputs. Therefore, the first prompt integrates the task instruction

```
"""You are provided with an ontology description and a text input. Create instances extracted from
the text based on the ontology description.\n

Here is the current ontology description:
{ontology_description}\n

Input Text:
{text}\n"""
```

(a) Simple zero-shot prompt

```
"""You are provided with an ontology description and a text input. Create instances extracted from
the text based on the ontology description and the provided following template.\n

Here is the current ontology description:
{ontology_description}\n

Here is the given template to follow:
{template}\n

Input Text:
{text}\n"""
```
A

```
:<RestorationMeasureInstance> a :<RestorationMeasureClass>;
                              :associatedTo :<StructureInstance> ;
                              :isManagedBy :<ProjectOwnerInstance> ;
                              :hasMainContractor :<MainContractorInstance> ;
                              :startsAt <"StartDateTime">^^xsd:dateTime;
                              :endsAt <"EndDateTime">^^xsd:dateTime ;
                              :hasMaxLowWaterFlow <"theMaxLowWaterFlow">^^xsd:float ;
                              :hasMinLowWaterFlow <"theMinLowWaterFlow">^^xsd:float> ;
                              :containsTechnicalElement TetraOnto:<TechnicalElementInstance> ;
                              :numberOfPools <NumberOfTechnicalElements> ;
                              :averageSlope <AverageSlope> .

:<StructureInstance> a:structure , :<SubClassOfStructureToBelong> ;
                     :isLocatedOn :<GeographicZoneInstance> ;
                     :hasHeight <heightOfTheStructure> ;
                     :isImpassable <xsd:boolean> .

:<GeographicZoneInstance> a :GegraphicZone .

:<ProjectOwnerInstance> a :projectOwner .

:<MainContractorInstance> a :mainContractor.

:<TechnicalElementInstancet> a:technicalElement ,
                 <add information with respect to the ontology description> .
```
B

(b) Zero-shot prompt with template (A): Task description, (B): Template

Fig. 3. Zero-shot: Direct Prompting

("Individual extraction"), a detailed description of the target case-base (the ontology), an example of annotated text with the extracted individuals, and the input text. This configuration enables the model to identify relevant instances based on the provided example. Therefore, the first prompt integrates the task instruction ("Individual extraction"), a detailed description of the target case-base (the ontology), a concise example of annotated text with the extracted individuals, and the input text. The second prompt extends the first by incorporating additional instructions to convert the extracted individuals into Turtle format. It leverages a more elaborate Turtle example to guide this transformation, as this format requires greater structural detail compared to the simpler annotated text. This layered approach enhances output consistency by ensuring both precise extraction of individuals and their accurate structuring in the required Turtle format.

4 Results and Discussion

This section presents our experiments based on feedback from hydrological restoration operations. The data is sourced from an csv file, where each row represents a feedback entry detailing a restoration operation, including key information such as the context and the type of intervention. In this study, we have used recent open-source models, particularly *Mistral:7b v0.3*, *Qwen:7b v2*, *Qwen:14b v2.5*, *Llama:3b v3* and *LLaMA:8b v3*, which allow full reproducibility and seamless integration into customizable knowledge extraction workflows. Although cutting-edge proprietary models like *GPT-4o* or *Claude 3* demonstrate exceptional performance, their limited accessibility, closed architectures, and lack of transparency pose constraints for automatic case-base construction. All selected open-source LLMs, were executed locally using the Ollama[1] server, which facilitates seamless deployment of large language models in a self-hosted environment.

The generative knowledge extraction process is evaluated by comparing the performance of different LLMs through the calculation of precision (P), recall (R), and F-measure ($F1$), defined respectively in formulas[2] (2), (3) and (4).

$$P = \frac{VP}{VP + FP}, \quad (2) \qquad R = \frac{VP}{VP + FN}, \quad (3) \qquad F1 = 2 \times \frac{P \times R}{P + R} \quad (4)$$

Tables 1 and 2 present the performance of different large language models in extracting triplets from 15 restoration feedback texts, including 10 French texts from [28] and 5 English texts from [29]. Table 1 compares simple zero-shot prompting with zero-shot prompting utilizing a template, while Table 2 compares zero-shot prompting with one-shot prompting. As illustrated in Table 1, incorporating a template into the zero-shot prompt significantly enhances extraction performance. The results show an increase in precision, recall and F-measure, indicating that the structured guidance provided by the template helps the model generate more accurate and relevant triplets. Larger and more recent models demonstrate superior performance with the template-guided zero-shot prompt. In particular, *Qwen2.5:14b* achieves a precision of 0.89, a recall of 0.94, and an F-measure of 0.91, although its average execution time remains relatively high at 1 min and 27 s. Its extensive size (14 billion parameters) allows it to better capture and leverage contextual information from the prompt, leading to more accurate triplet extraction while reducing hallucinations and omissions. In contrast, intermediate and especially smaller models exhibited lower performance with the simple zero-shot prompt. For instance, the low precision (0.21), recall (0.27), and F-measure (0.23) obtained by *Llama3.2:3B* can be attributed to its

[1] https://ollama.com/.

[2] True Positive (TP) is a correct assertion, False Positive (FP) is an incorrect assertion, and False Negative (FN) is a missing assertion.

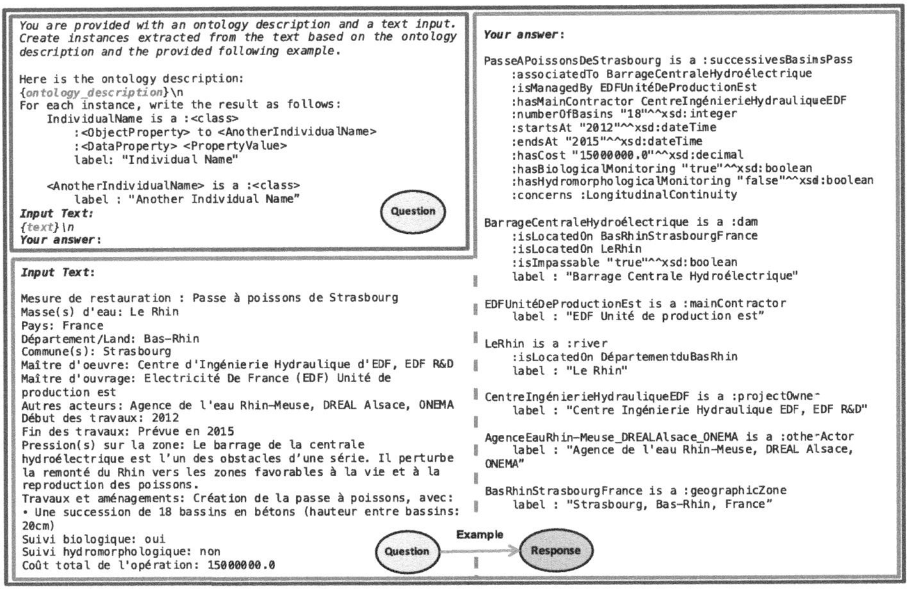

(a) The one-shot prompt first layer

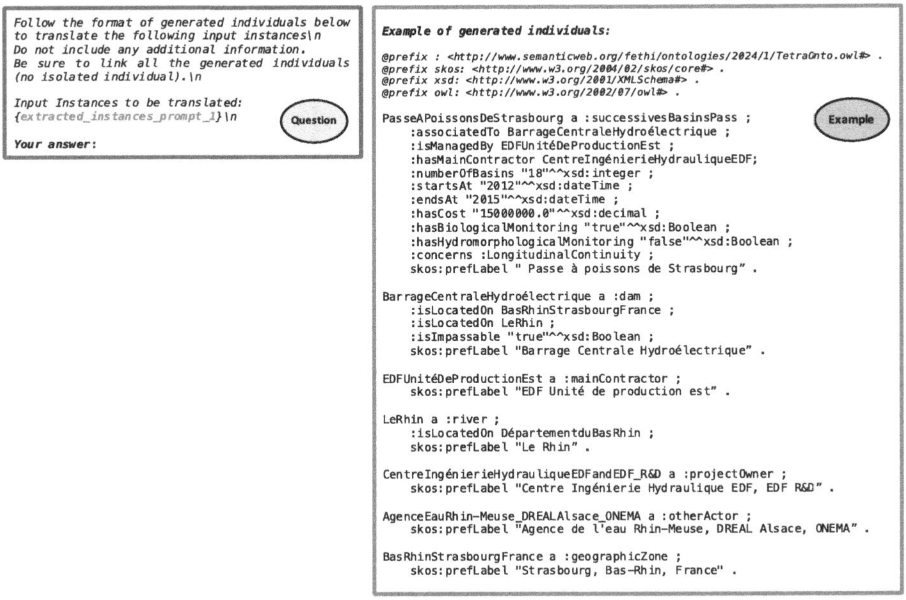

(b) The one-shot prompt second layer

Fig. 4. One-shot: ICL layered prompting structure

limited capacity (3 billion parameters) to effectively capture and interpret contextual cues from the prompt. However, this model stands out for its remarkable execution time (25 s), making it potentially suitable for simple tasks requiring fast responses. Nevertheless, its performance remains limited for complex inputs (O+TD+IT).

Table 1. Simple zero-shot prompt *Vs.* zero-shot prompt with template

	simple zero-shot				zero-shot with template			
	P	R	F1	Time	P	R	F1	Time
Mistral:7b	0.53	0.54	0.53	42 s	0.75	0.90	0.82	46 s
Llama:8b	0.60	0.61	0.60	41 s	0.84	0.90	0.87	44 s
Llama:3b	0.21	0.27	0.23	**24 s**	0.73	0.85	0.78	**25 s**
Qwen:7b	0.45	0.43	0.43	36 s	0.77	0.89	0.82	37 s
Qwen:14b	0.75	0.68	0.71	1 mn 16 s	**0.89**	**0.94**	**0.91**	1 mn 27 s

Similarly, Table 2 demonstrates that one-shot prompting further enhances performance compared to zero-shot prompting, as the provided example helps the model better understand the extraction task and align its output with the expected format. With the layered one-shot prompt, which includes an example, the *Qwen2.5:14b* model remains the top performer, achieving an F-measure of 0.90, although the execution time increases to 2 min and 21 s. This further underlines the model's ability to effectively integrate complex contexts, such as layered prompts that include an example. As also shown in this table, the performance of *Qwen:7b*, *Mistral:7b* and *Llama3.1:8b* decreases slightly for this type of prompt, compared to the template-driven zero-shot prompt (Table 2). This degradation could be related to the architecture's limited number of parameters to cover the full context (O+TD+IT+EX) of the one-shot prompt. However, *Llama3.1:8b*, with its 8 billion parameters, shows a certain one-shot robustness while maintaining a reasonable execution time of 58 s. Finally, while the *Llama3.2:3b* model performs better with the one-shot prompt compared to the simple zero-shot prompt, it shows a significant decrease in performance when compared to the template-guided zero-shot prompt. This reflect the increased difficulty for this type of model to integrate and exploit the provided example, due to its reduced size (3 billions parameters). However, it retains a significant advantage with the lowest average execution time (43 s) over the other models.

In summary, the analysis of the results shows that large models, such as Qwen2.5, excel at accurately extracting triplets across all prompt types, though at the cost of increased computation time. The integration of a template in zero-shot prompting helps focus the model's reasoning strictly within the defined context, thereby limiting hallucinations and minimizing both formatting errors (e.g., malformed structural outputs) and semantic errors (e.g., incorrect or missing entities). This improvement is largely due to the template's structured guidance, which includes most of the target triplets, ensuring alignment with the

Table 2. Simple zero-shot prompt *Vs.* one-shot prompt

	simple zero-shot				one-shot			
	P	R	F1	Time	P	R	F1	Time
Mistral:7b	0.53	0.54	0.53	42 s	0.74	0.77	0.69	1 mn 32 s
Llama:8b	0.60	0.61	0.60	41 s	0.83	0.75	0.78	58 s
Llama:3b	0.21	0.27	0.23	**24 s**	0.69	0.70	0.69	**43 s**
Qwen:7b	0.45	0.43	0.43	36 s	0.69	0.65	0.66	1 mn 40 s
Qwen:14b	0.75	0.68	0.71	1 mn 16 s	**0.93**	**0.89**	**0.90**	2 mn 21 s

expected output. Similarly, one-shot prompting outperforms basic zero-shot by providing an illustrative example, guiding the model in both structure and content. Notably, larger LLMs demonstrate better performance than smaller ones, as their greater capacity enables them to more effectively integrate all contextual information. However, results also reveal that extraction quality is generally higher for English texts, while French inputs tend to produce more inconsistencies, likely due to uneven language exposure during model training. Moreover, the performance of example-based prompting appears sensitive to the quality and specificity of the examples provided. Initial observations suggest that variations in example clarity, ontology coverage, and alignment with the task can lead to fluctuations in precision, recall, and F1-score. A systematic investigation of how example quality and design influence the output—especially when multiple examples are used—remains an important area for future work. Such an analysis would help identify whether certain errors originate from example ambiguity, incomplete coverage of ontology elements, or prompt design limitations.

5 Conclusion

In this paper, we have emphasized the need to integrate knowledge from unstructured texts describing hydro-ecosystem restoration experiences into a structured case-base. This case-base is intended to serve as a support for a CBR framework, enabling the retrieval of past cases to inform decision-making for new restoration challenges. However, the instanciation of this case-base from unstructured textual data poses significant challenges due to inconsistencies, implicit information, and varied terminology. To address this, we proposed leveraging LLMs for generative knowledge extraction, effectively populating the ontology. Our results demonstrate that LLMs can extract triplets with high precision, facilitating the automatic instantiation of the case-base.

In future work, we aim to further explore the potential of LLMs in this context, including the fine-tuning of a model specifically adapted to the particularities of hydro-ecosystem restoration. While our current results—particularly with Qwen 14B using a zero-shot template approach—demonstrate that well-crafted prompts can yield strong performance, fine-tuning offers a complementary path for improvement. It may enhance the model's robustness across varied textual formats, reduce sensitivity to prompt design, and improve generalization to multilingual inputs. This customization is expected to increase the accuracy and semantic consistency of extracted knowledge, ultimately improving the quality and completeness of the case-base.

Future research will also consider alternative strategies that bypass explicit information extraction and structuring, such as directly retrieving and presenting raw problem-solution pairs using Retrieval-Augmented Generation (RAG) frameworks [30]. While these methods are promising for quick deployment, we argue that structured representations—despite the added complexity—enhance transparency, reusability, and reasoning capabilities. A comparative evaluation between structured and unstructured approaches will be valuable to assess trade-offs in precision, flexibility, and explainability.

Acknowledgements. This work is funded by the ANR-DLR Tetra (ANR-22-FAI2-0006-02).

References

1. Aamodt, A., Plaza, E.: Case-based reasoning: foundational issues, methodological variations, and system approachs. AICOM **7**(1), 39–59 (1994)
2. Zaman, G., Mahdin, H., Hussain, K., Rahman, A.: Information extraction from semi and unstructured data sources: a systematic literature review. ICIC Expr. Lett. **14**(6), 593–603 (2020)
3. Xu, D., et al.: Large language models for generative information extraction: a survey. Front. Comp. Sci. **18**(6), 186357 (2024)
4. Sahbi, A.N.E., Alec, C., Beust, P.: Peuplement automatique d'ontologie: l'IA générative est-elle plus efficace qu'une approche sémantique? In: 24ème conférence francophone sur l'Extraction et la Gestion des Connaissances (EGC) (2024)
5. Kumar, S., et al.: Semantic information extraction from multi-corpora using deep learning. Comput. Mater. Continua **70**(3) (2022)
6. Sambandam, P., Yuvaraj, D., Padmakumari, P., Swaminathan, S.: Spiking equilibrium convolutional neural network for spatial urban ontology. Neural Process. Lett. **55**(6), 7583–7602 (2023)
7. Smith, E., Papadopoulos, D., Braschler, M., Stockinger, K.: Lillie: information extraction and database integration using linguistics and learning-based algorithms. Inf. Syst. **105**, 101938 (2022)
8. Alec, C.: Peuplement d'ontologie à partir de petites annonces immobilières. Ingénierie des Connaissances 160 (2023)
9. Makki, J., Alquier, A.M., Prince, V.: Ontology population via NLP techniques in risk management. Int. J. Humanit. Soc. Sci. (IJHSS) **3**(3), 212–217 (2009)
10. Sakor, A., et al.: Knowledge4covid-19: a semantic-based approach for constructing a covid-19 related knowledge graph from various sources and analyzing treatments' toxicities. J. Web Semant. **75**, 100760 (2023)
11. OpenAI and others: GPT-4 technical report. arXiv:2303.08774 (2023)
12. Touvron, H., et al.: Llama 2: open foundation and fine-tuned chat models. arXiv:2307.09288 (2023)

13. AnthropicAI: Introducing Claude (2023). https://www.anthropic.com/index/introducing-claude
14. Chowdhery, A., et al.: Palm: scaling language modeling with pathways. J. Mach. Learn. Res. **24**(240), 1–113 (2023)
15. Bai, J., et al.: Qwen technical report. arXiv:2309.16609 (2023)
16. Cabot, P.L.H., Navigli, R.: Rebel: relation extraction by end-to-end language generation. In: Findings of the Association for Computational Linguistics: EMNLP 2021, pp. 2370–2381 (2021)
17. Huang, K.H., Tang, S., Peng, N.: Document-level entity-based extraction as template generation. arXiv preprint arXiv:2109.04901 (2021)
18. Yan, H., Gui, T., Dai, J., Guo, Q., Zhang, Z., Qiu, X.: A unified generative framework for various NER subtasks. arXiv preprint arXiv:2106.01223 (2021)
19. Ghanem, H., Cruz, C.: Fine-tuning vs. prompting: evaluating the knowledge graph construction with LLMs. In: 3rd International Workshop on Knowledge Graph Generation from Text (Text2KG), Co-located with ESWC 2024, pp. 26–30 (2024)
20. Gillani, K., Novak, E., Kenda, K., Mladenić, D.: Knowledge graph extraction from textual data using LLM. In: Information Society Conferences 2024 (2024)
21. Ionut Remus Iga, V., Cosmin Silaghi, G.: Assessing LLMs suitability for knowledge graph completion. arXiv e-prints pp. arXiv–2405 (2024)
22. Brand, F., Malburg, L., Bergmann, R.: Large language models as knowledge engineers. In: Proceedings of the Workshops at the 32nd International Conference on Case-Based Reasoning (ICCBR-WS 2024) co-located with the 32nd International Conference on Case-Based Reasoning (ICCBR 2024), Merida, Mexico, vol. 1 (2024)
23. Li, B., et al.: Evaluating ChatGPT's Information Extraction Capabilities: An Assessment of Performance, Explainability, Calibration, and Faithfulness. arXiv:2304.11633 (2023)
24. Brown, T.B.: Language models are few-shot learners. arXiv:2005.14165 (2020)
25. Polat, F., Tiddi, I., Groth, P.: Testing prompt engineering methods for knowledge extraction from text. Semantic Web, Under Review (2024)
26. Saetia, C., Phruetthiset, J., Chalothorn, T., Lertsutthiwong, M., Taerungruang, S., Buabthong, P.: Financial product ontology population with large language models. In: Proceedings of TextGraphs-17: Graph-Based Methods for Natural Language Processing, pp. 53–60 (2024)
27. Kouhoue, J.M., Lefrançois, M., Lesage, A., Lonlac, J., Doniec, A., Lecoeuche, S.: Ontologie de maintenance des bâtiments et capacités des Larges Modèles de Langage (LLM) pour le peuplement. In: 35es Journées francophones d'Ingénierie des Connaissances, pp. 103–106 (2024)
28. Schmitt, L., Beisel, J.N.: Les projets de restauration du Rhin Supérieur: vers la mise en place d'un observatoire transfrontalier et transdisciplinaire. In: Final Proceedings of International Conference on Integrative Sciences and Sustainable Development of Rivers, vol. 3 (2015)
29. US Forest Service, National Stream & Aquatic Ecology Center: FishXing: Case Studies (2024). https://www.fs.usda.gov/biology/nsaec/fishxing/case.html
30. Wiratunga, N., et al.: CBR-RAG: case-based reasoning for retrieval augmented generation in LLMs for legal question answering. In: International Conference on Case-Based Reasoning, pp. 445–460. Springer (2024)

Explaining Translational Embedding Models in Recommender Systems Using Knowledge Graphs and Language Models

Mario González-Monge(✉), Belén Díaz-Agudo, and Juan A. Recio-Garcia

Department of Software Engineering and Artificial Intelligence, Instituto de Tecnologías del Conocimiento, Universidad Complutense de Madrid, Madrid, Spain
mario.gl.monge@gmail.com

Abstract. We propose a modular and scalable architecture for building explainable recommendation systems that leverages knowledge graphs, translational embeddings, and LLMs. First, enriched knowledge graphs are constructed, followed by embedding-based relationship capture. Rather than a post-hoc addition, explanations are integrated into the core recommendation process. Visual explanations highlight relevant paths in the knowledge graph that connect users to recommended items, while natural language explanations, generated through an LLM, provide intuitive justifications that users can easily understand. A MovieLens 1M case study, enhanced with DBpedia, demonstrates strong experimental results and qualitative evidence of coherent, justifiable recommendations, particularly in sparse data scenarios. This highlights the potential of our approach for improving explainable recommender systems.

Keywords: Recommender Systems · Explainable AI (XAI) · Explainable CBR (XCBR) · Knowledge Graphs · Translational Embeddings · Case-based Reasoning · Large Language Models (LLMs)

1 Introduction

Recommender systems are often viewed as black boxes, where users have limited insight into the underlying processes that drive recommendations. This lack of transparency makes it challenging for users to understand why specific items are being suggested, which can impact trust and satisfaction with the system. In the context of movie recommendations, for example, users are more likely to engage with suggestions when they understand the reasoning behind them, whether based on shared characteristics with previously enjoyed content or connections through common creators, genres, or themes. Previous research has demonstrated that explanations enhance user engagement and trust, where CBR style explanations can be particularly effective in improving user satisfaction [18]. However, many authors [9,17] agree that displaying the best case is not always sufficient explanation. That is especially true when the goal of the explanation

© The Author(s), under exclusive license to Springer Nature Switzerland AG 2025
I. Bichindaritz and B. López (Eds.): ICCBR 2025, LNAI 15662, pp. 81–95, 2025.
https://doi.org/10.1007/978-3-031-96559-3_6

is to provide transparency and when the solution is not a simple reuse of a similar experience but it emerges from complex retrieval or adaptation processes. In this situation, specific explanation knowledge, apart from the cases, is required [1,13,17], and explanations may make explicit details about the features that the query has in common with the retrieved cases, why some similarities and differences are more relevant than others for the solution and why the system performs a certain adaptation. This aligns with recent findings which emphasize the importance of knowledge graphs in extracting reasoning paths between new recommendations and historical users' interactions [2,3]. Here, we can highlight recent findings on translational-based knowledge graph embeddings, like TransE and TransD, that model relationships as vector translations in an embedding space [4,11]. These methods significantly improve recommender system performance, showing substantial gains in accuracy metrics while addressing data sparsity and cold start problems [5,15,27].

This paper presents a novel approach that addresses these challenges by combining three key technologies: knowledge graphs, translational embeddings, and large language models (LLMs). Our main contributions are as follows.

- A modular and scalable architecture that integrates heterogeneous data sources through knowledge graphs, providing a rich foundation for generating contextual recommendations.
- An innovative dual-layer explainability mechanism that combines *visual path-based explanations* with natural language justifications. These visual path explanations highlight the relevant connections between users, items, and contextual entities within the knowledge graphs that justify the reasoning behind the recomendation, making it more transparent and accessible to users.
- Implementation and evaluation of translational embedding models (TransE and TransD) to measure the impact of different state-of-the-art models, that effectively capture complex relationships within the knowledge graph, enabling more nuanced recommendations.

The paper presents a case study that utilizes knowledge graphs built from MovieLens 1M data, enriched with DBpedia information. This integration offers a strong semantic framework that captures not only direct user-item interactions but also broader contextual relationships. The system uses translational embeddings to represent these relationships in a continuous vector space, facilitating more effective and contextually relevant similarity calculations and recommendations. Explanations are not an afterthought; instead, they are embedded within the core recommendation process. Visual explanations highlight key paths in the knowledge graph connecting users to recommended items, while natural language explanations, generated by LLMs, provide clear and intuitive justifications for users.

Experimental results demonstrate that our system not only achieves competitive performance on standard metrics but also provides meaningful explanations that enhance user understanding. Even in cases with sparse user data, the system generates coherent and well-justified recommendations, showcasing its robustness and practical utility.

The remainder of this paper is organized as follows: Sect. 2 reviews related work in recommendation systems, knowledge graphs, and explainability. Section 3 details our proposed framework, including the system architecture and knowledge graph construction. Section 4 describes our explainability mechanisms. Section 5 presents experimental results and analysis. Finally, Sect. 6 discusses our findings and future directions.

2 Related Work

Traditional recommendation systems have evolved significantly from simple collaborative filtering approaches to more sophisticated methods that incorporate diverse data sources and complex relationships [7,24]. In the context of CBR, recommendation systems can be viewed as a specialized form of case retrieval, where past user interactions serve as cases for generating new recommendations [16]. Recent advances have focused on integrating deeper semantic understanding and contextual information to improve recommendation quality [14]. Here, knowledge graphs have emerged as powerful tools for enhancing recommendation systems by capturing complex relationships between entities. Recent work by [21] introduced Knowledge Graph Attention Network (KGAT), demonstrating how graph attention mechanisms can leverage both collaborative signals and knowledge-aware connectivity to generate more accurate recommendations. Similarly, [22] proposed Neural Graph Collaborative Filtering (NGCF), which explicitly models user-item interactions through graph neural networks.

A key issue in knowledge graphs is the representation and exploitation of the semantic relationships. The development of translational embedding models has provided efficient methods for representing knowledge graph relationships in continuous vector spaces. *TransE* [4] pioneered this approach by modeling relationships as translations in the embedding space. Specifically, it represents entities as vectors and relationships as translations, ensuring that the vector representation of a head entity, when translated by the relation vector, is close to the vector of the tail entity. Subsequent models like *TransD* [11] have introduced more sophisticated relationship modeling capabilities. These advances have particular relevance for recommendation systems, as they enable more nuanced capturing of user-item relationships and contextual information.

2.1 Explanability in Recommender Systems

Explainability in recommendation systems has gained increasing attention, particularly as systems become more complex. Traditional approaches to explanation often relied on simple similarity-based justifications, but recent work has explored more sophisticated methods. Research by [23] has shown how paths in knowledge graphs can provide interpretable explanations for recommendations, allowing users to understand the chain of relationships leading to a suggestion. Path based explanations are also used in [8] where formal concept analysis is used to build an explanation lattice. Models like [28] have demonstrated how neural architectures can be adapted to generate natural language explanations alongside recommendations.

The recent emergence of LLMs has opened new possibilities for generating natural and contextually relevant explanations in recommendation systems. Recent work by [25] has explored how LLMs can be leveraged to generate personalized explanations for recommendations, moving beyond template-based approaches to more dynamic and context-aware explanations.

Despite these advances, several significant challenges remain in the field of explainable recommendations. These include balancing the computational costs of explanation generation with real-time recommendation needs, developing comprehensive metrics that assess both recommendation quality and explanation effectiveness, adapting explanations to diverse user preferences and cognitive styles, and effectively integrating multiple explanation modalities while maintaining coherence and usefulness. Our work explores these challenges by proposing a unified framework that leverages knowledge graphs, translational embeddings, and LLMs to generate both effective recommendations and meaningful explanations. This approach builds upon existing work by leveraging established embedding methods for recommendation but introduces novelty through its explainability framework. Specifically, our contribution lies in the generation and integration of explanations, combining visual path-based reasoning with LLM-generated natural language justifications.

3 Proposed Framework

Our framework follows a modular and scalable architecture designed to facilitate the integration of heterogeneous data sources and support flexible experimentation with different recommendation strategies. The system comprises four main components, as illustrated in Fig. 1: *Knowledge Graph Construction*, *Embedding Generation*, *Recommendation Engine* and *Explainability Mechanisms*.

The architecture is implemented using FastAPI, providing a RESTful interface that enables dynamic configuration and real-time interaction with the system. Each component is designed to be independently scalable and maintainable, allowing for future extensions and improvements.

3.1 Knowledge Graph Construction

The knowledge graph forms the foundation of our system, integrating information from multiple sources to create a rich semantic representation of the recommendation domain. Our implementation focuses on movie recommendations, combining data from two primary sources:

- **MovieLens 1M:** Provides core user-item interactions, including ratings, user demographics, and basic movie metadata.
- **DBpedia:** Enriches movie entities with additional contextual information such as directors, actors, genres, and production details.

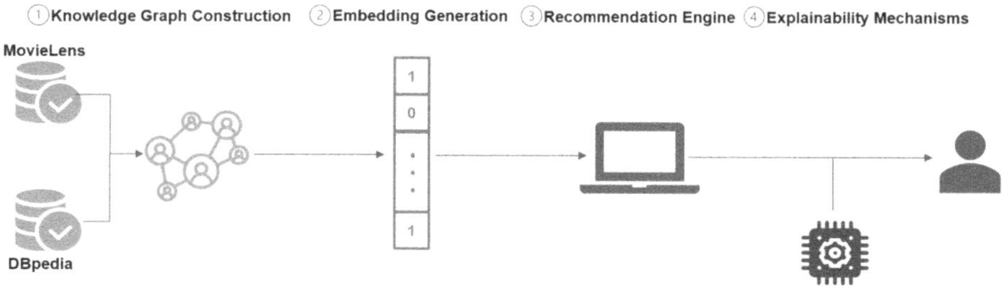

Fig. 1. System architecture showing the main components and data flow.

The graph construction process follows a three-step approach. First, integrating data by mapping MovieLens entities to DBpedia URIs through correspondence tables. Second, defining relationships by establishing typed edges between entities, where each edge represents a specific interaction or semantic connection. User-related relationships originate from user nodes, while item-item relationships capture domain-specific knowledge such as genre or actor connections. This structure ensures that both user preferences and item characteristics are effectively represented in the knowledge graph. Finally, optimizing the graph by implementing constraints such as limiting LIKED relationships to 5 per user and LIKED_GENRE connections to 2 per user. These constraints help control graph density, reducing noise and ensuring that recommendations are based on meaningful interactions rather than overfitting to highly active users.

3.2 Embedding Generation

To capture the semantic relationships encoded in the knowledge graph, we implement two translational embedding models:

TransE. is a model for representing knowledge graphs where relations between entities are modeled as linear translations in a low-dimensional vector space [4]. Its *score* function:

$$f(h, r, t) = \|\mathbf{h} + \mathbf{r} - \mathbf{t}\|_2 \tag{1}$$

evaluates the validity of triples $\langle h, r, t \rangle$, where $\mathbf{h}$, $\mathbf{r}$, and $\mathbf{t}$ represent the head entity, relationship, and tail entity embeddings respectively, minimizing the distance in positive triples and maximizing it in negative ones during training.

The fundamental intuition behind TransE lies in conceptualizing relationships as geometric displacements in a continuous space. For example, if h represents a user and t a movie, the LIKED relation (r) will adjust the vectors so that the sum of $\mathbf{h}$ and $\mathbf{r}$ approximates $\mathbf{t}$ as closely as possible, thus reflecting the probability of the relation being valid through the distance between vectors.

TransD. Despite its effectiveness in capturing relational patterns while being computationally efficient, TransE struggles with modeling complex relationships, such as one-to-many or many-to-many interactions, as mentioned in [11]. The scoring function used in TransE assumes a single vector space shared by all entities and relations, which causes overlaps in representations and reduces its effectiveness when handling the diversity among graph relationships. To address this problem, TransD [11] emerged as an improvement. Unlike TransE, which embeds all entities and relations in the same space, TransD assigns distinct representations to each entity and relation by introducing dynamic projection matrices. These matrices enable entities to have different representations depending on the relation they participate in, allowing for a more flexible and accurate modeling of complex interactions within the knowledge graph.

Formally, TransD extends TransE by introducing projection matrices for each entity-relation pair:

$$\mathbf{M}_{rh} = \mathbf{r}_p\mathbf{h}_p^T + \mathbf{I}_{m\times n} \quad \mathbf{M}_{rt} = \mathbf{r}_p\mathbf{t}_p^T + \mathbf{I}_{m\times n} \tag{2}$$

$$h_\perp = M_{rh}h, \quad t_\perp = M_{rt}t. \tag{3}$$

$$f(h,r,t) = \|\mathbf{h}_\perp + \mathbf{r} - \mathbf{t}_\perp\|_2, \tag{4}$$

where:

- $\mathbf{h}, \mathbf{h_p}, \mathbf{t}, \mathbf{t_p} \in \mathbb{R}^n$ represent the embeddings of the head and tail entities, along with their corresponding projection vectors. The parameter n denotes the dimensionality of the entity embedding space in TransD.
- $\mathbf{r}, \mathbf{r_p} \in \mathbb{R}^m$ represent the embedding of the relation and its associated projection vector. The parameter m specifies the dimensionality of the relational embedding space in TransD.
- $\mathbf{I}_{m\times n}$ is the identity matrix, ensuring that the transformation maintains the proper dimensional consistency in the projected space.

Both models are trained using margin-based ranking loss with negative sampling:

$$L = \sum_{(h,r,t)\in S} \sum_{(h',r,t')\in S'} [\gamma + f(h,r,t) - f(h',r,t')]_+ \tag{5}$$

where f is the score function in Eq. 4. S represents the set of positive, real triplets and S' represents the set of negative triplets, generated by corrupting the head or the tail entity in the original triplets.

The embedding training phase is performed on the entire knowledge graph, meaning that all users and items are represented in the vector space. However, when learning rating-based models, only the ratings from the training set are used to compute predictions, ensuring that the test set remains unseen during training.

3.3 Recommendation Engine

This section details the implementation of three recommendation approaches using the previously discussed embedding-based similarity function: item-based, user-based, and hybrid methods. Although more complex techniques like matrix factorization or deep learning models exist, we have opted for these methods due to their greater interpretability and better alignment with the specific needs of our case study, especially considering the available data.

Item-Based Recommendations. For a user u and item i, the prediction is calculated as:

$$\hat{r}_{u,i}^{\text{item}} = \frac{\sum_{j \in I(u)} s(i,j) r_{u,j}}{\sum_{j \in I(u)} s(i,j)} \tag{6}$$

where $s(i,j)$ is the similarity between items i and j, computed using the dot product of their embedding vectors. $r_{u,j}$ is the rating given to item j by user u. $I(u)$ represents the set of items rated by user u, but only ratings from the training set are used during model training. The item-based method is effective for scenarios where user preferences are strongly tied to specific items, as it focuses on the similarities between items based on past interactions.

User-Based Recommendations. Similarly, user-based predictions are computed as:

$$\hat{r}_{u,i}^{\text{user}} = \frac{\sum_{v \in U(i)} s(u,v) r_{v,i}}{\sum_{v \in U(i)} s(u,v)} \tag{7}$$

where $U(i)$ is the set of users who have rated item i. The user-based method, on the other hand, works well when there are clear patterns in user behavior, allowing for the identification of similar users and their preferences.

Hybrid Recommendations. The hybrid approach combines both methods using a weighted average:

$$\hat{r}_{u,i}^{\text{hybrid}} = \alpha \hat{r}_{u,i}^{\text{item}} + (1 - \alpha) \hat{r}_{u,i}^{\text{user}} \tag{8}$$

where $\alpha \in [0, 1]$.

To address rating scale bias, we implement z-score normalization:

$$r'_{u,i} = \frac{r_{u,i} - \mu_u}{\sigma_u} \tag{9}$$

This method leverages the strengths of both item-based and user-based approaches.

4 Explainability Mechanisms

A key contribution of our work is the development of a dual-layer explainability system that combines *visual path-based explanations* with *natural language justifications*. This approach provides users with both structural understanding through graph visualization and intuitive explanations through natural language, enhancing the transparency and interpretability of recommendations. Users can interact with different paths in the visual representation and focus on specific aspects of the recommendation that interest them. The system adaptively adjusts explanations based on the users' preferences, shared history with similar users, items' context, and path complexity.

4.1 Visual Path-Based Explanations

The visual explanation component leverages the structure of our knowledge graph to identify and visualize meaningful paths between users and recommended items. To generate these explanatory paths, we first transform the directed knowledge graph into an undirected graph by creating inverse relationships, ensuring path discovery between any user-item pair. We then apply Dijkstra's algorithm to find the shortest paths between users and recommended items. The discovered paths are filtered based on their length, relationship types, and diversity to ensure meaningful and interpretable explanations.

The visual representation renders these paths as interactive subgraphs, where nodes represent different entities such as users, movies, actors, directors, and genres. Relationships between entities are shown as labeled edges, indicating different types of relationships.

Figure 2 demonstrates our integrated approach through a concrete example. The visualization shows a recommendation path connecting a user to a movie through shared actors and genres, while the accompanying natural language explanation provides context: "We recommend [Movie X] because you enjoyed [Movie Y], which shares the same director. Both films are [Genre Z], a genre you've rated highly in the past."

After the system finds contextual paths connecting the user to the recommended movie through the recommender knowledge graph and an auxiliary knowledge graph based solely on contextual information about the item, a prompt combining all the information captured in the paths is generated.

4.2 Natural Language Explanations

To complement the visual explanations, we incorporate a natural language generation system using a selection of state-of-the-art language models. For each discovered path, we generate explanation templates that capture various aspects of the recommendation rationale, including direct user preferences, transitive relationships, genre preferences, and collaborative patterns. These templates form the basis for generating personalized explanations that resonate with users' understanding.

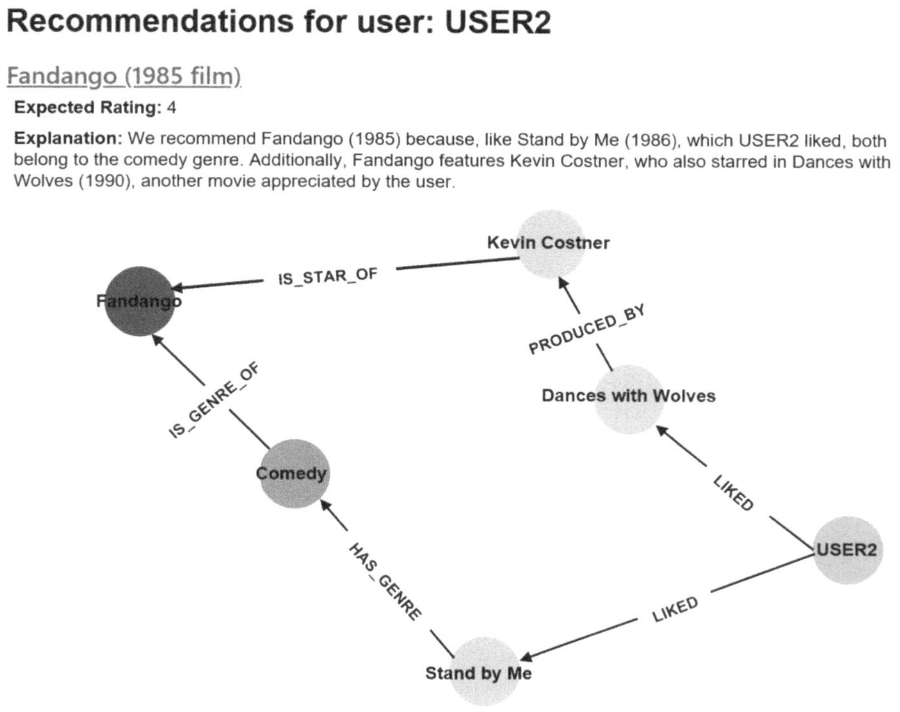

Fig. 2. Example of a visual path-based explanation showing the connection between a user and a recommended movie through shared genres and actors.

The LLM integration starts with prompts that blend path information from the knowledge graph, user history, and recommendation context. These prompts are created by combining a general template with extracted data from various knowledge graph paths, which the LLM then processes to generate personalized, concise contextual explanations. After careful consideration and testing, we explored models such as ALBERT, Flan-T5, and LLaMA 3.1-8B-Instruct before selecting "gpt-4o-mini-2024-07-18", which demonstrated the best balance of high-quality results, efficiency, and response time.

Figure 3 exemplifies how the system generates a prompt for the natural language explanation in Fig. 2. This prompt captures relevant information that the LLM can present in a more user-ready format, capturing all the relevant context within the visual representation. The response generated from this prompt is shown in Fig. 2 and, as with all explanations in natural language, it is integrated as part of the report presented to the user.

This integrated approach to explanation generation provides users with both intuitive understanding through natural language and detailed insights through visual path exploration. The combination of these complementary explanation modes enhances the transparency and trustworthiness of the recommendation

Example Prompt

Using the information from the following paths in the knowledge graph:
Main path connecting the user to the recommended movie:

- USER2 -(LIKED)-> *Stand by Me* (1986)
- *Stand by Me* (1986) -(HAS_GENRE)-> Comedy
- Comedy -(IS_GENRE_OF)-> *Fandango* (1985)

Additional path providing complementary information:

- USER2 -(LIKED)-> *Dances with Wolves* (1990)
- *Dances with Wolves* (1990) -(PRODUCED_BY)-> Kevin Costner
- Kevin Costner -(IS_STAR_OF)-> *Fandango* (1985)

Write a concise and clear explanation that combines both sources of information to justify the recommendation.

Fig. 3. Example of a prompt used in the system integrating various paths between the user and the recommended movie

system, allowing users to understand both the high-level reasoning and the detailed connections that lead to specific recommendations.

The explanations are designed to be both informative and engaging, helping users build trust in the system while providing them with valuable insights about their preferences and the relationships between different items in the recommendation space. By making these connections explicit and understandable, our system helps users make more informed decisions about the recommendations they receive.

5 Experimental Evaluation

5.1 Experimental Setup

We evaluate our framework using the MovieLens 1M dataset, which contains *1,000,209 ratings from 6,040 users on 3,900 movies.* The ratings are provided on a scale from 1 to 5, accompanied by user demographic information and basic movie metadata. To enrich this dataset, we integrate additional information from DBpedia, including director and actor information, production details, extended genre classifications, and comprehensive release information.

Our evaluation protocol follows a systematic approach to ensure reliable results. We generate embeddings for all entities in the knowledge graph, capturing relationships between users, movies, and additional attributes. The recommendation models are then trained separately on user rating data to learn personalized preferences. We split the dataset into an 80% training set and a 20% test set. When constructing the knowledge graph, we apply strategic limitations to maintain data quality, restricting each user to a maximum of 5 LIKED relationships and 2 LIKED_GENRE connections, while retaining complete attribute information for all movies.

For embedding generation, we employ a configuration optimized through preliminary experiments: 128-dimensional embeddings, 5 negative samples per positive instance, a margin of 2.0, and a batch size of 64. These parameters were selected to balance computational efficiency with model performance.

We benchmark our approach against several state-of-the-art models in the field. These include CKE (Collaborative Knowledge-based Embedding) [26], SHINE (Signed Heterogeneous Information Network Embedding) [19], DKN (Deep Knowledge-aware Network) [20], PER (Path-Enhanced Recommendations) [12], Wide&Deep (Neural Recommendation with Wide and Deep Learning) [6], and HI2Rec (Hierarchical Interest-based Recommendation) [10].

Table 1. Performance Comparison with Baseline Models

Model	NDCG@10	Precision@10	Recall@10	F1@10
Our Model	0.186	0.142	0.156	0.148
CKE	0.172	0.138	0.149	0.143
SHINE	0.168	0.135	0.147	0.140
DKN	0.165	0.133	0.145	0.138
PER	0.189	0.145	0.158	0.151
Wide&Deep	0.175	0.140	0.152	0.145
HI2Rec	0.192	0.147	0.160	0.153

5.2 Results and Analysis

Additionally, we evaluate the impact of each phase of our system on the overall quality of the generated recommenders using two categories of metrics. To measure rating prediction accuracy, we use Mean Absolute Error (MAE) and Root Mean Square Error (RMSE). For assessing ranking performance, we apply ranking metrics like Precision@k, Recall@k, NDCG@k, and F1@k, which offer a comprehensive view of the system's effectiveness in ranking relevant items. Table 1 presents the comparative performance across different metrics, demonstrating our model's competitive performance against established baselines.

Our analysis reveals several key insights about system components. All analyses were carried out using a relative approach. We establish baseline reference models and compare the given modifications relative to the baseline reference. This procedure allows us to examine the real impact of each component of the architecture and how the different decisions influence the final recommendation.

Figure 4a shows that the inclusion of user information in the knowledge graph significantly improves performance across all metrics, while our approach to limiting relationship counts maintains graph quality without degrading performance. Regarding embedding models, Fig. 4b confirms that TransD consistently

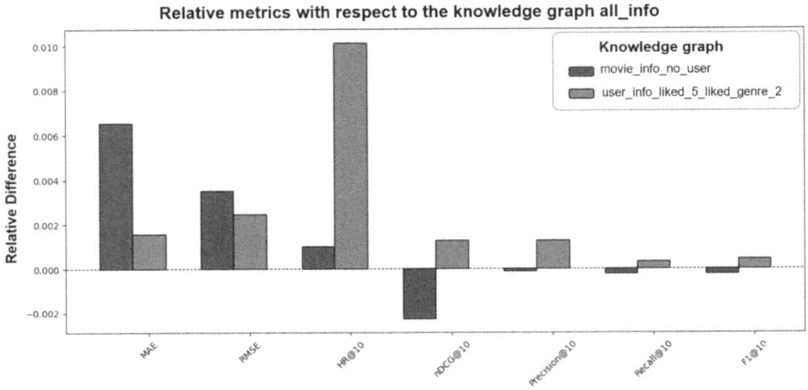

(a) Knowledge graph information impact

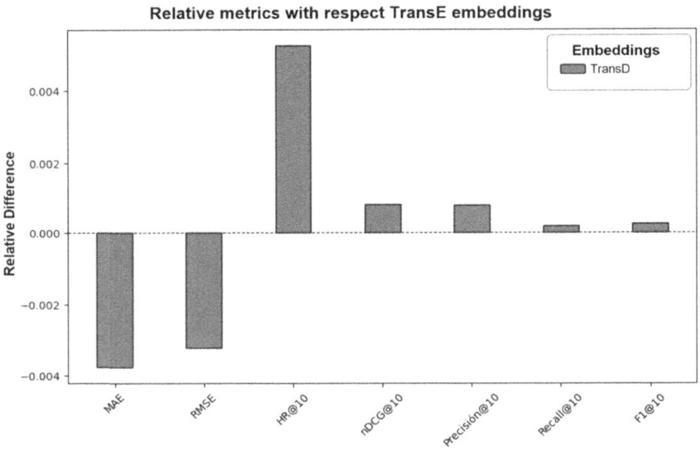

(b) Relative recommender performance between TransD and TransE

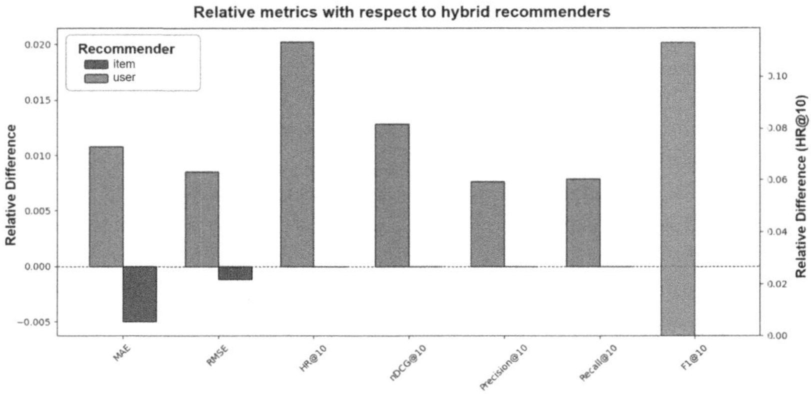

(c) Recommender's type impact relative to the hybrid approach

Fig. 4. Impact analysis of the different components of the architecture outperforms TransE across all metrics, obtaining lower MAE and RMSE results and improving all ranking metrics.

In comparing recommendation approaches, we find that item-based models excel in rating prediction (MAE and RMSE), while user-based models show superior performance in ranking metrics, as shown in Fig. 4c. This analysis allows users to choose the recommender's type based on the strengths they want to prioritize, whether it be accurate rating predictions or better ranking performance.

Our evaluation reveals that the combination of knowledge graphs and translational embeddings provides robust recommendation performance across various scenarios. The dual-layer explanation system effectively communicates recommendation rationale, while maintaining good performance even with limited user data. However, we identify several areas for future improvement, including the computational cost of path generation for large-scale deployments, the need for more sophisticated explanation personalization, and opportunities for implementing more advanced embedding techniques.

6 Conclusion and Future Work

This paper presents a novel approach to explainable recommendations that combines knowledge graphs, translational embeddings, and LLMs. Our framework addresses the need for transparency in recommendation systems while maintaining competitive performance against state-of-the-art baselines.

The primary contributions of this work include the development of a modular and scalable architecture for knowledge graph-based recommendations, the implementation of a dual-layer explainability mechanism, and the demonstration of effective recommendation generation even in challenging scenarios with limited user data. Our experimental results show that the integration of knowledge graphs with translational embeddings provides a robust foundation for generating recommendations. The TransD model, in particular, demonstrates superior performance compared to simpler translational approaches, effectively capturing complex relationships within the knowledge graph. Additionally, the creation of rich-context knowledge graphs including user information proves to strengthen the final recommendations given to users. Moreover, our dual-layer explainability system, combining visual path-based explanations with natural language generation, offers users both structural understanding and intuitive explanations of recommendations.

The case studies presented demonstrate our system's effectiveness in handling various challenging scenarios, including users with limited interactions and diverse preferences. The ability to generate meaningful explanations in these cases highlights the robustness of our approach and its practical utility in real-world applications.

Our current implementation yields promising results, highlighting several directions for future research, for example, the application of more advanced embedding techniques, such as graph neural networks or attention-based models, to capture deeper relationships within the knowledge graph. There is also significant potential for enhancing the personalization of explanations. This could involve adapting the complexity and style of explanations based on user preferences, interaction history, and cognitive styles. Research into dynamic explanation generation that considers user feedback and learning patterns could lead to more effective and engaging explanations. Another promising direction involves deeper integration with explanation-by-example techniques, particularly in the context of explanation generation. This could include developing methods to leverage past successful explanations as templates for new recommendations, adapting them based on current context and user feedback.

Acknowledgements. Supported by the UCM (Research Group 921330) and the AUDITIA-X project PID2023-150566OB-I00, funded by the Ministry of Science and Innovation of Spain (https://gaia.fdi.ucm.es/research/auditia-x/). Partially supported by the BOSCH-UCM Honorary Chair on Artificial Intelligence.

References

1. Armengol, E., Plaza, E.: Using symbolic descriptions to explain similarity on CBR. In: Proceedings of the 8th International Conference of the ACIA, Alguer, Italy, pp. 239–246 (2005)
2. Balloccu, G., Boratto, L., Fenu, G., Marras, M.: Post processing recommender systems with knowledge graphs for recency, popularity, and diversity of explanations. In: ACM SIGIR Conference on Research and Development in Information Retrieval, pp. 646–656. SIGIR 2022, ACM, July 2022
3. Balloccu, G., Boratto, L., Fenu, G., Marras, M.: Reinforcement recommendation reasoning through knowledge graphs for explanation path quality (2022)
4. Bordes, A., Usunier, N., Garcia-Duran, A., Weston, J., Yakhnenko, O.: Translating embeddings for modeling multi-relational data. In: Burges, C., Bottou, L., Welling, M., Ghahramani, Z., Weinberger, K. (eds.) Advances in Neural Information Processing Systems. vol. 26. Curran Associates, Inc. (2013)
5. Cao, Y., Wang, X., He, X., Hu, Z., Chua, T.S.: Unifying knowledge graph learning and recommendation: towards a better understanding of user preferences. In: The World Wide Web Conference, pp. 151–161. WWW 2019, Association for Computing Machinery, New York, NY, USA (2019)
6. Cheng, H.T., et al.: Wide & deep learning for recommender systems (2016). https://arxiv.org/abs/1606.07792
7. Debbah, A., Lagrini, S.: Latest advances in deep learning-based recommender systems. Int. J. Reason. based Intell. Syst. **16**(3), 249–266 (2024)
8. Diaz-Agudo, B., Caro-Martinez, M., Recio-Garcia, J.A., Jorro-Aragoneses, J., Jimenez-Diaz, G.: Explanation of recommenders using formal concept analysis. In: Bach, K., Marling, C. (eds.) ICCBR 2019. LNCS (LNAI), vol. 11680, pp. 33–48. Springer, Cham (2019). https://doi.org/10.1007/978-3-030-29249-2_3
9. Doyle, D., Cunningham, P., Bridge, D., Rahman, Y.: Explanation oriented retrieval. In: Funk, P., González Calero, P.A. (eds.) ECCBR 2004. LNCS (LNAI), vol. 3155, pp. 157–168. Springer, Heidelberg (2004). https://doi.org/10.1007/978-3-540-28631-8_13
10. He, M., Wang, B., Du, X.: Hi2rec: exploring knowledge in heterogeneous information for movie recommendation. IEEE Access **PP**, 1 (2019)

11. Ji, G., He, S., Xu, L., Liu, K., Zhao, J.: Knowledge graph embedding via dynamic mapping matrix, pp. 687–696 (2015)
12. Liu, J., Shi, C., Yang, C., Lu, Z., Yu, P.S.: A survey on heterogeneous information network based recommender systems: concepts, methods, applications and resources. AI Open **3**, 40–57 (2022)
13. Maximini, R., Freßmann, A., Schaaf, M.: Explanation service for complex CBR applications. In: 7th ECCBR, Madrid, Spain, pp. 302–316 (2004)
14. Muthivhi, M., van Zyl, T.L., Wang, H.: Multi-modal recommendation system with auxiliary information (2022). https://arxiv.org/abs/2210.10652
15. Nguyen, L.V., Vo, Q.T., Bui, C.V., Phan, T.T.H., Lee, O.J.: Knowledge graph-based recommender systems: a case study on movie domain. In: 2024 15th International Conference on Information and Communication Technology Convergence (ICTC), pp. 1026–1029 (2024)
16. Ricci, F., Rokach, L., Shapira, B., Kantor, P.B. (eds.): Recommender Systems Handbook. Springer, Boston, MA (2011). https://doi.org/10.1007/978-0-387-85820-3
17. Roth-Berghofer, T.: Explanations and case-based reasoning: foundational issues. In: 7th ECCBR, Madrid, Spain, pp. 389–403 (2004)
18. Tintarev, N., Masthoff, J.: Explaining recommendations: design and evaluation. In: Ricci, F., Rokach, L., Shapira, B. (eds.) Recommender Systems Handbook, pp. 353–382. Springer, Boston, MA (2015). https://doi.org/10.1007/978-1-4899-7637-6_10
19. Wang, H., Zhang, F., Hou, M., Xie, X., Guo, M., Liu, Q.: Shine: signed heterogeneous information network embedding for sentiment link prediction. In: Proceedings of the Eleventh ACM International Conference on Web Search and Data Mining, pp. 592–600. WSDM 2018, ACM (2018)
20. Wang, H., Zhang, F., Xie, X., Guo, M.: DKN: deep knowledge-aware network for news recommendation (2018). https://arxiv.org/abs/1801.08284
21. Wang, X., He, X., Cao, Y., Liu, M., Chua, T.S.: KGAT: knowledge graph attention network for recommendation. In: Proceedings of the 25th ACM SIGKDD International Conference on Knowledge Discovery & Data Mining, pp. 950–958. KDD 2019, ACM (2019)
22. Wang, X., He, X., Wang, M., Feng, F., Chua, T.S.: Neural graph collaborative filtering. In: Proceedings of the 42nd International ACM SIGIR Conference on Research and Development in Information Retrieval, pp. 165–174. SIGIR 2019, ACM, July 2019
23. Wang, X., Wang, D., Xu, C., He, X., Cao, Y., Chua, T.S.: Explainable reasoning over knowledge graphs for recommendation (2018). https://arxiv.org/abs/1811.04540
24. Wang, Y., Ma, X., Zhu, M.: A knowledge graph algorithm enabled deep recommendation system. PeerJ. Comput. Sci. **10**, e2010 (2024)
25. Wu, L., et al.: A survey on large language models for recommendation (2024). https://arxiv.org/abs/2305.19860
26. Zhang, F., Yuan, N., Lian, D., Xie, X., Ma, W.Y.: Collaborative knowledge base embedding for recommender systems, pp. 353–362, August 2016
27. Zhang, J.C., Zain, A.M., Zhou, K.Q., Chen, X., Zhang, R.M.: A review of recommender systems based on knowledge graph embedding. Expert Syst. Appl. **250**, 123876 (2024)
28. Zhang, Y., Chen, X.: Explainable recommendation: a survey and new perspectives. Found. Trends® Inf. Retr. **14**(1), 1–101 (2020)

Fuzzy Symbolic Reasoning for Few-Shot KBQA: A CBR-Inspired Generative Approach

Xinyu Hu[1,2], Li Tong[2], Jian Yang[3], Lingtao Xue[2,4], Kai Huang[5], and Gang Xiao[2(✉)]

[1] School of System Science and Engineering, Sun Yat-sen University, Guangzhou, China
huxy53@mail2.sysu.edu.cn

[2] National Key Laboratory for Complex Systems Simulation, Beijing, China
searchware@qq.com

[3] China Electronics Corporation, Shenzhen, China

[4] School of Computer Science and Technology, Xidian University, Xi'an, China
lingtaoxue@stu.xidian.edu.cn

[5] School of Computer Science and Technology, Sun Yat-sen University, Guangzhou, China
huangk36@mail.sysu.edu.cn

Abstract. Knowledge base question answering (KBQA) aims to retrieve and reason over structured data to answer natural language questions. Traditional semantic parsing approaches often struggle in few-shot scenarios due to limited annotated data and reliance on rigid query structures, while retrieval-augmented generation (RAG) methods lack explicit symbolic reasoning and are prone to factual errors. We propose FSR-KBQA, a fuzzy symbolic reasoning framework inspired by case-based reasoning, which enables large language models to perform stepwise inference over retrieved knowledge using approximate symbolic programs. This design enhances robustness and interpretability without requiring precise logical forms. Experiments on KQA Pro and GrailQA show that FSR-KBQA achieves strong accuracy and generalization, reaching 68.25% on KQA Pro with Llama-3.1 (70B), and surpassing GPT-4 on GrailQA despite using smaller, open-weight models. These results demonstrate the effectiveness of fuzzy symbolic reasoning as a scalable approach for few-shot KBQA, and we release code and resources at https://github.com/Husense6/FSR-KBQA.

Keywords: Knowledge Base Question Answering · Fuzzy Symbolic Reasoning · Case-Based Reasoning · Few-shot Learning · Generative AI

1 Introduction

Knowledge base question answering (KBQA) retrieves structured knowledge from knowledge bases (KBs) to provide accurate and interpretable answers. This

© The Author(s), under exclusive license to Springer Nature Switzerland AG 2025
I. Bichindaritz and B. López (Eds.): ICCBR 2025, LNAI 15662, pp. 96–110, 2025.
https://doi.org/10.1007/978-3-031-96559-3_7

is essential in domains requiring factual reliability and logical reasoning, such as medicine, law, and science [13].

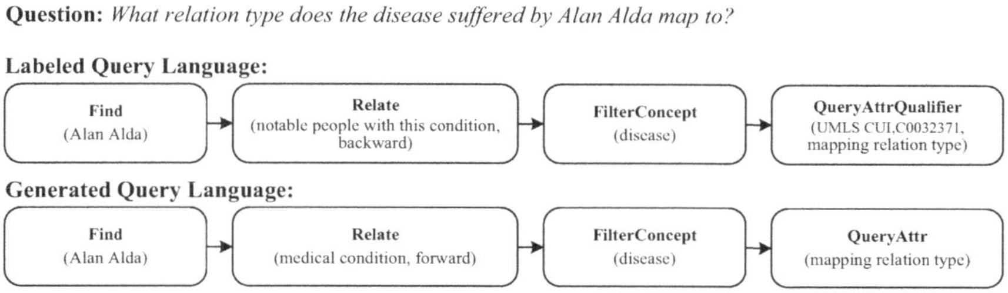

Fig. 1. Error case of traditional KBQA models

Traditional KBQA systems [29,31] rely on semantic parsing to convert natural language questions into structured queries like SPARQL or KoPL. However, in few-shot scenarios with limited supervision, parsing often suffers from low accuracy, leading to retrieval failure due to incorrect relation direction, missing attributes, or incomplete constraints.

Figure 1 presents a representative failure case of semantic parsing. While the generated query maintains a structurally valid and seemingly logical form, it introduces subtle but critical errors: the relation direction is reversed (using a forward relation instead of the labeled backward one), and the query omits a qualifier that precisely defines the mapping relation type. These omissions, though minor in form, prevent the query from being correctly executed on the knowledge base, resulting in reasoning failure. Such issues are particularly frequent in few-shot scenarios, where parsing robustness is limited by data scarcity.

Recent work applies large language models (LLMs) and retrieval-augmented generation (RAG) to KBQA [2,16]. While LLMs improve generality, RAG lacks explicit symbolic reasoning and often produces hallucinated or logically inconsistent responses— particularly for multi-hop or qualifier-dependent queries.

To address these issues, we propose FSR-KBQA, a fuzzy symbolic reasoning framework inspired by case-based reasoning (CBR) [1]. CBR solves new problems by adapting solutions from similar past cases. In our framework, retrieved knowledge serves as "past experience," and large language models act as the reasoning engine that adapts and recombines these experiences to answer new questions. Instead of executing rigid structured queries, FSR-KBQA allows LLMs to generate approximate symbolic representations, which guide stepwise reasoning over the retrieved facts. This design enables flexible inference over structured knowledge, analogous to how CBR applies imperfect yet contextually relevant prior knowledge. It improves robustness to handle parsing errors and enhances adaptability in few-shot settings, effectively bridging symbolic reasoning and generative capabilities.

Our contributions are as follows:

- We propose FSR-KBQA, a novel framework that enables LLMs to perform symbolic reasoning via approximate representations, reducing reliance on precise semantic parsing.
- We introduce fuzzy symbolic reasoning to enhance KBQA robustness, enabling flexible stepwise inference over retrieved knowledge while maintaining interpretability.
- We achieve state-of-the-art few-shot performance, with 68.25% accuracy on KQA Pro [3] using Llama-3.1 (70B), and strong generalization on GrailQA, demonstrating the scalability and effectiveness of our approach.

2 Related Works

2.1 Traditional KBQA Techniques

Traditional KBQA methods can be broadly categorized into semantic parsing-based (SP-based) and information retrieval-based (IR-based) approaches [13].

SP-based methods convert questions into logical forms such as SPARQL, S-expression [8], or KoPL [3], and execute them over knowledge bases. Although effective under full supervision, these methods heavily rely on annotated question-program pairs. To reduce supervision costs, various strategies have been explored, including reinforcement learning [10,19,21,32], intermediate representations [4,14,17], subquery decomposition [11], and syntax-enhanced modeling [12]. Ensemble strategies [7] have also improved robustness. Nevertheless, these methods remain sensitive to parsing errors and struggle under few-shot supervision.

IR-based methods retrieve subgraphs based on detected entities and relations, then reason over them. Advances include improved entity representations [6], noise filtering [9,28], and optimized retrieval [22,30]. Despite improvements, IR-based models still rely on complete subgraphs and often degrade in low-resource scenarios.

2.2 LLM-Based KBQA Techniques

Recent work has applied large language models (LLMs) to KBQA, particularly in few-shot settings [23]. Some treat LLMs as semantic parsers via in-context learning [2,16], while others adopt retrieval-augmented generation (RAG) [15]. Techniques such as chain-of-thought prompting [26], knowledge-grounded instruction tuning [24], and agent-based frameworks [27] have further enhanced multi-step reasoning. However, these methods often lack symbolic transparency, limiting their effectiveness on complex queries.

To bridge this gap, symbolic reasoning has been integrated with LLMs. Zhang et al. [33] propose a rule-guided framework to flexibly control logical form generation, while Das et al. [5] introduce case-based reasoning (CBR) to adapt past reasoning patterns for few-shot generalization.

Building on these insights, we propose a hybrid framework that combines approximate symbolic representations, retrieval-grounded knowledge, and stepwise LLM reasoning, achieving robustness and interpretability in few-shot KBQA.

3 FSR-KGQA Framework

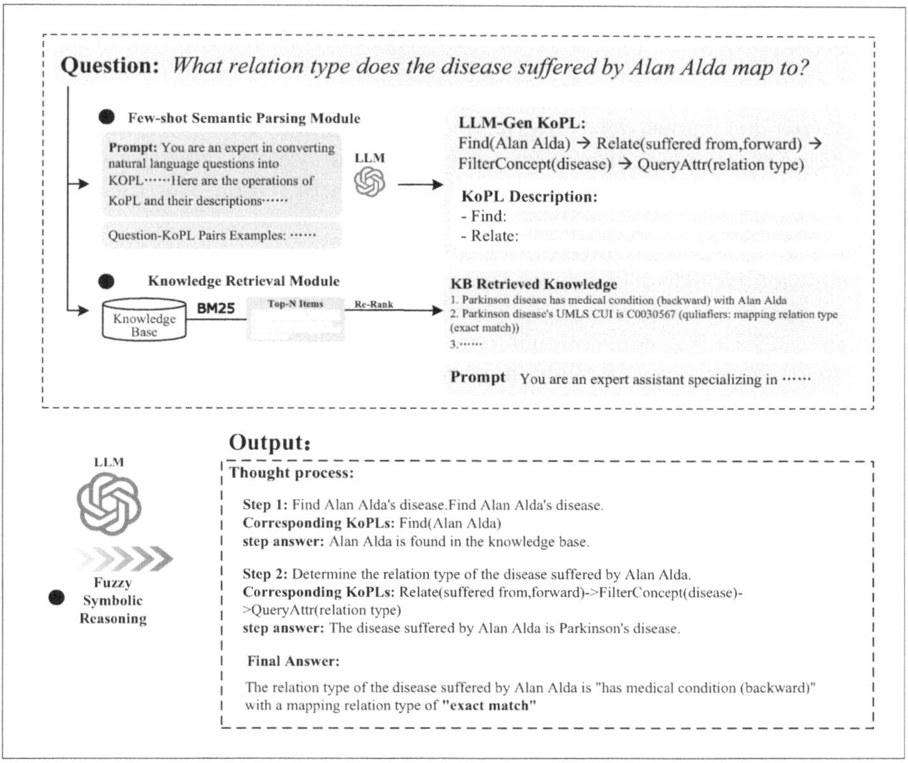

Fig. 2. FSR-KBQA Framework

3.1 Problem Definition

Given a natural language question Q and a structured knowledge base K composed of entity-relation triples $K = \{(e_i, r, e_j) \mid e_i, e_j \in E, r \in R\}$, the goal of KBQA is to derive an accurate answer A through reasoning over relevant knowledge.

Traditional methods typically translate Q into a formal query and execute it over K. In contrast, we aim to generate an approximate symbolic representation $S(Q) = (f_1, f_2, \dots, f_n)$, where each f_i is a symbolic operation (e.g., entity lookup, relation filtering, logical inference).

Based on $S(Q)$, relevant knowledge facts $R(Q) = (k_1, \ldots, k_m)$ are retrieved from K. Instead of executing $S(Q)$ directly, we use a language model to perform symbolic reasoning over $R(Q)$ guided by $S(Q)$:

$$A = \text{LLM}(S(Q), R(Q))$$

This formulation enables robust inference under few-shot conditions by avoiding reliance on strict query execution.

3.2 Overview

The overall architecture of FSR-KBQA consists of three main components: semantic parsing, knowledge retrieval, and fuzzy symbolic reasoning. As shown in Fig. 2, these components transform a user question into symbolic steps, retrieve relevant knowledge, and guide the language model to reason over the retrieved content.

The semantic parser converts the input question into a KoPL-like symbolic representation, which decomposes the querying process into several reasoning steps, making it more human-friendly and interpretable compared to other query languages [3]. Unlike conventional parsers that aim for strict query correctness, our parser produces flexible, approximate structures that act as reasoning instructions. The knowledge retriever selects top-k relevant facts from the KB using both keywords and symbolic hints. By incorporating lexical and semantic matching, this module ensures that useful information is provided even if parsing is imperfect. Finally, the FSR engine integrates retrieved knowledge with symbolic steps to perform stepwise reasoning using the LLM. Symbolic instructions act as Chain-of-Thought prompts, enabling interpretable and robust inference. Together, these components enable reasoning that is tolerant to input ambiguity and effective even under limited supervision.

3.3 Semantic Parsing Module

The semantic parsing module converts natural language questions into symbolic representations similar to KoPL programs. We adopt a prompt-based approach using few-shot in-context learning, where a small set of representative question-program pairs are embedded into the prompt to guide the LLM in generating stepwise symbolic instructions.

These symbolic programs are not required to be syntactically complete or executable; instead, they serve as fuzzy but structured reasoning templates. For instance, the model may omit certain qualifiers or mislabel relation directions, yet still provide sufficient signals to support subsequent symbolic reasoning. To construct prompts, we select 10 diverse examples from the KQA Pro training set, covering query types such as entity relations, attribute retrieval, and multi-hop constraints. This fuzzy symbolic parsing design reduces reliance on strict syntax, and improves adaptability to novel query forms, laying the foundation for downstream reasoning to recover from parsing imperfections.

3.4 Knowledge Retrieval Module

This module retrieves relevant facts from the knowledge base based on both the input question and the symbolic representation. To improve alignment between structured KB entries and natural language queries, we first preprocess all triples by converting them into natural language-style textual descriptions. This transformation facilitates better semantic compatibility between symbolic elements and the retrieval index. During retrieval, we extract lexical features—such as entities and relations— from both the input question and the fuzzy symbolic instructions. An initial BM25-based retrieval [20] is performed over the textualized KB to obtain candidate facts. These are then re-ranked using mBERT [18], enabling semantic-level matching beyond exact keyword overlap.

This two-stage retrieval strategy enhances robustness to imperfect symbolic parsing. Even if certain attributes or relation directions are missing or misaligned, the re-ranking process can recover relevant knowledge based on latent semantic cues. By integrating symbolic signals and semantic matching, the retrieval module ensures high-quality grounding for downstream reasoning, even under low-resource or noisy-input conditions.

3.5 LLM-Based Reasoning Engine

The reasoning engine performs symbolic reasoning over retrieved knowledge, guided by the approximate symbolic instructions. We design the reasoning process as a structured prompting workflow, where the LLM receives four key components: the original question, the symbolic representation, its KoPL-step semantic explanation, and the top-k retrieved facts. These elements are concatenated into a single input prompt, allowing the LLM to perform step-by-step reasoning in a Chain-of-Thought style. At each step, the LLM generates intermediate conclusions based on symbolic operations and supporting facts, producing an interpretable trace that leads to the final answer. This structure improves transparency and helps mitigate error propagation.

To enhance robustness, the LLM is permitted to incorporate its internal knowledge only when retrieved content is missing or incomplete, ensuring that the reasoning remains factually grounded and logically consistent. This module enables flexible yet interpretable inference over structured knowledge, and completes the loop of fuzzy symbolic reasoning by adapting to imperfections in both parsing and retrieval.

4 Experiment Setup

4.1 Datasets

We evaluate our approach on two widely used KBQA benchmarks: KQA Pro [3] and GrailQA [8].

KQA Pro contains over 117,000 questions annotated with KoPL programs, designed to cover diverse reasoning types such as multi-hop, attribute comparison, and logical inference. It is built upon a cleaned subset of Wikidata and does

Table 1. Statistics of Datasets

Dataset	#Total Size	#Used
KQA Pro	117970	11797
GrailQA	64,331	6763

not require explicit entity linking. Since the test set is not publicly available, we follow standard practice and use the validation set for evaluation.

GrailQA includes over 60,000 question-program pairs across a wide range of relations and schemas. It emphasizes generalization across unseen entities and query structures. We use its validation set for consistency with prior work.

These two datasets differ in scale, complexity, and schema design, providing a comprehensive basis for evaluating the effectiveness and generalization of FSR-KBQA. The statistics of these datasets are summarized in Table 1.

4.2 Underlying Models and Baselines

We use instruction-tuned Llama models [25] as the backbone, evaluating both 8B and 70B variants in a few-shot, plug-and-play setting. All models are deployed using quantized Q4 K M versions for computational efficiency.

We compare FSR-KBQA against the following baseline groups:

Fully-Supervised (FS): We include BART Program [21] trained on gold logical forms as a strong supervised baseline.

Direct QA: We test ChatGPT, GPT-4, and Llama 3.1 models under direct question-answering, without symbolic parsing or retrieval.

Few-Shot LLM-Based: These approaches prompt LLMs to generate symbolic programs from a few in-context examples. We include FlexKBQA [16] and SymKGQA [2], as well as our own method using both generated and gold KoPL.

This setup allows us to evaluate both absolute performance and robustness under low-resource conditions.

4.3 Evaluation Method

To accommodate the flexibility of natural language outputs from LLMs, we adopt an extended answer matching protocol rather than strict string matching. Following [23], we apply a three-step fuzzy matching strategy: (1) candidate spans are extracted from LLM outputs via constituency parsing; (2) gold answers are expanded using multilingual aliases from the KB; (3) semantic similarity between predictions and references is computed using a multilingual BERT model.

This evaluation is applied to non-numeric, non-boolean, and non-date answers, where surface-level variation is common. For exact-type answers (e.g., numbers, dates, booleans), string match is used. This protocol ensures a fair and semantically grounded evaluation of LLM-based symbolic reasoning in KBQA.

4.4 Implementation Details

All experiments are conducted on NVIDIA A100 GPUs. We use instruction-tuned LLMs without any task-specific finetuning, and deploy the reasoning module through the OLlama engine under a zero-shot setting.

To facilitate retrieval, the knowledge base is preprocessed by converting structured triples into natural language-style texts. Initial retrieval is performed via BM25 with Elasticsearch, using keywords from both the raw question and symbolic instructions. The top-k candidates are then re-ranked using mBERT embeddings to improve contextual relevance.

Symbolic reasoning is implemented through template-based prompting. For each instance, the input question, fuzzy symbolic program, stepwise action descriptions, and retrieved knowledge items are concatenated into a single prompt for inference. The pipeline is model-agnostic and training-free, supporting flexible integration with various LLMs and knowledge base formats.

Table 2. Experimental Results on KQA Pro Validation Set

Method	Models	ACC (%)
BART_Program (FS)	-	91.23
Direct QA	ChatGPT	52.61
	GPT-4	57.20
	Llama 3.1-inst (8b)	42.85
	Llama 3.1-inst (70b)	44.99
FlexKBQA	gpt-3.5-turbo (zero shots)	33.28
	gpt-3.5-turbo (100 shots)	46.83
SymKGQA	CodeLlama (10 shots)	50.9
	CodeLlama (100 shots)	51.1
FSR-KBQA (ours)	Llama 3.1-inst (8b)	61.12
	Llama 3.1-inst (70b)	**68.25**
FSR-KBQA† (w/ gold KoPL)	Llama 3.1-inst (70b)	**69.10**

5 Experiments

5.1 Baseline Comparisons

We evaluate FSR-KBQA against a wide range of baselines on the KQA Pro validation set, including fully-supervised models, direct question-answering (QA)

Table 3. Ablation Study Results on KQA Pro Validation Set

Model Variant	70B		8B	
	#Correct	Acc (%)	#Correct	Acc (%)
FSR-KBQA (full)	**8051**	**68.25**	**7210**	**61.12**
w/o Symbolic	7669	65.01	6886	58.37
w/o Retrieval	5213	44.19	4782	40.54
Direct QA (Llama 3.1)	5307	44.99	5055	42.85

approaches, and few-shot symbolic reasoning methods. As shown in Table 2, the fully-supervised BART Program achieves the highest accuracy (91.23%) by leveraging gold-standard logical forms, but its applicability is limited by the need for extensive annotations. In contrast, direct QA models such as ChatGPT (52.61%), GPT-4 (57.20%), and Llama-3.1 (70B: 44.99%) generate answers directly from questions without explicit reasoning steps, resulting in substantially lower performance due to their inability to handle structured constraints or multi-hop logic.

Few-shot symbolic reasoning approaches offer a more structured alternative by prompting LLMs to generate logical programs from limited in-context examples. FlexKBQA and SymKGQA demonstrate moderate improvements over direct QA, but still suffer from parsing errors and poor robustness in complex queries. FSR-KBQA outperforms all few-shot and direct methods, achieving 68.25% accuracy with Llama-3.1 (70B), even without gold KoPL. The performance further increases only marginally (to 69.10%) when gold symbolic input is provided, suggesting that our model can effectively operate on fuzzy, approximate programs. These results highlight the effectiveness of fuzzy symbolic reasoning in bridging the gap between rigid program execution and flexible language generation, particularly under few-shot conditions.

5.2 Ablation Study

To evaluate the contribution of each component in our framework, we conduct ablation experiments under both Llama-3.1 70B and 8B settings. As shown in Table 3, removing either symbolic reasoning or knowledge retrieval leads to noticeable performance drops, confirming their complementary roles within the FSR-KBQA architecture. Without retrieval, the model relies solely on symbolic prompts, resulting in brittle reasoning due to the lack of factual grounding. Conversely, removing symbolic structure while retaining retrieval causes the model to treat facts as unstructured input, weakening multi-step coordination and interpretability.

Compared to the direct QA baseline, both components independently improve performance, but the full FSR-KBQA setup—combining fuzzy symbolic instructions and retrieval-enhanced context—achieves the highest accuracy. This validates our central hypothesis: approximate symbolic reasoning acts as a flexible yet structured scaffold, while retrieval serves as contextual memory. Their integration, inspired by case-based reasoning, enables accurate and interpretable reasoning in few-shot KBQA.

Table 4. Accuracy by Answer Type on KQA Pro Validation Set

Model	MISC	WHY	LOC	DATE	PER	BOOL	NUM	ORG
ChatGPT	54.57	0.00	62.36	31.86	48.15	71.88	31.94	70.97
Llama	41.63	0.00	47.79	30.12	39.12	64.67	18.00	54.30
w/o Retrieval	43.46	33.33	50.17	33.51	43.84	69.04	17.16	65.05
w/o Symbolic	63.47	33.33	69.50	63.45	74.62	79.44	**40.86**	79.03
FSR-KBQA	**67.51**	**66.67**	**71.43**	**70.57**	**79.60**	**82.18**	40.58	**82.26**

Table 5. Accuracy by Reasoning Type on KQA Pro Validation Set

Model	Multi-hop	Qualifier	Comparison	Logical	Count	Verify
ChatGPT	46.72	48.90	**81.92**	66.28	37.94	62.61
Llama	34.88	39.98	74.26	54.56	19.27	56.39
w/o Retrieval	38.56	42.94	75.23	56.78	17.83	61.16
w/o Symbolic	68.86	75.09	70.40	68.57	**30.35**	76.71
FSR-KBQA	**72.42**	**77.87**	75.93	**72.67**	28.38	**79.20**

5.3 Category Classification Statistics

To further analyze the strengths of FSR-KBQA, we compare its performance with baseline models across different answer types and reasoning types, as shown in Tables 4 and 5.

Table 6. Generalization Bility Validation on the GrailQA Dataset

Method	**Models**	**ACC (%)**
SOTA (FS)	Qqq	76.31
Direct QA	ChatGPT	46.77
Direct QA	GPT-4	51.40
FSR-KBQA	Llama 3.1-inst (70b)	47.58
FSR-KBQA	Llama 3.1-inst (8b)	56.96

FSR-KBQA consistently achieves the highest accuracy across almost all answer types, including challenging categories such as `WHY`, `DATE`, and `NUM`. These categories typically require implicit causal reasoning, temporal comparison, or numerical inference, where traditional symbolic parsing or generative methods struggle due to rigid structure or hallucination. The strong performance of FSR-KBQA in these cases demonstrates the model's ability to flexibly integrate fuzzy symbolic instructions with fact-grounded reasoning.

For reasoning types, FSR-KBQA shows clear advantages in complex multi-hop, qualifier-dependent, and logical questions. Compared to symbolic-only variants, it benefits from factual grounding through retrieval; compared to retrieval-only models, it maintains structural reasoning traces via symbolic prompts. This aligns with our CBR-inspired design, where symbolic steps serve as interpretable adaptation strategies, and retrieval provides concrete "case memory" to support factual inference.

Although direct QA models such as ChatGPT perform competitively in some shallow categories (e.g., `Comparison`), they underperform in logic-intensive or schema-dependent settings, highlighting the need for structured reasoning. FSR-KBQA's robustness across reasoning types illustrates the effectiveness of combining symbolic structure with retrieval in few-shot KBQA.

5.4 Generalization Ability Validation

To evaluate the generalization capability of our approach beyond a single dataset, we conduct additional experiments on the GrailQA validation set. Unlike KQA Pro, GrailQA features a broader schema with a larger number of unseen entities and relation types, making it a suitable benchmark for testing few-shot adaptability.

As shown in Table 6, direct QA models such as GPT-4 achieve 51.40% accuracy, outperforming ChatGPT and other generative baselines. Our FSR-KBQA approach, using Llama-3.1 (70B), achieves 56.96% accuracy, surpassing GPT-4 despite relying only on open-weight models and a plug-and-play setup. This result highlights the transferability of our framework across knowledge schemas and query formats. The integration of approximate symbolic instructions with retrieved factual knowledge allows the model to generalize to new relations and compositional structures without requiring additional training.

Moreover, the performance is achieved using a significantly smaller model than GPT-4, indicating that architectural design—rather than sheer parameter count—is the key to generalization in few-shot KBQA. The modular and interpretable nature of FSR-KBQA provides a scalable foundation for knowledge-based reasoning under resource-constrained conditions.

6 Case Study

To qualitatively illustrate the reasoning behavior of FSR-KBQA, we compare it with a RAG-based model on two representative examples from KQA Pro, both involving multi-hop and constraint-based queries (Table 7).

Table 7. Case Study Results of FSR-KBQA

Case 1: What city is where film director John Abraham died and is located in India, which has diplomatic ties to Seychelles?	
FSR-KBQA	**Step 1:** What is the place of death of film director John Abraham? **Corresponding KoPLs:** Find(John Abraham) → Relate(place of death, forward) **Step answer:** Kozhikode. **Step 2:** Does India have diplomatic ties to Seychelles? **Corresponding KoPLs:** Find(India) → And() → QueryRelationQualifier(country, point of interest) **Step answer:** Yes, they have diplomatic relations. **Answer: Kozhikode** is the city in India where film director John Abraham died and has diplomatic ties with Seychelles.
RAG	**Reasoning Process:** We are looking for a city in India where film director John Abraham died. The information about John Abraham's death is not explicitly mentioned in the KB knowledge. However, we know that John Abraham has residence (forward) with India and film director has occupation (backward) with John Abraham. Answer: Based on the available information, we can infer that the city where John Abraham resided or worked would be the one related to his life events. Since Thiruvananthapuram is mentioned as the place of death for John Abraham in external knowledge, the answer is: Thiruvananthapuram" **Answer:** Thiruvananthapuram
Case 2: What is the topic of the statement that Jordan shares a border with Israel (whose nominal GDP is 109957321960.084 United States dollars)?	
FSR-KBQA	**Step 1:** Find all entities that have a nominal GDP of 109957321960.084 United States dollars and are related to Israel. **Corresponding KoPLs:** FilterStr(country,Israel) → QueryAttr(nominal GDP) → VerifyNum(109957321960.084 United States dollar,=) **Step answer:** The entity is Israel. **Step 2:** Find the entities that have a border with Israel. **Corresponding KoPLs:** Relate(border with,forward) → Find(Jordan) **Step answer:** The entity is Jordan. **Step 3:** Verify if Jordan shares a border with Israel and find the topic of this statement. **Corresponding KoPLs:** And() → QueryRelationQualifier(topic) **Step answer:** Yes, Jordan shares a border with Israel. The topic of this statement is "Israel-Jordan border" **Answer:** The topic of the statement that Jordan shares a border with Israel (whose nominal GDP is 109957321960.084 United States dollars) is **Israel-Jordan border**
RAG	**Reasoning Process:** The statement "Jordan shares a border with Israel (whose nominal GDP is 109957321960.084 United States dollars)" involves information about Jordan's borders and Israel's nominal GDP. According to the provided knowledge, there are multiple entries confirming that Jordan shares a border with Israel, but only one entry related to Israel's nominal GDP in a specific year. **Answer:** The topic of the statement is geography (specifically international borders) and economics (nominal GDP).

In the first case, the question requires entity disambiguation and geopolitical qualification: *"What city is where film director John Abraham died and is located in India, which has diplomatic ties to Seychelles?"* FSR-KBQA accurately identifies the correct person entity, retrieves the place of death, and verifies India's diplomatic relation through explicit symbolic reasoning steps. RAG, however, fails to ground entity context and infers the answer based on loosely associated text patterns, leading to an incorrect result.

The second case involves qualifier reasoning and numerical filtering: *"What is the topic of the statement that Jordan shares a border with Israel (whose nominal GDP is 109... USD)?"* FSR-KBQA decomposes the query into symbolic steps—GDP filtering, border relation lookup, and qualifier extraction—resulting in a precise and interpretable answer. RAG, in contrast, retrieves relevant facts but fails to resolve constraints compositionally, producing an abstract category rather than a specific topic.

These examples demonstrate that FSR-KBQA not only performs accurate fact retrieval, but also maintains symbolic structure throughout the reasoning process, enabling reliable answers in constraint-sensitive and knowledge-intensive QA tasks.

7 Conclusion

This paper presents FSR-KBQA, a fuzzy symbolic reasoning framework for few-shot knowledge base question answering, inspired by case-based reasoning. The framework integrates approximate symbolic parsing with retrieval-augmented inference, allowing large language models to perform stepwise reasoning over structured knowledge without relying on precise semantic parsing. Experiments on KQA Pro and GrailQA demonstrate that FSR-KBQA achieves strong performance and generalization, outperforming existing few-shot and direct QA models while using smaller, open-weight LLMs. These results validate fuzzy symbolic reasoning as a scalable and interpretable alternative to rigid query execution, effectively bridging symbolic structure with neural generation. Future work will explore extending this framework to open-domain QA, incorporating commonsense reasoning, and enhancing tool-augmented symbolic planning.

References

1. Aamodt, A., Plaza, E.: Case-based reasoning: Foundational issues, methodological variations, and system approaches. AI Commun. **7**(1), 39–59 (1994)
2. Agarwal, P., Kumar, N., Bedathur, S.: SymKGQA: few-shot knowledge graph question answering via symbolic program generation and execution. In: Proceedings of the 62nd Annual Meeting of the Association for Computational Linguistics (Volume 1: Long Papers), pp. 10119–10140 (2024)
3. Cao, S., et al.: KQA pro: a dataset with explicit compositional programs for complex question answering over knowledge base. In: Proceedings of the 60th Annual Meeting of the Association for Computational Linguistics (Volume 1: Long Papers), pp. 6101–6119 (2022)
4. Chen, Y., Li, H., Qi, G., Wu, T., Wang, T.: Outlining and filling: hierarchical query graph generation for answering complex questions over knowledge graphs. IEEE Trans. Knowl. Data Eng. **35**(8), 8343–8357 (2022)
5. Das, R., et al.: Knowledge base question answering by case-based reasoning over subgraphs. In: International Conference on Machine Learning, pp. 4777–4793. PMLR (2022)

6. Feng, Y., You, H., Zhang, Z., Ji, R., Gao, Y.: Hypergraph neural networks. In: Proceedings of the AAAI Conference on Artificial Intelligence, vol. 33, pp. 3558–3565 (2019)
7. Gao, F., et al.: Self-supervised BGP-graph reasoning enhanced complex KBQA via SparQL generation. Inf. Process. Manage. **61**(5), 103802 (2024)
8. Gu, Y., et al.: Beyond IID: three levels of generalization for question answering on knowledge bases. In: Proceedings of the Web Conference 2021, pp. 3477–3488 (2021)
9. Han, J., Cheng, B., Wang, X.: Two-phase hypergraph based reasoning with dynamic relations for multi-hop KBQA. In: Proceedings of the Twenty-ninth International Conference on International Joint Conferences on Artificial Intelligence, pp. 3615–3621 (2021)
10. Hua, Y., Li, Y.F., Qi, G., Wu, W., Zhang, J., Qi, D.: Less is more: data-efficient complex question answering over knowledge bases. J. Web Semant. **65**, 100612 (2020)
11. Ji, G., Wang, S., Zhang, X., Feng, Z.: A fine-grained complex question translation for KBQA. In: ISWC (Demos/Industry), pp. 194–199 (2020)
12. Kapanipathi, P., et al.: Leveraging abstract meaning representation for knowledge base question answering. In: Annual Meeting of the Association for Computational Linguistics (2021)
13. Lan, Y., He, G., Jiang, J., Jiang, J., Zhao, W.X., Wen, J.R.: Complex knowledge base question answering: a survey. IEEE Trans. Knowl. Data Eng. **35**(11), 11196–11215 (2022)
14. Lan, Y., Jiang, J.: Query graph generation for answering multi-hop complex questions from knowledge bases. In: Proceedings of the 58th Annual Meeting of the Association for Computational Linguistics, pp. 969–974 (2020)
15. Lewis, P., et al.: Retrieval-augmented generation for knowledge-intensive NLP tasks. Adv. Neural. Inf. Process. Syst. **33**, 9459–9474 (2020)
16. Li, Z., et al.: FlexKBQA: a flexible LLM-powered framework for few-shot knowledge base question answering. In: Proceedings of the AAAI Conference on Artificial Intelligence, vol. 38, pp. 18608–18616 (2024)
17. Nie, L., et al.: GrapHQ IR: unifying the semantic parsing of graph query languages with one intermediate representation. In: Proceedings of the 2022 Conference on Empirical Methods in Natural Language Processing, pp. 5848–5865 (2022)
18. Papadimitriou, I., Chi, E.A., Futrell, R., Mahowald, K.: Deep subjecthood: higher-order grammatical features in multilingual BERT. In: Proceedings of the 16th Conference of the European Chapter of the Association for Computational Linguistics: Main Volume, pp. 2522–2532 (2021)
19. Qiu, Y., Wang, Y., Jin, X., Zhang, K.: Stepwise reasoning for multi-relation question answering over knowledge graph with weak supervision. In: Proceedings of the 13th International Conference on Web Search and Data Mining, pp. 474–482 (2020)
20. Robertson, S., Zaragoza, H.: The probabilistic relevance framework: BM25 and beyond. Found. Trends Inf. Retr. **3**(4), 333–389 (2009). https://doi.org/10.1561/1500000019
21. Saha, A., Ansari, G.A., Laddha, A., Sankaranarayanan, K., Chakrabarti, S.: Complex program induction for querying knowledge bases in the absence of gold programs. Trans. Assoc. Comput. Linguist. **7**, 185–200 (2019)

22. Sun, H., Bedrax-Weiss, T., Cohen, W.: PullNet: open domain question answering with iterative retrieval on knowledge bases and text. In: Proceedings of the 2019 Conference on Empirical Methods in Natural Language Processing and the 9th International Joint Conference on Natural Language Processing (EMNLP-IJCNLP), pp. 2380–2390 (2019)
23. Tan, Y., et al.: Can ChatGPT replace traditional KBQA models? An in-depth analysis of the question answering performance of the GPT LLM family. In: International Semantic Web Conference, pp. 348–367 (2023)
24. Tian, Y., Set al.: Augmenting reasoning capabilities of LLMs with graph structures in knowledge base question answering. In: Findings of the Association for Computational Linguistics: EMNLP 2024, pp. 11967–11977 (2024)
25. Vavekanand, R., Sam, K.: LLaMA 3.1: an in-depth analysis of the next-generation large language model (2024)
26. Wang, K., et al.: Knowledge-driven cot: exploring faithful reasoning in LLMs for knowledge-intensive question answering. arXiv preprint arXiv:2308.13259 (2023)
27. Xiong, G., Bao, J., Zhao, W.: Interactive-KBQA: multi-turn interactions for knowledge base question answering with large language models. In: Proceedings of the 62nd Annual Meeting of the Association for Computational Linguistics (Volume 1: Long Papers), pp. 10561–10582 (2024)
28. Yasunaga, M., Ren, H., Bosselut, A., Liang, P., Leskovec, J.: QA-GNN: reasoning with language models and knowledge graphs for question answering. In: Proceedings of the 2021 Conference of the North American Chapter of the Association for Computational Linguistics: Human Language Technologies, pp. 535–546 (2021)
29. Ye, X., Yavuz, S., Hashimoto, K., Zhou, Y., Xiong, C.: RNG-KBQA: generation augmented iterative ranking for knowledge base question answering. In: Proceedings of the 60th Annual Meeting of the Association for Computational Linguistics (Volume 1: Long Papers), pp. 6032–6043 (2022)
30. Zhang, J., et al.: Subgraph retrieval enhanced model for multi-hop knowledge base question answering. In: Proceedings of the 60th Annual Meeting of the Association for Computational Linguistics (Volume 1: Long Papers), pp. 5773–5784 (2022)
31. Zhang, L., et al.: FC-KBQA: a fine-to-coarse composition framework for knowledge base question answering. In: The 61st Annual Meeting Of The Association For Computational Linguistics (2023)
32. Zhang, Q., Weng, X., Zhou, G., Zhang, Y., Huang, J.X.: ARL: an adaptive reinforcement learning framework for complex question answering over knowledge base. Inf. Process. Manage. **59**(3), 102933 (2022)
33. Zhang, Z., Wen, L., Zhao, W.: Rule-KBQA: rule-guided reasoning for complex knowledge base question answering with large language models. In: Proceedings of the 31st International Conference on Computational Linguistics, pp. 8399–8417 (2025)

Context Driven Multi-query Resolution Using LLM-RAG to Support the Revision of Explainability Needs

Lasal Jayawardena[1](✉), Anne Liret[2], Nirmalie Wiratunga[1], Ikechukwu Nkisi-Orji[1], and Bruno Fleisch[2]

[1] Robert Gordon University, Aberdeen, UK
{l.jayawardena,n.wiratunga,i.nkisi-orji}@rgu.ac.uk
[2] British Telecommunications Group, BT France, Puteaux, France
{anne.liret,bruno.fleisch}@bt.com

Abstract. The revision step in the Case-Based Reasoning (CBR) cycle ensures that cases are adaptable and that updates can be integrated meaningfully based on evaluation metrics. However, the effectiveness of this step heavily depends on how new knowledge is acquired to support revision. In the iSee project, where CBR is used for explanation strategy recommendations, revision knowledge is typically derived from end-user feedback following an interactive, user-centric explanation experience. This raises the research question: how can we discover this knowledge from user interactions, and how can Large Language Models (LLMs) with Retrieval-Augmented Generation (RAG) enhance the explanation experience while capturing useful knowledge for the discovery? In this paper, we propose a methodology for detecting the evolution of user explanation intent (an indicator for the need for revision) through LLM-RAG enhanced interactions. Finally, experimental results evaluate the success of the proposed methodology, assessing its validity and, in particular, the reasonability of the LLM-RAG approach. Experimental results across multiple real-world use cases demonstrate that our methodology produces highly coherent and context-aware explanations, improving overall explanation clarity, and effectively identifies when explanation strategies require revision.

Keywords: Interactive Explanations · Large Language Model · Reasonability · Explainability Intent · Explanation Experience

1 Introduction

Explainable Artificial Intelligence (XAI) plays a key role in ensuring that we can place trust in AI decisions when they impact crucial areas, such as predicting the presence of a tumour [2], making a decision in a trial [21], or detecting possible attacks on citizen security [28]. Since early 2020, legal regulations framework have mandated that AI-based systems must produce meaningful, transparent

© The Author(s), under exclusive license to Springer Nature Switzerland AG 2025
I. Bichindaritz and B. López (Eds.): ICCBR 2025, LNAI 15662, pp. 111–125, 2025.
https://doi.org/10.1007/978-3-031-96559-3_8

and accurate explanation for the results they expose to human users [16]. However such explanations are generally multifaceted, as users' intents span across multiple explanation needs including task performance improvement, actionability, trust, learning, or transparency. Evaluating the quality of these explanations remains a challenge [8]. To achieve this, the iSee platform [3] incorporates methods for assessing the effectiveness of an explanation strategy tailored to AI scenarios, alongside knowledge structures that describe the user context. These knowledge structures enable systematic comparison of user context descriptions facilitating the identification of similar scenarios, the understanding of differences in context, and exploiting it to manage adaptation to variations in user explanation needs. The explanation strategies are collected through the development of several real-world use cases. In this way, the generated catalog of strategies can be transferred to other AI solutions. From this catalog, iSee applies a Case-Based Reasoning (CBR) [1] methodology to retrieve the most suitable explanation strategy that it has learned for the given domain and task and then adapts it to meet the end-user's requirements.

Work combining CBR and LLM have started to emerge over recent years [26]. LLMs, with their ability to process and generate human-like text, can enrich CBR systems by providing more natural language explanations, however ensuring that the LLM generates grounded, complete and coherent response remains a challenge. For this reason LLM based Retrieval-Augmented Generation (RAG) is used to refine the contextual knowledge used when generating responses. To assess the coherence, relevance and clarity of the response provided by the LLM-RAG, the Reasonability measure has gained attention as a useful means to ensure that the integration of external knowledge sources to LLM-RAG does not compromise the validity of the response and helps to evaluate how the responses align with human judgment [11].

Previous research work studied the benefits of iSee in evaluating the quality of explanations [3]. The findings indicate that using a structured, hierarchical structure, such as a behavior tree is effective in managing interactive explanation dialogues. They also highlight the need for more flexible conversation turns to accommodate user clarification needs. Accordingly, this paper makes the following contributions to iSee and XAI-CBR literature.

- An enhanced explanation strategy model with open free-text questions to allow users to express their clarification needs in their own words.
- An LLM-RAG approach that guides clarification responses interactive XAI by providing relevant context tailored to the end-user's experience. Specifically the context uses the iSee ontology and the instantiated knowledge accumulated through the traversal of the behaviour tree during the Explanation Experience.
- A metric to evaluate the reasonableness of LLM-RAG generated responses.
- A revision knowledge discovery method that identifies evolving user intent from end-user interactions to inform the revision of explanation strategies.

The rest of the paper presents the interactive clarification method in Sect. 3, and a methodology to assess the relevance of the new knowledge discovered from iSee clarification interactions with end users. Experimental results on three real-world use cases and one academic use case are described in Sect. 4 and conclusion and future work are discussed in Sect. 5.[1].

2 Related Work

The iSee platform enables AI developers to reuse satisfactory explanation strategies for a given AI scenario [12,23,25]. Design-users define the contextual requirements, including the domain, dataset, model to be explained, as well as the different stakeholder groups), and End Users interact through a conversational dialog manager (chatbot) with the different explainer algorithms within the strategy, and provide evaluation feedback about their explanation experience. This user-centered feedback helps Design Users refine the original explanation strategy to enhance the explanation experience. All aspects of the experience (the contextual requirements supplied by the design-user, the recommended explanation strategy, and end-user feedback) are then stored as a case to support reuse and revision tasks of the CBR iSee cycle [3].

An explanation strategy in iSee framework, i.e., the case solution is modelled using a Behaviour Tree (BT) [4]. An example of explanation strategy using Behaviour Tree is detailed in [3]. This tree structure is a Directed Acyclic Graph (DAG), formed of multiple user question-explanation strategy sub-trees, to enable the reuse of common sub-trees without duplicating nodes. Each sub-tree is formed on the basis of an "intent" question category and a combination of explanation methods. In this work we introduce a new concept into the Behavior Tree to represent the need for clarifications expressed by the end user. For example, within a behaviour tree, if a factual explainer such as LIME addresses a user's initial intent question ("Why did I receive this outcome?"), a linked clarification node can handle subsequent queries, such as "How were those attribution weights computed?". At which point we can trigger a LLM-RAG response using an LLM. In this way, a BT provides a structured and controlled approach, enabling systematic handling of various types of user questions by mapping them either to explainer nodes or LLM-RAG clarification nodes.

It is particularly important to prove that introducing LLM-RAG does not compromise the quality of explanation strategies, while ensuring that the clarifications provided about iSee explanations knowledge are complete and aligned with user requests. There is a rising trend toward using LLMs as judges for evaluation due to alignment performed on LLMs on human feedback [15,29] and human evaluations are often not scalable enough for complex, high-volume tasks. Recent studies have demonstrated that LLM-based evaluators can provide consistent, context-aware assessments while bypassing the high costs and limited throughput of manual human judgment. These approaches leverage in-context learning and advanced prompt engineering so that the LLMs can mimic human-like reasoning when scoring outputs [11]. In our work we will study how to apply

[1] Results and code used in the paper are available at https://github.com/LasalJayawardena/Context-Driven-Multi-Query-Resolution/.

this task to the domain of explanation experience sharing by human users and for human users, and to which level the metrics facilitate the evaluation of clarity and coherence of LLM-generated responses in iSee.

3 Methodology

In this section, we formalise the proposed methodology that enhances the *iSee* platform with large LLM capabilities for interactive clarifications and adaptive explanation strategies. The approach draws upon established principles from the CBR cycle, especially focusing on the *revision* of explanatory knowledge, and augments a previously static Behaviour Tree with a new Clarification Node driven by an agentic workflow. We also introduce the notion of a *Reasonability Score* to quantitatively assess explanation quality, and employ a Markov chain analysis to capture and model user intent evolution.

3.1 Overview of the iSee CBR Cycle

The *iSee* platform follows a CBR-inspired cycle for designing and refining explanation strategies. Formally, let

$$\mathcal{E} = \{\text{XS}_1, \text{XS}_2, \ldots, \text{XS}_m\} \tag{1}$$

be the set of available *explanation strategies* (XS) in the system. Each strategy XS_k is an instantiated flow of explanatory components tailored to particular user personas and goals. The CBR cycle typically involves:

1. **Retrieve:** Selecting the most relevant $\text{XS}_k \in \mathcal{E}$ based on the user's persona and intent.
2. **Reuse:** Adapting XS_k to address specific user queries.
3. **Revise:** Incorporating new insights (e.g., user feedback or clarifications) to refine XS_k.
4. **Retain:** Storing improved XS_k in the repository of explanation strategies for future reuse.

While previous versions of *iSee* relied on a *XEQ ("seek") Questionnaire* [24] and manual inspection to identify when to revise XS_k, this work introduces the *Clarification node* in the behaviour tree, enabling an interactive clarification process that enables the implicit discovery of revision knowledge applicable to the explanation strategy. Whenever user intent changes, the Clarification node drives the CBR **Revise** step: each clarification exchange is captured as revision knowledge and can be integrated back into the explanation strategy, updating the behaviour-tree's interaction to better match the user's evolving needs in the future.

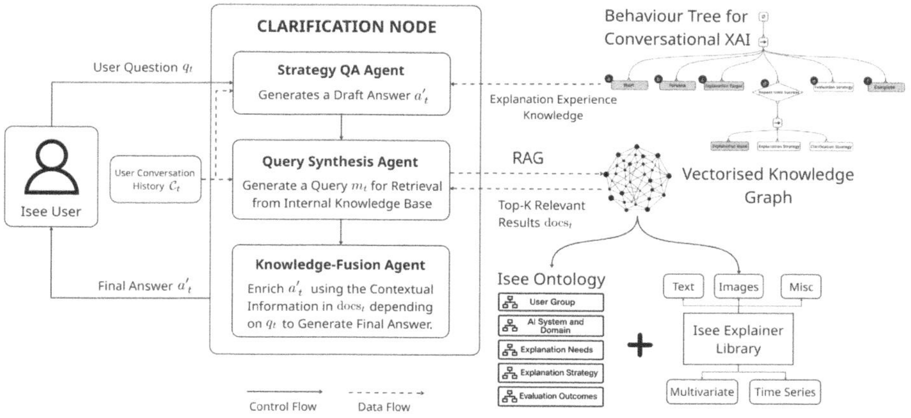

Fig. 1. An illustration of the iSee LLM Clarification Node agentic flow.

3.2 Clarification Node in the Behaviour Tree

A *Behaviour Tree* T defines the conversational and explanatory flow of *iSee*. In prior work, T was relatively static, offering limited user-driven revisions. We denote T as a directed acyclic graph of nodes:

$$T = (N, E), \tag{2}$$

where $N = \{n_1, n_2, \ldots, n_\ell\}$ is the set of nodes and E is the set of directed edges encoding transitions. We introduce a special node $n_{\text{clar}} \in N$, which is triggered whenever the user requests additional detail or signals uncertainty. Formally, we define a trigger function Φ that transitions from a standard explanatory node n_j to n_{clar}:

$$\Phi : N \times \{\text{user feedback}\} \;\mapsto\; n_{\text{clar}} \quad \text{(if clarification needed).} \tag{3}$$

Once at n_{clar}, the system spawns an *agentic workflow* (see Fig. 1). The user may engage in multiple rounds of clarification until satisfied, denoted by $q_0, q_1, \ldots, q_r$, where q_t is the t-th clarification question. The agentic workflow draws on state of art agentic design methodologies [22] and utilises *three agents*, underpinned by a shared instruct-tuned LLM, as follows:

1. **Strategy QA Agent**: This agent leverages the Behaviour Tree T (and any conversation state $\mathcal{C}_t$) to generate an initial, context-aware *draft* answer:

$$a'_t \;=\; \text{StrategyQA}\big(q_t,\; T,\; \mathcal{C}_t\big). \tag{4}$$

Here, a'_t aligns with the user's intent as captured in T. It does not incorporate any newly retrieved knowledge, relying solely on the conversation history and previous interactions in T.

2. **Query Synthesis Agent**: The system next identifies potential additional knowledge from the iSee knowledge bases $\mathcal{K}$, which is a collection of internal Isee usecase, explainers and dataset information, that may enrich or clarify the draft answer. The Query Synthesis Agent extracts metadata such as dataset types, relevant explainer methods, or domain facts from the user query q_t and relevant context C_t into a structured format for retrieval. The metadata may include the *dataset categories* (e.g., "image," "tabular"), recommended *explainers* (e.g., SHAP, LIME, GradCAM), or domain-specific facts (e.g., "X-ray guidelines"). This process is guided by the few-shot examples E_{fewshot} which is a representative collection of examples of potential metadata that could be extracted:
$$m_t = \text{QuerySynthesis}\big(q_t,\ \mathcal{C}_t,\ E_{\text{fewshot}}\big). \tag{5}$$
The system uses m_t along with the original query q_t to call a two-step RAG function:
$$\text{docs}_t = \text{RAG}\big(m_t,\ q_t,\ \mathcal{K}\big), \tag{6}$$
which retrieves the top-k relevant results from $\mathcal{K}$. The system applies an empirically selected semantic similarity threshold, based on cosine similarity with the user query q_t, to filter out less relevant items. In addition, the metadata m_t filters or reorders candidate results, further improving retrieval accuracy. If no relevant external context is found, docs_t remains empty.
3. **Knowledge-Fusion Agent**: Finally, the system optionally fuses any newly retrieved information (docs_t) with the draft answer a'_t:
$$a_t = \text{KnowledgeFusion}\big(a'_t,\ \text{docs}_t,\ q_t\big), \tag{7}$$
Even when docs_t is non-empty, the KnowledgeFusion$(\cdot)$ function may still opt to discard or ignore certain information. Specifically, it inspects each item in docs_t to determine whether it adds clarity or usefulness to the user's query q_t. If the retrieved content proves relevant, it is merged into a'_t; otherwise, the agent simply returns a'_t unchanged, ensuring that output formatting and other alignment constraints are satisfied.

Hence, for each clarification query q_t, the final response a_t follows the chain:
$$q_t \xrightarrow{\text{Strategy QA}} a'_t \xrightarrow{\text{Query Synthesis}} m_t \xrightarrow{\text{RAG}} \text{docs}_t \xrightarrow{\text{Knowledge-Fusion}} a_t$$

This workflow ensures that the user's clarification remains centered on the original explanation path while only selectively incorporating external knowledge. The motivation for using a multi-agent workflow is that relying on a single agent for all tasks can cause the agent to deviate from paying attention to relevant parts of the Behavior Tree T and conversation context $\mathcal{C}_t$, often producing more generic or less context-specific responses. Moreover, repeated or unexpected reliance on the *Query Synthesis Agent* can signal that the user's *explanation intent* has diverged from the originally designed strategy, prompting the need to track these changes. Such shifts are formally detected to trigger the *revision* step of the CBR cycle, where the explanation strategy is updated to reflect newly discovered user needs.

3.3 Revision Knowledge Discovery

To quantify the clarity and utility of each generated clarification, we propose a *Reasonability Score R*. Reasonability Score is defined in the Literature [11] as a measure comparing clarity of LLM responses. The idea is to use other large language models as impartial judges. Suppose an answer a_t is produced in response to the clarification query q_t under conversation context $\mathcal{C}_t$ and with access to knowledge base $\mathcal{K}$. We define:

$$R(a_t) \;=\; \frac{1}{|M|} \sum_{m \in M} \text{Score}_m\big(q_t, \mathcal{C}_t, \mathcal{K}, a_t\big), \tag{8}$$

where M is a set of LLM *judges*, and $\text{Score}_m\big(q_t, \mathcal{C}_t, \mathcal{K}, a_t\big) \in [0, 10]$ is the individual judge's rating of how coherent, correct, and context-aligned the answer a_t is, given the query q_t, the conversation context $\mathcal{C}_t$, and relevant knowledge base information $\mathcal{K}$. We typically use $|M| \geq 30$ for robust averaging. In practice:

1. Each model $m \in M$ is prompted with q_t, $\mathcal{C}_t$, $\mathcal{K}$, and a_t, and asked to produce a numerical rating reflecting the answer's coherence, factual correctness, and alignment with the conversation context and knowledge base.
2. The average $R(a_t)$ over all models in M is taken as the final *Reasonability Score*.
3. A 95% confidence interval is computed to measure variability across different judging models.

This score serves as a core part of the *revision knowledge* in the CBR cycle, informing whether XS_k should be updated to produce clearer or more comprehensive explanations. The application of Reasonability score methodology to iSee platform will be described under the Evaluation section.

Beyond individual clarifications, users' *intents* often shift during the conversation. We denote the set of possible user intents as

$$\mathcal{I} \;=\; \{\iota_1, \iota_2, \ldots, \iota_n\}. \tag{9}$$

At each clarification step t, we observe a random variable X_t that represents the user's intent:

$$X_t \;\in\; \mathcal{I}, \tag{10}$$

with $X_t = \iota_i$ meaning the user's intent at step t is ι_i. As clarifications progress $(t = 0, 1, \ldots, r)$, we track X_t either through explicit user statements or inferred signals (e.g. from the user's query content).

Transition Dynamics. We model the intent evolution $\{X_t\}$ as a discrete-time Markov chain with transition probabilities

$$P_{ij} \;=\; \Pr\big(X_{t+1} = \iota_j \,\big|\, X_t = \iota_i\big), \tag{11}$$

where P_{ij} is the probability of moving from intent ι_i to ι_j in one clarification step.

Over multiple user sessions, we estimate P_{ij} empirically by counting intent transitions:

$$\hat{P}_{ij} \approx \frac{\text{Number of transitions } (\iota_i \rightarrow \iota_j)}{\sum_{k=1}^{n} \text{Number of transitions } (\iota_i \rightarrow \iota_k)}. \tag{12}$$

In many cases, certain states (e.g. *transparency*) may be more recurrent or lead to frequent transitions (e.g. *transparency* $\rightarrow$ *debugging*), reflecting the evolving needs of the user.

Finally, the platform unifies:

1. **Clarification Node Interactions:** $\{q_0, q_1, \ldots, q_r\}$ which is the set of clarification queries and their corresponding answers $\{a_0, a_1, \ldots, a_r\}$, each evaluated with a *Reasonability Score* $R(a_t)$.
2. **User Intent Evolution:** The Markov chain transitions P_{ij} derived from user sessions.

Collectively, these form the *revision knowledge* needed to update or replace XS_k. Formally, let

$$\Omega\big(\text{XS}_k, \{q_t, a_t, R(a_t)\}_{t=0}^{r}, P\big) \;\mapsto\; \text{XS}'_k, \tag{13}$$

be the *revision function*, which outputs an updated strategy XS'_k by:

1. *Incorporating* high-level user requests identified in q_t.
2. *Adjusting* explanatory steps that yield persistently low $R(a_t)$ scores.
3. *Realigning* to user intents suggested by the transition probabilities P_{ij}.

This end-to-end workflow can automate the adaptation of explanation strategies to evolving user needs, while preserving the core CBR principle of *learning from experience.*

4 Evaluation and Use Cases

Previous experiments revealed that the explanation strategy used by the iSee chat interface was not always presented in a manner that was easily understood by humans. This highlighted the need for more readable explanations and the ability for end-users to request additional details about the explanation or the result.

We evaluated the effectiveness of the tools presented in this paper by elaborating relevant elements that align with user clarification requests regarding explanation strategies, and in identifying when user requirements or intents evolve during conversations.

The research questions are:

- **Meaningfulness**: Do users perceive the explanation conversational experience as more qualitative when using the clarification step?
- **Adaptation of explanation needs**: Can we construct a task that detects changes in explanation strategy goal and allow revising the explanation strategy context based on end user feedback?

We conducted evaluation experiments with a diverse group of 10 participants, including engineers, managers, and desk agents. Although not all were experts in AI or the specific domain used in the experiment, they all had experience in information technology and a technical background. The participants were asked to use iSee tools in one to four real-world use cases.

To address ethical concerns, we informed the users about the nature of the experiment, its goals, the tasks they needed to perform, and how the results would be used. No personal data was collected, ensuring the participants' autonomy, privacy, and confidentiality, and providing them with trustworthy information. The study followed the same protocol as described in [3].

4.1 Summary of the Use Cases

3 real world and 1 academic use cases have been proposed to the end user community of 10 people. The use cases are from different industrial sectors:

- **Telecommunication sector**: The AI task is the classification of field work scenario based on engineering task notes. The goal of the AI system is to recommend the most suitable next task to network planner from unstructured textual notes. 2 persona were designed: Telecom Planner where we set the goal of explanation to be understanding the reasoning behind the recommender (transparency) and Engineer were we set the goal of explanation to be evaluating whether the AI system works as expected (debugging).
- **Medical sector**: The AI task is the analysis of x-ray images from medical imaging equipment to support a medical expert or a manager. The goal of the AI system is to detect whether a fracture is present. 2 persona were designed: Clinician where we set the goal of the explanation to be supporting in assessing the result and deciding the next task (accountability) and Manager where we set the goal of the explanation to be understanding the reason why the AI system produces its result and how accurate the system is (transparency and performance).
- **Manufacturing sector**: The AI task is the analysis of equipment images to detect faulty produced assets in a production line. The goal of the AI model is to detect defects in the manufactured components using computer vision techniques. 2 Persona were designed: Auditor where we set the goal of explanation to be justifying the decision of acceptance or rejection of the component (actionability and transparency) and Engineer where the goal of explanation was set as informing about the goodness of the AI system (performance).
- **Finance Loan sector**: the AI task is the recommendation about the likelihood of a loan request to be approved based on requestor profile. One user was designed, with a goal of explanation set to improve trust in the AI system result.

4.2 Reasonability Evaluation Using LLMs

Given the limitations of conventional readability metrics, we adopted a more nuanced evaluation strategy. Our approach involved evaluating explanations using multiple LLM-generated Reasonability Scores, allowing nuanced judgment on the quality and relevance of explanations.

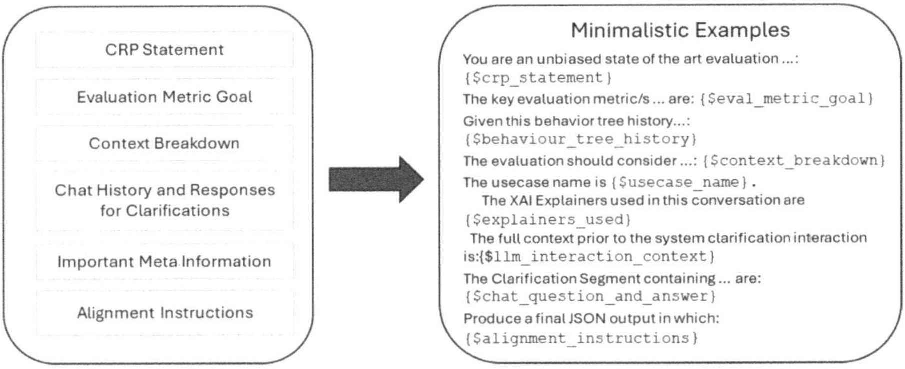

Fig. 2. Reasonability Assessment Prompt.

Evaluation Approach

- **Test Models:** In the evaluation, over 100 LLMs were tested, however, only 70 LLMs were comprehensively reported, as they were able to generate reasonability scores for all question-response pairs, whereas the others could not. From the total LLM collection 40% were closed source and 60% were open source. Open source LLM model variants such as LLAMA V1 [20], LLAMA V2 [20], LLAMA 3 [7], DeepSeek R1 [6], DeepSeek V2 [5], Flacon 3 Family[2], Gemma V1 [19], Gemma 2 [18], IBM Granite [13], Mistral [9], Mixtral [10], Nemotron [17], and Qwen 2.5 [27] were used. Closed source model variants such as OpenAI GPT-4 [14], OpenAI GPT-O reasoning models, Anthropic Claude[3], Google Gemini (including reasoning variants)[4], and Mistral[5] were used.
- **Reasonability Score:** Each explanation was assessed using an LLM-as-a-Judge approach, with LLMs generating a quantitative reasonability score (0–10 scale) for each model. The prompt used for the evaluation is outlined in Fig. 2.

[2] https://huggingface.co/blog/falcon3.
[3] https://www.anthropic.com/claude.
[4] https://gemini.google.com.
[5] https://mistral.ai.

- **Confidence and Impartiality Analysis:** To robustly determine fairness and consistency, median scores were calculated and impartial models were identified. Five randomly sampled questions and the relevant results are shown in Table 1 The most impartial LLM for all questions based on median was identified to be *Qwen-2.5-32B*.

Table 1. Reasonability Scores for 5 Randomly Sampled Questions asked

Question (Verbatim)	Avg with CI	Median	Std Dev
Don't give me the value in terms of the model parameters/features, give me the data value.	6.89 ± 0.47	7.00	2.01
Give me insights about how LIME explain that the result will be the same for similar instance	8.45 ± 0.15	8.00	0.63
Que signifie une influence negative sur le resultat? (*French in text*)	8.71 ± 0.20	9.00	0.84
What is the mat behind it	6.94 ± 0.46	8.00	1.97
Give me 2 other types of explanation of the result	8.71 ± 0.21	9.00	0.90

4.3 User Intent Evolution with Markov Chain Analysis

Beyond individual explanation clarity, our study also aimed to capture how user intents evolve over multiple clarification interactions. We collected user-chat sequences and labeled each clarification turn with a specific intent - the value being taken among the set of 16 possible intent values defined in iSee platform [8]. These labeled sequences were then used to construct a Markov chain model, where each state corresponds to an explanation intent, and transitions reflect how a user's intent changes from one clarification turn to the next.

Ordered Intent Sequences. Below is a sample of the how user intent shifts within a conversation:

- Chat 1: `Transparency` → `Performance` : `Transparency`
- Chat 2: `Actionability` : `Education`
- Chat 3: `Transparency` → `Transparency` : `Transparency`

  ⋮

- Chat 27: `Performance` → `Transparency` : `Comprehensibility` → `Comprehensibility` → `Transparency`
- Chat 28: `Debugging` : `Comprehensibility`
- Chat 29: `Transparency` : `Transparency`

The ":" indicates the starting point of the LLM clarification interaction.

In the examples above, we observe that on interaction 27, the end user shifted expectations from the explanations and clarifications produced by the tool. The intent then moved towards comprehensibility which indicates a need for structured and consistently formatted responses, while finally user was again focusing on transparency goal once having read more structured clarifications from the chatbot. Moreover in interaction 2, we observe that use case originally was designed with an actionable explanation need, whereas, user clarification questions suggest that end user was moving explanation needs toward a need for learning new knowledge about the explanation methods themselves.

Full Sequence Analysis: By aggregating all chats, we derived a transition matrix capturing the frequency with which one intent leads to another. Figure 3 depicts the probability transition matrix for the most frequently observed intents.

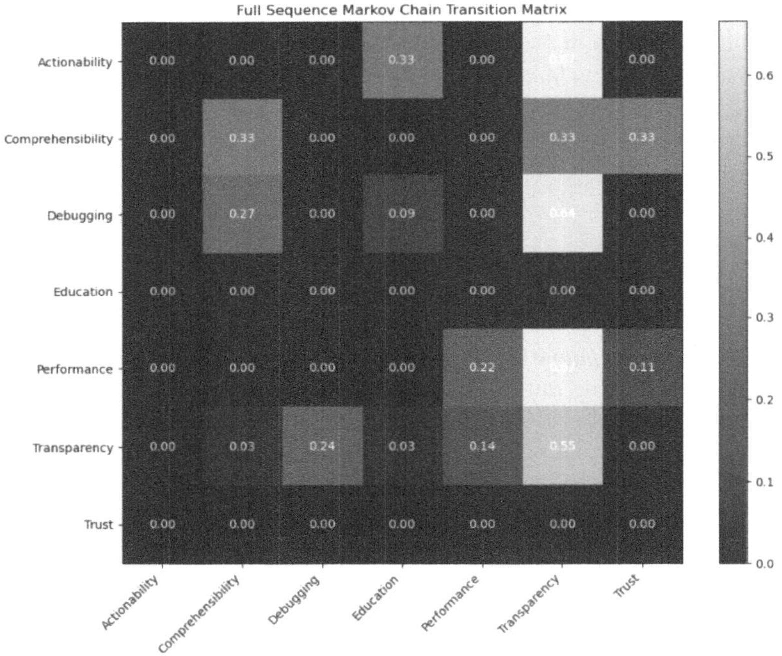

Fig. 3. Markov Chain Probability Transition Matrix.

4.4 Insights and Observations

A statistical analysis of the reasonability scores was performed, computing average scores, variance, standard deviation, and confidence intervals for each question. In addition, Shannon Entropy, Simpson Index, and Gini Coefficient were also computed for sampling purposes. Notable insights include:

- **Average Scores** ranged from 3.31 (for a low-complexity question about sensor measurement) to as high as 9.05 (for a question regarding precision and recall). On average, the reasonability scores were closer to 8 out of 10 or more for the clarification questions asked by the user.
- The highest scoring explanations included detailed clarifications on concepts such as SHAP vs. LIME (average score: 9.03), suggesting users found comparative and well-structured explanations more reasonable.
- Explanations requiring basic conceptual understanding, such as *"what is fluidity"*, scored slightly lower (average 7.87), suggesting potential areas for improvement in simpler, foundational explanations.
- **Impartiality:** Models frequently identified as impartial included *Qwen-2.5-32b, Mistral-Large*, and *Anthropic-claude-3-sonnet.*
  An additional Markov chain analysis of user intent transitions revealed that **Transparency** often serves as a central pivot: users repeatedly transition from and back to `Transparency`. Frequent moves between `Performance` and `Transparency` suggest that users initially seek general explanations, then deeper performance insights, and subsequently request clarifications about how decisions are made. The recurring transitions between `Debugging` and `Transparency` indicate that once users identify potential system issues, they often return to requesting transparent details for verification or deeper understanding.
  These patterns show that clarifications lead users to explore multiple facets of explanation, ranging from performance-oriented queries to debugging or trust concerns, highlighting the importance of adaptive, multi-intent explanation strategies. One of the most interesting revelations is the evolution of original intents to intents which were not modelled by the design user, for example `Actionability` to `Education`.

5 Conclusions and Future Research Directions

We proposed a methodology that enhances the iSee platform with LLM-RAG capabilities for interactive clarifications and adaptive explanation strategies. We also introduced the Reasonability Score to quantitatively assess explanation quality and employ a Markov chain analysis to capture and model the evolution of user explanation needs (intent), ultimately informing the revision task of the CBR cycle of iSee. The resulting workflow sets the grounds for automating the adaptation of explanation strategies to evolving user needs, while preserving the core CBR principle of *learning from experience.*

Finally we analysed how the resulting LLM-RAG has helped clarifying the explanation produced by iSee and improved explanation experience of the end user overall. We analysed the groundness of the proposed methodology and especially the proposed LLM-RAG reasonability that we compared to 100 other

LLMs in the Literature. The evaluation experiments (4 use cases) underscores the need for sophisticated reasonability scoring using LLMs and suggest reasonability of our LLM-RAG is on the higher end. Markov chain analysis provided insights into user intent evolution, emphasising user demands for transparency and debugging-focused explanations. The overall methodology enabled the feasibility of discovering when end users change their intent.

This work opens more research directions related to the use of LLM with CBR systems, including 1) The auto-adaption of the explanation flow based on user interaction patterns, 2) the dynamic exploration of other explainers within the iSee dialog manager, and 3) Further investigation of open-source, smaller parameter models for scalable explainability systems.

References

1. Aamodt, A., Plaza, E.: Case-based reasoning: foundational issues, methodological variations, and system approaches. AI Commun. **7**(1), 39–59 (1994)
2. Bera, K., Braman, N., Gupta, A., Velcheti, V., Madabhushi, A.: Predicting cancer outcomes with radiomics and artificial intelligence in radiology. Nat. Rev. Clin. Oncol. **19**(2), 132–146 (2022)
3. Caro-Martínez, M., Recio-García, J., Díaz-Agudo, B., et al.: iSee: a case-based reasoning platform for the design of explanation experiences. Knowl.-Based Syst. **302**, 112305 (2024)
4. Colledanchise, M., Ögren, P.: Behavior Trees in Robotics and AI: An Introduction. CRC Press (2018)
5. DeepSeek-AI: DeepSeek-V2: A Strong, Economical, and Efficient Mixture-of-Experts Language Model (2024). _eprint: 2405.04434
6. DeepSeek-AI: DeepSeek-R1: Incentivizing Reasoning Capability in LLMs via Reinforcement Learning (2025). _eprint: 2501.12948
7. Grattafiori, A., et al.: The Llama 3 Herd of Models (2024)
8. Hoffman, R.R., Mueller, S.T., Klein, G., Litman, J.: Measures for explainable AI: explanation goodness, user satisfaction, mental models, curiosity, trust, and human-AI performance. Frontiers Comput. Sci. **5** (2023)
9. Jiang, A., et al.: Mistral 7B (2023)
10. Jiang, A., et al.: Mixtral of Experts (2024)
11. Li, H., et al.: LLMs-as-Judges: A Comprehensive Survey on LLM-based Evaluation Methods (2024). arXiv:2412.05579
12. Martin, K., Wijekoon, A., Wiratunga, N., et al.: iSee: intelligent sharing of explanation experiences. In: CEUR Workshop Proceedings (2022)
13. Mishra, M., et al.: Granite Code Models: A Family of Open Foundation Models for Code Intelligence (2024)
14. OpenAI: GPT-4 Technical Report (2023). arXiv Version Number: 3
15. Ouyang, L., et al.: Training language models to follow instructions with human feedback. In: Proceedings of the 6th International Conference on Neural Information Processing Systems. NIPS 2022. Curran Associates Inc., Red Hook (2022)
16. Panigutti, C., et al.: The role of explainable AI in the context of the AI act. In: Proceedings of the 2023 ACM Conference on Fairness, Accountability, and Transparency, FAccT 2023, pp. 1139–1150. Association for Computing Machinery (2023)

17. Parmar, J., et al.: Nemotron-4 15B Technical Report (2024). arXiv:2402.16819
18. Team, G., et al.: Gemma 2: Improving Open Language Models at a Practical Size (2024)
19. Gemma Team, et al.: Gemma: Open Models Based on Gemini Research and Technology (2024). arXiv:2403.08295
20. Touvron, H., et al.: Llama 2: Open Foundation and Fine-Tuned Chat Models (2023)
21. Ulenaers, J.: The impact of artificial intelligence on the right to a fair trial: Towards a robot judge? Asian J. Law Econ. **11**(2) (2020)
22. Wang, L., Ma, C., Feng, X., et al.: A survey on large language model based autonomous agents. Front. Comput. Sci. **18**(6) (2024). http://dx.doi.org/10.1007/s11704-024-40231-1
23. Wijekoon, A., Wiratunga, N., Corsar, D., et al.: iSee: advancing multi-shot explainable AI using case-based recommendations. In: ECAI 2024, 27th European Conference on Artificial Intelligence, including 13th Conference on Prestigious Applications of Intelligent Systems (PAIS 2024), in series "Frontiers in Artificial Intelligence and Applications", pp. 4626–4634 (2024)
24. Wijekoon, A., Wiratunga, N., Corsar, D., et al.: XEQ Scale for Evaluating XAI Experience Quality (2025)
25. Wijekoon, A., Wiratunga, N., Palihawadana, C., et al.: iSee: intelligent sharing of explanation experience by users for users. In: Companion Proceedings of the 28th International Conference on Intelligent User Interfaces, pp. 79–82 (2023)
26. Wiratunga, N., Abeyratne, R., Jayawardena, L., et al.: CBR-RAG: case-based reasoning for retrieval augmented generation in LLMs for legal question answering. In: Case-Based Reasoning Research and Development. Lecture Notes in Computer Science, vol. 14775, pp. 445–460. Springer, Cham (2024)
27. Yang, A., et al.: Qwen2.5 Technical Report (2025). arXiv:2412.15115
28. Zhang, Z., et al.: Artificial intelligence in cyber security: research advances, challenges, and opportunities. Artif. Intell. Rev. 1–25 (2022)
29. Zheng, L., Chiang, W.L., Sheng, Y., Zhuang, S., et al.: Judging LLM-as-a-judge with MT-bench and chatbot arena. In: Proceedings of the 37th International Conference on Neural Information Processing Systems. NIPS 2023. Curran Associates Inc., Red Hook (2023)

LLsiM: Large Language Models for Similarity Assessment in Case-Based Reasoning

Mirko Lenz[1,2](✉), Maximilian Hoffmann[1,2], and Ralph Bergmann[1,2]

[1] Artificial Intelligence and Intelligent Information Systems, Trier University, Universitätsring 15, 54296 Trier, Germany
info@mirko-lenz.de, {hoffmannm,bergmann}@uni-trier.de

[2] German Research Center for Artificial Intelligence (DFKI), Branch Trier University, Behringstraße 21, 54296 Trier, Germany
{mirko.lenz,maximilian.hoffmann,ralph.bergmann}@dfki.de

Abstract. In Case-Based Reasoning (CBR), past experience is used to solve new problems. Determining the most relevant cases is a crucial aspect of this process and is typically based on one or multiple manually-defined similarity measures, requiring deep domain knowledge. To overcome the knowledge-acquisition bottleneck, we propose the use of Large Language Models (LLMs) to automatically assess similarities between cases. We present three distinct approaches where the model is used for different tasks: (i) to predict similarity scores, (ii) to assess pairwise preferences, and (iii) to automatically configure similarity measures. Our conceptual work is accompanied by an open-source Python implementation that we use to evaluate the approaches on three different domains by comparing them to manually crafted similarity measures. Our results show that directly using LLM-based scores does not align well with the baseline rankings, but letting the LLM automatically configure the measures yields rankings that closely resemble the expert-defined ones.

Keywords: Case-Based Reasoning · Large Language Models · Similarities · Ranking · Evaluation

1 Introduction

Case-Based Reasoning (CBR) [1,29] is based on the core principle that similar problems have similar solutions [28]. Given some new problem, CBR systems determine the most relevant past cases and reuse their solutions with the goal of maximizing the *utility* of the solution for the user. In real-world applications, the notion of utility is hard to assess objectively and thus often approximated via the concept of *similarity*. The computation of similarities within parts of a CBR application (e.g., during case retrieval) is conducted via similarity *measures*. Depending on the complexity of the case representation, defining an appropriate similarity *configuration* is a challenging task that may involve domain knowledge and close collaboration with domain experts. This *knowledge-acquisition bottleneck* can potentially hinder the deployment of CBR systems [13].

© The Author(s), under exclusive license to Springer Nature Switzerland AG 2025
I. Bichindaritz and B. López (Eds.): ICCBR 2025, LNAI 15662, pp. 126–141, 2025.
https://doi.org/10.1007/978-3-031-96559-3_9

At the same time, the field of Machine Learning (ML) has made significant advancements in recent years, particularly with the rise of Deep Learning (DL) and Large Language Models (LLMs) [8]. These models are widely used in various domains and often serve as baselines for the development of new ML techniques. With CBR being a problem-solving methodology that is open for new developments, such techniques have already been investigated by the community—for instance, as an embedding-based similarity method for texts [6] or an explanation technique for procedural cases [24]. Such hybrid approaches allow to combine the powerful text generation and understanding capabilities of LLMs with the structured domain knowledge and symbolic reasoning capabilities of CBR systems. Compared to traditional supervised ML approaches that require extensive amounts of labeled training data, LLMs use few-shot or even zero-shot learning to generate predictions based on a few examples or even just the prompt. This means that the information available in a CBR system, such as the case base and the vocabulary, can be used to guide the model in generating the desired output, accelerating the development of robust CBR systems.

This paper aims to explore the potential of LLMs for similarity assessment and case retrieval in CBR systems. We see an opportunity in using LLMs to automatically assess similarities between cases, thereby reducing the knowledge-acquisition effort. Besides directly generating similarity scores, the models may also be valuable for configuring established CBR applications—for instance, by selecting appropriate measures for certain attributes. Preliminary work in this direction has already been done by Wilkerson and Leake [36], who conducted several experiments with LLMs to assess similarities in a CBR system. While their results indicate limited usefulness of LLMs for this task, we argue that integrating more advanced prompting techniques and abstracting from traditional similarity-based retrieval can enhance their effectiveness—especially when dealing with different model sizes. To address this research gap, our paper contains the following contributions: (i) Three distinct retrieval strategies tailored for different types of LLMs, (ii) an experimental evaluation on three different domains with a selection of proprietary and open-weight models, and (iii) an open-source Python implementation of the approaches with a command-line interface.

The remainder of this paper is structured as follows: Sect. 2 introduces foundations regarding similarity measures, followed by an overview of related work in Sect. 3. Section 4 presents our approaches that are evaluated in Sect. 5. Finally, Sect. 6 concludes the paper and presents future work.

2 Foundations

In this section, we provide an overview of the basic concepts relevant to our work. After a brief introduction to traditional similarity-based retrieval and its potential shortcomings in Sect. 2.1, we discuss alternative retrieval techniques involving pairwise case preferences and rankings in Sect. 2.2. Additionally, we present the potential of LLMs to reduce the knowledge-acquisition effort in CBR systems by automatically learning similarity measures from data in Sect. 2.3.

2.1 Similarity-Based Retrieval

This paper takes a more general view on the retrieval process—simply speaking, as a selection of the most relevant cases of a case base w.r.t. to a query. In the traditional CBR process, the retrieval step selects the most relevant cases from the case base based on their similarity to the query. Thereby, the similarity between cases acts as a proxy for their utility which, in turn, determines the reusability of a case to solve the current problem [28,29].

This traditional approach comes with some shortcomings. One of the main issues is the complex and time-consuming process of defining the similarity measures, known as the knowledge-acquisition bottleneck [13]. It requires a deep understanding of the domain and the use case to define proper similarity measures which is often not available or difficult to obtain. While the knowledge-acquisition bottleneck refers to all types of knowledge in a CBR system [29], it can be particularly pronounced for the similarity knowledge. Additionally, the concrete similarity values themselves come with some challenges that further increase the manual effort [15]. First, they are not directly interpretable, making it difficult to understand the reasoning behind the retrieval process and even hindering domain experts from working with them. Second, the similarity values are often not consistent across different cases, similarity measures, and similarity models, leading to unreliable retrieval results. For example, the similarities of a Levenshtein measure are usually not comparable to scores based on embeddings. Finally, the values are only meaningful in relation to each other—for instance, a case with a similarity of 0.8 is more useful relative to a case with a similarity of 0.4, but may not actually provide twice the utility for solving the problem.

2.2 Abstracting from Similarities

There are several ways of overcoming the aforementioned challenges with traditional similarity-based retrieval. One approach is to abstract from similarities by using *preference relations* [15] and, more general, case ranking techniques [11]. Thereby, the goal is to determine the most relevant cases for a given query based on their relative preferences rather than their absolute similarity values. For example, given two cases c_i and c_j, the preference relation $c_i \succ c_j$ indicates that case c_i is preferred over case c_j for the given query. This allows for a more intuitive understanding of the retrieval process, as it focuses on the relative importance of cases rather than their absolute similarity values. Determining preferences rather than specific similarity values usually aligns better with the human perception of ranking and retrieval [15], as pairwise similarities can be hard to interpret and only meaningful in comparison to other pairwise similarities. On the other hand, pairwise preference are often interpretable on their own ("A is more relevant than B") and, thus, easier to determine for domain experts.

As pairwise preferences do not provide a complete ranking of the cases, they need to be aggregated to create a ranked list of cases. This step is usually referred to as *rank aggregation* and is a common task in various fields, including information retrieval, recommender systems, and social choice theory [15]. Rank aggregation can be performed using various techniques [2]—we want to point out specific rank aggregation techniques from the field of information retrieval for the web which are subsumed under the term *centrality* measures [11]. Centrality measures assess node importance in networks, offering a way to combine multiple rankings into a single consensus. In rank aggregation, items are nodes and their pairwise comparisons form edges, so measures like degree, closeness, betweenness, and eigenvector centrality (e.g., PageRank [25]) reveal consistently influential items. We see strong potential of using centrality measures in CBR, because a list of pairwise case preferences closely resembles a network of nodes and edges and runtime optimizations such as power iteration [25] can be employed for efficient computation even on large case bases.

2.3 Automatic Learning with LLMs

Whether the retrieval process is based on similarity values or preferences, the usage of ML techniques can help to reduce the knowledge-acquisition effort in CBR systems. Several approaches have been proposed in the past [14,23,37] with the most recent and prominent approaches being based on DL techniques—more specifically, on LLMs [7,19,35,36].

LLMs are neural networks specifically designed to process and generate natural language. A comprehensive introduction to the topic is beyond the scope of this paper—instead, we give a brief overview. These models are built on the transformer architecture, leveraging the attention mechanism to process an input sequence of text [33]. OpenAI's Generative Pre-trained Transformer (GPT) [27] series, widely recognized through ChatGPT, employs a decoder-only architecture that generates the next token based on the preceding sequence. Rather than fine-tuning the model for specific tasks, prompting techniques can be used to steer the model toward the desired output. This can be achieved through few-shot learning, where examples of input-output pairs are provided, or zero-shot learning, which relies solely on user input without example outputs [8].

Among other aspects, LLMs can help mitigate the knowledge-acquisition bottleneck by capturing domain expertise from large text corpora. Their learned representations allow CBR engineers to create, refine, or expand case structures, vocabularies, and similarity measures. This reduces the need for deep domain knowledge and accelerates the development of robust CBR systems.

3 Related Work

Research on the synergies between CBR and LLMs is a prominent topic in the CBR community, resulting in dedicated workshops at ICCBR 2024 and 2025 and a research manifesto of many researchers from the community [3]. One of the motivations is to combine the strengths of LLMs and CBR methods to overcome the respective weaknesses based on the concept of neuro-symbolic Artificial Intelligence (AI) [18,30]. Most approaches can either be categorized as LLMs improving CBR or CBR improving LLMs [3]. Approaches of the first category are mostly focused on the knowledge engineering process, specifically using the rich capabilities of LLMs to deal with textual data—for instance, modeling of planning knowledge [7], adaptation of arguments [19], or case elicitation [35]. Approaches of the second category are mostly focused on integrating the symbolic knowledge and reasoning capabilities of CBR systems into the text generation process of LLMs—for instance, to enhance LLMs with a Retrieval-Augmented Generation (RAG) [21] process guided by a CBR system [38], to use the CBR knowledge as persistent memory for LLMs improving their performance in specific tasks [34], and other use cases [12,24,32]. Our paper mostly fits in the former category, addressing opportunities 5.4, 6.1, and 6.2 of Bach et al. [3].

The work of Wilkerson and Leake [36] is the one most closely related to our work. They discuss the use of LLMs for similarity-based retrieval and case adaptation and compare several scenarios where they vary the information that is provided to the model. This information contains the case features but, depending on the prompting strategy, also the best results of a k-NN retrieval conducted before prompting. The experiments show that LLMs generally perform poorly in similarity assessment and case ranking but additional knowledge such as the k-NN retrieval results can improve their performance. Our approach differs from this work mainly in two aspects: First, we take a more general view on the retrieval process, simply speaking, as a selection of the most relevant cases of a case base w.r.t. to a query. More specifically, we abstract the task of the LLM from predicting similarities to predicting pairwise preferences, rankings and similarity measures, which is the base of the three LLM-based approaches we propose. Second, we focus strongly on reducing the knowledge-acquisition effort and, thus, design the approaches to function without the need for manually defined similarity measures. While a hybrid approach as proposed by Wilkerson and Leake [36] is a valid idea—for instance, if an existing CBR system is to be improved, we want to reduce the effort of defining the similarity measures in the first place. This lowers the barrier of entry for inexperienced CBR engineers and is especially important for domains where the knowledge-acquisition bottleneck is particularly strong. The common problem of LLMs returning inconsistent or even contradictory information is also considered in our work: We propose a method that outputs a similarity configuration which can then serve as a "first draft" for experienced CBR engineers to come to a final configuration faster.

4 Assessing Similarities via LLMs

Our approaches for assessing similarities using LLMs are motivated by the shortcomings of traditional similarity-based retrieval (see Fig. 1a): CBR engineers analyze the respective domain with the available cases and possibly consult domain experts to come up with the required definitions. It may happen that multiple iterations are needed to find a suitable configuration—potentially delaying the deployment of the CBR system if the domain is not well understood or the domain expert is not available. All of this can be done *offline* with the acquired knowledge being incorporated into the application. For subsequent queries, the

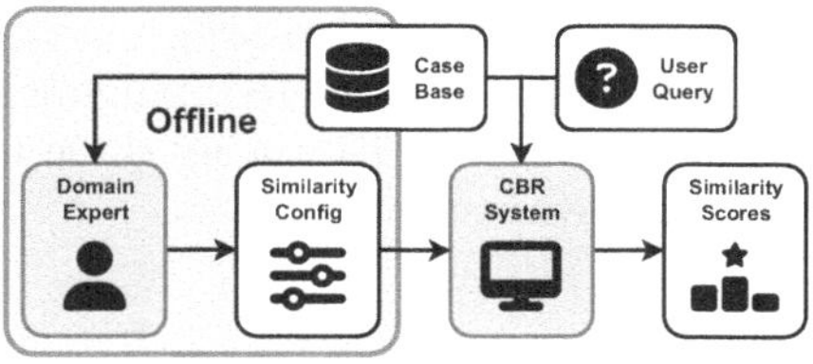

(a) Manual configuration.

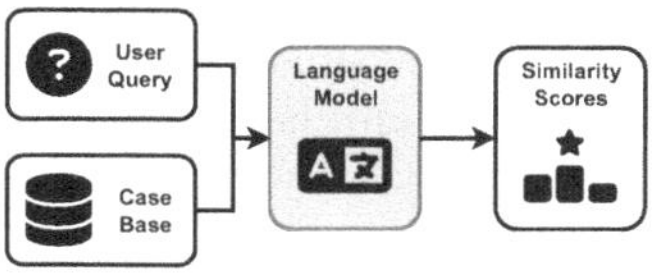

(b) Naive assessment.

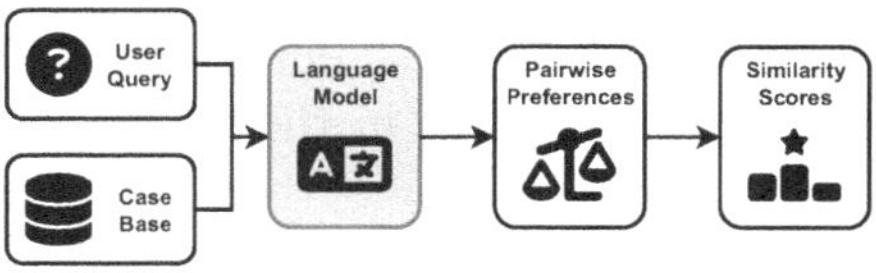

(c) Preference-based assessment.

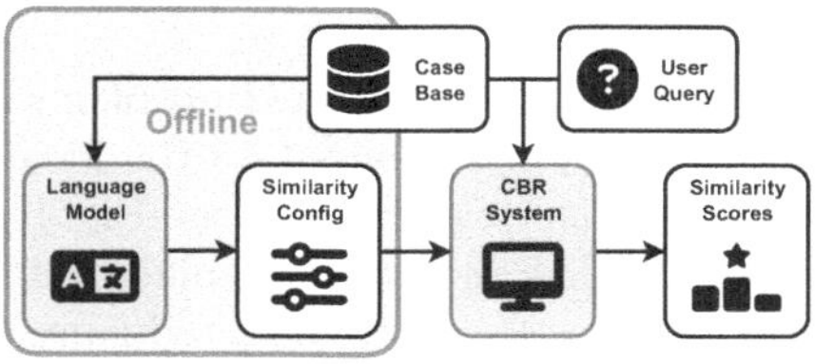

(d) Automated builder.

Fig. 1. Approaches for assessing similarities using LLMs.

CBR system then uses this configuration to compute the similarities to all available cases in an *online* phase. The runtime of this process depends on the complexity of the underlying similarity measures.

4.1 Naive Similarity Assessment

The naive way of introducing LLMs into the traditional similarity-based retrieval process is to let them *directly* predict the similarities between the query and all available cases (see Fig. 1b). One way of achieving that is to send query-case pairs to the LLM and let it predict some score for each pair—just like the idea of Wilkerson and Leake [36]. However, requesting individual similarity scores may not lead to a sensible ranking of the cases because the model does not have any information about the other cases in the case base. To solve this, we use a feature called *structured output* that is available in some LLMs such as those offered by OpenAI.[1] This allows us to provide a JSON schema of the expected response format that we want the model to follow—making it possible to pass the entire case base in the same context as the query. We propose two variants of this approach to deal with the fact that generating floating point numbers is not a trivial task for LLMs: (i) In the *similarity-based* variant, we define the expected output as a list of similarity scores in the range $[0, 1]$ for each case in the case base. (ii) In the *ranking-based* variant, we define the expected output as a list of case IDs sorted by their similarity to the query. Since our end goal is to have similarity scores and not only a ranking, we use Equation (1) to convert the ranking to similarity scores. Here, $\text{rank}(q, c_i)$ is the rank of case c_i w.r.t. query q

[1] https://platform.openai.com/docs/guides/structured-outputs.

and $|C|$ is the number of cases in the case base. As a result of this transformation, the similarity scores are evenly distributed, making it impossible to distinguish between cases with small or large differences in similarity. If capturing these is important, the similarity-based variant should be used instead.

$$\mathrm{sim}(q, c_i) = 1 - \frac{\mathrm{rank}(q, c_i) - 1}{|C| - 1} \tag{1}$$

4.2 Preference-Based Similarity Assessment

Due to the aforementioned problems with LLM-generated similarity scores, the second approach is based on the idea of replacing the absolute similarity values with *pairwise preferences* (see Fig. 1c) which are well-known in the CBR community [15]. Pairwise preferences add an additional layer of abstraction to the similarity assessment, thus, reducing the complexity of the task from predicting a coherent ranking or similarity scores to correctly predicting which of two cases is more relevant to the query. Enumerating all possible pairs of cases leads to a combinatorial explosion of the requests sent to the LLMs, so we propose two variants of this approach: (i) In the *isolated* variant, we send a triple (q, c_i, c_j) to the LLM and ask it to predict whether c_i or c_j is more relevant to q. (ii) In the *batched* variant, we send the query and all available cases to the LLM and request the preferences for all pairs of cases. The isolated variant can be applied to any LLM, but the batched variant requires a model that can handle larger contexts and is able to return structured outputs. Similar to the naive approach, the batched variant is prone to missing or extra pairs in the output—the isolated is not because there is exactly one request for each pair. This problem can be mitigated by computing all possible case pairs as an explicit list in advance and appending them to the prompt. In addition, we send retry requests with relevant cases for all missing pairs to not overload the LLM with irrelevant data.

As a list of case pairs with predicted preferences does not provide a complete ranking of the cases, rank aggregation is employed (see Sect. 2.2). We propose to use graph centrality measures for this purpose that can be adapted to case retrieval by transforming the pairwise preference into a directed graph G where each case is represented as a node and each preference as a directed edge from the more relevant case to the less relevant one. Depending on the use case, different metrics may be useful to turn this graph into a case ranking—for instance, the link analysis algorithms PageRank [25] and HITS [17]. These have been developed for ranking web pages, so they are well-suited to deal with incomplete or even contradictory information. This graph representation also allows for another optimization of the batched variant: After the first request to the LLM, we check for implicit/transitive preferences in the response and explicitly add them to the graph. For instance, if the LLM predicts the preferences $c_i \succ c_j$ and $c_j \succ c_k$, we add $c_i \succ c_k$ to the graph. This reduces the number of pairs to be sent to the LLM in the second request, making it faster and cheaper. We repeat the inference process after the second request to avoid sparse data and consequently produce a more complete graph.

4.3 Automated Similarity Builder (SimBuilder)

All techniques discussed above are only involved in the online phase, meaning that the LLM is invoked for each individual query. This does not match the traditional way of configuring similarity measures in CBR systems, where the configuration is done once and reused for all queries. To bridge this gap, we propose a third approach called SimBuilder shown in Fig. 1d where the domain expert is replaced by an LLM that is instructed to create a similarity configuration based on the available cases—enabling to shift the LLM inference to an offline phase. It is assumed that there exists a set of simple, atomic similarity measures in the underlying CBR system. The LLM is tasked to select, combine, and parameterize these measures based on the available cases, creating an elaborate similarity measure on the case level. The two main challenges are to expose the available similarity measures to the LLM in an understandable manner and to represent the necessary parameters—such as min/max values for interval-based measures—for each function. The bridge between the underlying CBR system and its similarity metrics and the model can be achieved via *function/tool calling* as offered by an increasing number of LLMs. Similar to the structured outputs used in some of the other approaches, this feature allows exposing functions to the model in a structured way and receive parameters to call them locally—these can be different for each similarity measure and control their behavior. For instance, an interval-based measure could have min/max values as parameters, while a taxonomy-based measure could expect a tree structure as input. The central difference to a structured output is that function calling allows to provide multiple JSON schemas in the same request and let the model decide which one to use. We filter the available measures based on the case representation since it would not make sense to use a taxonomy-based measure for numerical values or an edit distance for textual attributes. Then, the LLM is prompted to select the best function and predict values for all available parameters of the method—allowing to execute it locally later in the online phase. For example, given an attribute "miles" of a car, the LLM could decide to use an interval-based similarity measure and provide the parameters "min" and "max" as 0 and 100, 000, respectively. This enables the model to create a more tailored similarity configuration that aligns with the specific characteristics of the data.

5 Experimental Evaluation

Having introduced the different techniques for using LLMs for assessing the similarity in CBR applications, we evaluate them in this section. We first discuss our hypotheses, outline the experimental setup—including descriptions of the three domains at hand—and then present the results of our experiments. The overall goal of our experiments is to assess the *effectiveness* (i.e., accurate similarities) and *efficiency* (i.e., fast computations and low cost) of the proposed approaches. Thus, we compare the LLM-based approaches to the traditional way of configuring similarity measures in CBR systems.

H1. The naive ranking method is more effective than the naive similarity method as LLMs typically struggle to generate precise numerical values.
H2. The preference-based method is more effective than both naive methods because pairwise assessments are more tolerant to potential errors introduced by LLMs. Moreover, the batched variant is more effective than the isolated one as the larger amount of context allows for better informed decisions.
H3. The SimBuilder approach is more efficient than the naive and preference-based methods because the LLM inference can be done in advance. It is also more effective because it can be used with larger LLMs that better understand the semantics of the cases provided.

5.1 Experimental Setup

In this section, we describe the experimental setup of our experiments—that is, the selection of datasets, evaluation metrics, and language models as well as notes regarding our publicly available implementation.

Datasets. A total of three datasets is used in our experiments, each representing a different domain and case representation. The *cars* corpus [22] with 100 cases uses a simple attribute-value representation with numerical and textual attributes. The *recipes* corpus [5] with 40 cases contains semantic graphs representing cooking recipes. The graphs consist of three different types of nodes with different attributes. Finally, the *argumentation* corpus [26] with 110 cases contains argumentative microtexts represented as semantic graphs according to the Argument Interchange Format (AIF) [10] standard. While the first two datasets do not provide a distinct set of queries, the argumentation dataset contains 24 queries and corresponding gold standard relevance assessments [6]. The argumentation dataset is also notable for its heavy use of larger textual attributes, making it infeasible to use taxonomy-based or edit-based distances and instead relying on embeddings.

Evaluation Metrics. In our work, we are interested in the difference between multiple rankings, so standard metrics like precision and recall are not suitable. Instead, we use completeness (CP) and correctness (CR) as proposed by Cheng et al. [9] which are based on comparing available *orders* in the form of concordant and discordant pairs. CP $\in [0, 1]$ measures how many elements of the ground truth ranking are also in the generated ranking while CR $\in [-1, 1]$ indicates whether the generated ranking aligns well (1) or poorly (0) with the ground truth ranking, or even contradicts it (-1). In addition, we compute the normalized cumulative discounted gain (nDCG) [16] by using the inverse ranks as query relevance scores. Compared to CR, this metric incorporates the rank of the cases, meaning that higher importance is given to the top-ranked cases. Another relevant factor is the runtime t of the experiments.

To compute these metrics, we need a ground truth ranking of the cases for each query. As such an expert ranking is not available for some of our datasets, we use the *manual similarity* configuration to obtain the ground truth $\text{rank}(q, c_i)$

Table 1. Overview of the different approaches and the characteristics of the tested models. Parameters are measured in billions and price in USD per million input tokens as reported by OpenRouter.ai.

Size	Params	Price	Models	Approaches
Small	<4	<0.01	Llama-3.2-3b	preferences-isolated
Medium	40–120	0.1–0.2	GPT-4o-mini, Llama-3.3-70b	naive, preferences-batched
Large	>400	>0.8	GPT-4o, o3-mini, DeepSeek-V3, DeepSeek-R1, Llama-3.1-405b	SimBuilder

for each query. In addition, we compute a variant where the rank is normalized to the range $[0, k]$ to ignore smaller and less relevant differences in the ranking via Equation (2) where $\lfloor \cdot \rceil$ denotes rounding to the nearest integer.

$$\text{rank}'_k(q, c_i) = \left\lfloor \frac{\text{sim}(q, c_i) - \min \text{sim}(q, C)}{\max \text{sim}(q, C) - \min \text{sim}(q, C)} \times k \right\rceil \tag{2}$$

Language Model Selection. For our experiments, we distinguish between three classes of LLMs—small, medium, and large—as shown in Table 1. Depending on the specific use case at hand, these boundaries may be adjusted—here they serve as categories to select cost-effective models for the different approaches. In addition to the model size, we also report the price as it is a crucial aspect for real-world applications. Initial experiments showed that preferences-isolated is the most expensive and slowest approach—for each query, all possible query-case pairs are requested separately—so we use a single small model to evaluate it. For the preferences-batched and both naive approaches, the case base is sent once to the model for each query, so we can use medium-sized LLMs for them (but not large ones due to the cost). The SimBuilder approach, on the other hand, can be used with larger models. Here, the case base is sent to the LLM once to create the similarity configuration in the offline phase.

Implementation. We provide an open-source implementation[2] in Python that builds on top of CBRkit [20]. It offers a declarative way of configuring similarity measures and supports various case representations, including attribute-value and graphs. To convert pairwise preferences to similarity scores, we use the arithmetic mean of the two centrality measures PageRank and HITS. Initial experiments showed that sparse graphs as returned by some LLMs lead to many identical similarity scores, meaning that the ranking of the affected cases is arbitrary—combining multiple centrality measures helped mitigate this problem. We also experimented with individual centrality measures, but did not observe large differences in the results. For the SimBuilder, we convert the available similarity functions to JSON in a generic way—currently supporting attribute-value and graph-based representations. Some of these measures accept rather complex parameters, so we wrap those in a custom function that only exposes a subset to the LLM. In case a request fails—for instance, due to an invalid response—we retry the generation.

[2] https://github.com/wi2trier/llsim (MIT license).

Table 2. Cars results using baseline retrieval as ground truth.

Experiment	CP		CR		nDCG		t
	rank	rank'_5	rank	rank'_5	rank	rank'_5	
builder-deepseek-r1	1.000	1.000	0.733	0.907	0.991	0.994	0.463
builder-deepseek-v3	1.000	1.000	0.754	0.920	0.991	0.995	0.485
builder-gpt-4o	1.000	1.000	0.802	0.941	0.994	0.996	0.803
builder-llama-405b	1.000	1.000	0.757	0.923	0.993	0.996	0.438
builder-o3-mini	1.000	1.000	0.787	0.943	0.994	0.996	0.562
naive-rank-gpt-4o-mini	0.335	0.342	0.263	0.352	0.586	0.595	15.9
naive-rank-llama-70b	0.745	0.746	0.164	0.235	0.738	0.754	1936
naive-sim-gpt-4o-mini	0.067	0.069	0.157	0.266	0.324	0.339	51.3
naive-sim-llama-70b	0.642	0.640	0.016	0.166	0.684	0.693	2704
preferences-gpt-4o-mini	0.868	0.871	-0.018	-0.025	0.799	0.807	462
preferences-llama-3b	0.980	0.980	0.069	0.100	0.855	0.874	8673
preferences-llama-70b	0.385	0.385	-0.351	-0.333	0.386	0.396	4128

Table 3. Recipes results using baseline retrieval as ground truth.

Experiment	CP		CR		nDCG		t
	rank	rank'_5	rank	rank'_5	rank	rank'_5	
builder-deepseek-r1	1.000	1.000	0.669	0.854	0.980	0.991	149
builder-deepseek-v3	1.000	1.000	0.438	0.623	0.927	0.953	133
builder-gpt-4o	1.000	1.000	0.713	0.883	0.982	0.992	198
builder-llama-405b	1.000	1.000	0.658	0.841	0.975	0.989	173
builder-o3-mini	1.000	1.000	0.663	0.832	0.976	0.988	197
naive-rank-gpt-4o-mini	0.704	0.702	-0.051	-0.061	0.719	0.745	13.5
naive-rank-llama-70b	0.866	0.867	-0.039	-0.033	0.734	0.751	844
naive-sim-gpt-4o-mini	0.594	0.597	-0.136	-0.126	0.648	0.683	36.0
naive-sim-llama-70b	0.827	0.821	-0.063	-0.047	0.705	0.717	1185
preferences-gpt-4o-mini	0.940	0.948	-0.000	0.001	0.799	0.811	305
preferences-llama-3b	0.949	0.954	-0.030	0.020	0.785	0.810	857
preferences-llama-70b	0.809	0.813	-0.139	-0.141	0.696	0.702	4068

5.2 Results and Discussion

Based on the setup described in the previous section, we now present the results of our experiments for the three domains, starting with those using the baseline retrieval as ground truth. For all datasets combined, the cost of our experiments for the naive and preference-based techniques totaled to a few dollars per model. Even though using the larger models, the SimBuilder was actually cheaper and used less than one dollar per model. Its offline runtime—which is not included in the tables as it is upfront and does not affect the actual retrieval—ranges from 5 to 500 s depending on the domain and model.

Baseline Retrieval. The results for the cars and recipes domains are shown in Table 2 and Table 3, respectively. For the naive and preference-based approaches, the completeness is less than one, indicating missing or invalid LLM responses.

Table 4. Argumentation results using expert rating as ground truth.

Experiment	CP	CR	nDCG	t
baseline	1.000	0.187	0.841	177
builder-deepseek-r1	1.000	0.220	0.899	130
builder-deepseek-v3	1.000	0.220	0.899	166
builder-gpt-4o	1.000	0.220	0.899	142
builder-llama-405b	1.000	0.220	0.899	145
builder-o3-mini	1.000	-0.836	0.379	30.2
naive-rank-gpt-4o-mini	0.417	0.008	0.338	27.8
naive-rank-llama-70b	0.703	0.101	0.402	822
naive-sim-gpt-4o-mini	0.260	-0.472	0.302	47.5
naive-sim-llama-70b	0.680	-0.159	0.318	733
preferences-gpt-4o-mini	0.935	0.055	0.335	551
preferences-llama-3b	0.986	-0.142	0.338	2547
preferences-llama-70b	0.628	0.014	0.283	4941

The cars dataset (which contains more than double the number of cars compared to the recipes dataset) yields completeness scores below 0.1, meaning that the model excluded most of the cases from the output. The correctness scores for these techniques are mostly close to zero, indicating random rankings. Overall, the scores are higher for the less complex cars dataset—the graph-based representation of the recipes could make it harder for the LLM to understand the semantics of the cases. The SimBuilder approach however achieves a completeness of 1.0 for all models and a correctness of around 0.75 for the cars dataset and 0.5 for the recipes dataset. As such, the generated similarity configuration seems to closely match the expert-driven definitions. We consider this to be a very promising result, especially given the fact that both domains make use of rather complex taxonomy-based similarity functions that require a lot of domain knowledge to configure. Analyzing the effect of rank'_5 (i.e., not requiring strict adherence to the baseline), we see overall improved scores for all approaches. The metrics for the argumentation domain are missing here as we focus on the expert ratings in the next section for this corpus. We still ran the experiment for this corpus and observed similar results as for the recipes dataset.

Expert Ratings. The results for the argumentation domain shown in Table 4 are based on expert ratings as ground truth. Consequently, we do not report the rank' scores as no transformation from similarity scores to ranks is needed. We observe that even the manually defined *baseline* configuration does not achieve a correctness or nDCG of 1.0—meaning that in real-world scenarios, it may not be possible to achieve a perfect ranking of the cases, even with lots of domain knowledge. Overall, the findings are consistent with the previous results with one notable exception: When used with the reasoning model o3-mini, the SimBuilder achieves the worst correctness score of all approaches. All other SimBuilder experiments result in the exact same configuration as the expert one, so the different scores are solely caused by variations of the underlying A* algorithm (e.g., the order in which mapping candidates are evaluated [4]).

Hypotheses. Regarding the hypotheses, we see that the naive ranking method is indeed more effective than the naive similarity method, meaning that H1 can be accepted. However, the preference-based technique is not universally more effective than the naive ones. The isolated variant tends to outperform the batched one, ultimately leading to the rejection of H2. Finally, the SimBuilder is more effective than all other approaches, but not necessarily more efficient. For the simple representation of the cars dataset, the SimBuilder is the fastest, but that is not the case for the graph-based recipes and argumentation datasets. Thus, we can only partially accept H3.

6 Conclusion, Limitations and Future Work

In this paper, we present three different approaches for using LLMs in similarity-based retrieval of CBR applications. LLMs are used to assess pairwise similarities between cases directly, to assess pairwise preferences between cases, and to generate an expert-like similarity configuration via the SimBuilder approach. We evaluate them on three different domains using a selection of LLMs to assess their effectiveness and efficiency. The results show that the SimBuilder performs best and is capable of almost perfectly matching the ranking obtained via manually crafted similarity configurations, while the other two approaches struggle to achieve similar results.

We see limitations of our work regarding scaling to large case bases and the availability of atomic similarity measures: First, scaling to larger datasets could be challenging with the limited context size of LLMs—especially for preferences-batched and the naive approaches. This could be tackled through chunking where the case base is split into smaller parts and that are processed separately and then aggregated later on. Such strategies are already implemented in CBRkit and showed decent results in initial experiments. Second, using the SimBuilder approach requires a set of atomic similarity measures to use as building blocks for the generated similarity configuration. This could hinder its applicability in some CBR systems, but there already exist CBR frameworks with a decent amount of such ready-to-use functions [31].

In future work, we plan to extend our work in several ways. Extending the evaluation to other domains and case representations to assess the generalizability of the approaches is an important next step. We also think that it would be interesting to evaluate the approaches with user-defined similarities or preferences, serving as a more realistic ground truth. Additionally, experimenting with fine-tuned LLMs to improve the performance of the approaches is a possible direction for future work. This could be especially useful for the SimBuilder approach, where the LLM could be fine-tuned on different case representations and similarity models to create a very specialized model. As another means of future work, we plan to use the approach as part of a RAG process [38]. Compared to classical RAG, the approach can work on structured data such as databases by using local similarities instead of simply converting the data into strings and relying on a vector store. This would allow us to use the LLM as a generator of the initial solution and the CBR system as a means of refining the solution by retrieving similar cases and adapting them to the current problem.

Acknowledgments. This work is funded by the *Federal Ministry of Education and Research* under grant № 02WAZ1745A (SOWEKI), the association *Eifelkreis Digital* with its project KITEi, and the *Studienstiftung*.

References

1. Aamodt, A., Plaza, E.: Case-based reasoning - foundational issues, methodological variations, and system approaches. AI Commun. (1994)
2. Allwein, E.L., Schapire, R.E., Singer, Y.: Reducing multiclass to binary: a unifying approach for margin classifiers. J. Mach. Learn. Res. 113–141 (2000)
3. Bach, K., et al.: Case-Based Reasoning Meets Large Language Models: A Research Manifesto for Open Challenges and Research Directions (2025). https://hal.science/hal-05006761. Working Paper
4. Bergmann, R., Gil, Y.: Similarity assessment and efficient retrieval of semantic workflows. Inf. Syst. 115–127 (2014)
5. Bergmann, R., Grumbach, L., Malburg, L., Zeyen, C.: ProCAKE: a process-oriented case-based reasoning framework. In: Workshops Proceedings for the Twenty-Seventh ICCBR, pp. 156–161. CEUR (2019)
6. Bergmann, R., Lenz, M., Ollinger, S., Pfister, M.: Similarity measures for case-based retrieval of natural language argument graphs in argumentation machines. In: Proceedings of the 32nd FLAIRS Conference, pp. 329–334. AAAI Press (2019)
7. Brand, F.: Modeling and acquiring knowledge with large language models: a study in the cyber-physical domain. Master's thesis, Trier University (2024)
8. Brown, T., et al.: Language models are few-shot learners. In: Advances in Neural Information Processing Systems, pp. 1877–1901. Curran Associates, Inc. (2020)
9. Cheng, W., Rademaker, M., De Baets, B., Hüllermeier, E.: Predicting partial orders: ranking with abstention. In: Machine Learning and Knowledge Discovery in Databases, pp. 215–230. Springer (2010)
10. Chesñevar, C.I., et al.: Towards an argument interchange format. Knowl. Eng. Rev. 293 (2006)
11. Dwork, C., Kumar, R., Naor, M., Sivakumar, D.: Rank aggregation methods for the web. In: Proceedings of the Tenth International World Wide Web Conference, WWW 10, Hong Kong, China, 1–5 May 2001, pp. 613–622. ACM (2001)
12. Feng, B., Gao, H., Zhang, P., Zhang, J.: CBR-REN: a case-based reasoning driven retriever-generator model for hybrid long-form numerical reasoning. In: Case-Based Reasoning Research and Development - 32nd ICCBR, pp. 111–126. Springer (2024)
13. Hanney, K., Keane, M.T.: The adaptation knowledge bottleneck: how to ease it by learning from cases. In: Case-Based Reasoning Research and Development, pp. 359–370. Springer (1997)
14. Hoffmann, M., Bergmann, R.: Using graph embedding techniques in process-oriented case-based reasoning. Algorithms 27 (2022)

15. Hüllermeier, E., Schlegel, P.: Preference-based CBR: first steps toward a methodological framework. In: Ram, A., Wiratunga, N. (eds.) ICCBR 2011. LNCS (LNAI), vol. 6880, pp. 77–91. Springer, Heidelberg (2011). https://doi.org/10.1007/978-3-642-23291-6_8
16. Järvelin, K., Kekäläinen, J.: Cumulated gain-based evaluation of IR techniques. ACM Trans. Inf. Syst. 422–446 (2002)
17. Kleinberg, J.M.: Authoritative sources in a hyperlinked environment. J. ACM 604–632 (1999)
18. Leake, D., Crandall, D.: On bringing case-based reasoning methodology to deep learning. In: Watson, I., Weber, R. (eds.) ICCBR 2020. LNCS (LNAI), vol. 12311, pp. 343–348. Springer, Cham (2020). https://doi.org/10.1007/978-3-030-58342-2_22
19. Lenz, M., Bergmann, R.: Case-based adaptation of argument graphs with wordnet and large language models. In: Case-Based Reasoning Research and Development, pp. 263–278. Springer (2023)
20. Lenz, M., Malburg, L., Bergmann, R.: CBRkit: an intuitive case-based reasoning toolkit for python. In: Case-Based Reasoning Research and Development, pp. 289–304. Springer (2024)
21. Lewis, P., et al.: Retrieval-augmented generation for knowledge-intensive NLP tasks. In: Advances in Neural Information Processing Systems, pp. 9459–9474. Curran Associates, Inc. (2020)
22. Malburg, L., Hoffmann, M., Trumm, S., Bergmann, R.: Improving similarity-based retrieval efficiency by using graphic processing units in case-based reasoning. In: Proceedings of the Thirty-Fourth FLAIRS, Florida, USA, 17–19 May 2021 (2021)
23. Mathisen, B.M., Aamodt, A., Bach, K., Langseth, H.: Learning similarity measures from data. Prog. Artif. Intell. 129–143 (2020)
24. Minor, M., Kaucher, E.: Retrieval augmented generation with LLMs for explaining business process models. In: Case-Based Reasoning Research and Development, pp. 175–190. Springer (2024)
25. Page, L., Brin, S., Motwani, R., Winograd, T.: The PageRank Citation Ranking: Bringing Order to the Web. Technical report, Stanford InfoLab (1999)
26. Peldszus, A., Stede, M.: An annotated corpus of argumentative microtexts. In: Argumentation and Reasoned Action: Proceedings of the 1st European Conference on Argumentation, pp. 801–816. College Publications (2016)
27. Radford, A., Narasimhan, K., Salimans, T., Sutskever, I.: Improving language understanding by generative pre-training (2018)
28. Richter, M.M.: Foundations of similarity and utility. In: Proceedings of the Twentieth International Florida Artificial Intelligence Research Society Conference, 7–9 May 2007, Key West, Florida, USA, pp. 30–37. AAAI Press (2007)
29. Richter, M.M., Weber, R.: Case-Based Reasoning: A Textbook. Springer (2013)
30. Sarker, M.K., Zhou, L., Eberhart, A., Hitzler, P.: Neuro-symbolic artificial intelligence. AI Commun. 197–209 (2021)
31. Schultheis, A., Zeyen, C., Bergmann, R.: An overview and comparison of case-based reasoning frameworks. In: Case-Based Reasoning Research and Development, pp. 327–343. Springer (2023)
32. Sourati, Z., Ilievski, F., Sandlin, H.Â., Mermoud, A.: Case-based reasoning with language models for classification of logical fallacies. In: Proceedings of the Thirty-Second IJCAI, pp. 5188–5196 (2023)
33. Vaswani, A., et al.: Attention is all you need. In: Advances in Neural Information Processing Systems. Curran Associates, Inc. (2017)

34. Watson, I.: A Case-Based Persistent Memory for a Large Language Model (2023)
35. Weitl-Harms, S., Hastings, J.D., Powell, J.H.: Toward automated knowledge discovery in case-based reasoning. In: Proceedings of the Thirty-Seventh FLAIRS 2024, Sandestin Beach, FL, USA, 19–21 May 2024. AAAI Press (2024)
36. Wilkerson, K., Leake, D.: On implementing case-based reasoning with large language models. In: Case-Based Reasoning Research and Development, pp. 404–417. Springer (2024)
37. Wilkerson, Z., Leake, D., Crandall, D.J.: On combining knowledge-engineered and network-extracted features for retrieval. In: Case-Based Reasoning Research and Development - 29th ICCBR 2021, pp. 248–262. Springer (2021)
38. Wiratunga, N., et al.: CBR-RAG: case-based reasoning for retrieval augmented generation in LLMs for legal question answering. In: Case-Based Reasoning Research and Development, pp. 445–460. Springer (2024)

Offline-to-Online: Case-Based Knowledge Distillation with Large Language Models for Reinforcement Learning

Hongzhe Liu[1], Quan Liu[1(✉)], Lan Wu[1], Meilong Shi[1], and Zhiming Cui[2]

[1] School of Computer Science and Technology, Soochow University, Suzhou, China
{hzliu1019,20217927001,20215227110}@stu.suda.edu.cn, quanliu@suda.edu.cn

[2] School of Electronic and Information Engineering, Suzhou University of Science and Technology, Suzhou, China
zmcui@usts.edu.cn

Abstract. The integration of Large Language Models (LLMs) into Reinforcement Learning (RL) presents a promising approach to enhancing agent performance by leveraging the world knowledge embedded in LLMs. However, existing approaches face significant challenges, including high computational costs, over-dependence on pre-trained knowledge, and limited adaptability to dynamic environments. In this paper, we propose Offline-to-Online: Case-Based Knowledge Distillation with Large Language Models for Reinforcement Learning (OCaL-RL). Our framework features an LLM-driven case-based reasoning system, which constructs a case repository of simulated experiences enriched with world knowledge. The agent first retrieves and leverages relevant cases for initial policy optimization and then refines its policies based on real environmental interactions, ensuring both knowledge efficiency and adaptability. This case-driven paradigm enables RL agents to dynamically retrieve, adapt, and refine distilled policies, balancing pre-trained knowledge and real-time learning. Experiments in challenging MiniGrid environments demonstrate that OCaL-RL outperforms strong baselines in both return rate and success rate.

Keywords: Cased-base reasoning · Large language models · Reinforcement learning · Offline-to-online · Knowledge distillation

1 Introduction

The integration of Case-Based Reasoning (CBR) and Reinforcement Learning (RL) has shown significant potential in improving policy reuse and adaptation by leveraging past experiences [1]. In text-based RL, CBR-inspired approaches enhance generalization by enabling on-policy neural agents to retrieve and apply successful past experiences [2]. However, a key challenge in case-based RL lies in the efficient design and utilization of policy repositories, as suboptimal retrieval and adaptation of stored policies often lead to degraded performance.

© The Author(s), under exclusive license to Springer Nature Switzerland AG 2025
I. Bichindaritz and B. López (Eds.): ICCBR 2025, LNAI 15662, pp. 142–156, 2025.
https://doi.org/10.1007/978-3-031-96559-3_10

Large Language Models (LLMs) present a promising avenue for addressing these challenges by encoding extensive world knowledge and strong reasoning capabilities. Advanced models such as GPT-3 and GPT-4 have demonstrated effectiveness in guiding decision-making and improving agent learning [3]. By integrating LLMs, RL agents can accelerate learning and enhance planning in complex environments [4,5]. However, direct reliance on LLMs for real-time decision-making is computationally expensive and may limit the agent's ability to explore and adapt autonomously.

The offline-to-online RL paradigm mitigates sample inefficiencies by leveraging offline data, such as expert demonstrations or pre-trained models, to improve training efficiency [6,7]. By initializing learning with prior knowledge and gradually adapting to real-world interactions, this approach enhances sample efficiency. However, its effectiveness is constrained by the quality and diversity of offline data, making it challenging to generalize in dynamic environments.

Knowledge distillation provides an effective mechanism for transferring knowledge from a larger teacher model to a smaller student model, improving efficiency and generalization [8]. In RL, distilling high-level reasoning from LLMs into agent policies can reduce exploration costs and improve sample efficiency [9]. However, existing approaches often lack structured knowledge organization, leading to inefficient policy adaptation.

In this paper, we propose **OCaL-RL** (**O**ffline-to-Online: **Ca**se-Based Knowledge Distillation with **L**arge Language Models for **R**einforcement **L**earning), a novel framework that bridges LLMs and RL through a CBR paradigm. Unlike prior approaches that rely on LLMs solely for policy generation, we design an LLM-driven CBR system that constructs a structured case repository enriched with world knowledge. This repository serves as a foundation for offline training, enabling a Proximal Policy Optimization (PPO)-based student agent to retrieve, adapt, and refine policies. As training transitions to the online phase, the agent progressively integrates real-world feedback, ensuring a smooth shift from pre-distilled knowledge to adaptive decision-making. This approach enhances sample efficiency while maintaining a balance between LLM-guided knowledge and autonomous exploration.

Our key contributions are as follows:

- **Case-Based Offline-to-Online Learning**: We introduce a structured case-driven learning paradigm, where retrieved cases from the LLM-constructed repository guide the PPO-based agent, improving learning efficiency while reducing reliance on real-time LLM queries.
- **Case-Based Knowledge Distillation**: We develop OCaL-RL, a framework that distills world knowledge into a structured case repository, enabling RL agents to retrieve, adapt, and refine stored experiences for more effective policy learning.
- **Dynamic Policy Adaptation**: Our approach ensures that the student agent progressively transitions from pre-distilled cases to real-time interactions, maintaining both generalized world knowledge and task-specific adaptability.

2 Related Work

2.1 CBR for RL

CBR has been used to efficiently switch between previously stored RL policies [1]. Most imitation learning methods follow expert demonstrations step-by-step [10], while hierarchical approaches mitigate this by learning sub-goal policies guided by a meta-policy [11]. In text-based RL, a CBR-inspired method enhances on-policy neural agents by collecting and reusing past positive experiences for better generalization [2]. Additionally, a temporal coherence-based algorithm learns high-level policies by judging state similarity, achieving near-optimal policies with minimal expert data and outperforming action-level imitation [12].

2.2 LLMs for RL

The incorporation of LLMs into RL has gained considerable interest, primarily because of the potential advantages it offers in improving the performance of RL agents [4,5]. By integrating LLMs, these agents can significantly enhance their abilities in various complex tasks, such as long-term planning, logical reasoning, and sophisticated decision-making [13]. LLMs can enable agents to better understand and process natural language instructions, learn from textual descriptions, and even make sense of ambiguous or incomplete information [14]. The integration of LLMs into RL has garnered significant attention due to their potential to enhance agent capabilities in planning, reasoning, and decision-making [15].

2.3 Offline-to-Online Framework for RL

The offline-to-online framework in RL has become a vital area of study [6,7]. In offline RL, agents learn from pre-collected datasets without real-time environmental interaction, enabling efficient use of historical data and potentially yielding good initial policies [16]. However, due to distributional shift between offline data and real-time environment dynamics, offline-learned policies may not perform optimally online. To solve this, several methods have been suggested. Some cautiously fine-tune offline policies with online interactions, like using importance sampling to correct distributional differences and adapt policies gradually [17]. Other methods combine offline and online learning, using the offline policy as a starting point and enhancing it with online exploration [18]. Additionally, uncertainty estimation is incorporated to balance exploration and exploitation during the offline-to-online transition, which allows agents to estimate action uncertainty from offline data and decide whether to explore or exploit [19].

2.4 Knowledge Distillation for RL

The teacher-student framework in RL was introduced by Torrey and Taylor [20], where the teacher suggests actions to the student. Knowledge distillation, introduced for model compression [8], transfers knowledge from a high-capacity teacher model to a smaller student model. In RL, prior research has used teacher agents to guide specialized RL agents, improving the inefficiencies of tabula rasa RL. Approaches such as Jump-start RL [21] and Kickstarting RL [22] utilize teacher guidance through demonstrations, scalar feedback, and action advice to accelerate learning. Matthews et al. [23] further extended this to hierarchical policies, transferring pre-trained low-level skill policies as teachers.

3 Preliminaries

We model the sequential decision-making process as a Markov Decision Process (MDP), denoted as $\langle S, A, T, R, \gamma \rangle$, where S is the state space, A is the action space, T is the transition function, R is the reward function, and $\gamma \in [0, 1]$ is the discount factor controlling the trade-off between immediate and future rewards.

The goal in RL is to learn an optimal policy $\pi : S \to P(A)$ that maximizes the expected cumulative return:

$$\max_{\pi} \mathbb{E} \left[\sum_{t=0}^{\infty} \gamma^t r_t \right], \tag{1}$$

where r_t is the reward at time step t. The policy π is parameterized by θ, with $\pi(a|s; \theta)$ representing the probability of taking action a in state s.

RL algorithms optimize θ by minimizing a surrogate loss function $L_{RL}(\theta)$, estimated using trajectories $\langle s_t, a_t, r_t \rangle$ representing agent-environment interactions.

PPO [24] is an actor-critic method that optimizes the policy using the advantage function $A(s_t, a_t) = Q(s_t, a_t) - V(s_t)$. The PPO objective is:

$$\begin{aligned} J(\theta) = \mathbb{E}_{s,a} \Bigg[\min \Bigg(& \frac{\pi_\theta(a|s)}{\pi_{\theta_{old}}(a|s)} A_{\pi_{\theta_{old}}}(s, a), \\ & \text{clip} \left(\frac{\pi_\theta(a|s)}{\pi_{\theta_{old}}(a|s)}, 1 \pm \epsilon \right) A_{\pi_{\theta_{old}}}(s, a) \Bigg) \Bigg], \end{aligned} \tag{2}$$

where the clip operator bounds the policy update to avoid destabilizing changes. This clipped objective ensures stable learning and has made PPO a widely used RL algorithm due to its simplicity and effectiveness.

4 Methods

4.1 Overview of the OCaL-RL Framework

As illustrated in Fig. 1, the OCaL-RL framework introduces a CBR paradigm into RL by leveraging an LLM-based teacher agent and a PPO-based student agent. The teacher agent serves as a knowledge repository, encoding generalized policies extracted from diverse observations. These precomputed guidance policies are stored in a teacher buffer and retrieved adaptively to support the student agent's decision-making. Over time, the student agent progressively refines its policy through experience, allowing it to surpass the teacher's initially prescribed policies.

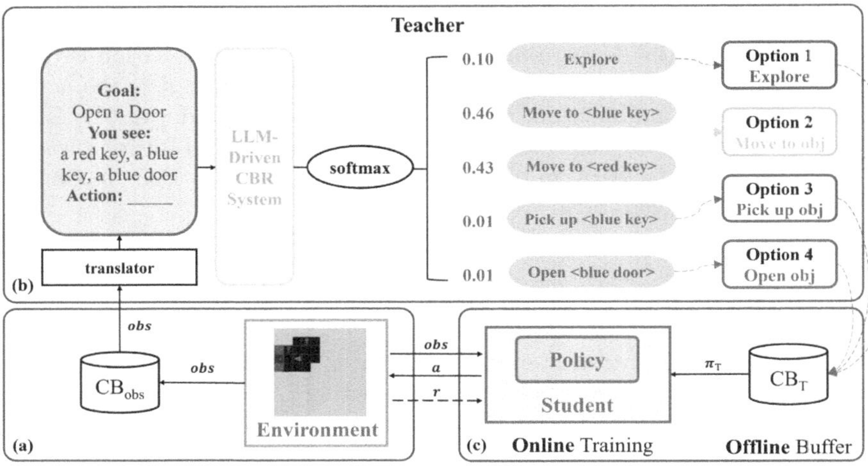

Fig. 1. An illustration of the OCaL-RL framework applied to the MiniGrid environment, demonstrating its case-based learning process. (a) The agent explores the environment to retrieve a key and unlock a door. It encounters a red key, a blue key, and a blue door, with the gray areas representing unexplored regions. The student agent interacts with the environment using an initial policy and systematically collects diverse observations obs_i, which are stored in the case buffer CB_{obs}. (b) An LLM acts as a CBR system, retrieving relevant knowledge based on the textual description of each observation and generating action recommendations. These recommendations are stored as reference cases in a teacher buffer CB_T for offline reuse. (c) The PPO-based student agent refines its policy iteratively by integrating environmental feedback and adapting the teacher's case-based guidance. Over time, the student agent transitions from relying on retrieved cases to independently deriving optimal policies. (Color figure online)

4.2 Offline Case-Based Knowledge Distillation via LLM-Based Teacher Agent

Case Retrieval: Pre-storing Observations for LLM Guidance. To construct a comprehensive knowledge base, the student agent initially explores the environment using a basic policy, storing encountered observations obs_i in an observation case buffer CB_{obs}, where $i \in \{1, 2, \ldots, M\}$. This ensures that the LLM has access to a diverse set of cases representing different environmental conditions, supporting the generation of adaptive guidance.

Policy Generation: LLM-Driven Action Recommendations. For each stored observation, the LLM-driven system acts as a teacher agent, synthesizing a soft decision policy by retrieving and reasoning over a set of predefined high-level options. Given an observation description $c(obs)$, the LLM selects an appropriate decision model π_k from a case library of policies $\Pi = \{\pi_k : k \in \{1, 2, \ldots, K\}\}$, assigning action probabilities as:

$$P_{\text{LLM}}(a_i|c(obs)) = \frac{\exp(score_i)}{\sum_{j=1}^{M} \exp(score_j)}, \tag{3}$$

where $score_i$ represents the confidence of the LLM in selecting action a_i. These action probabilities are then mapped to the K available policies, resulting in $P_{\text{LLM}}(k \mid c(obs))$. It forms a case-adaptive teacher policy:

$$\pi_T(\cdot|obs) = \sum_k P_{\text{LLM}}(k|c(obs))\pi_k(\cdot|obs). \tag{4}$$

The generated teacher policies are stored in a case buffer CB_T to facilitate subsequent offline knowledge transfer.

4.3 Online Case Adaptation via PPO-Based Student Agent

The training process is summarized in Algorithm 1.

Adaptive Teacher-Student Integration via KL-Divergence. To facilitate case-based adaptation, the student agent dynamically adjusts its reliance on the teacher's policy based on their divergence. The KL divergence between the student policy $\pi_\theta(\cdot|s)$ and the teacher policy $\pi_T(\cdot|s)$ is computed as:

$$D_{KL}(\pi_\theta||\pi_T) = \sum \pi_\theta(\cdot|s) \log \frac{\pi_\theta(\cdot|s)}{\pi_T(\cdot|s)}. \tag{5}$$

Algorithm 1. Online case adaptation via PPO-based student agent

Require: Teacher policy buffer CB_T, iterations N, optimization steps per iteration M, temperature τ, learning rate α, clip parameter ϵ, loss weights $\lambda_V, \lambda_E, \lambda_D$

1: **for** $i = 1, 2, \ldots, N$ **do**
2: Collect trajectory $\{s_t, a_t, r_t\}$ using student policy π_θ
3: Estimate advantages $A_t = R_t - V_\theta(s_t)$
4: Store previous policy $\pi_{\text{old}} = \pi_\theta$
5: **for** $j = 1, 2, \ldots, M$ **do**
6: Retrieve teacher policy π_T from CB_T
7: Compute KL divergence $D_{KL}(\pi_\theta || \pi_T)$ and case-adaptive scaling factor λ according to Equation 5 and 6
8: Compute combined policy ratio according to Equation 8
9: Compute policy loss, value loss, entropy loss and distillation loss according to Equation 7, Equation 9, Equation 10 and Equation 11
10: Combine total loss:

$$L_{\text{Total}}(\theta) = L_{\text{P}}(\theta) + \lambda_V L_{\text{V}}(\theta) + \lambda_E L_{\text{E}}(\theta) + \lambda_D L_{\text{D}}(\theta)$$

11: Update student policy:

$$\theta \leftarrow \theta - \alpha \nabla_\theta L_{\text{Total}}(\theta)$$

12: **end for**
13: **end for**

To regulate the influence of teacher guidance, a case-adaptive scaling factor λ is introduced:

$$\lambda = \frac{D_{KL}(\pi_\theta || \pi_T)}{D_{KL}(\pi_{\theta_{old}} || \pi_T) + \delta}, \tag{6}$$

where δ prevents instability. This adaptive mechanism enables the student to rely more on teacher guidance when its policy deviates significantly, while gradually shifting toward self-reliant decision-making as learning progresses.

Case-Based Policy Update with Knowledge Refinement. The student agent updates its policy using PPO, incorporating both environmental feedback and case-driven teacher guidance. The policy loss is formulated as:

$$L_{\text{P}}(\theta) = \hat{\mathbb{E}}_t \left[\min\left(r_t(\theta) A_t, \text{clip}(r_t(\theta), 1-\epsilon, 1+\epsilon) A_t\right)\right], \tag{7}$$

where the modified ratio accounts for teacher influence:

$$r_t(\theta) = \frac{\pi_\theta(a_t|s) + \lambda \pi_T(a_t|s)}{\pi_{\theta_{old}}(a_t|s) + \lambda}. \tag{8}$$

Value and Entropy Loss. The value loss is computed using the difference between the predicted value and the actual return R_t:

$$L_{\text{V}}(\theta) = \mathbb{E}_t \left[(V_\theta(s_t) - R_t)^2\right]. \tag{9}$$

The entropy loss is used to encourage exploration:

$$L_{\mathrm{E}}(\theta) = -\mathbb{E}_t \left[\sum_a \pi_\theta(a|s_t) \log \pi_\theta(a|s_t) \right]. \tag{10}$$

Distillation and Knowledge Retention. To retain critical knowledge, a distillation loss is introduced:

$$L_{\mathrm{D}}(\theta) = \mathrm{KL}\left(\frac{\pi_\theta(a|s)}{\tau} \parallel \frac{\pi_T(a|s)}{\tau} \right) \times (\tau^2), \tag{11}$$

where temperature τ controls the smoothness of policy alignment. The total loss is then formulated as:

$$L_{\mathrm{Total}}(\theta) = L_{\mathrm{P}}(\theta) + \lambda_{\mathrm{V}} L_{\mathrm{V}}(\theta) + \lambda_{\mathrm{E}} L_{\mathrm{E}}(\theta) + \lambda_{\mathrm{D}} L_{\mathrm{D}}(\theta). \tag{12}$$

where λ_{V} and λ_{E} are hyperparameters, and λ_{D} decays as the number of iterations increases:

$$\lambda_{\mathrm{D}} = \begin{cases} \lambda_0 - ki & \text{if } i < \gamma \\ 0 & \text{otherwise} \end{cases}, \tag{13}$$

where i represents the index of the training iteration, k, which represents the decay rate, is calculated as $k = \lambda_0/N$, and λ_0 is the initial value of λ.

5 Experiments

5.1 Simulation Environments

MiniGrid, the minimal grid world environment [25], is a classic sparse-reward RL environment with a discrete action space. The environment used in this work is a box-world, which includes the following three variations:

- *SingleDoorKey* requires the agent to find and use a key to open a single door. The layout is simple and straightforward, making it ideal for testing basic RL algorithms, especially in sparse reward scenarios.
- *SingleDoorKeyWithTrap* builds on the *SingleDoorKey* setup but adds traps. In addition to finding the key and opening the door, the agent must avoid falling into traps.
- *MultipleDoorsKeys* features multiple doors and keys, and the agent must find the correct key to open each corresponding door.

5.2 Baseline Methods

In the experiments, we include three baseline approaches to assess the performance of OCaL-RL:

- **LLM only** provides the teacher's buffer CB_T for each state, and based on the corresponding teacher policy in CB_T, selects the appropriate action to interact with the environment.
- **Baseline RL** serves as a Tabula Rasa RL benchmark, trained from scratch using the PPO algorithm [24]. The structure of the policy model and the training loss function are configured identically to those of our student agent in OCaL-RL.
- **RL with Teacher** is a PPO-based student model that receives continuous guidance from the teacher's policy throughout training. At each step, the student uses the teacher's policies stored in buffer CB_T to guide its actions.
- **LLM4Teach** is a novel framework that leverages an always-online LLM-based teacher agent to provide instructions for training a specialized RL-based student agent [14].

Case Prompt

Problem Representation:
In a locked 2D grid room, an agent's goal is to open a door. The door can only be opened with a key of the same color. The agent can perform the following actions: explore, move to an object, pick up an object, drop an object, or open an object. The agent can hold only one object at a time.

Case-Based Reasoning:

User: Agent sees red door, holds nothing
Assistant:
1. What the agent sees and holds: The agent sees a red door, and it holds nothing.
2. What should the agent do: The agent needs to find a key to open the red door. If holding anything, it should explore the room to look for the key.
3. Action: [explore]

Case Example

Observation: Agent sees a red key, a blue key, and a blue door. The agent holds nothing.

Case-Based Recommendation:
1. What the agent sees and holds: The agent sees a red key, a blue key, and a blue door. The agent holds nothing.
2. What should the agent do: The agent should pick up the blue key to open the blue door.
3. Actions: [pick up <blue key>, move to <blue door>, open <blue door>]

Fig. 2. The flowchart illustrates the CBR process within the LLM-driven decision-making system for reinforcement learning. It outlines how the agent retrieves and applies past cases to determine appropriate actions in a structured manner.

5.3 Experimental Setting

For each task, we define five specialized high-level options: {explore, move to, pick up, drop, open}. Except for "explore", all options are condition-dependent. For instance, the *pick up* option requires targeting a specific object, such as "pick up the blue key". These expert-designed options are derived from the foundational *SingleDoorKey* task, and each option policy deterministically outputs a Dirac delta distribution over actions based on the current state.

To construct the teacher agent, we adopt a case-based reasoning (CBR) system powered by ChatGLM-turbo [26], which serves as a high-capacity reasoning engine. We leverage Chain-of-Thought (CoT) prompting [27] to guide the model through multi-step decision-making in a structured and interpretable manner. The CoT pipeline comprises three main stages:

- **Case Retrieval & Summarization:** The system retrieves relevant prior cases from a repository and summarizes key environmental features.
- **Contextual Reasoning:** Using both retrieved cases and the current task context, the LLM infers the most plausible high-level option.
- **Recommendation Generation:** The system produces a final recommendation that aligns with task constraints and objectives.

To enhance consistency and ensure correct formatting, each prompt incorporates an illustrative example that serves as a reference for structuring the response. An example of a generated dialogue under this prompt design for the *MultipleDoorsKeys* task is shown in Fig. 2.

Table 1. Summary of experimental results across tasks.

Task	Method	Performances	
		Avg. Return	Avg. Success Rate
SingleDoorKey	LLM only	**0.87**	**100.0%**
	Baseline RL	0.03	7.6%
	RL with Teacher	0.83	98.8%
	LLM4Teach	0.67	81.1%
	OCaL-RL	0.79	94.7%
SingleDoorKeywithTrap	LLM only	0.48	54.6%
	Baseline RL	0.00	0.5%
	RL with Teacher	0.60	75.0%
	LLM4Teach	0.52	66.8%
	OCaL-RL	**0.62**	**77.9%**
MutipleDoorsKeys	LLM only	0.40	46.8%
	Baseline RL	0.02	4.7%
	RL with Teacher	0.37	53.9%
	LLM4Teach	0.53	67.1%
	OCaL-RL	**0.63**	**78.7%**

5.4 Summary of Experimental Results Across Tasks

As shown in Table 1, OCaL-RL consistently outperforms traditional RL methods across all tasks. In the *SingleDoorKey* task, LLM-only achieves the highest performance (return: 0.87, success rate: 100%), while Baseline RL performs poorly (0.03, 7.6%). OCaL-RL significantly improves performance (0.79, 94.7%), surpassing Baseline RL and LLM4Teach (0.67, 81.1%), though slightly behind RL with Teacher (0.83, 98.8%).

In the more complex *SingleDoorKeyWithTrap* and *MultipleDoorsKeys* tasks, OCaL-RL maintains superior results (returns: 0.62, 0.63; success rates: 77.9%, 78.7%). While LLM4Teach shows competitive performance (66.8%, 67.1%), it remains less effective due to limited adaptability in dynamic environments. These results highlight OCaL-RL's ability to enhance RL through offline-to-online learning, leveraging LLMs for structured case-based policy learning and improved adaptability in complex tasks.

5.5 Performance Trends of All Methods on Each Task

Our experiments on *SingleDoorKey*, *SingleDoorKeyWithTrap*, and *MultipleDoorsKeys* reveal distinct performance trends, as shown in Fig. 3. In *SingleDoorKey*, LLM-only achieved the highest performance, followed by RL with Teacher, while OCaL-RL, LLM4Teach, and Baseline RL lagged behind. Baseline RL showed some effectiveness in this relatively simple environment, where exploration requirements are limited and optimal policies can be discovered with basic trial-and-error learning. However, in more complex tasks such as *SingleDoorKeyWithTrap* and *MultipleDoorsKeys*, its performance deteriorated significantly due to its lack of prior knowledge and poor generalization in environments that demand structured exploration and long-term planning.

In *SingleDoorKeyWithTrap*, OCaL-RL surpassed all methods after 6000 iterations, outperforming LLM4Teach and RL with Teacher, demonstrating the importance of student training for effective exploration. In the more complex *MultipleDoorsKeys* task, OCaL-RL excelled by effectively leveraging prior knowledge, followed by LLM4Teach. RL with Teacher performed comparably to LLM-only but fell short due to limited self-training capabilities.

5.6 Visual Analysis of Student and Teacher Policies

To better understand the interaction between student and teacher policies in the *SingleDoorKeyWithTrap* task, we conducted a 2D and 3D t-SNE visualization analysis. At the 0th iteration, the student policy is far from the teacher policy and requires training. As the iterations progress, the student policy gradually moves closer to the teacher policy. By the 3000th iteration, when learning from the teacher is halted, the student policy is closest to the teacher policy. This alignment highlights the effectiveness of the OCaL-RL framework in leveraging offline teacher-generated knowledge to guide the student agent, thereby enhancing its learning efficiency, as shown in Fig. 4.

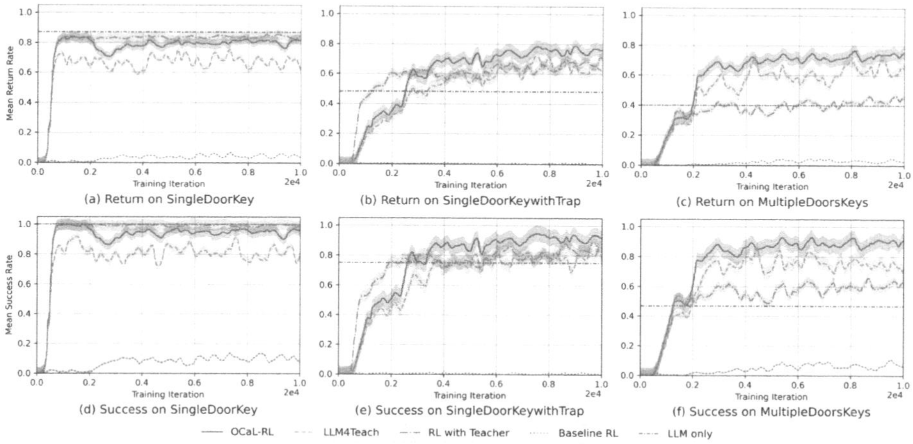

Fig. 3. Performance trends of all methods on each task.

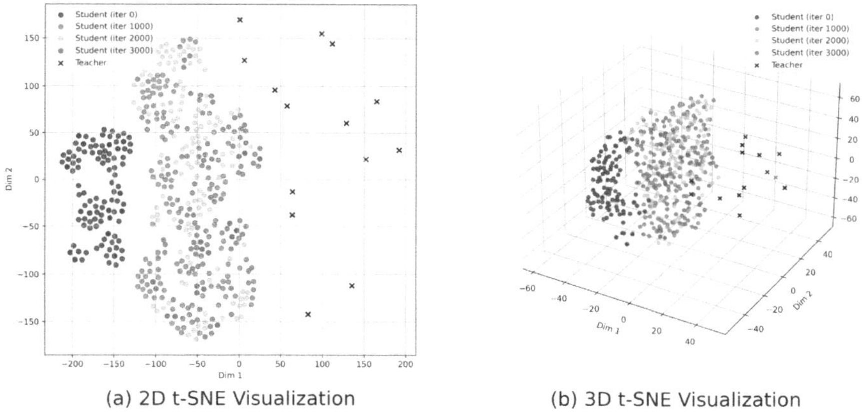

Fig. 4. Visual analysis of student and teacher policies.

5.7 Ablation Study on Transition Timing

To evaluate the impact of transition timing between teacher-guided and autonomous learning, we conducted an ablation study on the breakpoint γ using the *MultipleDoorsKeys* task, as shown in Fig. 5. When $\gamma = 1000$, $\gamma = 2000$, or $\gamma = 4000$, performance significantly declined once the student transitioned away from teacher supervision, ultimately leading to failure. Conversely, when $\gamma = 20000$, where the student agent relied heavily on teacher guidance throughout training, moderate improvements were observed, though performance remained suboptimal. The best results were achieved with $\gamma = 3000$, where a balanced

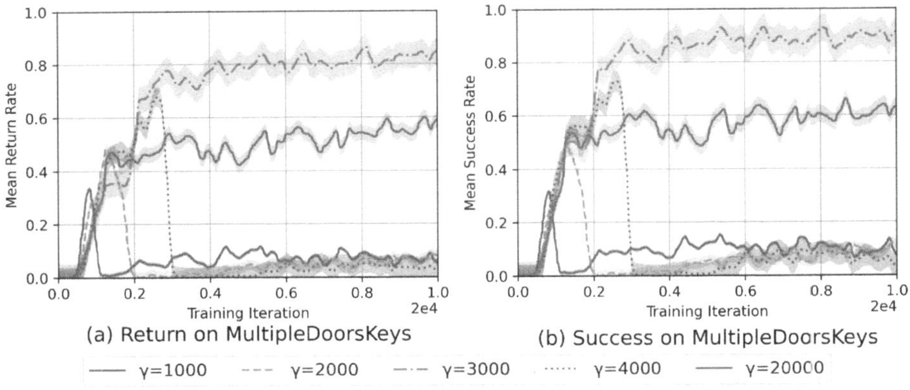

Fig. 5. Ablation study on transition timing.

transition from teacher-driven to independent learning facilitated effective adaptation and policy refinement. This underscores the importance of carefully structuring the transition phase in case-based RL to optimize long-term agent performance.

6 Conclusion

In this paper, we propose OCaL-RL, a novel Offline-to-Online reinforcement learning framework that integrates CBR with LLM to enhance policy learning. At the core of our approach is an LLM-driven CBR system, which constructs a structured case repository of simulated experiences enriched with world knowledge. Our framework enables a PPO-based student agent to retrieve, adapt, and refine stored policies, ensuring a seamless transition from offline policy distillation to online adaptation. This case-driven paradigm not only improves sample efficiency but also enhances adaptability to real-world environments. By leveraging CBR, OCaL-RL allows agents to dynamically reuse past knowledge, facilitating more efficient decision-making and better generalization. Experimental results in MiniGrid environments demonstrate that OCaL-RL consistently outperforms strong baselines in both return rate and success rate, validating its effectiveness. Future research will focus on extending this framework to more complex tasks and further refining case retrieval and adaptation mechanisms.

References

1. Bianchi, R.A., Ros, R., Lopez de Mantaras, R.: Improving reinforcement learning by using case based heuristics. In: International Conference on Case-Based Reasoning, pp. 75–89. Springer (2009)
2. Atzeni, M., Dhuliawala, S., Murugesan, K., Sachan, M.: Case-based reasoning for better generalization in textual reinforcement learning. arXiv preprint arXiv:2110.08470 (2021)

3. Liu, Y., et al.: Summary of chatgpt-related research and perspective towards the future of large language models. Meta-Radiol. 100017 (2023)
4. Zhang, F., et al.: Improving sample efficiency of reinforcement learning with background knowledge from large language models, arXiv preprint arXiv:2407.03964 (2024)
5. Yan, X., et al.: Efficient reinforcement learning with large language model priors, arXiv preprint arXiv:2410.07927 (2024)
6. Nair, A., et al.: AWAC: accelerating online reinforcement learning with offline datasets, arXiv preprint arXiv:2006.09359 (2020)
7. Zhang, H., et al.: Policy expansion for bridging offline-to-online reinforcement learning, arXiv preprint arXiv:2302.00935 (2023)
8. Hinton, G.: Distilling the knowledge in a neural network, arXiv preprint arXiv:1503.02531 (2015)
9. Tseng, W.-C., et al.: Offline multi-agent reinforcement learning with knowledge distillation. Adv. Neural. Inf. Process. Syst. **35**, 226–237 (2022)
10. Wender, S., Watson, I.: Combining case-based reasoning and reinforcement learning for unit navigation in real-time strategy game AI. In: Lamontagne, L., Plaza, E. (eds.) ICCBR 2014. LNCS (LNAI), vol. 8765, pp. 511–525. Springer, Cham (2014). https://doi.org/10.1007/978-3-319-11209-1_36
11. Lee, Y., Hu, E.S., Yang, Z., Lim, J.J.: To follow or not to follow: selective imitation learning from observations, arXiv preprint arXiv:1912.07670 (2019)
12. Nüßlein, J., Illium, S., Müller, R., Gabor, T., Linnhoff-Popien, C.: Case-based inverse reinforcement learning using temporal coherence. In: International Conference on Case-Based Reasoning, pp. 304–317. Springer (2022)
13. Liu, Z., et al.: Knowing what not to do: Leverage language model insights for action space pruning in multi-agent reinforcement learning, arXiv preprint arXiv:2405.16854 (2024)
14. Zhou, Z., et al.: Large language model as a policy teacher for training reinforcement learning agents, arXiv preprint arXiv:2311.13373 (2023)
15. Tan, W., et al.: True knowledge comes from practice: aligning LLMs with embodied environments via reinforcement learning, arXiv preprint arXiv:2401.14151 (2024)
16. Lee, A.X., et al.: How to spend your robot time: Bridging kickstarting and offline reinforcement learning for vision-based robotic manipulation. In: 2022 IEEE/RSJ International Conference on Intelligent Robots and Systems (IROS), pp. 2468–2475. IEEE (2022)
17. Xie, T., et al.: Policy finetuning: bridging sample-efficient offline and online reinforcement learning. In: Advances in Neural Information Processing Systems, vol. 34, pp. 27395–27407 (2021)
18. Lei, K., et al.: Uni-o4: unifying online and offline deep reinforcement learning with multi-step on-policy optimization, arXiv preprint arXiv:2311.03351 (2023)
19. Wang, S., et al.: Train once, get a family: State-adaptive balances for offline-to-online reinforcement learning. In: Advances in Neural Information Processing Systems, vol. 36 (2024)
20. Torrey, L., Taylor, M.: Teaching on a budget: agents advising agents in reinforcement learning. In: Proceedings of the 2013 International Conference on Autonomous Agents and Multi-Agent Systems, pp. 1053–1060 (2013)
21. Uchendu, I., et al.: Jump-start reinforcement learning. In: International Conference on Machine Learning, pp. 34556–34583. PMLR (2023)
22. Schmitt et al.: Kickstarting deep reinforcement learning, arXiv preprint arXiv:1803.03835 (2018)

23. Matthews et al.: Hierarchical kickstarting for skill transfer in reinforcement learning, arXiv preprint arXiv:2207.11584 (2022)
24. Schulman, J., et al.: Proximal policy optimization algorithms, arXiv preprint arXiv:1707.06347 (2017)
25. Chevalier-Boisvert et al.: Minigrid & miniworld: modular & customizable reinforcement learning environments for goal-oriented tasks. In: Advances in Neural Information Processing Systems, vol. 36 (2024)
26. Du, Z., et al.: GLM: general language model pretraining with autoregressive blank infilling, arXiv preprint arXiv:2103.10360 (2021)
27. Wei, J., et al.: Chain-of-thought prompting elicits reasoning in large language models. In: Advances in Neural Information Processing Systems, vol. 35, pp. 24824–24837 (2022)

Utilizing the Structure of Process Models for Guided Generation of Explanatory Texts

Tolga Tel(✉) and Mirjam Minor

Goethe University Frankfurt, Department of Business Informatics, Frankfurt, Germany
tel@em.uni-frankfurt.de, minor@cs.uni-frankfurt.de

Abstract. This paper explores a hybrid approach combining the strengths of traditional algorithms and Large-Language Model (LLM) powered Retrieval Augmented Generation (RAG) systems. While LLMs excel at generating human-like text and processing unstructured data, they can be unreliable for structured data extraction. To address the challenge of explaining complex business process models, we first use algorithms to extract key information. Then, a case-based RAG system generates textual descriptions. We investigate two methods: a) generating individual element descriptions and ordering them, and b) enhancing coherence through a harmonization step to produce a more unified explanation. A significant contribution of our work lies in the achievement of improved scalability. Unlike existing methods that often suffer from performance degradation when handling larger process models, our hybrid approach demonstrates a remarkable degree of consistency, maintaining accuracy even as the model complexity increases. Furthermore, we have successfully minimized the required context window for the LLM. By relying on the data extracted by the algorithms, we significantly reduce the amount of information the LLM needs to process simultaneously. This reduction in context window size not only improves efficiency but also mitigates the risk of information loss or "hallucinations" that can occur when LLMs are tasked with processing excessively large inputs. Therefore, our approach provides a trustworthy and robust solution for generating accessible explanations of complex business processes.

Keywords: Process-Oriented CBR · Generative AI · Guided Generation · Structural Knowledge · Model-To-Text

1 Introduction

Business Process Model and Notation (BPMN) has become the standard for visualizing and communicating business processes. Weske claims that business processes are "essential to understanding how companies operate" [16]. The research field of process-oriented case-based reasoning (PO-CBR) [13] addresses those business needs. PO-CBR has achieved considerable success in assisting business process professionals with case-based methods. However, many application

© The Author(s), under exclusive license to Springer Nature Switzerland AG 2025
I. Bichindaritz and B. López (Eds.): ICCBR 2025, LNAI 15662, pp. 157–171, 2025.
https://doi.org/10.1007/978-3-031-96559-3_11

domain experts and other users lack knowledge on process modeling languages. They are struggling to understand the graphical process models.

Our methodology, which we term guided generation, addresses the challenge of LLM reliability in specific tasks. The paper is an extension of previous work in which CBR retrieval has been used to improve LLMs to explain business processes [12]. In contrast to the preliminary approach, the case representation and the similarity function have been enhanced structurally, and thus improved considerably. We employ significant pre-processing to integrate the precision of traditional algorithms where they are proven effective. This allows the LLM to focus on its strengths like generating creative and contextually rich outputs, while relying on robust algorithmic foundations for information extraction. The pre-processing step provides a structural analysis of business process models. The case base resulting from the pre-processing serves as a data pool to guide the generation. Our novel approach is a contribution to combining generative AI and CBR methods on equal terms, with a special focus on using case-based knowledge structures for guided generation [1].

The complexity in many real-world BPMN models often presents a challenge for understanding and interpreting these diagrams. Current approaches to explaining BPMN models suffer from several limitations, which hinders the practical application and widespread adoption. The reliance on large context windows in current approaches [7,12] poses a significant bottleneck, that needs to be addressed [7]. Processing larger BPMN models as a single input demands computational resources and can lead to a loss of information or failure. Scalability is a crucial factor for handling a growing volume of BPMN models. Current methods often struggle to maintain performance and accuracy when applied to large, complicated models. A robust explanation framework must be capable to efficiently process and interpret models of varying sizes and complexities. The consistency of explanation results is crucial for a trustworthy solution. Existing approaches can produce explanations, which especially for larger BPMN models, do not explain all elements reliably. To address these limitations, we have chosen a case-based retrieval augmented generation (RAG) system. The RAG system combines a retriever module with a generator module and utilizes case based knowledge to leverage its understanding of describing a BPMN model.

We utilize guided generation in our approach to prioritize scalability and consistency of the explanations, by generating short descriptive texts for each element in the process model individually. With efficient pre-processing and the use of structural knowledge, we aim to provide clear, concise and consistent explanations, that are accessible without needing substantial computational resources and reduce hallucinations. We chose two different variants for this problem:

a) Without harmonizing the generated text snippets.
b) With harmonizing the generated text snippets.

The results for both variants are convincing and an improvement over previous work [12] while still leaving room for future work and improvement.

The remainder of the paper is organized as follows. Some foundations of LLMs and BPMN are reported as background for the work in Sect. 2. Related work is discussed in Sect. 3. The two approaches a) and b) are presented at a conceptual level in Sect. 4 and evaluated by means of a prototypical implementation with a repository of real process models in Sect. 5. Future work is found in Sect. 6 and a conclusion is drawn in Sect. 7.

2 Foundations

LLMs address text generation by a probabilistic model $P(y|x;\theta)$ that predicts an output y for an input x [11]. The parameters θ of the model are learned in a pre-training process. Instead of learning the conditional probability distribution for (x, y)-pairs directly, the model is pre-trained for the probability $P(x;\theta)$ of text x itself from large amounts of text. In a standard language model such as GPT the text is predicted in an autoregressive fashion, predicting the linguistic tokens in the sequence one at a time. This is usually done from left to right [11].

During pre-training [15], each linguistic token u_i from a universe $U = \{u_1, u_2, ...u_n\}$ is assessed within the context of its k predecessor tokens: $P(u_i|u_{i-k}, ..., u_{i-1})$. The target function is to maximize the following likelihood:

$$L(U) = \sum_i \log P(u_i|u_{i-k}, ..., u_{i-1};\theta)$$

for the context window size of k tokens where P is modeled using a neural network with parameters θ. For details of the pre-training, we refer to the literature [15].

The consortium OMG has established the standard BPMN [5] for modeling languages. BPMN offers a standardized graphical notation for visualizing business processes. Its primary goal is to bridge the gap between business and technical users, providing a notation that is both understandable to business analysts and precise enough for technical developers.

This flowchart-like notation empowers stakeholders to design, manage, and realize business processes efficiently. Its independence from specific implementation environments ensures flexibility and adaptability. An example for a small BPMN model can be found in Fig. 2 (c).

By creating a common language, BPMN facilitates seamless communication between business and technical teams, streamlining the process of translating business requirements into executable software.

3 Related Work

In this paper, we build on an extension of the groundwork laid in [12], where a process-oriented case-based reasoning approach, supported by the capabilities of retrieval augmented generation, was employed to generate coherent, informative textual descriptions for Business Process Models. Here, we further explore and refine this approach, aiming to enhance precision and scalability of generated textual descriptions within diverse BPMN models.

In [7] textual process descriptions are extracted from process models for different applications. The authors compare different traditional deterministic and LLM-based extraction methods. Even though LLMs produce human-like process descriptions, they lack real comprehension of the analyzed process models. In contrast, our approach uses a structural analysis of the process models and experiential knowledge from a case base to ensure that the generated texts cover the entire process model.

The paper [8] introduces a framework using LLMs to improve the interpretability of complex business process models. The authors investigate different ways to abstract process models for LLMs and use advanced prompting techniques. The results indicate that their framework enhances process model accessibility and interpretability via AI. However, our work differs in the preprocessing step, where structural information is used to get information that is not directly written into the original BPMN format to minimize information loss in the abstraction process.

In [4] the authors address the challenge of describing complex, aggregated causal maps, which are representations of group mental models, for community members. While these maps capture valuable collective knowledge, their diagrammatic format and lack of transparency can be barriers for the users. The authors developed a method that automatically translates causal maps into coherent narratives using LLMs. They evaluated various community detection algorithms and LLMs to find the optimal combination, successfully producing readable text comparable to human-written paragraphs without losing information from the original causal map. Similar to the process models that are the target of our work, causal maps are structured knowledge. However, the topology of causal maps is rather simplistic compared to real-world business process models.

A couple of case-based retrieval approaches for improving LLMs have been published recently [2,17,18]. They all have in common that they don't address process-oriented knowledge. LLMs like ChatGPT can make mistakes. Retrieval Augmented Generation improves accuracy by giving LLMs extra knowledge from external sources. The paper [17] explores using cases instead of simple text snippets in RAG, and prompting LLMs to use case-based reasoning. They tested four scenarios: (1) LLM adapting a given case, (2) LLM selecting and adapting a case, (3) LLM selecting two similar cases and combining them, and (4) LLM selecting the most similar and most different cases and combining them. Their results show that providing LLMs with cases benefits the accuracy.

Retrieval augmented generation can enhance LLM output by adding prior knowledge as context. This is useful for tasks that are knowledge intensive. In [18] this system is used for legal question-answering. Case-Based Reasoning can structure retrieval in RAG with retrieval, indexing, and similarity methods to give LLM queries relevant cases as context. This makes prompts richer and improves answer quality, especially in legal tasks, by ensuring similarity between questions and evidence.

The paper [2] introduces a multi-modal Case-Based Reasoning approach to explain image classification results. It generates natural language explanations using a Visual Question Answering (VQA) model, retrieves relevant explanations based on semantic similarity, and then filters them according to the desired explanation goal, such as education or persuasiveness.

4 Guided Generation by Structural Case Knowledge

To prepare the BPMN model for analysis, we perform a multi-step pre-processing seen in Fig. 1. The goal of pre-processing is to determine the order in which the process elements should be explained as well as to decompose the entire process model into units that can be explained step by step. Thus, the query BPMN model is analyzed in two branches in parallel, as depicted in Fig. 1. In the right branch, the control flow of the process model is investigated to determine the order of explanation ('Node Ordering'). The other branch is for the segmentation of the process model into elements that are to be explained. After the pre-processing, the structural knowledge from the pre-processing on elements and their order is used for the remainder of the guided generation procedure. The LLM is called for each process element with an in-context example from the case base to generate an explanatory text fragment. Finally, the text collector assembles and consolidates the particular text fragments into an explanation of the entire process.

The BPMN is given in an XML-format which is first decomposed to extract all elements (e.g. tasks, gateways, events) and their connections (e.g. sequence-flows, message-flows). These objects are parts of a graph, that can be analyzed regarding certain properties. These elements are then converted into string representations that include their ID, name, neighborhood and other properties. This leads to the possibility of verbalizing each element individually and thus achieve a high scalability for the size of the BPMN model.

The RAG system consists of a retriever module and a generator module. The input of the RAG system is an element and its neighborhood in the BPMN model. The output is a short text describing that element to a user, who is not familiar with process modeling. An example on the representation of a task with the corresponding graphical visualization is given in Fig. 2. Here (b) visualizes a task "Check Text" and its local neighborhood in the BPMN model. The information that is gained in pre-processing is shown in (a). Then (c) shows the text that is generated by the LLM to describe the task "Check Text".

Our approach considers two variants of text collection, referred to as 'Structured-Case-Knowledge' a) and b). Variant a) simply puts the generated text fragments into the correct order as given by 'Find Node Order'. Variant b) extends a) by an additional post-processing step to smoothen the text passages, for instance to eliminate redundancies. In Subsect. 4.1 we explain details on our approach a) and in Subsect. 4.2 we explain the addition in approach b).

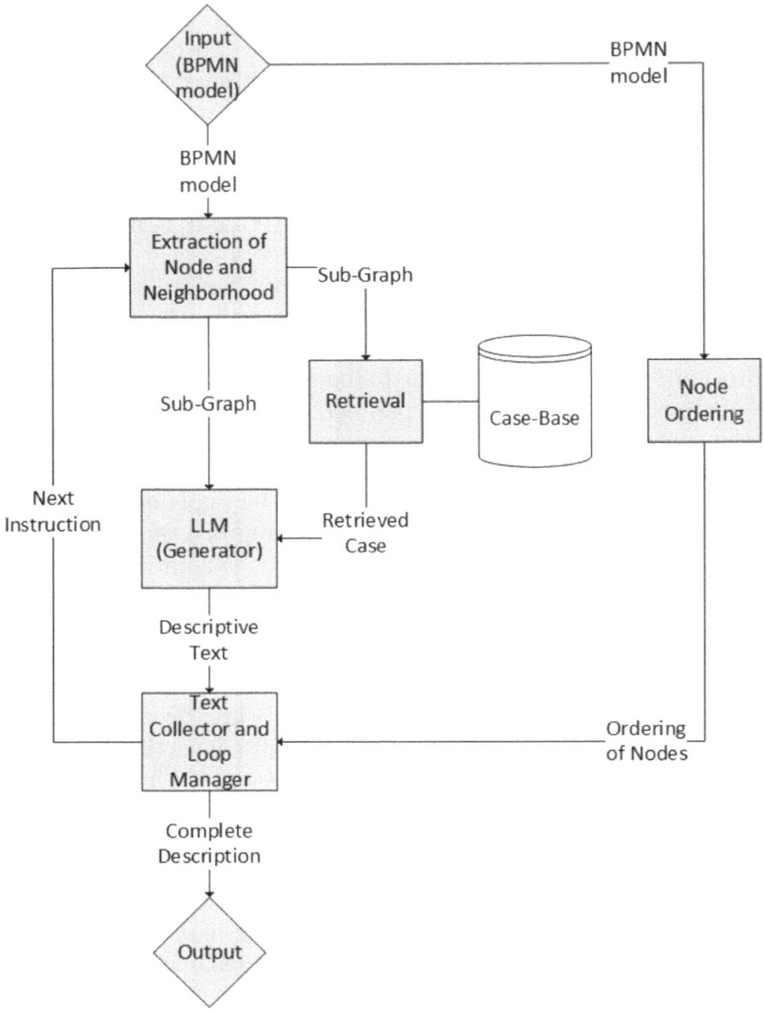

Fig. 1. Guided Generation Procedure

4.1 RAG with Case-Based Retrieval

Our case-base stores individual cases, each comprising a problem, which is a structural element resulting from the analytical step seen in Fig. 2 (a), and its corresponding solution, a textual description of the central element seen in Fig. 2 (c). Unlike the approach in [12], our cases are granular, focusing on a single model element and its immediate neighbors, rather than the entire process model. The design of the textual representations prioritizes conciseness to decrease potential information loss that is associated with limited context windows in LLMs. The cases were either taken from larger cases in [12] or are artificially constructed cases to build a comprehensive case base.

```
ID: Activity_1fnmfcj
Name: Check Text
Node Type: task
Incoming Flows: ['Flow_0184i9h']
Outgoing Flows: ['Flow_19hfo0i']
Previous Elements: ['StartEvent_1']
Next Elements: ['Gateway_0ocj6vg']

ID: Flow_0184i9h
Flow Type: SequenceFlow
Source: StartEvent_1
Target: Activity_1fnmfcj

ID: Flow_19hfo0i
Flow Type: SequenceFlow
Source: Activity_1fnmfcj
Target: Gateway_0ocj6vg

ID: StartEvent_1
Node Type: startEvent

ID: Gateway_0ocj6vg
Node Type: exclusiveGateway
```

(a) Extracted Information after Pre-Processing

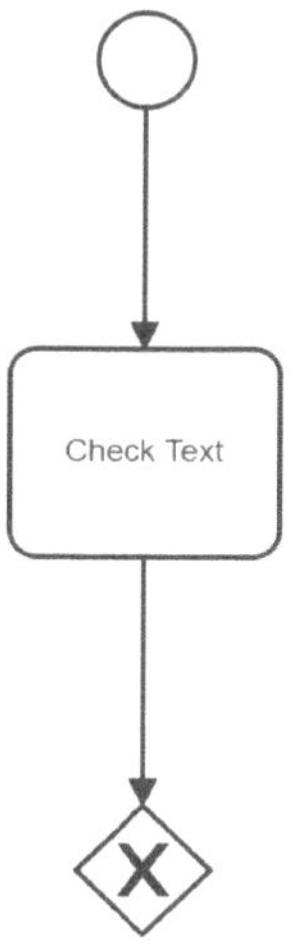

(b) Visualization of the neighborhood in BPMN

After the start event, the next element is a task named "Check Text" which involves checking some text and is done by an unspecified entity. This task has an incoming sequence flow "Flow_0l84i9h" from the start event and an outgoing sequence flow "Flow_19hfo0i" leading to an exclusive gateway. The Check Text task comes before a decision point represented by the gateway.

(c) Explanatory text for sample task "Check Text"

Fig. 2. Sample task "Check Text" and its neighborhood

The retrieval operates with a taxonomy-based similarity function for BPMN process elements to find a case that is most closely aligned with the input. In the tree seen in Fig. 3, the similarity is highest for the case, that has the lowest common ancestor with the element analyzed. For example, if the case-base includes a case for a userTask and a case for an endEvent, the similarity function will tend towards the endEvent if the analyzed element is a startEvent. Both input and cases are structured as element-centered representations, incorporating the elements local network neighborhood. The case from the case-base is added to the prompt seen in Fig. 4 as an exemplary description for the placeholder *documents*. The retrieval process is done for each element in the BPMN-model individually s.t. in the end a short text is generated for each element.

```
Elements
├── Gateways
│   ├── Split
│   │   ├── exclusiveGateway
│   │   ├── inclusiveGateway
│   │   └── ...
│   └── Join
│       ├── exclusiveGateway
│       ├── inclusiveGateway
│       └── ...
├── Events
│   ├── endEvent
│   ├── startEvent
│   └── ...
└── Tasks
    ├── Task
    ├── manualTask
    └── ...
```

Fig. 3. Taxonomy Tree

4.2 Harmonization

The direct verbalization of individual elements into standalone textual descriptions leads to a final text that, while being informative, has a lack of cohesion and a repetition of many contents. While straightforward, this approach fails to capture the complete context of the BPMN model. This leads to a fragmented and less accessible representation. The impact is a significant decline in readability, which makes it difficult for the user to grasp the overall structure and functionality of the process.

To counteract these problems, we introduce a post-processing stage powered by an additional LLM. This LLM will act as a harmonizing tool, which integrates the individual element descriptions into a coherent narrative. By analyzing the semantic relationships between elements and their properties, the LLM is designed to eliminate redundancies and establish logical connections and ensure a smooth flow of information.

5 Experimental Evaluation

The case-based Retrieval-Augmented Generation (RAG) methods were tested using a repository of BPMN process models. A human expert then assessed the performance based on specific evaluation criteria. The following hypotheses were formulated for our experimental evaluation:

H1 Guided generation by structural case knowledge improves the quality of explaining larger business process models.
H2 Harmonization step improves the comprehensibility of the generated output.

5.1 Experimental Data

The data underlying the experiments comes from two repositories of process models in BPMN taken from two Master theses [3,6]. The process models describe real business processes from different organisations and application fields, including human resource processes, insurance processes, and production processes. 15 BPMN models have been selected to achieve examples of higher model complexity in terms of number of tokens, number of model elements and types of elements. Previous evaluation from [12] is used as a reference.

All BPMN flow objects, i.e. events, activities and gateways are counted as model elements. BPMN types such as an XOR split gateway and an AND split gateway are counted as types of elements.

5.2 Evaluation Criteria and Performance Metrics

Similar to the paper [12] we have defined evaluation criteria to assess the experimental results in a semi-automated manner. Some performance metrics are specified based on the well-known precision and recall formulas introduced by Lesk and Salton in the field of information retrieval in the sixties [9]. The precision metrics identify "hallucinations" by the LLM, which may describe model contents that actually do not occur in the given BPMN model.

Two pairs of metrics aim to measure the accuracy the explanatory texts achieve in terms of covering the model elements `el` and the types of elements `ty` that occur in a process model. A model element mentioned in the explanation, such as the activity "Check Text", is considered relevant if it occurs also in the BPMN model. Irrelevant elements are those that have been hallucinated by the LLM. The following accuracy metrics are taken from the literature [12]. Similar accuracy metrics were also used in [18] to compute F1 scores for a retrieval analysis.

$$precision_{el} = \frac{|relevant\ el\ in\ explanation|}{|el\ in\ the\ explanation|} \quad recall_{el} = \frac{|relevant\ el\ in\ explanation|}{|el\ in\ the\ model|} \tag{1}$$

$$precision_{ty} = \frac{|relevant\ ty\ in\ explanation|}{|ty\ in\ the\ explanation|} \quad recall_{ty} = \frac{|relevant\ ty\ in\ explanation|}{|ty\ in\ the\ model|} \tag{2}$$

Further, the extent to which users can easily follow the generated explanation strongly depends on the order of explanatory passages within the text. Thus, the next pair of metrics measures whether the model elements are described at the expected position (`pos`) within the text following the control flow in the given BPMN model.

To evaluate element sequence accuracy, a human expert defines an 'optimal' ordering. We then calculate the positional error for the generated text by measuring the edit-distance of the ordering to the expert-defined sequence. The variant used in this evaluation is the Levenshtein distance [10]. For example, the sequences A, B, C, D and B, C, D, A have an edit-distance of 2 because it is sufficient to *remove* the letter A and *insert* it at the right position. Both operations *remove* and *insert* have a cost of 1, so using two operations ultimately costs 2.

5.3 Implementation with Haystack

The implementation of our RAG approaches is based on open source AI framework called Haystack [14]. We used Haystack to create a custom RAG Pipeline with pre-processing, that is explained in Sect. 4. Instead of using an embedding model, which is usual for a RAG-based approach, a custom component in the pipeline ensures a taxonomy based retrieval.

The prompt builder receives the extracted information about an element its local neighborhood in the process, and a retrieved case as an example. It combines these elements into a single prompt seen in Fig. 4, which is then sent to the generator module. This prompt structure remains consistent across all elements, with only the specific node, its local neighborhood, and the retrieved case varying.

```
# Prompt
messages = [
    ChatMessage.from_system("""
        You are an expert Q&A system with expert knowledge on business process models.
        Assume you are given information about an element in a business process model
        and its surroundings and need to verbalize it.
        To help you with the verbalization, an example 'Example' is given beforehand.
    """
    ),
    ChatMessage.from_user("""
         Please describe the given element "{{ query.id }}" of the model "Explain".
         Only use up to three sentences and only use plain text without bullet
         points or formatting.

         Exemplary textual process description for model part of "Example": {{ documents }}

         Given element "{{ query.id }}" of process model "Explain":
         {{ query.info_to_string() }}

         Surroundings in model "Explain":
         {{ context }}
    """
    )
]
```

Fig. 4. Prompt for generating descriptive texts.

The generator module was instantiated with the Llama 3.1 8B model[1], a quantized implementation designated Q4_K_M, accessed through the Ollama[2] extension integrated into the Haystack pipeline. To achieve deterministic output and maximize result reproducibility, the temperature parameter was configured to 0.

To effectively manage the sequence of RAG operations, a custom component within the Haystack framework was developed. This custom component gathers the textual outputs produced by the generator module for each element. This component also has a role of a task scheduler, which initiates the next RAG call for the following elementin the BPMN model. This design ensures that the RAG process is performed in an orderly and efficient manner, with each node receiving the necessary contextual information.

These components are used in a Haystack *Pipeline*, which defines the connection of different components, which are used in our approach. Haystack offers a flexible system for building complex pipelines using LLMs. Its core feature is the ability to create pipelines as directed multi-graphs, allowing for diverse connections between components. This means pipelines are not limited to linear data flows. They can include branching for concurrent processing, loops for iterative tasks like self-correction, and conditional routing for complex decision-making.

5.4 Experimental Setup

We conducted all experiments using the Haystack implementation. The context window was limited to 2048 tokens, accommodating all prompt sizes used in our experiments. The case base has been created by choosing a variety of different elements from different BPMN models, which are not included in the test data. For each element in the case base, a human expert created a short explanatory text.

5.5 Experimental Results

The experimental results for approach a) and b) show that it is possible to analyze a BPMN model of any size. This advancement allows for the analysis of BPMN models previously inaccessible, as demonstrated by a comparison with results from the RAG with LLMs variant in [12] in table 1. Additionally the size of the BPMN does not influence the $F1_{el}$ score nor the $F1_{ty}$ as seen in table 1 and 2. The approach b) involves the harmonization of the results in approach a). We chose a rather small harmonization step, where the primary goal is a minimal loss of information, while improving the readability. Tables 1 and 2 indicate that the information loss is minimal. The vast majority of BPMN elements, such as tasks, gateways, and events, were accurately identified and represented with their corresponding types. For most BPMN models, we can see an improvement to the results in [12]. Both, variants a) and b) consistently outperform the previous results and thus also the results of a plain LLM, which was also analyzed in [12].

---

[1] https://ai.meta.com/blog/meta-llama-3-1/, last access: 03-15-2025.

[2] https://ollama.com/, last access: 03-15-2025.

Table 1. High complexity

Model	4–1	6–1	6–4	8–4	8–5	8–6	8–7	10–2
$F1_{el}$	0.9733	0.9932	0.9926	0.9862	0.9909	0.9677	0.9935	0.9697
$F1_{ty}$	0.92	1	0.96	0.92	0.95	0.96	0.95	1
$F1_{el}$ harm.	0.9664	0.9932	0.9851	0.9862	0.9864	0.9677	0.9935	0.9697
$F1_{ty}$ harm.	0.92	1	0.96	0.92	0.95	0.96	0.95	1
$F1_{el}$ [12]	-	-	0.8189	-	-	-	-	-
$F1_{ty}$ [12]	-	-	0.8	-	-	-	-	-

Table 2. Medium complexity

Model	1–1	1–2	1–3	1–4	9–4	10–3	10–12
$F1_{el}$	0.9639	0.9583	0.9913	0.9592	0.9600	0.9612	0.9538
$F1_{ty}$	0.93	0.95	0.95	0.90	0.95	1	0.95
$F1_{el}$ harm.	0.9512	0.9474	0.9828	0.9592	0.9600	0.9612	0.9538
$F1_{ty}$ harm.	0.93	0.95	0.95	0.90	0.95	1	0.95
$F1_{el}$ [12]	0.9367	0.7765	0.84	0.9011	0.8378	0.7678	1
$F1_{ty}$ [12]	1	0.8182	0.7778	0.8696	0.75	0.667	1

Despite our pre-processing producing valid orderings for how to traverse a process model, we let a human choose an optimal order for the explanation. The edit-distances between explanation and'optimum' are given in table 3.

Table 3. Edit-distance to ordering by a human expert

Model	1–1	1–2	1–3	1–4	4–1	6–1	6–4	8–4	8–5	8–6	8–7	9–4	10–2	10–3	10–12
Edit-distance	4	8	8	10	6	10	10	22	6	2	2	8	30	6	4

Our edit distance metric can inflate error estimations because it doesn't account for multiple equally valid orderings. In particular, when network flows diverge (e.g. at gateways), the sequence of branch explanations becomes less critical. Models with numerous gateways, like 8–4 and 10–2, have a high edit distance primarily because they possess many such'optimal' orderings. However, our evaluation only recognizes a single correct order, leading to an overestimation of error for these complex BPMN models.

6 Future Work

The algorithm currently employed to determine the sequential order of nodes within Business Process Model and Notation (BPMN) diagrams operates on a relatively simplistic idea. While this approach is working as intended for BPMNs that are modeled strictly to best practices, its limitations become apparent when bad modeling practices like multiple end-events occur. It is crucial to acknowledge that in practical applications, a significant proportion of BPMN models diverge from the idealized standards of perfect modeling. An important objective for future development is the creation of a more robust and sophisticated algorithm for an understandable order of nodes.

The current concept for harmonization includes a pairwise aligning of texts for pairs of texts in the final output. That means, that text 1 is aligned with text 2 and text 3 is aligned with text 4. However, it has become apparent that this method, relying solely on sequential alignments, is significantly less than ideal. The resulting final output often exhibits inconsistencies and a lack of overall coherence. Therefore, a crucial objective is to develop and implement a more sophisticated and effective approach to harmonization. This new approach must be capable of producing a much higher degree of consistency across the entirety of the generated texts, avoiding the limitations inherent in the current pairwise alignment strategy. Additionally for the concept of eliminating redundancies in BPMN description, a promising direction for future development lies in implementing a system that intelligently tracks and manages the introduction of objects. Specifically, this system would focus on identifying and marking the initial occurrence of each unique object within the BPMN diagram. The core principle behind this approach is to acknowledge that once an object's purpose and characteristics have been thoroughly explained at its point of introduction, repeating that explanation in later instances becomes redundant.

In order to advance the precision and robustness of our system, future research should prioritize the development of a more sophisticated methodology for identifying and quantifying errors within the ordering process. Specifically, the current error detection mechanisms require refinement to better address the problems arising from scenarios where multiple distinct orderings can be legitimately considered optimal. Our current approach sometimes fails to adequately capture the nuanced deviations from these diverse, but equally valid, solutions. To mitigate this, we propose the exploration of an error measurement that works beyond a single, predetermined "correct" ordering.

7 Conclusion

This paper introduces a novel, guided generation approach designed to enhance RAG systems, specifically within the context of generating accurate explanatory text for larger business process models. Leveraging the robust Haystack framework and the advanced capabilities of the Llama 3.1 LLM, our approach aims to address the challenges associated with producing consistent and reliable textual descriptions of intricate process flows. To work with the inherent complexity of larger BPMN models, we implemented a strategy of decomposing the overall process into smaller, more manageable sub-graphs. Each sub-graph serves as the basis for generating an explanation for an individual element within the broader process model. This modular approach allows the LLM to concentrate on specific segments of the BPMN, fostering a more granular and accurate representation of the process logic.

Recalling our hypotheses for Sect. 5, our experimental findings demonstrate a significant improvement in the consistency of generated explanations, particularly concerning the accurate representation of each element within the BPMN. By focusing on sub-graphs, we ensure that all components of the process model are consistently and reliably described in the generated text.

Furthermore, a crucial outcome of our study is the observation that the quality of the generated explanatory texts remains robust and consistent, irrespective of the complexity of the underlying BPMN model. This result indicates that our guided generation approach effectively mitigates the challenges posed by intricate process structures, enabling the production of high-quality explanations even for highly complex business processes. This robustness is essential for practical applications, as it ensures that the RAG system can reliably provide clear and accurate explanations across a wide range of BPMN models, regardless of their size or complexity.

The consistency of LLM-generated explanations for BPMN models is significantly enhanced through pre-processing and the use of a structured textual representation of key model features. The decomposition of process models into smaller manageable segments, coupled with individual element descriptions improves performance when working with larger BPMN models. This modular approach mitigates the limitations imposed by the LLM's context window, allowing for more accurate interpretations of processes. The consequence of this behavior is a noticeable reduction in the diversity of generated text. Specifically, repeated attempts to regenerate the output yield minimal variations, indicating a tendency for the model to produce highly similar, if not identical, responses.

Our harmonization is preliminary, with the texts remaining very similar to the originals. We've avoided significant information loss, but the overall benefit of our harmonization approach is still under evaluation.

The analysis of the descriptive patterns reveals a variability in its approach to representing flow objects. While the LLM occasionally mentions the ID of the flow object, it sometimes relies on describing a flow object by referencing its source or target. This introduces an interesting variability into the descriptive texts.

References

1. Bach, K.: Case-based reasoning meets large language models: a research manifesto. arXiv pre-print (to be done) (2025)
2. Bastardo-Rojas, A., Caro-Martinez, M.: Visual question answering to generate case-based explanations for image classification in the internet of things. In: International Conference on Case-Based Reasoning (to be done) (2025)
3. Friedrich, F.: Automated Generation of Business process Models from Natural Language Input. Diplomarbeit, Humboldt-Universität zu Berlin (2010)

4. Gandee, T.J., Giabbanelli, P.J.: Combining natural language generation and graph algorithms to explain causal maps through meaningful paragraphs. In: ISaeki, M., et al. Advances in Conceptual Modeling. ER 2024. LNCS, vol. 14932, pp. 359–376. Springer, Cham (2024). https://doi.org/10.1007/978-3-031-75599-6_25
5. Group, O.M.: Business process model and notation (2014). https://www.omg.org/spec/BPMN/2.0.2#document-metadata
6. Hoffmann, D.: Ontology-Based Transfer Learning for the Digitization of Administrative Processes. Master thesis, Goethe University, Frankfurt (2022)
7. Klievtsova, N., Mangler, J., Kampik, T., Rinderle-Ma, S.: Utilizing process models in the requirements engineering process through model2text transformation. In: 2024 IEEE 32nd International Requirements Engineering Conference (RE), pp. 205–217. IEEE (2024). https://ieeexplore.ieee.org/abstract/document/10628509/
8. Kourani, H., et al.: Leveraging large language models for enhanced process model comprehension. arXiv preprint arXiv:2408.08892 (2024)
9. Lesk, M.E., Salton, G.: Relevance assessments and retrieval system evaluation. Inf. Storage Retr. **4**(4), 343–359 (1968)
10. Levenshtein, V.I., et al.: Binary codes capable of correcting deletions, insertions, and reversals. In: Soviet Physics Doklady, vol. 10, pp. 707–710. Soviet Union (1966)
11. Liu, P., Yuan, W., Fu, J., Jiang, Z., Hayashi, H., Neubig, G.: Pre-train, prompt, and predict: a systematic survey of prompting methods in natural language processing. ACM Comput. Surv. **55**(9), 1–35 (2023)
12. Minor, M., Kaucher, E.: Retrieval augmented generation with LLMs for explaining business process models. In: Recio-Garcia, J.A., Orozco-del-Castillo, M.G., Bridge, D. (eds.) Case-Based Reasoning Research and Development. ICCBR 2024. LNCS, vol. 14775, pp. 175–190. Springer, Cham (2024). https://doi.org/10.1007/978-3-031-63646-2_12
13. Minor, M., Montani, S., Recio-García, J.A.: Editorial: process-oriented case-based reasoning. Inf. Syst. **40**, 103–105 (2014)
14. Pietsch, M., et al.: Haystack: the end-to-end NLP framework for pragmatic builders (2019). https://github.com/deepset-ai/haystack
15. Radford, A., Narasimhan, K., Salimans, T., Sutskever, I.: Improving language understanding by generative pre-training. Technical report (2018). https://openai.com/research/language-unsupervised. Accessed 23 Apr 2024
16. Weske, M.: Business Process Management Concepts, Languages, 2nd EDN. Architectures. Springer, Berlin (2012)
17. Wilkerson, K., Leake, D.: On implementing case-based reasoning with large language models. In: International Conference on Case-Based Reasoning, pp. 404–417. Springer (2024)
18. Wiratunga, N., et al.: CBR-RAG: case-based reasoning for retrieval augmented generation in LLMs for legal question answering. In: International Conference on Case-Based Reasoning, pp. 445–460. Springer (2024)

Case-Based Reasoning in Generative Agents: Review and Prospect

Haoxi Zhan, Youlin Wu, Jian Ding, Bo Xu, Liang Yang, and Hongfei Lin(✉)

Dalian University of Technology, Dalian 116024, Liaoning, China
{zhanhaoxi,wuyoulin,91mr_ding}@mail.dlut.edu.cn,
{xubo,liang,hflin}@dlut.edu.cn

Abstract. With the rapid pervasion of Generative AI across academia, industry, and society, researchers and the public alike have begun to envision the future of generative agents and their potential role in achieving Artificial General Intelligence (AGI). However, while representative generative AI algorithms have demonstrated impressive language capabilities, they still fall short in complex reasoning tasks. Recent findings in cognitive neuroscience suggest significant differences in the cognitive mechanisms underlying language and reasoning abilities within the human brain. Therefore, AI techniques such as Case-Based Reasoning (CBR), Expert Systems, and Knowledge Representation retain their unique advantages. Case-Based Reasoning, due to its emulation of human memory mechanisms, occupies an important and distinct position in cognitive processes. We argue that CBR will play an indispensable role in future intelligent agents. In this paper, we adopt an interdisciplinary perspective to review relevant research and perspectives from psychology, cognitive science, psychiatry, and artificial intelligence. Building upon this review, we envision future generative agents with case-based reasoning at their core. We propose a technical framework for CBR-based generative agents and discuss potential research avenues.

Keywords: case-based reasoning · generative agent · large language models

1 Introduction

Since its inception in the 1950 s [36], Artificial Intelligence (AI) has experienced several ups and downs. Throughout this history, numerous methodologies have been developed to advance AI technology. In the past decade, artificial intelligence, especially deep learning, has made remarkable advancements in many classic learning tasks. AI algorithms have been widely applied in industrial applications such as face recognition [49], biomedical engineering [42], and sentiment analysis [12]. With the launch of ChatGPT in 2022 and the subsequent popularization of Large Language Models (LLMs), artificial intelligence is increasingly integrated into the daily routines and professional activities of the general public.

© The Author(s), under exclusive license to Springer Nature Switzerland AG 2025
I. Bichindaritz and B. López (Eds.): ICCBR 2025, LNAI 15662, pp. 172–186, 2025.
https://doi.org/10.1007/978-3-031-96559-3_12

In this context, LLM-based generative agents that are capable of communicating with users while performing a set of tasks are becoming a new hotspot for the AI industry. Market analyses [23] and media sources [33] suggest that Agentic AI will lead to the next breakthrough of artificial intelligence, with the potential to alter how we work and live fundamentally.

Having strong zero- and few-shot learning abilities [51], large language models exhibit impressive language skills and considerably improve the generalization capabilities of deep learning algorithms. LLMs are capable of solving tasks in different disciplines such as language, mathematics, programming, and medicine [5]. Although not reliable enough, they have shown fundamental reasoning skills in zero-shot and few-shot settings [55]. Prompt engineering techniques such as Chain-of-Thought (CoT) [50] have been proposed to enhance the reasoning ability of LLMs. Consequently, LLMs are supposed to play a vital role in generative agents. Some position papers envision large language models as the brain of generative agents, viewing them as the central control unit for future general intelligent agents [54].

However, despite their excellent language capabilities, LLMs still have shortcomings in reasoning. Sometimes, they need to be combined with symbolic AI methods to construct Neuro-Symbolic AI systems for effective problem-solving. LLM-symbolic AI systems have achieved remarkable results in tasks such as puzzle solving [27], logical reasoning [37], automatic planning [2], and proof explanation [39], highlighting the potential synergy between LLMs and other AI approaches. While other forms of artificial intelligence can be utilized as tools by large language models within generative agent systems where LLMs function as the central control unit. Under this paradigm, the LLMs assume a dominant role, reducing other AI methods to tools comparable to conventional, non-intelligent computer programs. This paradigm is inconsistent with the cognitive properties of humans, who are characterized by a multitude of learning and reasoning abilities [43].

Grounded in the study of human cognitive capacities like memory, analogical reasoning, and problem-solving, case-based reasoning (CBR) offers distinct advantages in integrating multiple AI techniques. CBR excels in problem-solving and maintains close relationships with learning techniques [1]. Based on this understanding, in this position paper, we propose using CBR as the central unit for generative agents. We undertake a comprehensive review of existing surveys and positions for generative agents and examine relevant research literature in multiple areas including psychiatry, psychology, cognitive science, and software engineering. Based on this analysis, we elaborate on our position from the perspectives of both cognitive aspects and engineering implementation, outlining a general framework for case-based generative agents and presenting a roadmap for the proposed research avenue.

In summary, we focus on addressing the following questions in this position paper:

- **Q1**: How does the research community currently view the construction of generative agents? What technical frameworks have been proposed?

- **Q2**: Are LLMs capable of providing the necessary reasoning capabilities for future intelligent agents? How might generative deep learning models, such as LLMs, and other AI paradigms contribute to the functionality of generative agents?
- **Q3**: Why do we propose case-based reasoning as the central control unit for generative agents? What is the cognitive evidence for this?
- **Q4**: According to our roadmap, what components should be included in future case-based generative agents? How should these components be integrated?

2 Existing Frameworks for Generative Agents

Table 1. Representative surveys and technical frameworks for generative agents. Due to the focus of this position paper, for the surveys that cover multiagent systems, we only consider their proposed components for single agents in this table.

Survey	Focus	Proposed Components
[19]	Multiagent	Decision-Making thought, Tool use, and Memory
[54]	Agent and multiagent	Brain, Perception, and Action
[48]	Agent	Profiling, Memory, Planning, and Action
[17]	Domain-Specific Agents	Perception, Reasoning and Decision Making, Adaptive Learning, and Personalizing
[11]	Agent	Configurator, Perception, Short-term memory, Actor, World model, and Cost

To address research question **Q1**, we review representative surveys and position papers on generative agents, briefly discussing and analyzing their proposed technical frameworks. The selected papers and their corresponding frameworks are reported in Table 1.

Guo et al. reviewed LLM-based agents from the perspective of multiagent systems [19]. Their framework for LLM-based intelligent agents consists of three components: Decision-Making Thought, Tool-use, and Memory. Leveraging techniques like prompt engineering, self-reflection, and in-context learning, LLMs can fulfill most agentic functionalities. Vector databases are suggested to simulate long-term memory, addressing the LLMs' shortcomings in retaining information over extended contexts [19]. Xi et al. present a clear and concise roadmap for generative agents, framing them in terms of three modules: brain, perception, and action [54]. In their roadmap, a generative agent's brain comprises memory (memory and knowledge) and decision-making (reasoning and planning). They propose that the core component of a generative agent's brain is a LLM. By incorporating multimodal functionalities and the ability to call upon external tools, the LLM gains the capacity for both perception and action [54]. Wang et al.'s generative agent model consists of four components. In addition to the typical memory, planning, and action modules, they incorporate a profiling module, recognizing that generative agents often need to conform to specific roles. This module constrains the agent's behavior according to characteristics like personality and stance [48].

For social simulation agents, Gao et al. recognize four essential abilities: perception, reasoning and decision making, adaptive learning, and personalizing [17]. They envision generative agents continuously adapting to their environment, deviating from their initially defined decision-making strategies as needed. Dawid and LeCun propose an energy-based agent framework that consists of modules for configurator, perception, short-term memory, actor, world model, and cost [11]. Their framework explicitly adopted a connectionist approach.

In summary, existing surveys and position papers have proposed frameworks and roadmaps for generative agents. However, these frameworks generally rely heavily on LLMs, lacking integration with other AI paradigms.

3 The Limitation of LLM Reasoning

In this section, we address our position on research question **Q2** that investigates the roles of LLMs and other AI paradigms in future intelligent agents. Based on research in psychology and cognitive science, human reasoning is multifaceted. Furthermore, the human brain does not process language and logical reasoning in a unified area. Therefore, holding this interdisciplinary viewpoint, we believe that relying solely on LLMs for reasoning in generative agents will likely encounter a technical bottleneck. We argue that generative agents should incorporate multiple AI paradigms to provide comprehensive reasoning and thinking capabilities.

3.1 The Separate Nature of Language and Reasoning

Languages, specifically natural languages, are tools for humans to convey meaning and thought. Thus, language is inextricably linked to human cognition. However, language skills are not equal to thinking skills either. A good writer does not necessarily have an algebraic mind, and a mathematician or logician is not necessarily a good writer. Hence, an important topic of cognitive science is to investigate whether language and reasoning are separable. The Supramodal Hierarchical Parser (SHP) hypothesis claims that a unified cortical area to process and represent abstract hierarchical structures might exist in the human brain [47]. With the advancement of cognitive neuroscience, there is growing evidence that language comprehension and reasoning operate independently in the human brain, with the SHP hypothesis being denied by multiple results.

First, neuropsychological evidence from clinical neurology suggests that the language and mathematical abilities of patients are not necessarily linked. A patient with left temporal lobe atrophy was reported to have lost semantic memory while retaining his numerical knowledge [7]. A second patient, presenting with asymmetrical atrophy of both temporal lobes but with intact parietal lobes, exhibited severe deficits in language comprehension, language production, and semantic memory, while demonstrating superior performance on nearly all numerical cognitive tasks [57].

Second, utilizing the fMRI brain imaging technique, researchers can detect the active areas of the human brain when performing different tasks. Rodriguez-Moreno and Hirsch [40] find that the activated brain area related to visual and auditory deductive reasoning is different from the language area. Based on a series of fMRI studies, Monti and Osherson [35] conclude that the role of language in reasoning is limited to the encoding of language to inferential-suitable mental representations. Similar patterns are also found in mathematical tasks. Maruyama et al. [34] let volunteers parse algebraic expressions like "$(3-2)+4(1+$" and the fMRI analysis reveals minor contributions from the language area. Amalric and Dehaene [3] also report that when mathematicians judge mathematical statements in algebra, analysis, topology, and geometry, a distinct brain area separate from the language area is activated.

The aforementioned findings indicate the dissociation between language and reasoning in human brains.

3.2 The Cortical Separation of Other Cognitive Tasks

In addition to reasoning capabilities, action modules are typically included within generative agent frameworks. As humans frequently use language to articulate their plans, language and action are often considered to be tightly coupled. It was once conjectured in the theory of embodied cognition that natural language processing is strongly related to mental simulations of actions [15].

However, it is revealed that cortical profiles for language and action are separated even in the same brain area [56]. Formal analysis at the mathematical level has also confirmed that hierarchical structures for language and action possess fundamentally different algebraic structures [10].

Even within the different stages of the same cognitive task, entirely separate cortical areas may be involved. Studies have found that the controlled semantic retrieval and integration processes within analogical reasoning activate distinct subregions of the prefrontal cortex [6]. A recent study has revealed that during action processing, action access and execution also involve different neural mechanisms, localized to the pBA44 and BA6 areas, respectively [38].

3.3 Dual-Process Models for Human Cognition

In the human cognitive process, the occupation of cognitive resources varies according to the task. Such phenomena are described by dual-process theories in psychology. Cognitive procedures that require little attention and are carried out automatically without interfering with other cognitive tasks are defined as automatic processing. On the other hand, controlled processing refers to cognitive activities that are limited in capacity and performed under the intentional control of the subject [41]. In this dichotomy, the types of tasks are not completely fixed. Consistent training can turn a controlled task that requires significant attention into an automatic processing procedure. For instance, children who accept long-term training in Abacus-based Mental Calculation (AMC) develop automatic processing for abacus numbers [13].

A similar dual-process model that also takes into account the level of automation in task performance is suggested for reasoning. Stanovich and West [45] categorized human reasoning into 2 systems, a concept further advanced by Kahneman in his book "Thinking, Fast and Slow" [30]. In this model, System 1 reasoning is characterized as automatic and intuitive without cognitive control. System 2 reasoning, which combines the properties of controlled processing, includes diverse reasoning procedures that demand attention. This theory has a significant impact on the AI community and is commonly used as an analogy to illustrate the relationship between symbolic and subsymbolic AI systems [20].

Besides the Stanovich-West dual-process theory [45], various other dual-process theories of human reasoning exist in psychology. An early dual-process theory is proposed by Austrian psychiatrist Sigmund Freud [16]. He defined two distinct processes: the primary process and the secondary process. While primary process thinking is primitive, illogical, and pleasure-seeking, the advanced secondary process involves making conscious decisions. Evans [14] develops a distinction between two kinds of rationality. Rationality_1 reasons to achieve specific goals, while Rationality_2 reasons in a normative way similar to formal logic. Sloman [43] develops a computational theory that divides human reasoning into an associative system and a rule-based system. The associative system is intuitive and reasons according to similarity and temporal structures while the rule-based system utilizes logic rules. Another similar theory was developed by Swiss psychiatrist Carl Jung. His theory of cognitive functions divides human cognitive processes into four distinct functions: sensing and intuition, classified as irrational functions, and feeling and thinking, classified as rational functions [29]. The language, visual, and auditory capabilities exhibited by LLMs, including multimodal ones, are evidently subordinate to irrational functions.

Although LLMs demonstrate a degree of reasoning ability, it remains questionable whether they are able to adequately represent System 2 thinking, especially considering the separation of language and reasoning in human cognition. Based on these dual-process models, an intuitive hypothesis suggests that generative agents require components responsible for both System 1 and System 2.

3.4 On the Indispensability of System 2 Thinking

In contrast to the other dual-process theories mentioned above, Jung's theory distinguishes between rational and irrational cognitive functions based solely on the nature of the functions themselves, rather than on factors such as proficiency or the capacity for automation. We believe that understanding how humans, through repeated practice, gradually master specific cognitive tasks and process them more automatically holds important philosophical significance for the design and development of generative agents.

If we consider the reasoning capabilities exhibited by large language models as akin to System 1 thinking, or irrational functions within the Jungian framework, and if we consider more explicitly explainable and symbolically reasoned AI paradigms such as case-based reasoning, expert systems, and knowledge representation as akin to System 2 thinking, or rational functions within the Jungian framework, then the following philosophical question arises: Does the capacity of System 1 to execute a task, following extensive deep learning training, imply the complete redundancy of System 2 for that task?

Modern psychological research on intuition offers us some clues. Cognitive neuroscience reveals that the orbitofrontal cortex (OFC), which may form an initial coarse representation, is essential for human intuition [24]. As proficiency increases, humans can also develop quick intuitions regarding logical reasoning problems. Does this "logical intuition" have the capacity to replace conscious, deliberate logical reasoning? Research in experimental psychology has provided a negative answer to this question. Experiments on human reaction against pseudo-logical propositions indicate that logical intuition may not be linked to actual logical reasoning, but rather to superficial structural characteristics [18].

Research in developmental psychology further substantiates the indispensability of System 2 thinking. Studies indicate that training students to inhibit perceptual biases and encourage logical reasoning during cognitive tasks can facilitate a shift in their reasoning strategies. After the training, the participants tend to activate the left prefrontal network, illustrating a shift from reliance on perceptual biases to the utilization of logical reasoning [26]. Through inhibitory control, students can overcome heuristic biases and utilize System 2 more for accurate reasoning [25]. Beyond its benefits for logical thinking, inhibitory control also promotes creative problem-solving and plays a crucial role in idea generation [8].

3.5 Discussions

Evidence from psychology and cognitive science indicates a separation between language, reasoning, and other cognitive processes in the cerebral cortex. Furthermore, evidence suggests that while heuristic cognition can improve with training, it cannot truly replicate rational System 2 thinking. Instead, human cognition relies on inhibitory control to suppress heuristic biases when necessary. Based on this research, we believe large language model (LLM) reasoning training cannot simply replace classical AI paradigms like case-based reasoning, expert systems, and knowledge representation. We argue that LLMs are better suited for perceptual roles in generative agents, while case-based reasoning, expert systems, and knowledge representation can handle different types of reasoning tasks. Therefore, a key challenge for generative agents is how to effectively integrate the generative perceptual UI (LLMs) with various reasoning paradigms.

4 The Role of Case-Based Reasoning in Generative Agents

In this section, we discuss our approaches toward the research question **Q3** that deals with the unique role of CBR in future generative agents. With a perspective on integrating CBR and LLMs, some existing studies have explored the relationship between CBR and RAG [53], implemented CBR with LLMs [52], and discussed future research directions [4]. In this paper, we explore the role of CBR more from a psychological perspective and the overall architecture of future intelligent agents, rather than solely focusing on the combination of CBR and LLMs. In order to highlight the unique role of CBR, we review and analyze relevant research on working memory and intelligence from the field of psychology.

4.1 Working Memory and Intelligence

Working memory is a cognitive system that temporarily stores information needed for thinking and reasoning. It plays a crucial role in cognitive tasks like reasoning and decision-making. While multiple theories of working memory exist in cognitive psychology, it is generally considered to involve cognitive control, representation, and retrieval [46]. Working memory capacity is allocated dynamically in response to changing task demands. This necessitates the retrieval and maintenance of information highly relevant to the task, thus facilitating cognitive operations [21].

Working memory is considered to be a key factor of the general intelligence. Especially, the capacity of working memory is closely linked to intelligence. Early studies hinted that working memory capacity (WMC) is foundational to general intelligence. With the development of cognitive psychology, newer perspectives suggest that while working memory capacity is not fully correspond to general intelligence, there is a high correlation between the two [9]. A study that reviewed 14 datasets with over 3,000 samples found that working memory capacity and fluid intelligence (Gf) shared approximately 50% of their variance [31]. This suggests that working memory plays a fundamental role in human cognition.

it is a common observation that people who achieve high scores on one intelligence test often achieve high scores on other intelligence tasks as well. The process overlap theory provides an explanation for this phenomenon [32]. Working memory capacity largely reflects an individual's ability to maintain relevant information in mind while performing cognitive tasks [32]. The more complex and challenging a cognitive task, the more relevant information typically needs to be held in mind during the problem-solving process. The fundamental cognitive processes reflected in working memory capacity include encoding, storage, and retrieval of information [28]. These processes can help explain individual differences in intelligence.

Due to the limited capacity of working memory, it is essential to prioritize the retention of relevant information during cognitive processing. Studies on adults with varying circadian rhythms and ages have identified changes in inhibitory attention control over time and age as a key factor influencing working memory variations [22]. These findings suggest that inhibitory control plays a significant role in working memory capacity.

4.2 Discussions

Working memory, a temporary place for maintaining information for human cognition, is where information from perception and long-term memory meet. Besides maintaining perceived information, working memory also holds task-relevant material retrieved from long-term memory, such as past experiences, examples, and relevant rules.

Past experiences are held in working memory to facilitate reasoning. Among various AI paradigms, Case-Based Reasoning (CBR) most closely resembles working memory. Just as working memory is a key factor in the general intelligence of human beings, generative agents also need a key intellectual contributor as their central control unit. As far as we are concerned, CBR is the most suitable AI paradigm for this role. Specifically, CBR has the several following advantages:

- **Inhibitory Control**: Analogous to the critical role of inhibitory control in human working memory, generative agents require a mechanism for selecting appropriate reasoning pathways for a given task while suppressing irrelevant cases and reasoning strategies. CBR offers the most suitable framework for modeling such inhibitory control, allowing generative agents to leverage prior cases and experience to choose effective reasoning approaches while inhibiting unproductive ones.
- **Balance**: In contrast to most existing frameworks where other AI paradigms serve as plugins called by LLMs, in a generative agent where Case-Based Reasoning (CBR) acts as the central control unit, classical AI paradigms such as CBR, KR, and expert systems, as well as non-AI programs, can call upon LLMs by case matching and reusing. Our proposed framework affords diverse AI paradigms a more balanced status.
- **Agent Maintenance**: The case base of the central control unit can be updated continuously without the need for reinforcement learning, thereby providing the generative agent with new capabilities. Compared with the approaches to train LLMs for new tasks, our proposed Case-Based generative agent has the potential to lower the maintenance costs for generative agents.

5 Towards Case-Based Generative Agents

In this section, we present a case-based generative agent framework and present an initial exploration of its components to address research question **Q4**. Our proposed framework consists of four main components: a central control unit, perception modules, reasoning modules, and long-term memory modules.

5.1 Design Principles of the Framework

Beyond using CBR instead of LLM as the central control unit, our proposed framework on generative agents also differs significantly in design principles from most existing roadmaps introduced in Sect. 2.

First, adopting a cognitivist perspective, we define the modules of the generative agents according to the cognitive processes instead of the explicit functionalities. This approach minimizes the potential for functional redundancy between modules and facilitates their precise definition. For instance, consider the case where "action" is defined as a module. If the generative agent's task is text generation, the action module and the perception module would correspond to the same LLM component, leading to a significant overlap between modules. Similar issues could also be identified in the tool-calling module. Calling a perceptual tool by the LLM component embodies both tool usage and perception. Since nearly all components in our framework can interact, dedicated tool-calling modules would introduce significant redundancy. Consequently, our framework does not incorporate a designated "tool-calling" module.

Secondly, we believe each module within a generative agent framework should focus on a single task, rather than incorporating functionalities handled by other modules. This principle, inspired by the practices in software engineering to lower the coupling between classes [44], prevents high coupling between cognitive processes. If two distinct cognitive processes reside within the same module, updates to one could inadvertently affect the other. Therefore, instead of burdening LLMs with numerous cognitive processes, we tend to leverage their strength in perception while relying on other AI paradigms such as CBR, knowledge representation, and expert systems for System 2 reasoning tasks.

5.2 Components of Case-Based Generative Agents

Central Control Unit In our framework, the central control unit is the core component of the case-based generative agent, analogous to the working memory in human cognition. Within a case-based generative agent, the central control unit consistently employs CBR as its reasoning paradigm. Given the current state of the agent's task, the central control unit retrieves appropriate cases, experiences, and data from long-term memory. Under the guidance of the retrieved cases, it then performs inhibitory control and selects the appropriate reasoning and perception modules to execute the subsequent step in the task.

Perception Modules. Perception modules perform non-reasoning cognitive processes, analogous to System 1 thinking in the dual-process theory and irrational functions in the Jungian cognitive function theory. LLMs, with their excellent language capabilities, are the most crucial perception modules in generative agents. Other possible perception modules include computer vision algorithms, audio algorithms, environmental sensors and their associated algorithms, and file download algorithms. Perception modules interact with the user or environment and can understand and generate natural language, visual, and audio content.

Reasoning Modules. Reasoning modules perform logical thinking, analogous to System 2 thinking in dual-process theory and rational functions in Jungian cognitive function theory. Common reasoning modules might be CBR, knowledge representation, or expert systems. While there's no specific evidence that LLM reasoning is not pseudo-reasoning, in certain cases, the central control unit might also request LLMs to perform reasoning tasks.

Long-Term Memory. Long-term memory functions analogously to human long-term memory. It comprises multiple case bases and knowledge bases. Depending on the specific characteristics of the cases and the requirements of the various reasoning modules, cases and knowledge can be stored and retrieved using different formats, including text, graphs, first-order predicate logic, and tables.

5.3 The Framework for Case-Based Generative Agents

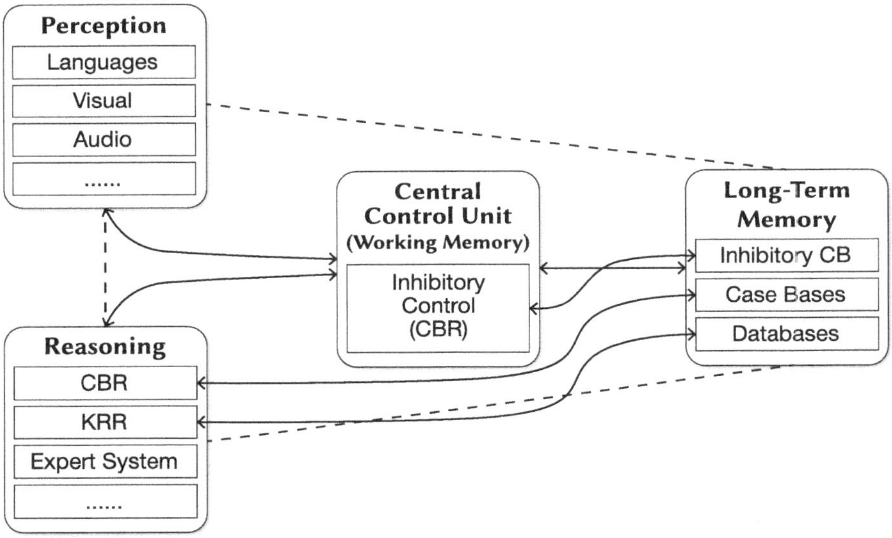

Fig. 1. The framework for case-based generative agents. Dashed lines indicate minimal direct connections, while solid lines represent the primary pathways for information exchange.

The complete framework for our case-based generative agent is illustrated in Fig. 1. The Central Control Unit, acting as the working memory, mediates information exchange between modules. While there is some data exchange between the perception, long-term memory, and reasoning modules – for example, language modules provide a foundational source of information for reasoning.

Dashed lines are used to connect the three modules to indicate minimal direct interaction, prioritizing communication through the Central Control Unit.

The Central Control Unit exercises inhibitory control over the execution of any potential cognitive task. It achieves this by querying the inhibitory case base and utilizing CBR to suppress modules inappropriate for the current task and activate those that are appropriate, along with the relevant data. A direct data link exists between the inhibitory control module and the inhibitory case base. Additionally, designated reasoning modules possess the capability to directly access their respective databases under specific conditions.

As an illustration, suppose a generative agent receives a mathematical reasoning task. The perception module's LLM processes the user's input and transmits it to the Central Control Unit. Using the inhibitory case base, the Central Control Unit performs case-based reasoning. Based on the results, the Central Control Unit suppresses the LLM-based System 1 heuristic generation and activates the KR reasoning functionality. The KR system performs symbolic reasoning based on formal logic, obtains the solution, and returns it to the Central Control Unit. The Central Control Unit then uses CBR again to suppress the reasoning module and activate the language generation capabilities of the perception module, producing a detailed explanation of the solution for the user.

6 Conclusion

In this position paper, we reviewed both classical and modern studies in artificial intelligence, psychology, psychiatry, and cognitive science to investigate the new opportunities for Agentic AI. Based on these insights, we argue that large language models and other AI paradigms are equally important for future generative agents. We propose a framework for case-based generative agents in which CBR is employed as the central control unit. This framework not only integrates various AI paradigms effectively but also follows the high-cohesion, low-coupling design practice from software engineering, extending the lifespan of large models and have to potential to reduce the cost of training.

Acknowledgements. We thank the reviewers for their useful feedbacks. This research is supported by National Natural Science Foundation of China (Grants No. 62376051 and 62076046).

References

1. Aamodt, A., Plaza, E.: Case-based reasoning: foundational issues, methodological variations, and system approaches. AI Commun. **7**(1), 39–59 (1994)
2. Agarwal, S., Sreepathy, A.: TIC: translate-infer-compile for accurate 'text to plan' using LLMs and logical intermediate representations. CoRR abs/2402.06608 (2024)
3. Amalric, M., Dehaene, S.: Origins of the brain networks for advanced mathematics in expert mathematicians. Proc. Natl. Acad. Sci. **113**, 4909–4917 (2016)

4. Bach, K., et al.: Case-based reasoning meets large language models: a research manifesto for open challenges and research directions. hal **hal-05006761** (2025)
5. Bubeck, S., et al.: Sparks of artificial general intelligence: Early experiments with GPT-4. CoRR **abs/2303.12712** (2023)
6. Bunge, S.A., Wendelken, C., Badre, D., Wagner, A.D.: Analogical reasoning and prefrontal cortex: evidence for separable retrieval and integration mechanisms. Cereb. Cortex **15**(3), 239–249 (2005)
7. Cappelletti, M., Butterworth, B., Kopelman, M.D.: Spared numerical abilities in a case of semantic dementia. Neuropsychologia **39**, 1224–1239 (2001)
8. Cassotti, M., Agogué, M., Camarda, A., Houdé, O., Borst, G.: Inhibitory control as a core process of creative problem solving and idea generation from childhood to adulthood. New Dir. Child Adolesc. Dev. **2016**(151), 61–72 (2016)
9. Conway, A.R., Kane, M.J., Engle, R.W.: Working memory capacity and its relation to general intelligence. Trends Cogn. Sci. **7**(12), 547–552 (2003)
10. Coopmans, C.W., Kaushik, K.R., Martin, A.E.: Hierarchical structure in language and action: a formal comparison. Psychol. Rev. **130**(4), 935–952 (2023)
11. Dawid, A., LeCun, Y.: Introduction to latent variable energy-based models: a path towards autonomous machine intelligence. CoRR **abs/2306.02572** (2023)
12. Diwali, A., Saeedi, K., Dashtipour, K., Gogate, M., Cambria, E., Hussain, A.: Sentiment analysis meets explainable artificial intelligence: a survey on explainable sentiment analysis. IEEE Trans. Affect. Comput. **15**(3), 837–846 (2024)
13. Du, F., Yao, Y., Zhang, Q., Chen, F.: Long-term abacus training induces automatic processing of abacus numbers in children. Perception **43**, 694–704 (2014)
14. Evans, J.S.B.T.: Bias and rationality. In: Rationality: Psychological and philosophical perspectives., pp. 6–30. International library of psychology., Taylor & Frances/Routledge, Florence, KY, US (1993)
15. Fischer, M.H., Zwaan, R.A.: Embodied language: a review of the role of the motor system in language comprehension. Quart. J. Exper. Psychol. **61**, 825–850 (2008)
16. Freud, S.: Die Traumdeutung. Franz Deuticke (1899)
17. Gao, C., et al.: Large language models empowered agent-based modeling and simulation: a survey and perspectives. Human. Soc. Sci. Commun. **11**(1), 1–24 (2024)
18. Ghasemi, O., Handley, S.J., Howarth, S., Newman, I.R., Thompson, V.A.: Logical intuition is not really about logic. J. Exp. Psychol. Gen. **151**(9), 2009–2028 (2020)
19. Guo, T., ET AL.: Large language model based multi-agents: a survey of progress and challenges. In: Proceedings of the Thirty-Third International Joint Conference on Artificial Intelligence, IJCAI 2024, Jeju, South Korea, August 3-9, 2024, pp. 8048–8057. ijcai.org (2024)
20. Hamilton, K., Nayak, A., Bozic, B., Longo, L.: Is neuro-symbolic AI meeting its promise in natural language processing? A structured review. CoRR **abs/2202.12205** (2022)
21. Hartmann, E.M., Gade, M., Steinhauser, M.: Adaptive control of working memory. Cognition **224**, 105053 (2022)
22. Hasher, L., Lustig, C., Zacks, R.T., et al.: Inhibitory mechanisms and the control of attention. Var. Work. Memory **19**, 227–249 (2007)
23. Hopkins, B.: Forrester's top 10 emerging technologies for 2024: as AI dominates, security becomes paramount (2024). https://www.forrester.com/blogs/top-10-emerging-technologies-for-2024/
24. Horr, N.K., Braun, C., Volz, K.G.: Feeling before knowing why: the role of the orbitofrontal cortex in intuitive judgments–an meg study. Cogn. Affect. Behav. Neurosci. **14**, 1271–1285 (2014)

25. Houdé, O., Borst, G.: Evidence for an inhibitory-control theory of the reasoning brain. Front. Hum. Neurosci. **9**, 148 (2015)
26. Houde, O., et al.: Shifting from the perceptual brain to the logical brain: the neural impact of cognitive inhibition training. J. Cogn. Neurosci. **12**, 721–728 (2000)
27. Ishay, A., Yang, Z., Lee, J.: Leveraging large language models to generate answer set programs. In: Marquis, P., Son, T.C., Kern-Isberner, G. (eds.) Proceedings of the 20th International Conference on Principles of Knowledge Representation and Reasoning, KR 2023, Rhodes, Greece, September 2-8, 2023, pp. 374–383 (2023)
28. Jonides, J., Lewis, R.L., Nee, D.E., Lustig, C.A., Berman, M.G., Moore, K.S.: The mind and brain of short-term memory. Annu. Rev. Psychol. **59**(1), 193–224 (2008)
29. Jung, C.G.: Analytical Psychology: It's Theory and Practice. Random House (1968)
30. Kahneman, D.: Thinking, Fast and Slow. Macmillan (2011)
31. Kane, M.J., Hambrick, D.Z., Conway, A.R.: Working memory capacity and fluid intelligence are strongly related constructs: comment on Ackerman, Beier, and Boyle (2005) (2005)
32. Kovacs, K., Conway, A.R.: Process overlap theory: a unified account of the general factor of intelligence. Psychol. Inq. **27**(3), 151–177 (2016)
33. Marr, B.: The third wave of AI is here: why agentic AI will transform the way we work (2024). https://www.forbes.com/sites/bernardmarr/2024/11/15/the-third-wave-of-ai-is-here-why-agentic-ai-will-transform-the-way-we-work/
34. Maruyama, M., Pallier, C., Jobert, A., Sigman, M., Dehaene, S.: The cortical representation of simple mathematical expressions. Neuroimage **61**, 1444–1460 (2012)
35. Monti, M.M., Osherson, D.N.: Logic, language and the brain. Brain Res. **1428**, 33–42 (2012)
36. Newell, A., Simon, H.A.: The logic theory machine-a complex information processing system. IRE Trans. Inf. Theory **2**(3), 61–79 (1956)
37. Pan, L., Albalak, A., Wang, X., Wang, W.: Logic-LM: empowering large language models with symbolic solvers for faithful logical reasoning. In: Bouamor, H., Pino, J., Bali, K. (eds.) Findings of the Association for Computational Linguistics: EMNLP 2023, Singapore, December 6-10, 2023, pp. 3806–3824. Association for Computational Linguistics (2023)
38. Papitto, G., Friederici, A.D., Zaccarella, E.: Distinct neural mechanisms for action access and execution in the human brain: insights from an FMRI study. Cerebral Cortex **34**(4), bhae163 (2024)
39. Quan, X., Valentino, M., Dennis, L.A., Freitas, A.: Verification and refinement of natural language explanations through LLM-symbolic theorem proving (2024)
40. Rodriguez-Moreno, D.V., Hirsch, J.: The dynamics of deductive reasoning: an FMRI investigation. Neuropsychologia **47**, 949–961 (2009)
41. Schneider, W., Shiffrin, R.M.: Controlled and automatic human information processing: 1. detection, search, and attention. Psychol. Rev. **84**(1), 1–66 (1977)
42. Sheng, N., et al.: A survey of deep learning for detecting miRNA- disease associations: databases, computational methods, challenges, and future directions. IEEE ACM Trans. Comput. Biol. Bioinform. **21**(3), 328–347 (2024)
43. Sloman, S.A.: The empirical case for two systems of reasoning. Psychol. Bull. **119**, 3–22 (1996)
44. Sommerville, I.: Software Engineering (ed.). America: Pearson Education Inc (2011)
45. Stanovich, K.E., West, R.F.: Individual differences in reasoning: implications for the rationality debate? Behav. Brain Sci. **23**(5), 645–665 (2000)

46. Sternberg, R.J.: The Cambridge Handbook of Intelligence. Cambridge University Press (2020)
47. Tettamanti, M., Weniger, D.: Broca's area: a supramodal hierarchical processor? Cortex **42**, 491–494 (2006)
48. Wang, L., et al.: A survey on large language model based autonomous agents. Frontiers Comput. Sci. **18**(6), 186345 (2024)
49. Wang, M., Deng, W.: Deep face recognition: a survey. Neurocomputing **429**, 215–244 (2021)
50. Wei, J., et al.: Chain-of-thought prompting elicits reasoning in large language models. In: Koyejo, S., Mohamed, S., Agarwal, A., Belgrave, D., Cho, K., Oh, A. (eds.) Advances in Neural Information Processing Systems 35: Annual Conference on Neural Information Processing Systems 2022, NeurIPS 2022, New Orleans, LA, USA, November 28 - December 9, 2022 (2022)
51. Wei, X., et al.: Zero-shot information extraction via chatting with ChatGPT. CoRR **abs/2302.10205** (2023)
52. Wilkerson, K., Leake, D.: On implementing case-based reasoning with large language models. In: International Conference on Case-Based Reasoning, pp. 404–417. Springer (2024)
53. Wiratunga, N., et al.: CBR-RAG: case-based reasoning for retrieval augmented generation in LLMs for legal question answering. In: International Conference on Case-Based Reasoning, pp. 445–460. Springer (2024)
54. Xi, Z., et al.: The rise and potential of large language model based agents: a survey. Sci. China Inf. Sci. **68**(2), 121101 (2025)
55. Xu, F., Lin, Q., Han, J., Zhao, T., Liu, J., Cambria, E.: Are large language models really good logical reasoners? A comprehensive evaluation from deductive, inductive and abductive views. CoRR **abs/2306.09841** (2023)
56. Zaccarella, E., Papitto, G., Friederici, A.D.: Language and action in Broca's area: computational differentiation and cortical segregation. Brain Cogn. **147** (2020)
57. Zamarian, L., Karner, E., Benke, T., Donnemiller, E., Delazer, M.: Knowing 7×8, but not the meaning of Elephant: evidence for the dissociation between numerical and non-numerical semantic knowledge. Neuropsychologia **44**, 1708–1723 (2006)

Theoretical or Methodological CBR Research

Evaluating Objective Metrics for Time Series Model Explainability

Jesus M. Darias(✉), Belén Díaz-Agudo, and Juan A. Recio-Garcia

Department of Software Engineering and Artificial Intelligence, Instituto de Tecnologías del Conocimiento, Universidad Complutense de Madrid, Madrid, Spain
{jdarias,belend,jareciog}@ucm.es

Abstract. Case-based Reasoning (CBR) relies on the quality of similarity metrics. Here, current developments in eXplainable Artificial Intelligence (XAI) aid in providing insights about their behavior and performance. While explainability for AI models has gained importance, XAI for time-series data models remains less developed compared to those for more common data types. The diversity of XAI approaches makes it challenging to identify fair metrics that effectively assess the quality of explanations. Furthermore, XAI methods are often highly customizable, and small changes in their parameters can significantly impact the quality of the explanations. In this work, we propose an adaptation of existing explainability metrics to extend their application to time series data models that can be used for the retrieval of cases. To validate the significance of the metrics, we propose a user-driven study to examine the correlation between human preferences and metric quality.

Keywords: eXplainable Artificial Intelligence · Case-Based Reasoning · Explainability Metrics · Time Series

1 Introduction

Modern AI systems process structured data, such as numerical values and categorical variables, as well as unstructured data, including text, images, and audio files. Besides, time series data are increasingly fundamental in various critical domains, such as finance, healthcare, Internet of Things (IoT), and predictive maintenance, where making timely and precise decisions is crucial. Time series models, with their ability to analyze temporal patterns and forecast future trends, have become indispensable in these fields. XAI (eXplainable AI) emerged recently as a set of techniques designed to make AI systems more transparent and interpretable. In doing so, XAI aims to bridge the gap between AI's capabilities and the need for human confidence in AI systems. While still in its early stages, XAI has gained significant momentum, with a wide range of tools and techniques introduced over the last few years, with libraries and platforms like [4,19]. Despite their widespread use and importance, however, XAI for time series data remains significantly underexplored compared to predictive AI

© The Author(s), under exclusive license to Springer Nature Switzerland AG 2025
I. Bichindaritz and B. López (Eds.): ICCBR 2025, LNAI 15662, pp. 189–203, 2025.
https://doi.org/10.1007/978-3-031-96559-3_13

systems that handle non-temporal data. For non-temporal data, there are some well-known explainers, such as LIME (Local Interpretable Model-agnostic Explanations) [15], SHAP (SHapley Additive exPlanations) [10], and counterfactual explanations. While this methods have been developed to explain individual predictions, other techniques focus on visualizing model behavior in general, or even simplifying deep networks [16]. Time series models often lack the interpretability and transparency required for stakeholders to fully trust and understand the decision-making process. This gap in explainability for time series models presents a critical challenge, especially in high-risk industries where decisions based on these models can have profound consequences. Therefore, advancing XAI for time series data is a crucial area of research to ensure these systems are both effective and trustworthy. While recent efforts such as TSInterpret [9], Time Interpret [6], and specific methods like LIMESegment [17] and WindowSHAP [11] have made progress in addressing the explainability of time series models, there remains a notable gap in comprehensive, widely adopted libraries that consolidate a broad range of XAI techniques tailored specifically for time series data.

Ensuring interpretability in time series AI models is particularly challenging, especially when evaluating the quality of generated explanations. While objective metrics offer a standardized way to assess clarity, relevance, and effectiveness, their outcomes can vary widely depending on the chosen metric (see Sect. 3). This challenge is further compounded by the lack of cross-compatible objective metrics tailored for time series, making it difficult to validate explanations without user input. While finding a one-size-fits-all metric solution is mostly unlikely, proposing fair and compatible metrics across different XAI approaches could be helpful to identify the most suitable technique for a given use case. Furthermore, defining such metrics could be beneficial for optimizing parameter configurations for different techniques.

The integration of XAI methods for time series analysis represents a significant advancement in CBR systems, particularly in enhancing the retrieval phase [14]. As CBR systems increasingly incorporate complex similarity measures and feature extraction techniques for temporal data, the black-box nature of these processes can obscure the rationale behind case selection. XAI approaches address this limitation by providing transparent interpretations of how temporal patterns are identified. This transparency enables domain experts to validate the relevance of retrieved cases, refine similarity metrics based on explainable feedback, and incorporate domain-specific temporal knowledge more effectively. Furthermore, XAI methods can highlight salient segments or features within time series data that drive the retrieval process, allowing for more targeted case adaptation and reuse.

In previous work [18], we have highlighted the relevance of combining CBR and XAI for time series forecasting and the challenges that this field raises. We have also introduced in [19] the use of CBR to retrieve and reuse previous experiences of explanations to help users better understand how AI models work. We have proposed capturing complete user-centered explanation experiences and representing complex strategies to recommend the explanation strategy that best suits a new explanation situation. To capture user explanation experiences and enrich our case base, we require specific metrics to assess the quality of AI explanations and determine whether they are useful for end-users in comprehending and trusting AI systems. In [3] we dealt with the problem of evaluating the quality of the output (i.e., the explanation itself). We have also addressed the challenge of evaluating final explanations generated by post hoc methods [2]. This is a complex process that requires a combination of objective and subjective metrics. Objective metrics such as insertion, deletion, fidelity, stability, sparsity, and diversity can be useful for comparing the quality of explanations provided by different explanation methods and identifying their strengths and weaknesses, but subjective evaluation is essential to understand how users actually perceive these explanations. The reliability of objective metrics depends on several factors, and they may not always represent a trustworthy reflection of user preferences.

In this paper, we have reviewed several XAI methods specifically designed for time-series models, which are later used to generate explanations for metric validation. We investigate the applicability of existing objective metrics to evaluate different XAI methods for time series and assess which metrics best capture explanation quality from a user perspective. We have proposed an adaptation for time series of objective metrics (used in [3]), leveraging existing metrics from the literature.

Section 2 provides an overview of existing XAI methods for time series, discussing their characteristics and known limitations. We also introduce general objective explainability metrics, outlining why they are not directly applicable to time-series explanations. In Sect. 3, we describe our proposed adaptations to these metrics for time-series data. The experimental setup and methodology are detailed in Sect. 4, while Sect. 5 presents and analyzes the results of our study. Finally, conclusions are discussed in Sect. 6.

2 Background

In this section we provide an overview of XAI methods for time series, highlighting their characteristics and known limitations. We also focus on the explainability metrics available in the literature for XAI in general.

2.1 XAI Methods for Timeseries

Interpretable machine learning for time-series data presents unique challenges due to the sequential nature and temporal dependencies of the input. Various explainability methods have been proposed, adapting established model-agnostic and model-specific techniques to handle these challenges. Below, we explore several key methods that have been developed to interpret time-series models.

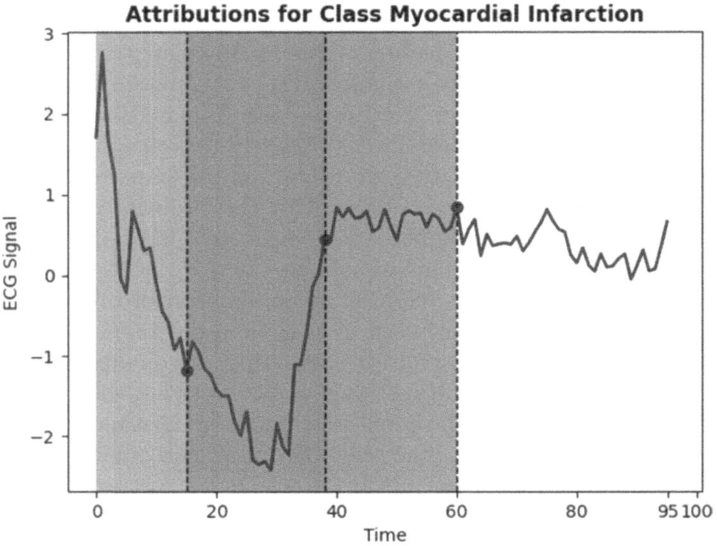

Fig. 1. LIMESegment example explanation. The blue line represents the time series, while green and red segments indicate positive and negative contributions to the target class, respectively. (Color figure online)

LIMESegment [17] builds upon the widely used Local Interpretable Model-agnostic Explanations (LIME) framework by introducing a segmentation-based adaptation for time-series data. Traditional LIME perturbs individual features in tabular datasets, but this approach is less effective for time-series models, which rely on temporal dependencies and sequential patterns. To address this, LIMESegment perturbs meaningful segments of the series rather than individual time points, generating local surrogate models that provide more interpretable explanations. A core innovation in LIMESegment is its NNSegment algorithm, which partitions a time series into contiguous, meaningful segments rather than treating each time step independently. These segments capture coherent patterns such as periodic fluctuations or significant peaks. The method allows user-defined segmentation granularity, offering flexibility while requiring careful tuning to ensure interpretability (Fig. 1).

Building on the idea of using LIME for time-series interpretation, Neves et al. [12] proposed an alternative method that perturbs fixed-size windows of the input series rather than dynamically segmenting it. Unlike LIMESegment, this method does not rely on a segmentation algorithm. Instead, it applies a binomial sampler to select windows for modification. One of the crucial aspects of any LIME-based approach is how perturbations are introduced. The authors tested three different perturbation strategies: zero, random, and mean perturbation. In the zero perturbation strategy, selected windows were replaced with zeros. In the random perturbation strategy, the windows were substituted with random values. Finally, in the mean perturbation strategy, the windows were assigned the average value computed from the training dataset. Among these strategies, mean perturbation yielded the most stable and effective explanations. However, since segmentation is predefined by fixed window sizes rather than learned dynamically, this approach does not fully capture temporal dependencies, as all segments have the same length.

A precursor to both LIMESegment and the Neves et al. approach, LEFTIST [8] was one of the first methods to adapt LIME for time-series interpretability. While it follows a similar perturbation-based framework, LEFTIST differs in that perturbations are created by replacing selected windows with data from randomly chosen instances in the training set. Despite being an important early effort, LEFTIST has several limitations. It uses fixed window sizes, which restrict flexibility, and lacks temporal awareness, as perturbations do not account for dependencies. Additionally, it suffers from high variability, with repeated explanations for the same instance often differing significantly due to the randomness in the perturbation strategy. Subsequent methods, such as LIMESegment, improved upon these aspects by introducing dynamic segmentation and more structured perturbation schemes.

Beyond perturbation-based techniques, gradient-based methods offer another approach to explainability by leveraging model gradients to identify important input features. These methods, such as Grad-CAM, Integrated Gradients, SmoothGrad, and GradientSHAP, highlight which parts of an input most influence a model's prediction. Unlike LIME-based methods, gradient-based explanations are inherently model-specific, meaning they are applicable only to differentiable models like neural networks. Additionally, they operate at the individual time-step level, rather than segmenting time-series data into broader windows. The TSInterpret package [9] provides an implementation of various gradient-based explainability techniques, making them accessible for time-series analysis (Fig. 2).

Alternatively, SHAP-based methods provide a widely used approach for explainability, but they often suffer from high computational costs when applied at fine-grained resolutions. WindowSHAP addresses this by aggregating time steps into larger windows, reducing the complexity of SHAP calculations while maintaining interpretability.

Three different windowing strategies are proposed in WindowSHAP. The stationary approach splits the series into fixed-length segments, similar to traditional LIME-based approaches. The sliding window method iterates a window of a fixed length across the series, allowing for overlapping representations that smooth transitions between feature importance scores. In contrast, the dynamic approach generates variable-length segments based on variation thresholds, adapting the segmentation process to changes in the time series data. By reducing granularity while retaining key patterns, WindowSHAP achieves a balance between explanation clarity and computational efficiency.

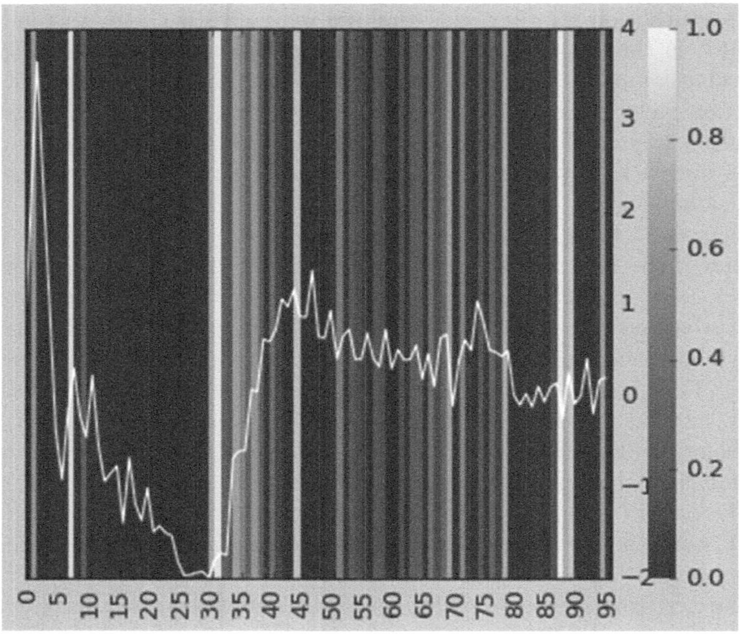

Fig. 2. GradientSHAP explanation example using TSInterpret.

2.2 Objective Explainability Metrics

Although various taxonomies classify explainability metrics, the most intuitive distinctions focus on user-centered (subjective) metrics and intrinsic properties of explanations (objective metrics). A comprehensive evaluation approach should incorporate both aspects, as suggested by Donoso-Guzmán et al. [5]. Moreover, prior research indicates that certain objective metrics exhibit a direct correlation with specific subjective metrics [3].

For feature-based explanations, where attributions are mapped to specific input features, the following objective metrics are particularly relevant:

- **Insertion**: This metric quantifies the increase in the probability of the predicted class as features are progressively added in importance order, according to the importance map of the explanation [13]. The process starts with an empty input, and features are introduced sequentially. Higher insertion values indicate that the most important features identified by the explanation strongly contribute to the model's prediction, leading to a rapid increase in confidence for the target class.
- **Deletion:** The deletion metric operates inversely to insertion. It measures the decrease in the probability of the predicted class as the most important features according to the explanation are gradually removed [13]. A sharp probability drop (i.e., a small area under the probability curve) suggests that

the identified features are crucial for the model's decision, indicating a high-quality explanation.

- **MuFidelity:** This metric evaluates the consistency of attribution scores by assessing how changes in input features influence the output of the model [1]. It is based on the premise that when a feature is replaced with a baseline value, the resulting change in the prediction should be proportional to the sum of the attribution scores assigned by the explanation. MuFidelity is computed by selecting random feature subsets, setting them to baseline values, and measuring the correlation between attribution scores and prediction variations. Higher MuFidelity scores indicate better alignment between the explanation and the model's actual behavior.

Certain libraries, such as Xplique [7], offer built-in implementations to calculate the above metrics. However, Xplique is primarily designed for image data, and no equivalent framework currently exists for time series explainability metrics. Additionally, the variety of explainability methods presents a challenge for fair comparisons, as different approaches may utilize different window sizes, segmentation strategies, or may not use any segmentation at all.

In the following section, we propose an adaptation of some of these metrics to ensure a standardized and equitable comparison across time-series explainability methods.

3 Metrics Adaptation

To highlight the importance of adapting explainability metrics in light of the variability among XAI methods, consider the following scenario. Imagine two explanations are generated for the same time series instance, both assigning identical attribution values to their respective time points. However, one explanation uses larger window sizes, while the other provides a more granular view. If explainability metrics are applied without considering this difference, they would likely favor the explanation with larger windows. This is because broader windows include more feature information, which can have a greater influence on the model's predicted value. As a result, this approach introduces an unfair bias against explanations that are more detailed or fine-grained. Such a discrepancy underscores the need to carefully adjust metrics to ensure that they evaluate explanations fairly and accurately, regardless of the window size used.

To address this issue, we normalize the impact of perturbing a window relative to its size, ensuring that each explanation contributes proportionally to the evaluation metric. This normalization process is defined as follows:

$$I'_i = \frac{I_i}{e_i - b_i} \tag{1}$$

where I'_i is the normalized importance score for segment i, I_i is the original importance score assigned to segment i, b_i and e_i are the starting and ending indices of segment i, respectively, and $e_i - b_i$ represents the segment size (number of time-points in the segment).

Another crucial aspect to consider is the calculation of the area under the curve (AUC) for insertion and deletion procedures. Since explanations may have varying window sizes, direct comparisons can be misleading. To create a fair evaluation framework, we first interpolate the explanation curve to a fixed number of evenly spaced points across the input domain. This standardizes the resolution of different explanations by mapping them to a common scale. We then compute the area under the interpolated curve using the trapezoidal rule, yielding an accumulated impact value for each fraction of the time series. By incorporating these adaptations, we ensure that explainability metrics provide an equitable comparison across explanations, regardless of their underlying segmentation strategies.

4 Experimental Procedure

To validate the significance of the proposed explainability metrics, we conducted a user study designed to investigate the relationship between explanation quality, measured using objective metrics, and user preferences. To minimize the influence of domain-specific knowledge, which could bias results in favor of experienced users, we devised a synthetic use case.

For this experiment, we first generated a synthetic dataset in which half of the time series followed a predefined pattern. Specifically, positive instances exhibited a characteristic pattern in which a peak (an abnormally high value) was followed by a valley (an abnormally low value), while negative instances did not follow this pattern and contained random variations. This dataset was then used to train a Long Short-Term Memory (LSTM) model to classify time series as either positive or negative. The trained model achieved a solid F1 score of 0.96.

To construct the user study, we randomly selected a subset of positive-class time series that were correctly classified by the model (i.e., true positives). For each selected series, explanations were generated using six different explainability methods: LIMESegment, NEVES, LEFTIST, Integrated Gradients, SmoothGrad, and Gradient SHAP. We then applied the Insertion and Deletion explainability metrics to assess the quality of these explanations. A global explainability score was computed as a normalized, equally weighted average of both metrics, following the formula:

$$\text{GlobalScore} = \frac{\text{InsertionMetric} + (1 - \text{DeletionMetric})}{2}$$

This score was used to rank the quality of each explanation. Next, we computed pairwise differences between explanations generated by methods belonging to the same family (i.e., perturbation-based methods: LIMESegment, NEVES, LEFTIST, and gradient-based methods: Integrated Gradients, SmoothGrad, Gradient SHAP). The top 15 explanation pairs with the highest differences in explainability scores were selected from each family for inclusion in the user study.

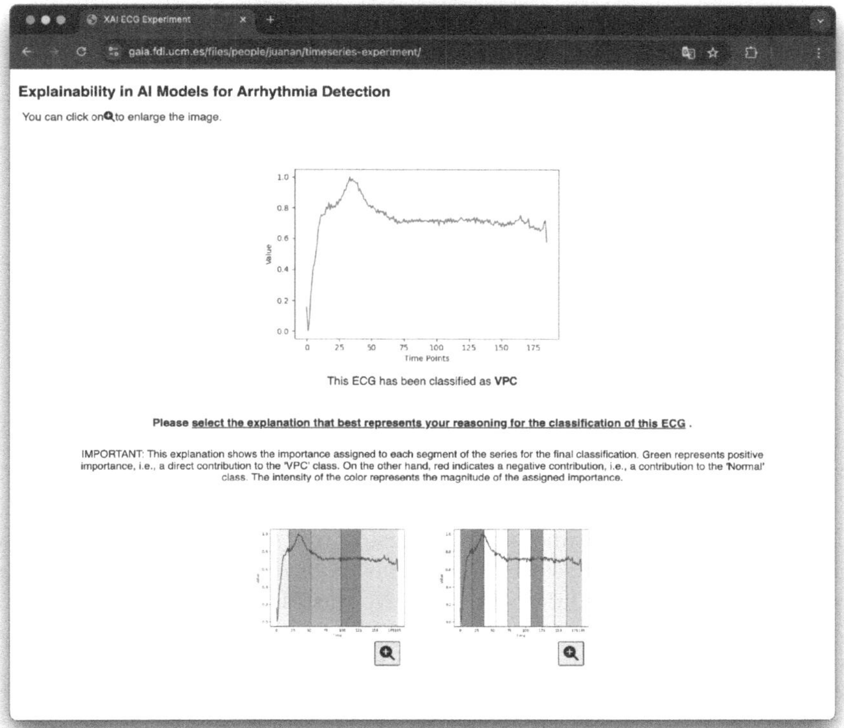

Fig. 3. Screenshot of explanation comparison extracted from the online survey. Participants were asked to choose their preferred explanation for the sample given.

A key factor in our evaluation was the format in which different explainability methods present their outputs. Perturbation-based methods and gradient-based methods produce explanations that differ significantly in their graphical styles. To avoid bias in user responses, as certain visual formats might appear inherently clearer or more intuitive, we limited direct comparisons to explanations within the same method family. This approach ensured that users assessed the explanations solely on their informativeness, rather than being influenced by differences in visualization styles.

The user experiment was conducted through an online survey, where participants with varying levels of expertise in AI and XAI were recruited to evaluate the explanations. The online survey collected a total of 464 responses, where participants compared pairs of explanations and selected the one they perceived as the most representative of a well-reasoned AI decision. As part of the survey, participants were also asked to indicate their expertise in these areas to determine whether it influenced their explanation preferences. Each survey question

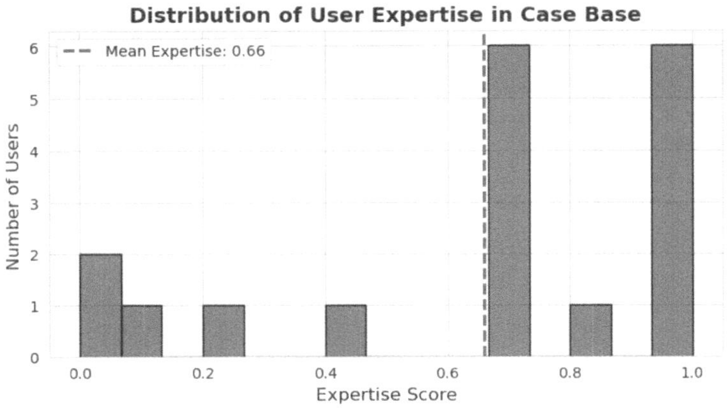

Fig. 4. Distribution of participants by expertise score, computed as a normalized measure of AI and XAI knowledge.

presented a true positive time series alongside two different explanations, and participants were asked to select the one they considered to be the most representative of a well-reasoned decision made by the AI model. This setup allowed us to gather insights into how users with different backgrounds perceive and interpret the explanations provided by the models.

Figure 3 shows a sample explanation comparison extracted from the experiment. The goal was to determine whether the user preferences aligned with the rankings derived from our proposed explainability metrics.

5 Results and Discussion

The online survey collected a total of 464 responses, where participants compared pairs of explanations and selected the one they perceived as the most representative of a well-reasoned AI decision. Notably, the majority of participants had a strong background in AI and XAI, which likely influenced their ability to assess explanations critically. This is reflected in the overall expertise distribution (see Fig. 4), where the mean expertise score, computed through a normalized combination of self-reported AI and XAI knowledge, was 0.66.

As for the comparison of selections against metrics, the overall correctness rate was 59.6%. This rate is defined as the percentage of times participant choices aligned with explanations favored by objective interpretability metrics. While this result exceeds random selection (50%), it suggests participants faced challenges in consistently identifying objectively superior explanations.

To investigate whether greater differences in explanation quality influenced correctness, we analyzed the top 25% of comparisons where the metric difference between explanations was the largest. In this subset (120 votes), correctness improved significantly to 72.5%, supporting the hypothesis that larger quality

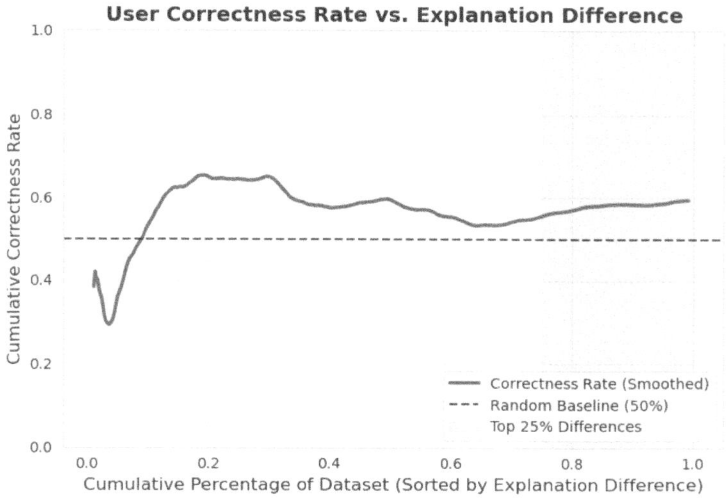

Fig. 5. Cumulative correctness rate as comparisons are included in the case base, sorted by increasing absolute metric difference. The early volatility likely reflects small-sample effects, while the overall trend suggests that larger differences in explanation quality lead to more consistent user agreement, especially when nearing the top third.

gaps enable users to more readily identify better explanations. This trend is further illustrated in Fig. 5, where correctness fluctuates initially but stabilizes as more data is considered, reinforcing the relationship between explanation quality gap and user agreement. When examining correctness rates by family of explainers, we observed notable variations. Perturbation-based methods had a correctness rate of only 56%, whereas gradient-based methods performed better, with a correctness rate of 64%. Our explanation for this discrepancy is that the mean absolute difference in objective metrics was substantially lower for perturbation-based explanations (7.6%) compared to gradient-based explanations (31%). This suggests that explanations generated by perturbation-based methods exhibited less distinguishable characteristics, making comparisons tasks more difficult for participants. Figure 6 shows the distribution of correct and incorrect answers per analyzed segment.

We further analyzed the impact of participant expertise in AI and XAI on correctness rates. Selecting the top 5 most knowledgeable participants and comparing them to the bottom 5, we found a striking difference: the most experienced users achieved a correctness rate of 73%, while the least experienced users had a correctness rate of only 46.7%, performing below random selection. This result highlights the crucial role of domain expertise in accurately assessing explanations and suggests that interpretability methods may be less effective for non-expert users (Fig. 7).

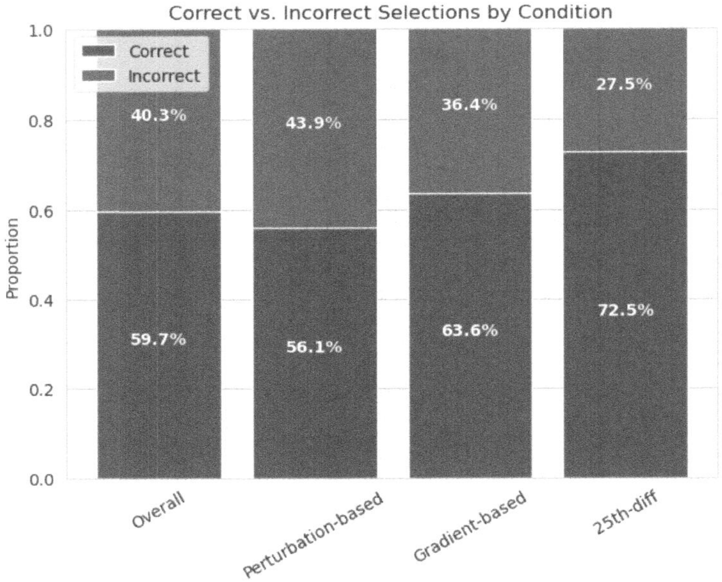

Fig. 6. Distribution of correct and incorrect selections by segment. The *25th-diff* label refers to the subsample of the top 25% of comparisons with the largest metric difference.

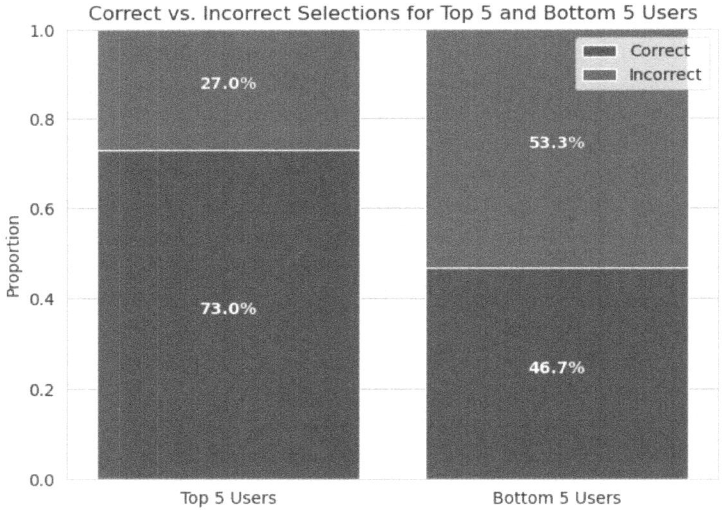

Fig. 7. Correctness distribution for the most and least experienced participants. The results indicate a clear gap in selection accuracy, with higher expertise correlating with better identification of the objectively superior explanations.

6 Conclusions

Explainable Artificial Intelligence methods for time series data have emerged as crucial components in enhancing CBR systems, particularly during the retrieval stage. As CBR systems rely fundamentally on identifying relevant cases that match current problems, the incorporation of transparent and interpretable time series similarity measures becomes paramount for users who must trust and validate system recommendations.

This study aims to validate the effectiveness of our adapted interpretability metrics by assessing whether human users generally agree with explanations that these metrics identify as optimal. Through an online survey, participants compared pairs of explanations and selected the one they found most representative of a well-reasoned AI decision-making. The results will help determine if our metrics successfully align with human preferences for the explanation of time series similarity measures.

Our findings suggest that while users performed better than random selection, non-expert users often struggled to recognize the better explanation according to objective metrics. This challenge was particularly evident for perturbation-based explainers, which had a lower agreement rate with the metrics compared to gradient-based methods. One possible explanation for this discrepancy is that the absolute difference in explanation quality was often more pronounced for gradient-based comparisons, making them easier to distinguish. In this line, we also found evidence that larger differences in explanation quality improve user agreement with the metrics. When analyzing the top 25% of comparisons with the greatest objective differences, correctness increased significantly. However, the most striking result was the impact of expertise: highly knowledgeable participants consistently selected the better explanation, while the least experienced users performed below random selection. This underscores the difficulty non-experts face in interpreting AI explanations and raises concerns about the accessibility of current XAI methods.

While these results offer valuable insights, they were not as conclusive as anticipated in fully validating the adapted metrics. A larger sample size would have provided a more comprehensive user profile and allowed for a deeper exploration of personalized explanation strategies. Specifically, with more participants, we could have created user-oriented clusters, tailoring explanations based on individual expertise levels. This would have enabled us to refine our evaluation further, ensuring that the adapted metrics are better aligned with varying user needs and backgrounds.

Ultimately, our findings highlight that objective interpretability metrics alone are not enough to ensure explanations are meaningful to all users. An approach, which considers the background of users and their cognitive profile, could provide a more effective path forward. By integrating both quantitative metrics and user-centered adaptation, future XAI methods may better align explanations with the needs of diverse audiences. This approach has the potential to enhance both the interpretability and trust in AI systems, ensuring that explanations are not only technically accurate but also resonate with users from different backgrounds and levels of expertise.

Acknowledgements. Supported by the AUDITIA-X project PID2023-150566OB-I00 funded by MCIN/AEI /10.13039/501100011033 and by ERDF/EU and the Complutense University of Madrid (GAIA research group 921330). Partially supported by the BOSCH-UCM Honorary Chair on Artificial Intelligence.

References

1. Bhatt, U., Weller, A., Moura, J.M.F.: Evaluating and Aggregating Feature-based Model Explanations (2020)
2. Caro-Martínez, M., Darias, J.M., Díaz-Agudo, B., Recio-García, J.A.: Use case-specific reuse of XAI strategies: design and analysis through an evaluation metrics library. In: Recio-García, J.A., Orozco-del-Castillo, M.G., Bridge, D. (eds.) Case-Based Reasoning Research and Development - 32nd International Conference, ICCBR 2024, Merida, Mexico, 1–4 July 2024, Proceedings. Lecture Notes in Computer Science, vol. 14775, pp. 81–95. Springer (2024). https://doi.org/10.1007/978-3-031-63646-2_6
3. Darias, J.M., Bayrak, B., Caro-Martínez, M., Díaz-Agudo, B., Recio-García, J.A.: An empirical analysis of user preferences regarding XAI metrics. In: Recio-García, J., Orozco-del-Castillo, M., Bridge, D. (eds.) Case-Based Reasoning Research and Development - 32nd International Conference, ICCBR 2024, Merida, Mexico, 1–4 July 2024, Proceedings. Lecture Notes in Computer Science, vol. 14775, pp. 96–110. Springer (2024). https://doi.org/10.1007/978-3-031-63646-2_7
4. Darias, J.M., Díaz-Agudo, B., Recio-García, J.A.: A systematic review on model-agnostic XAI libraries. In: Borck, H., Eisenstadt, V., Sánchez-Ruiz, A., Floyd, M. (eds.) Workshops Proceedings for the (ICCBR 2021), Salamanca (Spain)/Online, 13–16 September 2021. CEUR Workshop Proceedings, vol. 3017, pp. 28–39. CEUR-WS.org (2021). https://ceur-ws.org/Vol-3017/96.pdf
5. Donoso-Guzmán, I., Ooge, J., Parra, D., Verbert, K.: Towards a Comprehensive Human-Centred Evaluation Framework for Explainable AI (2023). https://arxiv.org/abs/2308.06274
6. Enguehard, J.: Time Interpret: a Unified Model Interpretability Library for Time Series (2023). https://arxiv.org/abs/2306.02968
7. Fel, T., et al.: Xplique: a deep learning explainability toolbox. In: Workshop on Explainable Artificial Intelligence for Computer Vision (CVPR) (2022)
8. Guillemé, M., Masson, V., Rozé, L., Termier, A.: Agnostic local explanation for time series classification. In: 2019 IEEE 31st International Conference on Tools with Artificial Intelligence (ICTAI), pp. 432–439 (2019). https://doi.org/10.1109/ICTAI.2019.00067
9. Höllig, J., Kulbach, C., Thoma, S.: Tsinterpret: a python package for the interpretability of time series classification. J. Open Source Softw. **8**(85), 5220 (2023). https://doi.org/10.21105/joss.05220
10. Lundberg, S.M., Lee, S.: A unified approach to interpreting model predictions. CoRR abs/1705.07874 (2017). http://arxiv.org/abs/1705.07874
11. Nayebi, A., Tipirneni, S., Reddy, C.K., Foreman, B., Subbian, V.: WindowSHAP: An Efficient Framework for Explaining Time-series Classifiers based on Shapley Values (2023). https://arxiv.org/abs/2211.06507

12. Neves, I., et al.: Interpretable heartbeat classification using local model-agnostic explanations on ECGs. Comput. Biol. Med. **133**, 104393 (2021). https://doi.org/10.1016/j.compbiomed.2021.104393. https://www.sciencedirect.com/science/article/pii/S0010482521001876
13. Petsiuk, V., Das, A., Saenko, K.: RISE: Randomized Input Sampling for Explanation of Black-box Models (2018)
14. Pradeep, P., Caro-Martínez, M., Wijekoon, A.: A practical exploration of the convergence of case-based reasoning and explainable artificial intelligence. Expert Syst. Appl. **255**, 124733 (2024). https://doi.org/10.1016/j.eswa.2024.124733. https://www.sciencedirect.com/science/article/pii/S0957417424016002
15. Ribeiro, M.T., Singh, S., Guestrin, C.: "Why should i trust you?" Explaining the predictions of any classifier. In: Proceedings of the 22nd ACM SIGKDD International Conference on Knowledge Discovery and Data Mining, pp. 1135–1144 (2016)
16. Rojat, T., Puget, R., Filliat, D., Ser, J.D., Gelin, R., Rodríguez, N.D.: Explainable Artificial Intelligence (XAI) on TimeSeries Data: A Survey. CoRR abs/2104.00950 (2021). https://arxiv.org/abs/2104.00950
17. Sivill, T., Flach, P.: LIMESegment: meaningful, realistic time series explanations. In: Camps-Valls, G., Ruiz, F.J.R., Valera, I. (eds.) Proceedings of The 25th International Conference on Artificial Intelligence and Statistics. Proceedings of Machine Learning Research, vol. 151, pp. 3418–3433. PMLR (2022). https://proceedings.mlr.press/v151/sivill22a.html
18. Valdez-Ávila, M.F., Bermejo-Sabbagh, C., Díaz-Agudo, B., Orozco-del-Castillo, M.G., Recio-García, J.A.: CBR-fox: a case-based explanation method for time series forecasting models. In: Massie, S., Chakraborti, S. (eds.) Case-Based Reasoning Research and Development - 31st International Conference, ICCBR 2023, Aberdeen, UK, 17–20 July 2023, Proceedings. Lecture Notes in Computer Science, vol. 14141, pp. 200–214. Springer (2023). https://doi.org/10.1007/978-3-031-40177-0_13
19. Wijekoon, A., et al.: iSee: advancing multi-shot explainable AI using case-based recommendations. In: Endriss, U., et al. (eds.) ECAI 2024 - 27th European Conference on Artificial Intelligence, 19–24 October 2024, Santiago de Compostela, Spain - Including 13th Conference on Prestigious Applications of Intelligent Systems (PAIS 2024). Frontiers in Artificial Intelligence and Applications, vol. 392, pp. 4626–4633. IOS Press (2024). https://doi.org/10.3233/FAIA241057

A Knowledge Representation Approach for Reasoning with Adaptation Rules

Nicolas François[1] and Jean Lieber[2](✉)

[1] Lycée public Chopin, 54000 Nancy, France
[2] Université de Lorraine, CNRS, LORIA, 54000 Nancy, France
jean.lieber@loria.fr

Abstract. The adaptation knowledge container of a CBR system is often represented by adaptation rules that can be learned from the case base using various approaches proposed in the CBR literature. However, the formal representation of such rules has been much less investigated. This paper introduces a formalism for representing such rules, given a formalism that can be used to express cases in an attribute-value formalism. One benefit of this study is a case retrieval algorithm for which the retrieved case is the best one with respect to adaptation (i.e. the one that requires the least adaptation effort as defined by the cost of adaptation rule sequences). Moreover, when attributes have Boolean range, its complexity is independent of the size of the case base.

Keywords: case-based reasoning · knowledge representation · adaptation · adaptation-guided retrieval

1 Introduction

Adaptation is considered, for some members of the case-based reasoning (CBR [10]) community as a key step for this type of reasoning. This paper follows that tradition and considers it from a perspective of knowledge representation: How can the representation of adaptation knowledge be useful for CBR?

To address this question, the starting point has been some work on adaptation knowledge learning (AKL). AKL has a long history in the field of CBR, at least since the seminal paper of K. Hanney and M. T. Keane [4]. In general, it is based on what is called the *difference heuristics* in [5]: the differences between pairs of cases in the case base are used to constitute a training set for a machine learning system. In particular, a notation has been introduced to represent such differences: it consists of expressions of the form a^v where a is a case attribute and v is a *variation symbol*. For example, in the cooking domain, to express that, in a dessert recipe, 2 eggs can be substituted by 1 banana, the following set of such expressions can be used:

$$\left\{\texttt{dessert}^{=1},\quad \texttt{\#eggs}^{-2},\quad \texttt{\#bananas}^{+1}\right\}$$

© The Author(s), under exclusive license to Springer Nature Switzerland AG 2025
I. Bichindaritz and B. López (Eds.): ICCBR 2025, LNAI 15662, pp. 204–219, 2025.
https://doi.org/10.1007/978-3-031-96559-3_14

Here, `dessert` is a Boolean attribute: it takes as potential values 0 and 1 (assimilated to *false* and *true*), whereas `#eggs` and `#bananas` are integer attributes.

This notation has been used in rather old studies [1] as well as in recent work [8]. To this notation (or syntax), a semantics can be associated, giving birth to logical formalisms, the *logics of variation*, in which adaptation rules can be represented: that is the first objective of this paper. Its second objective is to explain how such a logic can be beneficial to CBR.

Section 2 presents some preliminaries about CBR. The case base and the domain knowledge can be represented in a so-called *static logic*; Sect. 3 presents the static logic $(\mathcal{GL}, \models)$ that is expressive enough to represent attribute-value pairs (with Boolean and numerical attributes) and taxonomies (and beyond). Section 4 defines the variation logic $(\Delta\mathcal{GL}, \models)$, which is based on $(\mathcal{GL}, \models)$: its syntax, semantics, and basic properties. Section 5 presents how adaptation rules can be defined using this logic. Based on these notions, an algorithm for performing single case retrieval is presented in Sect. 6, which has two notable features. First, it guarantees that the retrieved case is the best case for adaptation (the best in a sense related to the effort of adaptation defined by the cost associated with the adaptation rules). Second, when every attribute has a Boolean range, its time complexity is independent of the size of the case base. Section 7 discusses this contribution, concludes, and briefly presents some future directions of work.

Remark. This paper contains some results without their proofs: these latters can be found in the extended version of this paper, which is available online [3].

2 Preliminaries

This section presents some notations and some assumptions, mainly about CBR.

2.1 Mathematical Notions and Notations

$\mathbb{B}$, the set of Booleans, is assimilated to the pair of integers $\mathbb{B} = \{0, 1\}$ (0 stands for false and 1, for true). $\mathbb{Z}$ is the set of integers (positive and negative). For $a, b \in \mathbb{Z}$ with $a \leq b$, $[\![a, b]\!] = \{n \in \mathbb{Z} \mid a \leq n \leq b\}$. $\mathbb{Q}$ is the set of rational numbers.

An *abelian group* is a pair $(\mathcal{G}, +)$ where $\mathcal{G}$ is a nonempty set and $+$ is an internal binary operation on $\mathcal{G}$ ($+ : (r, s) \in \mathcal{G} \mapsto r + s \in \mathcal{G}$) such that (1) it has an identity element denoted by 0 (for each $r \in \mathcal{G}$, $r + 0 = 0 + r = r$), (2) every $r \in \mathcal{G}$ has an inverse element s ($r + s = s + r = 0$), s is denoted by $-r$, (3) $+$ is associative ($(r+s)+t = r+(s+t)$ for every $r, s, t \in \mathcal{G}$), and (4) $+$ is commutative ($r+s = s+r$ for every $r, s \in \mathcal{G}$). For $r, s \in \mathcal{G}$, $r - s$ is an abbreviation of $r + (-s)$.

With the usual $+$ on numbers, $(\mathbb{Q}, +)$ and $(\mathbb{Z}, +)$ are groups. $(\{0, 1, 2\}, +)$ is not a group since $+$ is not internal (e.g. $2 \in \{0, 1, 2\}$ but $2 + 2 = 4 \not\in \{0, 1, 2\}$).

2.2 Notions, Notations and Assumptions About CBR

These preliminaries on CBR do not reflect the whole variety of CBR systems; in particular, in this paper, a case is considered as a problem-solution pair. A *problem* is, by definition, an element $\mathtt{x}$ of a given set $\mathcal{P}$. A *solution* is, by definition, an element $\mathtt{y}$ of a given set $\mathcal{S}$. It is assumed that a relation $\leadsto$ is defined on $\mathcal{P} \times \mathcal{S}$ that is not completely known to the CBR system, and that reads "has for solution". A *case* is an ordered pair $(\mathtt{x}, \mathtt{y}) \in \mathcal{P} \times \mathcal{S}$. A *correct case* is a case $(\mathtt{x}, \mathtt{y})$ such that $\mathtt{x} \leadsto \mathtt{y}$.

Process Model. A CBR session consists of solving a problem called *target problem* and denoted by $\mathtt{x}^{\mathtt{tgt}}$. A common process for CBR consists in (1) selecting a source case $(\mathtt{x}^s, \mathtt{y}^s)$ that is considered similar to $\mathtt{x}^{\mathtt{tgt}}$ (case retrieval), (2) modifying this retrieved case in order to propose a solution $\mathtt{y}^{\mathtt{tgt}}$ to $\mathtt{x}^{\mathtt{tgt}}$ (case adaptation), and other steps after these problem solving steps, which are not considered in this paper. In many systems, several cases are retrieved and then adapted; in this paper, only single case retrieval and single case adaptation are considered.

Knowledge Model. A CBR system is based on four knowledge containers. The case base $\mathtt{CB}$ is a finite set of correct cases. A case of $\mathtt{CB}$ is called *source case* and is denoted by $(\mathtt{x}^s, \mathtt{y}^s)$. It is assumed that each source case represents a *specific* problem-solving episodes.

Domain knowledge $\mathtt{DK}$ expresses knowledge about the vocabulary in which cases are expressed. It can be seen as a set of constraints on this vocabulary. For example, if "apple" and "fruit" belong to this vocabulary, the piece of domain knowledge "Every apple is a fruit." indicates that a case involving an apple that is not a fruit is incorrect.

The retrieval knowledge expresses the knowledge about case retrieval. It often takes the form of a dissimilarity measure $\mathtt{diss}$ between the source cases and the target problem: to $(\mathtt{x}^s, \mathtt{y}^s) \in \mathtt{CB}$ and $\mathtt{x}^{\mathtt{tgt}} \in \mathcal{P}$ is associated a nonnegative number $\mathtt{diss}((\mathtt{x}^s, \mathtt{y}^s), \mathtt{x}^{\mathtt{tgt}})$, and the retrieval aims at finding the $(\mathtt{x}^s, \mathtt{y}^s) \in \mathtt{CB}$ that minimizes this value.

The adaptation knowledge $\mathtt{AK}$ is used during adaptation. In this paper, it takes the form of a finite set of adaptation rules $\mathtt{ar}$. Generally speaking, such a rule can be interpreted as a mapping associating to $((\mathtt{x}^s, \mathtt{y}^s), \mathtt{x}^{\mathtt{tgt}}) \in (\mathcal{P} \times \mathcal{S}) \times \mathcal{P}$ a $\mathtt{y}^{\mathtt{tgt}} \in \mathcal{S} \cup \{\mathtt{failure}\}$. If $\mathtt{y}^{\mathtt{tgt}} = \mathtt{failure}$, that means that the adaptation rule is not applicable to the adaptation problem $((\mathtt{x}^s, \mathtt{y}^s), \mathtt{x}^{\mathtt{tgt}})$. In other situations, the case $(\mathtt{x}^{\mathtt{tgt}}, \mathtt{y}^{\mathtt{tgt}})$ is not necessarily correct: CBR is, in general, a hypothetical reasoning. To increase the chances of correctness, a positive value $\mathtt{cost}$ associated with $\mathtt{ar}$ is given: the lower $\mathtt{cost}$ is, the higher $(\mathtt{x}^{\mathtt{tgt}}, \mathtt{y}^{\mathtt{tgt}})$ is likely to be correct.

An adaptation can be performed in several steps, using *adaptation paths*, that is, sequences of adaptation rules [6]: given an adaptation problem $((\mathtt{x}^s, \mathtt{y}^s), \mathtt{y}^{\mathtt{tgt}})$, it can be solved using an adaptation path $\mathtt{AP} = \mathtt{ar}^1; \mathtt{ar}^2; \ldots; \mathtt{ar}^q$ if the sequential application of $\mathtt{ar}^k$ (k taking values 1 to q) starting from $(\mathtt{x}^s, \mathtt{y}^s)$ leads to the case $(\mathtt{x}^{\mathtt{tgt}}, \mathtt{y}^{\mathtt{tgt}})$. There may be several adaptation paths for a given adaptation problem, and the selection among them is made according to the cost. The cost of an adaptation path is assumed to be additive: `cost(AP)` is the sum of the cost of the $\mathtt{ar}^k$.

Knowledge Representation. CB and DK are knowledge containers about what *is*, or *is not*, a case: an $(\mathtt{x}^s, \mathtt{y}^s) \in \mathtt{CB}$ indicates that $\mathtt{y}^s$ *is* a (correct) solution of $\mathtt{x}^s$, whereas a piece of knowledge α from DK is a constraint on what a correct case has to be. By contrast, the retrieval knowledge is about comparing cases, and adaptation knowledge AK is about transformations, about how a case *changes* into another case.

For these reasons, two types of logic for representing knowledge in CBR are distinguished: the *static logics* for CB and DK, and the *variation logics* for adaptation knowledge.

In this paper, the static logic considered is $(\mathcal{GL}, \models)$, presented in Sect. 3 and used for both CB and DK. The variation logic $(\Delta\mathcal{GL}, \models)$ for representing adaptation knowledge is based on the former logic and is presented in Sect. 4.

3 The Static Logic $(\mathcal{GL}, \models)$

The static logic can be any classical logic used in knowledge representation, such as propositional logic, a description logic, etc. However, the study presented in this paper is about the logic $(\mathcal{GL}, \models)$ described below, together with a discussion about its expressivity. This logic is parametrized by $\mathcal{G}$ such that either $(\mathcal{G}, +)$ is an infinite abelian group (e.g. $\mathcal{G} = \mathbb{Q}$ or $\mathcal{G} = \mathbb{Z}$) or $\mathcal{G}$ is a subset of $\mathcal{H}$ such that $(\mathcal{H}, +)$ is an infinite abelian group (e.g. $\mathcal{G} = \mathbb{B}$: in this case, $(\mathcal{GL}, \models)$ corresponds to propositional logic).[1]

3.1 Syntax of $(\mathcal{GL}, \models)$

Let $\mathcal{V}$ be a given finite non-empty set of symbols: an $a \in \mathcal{V}$ is called a *variable*. An *atom* of $(\mathcal{GL}, \models)$ is an expression of the form $(a = r)$ where $a \in \mathcal{V}$ and $r \in \mathcal{G}$. A formula of $(\mathcal{GL}, \models)$ is an atom or one of the forms $\bot$, $\top$, $\neg\alpha$, $\alpha \wedge \beta$ and $\alpha \vee \beta$ where α and β are two formulas of this logic. Other connectives can be defined in the usual way as abbreviations. For example, the $\rightarrow$ connective is defined by $\alpha \rightarrow \beta = \neg\alpha \vee \beta$. $\mathcal{GL}$ is the set of formulas for this logic. The set of variables that occur in $\alpha \in \mathcal{GL}$ is denoted by $\mathcal{V}(\alpha)$.

A *literal* is either an atom (or positive literal) or of the form $\neg\alpha$ where α is an atom (negative literal). A *cube* is a conjunction of literals: it has the form $\ell_1 \wedge \ell_2 \wedge \ldots \wedge \ell_p$ where ℓ_k is a literal for $k \in [\![1, p]\!]$. A formula is under *DNF* (disjunctive normal form) if it is a disjunction of cubes: $\gamma_1 \vee \gamma_2 \vee \ldots \vee \gamma_q$ where γ_k is a cube for $k \in [\![1, q]\!]$.

1 The fact that $\mathcal{G}$ is infinite is a technical assumption useful for some proofs. In fact, it is not difficult to extend the approach to finite groups, although it would make the explanations more tedious.

3.2 Semantics of $(\mathcal{GL}, \models)$

An *interpretation* $\mathcal{I}$ is a mapping from $\mathcal{V}$ to $\mathcal{G}$. Let Ω be the set of all interpretations. For $\mathcal{I} \in \Omega$ and $\alpha \in \mathcal{GL}$, the relation "$\mathcal{I}$ is a model of α" (denoted by $\mathcal{I} \models \alpha$) is defined recursively as follows (for $a \in \mathcal{V}$, $r \in \mathcal{G}$ and $\alpha, \beta \in \mathcal{GL}$):

- $\mathcal{I} \models \bot$ never holds;
- $\mathcal{I} \models \top$ always holds;
- $\mathcal{I} \models (a = r)$ if $\mathcal{I}(a) = r$;
- $\mathcal{I} \models \neg\alpha$ if $\mathcal{I} \not\models \alpha$;
- $\mathcal{I} \models \alpha \wedge \beta$ if $\mathcal{I} \models \alpha$ and $\mathcal{I} \models \beta$;
- $\mathcal{I} \models \alpha \vee \beta$ if $\mathcal{I} \models \alpha$ or $\mathcal{I} \models \beta$.

For $\alpha \in \mathcal{GL}$, let $\mathcal{M}(\alpha)$ be the set of models of α. α is *satisfiable* (or *consistent*) if $\mathcal{M}(\alpha) \neq \varnothing$ and α is a *tautology* if $\mathcal{M}(\alpha) = \Omega$. For example, $\bot$ is unsatisfiable and $\top$ is a tautology. The relation $\alpha \models \beta$ means that $\mathcal{M}(\alpha) \subseteq \mathcal{M}(\beta)$. The relation $\alpha \equiv \beta$ means that $\mathcal{M}(\alpha) = \mathcal{M}(\beta)$. If $\mathcal{B}$ is a set of formulas, $\mathcal{M}(\mathcal{B}) = \bigcap\{\mathcal{M}(\alpha) \mid \alpha \in \mathcal{B}\}$. Then $\mathcal{B} \models \alpha$ means that $\mathcal{M}(\mathcal{B}) \subseteq \mathcal{M}(\alpha)$.

3.3 About the Expressivity of $(\mathcal{GL}, \models)$

Each variable a of $(\mathcal{GL}, \models)$ has the same range $\mathcal{G}$: for every $\mathcal{I} \in \Omega$, $\mathcal{I}(a) \in \mathcal{G}$. A slight modification of $(\mathcal{GL}, \models)$ consists in specifying the range of each variable (e.g. $\mathbb{B}$, $\mathbb{Z}$, $\mathbb{Q}$, an integer interval $[\![m, n]\!]$ or a rational interval $[r, s]$ — $m, n \in \mathbb{Z}$, $r, s \in \mathbb{Q}$). Therefore, this formalism contains attribute-value formalisms (with attribute ranges limited to numbers, Booleans, and enumerated type) and hierarchies (a hierarchy being represented by a set of implications, e.g. $(\mathtt{apple} = 1) \rightarrow (\mathtt{fruit} = 1)$ states that every apple is a fruit). For the sake of simplicity, in this study, we stick to static logic $(\mathcal{GL}, \models)$, considering that the extension with variable types should not be difficult to integrate.

3.4 Representing Cases in $(\mathcal{GL}, \models)$

According to Sect. 2, the sets $\mathcal{P}$ and $\mathcal{S}$ are assumed to be disjoint. This suggests partitioning the set of variables into $\{\mathcal{V}_\mathcal{P}, \mathcal{V}_\mathcal{S}\}$: $\mathcal{V}_\mathcal{P}$ (resp., $\mathcal{V}_\mathcal{S}$) is the set of *problem variables* (resp., *solution variables*). Thus, a problem (resp., a solution) is represented by a formula whose set of variables is in $\mathcal{V}_\mathcal{P}$ (resp., in $\mathcal{V}_\mathcal{S}$). So, a case $(\mathtt{x}, \mathtt{y}) \in \mathcal{P} \times \mathcal{S}$ can be written $\mathtt{x} \wedge \mathtt{y}$: finding the problem part $\mathtt{x}$ and the solution part $\mathtt{y}$ of $\mathtt{x} \wedge \mathtt{y}$ is easy since $\mathcal{V}_\mathcal{P} \cap \mathcal{V}_\mathcal{S} = \varnothing$.

Moreover, it has been assumed that the source cases $(\mathtt{x}^s, \mathtt{y}^s)$ represent specific pieces of experience. This means that for every $(\mathtt{x}^s, \mathtt{y}^s) \in \mathtt{CB}$, $\mathcal{M}(\mathtt{x}^s \wedge \mathtt{y}^s)$ is a singleton $\{\mathcal{I}^s\}$. Therefore, $\mathtt{x}^s$ and $\mathtt{y}^s$ can be written as atom conjunction on all variables of, respectively, $\mathcal{V}_\mathcal{P}$ and $\mathcal{V}_\mathcal{S}$: $\mathtt{x}^s \equiv \bigwedge_{a \in \mathcal{V}_\mathcal{P}} (a = \mathcal{I}^s(a))$ and $\mathtt{y}^s \equiv \bigwedge_{a \in \mathcal{V}_\mathcal{S}} (a = \mathcal{I}^s(a))$.

4 The Variation Logic $(\Delta\mathcal{GL}, \models)$

Given a static logic that can be used to represent cases and domain knowledge, a variation logic can be defined for representing, in particular, adaptation knowledge. This section describes the variation logic $(\Delta\mathcal{GL}, \models)$ built from the static logic $(\mathcal{GL}, \models)$: its syntax, its semantics, some of its properties, and some operators on these logics that are useful for representing adaptation rules.

4.1 Syntax of $(\Delta\mathcal{GL}, \models)$

To start with an example, let $\varphi = a^{+5} \wedge \neg b^{8\bullet} \wedge b^{\bullet 2}$ be a formula of this logic, for $\mathcal{G} = \mathbb{Z}$. φ indicates a change in the attribute a from a value r, for some $r \in \mathbb{Z}$, to the value $r + 5$, and a change in the attribute b from any value different from 8 to the value 2. The expressions $+5$, $8\bullet$, and $\bullet 2$ that occur in φ are called variation symbols.

More generally, the set of *variation symbols* is defined by:

$$\mathcal{D} = \{+r, \quad r\bullet, \quad \bullet r \mid r \in \mathcal{G}\}$$

An extra variation symbol $-r$ is defined as an abbreviation of $+(-r)$.

An *atom* of $(\Delta\mathcal{GL}, \models)$ is an expression of the form a^v where a is a variable and v is a variation symbol. A *formula* of $(\Delta\mathcal{GL}, \models)$ is an atom of this logic or of one of the forms $\bot$, $\top$, $\neg\varphi$, $\varphi \wedge \psi$ and $\varphi \vee \psi$ where φ and ψ are two formulas of this logic. The other connectives are defined as abbreviations. The set of formulas is denoted by $\Delta\mathcal{GL}$. A *variation formula* is an element of $\Delta\mathcal{GL}$. The set of variables that occur in $\varphi \in \Delta\mathcal{GL}$ is denoted by $\mathcal{V}(\varphi)$.

A *positive literal* of $(\Delta\mathcal{GL}, \models)$ is an atom a^v of this logic. A *negative literal* is of the form $\neg a^v$ where a^v is an atom. A *cube* of this logic is a conjunction of literals. $\bot$ is also considered as a cube ($\bot$ can be seen as the conjunction $A \wedge \neg A$ where A is a fixed and arbitrarily chosen atom).

4.2 Semantics of $(\Delta\mathcal{GL}, \models)$

Any variation symbol v is interpreted as a binary relation over $\mathcal{G}$. Formally, to every $v \in \mathcal{D}$ is associated $\langle v \rangle \subseteq \mathcal{G} \times \mathcal{G}$ defined in the following way (for $r \in \mathcal{G}$):

$$\langle +r \rangle = \{(x, y) \in \mathcal{G}^2 \mid y = x + r\} \quad \langle r\bullet \rangle = \{(r, x) \mid x \in \mathcal{G}\} \quad \langle \bullet r \rangle = \{(x, r) \mid x \in \mathcal{G}\}$$

Let $\Delta\Omega = \Omega \times \Omega$ be the set of interpretations used to define the semantics of $(\Delta\mathcal{GL}, \models)$: an interpretation of $\Delta\Omega$ is therefore an ordered pair $(\mathcal{I}, \mathcal{J})$ of Ω. In the following, $(\mathcal{I}, \mathcal{J})$ is simply written as $\mathcal{IJ}$.

The fact that $\mathcal{IJ} \in \Delta\Omega$ is a model of a $\varphi \in \Delta\mathcal{GL}$ is defined recursively as follows:

- $\mathcal{IJ} \models a^v$ if $(\mathcal{I}(a), \mathcal{J}(a)) \in \langle v \rangle$, for any atom a^v of $(\Delta\mathcal{GL}, \models)$;
- $\mathcal{IJ} \models \neg\varphi$ if $\mathcal{IJ} \not\models \varphi$, for $\varphi \in \Delta\mathcal{GL}$;

- $\mathcal{IJ} \models \varphi \wedge \psi$ if $\mathcal{IJ} \models \varphi$ and $\mathcal{IJ} \models \psi$, for $\varphi, \psi \in \Delta\mathcal{GL}$;
- $\mathcal{IJ} \models \varphi \vee \psi$ if $\mathcal{IJ} \models \varphi$ or $\mathcal{IJ} \models \psi$, for $\varphi, \psi \in \Delta\mathcal{GL}$.

The set of models of $\varphi \in \Delta\mathcal{GL}$ is denoted by $\mathcal{M}(\varphi)$. For a knowledge base $\mathcal{B}$ of $(\Delta\mathcal{GL}, \models)$, $\mathcal{M}(\mathcal{B}) = \bigcap\{\mathcal{M}(\varphi) \mid \varphi \in \mathcal{B}\}$. Then, the entailment is defined as usual: $\varphi \models \psi$ if $\mathcal{M}(\varphi) \subseteq \mathcal{M}(\psi)$ and $\mathcal{B} \models \varphi$ if $\mathcal{M}(\mathcal{B}) \subseteq \mathcal{M}(\psi)$. Finally, φ is *satisfiable* (or *consistent*) means that $\mathcal{M}(\varphi) \neq \varnothing$.

In the introduction, another variation symbol was used: $=r$ (for $r \in \mathcal{G}$). It has the following semantics (for $a \in \mathcal{V}$): $\mathcal{IJ} \models a^{=r}$ if $\mathcal{I}(a) = \mathcal{J}(a) = r$. Thus, $a^{=r}$ can be seen as an abbreviation of the cube $a^{r\bullet} \wedge a^{\bullet r} \wedge a^{+0}$.

4.3 Basic Properties of $(\Delta\mathcal{GL}, \models)$

Proposition 1. *Given a conjunction of two literals ℓ_1 and ℓ_2 on the same variable a, a third literal ℓ_3 can be deduced for some forms of the literals ℓ_1 and ℓ_2 (for $r, s \in \mathcal{G}$), thus $\ell_1 \wedge \ell_2 \equiv \ell_1 \wedge \ell_2 \wedge \ell_3$:*

$$\begin{array}{lll|}
a^{r\bullet} \wedge a^{\bullet s} \models a^{+(s-r)} & a^{+r} \wedge a^{s\bullet} \models a^{\bullet(r+s)} & a^{+r} \wedge a^{\bullet s} \models a^{(s-r)\bullet} \\
a^{r\bullet} \wedge \neg a^{\bullet s} \models \neg a^{+(s-r)} & a^{\bullet r} \wedge \neg a^{s\bullet} \models \neg a^{+(r-s)} & a^{+r} \wedge \neg a^{s\bullet} \models \neg a^{\bullet(r+s)} \\
a^{\bullet r} \wedge \neg a^{s\bullet} \models \neg a^{+(r-s)} & a^{r\bullet} \wedge \neg a^{\bullet s} \models \neg a^{+(s-r)} & a^{r\bullet} \wedge \neg a^{+s} \models \neg a^{\bullet(r+s)}
\end{array} \quad (1)$$

Definition 1 (Normal forms DNF and DNFNC). *A variation formula φ is in DNF (disjunctive normal form) if it is a disjunction of cubes: $\varphi = \theta_1 \vee \theta_2 \vee \ldots \vee \theta_p$ where θ_k is a cube.*

Let θ be a $(\Delta\mathcal{GL}, \models)$ cube with a sole variable a. θ is normal if one of the following conditions holds

(i) $\theta = \bot$;
(ii) θ contains exactly 3 positive literals, of the forms $a^{r\bullet}$, $a^{\bullet s}$ and a^{+t} with $r, s, t \in \mathcal{G}$ and $t = s - r$, and it does not contain any negative literal;
(iii) θ contains exactly 1 positive literal a^v and p negative literals ($p \in \mathbb{N}$) m_1, $m_2, \ldots, m_p$ that use variation symbols of a different form from the form of v (e.g. if $v = +r$ then $m_k = \neg a^w$ with $w \neq +s$ for any $s \in \mathcal{G}$); furthermore, for every negative literal $\neg a^w$, θ contains also the consequence $\neg a^x$ of $a^v \wedge \neg a^w$ according to Proposition 1 (e.g. if $v = +r$ and $w = s\bullet$, then $x = \bullet(s + r)$);
(iv) θ contains only negative literals of any kind.

Let θ be a $(\Delta\mathcal{GL}, \models)$ cube. For a, a variable occurring in θ, let θ_a be the conjunction of literals of θ with variable a. θ is a normal cube *if every θ_a is normal, for each a, variable of θ.*

A formula $\varphi \in \Delta\mathcal{GL}$ is under DNFNC (DNF with normal cubes) if it is under DNF and if every cube composing it is normal.

Proposition 2. *Every formula $\varphi \in \Delta\mathcal{GL}$ can be put under DNF and under DNFNC: there exists $\varphi_{\text{DNF}} \in \Delta\mathcal{GL}$ (resp. $\varphi_{\text{DNFNC}} \in \Delta\mathcal{GL}$) that is under DNF (resp. DNFNC) such that $\varphi \equiv \varphi_{\text{DNF}}$ (resp. $\varphi \equiv \varphi_{\text{DNFNC}}$).*

The fact that φ can be put in DNF is proven as it is proven, e.g., in propositional logic. The fact that any cube can be normalized relies in particular on Proposition 1.

As in many logics, the entailment problem and the satisfiability problem are tightly linked in $(\Delta\mathcal{GL}, \models)$. For example, $\{\varphi_1, \varphi_2\} \models \psi$ iff $\varphi_1 \wedge \varphi_2 \wedge \neg\psi$ is not satisfiable. Now, the satisfiability problem can be computed using the principles of the tableaux method (see e.g. [11]), which, with a logic using propositional connectives, amounts to build a DNF formula represented by a tree (each branch of the tree represents a cube). The following proposition is then useful for designing an algorithm based on the tableaux method for $(\Delta\mathcal{GL}, \models)$:

Proposition 3. *The following results can be used to determine whether a variation formula is satisfiable or not:*

(a) *For $\varphi \in \Delta\mathcal{GL}$, let φ_{DNF} be a formula under DNF such that $\varphi_{\text{DNF}} \equiv \varphi$. Then φ is satisfiable iff φ_{DNF} is satisfiable.*
(b) *Let $\varphi \in \Delta\mathcal{GL}$ be a formula under DNF: $\varphi = \theta_1 \vee \theta_2 \ldots \vee \theta_p$ where each θ_k is a cube of $(\Delta\mathcal{GL}, \models)$. Then φ is satisfiable iff at least one θ_k is satisfiable ($k \in [\![1, p]\!]$).*
(c) *Let θ be a normal cube of $(\Delta\mathcal{GL}, \models)$. For a, any variable occurring in θ, let θ_a be the conjunction of the literals of θ having a as variable. Then θ is satisfiable iff every θ_a is satisfiable.*
(d) *A normal cube θ_a with only one variable is satisfiable iff $\theta_a \not\equiv \bot$ (this means that if any of the conditions (ii), (iii) and (iv) of Definition 1 holds, then θ_a is satisfiable).*

4.4 Operators on $(\Delta\mathcal{GL}, \models)$

This section presents different operators on the logic $(\Delta\mathcal{GL}, \models)$ that are used in the next sections. Each of them has a semantical definition and satisfies the principle of irrelevance of syntax: if a formula occurring in the definition of an operator is replaced with an equivalent formula, then the result of applying the operator is unchanged up to the logical equivalence. Each of these operators is either defined within a classical definition or within a proposition which states its existence. The proofs of the propositions are given in the report [3]. Then, the ways the operators are computed are described when the formulas involved are cubes.

A variation formula φ can be seen as a representation of a binary relation on Ω, since $\mathcal{M}(\varphi) \subseteq \Omega \times \Omega$. The following proposition shows that the inverse of a relation $\mathcal{M}(\varphi)$ can be represented by a variation formula $\overleftarrow{\varphi}$.

Proposition 4. *For every $\varphi \in \Delta\mathcal{GL}$ there exists a variation formula denoted by $\overleftarrow{\varphi}$ such that*

$$\mathcal{M}(\overleftarrow{\varphi}) = \{\mathcal{JI} \mid \mathcal{IJ} \in \mathcal{M}(\varphi)\}$$

In other terms, $\mathcal{JI} \models \overleftarrow{\varphi}$ iff $\mathcal{IJ} \models \varphi$.

The computation of $\overleftarrow{\varphi}$ is linear: it consists in replacing every occurrence of a variation symbol v by $\overleftarrow{v}$ according to the following equalities:

$$\overleftarrow{{+}r} = {-}r \qquad \overleftarrow{r\bullet} = \bullet r \qquad \overleftarrow{\bullet r} = r\bullet \qquad\qquad (\text{for } r \in \mathcal{G})$$

For example, $\overleftarrow{a^{+1} \wedge a^{\bullet 2} \wedge c^{-2}} = a^{-1} \wedge a^{2\bullet} \wedge c^{+2}$.

Proposition 5. *For every* $\alpha, \beta \in \mathcal{GL}$ *there exists a formula of* $(\Delta\mathcal{GL}, \models)$ *denoted by* $\alpha \rhd \beta$ *and read "*α becomes β*", such that* $\mathcal{M}(\alpha \rhd \beta) = \mathcal{M}(\alpha) \times \mathcal{M}(\beta)$.
In other terms, $\mathcal{IJ} \models \alpha \rhd \beta$ *iff* $\mathcal{I} \models \alpha$ *and* $\mathcal{J} \models \beta$.

Now, let $\bigwedge_{i=1}^{p} \ell_i$ and $\bigwedge_{j=1}^{q} m_j$ be two cubes: $\ell_1, \ell_2, \ldots, \ell_p, m_1, m_2, \ldots, m_q$ are $p+q$ literals. The application of $\rhd$ on these cubes can be computed this way:

$$\left(\bigwedge_{i=1}^{p} \ell_i\right) \rhd \left(\bigwedge_{j=1}^{q} m_j\right) \equiv \left(\bigwedge_{i=1}^{p} \ell_i \rhd \top\right) \wedge \left(\bigwedge_{j=1}^{q} \top \rhd m_j\right) \tag{2}$$

Finally, it is sufficient to define $\alpha \rhd \beta$ when one of α and β is a literal and the other one is $\top$ (for $a \in \mathcal{V}$ and $r \in \mathcal{G}$):

$$\begin{array}{ll} (a = r) \rhd \top \equiv a^{r\bullet} & \neg(a = r) \rhd \top \equiv \neg a^{r\bullet} \\ \top \rhd (a = r) \equiv a^{\bullet r} & \top \rhd \neg(a = r) \equiv \neg a^{\bullet r} \end{array} \tag{3}$$

The operator $\rhd$ can be used for adaptation knowledge learning using the difference heuristics, as introduced in Sect. 1. Let us consider the following source cases expressed in $(\mathcal{GL}, \models)$ with $\mathcal{G} = \mathbb{Z}$ and where $\mathcal{V}_{\mathcal{P}} = \{a, b\}$ and $\mathcal{V}_{\mathcal{S}} = \{c, d\}$.

$$\begin{array}{rcl} \mathrm{x}^1 \wedge \mathrm{y}^1 & = & (a = 1) \wedge (b = 2) \wedge (c = 3) \wedge (d = 4) \\ \mathrm{x}^2 \wedge \mathrm{y}^2 & = & (a = 2) \wedge (b = 0) \wedge (c = 2) \wedge (d = 6) \\ \mathrm{x}^3 \wedge \mathrm{y}^3 & = & (a = 3) \wedge (b = 1) \wedge (c = 1) \wedge (d = 8) \end{array}$$

The variation from case $(\mathrm{x}^k, \mathrm{y}^k)$ to case $(\mathrm{x}^\ell, \mathrm{y}^\ell)$ is represented by $\Delta^{k\ell} = \mathrm{x}^k \wedge \mathrm{y}^k \rhd \mathrm{x}^\ell \wedge \mathrm{y}^\ell$. According to what is presented above, since the source cases $\mathrm{x}^s \wedge \mathrm{y}^s$ are conjunctions of positive literals of $(\mathcal{PL}, \models)$, the result $\Delta^{k\ell}$ is a conjunction of atoms of the forms $a^{r\bullet}$ and $a^{\bullet r}$ $(r \in \mathcal{G})$. Now, using the first entailment of (1), atoms of the forms a^{+r} are added to $\Delta^{k\ell}$, that highlight the variations. For example

$$\Delta^{12} \equiv a^{+1} \wedge a^{1\bullet} \wedge a^{\bullet 2} \wedge b^{-2} \wedge b^{2\bullet} \wedge b^{\bullet 0} \wedge c^{-1} \wedge c^{3\bullet} \wedge c^{\bullet 2} \wedge d^{+2} \wedge d^{4\bullet} \wedge d^{\bullet 6}$$

Using a frequent itemset extraction algorithm [7] on the training set $\{\Delta^{k\ell}\}_{k\ell}$ makes it possible to point out sets of atoms a^v occurring jointly in subsets of the training set. For example, for $(k, \ell) \in \{(1, 2), (2, 3)\}$, the itemset $\{a^{+1}, c^{-1}, d^{+2}\}$ can be made explicit, giving birth to the formula $\varphi = a^{+1} \wedge c^{-1} \wedge d^{+2}$ that can be used for representing an adaptation rule, as this can be seen further. Notice that $\overleftarrow{\varphi}$ can also be learnt, corresponding to $(k, \ell) \in \{(2, 1), (3, 2)\}$.

Proposition 6. *For every $\varphi \in \Delta\mathcal{GL}$, there exist $\mathsf{L}(\varphi) \in \mathcal{GL}$ and $\mathsf{R}(\varphi) \in \mathcal{GL}$ (the* left *and* right *projections of φ) such that:*

$$\mathcal{M}(\mathsf{L}(\varphi)) = \{\mathcal{I} \in \Omega \mid \textit{there exists } \mathcal{J} \in \Omega, \mathcal{I}\mathcal{J} \models \varphi\} \quad \textit{and}$$
$$\mathcal{M}(\mathsf{R}(\varphi)) = \{\mathcal{J} \in \Omega \mid \textit{there exists } \mathcal{I} \in \Omega, \mathcal{I}\mathcal{J} \models \varphi\}$$

$\mathcal{I}\mathcal{J} \models \varphi$ iff $\mathcal{I} \models \mathsf{L}(\varphi)$ and $\mathcal{J} \models \mathsf{R}(\varphi)$.

If α and β are two satisfiable formulas of $(\mathcal{GL}, \models)$ then $\mathsf{L}(\alpha \triangleright \beta) \equiv \alpha$ and $\mathsf{R}(\alpha \triangleright \beta) \equiv \beta$.

The computation of the let and right projections of a cube can be performed by putting this cube into normal form and using the following equivalences:

$$\text{if } \varphi = \bigwedge_{k=1}^{p} \ell_k \text{ is a normal cube, then } \mathsf{L}(\varphi) \equiv \bigwedge_{k=1}^{p} \mathsf{L}(\ell_k) \text{ and } \mathsf{R}(\varphi) \equiv \bigwedge_{k=1}^{p} \mathsf{R}(\ell_k)$$
$$\mathsf{L}(a^{+r}) \equiv \mathsf{R}(a^{+r}) \equiv \mathsf{L}(a^{\bullet r}) \equiv \mathsf{R}(a^{r\bullet}) \equiv \top$$
$$\mathsf{L}(\neg a^{+r}) \equiv \mathsf{R}(\neg a^{+r}) \equiv \mathsf{L}(\neg a^{\bullet r}) \equiv \mathsf{R}(\neg a^{r\bullet}) \equiv \top$$
$$\mathsf{L}(a^{r\bullet}) \equiv (a = r) \quad \mathsf{L}(\neg a^{r\bullet}) \equiv \neg(a = r) \quad \mathsf{R}(a^{\bullet r}) \equiv (a = r) \quad \mathsf{R}(\neg a^{\bullet r}) \equiv \neg(a = r)$$

Definition 2. *Let $\varphi \in \Delta\mathcal{GL}$ and $a \in \mathcal{V}$. a is said to be an* invariant variable *of φ if there exists $\psi \in \Delta\mathcal{GL}$ such that $\varphi \equiv \psi$ and $a \notin \mathcal{V}(\psi)$. The set of invariant variables of φ is denoted by $\mathsf{Inv}(\varphi)$. So, $\mathcal{V} \setminus \mathcal{V}(\varphi) \subseteq \mathsf{Inv}(\varphi) \subseteq \mathcal{V}$.*

A variable of a normal cube θ is invariant iff $a \notin \mathcal{V}(\theta)$. By contrast, there exist variation formulas φ such that $\mathsf{Inv}(\varphi) \neq \mathcal{V} \setminus \mathcal{V}(\varphi)$, for example $\varphi = (a^{+1} \wedge a^{+2}) \vee b^{4\bullet}$: $a \in \mathcal{V}(\varphi)$ but $a \in \mathsf{Inv}(\varphi)$ since $\varphi \equiv b^{4\bullet}$.

5 Representing Adaptation Rules

The $(\Delta\mathcal{GL}, \models)$ representation formalism has been designed to represent variations between source cases for the purpose of adaptation knowledge learning. If the output of such a learning process is a set of adaptation rules, these rules could be represented in this logic, and this is what is examined in this section.

5.1 Motivating Example and Introduction of the Ceteris Paribus

Let us consider again the adaptation rule of the cooking domain considered in the Introduction. Conjunctively written, it corresponds to the $(\Delta\mathcal{GL}, \models)$ cube, for $\mathcal{G} = \mathbb{Q}$: $\varphi = \texttt{dessert}^{=1} \wedge \texttt{\#eggs}^{-2} \wedge \texttt{\#bananas}^{+1}$. Now, consider a dessert recipe with 2 eggs, no banana, 50 grams of flour, and 20 grams of butter. This is represented by the $(\mathcal{GL}, \models)$ formula $\alpha = (\texttt{dessert} = 1) \wedge (\texttt{\#eggs} = 2) \wedge (\texttt{\#bananas} = 0) \wedge (\texttt{flour}_{\texttt{gram}} = 50) \wedge (\texttt{butter}_{\texttt{gram}} = 20)$ (not taking into account any other variable). How could the variation formula φ be applied to α?

To answer this question, the idea is first to define the variation formula θ that represents the transformation of α by φ: the expected result is then $\beta = \mathsf{R}(\theta)$. Let $\mathcal{I}\mathcal{J}$ be a model of θ. This transformation starts from α, so $\mathcal{I}$ should be a model of α, which is equivalent to write that (a) $\mathcal{I}\mathcal{J} \models \alpha \rhd \top$. Furthermore, θ should specialize φ, i.e. $\theta \models \varphi$, which entails that (b) $\mathcal{I}\mathcal{J} \models \varphi$. If (a) and (b) were the only conditions for $\mathcal{I}\mathcal{J}$ this would involve $\theta \equiv (\alpha \rhd \top) \wedge \varphi$ so, in this example, the result of the application would be $\beta = (\texttt{dessert} = 1) \wedge (\texttt{\#eggs} = 0) \wedge (\texttt{\#bananas} = 1)$. For variables $\texttt{flour}_{\texttt{gram}}$ and $\texttt{butter}_{\texttt{gram}}$, this raises a problem: they are not bound in β. Indeed, each of these variables is invariant in φ. Now, the following statement is made: if a variable is invariant in φ, then the application of φ on α should leave this variable unchanged. This suggests a third condition: (c) if $a \in \mathsf{Inv}(\varphi)$ then a is interpreted in α the same way as in β; formally $\{\mathcal{I}(a) \mid \mathcal{I}\mathcal{J} \in \mathcal{M}(\theta)\} = \{\mathcal{J}(a) \mid \mathcal{I}\mathcal{J} \in \mathcal{M}(\theta)\}$. If α, as in the example, is a cube, condition (c) means simply that if a literal ℓ with variable a occurs in α then β contains the same literal ℓ. Another way of formulating it consists of adding to φ the conjuncts a^{+0} for any $a \in \mathsf{Inv}(\varphi)$, leading to a formula denoted by $\mathsf{cp}(\varphi)$, formally defined below, in Definition 3.

So, taking into account the additional condition (c) leads to the following transformation θ and application β:

$$\begin{aligned}\theta = {} & \texttt{dessert}^{1\bullet} \wedge \texttt{dessert}^{=1} \wedge \texttt{\#eggs}^{2\bullet} \wedge \texttt{\#eggs}^{-2} \wedge \texttt{\#bananas}^{0\bullet} \wedge \texttt{\#bananas}^{+1} \\ & \wedge \texttt{flour}^{50\bullet}_{\texttt{gram}} \wedge \texttt{flour}^{+0}_{\texttt{gram}} \wedge \texttt{butter}^{20\bullet}_{\texttt{gram}} \wedge \texttt{butter}^{+0}_{\texttt{gram}} \\ \beta = {} & (\texttt{dessert} = 1) \wedge (\texttt{\#eggs} = 0) \wedge (\texttt{\#bananas} = 1) \\ & \wedge (\texttt{flour}_{\texttt{gram}} = 50) \wedge (\texttt{butter}_{\texttt{gram}} = 20)\end{aligned}$$

Now, the definition of $\mathsf{cp}(\varphi)$ can be given.

Definition 3. *Let $\alpha, \gamma \in \mathcal{GL}$, $\varphi \in \Delta\mathcal{GL}$, $\mathcal{W} \subseteq \mathcal{V}$ with $\mathcal{W} \neq \varnothing$. The* ceteris paribus[2] *of φ wrt $\mathcal{W}$ is defined by*

$$\mathsf{cp}_{\mathcal{W}}(\varphi) = \varphi \wedge \bigwedge \{a^{+0} \mid a \in \mathsf{Inv}(\varphi) \cap \mathcal{W}\}$$

$\mathsf{cp}(\varphi)$ *is an abbreviation of* $\mathsf{cp}_{\mathcal{V}}(\varphi)$ *(every variable is considered in* $\mathsf{cp}(\varphi)$*).*

5.2 Applying a Variation Formula on a Static Formula

From what precedes, the transformation of α by φ is $\theta = (\alpha \rhd \top) \wedge \mathsf{cp}(\varphi)$ and the result of this transformation is $\beta = \mathsf{R}(\theta)$. Now, a constraint can be added to the result of this transformation. If this constraint is represented by $\gamma \in \mathcal{GL}$, then it is possible to define the transformation and the application taking into account γ:

Definition 4. *Let $\alpha, \gamma \in \mathcal{GL}$ and $\varphi \in \Delta\mathcal{GL}$. The transformation on α of φ with constraint γ is the formula* $\mathsf{transf}(\alpha, \varphi, \gamma) \in \Delta\mathcal{GL}$ *defined by*

$$\mathsf{transf}(\alpha, \varphi, \gamma) = (\alpha \rhd \gamma) \wedge \mathsf{cp}(\varphi)$$

[2] The Latin expression *ceteris paribus* means "other things being equal".

The application on α *of* φ *with constraint* γ *is the formula* $\mathsf{appl}(\alpha, \varphi, \gamma) \in \mathcal{GL}$ *defined by*

$$\mathsf{appl}(\alpha, \varphi, \gamma) = \mathsf{R}(\mathsf{transf}(\alpha, \varphi, \gamma)) = \mathsf{R}((\alpha \rhd \gamma) \wedge \mathsf{cp}(\varphi))$$

The transformation (resp. application) on α of φ without any constraint is simply $\mathsf{transf}(\alpha, \varphi, \top)$ (resp. $\mathsf{appl}(\alpha, \varphi, \top)$).

5.3 Adaptation Rule Representation

Let $\mathtt{adPb} = ((\mathtt{x}^s, \mathtt{y}^s), \mathtt{x}^{\mathtt{tgt}}) \in \mathtt{CB} \times \mathcal{P}$ be an adaptation problem and $\mathtt{ar}$ be an adaptation rule. Three questions are raised: (Q1) Is $\mathtt{ar}$ applicable to solve $\mathtt{adPb}$? (Q2) If the answer to the previous question is yes, what is the result $\mathtt{y}^{\mathtt{tgt}} \in \mathcal{S}$ of applying $\mathtt{ar}$ on $\mathtt{adPb}$? (Q3) How reliable is the assertion "$\mathtt{y}^{\mathtt{tgt}}$ solves $\mathtt{x}^{\mathtt{tgt}}$"? To answer questions (Q1) and (Q2), a variation formula φ is used, as explained below. To answer (Q3), a positive number $\mathtt{cost}$ is given that characterizes the adaptation effort, that is, the risk taken by applying $\mathtt{ar}$ to an adaptation problem (the higher $\mathtt{cost}$, the more risky the adaptation is).

In the following, a proposal to formalize an adaptation rule and the way questions (Q1) to (Q3) are answered is given:

Definition 5. *An* adaptation rule *is a pair* $\mathtt{ar} = (\varphi, \mathtt{cost})$ *where* φ *is a variation formula and* $\mathtt{cost}$ *is a positive rational number called* cost *of* $\mathtt{ar}$.

Let $\mathtt{adPb} = ((\mathtt{x}^s, \mathtt{y}^s), \mathtt{x}^{\mathtt{tgt}})$ *be an adaptation problem. The application of* $\mathtt{ar}$ *on* $\mathtt{adPb}$ *is the following static formula:*

$$\beta = \mathsf{appl}(\mathtt{x}^s \wedge \mathtt{y}^s, \varphi, \mathtt{x}^{\mathtt{tgt}})$$

The rule $\mathtt{ar}$ *is said to be* applicable *on* $\mathtt{adPb}$ *if* β *is satisfiable.*

If $\mathtt{ar}$ *is applicable on* $\mathtt{adPb}$ *then the* application *of* $\mathtt{ar}$ *on* $\mathtt{adPb}$ *gives a satisfiable solution* $\mathtt{y}^{\mathtt{tgt}}$ *such that* $\beta \equiv \mathtt{x}^{\mathtt{tgt}} \wedge \mathtt{y}^{\mathtt{tgt}}$*. The value* $\mathtt{cost}$ *characterizes the reliability of the assertion "*$\mathtt{y}^{\mathtt{tgt}}$ *solves* $\mathtt{x}^{\mathtt{tgt}}$*" (the lower the cost, the more reliable this assertion is supposed to be).*

To take the example of Sect. 5.1, with $\mathtt{x}^s \wedge \mathtt{y}^s = \alpha$ and $\mathtt{x}^{\mathtt{tgt}} = (\mathtt{dessert} = 1) \wedge (\mathtt{\#eggs} = 0)$ ("I want a dessert without eggs.") then $\mathtt{ar} = (\varphi, \mathtt{cost})$ is applicable to the adaptation problem $\mathtt{adPb} = ((\mathtt{x}^s, \mathtt{y}^s), \mathtt{x}^{\mathtt{tgt}})$ and results in $\mathtt{y}^{\mathtt{tgt}} = (\mathtt{\#bananas} = 1) \wedge (\mathtt{flour}_{\mathtt{gram}} = 50) \wedge (\mathtt{butter}_{\mathtt{gram}} = 20)$.

6 An Algorithm for Retrieval and Adaptation

In this section, a case-based inference algorithm is presented for the particular $\mathcal{G} = \mathbb{B} = \{0, 1\}$ (subset of the group $(\mathbb{Z}, +)$).

Let $\mathtt{AK}$ be the set of adaptation rules: for $\mathtt{ar} \in \mathtt{AK}$, $\mathtt{ar} = (\varphi, \mathtt{cost})$ where $\varphi \in \Delta\mathcal{GL}$ and $\mathtt{cost} \in \mathbb{Q}$, $\mathtt{cost} > 0$. For practical purposes, it is assumed that, after a normalization process, $\mathtt{cost}$ is low compared to 1.

The measure of dissimilarity associated with AK, denoted by $\mathtt{diss}_{\mathtt{AK}}$, is the function that associates with $(\alpha, \beta) \in \mathcal{GL}^2$ the value $\mathtt{cost}(\mathtt{AP})$ where AP is the adaptation path of lowest cost relating α to β. Formally, an adaptation path from α to β is a sequence $\mathtt{AP} = \mathtt{ar}^1; \mathtt{ar}^2; \ldots; \mathtt{ar}^q$ of adaptation rules $\mathtt{ar}^k = (\varphi_k, \mathtt{cost}_k)$ such that, with $\alpha_0 = \alpha$, $\alpha_k = \mathsf{appl}(\alpha_{k-1}, \varphi_k, \top)$ for $k \in [\![1, q]\!]$, and α_q is consistent with β. Then $\mathtt{cost}(\mathtt{AP}) = \sum_{k=1}^{q} \mathtt{cost}_k$. If there is no similarity path from α to β then $\mathtt{diss}_{\mathtt{AK}}(\alpha, \beta) = \infty$. When $\mathtt{diss}_{\mathtt{AK}}(\alpha, \beta) = 0$, the corresponding adaptation path is empty ($q = 0$), thus $\alpha \wedge \beta$ is consistent.

To avoid the situation $\mathtt{diss}_{\mathtt{AK}}(\alpha, \beta) = \infty$ for two consistent static formulas α and β, some adaptation rules can be added to AK to obtain $\widehat{\mathtt{AK}}$ defined by

$$\widehat{\mathtt{AK}} = \left\{(a^{+1}, 1), (a^{-1}, 1) \mid a \in \mathcal{V}_{\mathcal{P}}\right\}$$

The additional adaptation rules $(a^{+1}, 1)$ and $(a^{-1}, 1)$ have a high cost of 1 (relatively to the costs of the other adaptation rules) and so are triggered mainly when α and β could not be related otherwise. They correspond to null adaptations (as *default* adaptations) since they have no impact of the interpretation of solution variables.

Now, the specifications of the retrieval and adaptation algorithms are given.

Input: CB, AK, $\mathtt{x}^{\mathtt{tgt}} \in \mathcal{GL}$.

Retrieval: Find $(\mathtt{x}^s, \mathtt{y}^s) \in \mathtt{CB}$ that minimizes $\mathtt{diss}_{\widehat{\mathtt{AK}}}(\mathtt{x}^s \wedge \mathtt{y}^s, \mathtt{tgt})$, and the corresponding adaptation path AP from $\mathtt{x}^s \wedge \mathtt{y}^s$ to $\mathtt{x}^{\mathtt{tgt}}$.

Adaptation: Apply AP to $\mathtt{x}^s \wedge \mathtt{y}^s$ to obtain a consistent formula β such that $\beta \models \mathtt{x}^{\mathtt{tgt}}$, and let $\mathtt{y}^{\mathtt{tgt}}$ be such that $\beta \equiv \mathtt{x}^{\mathtt{tgt}} \wedge \mathtt{y}^{\mathtt{tgt}}$. $\mathtt{y}^{\mathtt{tgt}}$ is the output solution.

A naive retrieval algorithm (with a discouraging complexity) consists in finding AP by a best-first search in a state space:

- A state is a pair (α, C) where $\alpha \in \mathcal{GL}$ is consistent, $C \in \mathbb{Q}$ and $C \geq 0$.
- The set of initial states is $\{(\mathtt{x}^s \wedge \mathtt{y}^s, 0) \mid (\mathtt{x}^s, \mathtt{y}^s) \in \mathtt{CB}\}$.
- A successor of a state (α, C) is a state (β, C') for which there exists $\mathtt{ar} = (\varphi, \mathtt{cost}) \in \widehat{\mathtt{AK}}$ such that $\beta = \mathsf{appl}(\alpha, \varphi, \top)$ and $C' = C + \mathtt{cost}$.
- A final state (α, C) is such that $\alpha \wedge \mathtt{x}^{\mathtt{tgt}}$ is consistent.
- The states (α, C) are searched by non-decreasing C.

An A* search algorithm can be used for this purpose [9].

Let q be the length of the similarity path AP relating the retrieved case to the target problem. Let b be the average branching factor of the search ($b \leq \left|\widehat{\mathtt{AK}}\right|$ but is much lower in practice if, on the average, only few adaptation rules are applicable on a cube of $(\mathcal{GL}, \models)$). Under the assumptions of Sect. 3.4, and assuming also that the variation formulas of adaptation rules are cubes, it can be proven that the complexity of the retrieval algorithm is in $O\left(|\mathtt{CB}| \cdot |\mathcal{V}| \cdot b^q\right)$, thus proportional to the size of the case base. Case adaptation is fast: it consists mainly in using the value β of the application of AP on the retrieved case.

A less naive algorithm consists in going the other way round: from $\mathtt{x}^{\mathtt{tgt}}$ to source cases. For an adaptation rule $\mathtt{ar} = (\varphi, \mathtt{cost})$, let $\overleftarrow{\mathtt{ar}} = (\overleftarrow{\varphi}, \mathtt{cost})$. This algorithm consists in modifying the best-first search of the naive algorithm as follows:

- The set of adaptation rules is $\{\overleftarrow{\mathtt{ar}} \mid \mathtt{ar} \in \widehat{\mathtt{AK}}\}$.
- The sole initial state is $\mathtt{x}^{\mathtt{tgt}}$.
- A final state (α, C) is such that there exists $(\mathtt{x}^s, \mathtt{y}^s) \in \mathtt{CB}$ such that $\mathtt{x}^s \wedge \mathtt{y}^s \wedge \alpha$ is consistent. This exact match search can be performed in $O(|\mathcal{V}_\mathcal{P}|)$ thanks to an organization of the case base in a binary tree of depth $|\mathcal{V}_\mathcal{P}|$ (this point is detailed in [3]).

The output of this search is a retrieved case $(\mathtt{x}^s, \mathtt{y}^s) \in \mathtt{CB}$ and an adaptation path $\mathtt{AP} = \mathtt{ar}^1; \ldots; \mathtt{ar}^q$ from $\mathtt{x}^{\mathtt{tgt}}$ to $\mathtt{x}^s \wedge \mathtt{y}^s$. Then, the inverse adaptation path $\overleftarrow{\mathtt{AP}} = \overleftarrow{\mathtt{ar}^q}; \ldots; \overleftarrow{\mathtt{ar}^1}$ is computed, resulting in the same adaptation path as the one produced by the naive algorithm. Finally, adaptation consists in sequentially applying $\overleftarrow{\mathtt{AP}}$ on $\mathtt{x}^s \wedge \mathtt{y}^s$ (in q steps) to obtain $\beta \equiv \mathtt{x}^{\mathtt{tgt}} \wedge \mathtt{y}^{\mathtt{tgt}}$.

The complexity of this algorithm is in $O(|\mathcal{V}_\mathcal{P}| \cdot |\mathcal{V}| \cdot b^q)$, thus independent of the size of the case base (whereas the naive algorithm complexity is $|\mathtt{CB}|$ times higher because of the $|\mathtt{CB}|$ initial states). This is due to the use of a $O(|\mathcal{V}_\mathcal{P}|)$ exact match step of the algorithm and this is where the application of this algorithm gives another complexity for $\mathcal{G} \neq \mathbb{B}$.

The fact that this algorithm fulfills the specification and thus, gives the same result as the naive algorithm, is related to the following result:

Proposition 7. *Let* α *and* γ *be two cubes of* $(\mathcal{GL}, \models)$ *and* φ *be a cube of* $(\Delta\mathcal{GL}, \models)$. *Then* $\mathsf{appl}(\alpha, \varphi, \gamma) \not\models \bot$ *iff* $\mathsf{appl}(\gamma, \overleftarrow{\varphi}, \top) \wedge \alpha \not\models \bot$.

7 Discussion and Conclusion

This paper has presented a formal approach to represent variations between cases and adaptation rules, with an algorithm for single retrieval and adaptation. The retrieval is adaptation-guided [12]: the retrieved case is necessarily adaptable to solve the target problem, but beyond that, the retrieved case is the one that requires the least adaptation effort according to the costs associated with adaptation knowledge. Moreover, if all the attributes have a Boolean range, the retrieval complexity is independent of the size of the case base. Finally, the retrieval knowledge is determined by the adaptation knowledge: it is defined by the dissimilarity measure $\mathtt{diss}_{\widehat{\mathtt{AK}}}$. Although the approach presented in this paper could be implemented without an explicit representation in the logical formalisms $(\mathcal{GL}, \models)$ and $(\Delta\mathcal{GL}, \models)$, studying case-based inference from a logical point of view has at least two advantages. First, it is useful for studying the properties of these inferences at a semantic level (e.g., the properties of the retrieval algorithm). Second, it makes it possible to go beyond attribute value representation (taking into account disjunctions and negations, in particular, which makes it possible to use generalized cases and complex adaptation rules).

This theoretical work can be continued in several directions.

A first direction of work is to confront this approach with practical applications and/or benchmarks, using an adaptation knowledge learning system to feed $\mathtt{AK}$.

This work has mainly considered three knowledge containers of a CBR system: $\mathtt{CB}$ and $\mathtt{AK}$, obviously, but also the retrieval knowledge $\mathtt{diss}_{\widehat{\mathtt{AK}}}$ that is determined by $\mathtt{AK}$. Now, little attention has been given to domain knowledge represented by the set of static formulas $\mathtt{DK}$. For static knowledge (in particular cases), it consists mainly in defining the inferences modulo $\mathtt{DK}$ ($\alpha \models_{\mathtt{DK}} \beta$ if $\mathtt{DK} \cup \{\alpha\} \models \beta$, α is $\mathtt{DK}$-satisfiable if $\mathtt{DK} \cup \{\alpha\}$ is satisfiable, etc.). How can static knowledge $\mathtt{DK}$ be used for inference in $(\mathcal{\Delta G L}, \models)$ and adaptation rules is a question still requiring some consideration.

Olaaaf is an adaptation engine based on belief revision in a logic where atoms are linear constraints and which is propositionally closed [2]. Olaaaf inference engine mainly relies on $\mathtt{DK}$, the domain knowledge, and $\mathtt{diss}$, a measure of dissimilarity between interpretations. Some adaptation rules are "simulated" in Olaaaf by adding pieces of knowledge to $\mathtt{DK}$ and/or by modifying $\mathtt{diss}$, although this aspect of Olaaaf has not yet been investigated in detail. By contrast, the approach proposed in this paper is centered on $\mathtt{AK}$ (and its representation) and the dissimilarity measure $\mathtt{diss}_{\widehat{\mathtt{AK}}}$ comes as a byproduct. A direction of work worth investigating aims to find an integrated view of these two logic-based approaches to adaptation.

References

1. d'Aquin, M., Badra, F., Lafrogne, S., Lieber, J., Napoli, A., Szathmary, L.: Case base mining for adaptation knowledge acquisition. In: Veloso, M.M. (ed.) Proceedings of the 20th International Joint Conference on Artificial Intelligence (IJCAI 2007), pp. 750–755. Morgan Kaufmann, Inc. (2007)
2. Diebold, E., et al.: Olaaaf: a general adaptation prototype. In Recio-Garcia, J.A., del Castillo, M.G.O., Bridge, D. (eds.) Case-Based Reasoning Research and Development. Lecture Notes in Computer Science, Merida, Mexico, vol. 14775, pp. 223–239. Springer (2024)
3. François, N., Lieber, J.: A knowledge representation approach for reasoning with adaptation rules (extended version). Technical report, Loria (2025). https://hal.science/hal-04961604
4. Hanney, K., Keane, M.T.: Learning adaptation rules from a case-base. In: Smith, I., Faltings, B. (eds.) Advances in Case-Based Reasoning – Proceedings of the Third European Workshop, EWCBR 1996. LNAI, vol. 1168, pp. 179–192. Springer, Berlin (1996)
5. Jalali, V., Leake, D., Forouzandehmehr, N.: Learning and applying adaptation rules for categorical features: an ensemble approach. AI Commun. **30**(3–4), 193–205 (2017)
6. Lieber, J., Napoli, A.: Using classification in case-based planning. In: Wahlster, W. (ed.) Proceedings of the 12th European Conference on Artificial Intelligence (ECAI 1996), Budapest, Hungary, pp. 132–136. Wiley (1996)
7. Luna, J.M., Fournier-Viger, P., Ventura, S.: Frequent itemset mining: a 25 years review. Wiley Interdisc. Rev. Data Mining Knowl. Discov. **9**(6), e1329 (2019)

8. Nauer, E., Lieber, J., d'Aquin, M.: Lazy adaptation knowledge learning based on frequent closed itemsets. In: Case-Based Reasoning Research and Development. Lecture Notes in Computer Science, Aberdeen, United Kingdom, vol. 14141, pp. 309–324. Springer (2023)
9. Pearl, J.: Heuristics: intelligent search strategies for computer problem solving. Addison-Wesley Longman Publishing Co., Inc. (1984)
10. Riesbeck, C.K., Schank, R.C.: Inside Case-Based Reasoning. Lawrence Erlbaum Associates, Inc., Hillsdale (1989)
11. Smullyan, R.M.: First-order logic. Courier Corporation (1995)
12. Smyth, B., Keane, M.T.: Using adaptation knowledge to retrieve and adapt design cases. Knowl.-Based Syst. **9**(2), 127–135 (1996)

Efficient Case Retrieval Using Dropout Similarity Highway Multigraphs

Thomas Gabel(✉)

Faculty of Computer Science and Engineering, Frankfurt University of Applied Sciences, 60318 Frankfurt am Main, Germany
tgabel@fra-uas.de

Abstract. The time required to retrieve a query's nearest neighbor may quickly become a CBR system's bottleneck when its case base contains a large volume of cases. Approximate retrieval techniques that build and employ complex index data structures can mitigate this issue by providing an acceptable tradeoff between time complexity and retrieval accuracy. In this paper, we propose a specialized multigraph-based index structure composed of multiple nested sub-case bases with individually labeled edge sets. We develop tailored algorithms for both constructing the index and utilizing it in a more efficient retrieval process, and we also evaluate our approach empirically using established benchmark datasets.

1 Introduction

A key merit of Case-Based Reasoning (CBR) is its ability to allow for "approximate reasoning" in a controlled manner [18]. This statement addresses the conceptually approximate nature of similarity- and utility-based matching. However, approximations may also come into effect on a rather technical level, when acknowledging that the time required for the matchmaking process can easily become a system's bottleneck. If it is possible to avoid an exhaustive similarity-based search over all cases and to perform similarity comparisons for only a tiny fraction of the data, while still reliably identifying approximate nearest neighbor(s), then processing datasets that are orders of magnitude larger becomes feasible. A common approach to achieve that is to create an index data structure from the case data and to exploit it when searching for the best match(es) to a new query. This is exactly the path we follow in the paper at hand. Our main contributions are (a) a structured two-stage construction process of a sophisticated graph-based index data structure using one bottom-up and one top-down pass, and (b) a straightforward adjustability of the complexity and size of the index structure using an exponential complexity decay via a simple parameterization, trading off time versus accuracy. Additionally, our approach ensures (c) linear space demand for the index and logarithmic time scaling during retrieval.

Accuracy and speed of case-based retrieval have been a topic of active research for decades. We devote Sect. 2 to a review of related work and foundations on approaches to efficient case retrieval. In Sect. 3, we propose a set of

© The Author(s), under exclusive license to Springer Nature Switzerland AG 2025
I. Bichindaritz and B. López (Eds.): ICCBR 2025, LNAI 15662, pp. 220–235, 2025.
https://doi.org/10.1007/978-3-031-96559-3_15

algorithms that accomplish both, the (a) construction of a multigraph structure whose vertices are selected in a dropout manner and whose edges, speaking metaphorically, resemble a highway system based on similarities, and (b) the efficient utilization of that index structure when performing approximate case-based retrieval. Section 4 presents the results of an empirical evaluation, analyzing our approach's capabilities regarding classification accuracy as well as nearest neighbor retrieval for a variety of established benchmark datasets. Furthermore, we examine its scalability in terms of runtime and memory requirements.

2 Foundations and Related Work

The main challenge of the CBR cycle's first phase, the retrieve phase, is to select a query's nearest neighbor or k nearest neighbors. The traditional approach of linearly iterating over a case base of n cases, calculating each case's similarity to the query, and remembering the k most similar ones, quickly comes to its limits when n grows large. Traditionally, the computational burden of this task has been addressed by two predominant classes of approaches: limiting the amount of cases stored and limiting the number of similarity calculations required.

Case Base Maintenance (CBM [14]), on the one hand, controls the number of cases in the case base, thus fundamentally reducing the overall number of similarity calculations needed. Grounded in the CBR cycle's retain phase, these methods deliberately decide which cases to store, keep, or remove, aiming at a high efficacy and efficiency of the system. Following the initial proposal of the nearest neighbor rule, many authors have proposed ideas to reduce the set of stored cases [1,20]. Since we will not address CBM in the remainder of this paper, we point to an excellent overview [11] of the history of CBM algorithms. Retrieval below linear time, on the other hand, is key to efficient CBR systems when coping with big data and large case bases. As this is more relevant to the paper at hand, we review that line of research more thoroughly in the following.

2.1 Sublinear Retrieval

Many methods exists that try to limit the number of cases whose similarity to the query must be calculated during a single retrieval. They typically build up a tree- or graph-based *index structure* before the actual retrieval takes place, then utilizing that index to efficiently guide the search towards similar cases.

Accurate Retrieval: Even with sophisticated index structures, the time complexity of nearest neighbor search degrades to linear as the data's intrinsic dimensionality increases [9]. Nevertheless, there are classical approaches that led to, e.g., query times in $O(\log n)$ under certain strong preconditions. In line with this, kd-trees yield near-logarithmic retrieval times, provided that the data dimensionality is low to moderate and the similarity measure satisfies certain conditions [24]. Cover trees [4] arrange the cases with nested trees (an idea that we will build upon, too), require a true metric as similarity measure and have mild time and memory demands, but a strong dependence on the dimensionality of the data. In recent years, more enhanced tree-based structures and optimized versions of classical ones were proposed, including dual trees and variants specifically tailored for GPU-based acceleration [15]. All of these techniques, however, revert to $O(n)$ query time, if some of their respective preconditions are violated, which is why research in recent years has mostly focused on *approximate* retrieval algorithms.

Approximate Retrieval: Algorithms that settle for finding a query's approximate nearest neighbor may be categorized into one of the following three classes: First, multi-stage retrieval techniques start with a coarse preselection and conclude with a refinement. Among those, locality sensitive hashing approaches (LSH [2]) have gained much popularity in recent years. They start with a hashing procedure for preselection before they perform a more detailed similarity evaluation and, in so doing, share considerable conceptual relatedness with MAC/FAC retrieval approaches traditionally anchored in cognitive modelling and early CBR research [5]. Second, product quantization approaches compress the given data to compact codes of quantized subvector indices [12], enabling an efficient though approximate (due to lossy compression) retrieval. These methods are conceptually more dissimilar from classical CBR since the results they return are not actually stored instances, but rather compression-generated prototypes. The third category adopts discrete index data structures (typically trees or graphs, see Sect. 2.2 below) which allow to efficiently express neighborhood relationships and, thus, to evaluate the similarity of much fewer cases to the query.

In particular, approximate k-NN algorithms that rely on proximity graphs have gained popularity in recent years, driven by the more and more common need to quickly match queries in large volumes of data or in high-dimensional vector embeddings. The algorithms we are proposing in the paper at hand also fall into this category which is why we explore related work on that topic next.

2.2 Proximity Graphs

Due to the exhaustive volume of research on proximity graphs we provide a coarse overview, only. A comprehensive survey can be found in [23].

Definition 1. *A* Proximity Graph *for a case base* $\mathcal{C} = \{c_1, \ldots, c_n\} \subsetneq \mathcal{M}$ *is a graph* $\mathcal{P} = (V, E)$ *with* $V = \mathcal{C}$ *the set of vertices and* E *the edges such that: For any similarity measure* $sim : \mathcal{M}^2 \to [0, 1]$*, any query* $q \in \mathcal{M}$ *and any* $c \in V$ *either* c *is the nearest neighbor of* q *within* $\mathcal{C}$*, i.e.* $sim(q, c) = \max_{c_i \in \mathcal{C}} sim(q, c_i)$*, or there exists an edge* $(c, c') \in E$ *with* $sim(q, c') > sim(q, c)$*.*

A proximity graph (PG) enables the use of an efficient greedy retrieval algorithm. Given a query q and a random start case, the search gets iteratively closer to the nearest neighbor by following only adjacent edges from $\mathcal{P}$ that lead to cases that are more similar to q than the current node, stopping when no more increase in similarity can be attained. An example for a PG in multi-dimensional vector spaces is the Delaunay graph which guarantees precise results under greedy search, but which is almost fully connected when the data dimensionality is high. Since the construction of PGs according to Definition 1 is costly ($O(n^2)$) and their retrieval time does not necessarily scale well, a whole body of research has focused on relaxing the proximity property from above, thus creating *approximate* proximity graphs (APG) in a much more efficient manner.

Relative neighborhood graphs (RNG [22]), for instance, have connections between two cases only, if there is no third case that is more similar to any of the former. While RNGs cut off many redundant connections, the time required for their full construction is in $O(n^3)$. In k-nearest neighbor graphs (KNNG [17]), by contrast, each case gets connected to its k nearest neighbors which yields a directed graph limiting strictly the number of cases to which each vertex is connected, but which may destroy the global connectivity of strict PGs. Numerous graph-based algorithms for the approximate search of nearest neighbors combine various components of Delaunay graphs, RNGs, and KNNGs to form more complex approaches that are scalable to very large data volumes [6,7,16]. The authors of [23] disentangle those developments and provide a thorough overview.

In what follows, we propose Dropout Similarity Highway Multigraphs, a graph-based index structure that yields an APG-like structure with logarithmic complexity scaling during case retrieval. We take inspiration from tree-based nearest neighbor search algorithms [4] and from graph-based ones [16] as well as from classical beam search [19] and more recent techniques like dropout [21].

3 Dropout Similarity Highway Multigraphs

Driving to a distant destination, humans typically take the nearest highway ramp, travel along the system of (interstate) highways, until more regional roads and, finally, tiny drives or alleys are needed to arrive at the target. Our approach for finding a query's (approximate) nearest neighbor is inspired by that analogy. We divide the set of cases into multiple subsets where for each case it is decided whether it gets connected to other (very similar) cases by small roads or, whether it has the privilege of being connected by some (generally longer) "highway segment" to (generally less similar) cases. This way, we form a system of "traffic" connections that we employ when searching for a query's nearest neighbor.

3.1 Outline

We aim at the construction of a labeled multigraph structure whose construction process consists of two parts (cf. Algorithm 1). In a first bottom-up stage, the vertices (so to say, the traffic hubs) of the multigraph are selected randomly in a nested order (line 1). This results in D subsets of the case base, each of which contains the next one. The details on this part are given in Sect. 3.3.

The second stage (line 2) deals with the edges (so to say, the highways and roads) and, in doing so, follows a top-down approach. Details on this part will be given in Sect. 3.4. In Sect. 3.2, we start by discussing a beam search adaptation for APGs that is utilized in the second stage. Algorithm 1 takes four parameters. Besides the case base $\mathcal{C}$ for which the graph-based index structure is to be created, δ is the defining parameter for the dropout idea, whereas m restricts the maximum degree of graph vertices and Ω influences the beam search algorithm mentioned. We will discuss those parameters in Sect. 3.5.

```
CONSTRUCT_DROPOUT_SIMHIGHWAY_MULTIGRAPH( C, δ, Ω, m)
Input: case base C, dropout factor δ ∈ [0,1), maximum beam width Ω
       and maximum vertex degree m
Output: dropout similarity highway multigraph S̃
1:  D_C := CREATE_CASE_DROPOUT_SEQUENCE(C, δ, Ω, m)      //call to Alg. 3
2:  S̃ := CREATE_DSHM_WITH_EDGES( D_C )                    //call to Alg. 4
3:  return S̃
```

Algorithm 1: Full Creation Procedure of a Dropout Similarity Highway

3.2 Beam Search in Approximate Proximity Graphs

As delineated above, greedy search in a *strict* proximity graph always yields the case from the case base with maximal similarity to the query. If the graph G used does not have the proximity property (cf. Definition 1), because G is just an approximation of $\mathcal{P}$ (e.g. a k-nearest neighbor graph or some approximation of that), then parts of the case base may be poorly or not at all connected to other parts, such that the search can get stuck in local optima.

An effective method to mitigate that problem is to apply a beam search approach with a large enough beam width ω [19]. In Algorithm 2, we delineate how beam search can generally be applied for a given query and an APG. Basically, a beam of width ω of the most promising cases is kept, from which all neighboring cases are considered. In so doing, the algorithm remembers which cases have already been visited and tries to finish the search as early as possible, returning the beam of the most similar cases found. For ease of presentation, we assume the similarity measure *sim* to be symmetric for the remainder of this paper. We also restrict our presentation to graphs with undirected edges, i.e. $(e, f) \in E \iff (f, e) \in E$.

3.3 Bottom-Up Selection of Multigraph Nodes

While the previously presented algorithm is merely a tool to be used later, we now turn to the actual construction of our multigraph index structures, starting with its vertices. The eligibility of cases to become "major hubs" follows a simple procedure that is inspired by the dropout approach known from neural network training [21] and has also some relatedness to the tree-based structures in [4].

Given a case base $\mathcal{C}$ and a dropout (or decay) factor $\delta \in [0, 1)$, a fraction of $\lfloor \delta \cdot |\mathcal{C}| \rfloor$ cases is selected randomly to form a subset of instances of "higher traffic importance". This procedure is applied repeatedly until only one case remains.

BEAM_SEARCH_APG(G, q, ω, S)
Input: approximate proximity graph $G = (\mathcal{C}, E)$ where $\mathcal{C}$ is the case base,
query $q \in \mathcal{M}$, beam width ω, search start vertices $S \subset \mathcal{C}$
Output: beam $\mathcal{B}$ of most similar cases to q
$\mathcal{V} := S$, $\mathcal{B} := S$, $\mathcal{E} := S$ *//visited cases, the beam, cases to be explored*
while $|\mathcal{E}| > 0$
  $e := \arg\max_{c \in \mathcal{E}} sim(q, c)$, $\mathcal{E} = \mathcal{E} \setminus \{e\}$ *//currently explored case*
  $w := \min_{c \in \mathcal{B}} sim(q, c)$ *//worst case's similarity within beam*
  if $sim(q, e) < w$ **then return** $\mathcal{B}$ *//everything in $\mathcal{B}$ has been evaluated*
  forall $\nu \in \{f \in \mathcal{C} | (e, f) \in E\}$ **do** *//iterate over proximity of e*
    if $\nu \notin \mathcal{V}$ **then**
      $w := \min_{c \in \mathcal{B}} sim(q, c)$ *//worst case's similarity within beam*
      if $sim(q, \nu) > w$ **or** $|\mathcal{B}| < \omega$ **then**
        $\mathcal{E} := \mathcal{E} \cup \{\nu\}$, $\mathcal{B} := \mathcal{B} \cup \{\nu\}$
        if $|\mathcal{B}| > \omega$ **then** *//keep beam width under control*
          $\mathcal{B} := \mathcal{B} \setminus \{\arg\min_{c \in \mathcal{B}} sim(q, c)\}$
      $\mathcal{V} := \mathcal{V} \cup \{\nu\}$ *//mark ν as visited*
return $\mathcal{B}$

Algorithm 2: Beam Search Applied to an Approximate Proximity Graph

Definition 2. *For a given dropout factor $\delta \in [0, 1)$ and a case base $\mathcal{C}$, the sequence $\mathcal{L} = (\mathcal{C}_0, \mathcal{C}_1, \ldots, \mathcal{C}_D)$ is called* Sub-Case Base Sequence, *if $\mathcal{C}_0 = \mathcal{C}$ and $\mathcal{C}_{i+1}$ is a random subset of $\mathcal{C}_i$ ($\mathcal{C}_{i+1} \subsetneq \mathcal{C}_i$) with $|\mathcal{C}_{i+1}| = \lfloor \delta \cdot |\mathcal{C}_i| \rfloor$ and $|\mathcal{C}_D| = 1$.*

As far as the traffic system metaphor is concerned, we might say that later entries in a sub-case base sequence correspond to sets of the more major hubs. In the preview picture (Fig. 1) those cases are plotted with a slightly larger diameter. Furthermore, any place that has access to a major highway can also have connections to roads of lower importance with rather small range reach. We will exploit that property in the sense that possible connections between the (few) major hubs allow us to get quickly to different (i.e. to dissimilar) parts of the search space. By construction it holds $D = \lceil \log_{\frac{1}{\delta}}(|\mathcal{C}|) \rceil = \lceil -\log_{\delta}(|\mathcal{C}|) \rceil$, so for smaller values of δ the sub-case base sequence is shorter.

We take the dropout idea a step further by attaching two properties to each sub-case base $\mathcal{C}_i$. First, if $c \in \mathcal{C}_i$ is a vertex in the graph, then we might be interested in limiting the number of edges it can have. Given the maximum vertex degree m (parameter to the main Algorithm 1) we define (exponentially decaying) dropout vertex maximum degrees for each sub-case base according to

$$m_i := max(D - i, \lfloor m\delta^i \rfloor). \tag{1}$$

The first entry in the max operator is added merely to ensure increasing connectivity from one sub-case base to the next, whereas the second actually realizes the dropout. Likewise, we restrict the beam width of the beam search within the different sub-case bases in just the same way. Given the maximum beam width Ω (parameter to Algorithm 1), we set sub-case base-specific beam widths to

$$\omega_i := max(1, \lfloor \Omega\delta^i \rfloor). \tag{2}$$

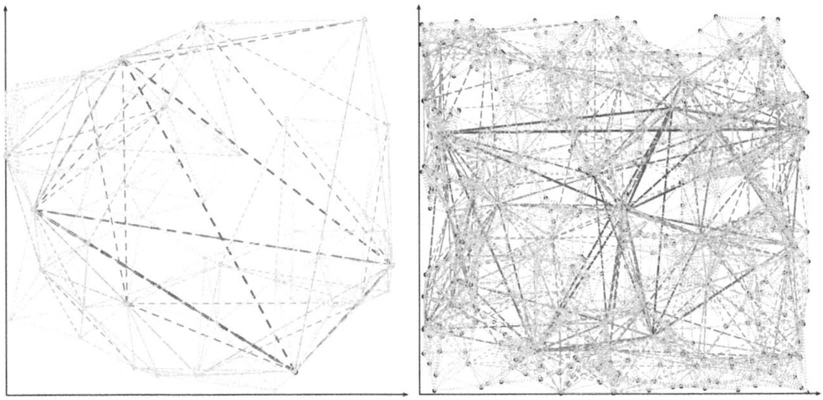

Fig. 1. Preview images of DSHMs in two two-dimensional toy domains with 100 (left) and 10000 (right) cases. Style and thickness of lines identify edge labels. There are 5 different labels in the left DSHM, and 9 in the right one. Each vertex may have up to $m = 10$ edges with the same label. Unlike in [7], both structures encode no information about the solution space (e.g. classes as indicated by the background color).

In fact, the exact values of m_i are defined proportional to the sizes of the corresponding sub-case bases. The same holds for the decaying beam widths ω_i facilitating the use of wider beams when searching through larger sub-case bases.

Definition 3. *Given a sub-case base sequence* $(\mathcal{C}_0, \mathcal{C}_1, \dots, \mathcal{C}_D)$ *for dropout factor* $\delta \in [0, 1)$, *we define a* Case Dropout Sequence $\mathcal{D}_\mathcal{C} = (C_0, \dots, C_D)$ *as a vector of three-tuples* $C_i = (\mathcal{C}_i, m_i, \omega_i)$ *whose 2nd and 3rd component are defined according to Eqs. 1 and 2 for a given max vertex degree* m *and max beam width* Ω.

For ease of notation, we use $m_i^\mathcal{D}$ and $\omega_i^\mathcal{D}$ as a shorthand when referring to the maximum vertex degree and beam width of the ith entry of $\mathcal{D}_\mathcal{C}$. The sequence of sub-case bases $\mathcal{C}_i$ in $\mathcal{D}_\mathcal{C}$ will serve as label set $\mathcal{L}$ in the to-be-constructed labeled multigraph. As an example, for $|\mathcal{C}| = 1024$ and $\delta = \frac{1}{4}$ we obtain $|\mathcal{L}| = D = 5$ with, e.g., $|\mathcal{C}_1| = 256$ or $|\mathcal{C}_3| = 16$. Using the illustrative metaphor, there are 1024 cases in $\mathcal{C}_0$ that have connections via an alley, 256 of the cases have connections via lanes, 64 via drives, whereas 16 are connected by larger roads and the four cases within $\mathcal{C}_4$ may become connected with one another using highways.

3.4 Top-Down Construction of Multigraph Edges

Next, we extend PGs by identifiable labeled edges in the graph structure. This means we allow for multiple edges between vertices, but make them distinguishable by attaching a label out of a set $\mathcal{L}$ of D different labels to each edge.

3.4.1 Notation

We define a *Dropout Similarity Highway Multigraph (DSHM)* as a labeled undirected multigraph as follows:

```
CREATE_CASE_DROPOUT_SEQUENCE( C, δ, Ω, m),
Input: case base C, dropout factor δ ∈ [0, 1)
       maximum vertex degree m, maximum beam width Ω
Output: case dropout sequence D_C
  D := 0, C_0 := C, D_C := (C_0) with C_0 := (C, m, Ω)      //first element of D_C
  while |C_D| > 1                                        //no more dropout possible
     C_{D+1} := ∅
     while |C_{D+1}| < ⌊δ · |C_D|⌋                         //create next sub-case base
        a := random case from C_D \ C_{D+1},  C_{D+1} := C_{D+1} ∪ {a}
     D := D + 1
  for i := 0 to D do
     m_i := max(D − i, ⌊mδ^i⌋), ω_i := max(1, ⌊Ωδ^i⌋)           //use Eq. 1+2
     C_i := (C_i, m_i, ω_i)                                   //next entry in D_C
     D_C := (C_0, ..., C_{i−1}, C_i)        //append C_i to the existing sequence D_C
  return D_C
```

Algorithm 3: Case Dropout Sequence Generation

Definition 4. *Let* $\mathcal{C}$ *be a case base and* $\mathcal{D}_\mathcal{C} = (C_0, \ldots, C_D)$ *its case dropout sequence with length* D*. Then, a* Dropout Similarity Highway Multigraph (DSHM) $\tilde{\mathcal{S}} = (\tilde{V}, \tilde{E}, \tilde{L})$ *is defined as a labeled undirected multigraph with* $\tilde{V} = \mathcal{C}$ *the set of vertices,* $\tilde{E}$ *a multiset of bidirectional edges, and* $\tilde{L} : \tilde{E} \to \mathcal{L}$ *a labeling function which maps to each edge a label out of a finite set* $\mathcal{L}$ *of* D *unique labels.*

We use the notation $\tilde{\mathcal{S}}|_l$ to indicate the sub-multigraph of $\tilde{\mathcal{S}}$ for some specific edge label $l \in \mathcal{L}$. Note that, due to the restriction to edge label l, $\tilde{\mathcal{S}}|_l$ represents an approximate PG (cf. Definition 1), no longer a DSHM. We formally obtain

$$\tilde{\mathcal{S}}|_l = (V_l, E_l) \text{ where } E_l = \{e \in \tilde{E} | \tilde{L}(e) = l\} \text{ and } V_l = \mathcal{C}_l \quad (3)$$

Metaphorically, we might say that, for instance, the induced sub-multigraph $\tilde{\mathcal{S}}|_l$ of $\tilde{\mathcal{S}}$ for label $l =$ "*interstate highway*" refers to an excerpt of the entire traffic system that covers cities connected to interstate highways, only.

3.4.2 Creation of a DSHM and Its Edges

The second stage of creating a full DSHM is delineated in Algorithm 4. This procedure takes as input a case dropout sequence $\mathcal{D}_\mathcal{C} = (C_0, \ldots, C_D)$, which is a vector of triples $C_l = (\mathcal{C}_l, m_l^\mathcal{P}, \omega_l^\mathcal{P})$ whose first elements are sub-case bases of $\mathcal{C}$. As pointed out earlier, the set of edge labels considered (line 1) corresponds to those sub-case bases $\mathcal{L} := \{\mathcal{C}_0, \mathcal{C}_1, \ldots, \mathcal{C}_D\}$. Recall the meaning of the 2nd and 3rd component of C_l: $\omega_l^\mathcal{P}$ indicates the applied beam width when performing beam search using edges with a specific label l on some subgraph $\tilde{\mathcal{S}}|_l$ of the DSHM, and $m_l^\mathcal{P}$ stands for the maximal degrees that vertices are allowed to have w.r.t. a specific edge label l. Note that the degree of a vertex c with respect to some edge label l is defined as $deg_l(c) = |\{(u, v) \in \tilde{E} | \tilde{L}((u, v)) = l, c \in \{u, v\}\}|$.

The algorithm starts by defining a DSHM $\tilde{\mathcal{S}}$ whose vertices are $\mathcal{C}_0$, i.e. the full case base $\mathcal{C}$, and which has no edges. It then (line 3) proceeds "top-down"

CREATE_DSHM_WITH_EDGES($\mathcal{D}_{\mathcal{C}}$)
Input: case dropout sequence $\mathcal{D}_{\mathcal{C}} = (C_0, \ldots, C_D)$ with length D
Output: similarity highway multigraph $\tilde{\mathcal{S}}$
1: $\mathcal{L} := \{\mathcal{C}_0, \mathcal{C}_1, \ldots, \mathcal{C}_D\}$ *//sub-case bases form the set of labels*
2: $\tilde{\mathcal{S}} := (\mathcal{C}_0, \tilde{E}, \tilde{L})$ with $\tilde{L} : \tilde{E} \to \mathcal{L}$ and $\tilde{E} = \emptyset$ *//initial DSHM without edges*
3: **for** $l = D$ **downto** 0 *//iterate over labels: from "highways" to "alleys"*
4: **forall** $c \in \mathcal{C}_l$ **do** *//all cases in current "type of road"*
5: $\mathcal{B} := \mathcal{C}_D$ *//start beam search with "main traffic hub"*
6: **for** $r = D$ **downto** l *//find neighbors of c in partially built DSHM*
7: $\mathcal{B} :=$ BEAM_SEARCH_APG(c, $\tilde{\mathcal{S}}|_r$, $\omega^{\mathcal{D}}_{r-l}$, $\mathcal{B}$) *//call to Alg. 2*
8: **while** $|\mathcal{B}| > 0$ **and** $deg_l(c) < m^{\mathcal{D}}_l$ *//process all neighbors in beam*
9: $b := \arg\max_{b \in \mathcal{B}} sim(c, b)$ *//best in beam*
10: $\tilde{E} := \tilde{E} \cup \{(c, b)\}$, $\tilde{L}((c, b)) := \mathcal{C}_l$ *//add bidirectional edge + set label*
11: $\mathcal{B} := \mathcal{B} \setminus \{b\}$ *//remove processed neighbor from beam*
12: **if** $deg_l(b) > m^{\mathcal{D}}_l$ **then** *//max degree of b exceeded*
13: $\tilde{E} := \tilde{E} \setminus \arg\min_{(b,x) \in \tilde{E}, \tilde{L}((b,x)) = \mathcal{C}_l, x \in \mathcal{C}_l} sim(x, c)$
14: **return** $\tilde{\mathcal{S}}$

Algorithm 4: Creation of a Similarity Highway Multigraph's Edges

through the case dropout sequence, starting with C_D and progressing downwards to level C_0. In iteration l the algorithm considers element $C_l = (\mathcal{C}_l, m^{\mathcal{D}}_l, \omega^{\mathcal{D}}_l)$ of $\mathcal{D}_{\mathcal{C}}$. Within each such iteration, each case from $\mathcal{C}_l$ is processed (line 4) which is why a number of cases are touched multiple times. Since $\mathcal{C}_{l+1} \subset \mathcal{C}_l$, each $c \in \mathcal{C}_{l+1}$ is processed once more when iterating over all elements of $\mathcal{C}_l$ (and again for $\mathcal{C}_{l-1}$ etc.). This may appear as a tremendous overhead, but due to the nestedness of the case dropout sequence the amount of work on individual cases is

$$\sum_{l=0}^{D} |\mathcal{C}_l| \underset{|\mathcal{C}_{l+1}| = \delta \cdot |\mathcal{C}_l|}{=} \sum_{l=0}^{D} \delta^l \cdot |\mathcal{C}_0| \underset{\delta \in [0,1)}{\simeq} \frac{|\mathcal{C}|}{1 - \delta}$$

and, thus, the overhead can simply be controlled by adjusting δ.

For each $c \in \mathcal{C}_l$ (line 4) two steps are made. First (lines 5–7), a graph-based nearest neighbor beam search for c is made, exploiting the so far created multigraph structure $\tilde{\mathcal{S}}$ in conjunction with the beam search Algorithm 2. Iteratively, a number of beam searches on sub-multigraphs of $\tilde{\mathcal{S}}$ are made, each time utilizing a different edge label $r \in \mathcal{L}$, starting with $r = D$ and proceeding top-down till reaching label l—the label for which the DSHM is currently extended. Each call to BEAM_SEARCH_APG receives the currently considered case c as query, the induced subgraph $\tilde{\mathcal{S}}|_r$ from $\tilde{\mathcal{S}}$ with respect to label r, a beam width $\omega^{\mathcal{D}}$ increasing for smaller values of r, and, most importantly, the result beam $\mathcal{B}$ of the preceding call as starting nodes for the next call to the beam search. This way, the search for nearest neighbors of c steps through $\tilde{\mathcal{S}}$ in a label-wise manner, finding in each step r the nearest neighbors to c within $\mathcal{C}_r$ and, using those as the seed for the search in the (by factor $\frac{1}{\delta}$) larger sub-case base $\mathcal{C}_{r-1}$.

The remaining lines (8–13) process the results from the previous search and extend $\tilde{\mathcal{S}}$. As long as there are still elements in the result set $\mathcal{B}$ and if the degree of the current case c w.r.t. label $\mathcal{C}_l$ is below the allowed maximum (which decays w.r.t. the sub-case base size of $\mathcal{C}_l$), the most similar case b from $\mathcal{B}$ is determined (line 9) and an undirected edge between c and b, which is labeled by $\mathcal{C}_l$, is added to the edges of $\tilde{\mathcal{S}}$ (line 10). Then, b is removed from $\mathcal{B}$. Finally, line 12 checks whether the recent extension of $\tilde{E}$ has caused b to have more edges with label $\mathcal{C}_l$ than permitted (the maximum $m_l^{\mathcal{P}}$ is taken from the l-th entry in the case dropout sequence, i.e. from $C_l = (\mathcal{C}_l, m_l^{\mathcal{P}}, \omega_l^{\mathcal{P}})$). If that is the case, then line 13 removes a $\mathcal{C}_l$-labeled edge between b and the case least similar to c.

RETRIEVE_USING_DSHM(q, $\tilde{\mathcal{S}}$, Ω, k)
Input: query q, dropout similarity highway multigraph $\tilde{\mathcal{S}} = (\mathcal{D}_C, \tilde{E}, \tilde{L})$,
maximum beam width Ω, number k of nearest neighbors to retrieve
Output: set of k nearest neighbors
1: $\mathcal{B} := \mathcal{C}_D$ *//where* $\mathcal{D}_C = (C_0, \ldots, C_D)$
2: **for** $l = D$ **downto** 0 *//knowing that length of* $\mathcal{D}_C$ *is* D
3: $\omega := max(1, \lfloor \Omega \left(\frac{|\mathcal{C}_{l+1}|}{|\mathcal{C}_l|}\right)^l \rfloor)$ $//|\mathcal{C}_{l+1}|/|\mathcal{C}_l| = \delta$
4: **if** $l = 0$ **and** $\omega < k$ **then** $\omega := k$ *//assert that at least* k *nghbs. are found*
5: $\mathcal{B}$:= BEAM_SEARCH_APG(q, $\tilde{\mathcal{S}}|_l$, ω, $\mathcal{B}$) *//call to Alg. 2*
6: **return** $\arg\max_{B \subset \mathcal{B}, |B|=k} \sum_{b \in B} sim(q, b)$

Algorithm 5: k-NN Retrieval Using a Dropout Similarity Highway Multigraph

3.4.3 Utilizing a DSHM for K-Nearest Neighbor Retrieval

Once, a full DSHM has been constructed, its usage during case-based retrieval for a new query q is straightforward. Algorithm 5 reveals that—very similar to lines 5–7 in Algorithm 4—a label-wise top-down beam search approach is taken, where the results from retrieving within one induced subgraph of the DSHM $\tilde{\mathcal{S}}$ are carried further as the seed to the search in the subgraph for the next label.

The maximum dropout beam width handed over as a parameter Ω may very well differ from the eponymous parameter used during DSHM construction. This way, it is, for example, possible, to do the retrieval on the basis of broader beams and, thus, to trade accuracy for computational efficiency. When reaching label $l = 0$ during search, line 4 additionally asserts that at least k entries will be contained in the result set by setting a lower bound to ω.

3.5 Discussion

Our algorithms are defined by a dropout-inspired divide-and-conquer approach, where the dropout factor δ serves as a key parameter. It determines the length of the case dropout sequence, the exponentially decaying maximum vertex degrees, and the beam widths in the multigraph structure. We consider $\delta = 0.5$ a reasonable default, as it halves the sizes of sub-case bases sequentially. The maximum vertex degree m affects the space requirements of the multigraph (proportional to

m) and must be sufficiently large to ensure connectivity within $\mathcal{C}_0$. Empirically, we found that the maximum beam width Ω during the construction influences graph quality and should not be set below m, making $\Omega = m$ a reasonable choice. The structure of a case dropout sequence implies that most cases are represented multiple times and have edges with varying labels. An efficient implementation represents the sub-case base sequence and all edges between cases using pointers. For a given $\delta \in [0, 1)$ and n cases the space requirements are in $O(\frac{mn}{1-\delta})$. By definition, the length D of the case dropout sequence is $\log_{\frac{1}{\delta}}(n)$. When taking the step from C_{l+1} to C_l the starting case(s) for searching through $\mathcal{C}_l$ are the result of a preceding search in a sparser case base and, thus, a good approximation to the outcome already. The backtracking nature of beam search adds a constant factor to the overall effort which is thus in $O(log(n))$ for the retrieval. As far as the construction of a DSHM is concerned, up to $2n$ retrievals in a partial DSHM must be made, yielding an overall time complexity of $O(n \log(n))$.

4 Experimental Evaluation

The main focus of our experiments is on the accuracy of approximate retrieval, its speed and memory demand, and the corresponding trade-off between them.

We selected the same established classification benchmark datasets as in [7] from the UCI Machine Learning Repository [13] omitting, however, very small datasets with less than 300 instances. We also used a larger nine-dimensional dataset (500k instances) from robotic soccer simulation (RSS) to classify an opponent agent's next action (e.g., kick, dash, or turn, cf. [8]), along with the widely used SIFT 1M dataset, which contains one million 128-dimensional image feature descriptors [10]. While the smaller UCI datasets evaluated DSHM's basic functionality, the million-scale datasets analyzed its scaling properties.

In all classification experiments, we used a knowledge-poor default similarity measure according to the local-global principle [3]. For each domain, we randomly split the data into 80% for constructing the DSHM and 20% for testing. To account for the stochastic nature of our algorithms, we repeated experiments 100 times, except for the largest volumes of data, and averaged performance indicators. The main metrics are classification error and speedup σ, defined as the ratio of total cases to those actually compared during retrieval with a DSHM using Algorithm 5. Thus, σ directly quantifies the speedup over linear search.

The SIFT domain includes a ground truth test set with 10k queries and their 100 true nearest neighbors among the one million cases. To align with the literature, we used a similarity measure that is compatible to the Euclidean distance and focused on 1-recall as performance indicator—the fraction of queries where our approach found the true nearest neighbor.

4.1 Classification Datasets

In our first experiments, we evaluated DSHMs with $\delta = 0.5$ for three different maximum vertex degrees m and beam widths Ω, comparing them to the best-performing linear k-NN retriever (optimal k was found to be $k^* = 13$). We determined classification error ε on the test set and the speedup σ achieved over sequential search. Table 1 lists the results plus an average over all of them. For reference, the last four columns show error values for related algorithms [7].

Table 1. Classification error ε (in %, averaged over 100 runs) and speedup σ (relative to linear retrieval) for DSHMs with varying maximum vertex degrees m and maximum beam widths Ω, compared to the best linear k-NN ($k^* = 13$) and four retrieval methods from [7]. Top two algorithms per domain are highlighted.

Domain	k-NN	DSHM with $k = 13$ and $m = \Omega := p\,\mathrm{BF}_t$							$\mathrm{IB2}_e$	BG_r	LBM_λ
	$k^* = 13$	$p = 15$		$p = 30$		$p = 100$		$t^* = 325$	$e^* = 94$	$r = 50$	$\lambda^* = 37$
	ε	ε	σ	ε	σ	ε	σ	ε	ε	ε	ε
Balance	17.12	16.56	*3.01*	16.80	*1.60*	**16.24**	*1.01*	19.13	45.75	25.18	**15.69**
BanknoteAuth	0.30	1.71	*15.68*	0.25	*9.31*	**0.10**	*2.87*	0.15	0.17	0.14	**0.12**
Car	9.18	10.52	*7.12*	9.50	*3.56*	9.62	*1.31*	**3.93**	14.57	**5.76**	6.59
Contraceptive	52.00	52.92	*8.29*	53.02	*3.94*	**51.49**	*1.43*	52.67	53.90	54.81	**51.11**
Ecoli	16.12	14.17	*3.92*	**14.02**	*2.58*	**13.88**	*1.10*	19.98	23.13	21.99	15.24
Flare	**17.52**	18.26	*11.51*	18.35	*5.87*	18.30	*1.81*	21.21	33.82	21.16	**17.12**
Haberman	**26.20**	**28.19**	*3.91*	**28.19**	*2.24*	**28.19**	*1.06*	35.17	38.12	36.66	33.39
MammogrMass	20.10	20.54	*7.03*	19.27	*4.36*	**18.97**	*1.68*	21.82	27.42	23.64	**19.14**
Monks	6.11	10.23	*2.62*	6.39	*1.50*	5.46	*1.00*	**0.00**	13.03	1.03	**0.22**
Pima	26.58	**25.16**	*5.64*	**24.90**	*3.09*	**24.90**	*1.31*	28.14	34.00	32.47	26.38
TicTacToe	**2.33**	3.56	*5.07*	3.24	*2.41*	2.98	*1.07*	**1.07**	16.02	2.46	4.61
Transfusion	**22.30**	22.34	*9.02*	**22.28**	*5.28*	22.48	*1.86*	29.03	33.51	30.98	24.08
VertebralCol	21.26	20.16	*3.49*	**20.00**	*2.13*	**20.00**	*1.14*	22.53	25.59	26.19	22.37
Wholesale	29.24	**29.20**	*4.60*	**29.20**	*2.77*	**29.20**	*1.25*	42.91	49.19	46.31	35.75
Yeast	**41.85**	42.83	*9.47*	42.43	*5.04*	**42.06**	*1.81*	43.92	51.60	47.98	42.17
Average	20.55	21.09	*6.70*	**20.53**	*3.72*	**20.26**	*1.45*	22.78	30.65	25.12	20.93

Figure 2 visualizes the impact of a DSHM construction algorithm's main parameters. Its left chart plots ε (averaged over 15 UCI domains) as $m = \Omega$ increases from 5 to 100 ($\delta = 0.5$). There is a strong correlation between the error ε and the speedup σ (dashed line). Notably, for $m = \Omega \geq 28$ the linear k^*-NN retriever ($k^* = 13$) is outperformed while still yielding a speedup of ≈ 4.

The right chart in Fig. 2 examines 250k RSS cases, highlighting the impact of varying δ. Here, m and Ω were set to 100. For DSHM-based 1-NN retrieval on test cases, classification error plateaus around $\delta = 0.3$. Beyond ~ 0.6, speedup degrades, and memory usage (measured by edge count) increases substantially.

4.2 Scaling Analysis

After analyzing our approach's basic functioning, we now examine its performance on larger, real-world datasets. Case-based classification should improve with more case data. This is confirmed by the solid graphs in Fig. 3. In 1-NN classification for the 3-class RSS dataset, DSHM-based retrieval surpasses linear retrieval in accuracy—while achieving a tremendous speedup. Having constructed a DSHM for $\sim 400k$ cases, the classification of a new query q requires

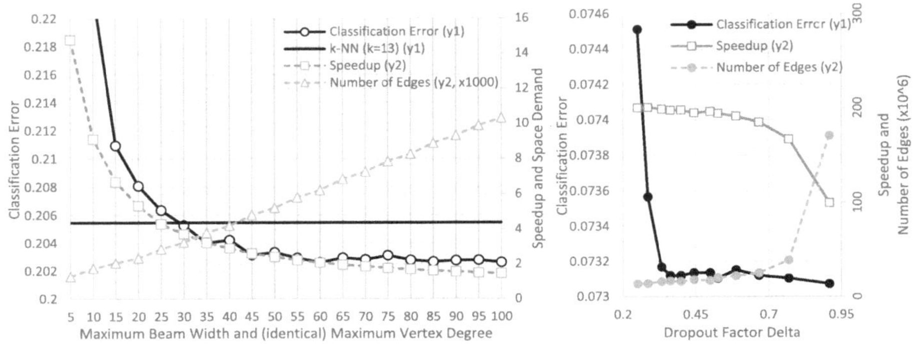

Fig. 2. Left: For a fixed dropout factor $\delta = 0.5$, the impact of the maximum vertex degree m and maximum beam width Ω is analyzed, averaged over 15 UCI domains. Right: For 250k RSS cases, $m = \Omega = 100$ is used with varying δ. Around $\delta = 0.5$, a strong trade-off between accuracy and speedup is achieved.

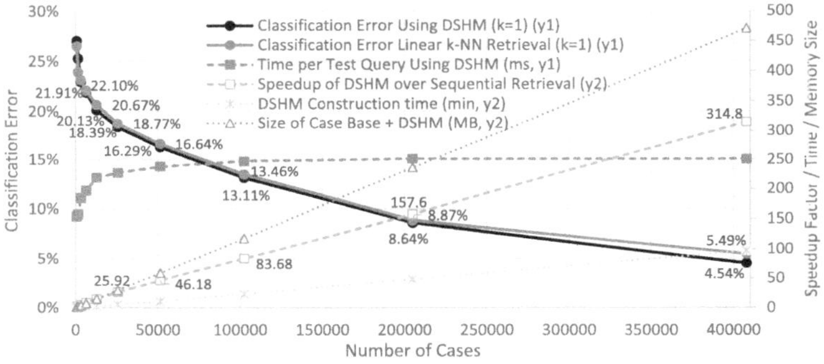

Fig. 3. Settling for fixed maximum vertex degrees ($m = 100$), maximum beam width ($\Omega = 100$) and dropout rate ($\delta = 0.5$), this series of experiments highlights the scaling behavior of DSHMs. We use DSHMs for classification on the basis of a 1-NN retrieval in the RSS domain and compare it to sequential retrieval. For $n = 400k$ cases, a speedup of more than 300 is achieved at linear space requirements.

only 1295 similarity calculations between q and cases/vertices from $\mathcal{C}$, which is a speedup of ~ 314. Although retrieval time depends on hardware, we clearly observe logarithmic scaling with case data, leading to a speedup growing linearly with $|\mathcal{C}|$. However, and this is a downside, memory consumption (index size) also increases linearly with the number of cases.

Unlike classification, which benefits from more cases, pure retrieval tasks (where cases lack a solution part) becomes harder with larger case volumes when focusing on 1-recall. Let $\tilde{S}$ be the DSHM for case base $\mathcal{C}$. The ground truth over $\mathcal{C}$ for a query q is defined as $g_q = \arg\max_{c \in \mathcal{C}} sim(q, c)$. Let $\mathcal{R}$ be the result of the retrieve Algorithm 5 for $\tilde{\mathcal{S}}$, q, and $k = 1$. We then say that the DSHM-based retrieval *recalls* successfully if $\mathcal{R} = g_q$. The fraction of queries

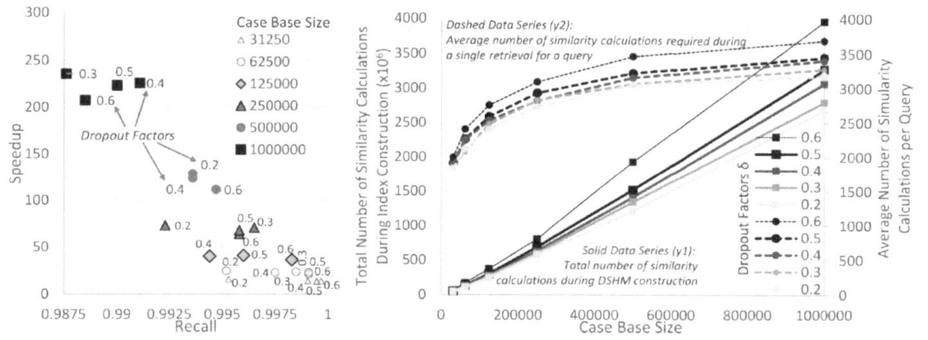

Fig. 4. Analysis for SIFT data with DSHM construction on up to 10^6 cases and testing on 10k ground truth queries. Left: Tradeoff between recall and speedup for $m = 100 = \Omega = 100$, with varying dropout factors δ and data sizes. Right: Same setting with $\Omega = 70$, showing time demand in terms of the number of required similarity calculations.

(from a ground truth set) meeting this condition is denoted as 1-recall. We stick to this performance measure, noting that relaxations to $k > 1$ (e.g., 10-recall) are also common in the literature. For a fixed maximum capacity determined by $m = 100$, the left part of Fig. 4 shows exemplarily, i.e. for individual runs, recall results for varying case base sizes and dropout factors. For moderate amounts of data nearly perfect recall is achieved with a speedup of 10-20. Generally, larger values of δ imply higher recall at lower speed and at the cost of more edges in the DSHM due to its longer case dropout sequence. The right part of Fig. 4 highlights the logarithmic scaling of DSHM-based retrieval time with case base size. For $1M$ cases and $\delta = 0.5$, only ≈ 3500 similarity calculations are needed while achieving a recall > 0.99. Moreover, the chart plots the total number of similarity calculations required to fully construct a DSHM. Since those similarity comparisons make up for the most of the time effort except for a constant factor, these graphs expose the linearithmic time complexity (cf. Sect. 3.5) of the DSHM construction procedure.

5 Conclusion

Retrieval efficiency in Case-Based Reasoning remains an important topic even after decades of research. In this paper, we have introduced the concept of dropout similarity highways multigraphs which we suggest to use as an efficient index structure during approximate case-based retrieval. The core idea of these multigraph structures is that multiple nested sub-case bases with their own labeled edge connection sets exist. These are exploited in a top-down manner to more quickly approach regions in the case base with more similar cases.

We have proposed appropriate index construction and retrieve algorithms and evaluated them using a selection of benchmark classification problems as well as two large-scale datasets in the million range. The methods we presented are applicable to various problem types, including classification and information retrieval. In both areas, we found that the performance, in terms of classification error and recall versus time complexity, is very good.

References

1. Aha, D., Kibler, D., Albert, M.: Instance-based learning algorithms. Mach. Learn. **6**, 37–66 (1991)
2. Andoni, A., Indyk, P., Laarhoven, T., Razenshteyn, I., Schmidt, L.: Practical and optimal LSH for angular distance. In: NeurIPS, Montreal, pp. 1225–1233 (2015)
3. Bergmann, R., Richter, M., Schmitt, S., Stahl, A., Vollrath, I.: Utility-oriented matching: a new research direction for CBR. In: GWCBR (2001)
4. Beygelzimer, A., Kakade, S., Langford, J.: Cover tree for nearest neighbor. In: Proceedings of ICML 2006, Pittsburgh, USA, pp. 97–104. ACM Press (2006)
5. Forbus, K., Gentner, D., Law, K.: MAC/FAC: a model of similarity-based retrieval. Cogn. Sci. **19**(2), 141–205 (1995)
6. Fu, C., Xiang, C., Wang, C., Cai, D.: Fast approximate NN search with the navigating spreading-out graph. Proc. VLDB Endow. **12**(5), 461–474 (2019)
7. Gabel, T., Sommer, F.: Case-based learning and reasoning using layered boundary multigraphs. In: ICCBR 2022, Nancy, France, pp. 193–208. Springer (2022)
8. Gabel, T., Sommer, F.: Instance-based opponent action prediction in soccer simulation using boundary graphs. In: RoboCup 2022, Bangkok. Springer (2022)
9. Indyk, P., Motwani, R.: Approximate nearest neighbors: towards removing the curse of dimensionality. In: ACM Symposium on the Theory of Computing (1998)
10. Jégou, H., Douze, M., Schmid, C.: Product quantization for nearest neighbor search. IEEE Trans. Pattern Anal. Mach. Intell. **33**(1), 117–128 (2011)
11. Juarez, J., Craw, S., Lopez-Delgado, J., Campos, M.: Maintenance of case bases: current algorithms after fifty years. In: Proceedings of the 27th International Joint Conference on Artificial Intelligence (IJCAI), Stockholm, pp. 5457–5463 (2018)
12. Kalantidis, Y., Avrithis, Y.: Locally optimized product quantization for approximate nearest neighbor search. In: CVPR, Columbus, pp. 2329–2336. IEEE (2014)
13. Kelly, M., Longjohn, R.: The UCI ML Repository. https://archive.ics.uci.edu
14. Leake, D., Wilson, D.: Categorizing case-base maintenance: dimensions and directions. In: Proceedings of 4th European Workshop on CBR, Dublin, pp. 196–207 (1998)
15. Li, S., Amenta, N.: Brute-force k-nearest neighbors search on the GPU. In: 8th International SISAP Conference, Glasgow, UK, pp. 259–270. Springer (2015)
16. Malkov, Y., Yashunin, D.: Efficient and robust approximate nearest neighbor search using hierarchical navigable small world graphs. IEEE Trans. Pattern Anal. Mach. Intell. **42**(4), 824–836 (2020)
17. Paredes, R., Chávez, E.: Using the k-nearest neighbor graph for proximity searching in metric spaces. In: Consens, M., Navarro, G. (eds.) SPIRE 2005. LNCS, vol. 3772, pp. 127–138. Springer, Heidelberg (2005). https://doi.org/10.1007/11575832_14
18. Richter, M., Weber, R.: Case-Based Reasoning. A Textbook. Springer (2013)
19. Russell, S., Norvig, P.: Artificial Intelligence: A Modern Approach. Pearson (2020)
20. Smyth, B., McKenna, E.: Building compact competent case-bases. In: Proceedings of ICCBR 1999, pp. 329–342. Springer (1999)
21. Srivastava, N., Hinton, G., Krizhevsky, A., Sutskever, I., Salakhutdinov, R.: Dropout: a simple way to prevent neural networks from overfitting. J. Mach. Learn. Res. **15**(1), 1929–1958 (2014)

22. Toussaint, G.: The relative neighbourhood graph of a finite planar set. Pattern Recognit. **12**(4), 261–268 (1980)
23. Wang, M., Xu, X., Yue, Q., Wang, Y.: A comprehensive survey and experimental comparison of graph-based approximate nearest neighbor search. Proc. VLDB Endow. **14**(11), 1964–1978 (2021)
24. Wess, S., Althoff, K., Derwand, G.: Using k-d trees to improve the retrieval step in CBR. In: Proceedings EWCBR 1993, Germany, pp. 167–181. Springer (1993)

Advanced Search Techniques for Determining Optimal Sequences of Adaptation Rules in Process-Oriented Case-Based Reasoning

Maxim Hotz[1,2], Lukas Malburg[1,2(✉)], and Ralph Bergmann[1,2]

[1] Artificial Intelligence and Intelligent Information Systems, University of Trier, 54296 Trier, Germany
{s4mahotz,malburgl,bergmann}@uni-trier.de

[2] German Research Center for Artificial Intelligence (DFKI), Branch University of Trier, Behringstraße 21, 54296 Trier, Germany
{maxim.hotz,lukas.malburg,ralph.bergmann}@dfki.de
https://www.wi2.uni-trier.de

Abstract. The application of adaptation knowledge still poses a major challenge in modern Case-Based Reasoning (CBR) systems. This is especially the case in the subdomain of Process-Oriented Case-Based Reasoning (POCBR), where cases represent procedural experimental knowledge. Current adaptation methods in this field make use of proprietary local search techniques to apply adaptation knowledge, which is inefficient and does not allow exploitation of advanced search and optimization techniques. Therefore, this work presents an approach to transform rule-based adaptation into a planning problem that is solvable with both Constrained Optimization Planning (COP) and Genetic Algorithms (GAs). The results of an experimental evaluation indicate that this transformation is feasible, although it does not achieve significant improvements in terms of adaptation quality without fine-tuning the default search parameters. However, integration into state-of-the-art planning frameworks builds the basis for using a variety of additional features and updates, enhancing the modeling and configuration process.

Keywords: Process-Oriented Case-Based Reasoning · Adaptive Workflow Management · Rule-Based Adaptation · Constrained Optimization Planning · Genetic Algorithms

1 Introduction

Case-Based Reasoning (CBR) [1,21] is a problem-solving methodology that employs experience-based learning and reusable knowledge for a wide variety of tasks. Within the CBR cycle, the *Reuse* phase plays a crucial role for synthetic tasks, particularly in Process-Oriented Case-Based Reasoning (POCBR) [4,18], where the cases are represented as semantically annotated workflow graphs. The

© The Author(s), under exclusive license to Springer Nature Switzerland AG 2025
I. Bichindaritz and B. López (Eds.): ICCBR 2025, LNAI 15662, pp. 236–251, 2025.
https://doi.org/10.1007/978-3-031-96559-3_16

complexity of these workflow representations means that stored cases rarely match queries completely, requiring the adaptation of retrieved cases by means of adaptation knowledge. Despite significant research efforts in the CBR research community (e.g., [8,10,11,26,28,29]), both the acquisition with regard to knowledge engineering and the application of adaptation knowledge remain the main challenges in modern CBR systems.

A common approach to address these challenges is to encode knowledge in the form of adaptation rules [13,15]. However, the process of applying knowledge stored in rules to achieve an optimal adaptation result is a non-trivial process whose execution has a major impact on the quality and performance of the final adaptation result. This is particularly evident in POCBR where structural adaptations [3, p. 221] are essential for qualitative results. In contrast to substitutional adaptation [3, p. 221], structural adaptation complicates the process of applying adaptation rules by introducing interdependencies between the applied rules. Moreover, the application of adaptation knowledge in both CBR and POCBR is oftentimes still performed manually by domain experts, which is a tedious, time-consuming, and error-prone task [17].

Currently, there are two key approaches that address this lack of automation in POCBR: an operator-based method [20] and its extension into a rule-based system using the rule engine *Drools*[1] [16]. Both have been successfully implemented into the POCBR framework *ProCAKE* [5], demonstrating the feasibility of the automatic adaptation process. However, these approaches rely on proprietary local search techniques to construct sequences of operators or rules, which cannot guarantee the discovery of optimal solutions within the search space. Therefore, the goal of this work is to combine the benefits of knowledge representation through adaptation rules with advanced search techniques commonly associated with planning and optimization. This is achieved by dividing this task into two steps: To identify planning approaches that are suitable for use in the adaptation process, a set of requirements is derived based on the literature and the inherent properties of adaptation in POCBR. Based on these requirements, we evaluate state-of-the-art approaches, such as model-based planning [23, pp. 366–369], state-based planning [23, pp. 372–376], or Mixed Integer Programming (MIP) [30]. In a second step, the two best suited approaches are selected to develop a concrete concept to perform the adaptation by means of these planning approaches. The employment of such techniques could not only significantly improve adaptation quality compared to currently applied approaches, but also produce improvements in terms of performance. Ultimately, successful utilization of advanced search and planning techniques in this context could leverage the rule-based representation of structural adaptation knowledge to its full potential.

The paper is structured as follows: Sect. 2 describes the foundations regarding adaptations in POCBR and covers related approaches that have already investigated automatic adaptation techniques. Section 3 outlines the requirements that a planning approach must meet to be considered suitable for this task. In Sect. 4,

[1] https://www.drools.org.

the concept for modeling rule-based adaptation in POCBR by the means of the selected planning approaches is presented. Section 5 covers the experimental evaluation of the concepts. Finally, Sect. 6 concludes this paper and discusses future research directions.

2 Foundations and Related Work

The foundations for this paper comprise the basics of rule-based adaptation in CBR and the corresponding rule formalism [3, pp. 142–144]. Furthermore, the *NEST* graph representation and the similarity assessment by Bergmann and Gil [4] are fundamental to this work. Hence, they are introduced in the following along with related approaches applying advanced search techniques in the context of CBR.

2.1 Rule-Based Adaptation in CBR

Adaptation rules in the context of CBR are classical rules whose preconditions describe the circumstances under which the conclusion is executed [3, pp. 142–144]. These rules encode knowledge about how a retrieved case can be adapted to better fit the query by transforming the solution part of a case into another solution. By doing so, the similarity to the query case is typically increased. Hence, they are applied for both substitutional and structural adaptation. Since typical case representations in CBR rely on attribute-value representations, rules usually address query and case attributes within their precondition and define how new attributes for the target case can be derived within their conclusion.

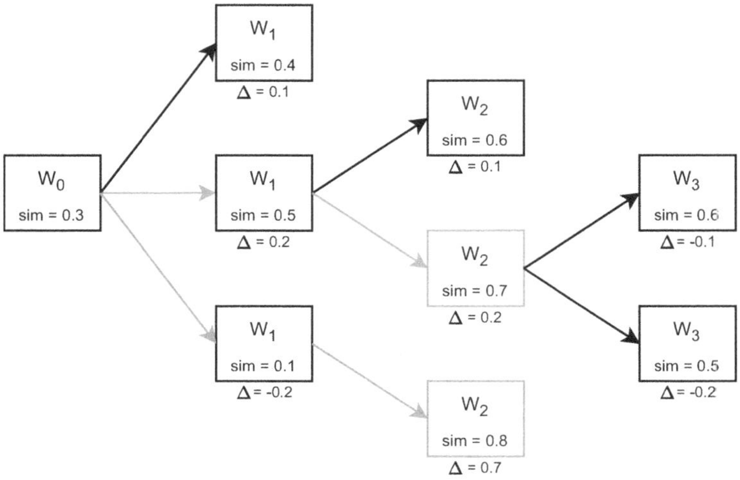

Fig. 1. Potential Search Paths Leading to Local or Global Maxima.

Since adaptation rules transform the case they are applied to toward the adaptation query, the adaptation problem can be considered as a search/planning task. To arrive at the optimal sequence of rules to apply, the search space has to be traversed by means of various search and planning strategies. In this context, the similarity between the adapted case and the query serves as a quality criterion or fitness function to guide the search. Figure 1 shows an exemplary search tree whose states are annotated with a similarity value and a delta that describes the change in similarity when traversing the search paths. The path marked in green reflects the path chosen by *Hill Climbing*, which is used in current adaptation approaches [16,19]. As it accepts no negative delta, i.e., worsening of the fitness function, it could get stuck in a local optimum. The orange path highlights the branch leading to the global optimum in this search space. To achieve this, temporary valleys of the fitness function have to be tolerated.

2.2 Adaptation of Semantic Workflows by Adaptation Rules

In contrast to CBR, cases in POCBR consist of procedural experimental knowledge [4,18] represented as semantic workflow graphs. In this work, the *NEST* graph [4] representation is used to represent these graphs. A *NEST* graph $W = (N, E, S, T)$ is a directed, semantically enriched graph with N being the set of nodes and E being the edges between them. S defines the semantic description that can be assigned to both nodes and edges by using a metadata language Σ. Finally, T assigns every node and every edge to a concrete type. To define similarity between graphs in this context, the knowledge-intensive similarity measure for semantic workflow graphs by Bergmann and Gil [4] is applied. This similarity measure is based on the best-possible mapping between the nodes and edges of two graphs, whereas only nodes and edges of the same type can be mapped. If such mapping exists, the similarity of the corresponding semantic descriptions between the mapped elements is calculated based on local similarity measures [4] and is finally aggregated according to the local-global principle. The adaptation of a *NEST* graph by adaptation rules comprises substitutional and structural adaptation elements, i.e., the exchange of semantic descriptions and the insertion or removal of nodes and edges. This notion of adaptation rules [16] differentiates between insert, delete, and exchange rules. Due to this complexity, the search space for determining an optimal sequence of rules is usually significantly larger compared to attribute-value case representations. Figure 2 depicts a *NEST* graph representing a cooking recipe alongside an exemplary insertion rule. The task nodes represent the preparation steps in the cooking recipe that are connected by control-flow edges defining the execution order. The data nodes represent ingredients that are produced or consumed by the task nodes in every step, which is indicated by the corresponding dataflow edges. If a user desires to add olives to his retrieved sandwich recipe, a corresponding adaptation rule can be applied such that the similarity between the adapted case and the query case is increased. As indicated in the graph, this insertion rule inserts a graph fragment, also called *streamlet* [19], consisting of the data node $d4$, the task node $t3$

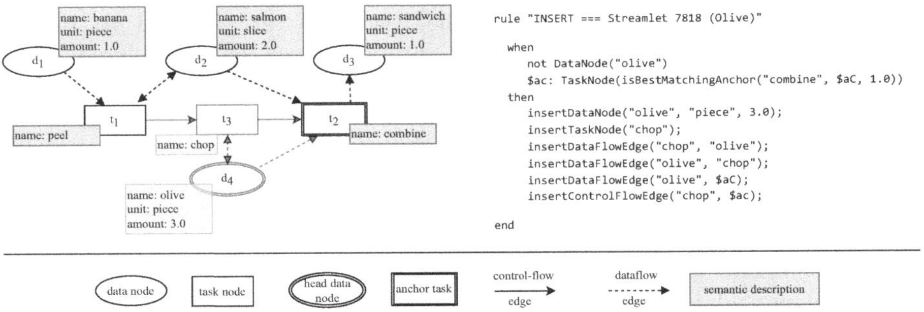

Fig. 2. *NEST* Graph with Insertion Rule. (Based on: [16])

and the corresponding edges between them into the graph at the position of the best-matching anchor candidate (see [19] for more details). This also holds for deletion rules, which determine a sufficiently similar streamlet from the graph that can be removed. Finally, exchange rules combine the principles of insertion and deletion rules, i.e., they delete a sufficiently similar streamlet from the graph and replace it by inserting a new streamlet at a suitable position.

2.3 Advanced Search Techniques in CBR

Related approaches in the field of advanced search techniques in CBR consist of studies like the one conducted by Salem and Mohamed [24] who present a method to optimize case adaptation using Genetic Algorithm (GA) applied to tablet formulation design in the pharmaceutical domain. However, they directly map the key-value-based case representation to a GA chromosome and thereby do not explicitly use adaptation knowledge. Leake and Ye [14] present the search-based *Robust Adaptation (ROAD)* approach to chain adaptation rules into potentially multiple adaptation paths that are pursued simultaneously. While their work provides backtracking and path resetting capabilities, they apply a greedy search for path construction. In the context of planning, Sánchez-Ruiz et al. [25] demonstrate that conventional CBR adaptation problems can be transformed into planning problems. More precisely, they employ planning operators based on Description Logics [2] that adapt both the problem and solution component of a case to exchange programming exercises in the Java programming education system JV^2M. However, most Description Logics are not as expressive [6] as first-order logic and, thus, may not be sufficient to represent more complex concepts that are required for semantic workflow graph adaptations, such as n-ary predicates. Müller and Bergmann [20], who introduce an operator-based adaptation approach for semantically enriched workflow graphs, present a more expressive approach suited to structural adaptations involving procedural knowledge. In their work, they use *Adaptation Operators* consisting of graph fragments to be inserted or removed from a workflow graph, transforming it toward the query while utilizing a knowledge-intensive similarity measure [4] to guide the search. However, they employ a proprietary local search mechanism to apply the operators. Based on this work, Malburg et al. [16] propose an approach to represent *Adaptation Operators* by means of Drools Rule Language (DRL) such that the adaptation process can be executed by a rule engine. While they succeed in transforming the operators into a rule-based representation, the search process during the application phase still uses a local search. Finally, Brand et al. [7] make an advance in employing a Reinforcement Learning (RL) agent [27] in the context of POCBR. However, the usage of RL for this purpose differs significantly from the conventional planning methods investigated in more detail in this paper.

The related approaches can be categorized into two distinct groups. The first category comprises studies employing advanced search techniques, such as GAs, in the adaptation phase of CBR. This means that they rely on attribute-value-based case representations, which limits their applicability in POCBR. The second category comprises studies that focus on extracting and applying complex adaptation knowledge in POCBR. Although these studies address the limitations mentioned above, they do not incorporate advanced search techniques. This reveals a significant research gap at the intersection of these two groups. Furthermore, by omitting the step of generating explicit adaptation knowledge, they lack explainability, making it difficult to validate the adaptation results.

3 Requirements Analysis of Planning Techniques for Rule-Based Adaptation in POCBR

In order to transform the adaptation problem into a planning problem, existing planning paradigms must be assessed regarding their suitability to achieve the overall goal of using planning techniques for adaptation rules. For this purpose, a set of requirements consisting of functional (FR) and non-functional (NFR) requirements is presented and applied to a variety of planning paradigms in the following. The set of requirements is derived on the basis of a comprehensive literature review.

[FR1] (Representation of Similarity). The planning approach should allow for the representation and incorporation of the complex similarity measure [4]. This is relevant not only for determining the proximity of the adapted case toward the query, but also to determine the applicability of a rule within its precondition. Hence, it should be possible to dynamically compute the similarity as a state-dependent metric during the planning process.

[FR2] (Representation of the Solution State). The planning approach should allow for the representation of the initial state and possible solution states of the adaptation problem. This involves not only the workflow representations themselves but also the constructs for holding the adaptation rules associated with the state of the planning problem, i.e., which rules have been applied to arrive at the current state and which ones are applicable in subsequent planning steps.

[FR3] (State-Based Decision Making). The planning approach should enable the computation of state-based metrics, i.e., the similarity assessment, either during the plan construction or afterward when evaluating the validity of a plan (see requirement FR5). This is necessary as applying a rule transforms the current state of the workflow into a successor state, meaning that the applicability of rules present in the rule base potentially changes in every adaptation/planning step/state.

[FR4] (Optimization). In POCBR, it is often not possible to adapt a retrieved workflow so that it fully matches the given query workflow specified in the goal state. For this reason, the planning approach should enable the use of a global optimization goal, e.g., maximizing the similarity of the workflow state to the query workflow.

[FR5] (Ensuring State-Consistency). The planning approach should provide a means to perform consistency checks of intermediate workflow states, i.e., the syntactical correctness of the workflow graph, and the applicability of the rule chosen in each adaptation step. These consistency checks are necessary because automatically learned rules can result in inconsistencies due to their intended broad applicability to different cases.

[NFR1] (Estimated Implementation Effort). In addition to the functional requirements, the implementation effort should not be excessive. This means that no modifications of the internal search and planning techniques should be necessary, and an out-of-the-box search or planning configuration should be applicable once the problem has been modeled.

3.1 Assessment of Planning Approaches

In this section, several state-of-the-art planning approaches are evaluated by applying the requirements outlined in the previous section. The selection of approaches is based on a preliminary assessment of the suitability for the task at hand, and at the same time, it tries to strike a balance by choosing approaches from different fields of planning, e.g., model-free and model-based approaches. The results of this assessment are summarized in Table 1.

State-Space Model (e.g., PDDL). Model-based languages like Planning Domain Definition Language (PDDL) [12] require the description of both the state space and the solution space of the planning problem beforehand. This would require the pre-computation of all similarities for using planners out-of-the-box and to enable them to make an informed choice about which rules are applicable in a planning step, which is not feasible for workflow graphs (FR1 ✗). For the same reason, FR2 is only partially fulfilled, as a state representation also comprises the applicability of rules (FR2 (✓)). FR3 is satisfied by the nature of the planning approach (FR3 ✓). FR4 is not met, as the lack of similarity representation means that no quality criterion is available to guide the search (FR4 ✗). Since the lack of similarity assessment does not allow the verification of the applicability of a rule during plan time, it cannot also be guaranteed that the resulting workflow is consistent (FR5 ✗). Since either the existing rule formalism or the internal planning heuristics would have to be adjusted to be compatible, the estimated implementation effort is assessed as high (NFR1 ✗).

Solution-Space Model (e.g., COP). Contrary to state-space models, solution-space models such as Constrained Optimization Planning (COP) [22] only require a set of global constraints to describe the solution-space. This allows for the representation of similarity dynamically during plan time (FR1 ✓) and consequently a suitable representation of solution states by means of constraints (FR2 ✓). Since COP follows a 'construct then evaluate' approach, state-based decision-making is not inherently given, but can be provided by employing incremental construction and scoring strategies (FR3 (✓)). Soft constraints encapsulating the similarity can be used as an optimization criterion guiding the search (FR4 ✓). Tightly coupled with the state-based decision-making, state consistency can only be achieved a-posteriori by plan validation (FR5 (✓)). Since the solution space of the adaptation problem is fully known in advance and no state-space modeling is required, the estimated implementation effort is assessed as manageable (NFR1 ✓).

Solution-Space Model (e.g., MIP). Similarly to COP, Mixed Integer Programming (MIP) [30] only requires that the solution space is modeled beforehand. However, constraints in MIP must adhere to a mathematical linear model, which lacks flexibility compared to the generic global constraints of COP. This makes the representation of a complex non-linear similarity measure unfeasible and would require an abstraction of similarity (FR1 (✓)). Consequently, the applicability of the rule formalism based on the concept of similarity is impaired (FR2 (✓)). Solutions are found by minimizing/maximizing global linear constraints, which do not allow state-based decision-making (FR3 ✗). Although MIP provides provably optimal solutions with respect to an optimization criterion, it is not applicable in the context of workflow adaptation due to the lack of an adequate optimization criterion (FR4 ✗). State consistency cannot be guaranteed at plan time, but must be verified during plan evaluation (FR5

Table 1. Comparison of Planning Approaches.

Requirements	Model-Based Planning			Model-Free Planning
	State-Space	Solution-Space		Population
	PDDL	COP	MIP	GA
[FR1] Sim. Representation	✗	✓	(✓)	✓
[FR2] State Representation	(✓)	✓	(✓)	✓
[FR3] Decision-Making	✓	(✓)	✗	✗
[FR4] Optimization	✗	✓	✗	✓
[FR5] State-Consistency	✗	(✓)	(✓)	(✓)
[NFR1] Est. Impl. Effort	✗	✓	✗	✓

✓ = *fulfilled,* (✓) = *partially fulfilled,* ✗ = *not fulfilled.*

(✓)). Due to the changes required for the rule- and similarity-formalisms, the expected implementation effort is assessed as high (NFR1 ✗).

Population-Based Planning (e.g., GA). Genetic Algorithms (GAs) [9] are a model-free approach to search/optimization problems that do not require explicit modeling of the problem domain. Hence, there is no limitation or requirement for the representation of similarity (FR1 ✓) nor the state representation itself (FR2 ✓). Every aspect of the problem domain can be encoded in genotypes/chromosomes and decoded afterward. However, this means that state-based decision-making is not provided (FR3 ✗). The fitness of a population or individual genotypes is used to guide the search as an optimization criterion (FR4 ✓). Similarly to COP, state consistency can only be achieved a-posteriori by plan validation (FR5 (✓)). Due to the lack of explicit modeling, the estimated implementation effort is assessed as low (NFR1 (✓)).

4 Applying Advanced Planning Techniques for Rule-Based Adaptation in POCBR

Based on the results of the scoring process, this section presents concrete concepts to solve adaptation tasks in POCBR by applying both GAs and COP. Since both paradigms share the same fundamental assumptions about the core components of a planning problem, i.e., initial state, goal state, actions, planning entities/variables, and quality criterion/fitness of the planning process can be represented by unified means.

In the context of POCBR, the retrieved workflow represents the initial state, while the query workflow represents the goal state. Adaptation rules correspond to the actions that a planner can choose to apply to improve the similarity toward the query workflow. Both COP and GA based approaches construct plans whose validity and fitness is checked after plan construction but still during plan time. Hence, the same fundamental concept for devising planning variables can be applied. The planning model can be created on a high level, meaning that the planner does not need to know explicitly which preconditions and conclusions the rules contain and how exactly their application changes the workflow state. This is a significant advantage over state-space modeling approaches like PDDL.

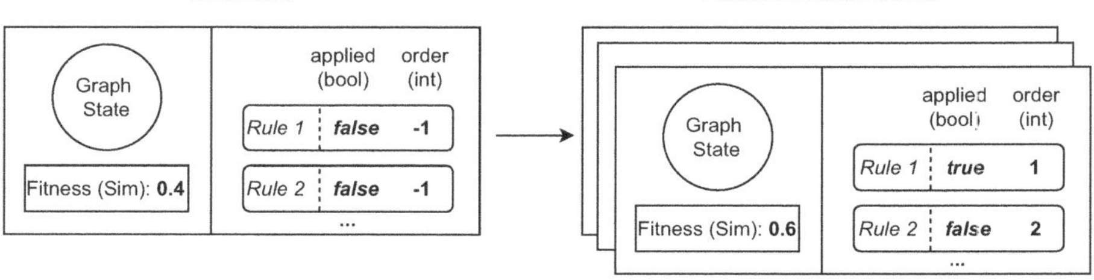

Fig. 3. Representation of Planning States.

Both rules and the workflow graph can be considered as black boxes for the planner, since the application of rules and the consistency of the workflow can be exposed to the planner by means of suitable object instance methods called during plan validation. Figure 3 shows this in more detail. A planning state contains the current state of the workflow graph, a collection comprising all available adaptation rules, and the fitness value of the current configuration. The rule formalism is extended by two planning variables. The variable *applied* is a Boolean value that determines whether the rule is applied or not. The variable *order* is an integer value that represents a non-consecutive total order in which the applied rules are ordered with $order \in \mathbb{N} \cap [0, |rules| - 1]$. Allowing a non-consecutive order relaxes the problem and thereby should have a positive impact on runtime. If a rule is not applied, its assigned order is ignored. The planning process itself thus consists of the manipulation of these two planning variables, either by means of metaheuristics in the context of COP or by mutations/cross-overs in the context of GAs.

COP solvers operate under the assumption that all relevant aspects regarding the problem state configuration can be expressed by means of a set of global constraints [22]. These constraints target constructed solutions and score them according to the principle of hard and soft constraints. Hard constraints are requirements that must be satisfied in order for a solution to be valid. In this context, the applicability of a rule or the final consistency of the resulting workflow graph can be considered as a hard constraint. In practice, this can be either accomplished by constraining solution states or by constraining the generation of planning moves before they are applied. Soft constraints are goals that can be violated, although leading to a penalty during score calculation. Alternatively, they can be used to reward solutions that display a great proximity to the goal state. In this use case, soft constraints are employed as a reward proportional to the similarity improvement toward the adaptation query. To navigate the search space, metaheuristics require a set of moves that can be applied in every planning step. By manipulating both *applied* and *order* a variety of moves can be constructed for the planner to explore (see Fig. 4). *Append* always adds a new rule at the last position of the rule chain. This is advantageous in terms of run time, as the validity of the pre-existing rule sequence remains unchanged. *Insert*, *Remove*, and *Swap* operate on arbitrary positions in the rule chain, meaning that the validity of all subsequent rules is potentially endangered. Finally, *InsertAndCutoff* represents a partial reset of the rule chain, which is intended to help escape local maxima.

Using Genetic Algorithms (GAs) requires encoding of adaptation rules or planning entities into a genotype compatible with mutation, selection, and crossover operations. For this purpose, a composite genotype consisting of two integer chromosomes is chosen. The *Selection Chromosome* corresponds to the *applied* variable of the COP approach, while the *Ordering Chromosome* corresponds to the *order* accordingly.

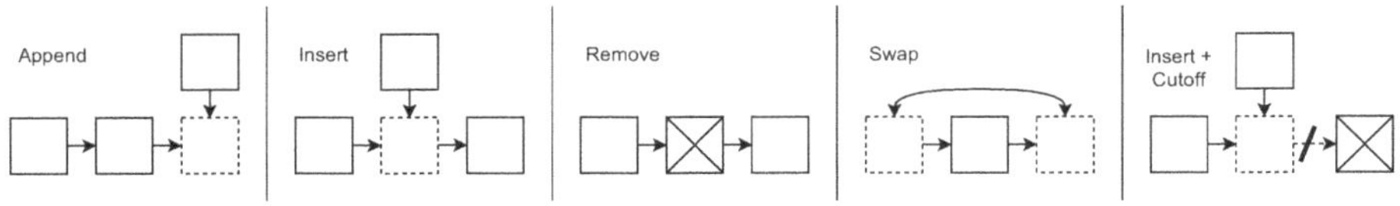

Fig. 4. Different Move Strategies for Constructing Rule Sequences.

5 Experimental Evaluation

In this section, both COP and GA approaches are evaluated in the domain of cooking recipes [5]. This is done by comparing the novel approaches with a current implementation [16] of rule-based adaptation. The goal of the experimental evaluation is to determine how well the respective approaches are capable of constructing optimal sequences of rules. For this purpose, the following hypotheses are investigated:

H1 The usage of advanced search techniques results in equal or better adaptation results than the current local search applied in rule-based adaptation.
H2 Advanced search techniques yield a higher rate of similarity improvement per second during the early stages of the adaptation process than the current local search applied in rule-based adaptation.
H3 Advanced search techniques achieve qualitatively better results with fewer available adaptation knowledge than the current local search applied in rule-based adaptation.
H4 More sophisticated move strategies for COP lead to better adaptation results.
H5 A combination of different move strategies for COP leads to better results than the isolated use of a single strategy.

Hypothesis H1 determines the differences in similarity values between the investigated methods and the current local search approach. Furthermore, Hypothesis H2 examines whether advanced search techniques lead to better results in a shorter period of time compared to the current approach, considering the steepness of the similarity delta. Since advanced search techniques are assumed to be superior w.r.t. balancing between exploration and exploitation of the search space, it is expected that they outperform the current approach in this regard. Analogously to H1, Hypothesis H3 examines the differences in similarity values over differently sized knowledge bases, as it is expected that the superiority of advanced search techniques should be independent of the amount of available knowledge. Finally, different move selection strategies for COP are investigated by Hypotheses H4 and H5. Here, it is assumed that the complexity of composite moves and the combination of such with atomic moves should help the planner navigate the search space more efficiently.

5.1 Experimental Setup

In this section, the experimental setup to validate the hypotheses is described. The concepts have been implemented in *Timefold*[2] (COP) and *Jenetics*[3] (GA) in combination with the POCBR framework *ProCAKE*[4] [5]. The experiment is based on a Leave One Out Cross Validation with a case base of 40 cooking workflow graphs. To perform the cross validation, each workflow serves as a query workflow for a retrieval on the remaining 39 workflows. The retrieved case workflow then becomes the starting point for the adaptation process. The adaptation knowledge consists of rules that have been learned from the remaining 39 workflows in advance. The experiment is conducted on different fractions of the total available knowledge so that the influence of different sized knowledge bases can be tested. Therefore, the rule base is randomly reduced to 20, 40, 60, and 80% of the total knowledge. To ensure stability, the experiment is repeated three times with different random seeds for the sampling process. Every adaptation run is terminated after a maximum of 10 min, during which the best fitness is tracked along with the gradient of fitness improvement in 25 s intervals. This described experiment is conducted for the current rule-based adaptation, *Jenetics*, and *Timefold*. Using *Timefold*, the following metaheuristics are used for the adaptation process with their default and/or recommended parameters independently[5]: *Hill Climbing (HC)*, *Diversified Late Acceptance (DLA)*, *Tabu Search (Tabu)*, and *Simulated Annealing (SA)*. Of those four search techniques, the two best performers are combined into a two-phase search configuration, each being assigned 5 min of search time. To ensure comparability with the current approach, all metaheuristics first only use *Append* moves (Strategy 1). In a second stage of the experiment, the best performing approach is also tested with *Insert* (Strategy 2), *InsertAndCutOff* (Strategy 3), and a combination of all the moves mentioned (Strategy 4). Moves such as *Swap* are omitted, as a first pre-evaluation has shown only limited potential to improve performance.

5.2 Experimental Results

Figure 5 illustrates the adaptation improvement in percent over time for the respective approaches. Although the current approach (*Baseline*) still achieves the best average improvement after the entire adaptation time span, a subset of the proposed approaches outperform the current approach in the early phase of the adaptation process. For example, after 50 s the *Baseline* reaches an average improvement of approximately 8.6% while both Timefold's *Hill Climbing* and the hybrid search achieve an average of 9.8%. As the *Reuse* phase in CBR should provide meaningful adaptation results as quickly as possible to increase the user

[2] https://timefold.ai/.
[3] https://jenetics.io/.
[4] https://procake.uni-trier.de.
[5] All evaluation results including the used search parameters, and further information for reproducibility can be found at: https://gitlab.rlp.net/procake/publications/optimal-adaptation-rule-sequences-iccbr-2025.

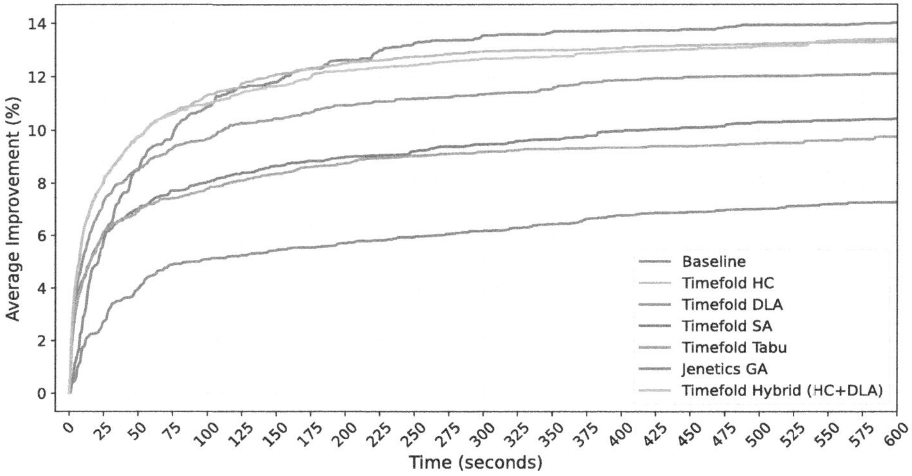

Fig. 5. Average Improvement over Time.

acceptance of a CBR system, this is an important observation (see H2). Consequently, Hypothesis H1 can be partially accepted. In terms of improvement in fitness over time, the gradient values of all metaheuristics (*Timefold*) temporarily exceed the *Baseline*. For example, Timefold's *Hill Climbing* achieves an improvement of 0.32% per second within the first 25 s, that drops down to 0.03% per second. Compared to that, the *Baseline* begins the adaptation process with an improvement of 0.23% per second and drops to 0.04% per second. Consequently, Hypothesis H2 can be accepted. Table 2 provides an overview of the final average adaptation improvements after the full 10-minute time span recorded for different fractions of available knowledge and move selection strategies. All presented differences are statistically significant ($p < 0.01$) using a two-way *ANOVA*. As there is no indication that the novel approaches lead to better results with fewer adaptation knowledge available, Hypothesis H3 is rejected. The investigation of different move strategies indicates that the *Append* (S1) strategy performs best overall. However, the improvements between the strategies *Insert* (S2) and *InsertAndCutoff* (S3) are significant. Based on these results, Hypothesis H4 can be partially accepted. Finally, the combination of all moves only beats S2, which means that Hypothesis H5 is also rejected.

Table 2. Averaged Results of the Experimental Evaluation.

Strat.		Base	HC	DLA	Tabu	SA	GA	Hybrid (HC + DLA)			
								S1	S2	S3	S4
Knowledge (%)	20	9.81	8.88	8.18	7.47	8.25	6.55	8.94	-	-	-
	40	12.22	11.61	10.45	8.35	9.50	6.85	11.85	-	-	-
	60	12.91	12.48	11.36	9.18	10.88	7.22	12.39	-	-	-
	80	13.47	13.13	11.69	9.48	10.86	7.35	13.41	-	-	-
	100	14.01	13.30	12.12	9.74	10.42	7.30	13.39	10.31	11.27	10.53

6 Conclusion and Future Work

In this paper, an approach is presented to treat rule-based adaptation in Process-Oriented Case-Based Reasoning (POCBR) as a planning problem. For this purpose, a set of requirements towards a planning approach is derived and used to filter state-of-the-art planning approaches w.r.t. their suitability for this task. Based on the results of this analysis, the adaptation problem is transformed such that both Constrained Optimization Planning (COP) and Genetic Algorithm (GA) approaches can be used. Although the practical experiment could not prove the meaningful superiority of the new techniques, the integration into state-of-the-art frameworks such as *Timefold* or *Jenetics* yields several advantages over the existing implementation, e.g., the ease of configuration or availability of efficient search algorithms and additional features. Furthermore, all results are obtained by using default parameters for the search techniques, as a more sophisticated configuration would exceed the scope of this paper.

In future work, we want to focus on hyperparameter tuning and benchmarking different search configurations so that adaptation performance can be improved. In terms of COP this comprises the parameters of the different metaheuristics and move selection strategies, but also the global hard and soft constraints. For example, it could be investigated whether penalizing rule chains that grow too long can have a positive impact on the adaptation result. In more general terms, this could also mean the usage of framework features like multi-threaded move evaluation, which is not employed in this work due to comparability reasons, but could improve performance. The results of the experimental evaluation also indicate that the usage of GAs in combination with built-in mutators/cross-over operations may not be sufficiently informed to achieve a meaningful advantage over a brute force search. At this point, custom mutators and/or cross-over operations should be employed. Furthermore, it should be investigated how different search techniques perform in other application domains with respectively more or less available adaptation knowledge, as there could be significant differences in the rate of similarity improvement. Since the proposed approach is directly applicable to less complex case representations, such as attribute-value-based CBR domains, we also want to test the suitability of the proposed approach in these domains in more detail in future work.

References

1. Aamodt, A., Plaza, E.: Case-based reasoning: foundational issues, methodological variations, and system approaches. AI Commun. **7**(1), 39–59 (1994)
2. Baader, F., et al.: The Description Logic Handbook: Theory, Implementation, and Applications. Cambridge University Press (2003)
3. Bergmann, R.: Experience Management: Foundations, Development Methodology, and Internet-Based Applications. Springer (2002)
4. Bergmann, R., Gil, Y.: Similarity assessment and efficient retrieval of semantic workflows. Inf. Syst. **40**, 115–127 (2014)
5. Bergmann, R., Grumbach, L., Malburg, L., Zeyen, C.: ProCAKE: a process-oriented case-based reasoning framework. In: 27th ICCBR Workshops (2019)
6. Borgida, A.: On the relative expressiveness of description logics and predicate logics. Artif. Intell. **82**(1–2), 353–367 (1996)
7. Brand, F., et al.: Using deep reinforcement learning for the adaptation of semantic workflows. In: 31st ICCBR Workshops, pp. 55–70 (2023)
8. Craw, S., Wiratunga, N., Rowe, R.: Learning adaptation knowledge to improve case-based reasoning. Artif. Intell. **170**(16–17), 1175–1192 (2006)
9. Forrest, S.: Genetic algorithms. ACM Comput. Surv. **28**(1), 77–80 (1996)
10. Hanney, K., Keane, M.T.: Learning adaptation rules from a case-base. In: Smith, I., Faltings, B. (eds.) EWCBR 1996. LNCS, vol. 1168, pp. 179–192. Springer, Heidelberg (1996). https://doi.org/10.1007/BFb0020610
11. Hanney, K., Keane, M.T.: The adaptation knowledge bottleneck: how to ease it by learning from cases. In: Leake, D.B., Plaza, E. (eds.) ICCBR 1997. LNCS, vol. 1266, pp. 359–370. Springer, Heidelberg (1997). https://doi.org/10.1007/3-540-63233-6_506
12. Haslum, P., et al.: An Introduction to the Planning Domain Definition Language, vol. 13. Springer (2019)
13. Leake, D.B., Kinley, A., Wilson, D.: Learning to improve case adaptation by introspective reasoning and CBR. In: Veloso, M., Aamodt, A. (eds.) ICCBR 1995. LNCS, vol. 1010, pp. 229–240. Springer, Heidelberg (1995). https://doi.org/10.1007/3-540-60598-3_21
14. Leake, D., Ye, X.: On combining case adaptation rules. In: Bach, K., Marling, C. (eds.) ICCBR 2019. LNCS (LNAI), vol. 11680, pp. 204–218. Springer, Cham (2019). https://doi.org/10.1007/978-3-030-29249-2_14
15. Leake, D.B., Ye, X., Crandall, D.J.: Supporting case-based reasoning with neural networks: an illustration for case adaptation. In: AAAI Spring Symposium: Combining ML with Knowledge Engineering, vol. 2846. CEUR-WS.org (2021)
16. Malburg, L., Hotz, M., Bergmann, R.: Improving complex adaptations in process-oriented case-based reasoning by applying rule-based adaptation. In: 32nd ICCBR, pp. 50–66. Springer (2024)
17. Minor, M., Bergmann, R., Görg, S., Walter, K.: Towards case-based adaptation of workflows. In: Bichindaritz, I., Montani, S. (eds.) ICCBR 2010. LNCS (LNAI), vol. 6176, pp. 421–435. Springer, Heidelberg (2010). https://doi.org/10.1007/978-3-642-14274-1_31

18. Minor, M., Montani, S., Recio-García, J.A.: Process-oriented case-based reasoning. Inf. Syst. **40**, 103–105 (2014)
19. Müller, G.: Workflow Modeling Assistance by Case-based Reasoning. Springer (2018)
20. Müller, G., Bergmann, R.: Learning and applying adaptation operators in process-oriented case-based reasoning. In: 23rd ICCBR, pp. 259–274. Springer (2015)
21. Richter, M.M., Weber, R.O.: Case-Based Reasoning - A Textbook. Springer (2016)
22. Rossi, F., Van Beek, P., Walsh, T.: Constraint programming. In: Handbook of Knowledge Representation, Foundations of Artificial Intelligence, vol. 3, pp. 181–211. Elsevier (2008)
23. Russell, S.J., Norvig, P.: Artificial Intelligence: A Modern Approach. Pearson (2016)
24. Salem, A., Mohamed, A.: Genetic Algorithms for Case Adaptation. In: 9th Nuclear Sciences and Applications Conference (2008)
25. Sánchez-Ruiz, A., et al.: Adaptation through planning in knowledge intensive CBR. In: 9th ECCBR, pp. 503–517. Springer (2008)
26. Smyth, B., Keane, M.T.: Retrieving adaptable cases: the role of adaptation knowledge in case retrieval. In: 1st EWCBR. LNCS, vol. 837, pp. 209–220. Springer (1993)
27. Sutton, R.S., Barto, A.G.: Reinforcement Learning - An Introduction. MIT Press (1998)
28. Wilke, W., Bergmann, R.: Techniques and knowledge used for adaptation during case-based problem solving. In: 11th IEA, pp. 497–506. LNCS, Springer (1998)
29. Wilke, W., Vollrath, I., Althoff, K.D., Bergmann, R.: A framework for learning adaptation knowledge based on knowledge light approaches. In: 5th GWCBR, pp. 235–242 (1997)
30. Wolsey, L.A.: Integer Programming. John Wiley & Sons (2020)

A Framework for Supporting the Iterative Design of CBR Applications

Guillermo Jimenez-Diaz[1(✉)], Mirko Lenz[2,3], Lukas Malburg[2,3], Belén Díaz-Agudo[1], and Ralph Bergmann[2,3]

[1] Department of Software Engineering and Artificial Intelligence, Instituto de Tecnologías del Conocimiento, Universidad Complutense de Madrid, Madrid, Spain
{gjimenez,belend}@ucm.es

[2] Artificial Intelligence and Intelligent Information Systems, Trier University, 54296 Trier, Germany
info@mirko-lenz.de, {malburgl,bergmann}@uni-trier.de

[3] German Research Center for Artificial Intelligence (DFKI) Branch Trier University, Behringstraße 21, 54296 Trier, Germany
{mirko.lenz,lukas.malburg,ralph.bergmann}@dfki.de
https://www.wi2.uni-trier.de

Abstract. Iterative design is a well-known methodology that involves prototyping, testing, analyzing, and refining products or processes. Rapid prototyping and evaluation are crucial, enabling designers to quickly identify and resolve issues and iteratively improve the design. However, effective iterative design relies on tools that accelerate both prototype creation and visual evaluation. This paper aims to address this challenge by presenting a framework specifically designed to enhance the iterative design process for CBR applications. In this context, we emphasize the manual and knowledge-intensive task of defining similarity measures. Furthermore, we introduce a proof-of-concept implementation of this framework based on the CBRkit toolkit and the SimViz visualization tool. We studied the capabilities to support the iterative design of CBR applications through a case study in the prototypical cars domain.

Keywords: Case-Based Reasoning · Iterative Design · CBR Frameworks · Rapid Prototyping · Visualization · Similarity · CBRkit · SimViz

1 Introduction

The Case-Based Reasoning (CBR) literature provides various frameworks designed to streamline the design and implementation of CBR applications (see [20] for a comprehensive review). One of the most challenging aspects of CBR development is gaining a deep understanding of the domain and constructing effective similarity measures that accurately capture its intricacies. Several approaches exist to tackle this problem [18]. A common method is manual programming, where domain experts define similarity functions based on predefined heuristics and rules. Another approach involves learning from data, where

© The Author(s), under exclusive license to Springer Nature Switzerland AG 2025
I. Bichindaritz and B. López (Eds.): ICCBR 2025, LNAI 15662, pp. 252–266, 2025.
https://doi.org/10.1007/978-3-031-96559-3_17

machine learning techniques are applied to automatically infer similarity measures from case examples. Regardless of the chosen option, modeling similarity measures is a critical and multifaceted task that requires an iterative modeling-testing loop. Visualizations play a key role in overcoming intrinsic modeling challenges by offering intuitive insights and improving the understanding of complex relationships within the data. As evidenced by previous approaches (e.g., [3,13,17]), visual tools facilitate expert-assisted methodologies that seamlessly integrate human expertise with computational techniques. By leveraging expert knowledge, these tools guide the development of similarity measures while iteratively refining them through systematic testing and feedback.

This paper aims to improve CBR development by integrating visualization techniques with CBR frameworks, helping developers and making CBR more accessible, especially to those outside the research community. To address the complexities of building CBR systems and designing effective similarity measures, we apply *iterative design* [6], a well-established methodology involving prototyping, testing, analyzing, and refining a product or process. This approach improves design quality and functionality by using system interaction as a research tool to continuously refine and evolve the project. Developers create a prototype, test and analyze it, refine it based on feedback, and repeat the cycle to converge toward an optimal solution.

Although individual CBR frameworks provide structured methodologies for designing CBR applications and there are some initial approaches to visualizing similarity measures during their construction [8,21], there is currently a lack of flexible solutions that integrate seamlessly into existing CBR frameworks. As a result, assessing the impact of modifications in similarity measures on similarity assessments remains a significant challenge. This issue is particularly critical in CBR, as the retrieval of relevant cases is heavily based on well-designed similarity measures, which, in turn, influence subsequent phases of the reasoning process.

Specifically, we demonstrate how the CBRkit framework [11] can be integrated with the SimViz approach [8] to facilitate the design of CBR systems in this paper. This integration involves identifying their inter dependencies, determining the necessary metadata for similarity measure computation, and exploring methods for visualizing and dynamically recalculating results when similarity measures are modified by the CBR developer. The emphasis of CBRkit on usability and integration capabilities, such as seamless compatibility with visualization tools like SimViz, makes it an ideal choice for researchers and practitioners aiming to build CBR systems. Through its streamlined design, CBRkit reduces the complexity of implementing CBR solutions while maintaining adaptability to diverse application scenarios.

The main contribution of this paper is the design and implementation of a framework to support the iterative design process for creating CBR similarity measures in CBR systems. This paper represents the integration effort between CBRkit [11] a flexible and modular framework designed to simplify the development and deployment of Case-Based Reasoning systems, and SimViz [8], an exploratory visualization tool aimed at understanding and identifying errors in both data and similarity measures. CBRkit supports customizable similarity measures and allows users to tailor the framework to specific domain requirements, and SimViz visualizations provide insight into the similarity between local and global attributes across different case representations. We propose an applied methodology using the CBRkit-SimViz tandem to ensure systematic development and evaluation for designing, prototyping, and evaluating CBR systems.

The paper is structured as follows: Sect. 2 reviews several CBR frameworks from a visualization perspective. Based on this literature review, in Sect. 3 we describe the proposed design framework and identify the requirements that should be met to support the CBR development cycle and enhance understanding of the domain, data, and similarity measures. Section 4 describes the architecture and implementation of the integrated system, focusing on the data flow between CBRkit (design and prototype) and SimViz (evaluate). We use the cars domain, which includes rich attribute diversity and relationships characteristic of many real-world similarity modeling challenges, for demonstrating a step-by-step CBR development cycle with SimViz visualization during the design phase. The cars domain has been extensively used in CBR research as a standard benchmark to illustrate core concepts and methodologies [12,15,24].

Section 5 concludes the paper by reviewing key lessons learned from the integration of these tools and outlining future research lines.

2 State-of-the-Art

Iterative design emerged as a need in the 1980s for the development of user interfaces and with the rise of the discipline of Human-Computer Interaction [6]. It attempts to solve the problems of designing new interfaces and adapting them to users, rather than training users to use them. The foundations of iterative design lie in the development of "cheap" prototypes whose purpose is to test a design idea. The performance of the prototype is evaluated with users, and a new design is proposed based on the evaluation findings. Iterative design methods have become standard in software development and management and are applied in different methodologies such as Spiral Development [5], Scrum [22], or Lean Software Development [19], among others. The iterative design cycle is more effective when the iterations are fast enough to determine whether a solution has value. Rapid prototyping and evaluation are crucial, enabling designers to quickly identify and address issues and iteratively improve the design. This requires tools that accelerate both prototype creation and the analysis of user feedback.

Visualization techniques play a vital role in this process, enabling users to quickly grasp the results of design choices, evaluate prototypes, and facilitate rapid adjustments. Effective evaluation requires the ability to visually access detailed information, connect disparate data points, identify patterns and deviations, and explore information from multiple perspectives [25]. In the context of CBR, the design of effective similarity measures is critical, and existing CBR frameworks enable the development of tailored CBR prototypes and further support this rapid iteration. Visualizations serve as powerful evaluation tools that help to understand information [1]. Interactive visualizations empower evaluators by allowing them to dynamically select, manipulate, and refine the displayed information, tailoring the visualization to their specific evaluation goals and enhancing its effectiveness.

In the following sections, we explore approaches and methods relevant to integrating visualization techniques for interactive design within CBR systems. This exploration is twofold: First, we examine the interactive design support provided by current CBR frameworks, based on Schultheis et al. [20]. Second, we discuss visualization approaches for interactive design, particularly during the key similarity measure modeling phase in CBR. Finally, we synthesize these contributions and identify the research gaps that motivate this paper.

2.1 Support of Interactive Design in CBR Frameworks

Schultheis et al. [20] present a review of open source CBR frameworks used to develop specific CBR applications. The authors compare the following CBR frameworks: *CloodCBR*, *eXiT*CBR*, *jColibri*, *myCBR*, and *ProCAKE*. In addition, they define a framework as "[...] a generic, domain-independent, and extensible software component that enables the implementation of specific applications." [20, p. 327]. All CBR frameworks have been compared in terms of supported CBR types and case representations, support to implement the knowledge containers, the CBR phases that can be applied, interfaces, and other additional features. In the following, we compare the results of the review, with a special focus on the visualization capabilities of the CBR frameworks and their support for interactive design. Based on this detailed analysis, we are able to identify current gaps in visualization techniques and derive requirements for developing suitable interactive design capabilities for CBR systems.

CloodCBR is a CBR framework that supports the development of textual and structural CBR applications. Regarding visualization capabilities, Schultheis et al. [20] determine that a web-based GUI is provided as a dashboard to visualize the CBR cycle. *eXiT*CBR* supports the development of structural CBR applications. A GUI is provided for configuration, to perform retrievals, data export, and the visualization of the results. *jColibri* is a Java-based CBR framework that supports the development of textual, structural, and conversational CBR applications. The framework provides a GUI for configuration and visualization tools for the case base. *myCBR* supports the development of textual and structural CBR applications. It is the only CBR framework that provides a GUI for modeling similarity measures and thus supports the interactive design of similarity measures. *ProCAKE* is a CBR framework that enables developers to create textual, structural, and process-oriented CBR applications. The framework provides a GUI for visualization and the creation of cases.

2.2 Approaches for Visualization of Similarity Measures

In addition to the support of interactive design to model similarity measures in CBR frameworks, there exist several visualization approaches and methods that can be beneficial for this purpose.

Schultheis et al. [21] present a visualization approach that helps to understand the similarity assessment of complex cases in the context of process-oriented CBR. For this purpose, three adopted visualization techniques have been used with the aim of supporting the design of similarity measures. Similarly, the SimViz approach [8] is a tool for visualizing similarity functions. It offers a web-based GUI for users to assess the similarity between cases in a case base, using various visualization techniques. Changing similarity measures triggers recalculations of similarity values. Bach and Mork [3] propose a similarity visualization method in CBR to aid in visualizing similarity measures during the retrieval phase.

Marin-Veites et al. [13] propose a visual explanation of the similarity scores for the query cases by comparing the global and local similarity measures of the attributes for end users in a medical domain. They use bar charts to compare the case similarity between the top 5 ranks of most similar cases and a query case. The visualization shows not only the global similarity, but also the local similarity scores that intervene in the similarity measure.

The works in [16,17,23] propose visualization methods based on the use of graphs and spring force models for visual exploration of case bases and the similarity measures applied to them. The distance between cases in a two-dimensional space represents their similarity, so similar cases will be drawn close together, and dissimilar cases should be drawn far apart. This visualization is useful to identify regions of similar cases and gaps without representative cases or outliers, but it only works for small case bases.

The work in [9] describes another alternative to provide visual explanations of the similarity scores between a query and the retrieved cases. These visualizations are based on scatter plots and rainbow boxes and are aimed at end users, i.e., medical experts of the CBR system. The complexity of the visualization used led the authors to simplify and reduce the dimensions and information displayed by the tool, which required a short training before using it.

In [14], the authors use visualization techniques to increase the explainability of the results of a CBR system. For this purpose, coordinate diagrams are used that represent the similarities between the cases.

2.3 Summary and Research Gaps

Schultheis et al. [20] note that while most CBR frameworks offer GUIs for visualization and configuration, they rarely support the interactive design of similarity measures. Although visualization techniques exist, they mainly focus on explaining similarities rather than guiding the design process. Moreover, these tools are often standalone, limiting integration with modern CBR frameworks. This lack of interactive design capabilities hinders broader applicability, both within and outside the CBR research community. To address these limitations, we propose a tightly integrated architecture that combines visualization techniques directly within CBR frameworks, enabling interactive similarity measure design tailored to various applications.

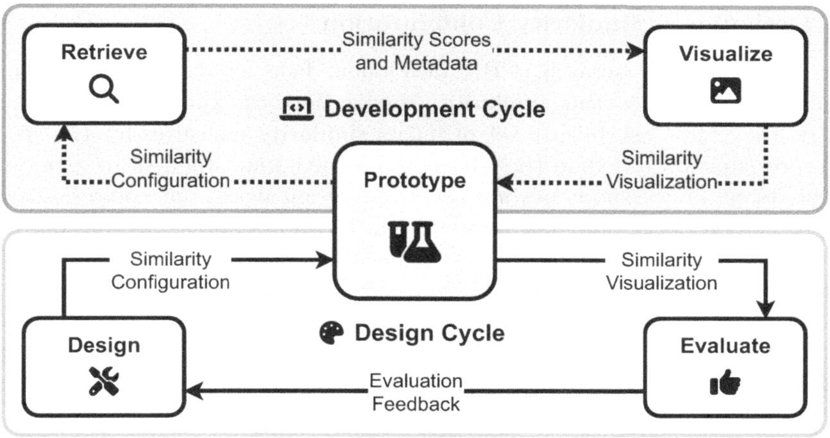

Fig. 1. Iterative CBR design process with integrated visualization.

3 Iterative Design Framework

The goal of this section is to propose an implementation-agnostic description of the proposed iterative process for designing CBR applications that can be used as a template for other work in this area. A reference implementation of this framework is provided in Sect. 4. Figure 1 shows an overview of the proposed iterative design process. Compared to the standard process described in Sect. 2, our approach focuses on the integration of CBR development frameworks and visualization tools to enable rapid prototyping. As a result, practitioners are no longer required to model rather complex similarity measures by hand, but can rely on visual guidance and feedback through the process. In order to enable these interactions, the framework needs to meet certain *constraints*—expressed as *requirements* in the context of our envisioned integration—that will be discussed as part of this framework description. These requirements have been derived based on current CBR frameworks supporting visualizations and additional standalone tools helping CBR developers during modeling similarity measures (see Sect. 2). In addition, the requirements reflect both our expertise as CBR researchers and our experience developing CBR applications, thereby representing the user group of CBR developers. In addition to *mandatory* requirements (MR), we propose a set of *optional* requirements (OR) that can further enhance the user experience, but may be omitted for certain use cases. We divide the proposed framework into three sections: (i) *Designing* a similarity configuration, (ii) visualization-aware *prototyping* as part of the development cycle, and (iii) end-to-end *evaluation*.

We want to emphasize that similarity is useful in different CBR tasks, not just in retrieval. It plays a crucial role in adaptation, reuse, and learning by ensuring that relevant cases are identified, appropriately modified, and integrated into the system effectively. As such, finding optimal similarity measures for a domain is a central task in the overall CBR design process.

3.1 Designing a Similarity Configuration

When starting from scratch, CBR developers face a cold start problem as they cannot rely on existing similarity visualizations or expert feedback. Consequently, they must establish a set of initial similarity measures for the specific case representation based on the data types involved and their prior experience. This bootstrapping issue is beyond the scope of our work, but could be tackled with the help of Large Language Models (LLMs)—for instance, by automatically selecting and parameterizing similarity measures of established CBR frameworks as proposed by Lenz et al. [10]. Having obtained an initial configuration, the CBR developer can draw on two crucial sources of knowledge during this phase: the evaluation of the similarity score and the feedback from the domain expert. Using these resources, they can refine the similarity configuration and initiate the next iteration of the design process.

MR1 (Similarity Configuration)**.** The framework must provide a description of the similarity configuration used by the CBR system prototype. This includes the functions used to determine local similarities and the aggregation method to calculate the global similarity score.

3.2 Visualization-Aware Prototyping

After an initial similarity configuration is established, the CBR developers can evaluate the retrieval performance using a CBR system prototype. Typically, this involves defining a query, executing it against the available case base, and examining the retrieved cases along with their corresponding numeric similarity values. This process can be tedious and time-consuming, with only little or no insight into the underlying computations. Instead, providing visual feedback on the similarity scores and the impact of individual similarity measures can significantly enhance the expert's understanding of the system's behavior. In this context, relying solely on the global aggregated similarity score is insufficient, and further data is needed to generate appropriate visual representations.

MR2 (Case Representation)**.** The framework must define a machine-readable representation of the case base and the queries. This makes it possible to analyze the data types and select appropriate visualizations.

MR3 (Similarity Scores)**.** The framework must generate data on the local similarity scores for each attribute of the retrieved cases in addition to the overall global score. This data will be used to generate visual representations to explore and analyze the similarity functions described in the previous stage.

OR1 (CBR Introspection)**.** The framework should provide information on all the CBR processes required to achieve the final solution. This enables fine-grained analysis of complex patterns, such as retrieval with MAC/FAC [7].

OR2 (Arbitrary Case Representation)**.** The framework should support not only simple attribute-value case representations, but also more arbitrary representations such as object-oriented structures, hierarchical data, graph-based structures, or even images.

OR3 (Interactivity). The framework should allow interactive configuration of the similarity measures. Instead of using hard-coded or built-in metrics, the user should be able to tweak the parameters and observe the impact on the computed scores in real time.

3.3 End-to-End Evaluation

The final step in the iterative design process is the evaluation of the system with domain experts. Having completed the prototyping phase, the CBR developer already has a working implementation at hand together with a corresponding similarity visualization. Contacting domain experts is resource intensive and time-consuming, so the CBR developer may decide to perform multiple rounds of prototyping first. However, actual feedback from people working in the field is invaluable and can help to identify issues that may not be apparent to the CBR developer. The generated visualization can be helpful for this task as it helps the CBR developer to explain the system's behavior to the domain expert, and, thus, provides an introspective view of the system's behavior. Afterward, the CBR developer can incorporate the suggestions into the similarity configuration as part of the next iteration of the design cycle.
MR4 (Interactive Visualization). The evaluation process must be supported with interactive features. Interactive visualization should be preferred to support the evaluation stage because it will ease the engagement of the different users involved in the evaluation process.
OR4 (Automated Evaluation). The framework should provide automated evaluation methods to assess the appropriateness of the computed similarities. This can, for instance, be achieved by comparing a retrieval result with a set of known relevant cases crafted by human experts. This allows a proper assessment of a good number of cases and helps in maintaining the case base.

4 Proof-of-Concept Implementation

Based on the proposed framework for supporting the iterative CBR design process, in this section, we present a proof-of-concept that instantiates the theoretical framework and works as an example of how to implement and use it in a real use case. For this purpose, we propose the integration of CBRkit [11], an easily applicable CBR framework for the prototyping stage, and SimViz [8], a visualization tool for the visual evaluation stage. In the following, we discuss the concrete integration between these two tools and their data flow to implement the proposed. In addition, we conduct a case study for evaluation and to demonstrate the suitability of their integration. For this purpose, we use the cars domain, and discuss step by step the iterative CBR design process using both tools.

4.1 CBRkit

CBRkit [11] is a Python-based framework for building CBR applications[1]. It is designed to be modular and flexible and uses a declarative approach to build

[1] Source code: https://github.com/wi2trier/cbrkit (MIT license).

custom pipelines for the different stages of the CBR cycle. The library comes with a set of built-in components such as similarity measures—making it easy to get started—but also allows for the creation of completely custom functions for more advanced use cases. Built-in functions are available for basic data types like strings or numbers, but also more complex ones like attribute-value data or graphs. CBRkit does not introduce a new abstraction layer through some similarity configuration format, instead it uses native Python code for declaratively defining the desired similarity measures. In addition to running CBR pipelines using these, it is also possible to expose them via a REST API, which allows for easy integration with other systems like SimViz.

The first version of CBRkit published in 2024 already met some of the requirements outlined in Sect. 3: It is possible to define CBR pipelines consisting of multiple retrieval and reuse stages—making it possible to apply MAC/FAC—which are then transparently exposed in the result object (OR1). Its way of defining similarity measures is flexible enough to allow for arbitrary case representations (OR2). In addition, the resulting similarity scores can be *structured* and contain additional metadata—for instance, local similarity scores for each attribute of the retrieved cases (MR3).

However, two mandatory and two optional requirements were still unmet. First, while easy to configure, the similarity measure definitions were not exposed in a machine-readable format in the result object (MR1). These measures are defined in plain Python code, making the extraction of the required information complex and not feasible without changes to the core of the library. This lack of abstraction also means that the similarity configuration cannot be dynamically changed (OR3). In addition, while CBRkit can handle arbitrary case representations, these are not passed to downstream components due to missing serialization techniques. Furthermore, automated evaluation is not possible due to the absence of interfaces for standardized evaluation metrics such as precision/recall or completeness/correctness (OR4). Lastly, the mentioned REST interface was a byproduct of the library, not a primary feature, leading to an overly verbose and difficult-to-consume API specification.

4.2 SimViz

SimViz[2] (**Sim**ilarity **V**isuali**Z**ation) is a tool that focuses on the interactive visualization of similarity measures and its application to different case bases [8]. SimViz can visualize structured cases based on attribute-value representations. It uses case base metadata with information about attribute data types to choose the appropriate visualization (MR2). In addition to basic datatypes (strings, numbers, and symbols), it provides specific visualizations for visual attributes (like colors and images) and symbols arranged in a taxonomy.

SimViz supports global-local similarity measures based on weighted similarity. It uses similarity configuration metadata about global and local similarity

[2] Source code: https://github.com/gjimenezUCM/simviz (Apache 2.0 License). Deployed version: https://gjimenezucm.github.io/simviz/.

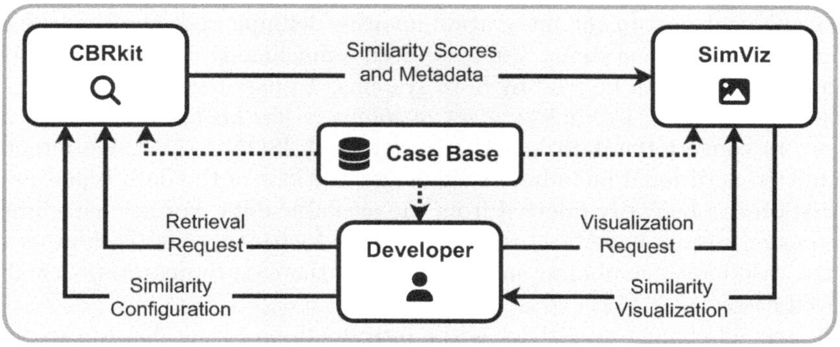

Fig. 2. Architecture of the integration between CBRkit and SimViz.

measures to display visual explanations about the case attributes, and the similarity measures employed (MR1). It also provides heatmaps and histograms to explore the distribution of similarity scores over a case base (MR3). More specifically, the global similarity score between two cases can be visually analyzed, showing how it is deconstructed into local similarity values and which functions are employed to compute them.

Since its early design, SimViz supports the interactive exploration of the case base and the similarity scores (MR4). First, users can click on the heatmap to select a particular pair of cases, or users can randomly select a pair of cases by clicking on a particular histogram bar or on a taxonomic concept. Moreover, users can explore the similarity distribution of an individual case against the other cases in the case base using an interactive stripe chart. Finally, SimViz partially supports the interactive configuration of the similarity measures (OR3). Users can modify the predefined weights of the local similarity measures and compare the effect of these changes on the global similarity value, recalculating it without the need of any additional prototyping tool.

Although SimViz meets all mandatory requirements, some optional ones are still missing. Designed primarily for similarity visualization, SimViz does not support introspection of other stages in the CBR process (OR1). Furthermore, requirement OR2 is only partially fulfilled. Although it includes visualization for taxonomies, images, and colors, SimViz cannot handle arbitrary case representations. We are working on supporting hierarchical data, with future plans to include its representation. Finally, automated evaluation is not supported as its interface does not visualize any standardized evaluation metrics (OR4).

4.3 Integration of CBRkit and SimViz

In this section, we detail the integration process of CBRkit and SimViz. CBRkit is used to design similarity measures and prototype the retrieval cycle to generate similarity scores, while SimViz utilizes these data, along with the case base and its case representation, to visualize and evaluate the similarity values and the similarity measures employed. Figure 2 illustrates the use of both tools to implement the proposed theoretical framework.

A significant part of the integration involves defining and adapting the data formats used by both systems. First, we need a machine-readable case representation (MR2) that can be read by both systems. To pass the retrieved cases and the underlying query to SimViz, a set of *dumpers* has been implemented, such as those to convert the data into the widely used JSON format. We intentionally omitted additional metadata, such as descriptions of the data types, as this information can be easily inferred from the available data. For use with SimViz, the exported results have been manually merged with the SimViz data used to load the case base—combining metadata about the case representation and the retrieved cases.

The second change in CBRkit is the introduction of a mechanism to gather information about the similarity configuration provided (MR1). Our goal was to transmit *everything* given by the user in a machine-readable format to downstream applications such as SimViz. To achieve that, *all* built-in similarity measures have been refactored to use a class-based interface that exposes the parameters of the measure set by the user via class attributes. By leveraging Python's magic methods, instances of these classes can still be called as if they were functions, allowing for a seamless transition from the original implementation. Besides the parameters, we automatically determine the name of the function and collect the docstring of the class as a description of the measure. This approach has been implemented in a generic way that works not only for the built-in metrics, but also for custom similarity functions defined by the user. Using these new capabilities, we can generate files containing the similarity configuration (MR1) and similarity scores (MR3) to be ingested by SimViz for visual evaluation. As SimViz expects the data in a specific format, we implemented an adapter to convert between the formats—making it possible for SimViz to directly work with the CBRkit results.

Next, we added an evaluation module (OR4) to CBRkit that is based on the `ranx` library [4]. In an effort to simplify integration with other systems, we also completely overhauled the REST API, which now offers a fully typed OpenAPI specification that can be used to generate client libraries for different programming languages. Currently, the evaluation module is not yet integrated into the REST API, but we see this as a first step towards a more automated evaluation of the CBR system.

The last missing piece is an interactive way to define similarity measures in CBRkit (OR3). One way to tackle this aspect would be to define a serialization format manually configuring CBRkit—leading to a high maintenance burden. A more elegant way is to automatically generate a schema from the set of available Python functions based on the available type annotations. Doing this in a generic way is not trivial, since CBRkit supports not only attribute-value representations, but also graphs or fully custom, domain-specific representations. We therefore decided to leave this requirement for future work and focus on the integration with SimViz first.

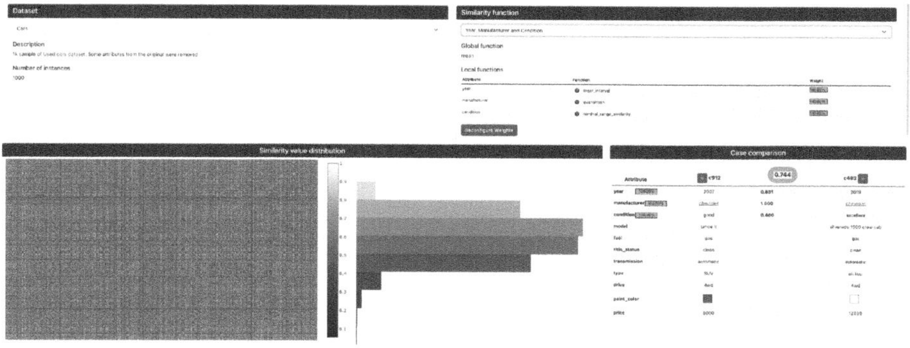

Fig. 3. Visualization of Case Representation With Attribute Weighting (Full image available at https://tinyurl.com/musaj774)

4.4 Case Study in the Cars Domain

To demonstrate the suitability of the proposed integration between a CBR framework and a visualization tool, we present a case study on the integration of CBRkit and SimViz. For this, we use the cars domain, which includes a dataset of 1,000 cars[3] The cars domain represents an exemplary case study for similarity modeling, embodying challenges common across real-world applications. This dataset requires sophisticated similarity measures that can appropriately handle different data types while capturing their relative importance in determining the overall similarity. Its 11 attributes and their metadata are crucial for the integration between CBRkit and SimViz. Below, we demonstrate how this integration can support the iterative design process in the cars domain.

We started the design process by analyzing the dataset and exploring the catalog of similarity measures provided by CBRkit. After that, we use CBRkit to implement a first version of a similarity measure that combines local similarities using a weighted mean. This measure combines diverse functions such as a linear similarity for the *year* attribute, Levenshtein for the *manufacturer* attribute, and a custom function for linear similarity in a set of values for the *condition* attribute. The similarity configuration and similarity scores data created using CBRkit are used in SimViz to visualize the designed similarity measures.

Figure 3 illustrates the dataset used, the case representation, including attribute weighting, and the similarity measures applied. The top section shows the used dataset (left) and the similarity configuration (right). The bottom section is for the interactive visualization of similarity scores data, showing the distribution of the similarity values in the case base (left), and a case comparison between two selected cases (right). In this context, it is visualized with which importance each attribute contributes to the final similarity value. Furthermore, it is also possible to focus on local similarity values and their corresponding similarity measures.

[3] The used cars dataset is available at https://doi.org/10.5281/zenodo.15006920.

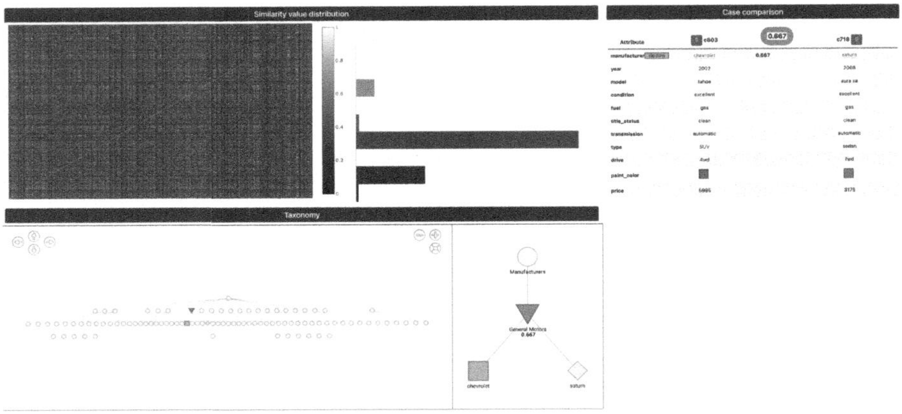

Fig. 4. Explanation of Local Similarities by Visualization (Full image available at https://tinyurl.com/mr3y4n2e).

The iterative process continues using the Similarity configuration panel provided by SimViz, where we can modify the predefined weights of the local similarity measures. This feature supports a fine-tuning of the similarities in the case base, visualizing the effect of these changes on the global similarity value.

The iterative process can return to the design stage in order to experiment with more complex similarity measures, using a taxonomy for the *manufacturer* attribute. In this case, we return to CBRkit to use the similarity measures that this framework implements for taxonomies to create new similarity configurations and data scores and visualize these new similarity functions. Back to SimViz to analyze them, Fig. 4 shows how SimViz supports the visualization of the taxonomy used for similarity calculation. To better understand the assessment of similarity between the two attribute values, i.e., *Chevrolet* and *Saturn*, the corresponding nodes in the taxonomy are highlighted. This helps both the CBR developer and the domain expert determine how the similarity originates.

5 Lessons Learned, Limitations, and Future Work

Developing effective similarity measures remains a challenge in CBR system design and implementation. Although existing CBR frameworks provide structured methodologies, they often lack the flexibility to integrate with visualization techniques and tools. CBRkit addresses this gap, standing out for their focus on usability and integration. In this paper, we show how the integration of CBRkit with a visualization tool such as SimViz makes it an ideal choice for researchers and practitioners. We demonstrate how CBRkit's streamlined design simplifies CBR solution implementation while maintaining adaptability for various applications. Our approach improves the interpretability of similarity measures, facilitating their iterative refinement, and ultimately making CBR systems more accessible to a broader audience. By visualizing the behavior of similarity measures, developers can gain more profound insight into their impact on case retrieval and system performance, leading to more effective design choices. Based on our experience during the integration of both tools, we identified several paths for future work:

Data-Driven Process. Currently, similarity measures must be manually defined in CBRkit based on a configuration. A more integrated approach would involve a common interchange format for CBRkit and SimViz, enabling automatic generation of similarity measures.

Orchestration. In its current state, both tools are loosely coupled: CBRkit generates files that are consumed by SimViz. A deeper integration could involve an orchestrated workflow in which SimViz initiates the similarity computation using CBRkit through an integrated user interface to configure the similarity configuration.

Data Format Standardization. To bridge the different case representation formats, we created an adapter. A better solution would be to standardize the data formats to meet both applications' requirements.

Limitations in Data Size. Large data files can result in high latency when running as a service. For example, the Cars 1k dataset generates similarity score files of around 200 MB. The API should support selectively querying only the relevant data to mitigate this issue.

Evaluation Metrics. While CBRkit includes an initial implementation of an evaluation module, it is not yet part of the integration. To fulfill OR4, it should allow loading a gold standard corpus and comparing the similarity scores with the expected results.

In future work, we will extend this integration by adding more visualization techniques and evaluating their effectiveness through empirical studies. In addition, we want to examine how large language models (LLMs) can be used to support similarity modeling by suitable explanations [2]. We also plan to expand visualization to other key CBR processes, particularly reuse and case base maintenance. Additionally, by providing an OpenAPI specification, we enable easy re-implementation by other libraries, fostering future integration of SimViz with other CBR frameworks and promoting a more collaborative, interoperable CBR ecosystem.

Acknowledgments. Supported by the UCM (Research Group 921330) and the AUDITIA-X project PID2023-150566OB-I00, funded by the Ministry of Science and Innovation of Spain (https://gaia.fdi.ucm.es/research/auditia-x/), the association *Eifelkreis Digital* with its project KITEi, and the *Studienstiftung*.

References

1. Azzam, T., et al.: Data visualization and evaluation. N. Dir. Eval. **2013**(139), 7–32 (2013)
2. Bach, K., et al.: Case-based reasoning meets large language models: a research manifesto for open challenges and research directions. HAL Science **hal-05006761v1** (2025). https://hal.science/hal-05006761, working paper or preprint

3. Bach, K., Mork, P.J.: On the explanation of similarity for developing and deploying CBR systems. In: 33rd FLAIRS, pp. 413–416. AAAI Press (2020)
4. Bassani, E.: Ranx: a blazing-fast Python library for ranking evaluation and comparison. In: Advance in Information Retrieval, pp. 259–264. Springer (2022)
5. Boehm, B.W.: A spiral model of software development and enhancement. Computer **21**(5), 61–72 (1988)
6. Buxton, W., Sniderman, R.: Iteration in the design of the human-computer interface. In: 13th HFAC, pp. 72–81 (1980)
7. Forbus, K.D., Gentner, D., Law, K.: MAC/FAC: a model of similarity-based retrieval. Cogn. Sci. **19**(2), 141–205 (1995)
8. Jiménez-Díaz, G., Díaz-Agudo, B.: Visualization of similarity models for CBR comprehension and maintenance. In: 32nd ICCBR, vol. 14775, pp. 67–80 (2024)
9. Lamy, J., Sekar, B.D., Guézennec, G., Bouaud, J., Séroussi, B.: Explainable artificial intelligence for breast cancer: a visual case-based reasoning approach. Artif. Intell. Medicine **94**, 42–53 (2019)
10. Lenz, M., Hoffmann, M., Bergmann, R.: LLsiM: large language models for similarity assessment in case-based reasoning. In: 33rd ICCBR in Biarritz, France. Springer (2025)
11. Lenz, M., Malburg, L., Bergmann, R.: CBRkit: an intuitive case-based reasoning toolkit for Python. In: 32nd ICCBR, vol. 14775, pp. 289–304. Springer (2024)
12. Malburg, L., Hoffmann, M., Trumm, S., Bergmann, R.: Improving similarity-based retrieval efficiency by using graphic processing units in case-based reasoning. In: 34th FLAIRS (2021)
13. Marín-Veites, P., Bach, K.: Explaining CBR systems through retrieval and similarity measure visualizations: a case study. In: 30th ICCBR. LNCS, vol. 13405, pp. 111–124. Springer (2022)
14. Massie, S., Craw, S., Wiratunga, N.: Visualisation of case-base reasoning for explanation. In: ECCBR 2004 Workshops, pp. 135–144 (2004)
15. Mathisen, B.M., Aamodt, A., Bach, K., Langseth, H.: Learning similarity measures from data. Prog. Artif. Intell. **9**(2), 129–143 (2020)
16. McArdle, G., Wilson, D.C.: Visualising case-base usage. In: 5th ICCBR Workshops, pp. 105–114. Springer (2003)
17. Namee, B.M., Delany, S.J.: CBTV: visualising case bases for similarity measure design and selection. In: 18th ICCBR, vol. 6176, pp. 213–227. Springer (2010)
18. Ontañón, S.: An overview of distance and similarity functions for structured data. Artif. Intell. Rev. **53**(7), 5309–5351 (2020)
19. Poppendieck, M., Poppendieck, T.: Lean Software Development: An Agile Toolkit. The Agile Software Development Series. Addison-Wesley (2010)
20. Schultheis, A., et al.: An overview and comparison of case-based reasoning frameworks. In: 31st ICCBR. LNCS, vol. 14141, pp. 327–343. Springer (2023)
21. Schultheis, A., et al.: Explanation of similarities in process-oriented case-based reasoning by visualization. In: 31st ICCBR, vol. 14141, pp. 53–68. Springer (2023)
22. Schwaber, K.: Agile Project Management with Scrum. Microsoft Press (2004)
23. Smyth, B., Mullins, M., McKenna, E.: Picture perfect - visualisation techniques for case-based reasoning. In: 14th ECAI, ECAI 2000, pp. 65–69. IOS Press (2000)
24. Verma, D., Bach, K., Mork, P.J.: Similarity measure development for case-based reasoning-a data-driven approach. In: 3rd NAIS Symposium. CCIS, vol. 1056, pp. 143–148. Springer (2019)
25. Ward, M.O., Grinstein, G., Keim, D.: Interactive Data Visualization. CRC Press (2015)

Two-Agent Case-Based Reasoning for Prediction

Pierre-Alexandre Murena(✉)

Hamburg University of Technology Research Group on Human-Centric Machine Learning Hamburg, Hamburg, Germany
pierre-alexandre.murena@tuhh.de

Abstract. Decision-making and prediction using Case-Based Reasoning involve two sequential steps: retrieval, where similar cases are selected, and adaptation, where these retrieved cases are used to infer a solution to the target problem. Traditionally, both steps are performed by a single agent, and prior research has emphasized the importance of adaptation-guided retrieval, i.e. considering the adaptation method when conducting retrieval. This paper explores an alternative setting, in which retrieval and adaptation are carried out by two distinct agents. A particularly relevant scenario arises when retrieval is performed by an AI agent, while adaptation is handled by a human. Since adaptation is conduced externally, adaptation-guided retrieval is only feasible if there is a model of how adaptation is performed. Two scenarios are examined: (1) when the retrieval agent knows the target solution and seeks to guide the adaptation toward it, and (2) when the retrieval agent does not have access to the target solution. Our approach is evaluated with a series of experiments on both a symbolic and a numerical task, using models of varying complexity. The results highlight the importance of inferring a correct model of the adaptation.

Keywords: Adaptation-guided Retrieval · Multi-agent · User modeling

1 Introduction

Despite the spread of technologies based on machine learning and artificial intelligence, many crucial decisions cannot be fully delegated to an artificial agent, in particular for ethical or safety reasons. In medical applications for instance, where human lives can be at stake, it is essential that a human expert has control over the final decisions. Therefore, the challenge moves from designing AI algorithms able to make perfect decisions, to designing AI agents able to make decisions in collaboration with human agents, to communicate efficiently with them and to explain their choices.

Case-based reasoning (CBR) [22] provides a reasoning paradigm where the solution to a new problem is obtained by exploiting known solutions to some memorized problems, called *cases*. Making a decision based on CBR follows two steps: *retrieval* of similar *cases* (i.e. problem-solution tuples) in the memory, called *case base*; and *adaptation* of the solutions to the new problem.

© The Author(s), under exclusive license to Springer Nature Switzerland AG 2025
I. Bichindaritz and B. López (Eds.): ICCBR 2025, LNAI 15662, pp. 267–281, 2025.
https://doi.org/10.1007/978-3-031-96559-3_18

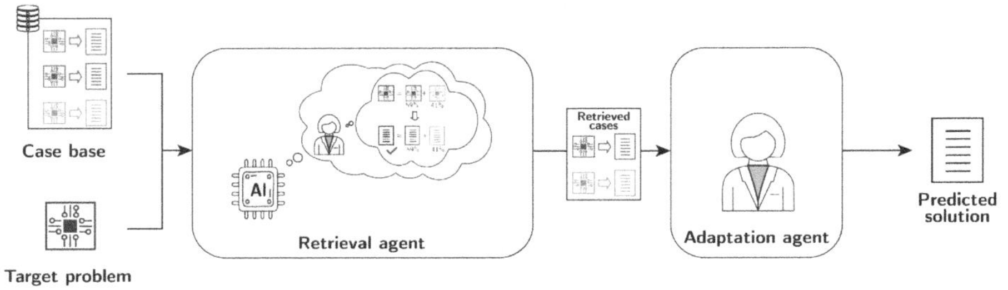

Fig. 1. In the standard CBR pipeline, a prediction for a new problem x^{tgt} is made by retrieving similar cases and adapting them to the problem of interest. Adaptation-guided retrieval has develops the idea that the retrieval process should account for the specific adaptation mechanism. However, a limitation, addressed in this paper, is that the adaptation model is supposed to be known. The framework we present assumes that a distinct agent (typically a human user) is in charge of the adaptation, which forces the retrieval agent to build and infer a model of how the adaptation is done.

This paradigm is strongly inspired by cognitive theories describing the role of memory in human cognition [23] and is meant to be common to humans and machines [13]. In practice however, human and artificial agents differ in their abilities and skills. We, humans, are not capable of consistently explore a large base of problem-solution instances (called *cases*). Instead, we prune this memory base according to our computational capabilities, which relates to the concept of *computational rationality* [9]. This task is elementary for a machine though. Conversely, adapting retrieved case relates to analogical reasoning, a form of reasoning which is a specificity of human cognition [8] and yet remains challenging for machines.

In this context, it seems reasonable to consider a collaboration where an AI agent would perform the retrieval task and a human agent the adaptation part. This collaboration is intrinsically complex: if the AI agent does retrieve cases based on its own criteria, the retrieved cases may not been optimally exploited by the human agent. For this reason, it is important for the AI agent to understand and anticipate how the human agent will do the adaptation. This paper proposes a first step into this direction, by exploring how an AI agent can be in charge of the retrieval, selecting cases from the case base not only for their intrinsic qualities, but also by estimating how the adaptation will treat them. This is done by endowing the AI agent with a *mental model* of the user, i.e. a forward model of how the user makes the final decision.

The remainder of this paper is organized as follows: Sect. 2 introduces the multi-agent framework and important setups within this framework. Section 3 proposes solutions under the simple assumption that the adaptation is known; these solutions are then used in Sect. 4 for the general case where this knowledge is not available. The proposed methods and hypotheses are discussed empirically in Sect. 5. The paper concludes by discussing similar works, in particular adaptation-guided retrieval and multi-agent CBR (Sect. 6) and by presenting some perspectives for future works (Sect. 7).

2 Setup of Two-Agent CBR for Prediction

2.1 Task Setup

Let $\mathcal{X}$ be a problem space and $\mathcal{Y}$ a solution space. A *case* is defined as a tuple $(x, y) \in \mathcal{X} \times \mathcal{Y}$. A *case base* is a finite subset of $\mathcal{X} \times \mathcal{Y}$. Given a fixed case base $CB \subset \mathcal{X} \times \mathcal{Y}$, the considered task is to find a solution $y \in \mathcal{Y}$ to a new problem $x^{\text{tgt}} \in \mathcal{X}$, which would be *consistent* with the case base. The problem x^{tgt} is called *target problem.*

The CBR approach to this task consists in splitting the resolution into two distinct steps. First, the *retrieval* consists in selecting a subset $r \subseteq CB$. The second step, called *adaptation* consists in using the information contained in the cases to predict the solution to x^{tgt}. These two components are formalized as two functions. The retrieval function $Ret : \mathcal{X} \to \mathcal{P}(CB)$ (where $\mathcal{P}(S)$ is the power set of a set S, i.e. the set of all subsets of S) takes the target question x^{tgt} as input, and outputs a subset of the case base. The adaptation function $Ad : \mathcal{X} \times \mathcal{P}(CB) \to \mathcal{Y}$ outputs the predicted solution to the target problem given the retrieved cases. Parametric families of retrieval and adaptation functions are considered in this paper, where the variable θ designates the parameter of the retrieval function Ret_θ) and ψ the parameter of the adaptation function Ad_ψ.

This work assumes a fixed case base, written CB. For this reason, the retention problem is not considered.

2.2 Two-Agent CBR Prediction

CBR prediction decomposes into two steps, namely retrieval and adaptation. In standard CBR, these two steps are performed by a single agent which is in charge of finding the solution to the problem using the entire case base. The predicted solution to the target problem x^{tgt} is then given by:

$$y^{\text{tgt}} = Ad_\psi(x^{\text{tgt}}, Ret_\theta(x^{\text{tgt}})) \tag{1}$$

In the proposed *Two-Agent CBR* (TA-CBR), retrieval and adaptation are performed by two distinct agents. In practice, this corresponds to two-agent interaction, where the first agent first applies Ret_θ and the second agent then applies Ad_ψ. In this interaction, the question is how each agent selects the parameter for its function.

It is essential to notice that, in this interaction, none of the agents has a full control over the task: the adaptation agent perceives from CB only the subset selected by the retrieval agent, and the retrieval agent does not have control over the final decision. In addition, the roles of the two agents are asymmetrical. The retrieval agent has only indirect control over the final prediction y^{tgt}, but the adaptation agent must only make sense of the selected cases.

The decision of the adaptation agent does not need to take the retrieval strategy into account, as it operates in the final step and uses the output of the retrieval agent. In Sect. 7, it will discussed how the adaptation agent could, in fact, adopt a fully strategic behavior by interpreting the retrieval agent's decision. However, this possibility falls outside the scope of this paper.

The decision of the retrieval agent is necessarily strategic, since it must anticipate the decision of the adaptation agent to predict the outcome y^{tgt}. Previous study in a context of a two-agent collaboration for function optimization demonstrated the importance of this anticipation [12]. In standard adaptation-guided retrieval [25], one single agent is responsible for both the retrieval and the adaptation: consequently, this agent knows which adaptation algorithm is actually used. This is not the case anymore in TA-CBR: the retrieval agent must have a model of the adaptation algorithm used by the adaptation agent.

2.3 Objective of the Agents

The strategic approach has one key prerequisite: the agents must have a goal. Without a goal, the two agents would merely produce a prediction y^{tgt} for the given problem x^{tgt}, without being able to assess its quality. In such a scenario, no strategy would be necessary, as there would be no objective to guide the process. Three possible objectives are identified.

Loss Minimization for a Training Set. The target problem is not known in advance, but a training dataset $\mathcal{D}^{\text{tr}} = \{(x_1^{\text{tr}}, y_1^{\text{tr}}), \dots, (x_N^{\text{tr}}, y_N^{\text{tr}})\}$ is available. The objective is to learn optimal parameters from this dataset and to use them for prediction with the target problem. Given a *loss* function $\ell : \mathcal{Y} \times \mathcal{Y} \to [0, \infty)$, the objective is to minimize the total prediction loss:

$$L(\theta, \psi) = \frac{1}{N} \sum_{n=1}^{N} \ell\Big(y_n, Ad_\psi(x_n, Ret_\theta(x_n))\Big) \tag{2}$$

Loss Minimization for a Known Solution. In certain scenarios, no training data is available, but the retrieval agent may have a visibility on the task and know the actual value of y^{tgt} for the given problem x^{tgt}. The objective is then to ensure that the value $\hat{y}^{\text{tgt}}$ predicted by the adaptation agent is as close as possible to y^{tgt}, with similarity measured for instance using the same loss function as previously. It requires to select cases that will guide the adaptation toward y^{tgt}.

Conditions on the Prediction. Even when y^{tgt} is not known, it might be the case that the agents have some specific conditions on the form of the solution that they want to satisfy. For instance, it could be desired that the output is in a specific range of values, or that it satisfies some fairness and ethical constraints. This objective can be expressed with a constraint satisfaction function $\mathcal{C} : \mathcal{Y} \to \mathbb{R}$, where the goal is to maximize $\mathcal{C}(Ad_\psi(x^{\text{tgt}}, Ret_\theta(x^{\text{tgt}})))$.

2.4 Adversarial and Collaborative Prediction

The two agents may not share a common objective. Such a setting, in which the objectives of the two agents do not necessarily align, is called *cooperative*.

It has two extreme cases: the adversarial setting, where the goals are completely opposed, and the collaborative setting, where the agents share the same goal.

In the worst case, the agents pursue opposite goals, effectively making the approach *adversarial*. A positive case is when one agent focuses on the accuracy of the prediction and the other agent on its fairness. More negatively, one agent can be malicious and try to force the other agent to make an incorrect prediction.

In a *collaborative* setting, both agents pursue the same objective, for instance accurate prediction. Even though none has full control over the full process, they still have aligned objectives. This is not enough for optimal choices [12], especially in cases where there is uncertainty about the other agent's strategy. The optimal case, where both agents know their respective parameters, has been implemented by Leake and Ye (2021) [15] in the form of an alternating optimization.

2.5 A Specific Application: Collaborative Human-AI CBR

The key motivation for introducing TA-CBR arises from the fundamental differences in computational capabilities between humans and machines. Machines excel at exploring, processing and analyzing vast amount of data, tasks that are infeasible for humans. Conversely, humans possess excellent skills in analogical reasoning and adapting knowledge to novel contexts [8], complemented by deep domain expertise that enables precise and context-aware adaptation. This contrast underscores the potential benefits of a collaborative approach in which an AI system handles retrieval, while a human expert is responsible for adaptation. Such a division of labor not only aligns with the respective strengths of AI and human cognition, but also presents a crucial advantage in human-AI interaction: it ensures that the final decision remains under human control and that the human agent remains the ultimate decision-maker.

3 Retrieval with a Fixed and Known Adaptation

In this section, the method Ad_ψ (including the parameter ψ) used for the adaptation is fixed and fully known from the retrieving agent. Two methods are proposed, corresponding to whether the retrieving agent knows the target solution (see Sect. 2.3). The method for unknown target solution is introduced, but will not be investigated in the empirical validation of this paper.

3.1 Known Target Solution

When the target solution is known to the retrieval agent, the problem becomes to select the right cases to retrieve, so that the adaptation leads to the most accurate solution. This task is related to machine teaching, the inverse problem of machine learning [26]. Using the loss function in the solution space defined in Sect. 2.3, the retrieval problem is the following:

$$\widehat{CB}_R = \arg\min_{X \subset CB} \ell\Big(y^{\text{tgt}}, Ad_\psi(x^{\text{tgt}}, X)\Big) \tag{3}$$

Solving this minimization problem is difficult, since its complexity is exponential with respect to the number of cases to retrieve.

3.2 Unknown Target Solution

In the second configuration, the retrieval ignores y^{tgt} but has access to a set of solved cases. A solution is to use these cases to learn the optimal retrieval parameters θ, by maximizing the prediction loss (Eq. 2):

$$\hat{\theta} = \arg\min_{\theta} \sum_{n=1}^{N} \ell\Big(y_n, Ad_{\psi}(x_n, Ret_{\theta}(x_n))\Big) \tag{4}$$

When the adaptation method is given as a numerical differentiable function, this minimization can be solved with a gradient method (as done by Leake et al. (2021) [15]) In real scenarios, especially when involving humans, the function Ad_{ψ} is actually a black-box function. Indeed, the adaptation method might be given only in the form of a simulator. The optimization cannot be done using gradient methods, but for instance using Bayesian optimization [7] for small dimensionality problems, or Particle swarm optimization [2] for larger dimensions.

4 Retrieval with Unknown Adaptation

In most applications, especially when the adaptation agent is a human user, the retrieval agent ignores the adaptation mechanism used by the adaptation agent. The methods of Sect. 3 must then be adapted to this situation. A Bayesian solution is proposed, where a belief is maintained over possible adaptation models Ad_{ψ}. This belief can be inferred from the observation of past adaptations (Sect. 4.1) and is then used to adapt the retrieval (Sects. 4.2 and 4.3).

4.1 Inference of the Adaptation Model

Consider a family of adaptations $\mathcal{M} = \{Ad_{\psi} \mid \psi \in \Psi\}$. Since the true adaptation mechanism is unknown, this choice of a family (and of a specific model within it) may be incorrect or sub-optimal. If it wants to account for the adaptation agent, the retrieval agent needs to infer which model in $\mathcal{M}$ best matches the observed behaviour of the adaptation agent. These observations are denoted as $\mathcal{O} = \{(x_1, y_1, r_1), \ldots, (x_N, y_N, r_N)\}$, where each tuple represents a problem x_n, the produced solution y_n based on retrieved cases r_n.

Instead of selecting a single best parameter ψ, Bayesian inference maintains a belief over the possible parameters in the form of a probability distribution $p(\psi)$. The objective of the inference is to compute the posterior distribution $p(\psi \mid \mathcal{O})$ which reflects how likelihy each model is after observing the adaptation data $\mathcal{O}$. This inference of the adaptation mechanism is a sub-problem of the inference task described in [16].

Using a Bayesian approach allows the retrieval agent to consider uncertainty about the adaptation mechanism. This is important because, when the available observations are insufficient to confidently identify a single best ψ, arbitrarily selecting one can lead to inaccurate simulates of the adaptation agent. Therefore, the retrieval should not only consider the most likely model but also remain robust to other plausible alternatives. How this uncertainty is taken into account in the retrieval process is the object of the following sections.

The posterior $p(\psi|\mathcal{O})$ is obtained via Bayes rule: $p(\psi|\mathcal{O}) \propto p(\mathcal{O}|\psi)p(\psi)$, where $p(\psi)$ is the prior, representing the belief over the models before observing any data, and $p(\mathcal{O}|\psi)$ is the likelihood, expressing how probable the observations are under a given a model. Bayesian inference requires a probabilistic version of the adaptation process: if Ad_ψ is deterministic, the likelihood can only be 1 (if it matches the exact observation) or 0 (if it does not), which is overly rigid and unrealistic in practical settings. To overcome this, a deterministic adaptation mechanism can be transformed into a probabilistic one by introducing noise. For example, if the adaptation outputs are d-dimensional real vector, normal noise can be added: $y \mid x, r \sim \mathcal{N}(Ad_\psi(x,r), \sigma^2 I)$, where I is the d-th dimensional identity matrix and σ^2 the intensity of the noise.

4.2 Known Target Solution and Unknown Adaptation

Since the adaptation is unknown, the same approach as in Sect. 3.1 cannot be directly applied. Instead of minimizing the loss for a given adaptation model, the expected loss must be considered:

$$\widehat{CB}_R = \arg\min_{X \subset CB} \mathbb{E}_{\psi \sim p(.|x_{1:N}, y_{1:N}, r_{1:N})} \left[\ell\left(y^{\text{tgt}}, Ad_\psi(x^{\text{tgt}}, X)\right)\right] \tag{5}$$

When ψ takes values from a finite set, the expected value can be computed exactly. Otherwise, it must be approximated, typically by sampling values of ψ from the posterior and summing over them using Monte-Carlo sampling.

4.3 Unknown Target Solution and Unknown Adaptation

Learning optimal retrieval parameters with unknown adaptation introduces challenges outlined here, with plans to address them in future works. The adopted method depends on the nature of the interaction, leading us to distinguish two cases: One where the posterior is inferred before the interaction, and one where it is updated during the interaction.

When the inference is done before the interaction, the posterior is fixed at the time of the training. Consequently, the retrieval parameter θ can be learned using Eq. 4, using the expected loss as in Eq. 5.

The second case, where the inference occurs during the interaction, is more challenging because the retrieval parameter θ must be re-trained at each interaction, after the posterior is updated. This iterative re-training renders the approach impractical for real-time applications. A promising solution, which will not be further explored in this paper, is to adopt meta-learning [5]. In this approach, a neural network is trained to predict the optimal θ given the value of the posterior, reducing the update of θ to a simple neural prediction.

5 Empirical Evaluation

This section describes the empirical results obtained to assess the strengths and limitations of the proposed framework. The code to reproduce the experiments can be found at https://github.com/ppaamm/TwoAgents-CBR.

5.1 Choice of the Datasets and Models

The methods are tested on two domains and datasets, with different constraints.

Finnish morphological analogies

Dataset. The dataset [16] consists of morphological transformations of words in Finnish, from the nominative to the illative case. A case is given by a noun in its nominative form of the noun (problem) and its corresponding illative form (solution). The dataset contains a large diversity of stem-to-radical transformations (e.g. “kissa $\rightarrow$ kissalla", “korpi $\rightarrow$ korvella", “rakkaus $\rightarrow$ rakkaudella" etc). All these transformations respect the rule of *vowel* harmony which states that the vowels a/o/u and ä/ö/y cannot coexist in a same word but have a one-to-one correspondence between them.

Adaptation. Given one retrieved case (x, y), the adapted solution y^{tgt} to x^{tgt} is obtained by solving the analogical equation $x : y :: x^{\mathrm{tgt}} : y^{\mathrm{tgt}}$ using the minimum complexity principle introduced by Murena et al. (2021) [16]. The adaptation is parametrized by $\psi \in \{0, 1\}$ which indicates whether to apply the rule of vowel harmony introduced earlier to the result of the analogical equation. When several source cases are available, a majority result is chosen, or, in case of equality, any of the majority results.

California Housing Dataset

Dataset. The dataset [17] consists of 20,640 instances of descriptions of housing blocks, associated to their median price. A case is given by the description of the block as an 8-dimensional vector (problem) and the median price (solution).

Adaptation. Given K retrieved cases $(x_1, y_1), \ldots, (x_K, y_K)$ and a diagonal matrix A with non-negative coefficients, the following adaptation rule is used:

$$Ad_B(x^{\mathrm{tgt}}, \{(x_1, y_1), \ldots, (x_K, y_K)\}) = \frac{\sum_{k=1}^{K} e^{-(x_k - x^{\mathrm{tgt}}) A (x_k - x^{\mathrm{tgt}})} y_k}{\sum_{k=1}^{K} e^{-(x_k - x^{\mathrm{tgt}}) B (x_k - x^{\mathrm{tgt}})}} \tag{6}$$

The vector w corresponding to the diagonal of A will be referred to as the *weight*.

5.2 Experiments

Experiment 1: Guided Retrieval with Known Adaptation. The first set of experiments focuses on the problem described in Sect. 3.1, where both the adaptation method and the target solution are known.

Experiment 1.1: Finnish morphological analogies. A case base CB consisting of $N_{\mathrm{CB}} \in \{20, 50, 100\}$ cases and a test set of $N_{\mathrm{test}} = 50$ problems is used. The experiment is conducted over 20 repetitions: in each repetition, the cases used for the case base CB and for the test set are sampled uniformly at random from the full dataset. The procedure is carried out for two conditions: $\psi = 0$ (no vowel harmony in the adaptation) and $\psi = 1$ (vowel harmony in the adaptation).

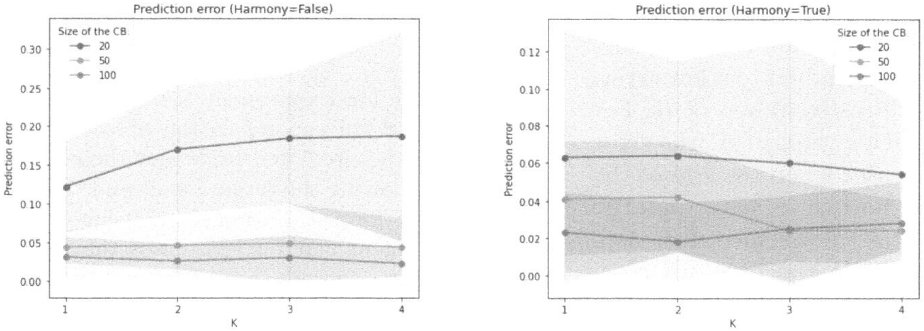

Fig. 2. Results for Experiment 1.1: When knowing the target result and the adaptation method for the Finnish morphological analogies, the retrieval agent can retrieve cases that lead to good prediction accuracy, independently on whether the adaptation agent knows vowel harmony. The precision accuracy increases with the size of the available case base, since a larger case base potentially covers more rules.

The results are displayed in Fig. 2. It can be observed that the number of errors increases as the size of the case base decreases, and that standard deviation is higher for smaller case bases. This aligns with the fact that a smaller case base is less likely to contain relevant cases for all test problems. Following the same reasoning, it becomes clear that the error rate will be lower when adaptation accounts for vowel harmony. When vowel harmony is ignored, retrieval must compensate for this lack of adaptation knowledge by including cases for all vowel groups. For instance, if vowel harmony is considered in adaptation, it is sufficient that the case base includes "kissa $\rightarrow$ *kissalla*" to correctly infer the transformation of "kuu" ("kuulla") and "kyy" ("kyyllä"). However, if vowel harmony is not incorporated into adaptation, retrieval must explicitly contain cases for all vowel groups to ensure accurate transformations.

Experiment 1.2: California housing dataset. A case base CB consisting of $N_{\mathrm{CB}} \in \{10, 20, 50\}$ cases and a test set of $N_{\mathrm{test}} = 100$ problems is used. The experiment is conducted over 20 repetitions: in each repetition, an adaptation weight w is drawn uniformly at random for the adaptation, and the cases used for the case base CB and for the test set are sampled uniformly at random from the full dataset.

The results are displayed in Fig. 3. The chosen accuracy measure is the absolute distance $|y^{\text{tgt}} - \hat{y}|$ between the predicted solution $\hat{y}$ and the true solution y^{tgt}. The provided accuracies are computed for the normalized dataset. Such as for Experiment 1.2, it can be observed that the guided retrieval succeeds in leading to a low error, for all tested values of K. For a specific value of K, the error decreases when the size of the case base increases, and the associated variance decreases too. As in the previous case, this is due to the representative capacity of the case base, which is higher for large case bases. The high variance for small case bases is caused by the stochasticity inherent to the random selection of the cases.

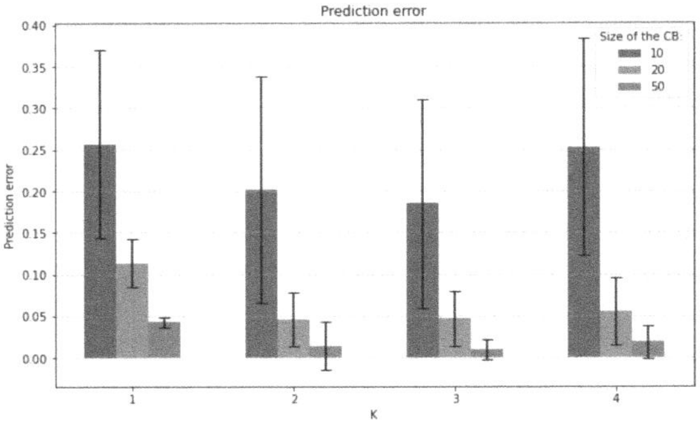

Fig. 3. Results for Experiment 1.2: The presented prediction error correspond to the absolute difference between the predicted price and the corrected price. When knowing the target result and the adaptation method for the California housing dataset, the retrieval agent can retrieve cases that lead to good prediction accuracy, especially when the case base is rich enough.

A qualitative analysis of the results shows an interesting phenomenon: the method tends to select a case with a solution similar to y^{tgt}. When $K \geq 2$, the other cases are chosen to be as distant as possible to the target case. This can be explained by the choice of the adaptation rule (Eq. 6): this adaptation gives a weight close to 0 to distant points, which eliminates their contribution.

Experiment 2: An Incorrect Knowledge of the Adaptation Method Leads to Sub-optimal Results. The second set of experiments addresses the same task, but assuming that the retrieval agent has an improper knowledge of the adaptation agent.

Experiment 2.1: Finnish Morphological Analogies. Experiment 1.1 is repeated, but this time using the incorrect adaptation method. For this experiment, a total case base consisting of $N_{\text{CB}} \in \{20, 30\}$ cases and a test set of $N_{\text{test}} = 50$ cases is used. The experiment is conducted 20 times. The results are displayed in Fig. 5 together with the results of Experiment 3. A significant gap can be observed between the results using the correct adaptation model and the incorrect adaptation model. With an incorrect model, the prediction error can exceed 0.5, depending on the composition of the case base. The gap is particularly important when the adaptation ignores vowel harmony: thinking it does not, the retrieval agent proposes cases that make sense only when knowing vowel harmony. When the adaptation agent knows vowel harmony, the difference is smaller and has a different origin: it cannot be explained by the choice of examples that the adaptation does not make sense of, but by the fact the retrieval will ignore cases that the adaptation would have been able to exploit.

Experiment 2.2: California housing dataset. A case base CB consisting of $N_{\text{CB}} \in \{10, 20, 30\}$ cases and a test set of $N_{\text{test}} = 50$ problems is used. The experiment is conducted 100 times: for each repetition, the cases used for the case base CB and for the test set are sampled uniformly at random from the full dataset, and two adaptation weights w_a and w_r are drawn uniformly at random. The weight w_a is used by the adaptation agent, and the weight w_r is used by the retrieval agent to simulate the adaptation. The distance $d(w_a, w_r) = \sqrt{\|w_r - w_a\|^2}$ is measured between these two weights. A small distance means that the retrieval agent is using a model of the adaptation which is close to the real adaptation process. For each repetition, the mean squared error (MSE) of the two-agent prediction on the test set is measured.

Figure 4 displays the MSE as a function of the weight distance for several values of K and sizes of the CB. When $K = 1$, the MSE seems not to depend on the distance. This can be easily explained by the choice of the adaptation model: indeed, the adaptation weight is used in the estimation of weights for the retrieved cases. When one single case is retrieved, the adaptation weight is unused, which confirms the observation. When $K \geq 2$, we can observe a global linear tendency, indicating that the MSE increases with the distance between weights. The coefficients of the interpolated linear model are reported in Table 1. We also observe that the variance of the results increases for smaller case bases: in that case, the retrieval is more constraint by the limited choice of cases will more critically try to to adjust the weighting of cases.

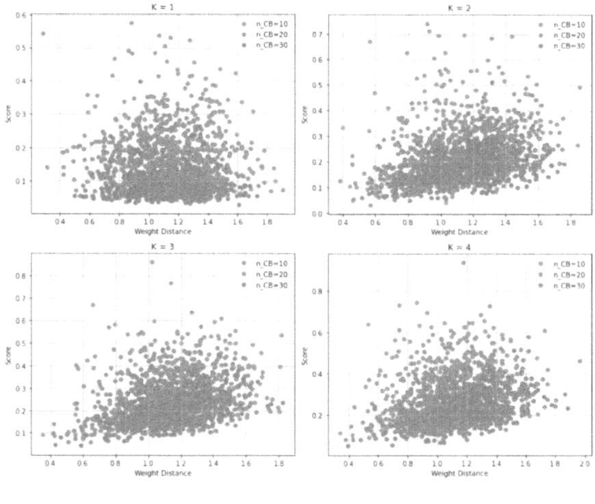

Fig. 4. Results for Experiment 2.2: The mean-squared error of the prediction increases with the distance between the true adaptation and estimated adaptation weights. As a global tendency, we observe that the MSE increases with the distance for $K \geq 2$.

Table 1. Linear Regression Results: Slope and Intercept for Different (K, n_{CB}) Values

K	1			2			3			4		
n_{CB}	10	20	30	10	20	30	10	20	30	10	20	30
Slope	0.0129	−0.0022	−0.0075	0.0856	0.1189	0.1255	0.1147	0.1390	0.1574	0.0859	0.1344	0.1512
Intercept	0.2087	0.1178	0.0865	0.1860	0.0608	0.0282	0.1823	0.0656	0.0108	0.2595	0.0933	0.0299

Experiment 3: Estimating the Adaptation Parameters Helps the Retrieval for Unknown Adaptation. The Finnish morphological analogies dataset is considered where the adaptation parameter ψ is not known. A case base CB consisting of $N_{\text{CB}} \in \{20, 30\}$ cases and a test set of $N_{\text{text}} = 50$ problems is considered. The inference of the adaptation parameter ψ is conducted on a training set $\mathcal{O}$ of $N_{\text{train}} = 20$ observations (problem, retrieved cases, adaptation solution). Note that the training set is used for the inference only, not for training the retrieval. The experiment is conducted 20 times: in each repetition, the cases used for the CB, for the training and test sets are sampled uniformly at random.

The posterior over ψ is first estimated, assuming a potential prediction error of 0.01, and the predictions are then computed, comparing the cases where the adaptation knows the correct adaptation, where it uses the incorrect adaptation, and where it infers it.

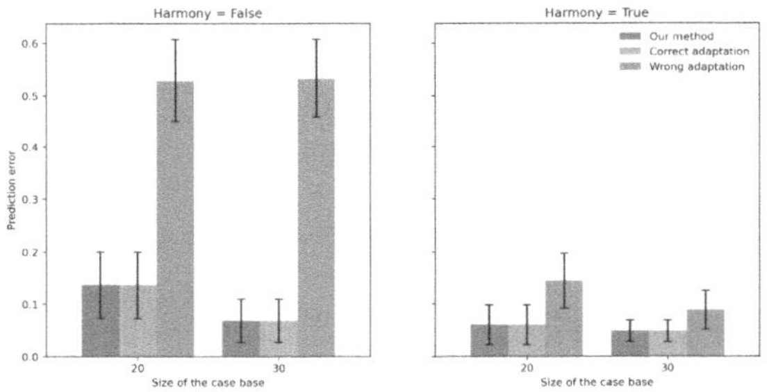

Fig. 5. Results for Experiment 3: When estimating the adaptation parameters, the prediction error is similar as when using the true model.

The results, displayed in Fig. 5, show that inferring the value of the adaptation model helps reaching results similar to the case where the retrieval knows the correct model. In this chosen example, the inference is easy and does not fail, but less perfect results are to be expected in more noisy scenarios.

6 Related Works

Adaptation-Guided Retrieval. Adaptation-guided retrieval follows the idea that the most similar case is not always the most appropriate for the adaptation [25]. Following this idea, several studies have aimed to incorporate adaptation knowledge into the retrieval [4,21]. Another technique consists in retrieving cases for which an ensemble of appropriate adaptations can be found [11]. As an alternative, Portinale (2019) [20] proposes to complement a standard kNN in the retrieval with a Markov Random Field representing the adaptability of the cases to the target problem. All these approaches assume that the adaptation process is known, which is not the case when the adaptation is performed by an external agent. More closely related to the proposed method, Leake and Ye (2021) [15] introduce an alternating optimization scheme to jointly learn the retrieval and adaptation parameters. However, their approach treats the CBR system as a single agent and does not support extension to multi-agent settings.

Multi-agent Systems and CBR. Several studies have investigated the integration of CBR with multi-agent systems, though from distinct perspectives. The typical approach is driven by applications involving multiple agents operating within an environment to accomplish one or different tasks collaboratively. For example, Fu & Fu (2012) [6], building on Kwon et al. (2007) [14], propose a multi-agent system for supply chain management, where agents take on roles such as component production, product manufacturing, order handing, and coordination. CBR is used as an external module to recommend collaborative management strategies. Similar ideas have been proposed for medical applications [3].

Shen et al. (2015) [24] propose a methodology similar to ours, where the various agents can interact with a CBR system to retrieve cases, and where the final decision is delegated to the human expert. The difference with this proposed work is that the retrieval is not adaptation-guided and that the CBR module does not aim to personalize strategically to the user.

Multi-agent systems can be used for a global management of a case-based reasoning system. For instance, Ayzenshtadt (2016) [1] proposes a multi-agent architecture where a query is distributed by a CBR manager among several retrieval agents. Similarly, distributed approaches of CBR describe the interactions of several agents which aim to solve a same problem. Collaborative Case-Based Reasoning [10] describes several CBR agents with various experience levels which are queried in parallel on the same problem. Similarly, in Cooperative CBR [18], agents interact with each other to solve tasks they are not capable of solving individually. This cooperation can be done in a fully distributed setting with several case bases [19]. In these methods however, the interaction is done at the level of the whole CBR agent, and not on individual sub-tasks.

7 Discussion and Conclusion

This paper introduced a scenario where case-based prediction is distributed between two agents: one responsible for the retrieval and one for the adaptation. This division of labor aligns naturally with cooperative settings in which human decision-makers are supported by AI agents.

This multi-agent setting necessitates that retrieval be adaptation-guided: selecting cases without considering the adaptation mechanism can lead to poor decisions. While this resembles adaptation-guided retrieval, a key distinction is that the retrieval agent lacks direct access to the adaptation mechanism. This constraint prevents joint training of the retrieval and adaptation, as done by Leake et al. (2021) [15], and instead requires inferring the adaptation mechanism from observations. Two main scenarios were introduced: (1) the retrieval agent knows the target solution and guides the adaptation agent toward it; and

(2) neither agent knows the solution. Due to space limitation, the experimental section focused on the first scenario, leaving the second for future work.

This first scenario relates to the problem of machine teaching [26] and has significant applications, particularly in education, fair decision-making or explainability. However, just as in machine teaching, this framework can also be misused, to manipulate decisions toward undesired or biased outcomes. Experimental results revealed that when the retrieval agent knows the solution, it tends to select cases that the adaptation agent will interpret correctly, potentially by exploiting model biases to maximize success. In some cases, it even selects highly irrelevant cases, knowing that they will be disregarded during the adaptation. Such behavior is unsuitable for an interaction with humans. Future works will need to incorporate additional constraints into the objective function to mitigate these undesired behaviors.

This limitation reflects a broader issue: the current setting does not fully capture the potential of multi-agent interaction. The paper assumes a passive adaptation agent that merely processes retrieved cases. In reality, a human adaptation agent may question the received cases and seek to understand their rationale. Just as the retrieval agent has a mental model of the adaptation agent, the adaptation agent forms a mental model of the retrieval agent. Although the adaptation agent makes the final decision, that decision is influenced by their perception of the retrieval agent's intent. This more complex perspective will be addressed in future work.

Acknowledgments. The author would like to acknowledge Jean Lieber for the insightful and inspiring discussions on adaptation-guided retrieval, as well as the anonymous reviewers for their constructive feedback.

Disclosure of Interests. The author has no competing interests to declare that are relevant to the content of this article.

References

1. Ayzenshtadt, V., Langenhan, C., Bukhari, S.S., Althoff, K.D., Petzold, F., Dengel, A.: Thinking with containers: a multi-agent retrieval approach for the case-based semantic search of architectural designs. In: ICAART (1), pp. 149–156 (2016)
2. Bonyadi, M.R., Michalewicz, Z.: Particle swarm optimization for single objective continuous space problems: a review. Evol. Comput. **25**(1), 1–54 (2017)
3. Dhatterwal, J.S., Malik, K., Das, P., Kaswan, K.S.: Medical diagnostic system using embedding jade in jcolibri. In: 2024 International Conference on Electrical Electronics and Computing Technologies (ICEECT), vol. 1, pp. 1–5. IEEE (2024)
4. Díaz-Agudo, B., Gervás, P., González-Calero, P.A.: Adaptation guided retrieval based on formal concept analysis. In: International Conference on Case-Based Reasoning, pp. 131–145. Springer (2003)
5. Finn, C., Rajeswaran, A., Kakade, S., Levine, S.: Online meta-learning. In: International Conference on Machine Learning, pp. 1920–1930. PMLR (2019)
6. Fu, J., Fu, Y.: Case-based reasoning and multi-agents for cost collaborative management in supply chain. Proc. Eng. **29**, 1088–1098 (2012)

7. Garnett, R.: Bayesian optimization. Cambridge University Press (2023)
8. Gentner, D., Smith, L.: Analogical reasoning. Encyclop. Human Behav. **2**, 130–136 (2012)
9. Gershman, S.J., Horvitz, E.J., Tenenbaum, J.B.: Computational rationality: a converging paradigm for intelligence in brains, minds, and machines. Science **349**(6245), 273–278 (2015)
10. Ginty, L.M., Smyth, B.: Collaborative case-based reasoning: applications in personalised route planning. In: International Conference on Case-based Reasoning, pp. 362–376. Springer (2001)
11. Jalali, V., Leake, D.: An ensemble approach to adaptation-guided retrieval. In: FLAIRS (2014)
12. Khoshvishkaie, A., Mikkola, P., Murena, P.A., Kaski, S.: Cooperative Bayesian optimization for imperfect agents. In: Joint European Conference on Machine Learning and Knowledge Discovery in Databases, pp. 475–490. Springer (2023)
13. Kolodner, J.: Case-based reasoning. Morgan Kaufmann (2014)
14. Kwon, O., Im, G.P., Lee, K.C.: Mace-SCM: a multi-agent and case-based reasoning collaboration mechanism for supply chain management under supply and demand uncertainties. Expert Syst. Appl. **33**(3), 690–705 (2007)
15. Leake, D., Ye, X.: Harmonizing case retrieval and adaptation with alternating optimization. In: International Conference on Case-Based Reasoning, pp. 125–139. Springer (2021)
16. Murena, P.A., Al-Ghossein, M.: Inferring case-based reasoners' knowledge to enhance interactivity. In: Case-Based Reasoning Research and Development: 29th International Conference, ICCBR 2021, Salamanca, Spain, September 13–16, 2021, Proceedings 29, pp. 171–185. Springer (2021)
17. Pace, R.K., Barry, R.: Sparse spatial autoregressions. Stat. Prob. Letters **33**(3), 291–297 (1997)
18. Plaza, E., Arcos, J.L., Martín, F.: Cooperative case-based reasoning. In: Workshop on Learning in Distributed Artificial Intelligence Systems, pp. 180–201. Springer (1996)
19. Plaza, E., Ontanón, S.: Ensemble case-based reasoning: collaboration policies for multiagent cooperative CBR. In: International Conference on Case-Based Reasoning, pp. 437–451. Springer (2001)
20. Portinale, L.: Approaching adaptation guided retrieval in case-based reasoning through inference in undirected graphical models. arXiv preprint arXiv:1905.12464 (2019)
21. Portinale, L., Torasso, P., Magro, D.: Selecting most adaptable diagnostic solutions through pivoting-based retrieval. In: Case-Based Reasoning Research and Development: Second International Conference on Case-Based Reasoning, ICCBR-97 Providence, RI, USA, July 25–27, 1997 Proceedings 2, pp. 393–402. Springer (1997)
22. Richter, M.M., Weber, R.O.: Case-based reasoning. Springer (2016)
23. Schank, R.C.: Dynamic memory: A theory of reminding and learning in computers and people. Cambridge university press (1983)
24. Shen, Y., Colloc, J., Jacquet-Andrieu, A., Lei, K.: Emerging medical informatics with case-based reasoning for aiding clinical decision in multi-agent system. J. Biomed. Inform. **56**, 307–317 (2015)
25. Smyth, B., Keane, M.T.: Adaptation-guided retrieval: questioning the similarity assumption in reasoning. Artif. Intell. **102**(2), 249–293 (1998)
26. Zhu, X., Singla, A., Zilles, S., Rafferty, A.N.: An overview of machine teaching. arXiv preprint arXiv:1801.05927 (2018)

Towards Non-programmed Robotic Manipulation of Novel Tasks Using GA-Driven CBR

Kent R. Østrem[1,4], Athanasios Lentzas[2], Ibrahim A. Hameed[3(✉)], and Evi Zouganeli[4]

[1] ABB, Fornebu, Norway
kent.robin.ostrem@no.abb.com
[2] Aristotle University of Thessaloniki, Thessaloniki, Greece
alentzas@csd.auth.gr
[3] Norwegian University of Life Sciences, Ås, Norway
ibrahim.abdelhameed@nmbu.no
[4] Oslo Metropolitan University, Oslo, Norway
evizou@oslomet.no

Abstract. A robotic manipulator, commonly employed for tasks such as object packing, sorting, and assembly, must be capable of handling items of varying shapes, sizes, weights, and colors. These tasks often require reprogramming especially when new manipulation challenges arise, making traditional approaches impractical. In this study, we propose the integration of two powerful decision-making and problem solving methodologies; Case-Based Reasoning (CBR) and Genetic Algorithm (GA) to enhance adaptability and efficiency of robotics manipulation for new manipulation tasks. CBR addresses new manipulation challenges by retrieving solutions from previously encountered cases that closely resemble the current problem. However, when the retrieved solution is suboptimal, conventional CBR methods typically require manual intervention to revise, adapt, and retain solutions, making this process slow and inefficient. To overcome these limitations, we propose the use of GA to iteratively refine and optimize retrieved solutions through GA operators such as selection, mutation, and crossover until convergence on an optimal or highly effective manipulation strategy is achieved. GA evaluates each candidate solution based on predefined fitness criteria, such as manipulation success rate, efficiency, and precision where most fitted solutions are retained in the case base. By integrating GA with CBR, the decision making process becomes significantly more efficient, as GA can automatically optimize, validate, and approve solutions without the need for human intervention, thereby accelerating new task execution. Furthermore, GAs provide a robust mechanism for handling complex and unforeseen manipulation tasks, enabling the system to adapt to highly dynamic tasks and environments and improve over time by automating case revision and retention process. This hybrid approach not only facilitates retrieval of past solutions but also continuously learns, optimizes, and retains new solutions, making the robotic system progressively smarter and more autonomous with each new manipulation challenge. Additionally, the proposed framework is scalable to increasingly complex

© The Author(s), under exclusive license to Springer Nature Switzerland AG 2025
I. Bichindaritz and B. López (Eds.): ICCBR 2025, LNAI 15662, pp. 282–297, 2025.
https://doi.org/10.1007/978-3-031-96559-3_19

tasks and environments, including scenarios involving large case bases and multiple collaborative robots operating within a shared workspace.

Keywords: GA · CBR · adaptive decision making · learning · task planning and execution · robotic manipulation · co-operation · optimization

1 Introduction

Robotic manipulators have become indispensable in modern industrial and domestic settings, performing complex tasks ranging from precision assembly to adaptive object handling [1–3]. While traditional programming approaches excel in structured environments, they struggle with the dynamic nature of real-world applications where objects vary in physical properties and task requirements change unexpectedly [1]. This limitation becomes particularly apparent in scenarios requiring rapid adaptation to new manipulation challenges, where conventional methods demand labor-intensive reprogramming cycles [3,4].

Case-Based Reasoning (CBR) has emerged as a promising solution for adaptive decision-making, leveraging historical success patterns through its four-phase cycle: retrieval, reuse, revision, and retention [4,5]. However, as identified in foundational CBR research, manual solution adaptation creates critical bottlenecks - particularly when facing novel manipulation scenarios that require complex, multi-parameter optimization [4]. Studies in robotic navigation demonstrate similar limitations, where purely case-based approaches struggle with environmental dynamics [6].

Genetic Algorithms (GA) offer complementary strengths through evolutionary optimization, to overcome limitations of CBR approach for automated solution refinement in manipulation tasks [7]. Recent implementations show GA's capability to optimize robotic trajectories while considering multiple constraints like torque limitations and obstacle avoidance [7,8]. The integration of CBR and GA enables robots to use historical experience visa CBR case-base and explore novel solutions through GA, creating systems that exceed the limits of either approach alone and the need for human intervention to adapt and refine retrieved solutions [9,10]. This combination proven effective in open-ended learning scenarios where task parameters and environmental conditions evolve continuously [11]. This work bridges these complementary paradigms through three key innovations:

1. **Automated solution refinement**: Use GA's operators to evolve retrieved CBR solutions, eliminating manual adaptation while maintaining case-based contextual relevance.
2. **Dynamic fitness evaluation**: Use of single- and multi-objective optimization to consider both operational efficiency (e.g., time, and energy) and task success metrics (e.g., precision, grasp stability, and task completion).
3. **Evolutionary case base maintenance**: Continuous solution improvement through automated retention of GA-optimized cases making CBR smarter overtime.

The integration enables robotic systems to progressively enhance their manipulation capabilities through successive task executions. As demonstrated in collaborative robotics research, this approach scales effectively across multi-robot systems and complex task environments [1]. By combining CBR's contextual awareness with GA's optimization power, the framework supports autonomous adaptation to objects with various physical properties and unforeseen environmental constraints [12]. The proposed system's architecture enable smooth integration with existing robotic middleware platforms while maintaining compatibility with various manipulator configurations. This positions the proposed hybrid CBR-GA approach as a foundational methodology for next-generation adaptive manipulation systems capable of operating in truly unstructured environments dealing with objects of various physical properties.

The article is structured to provide a comprehensive overview of integrating Case-Based Reasoning (CBR) and Genetic Algorithms (GA) for adaptive robotic manipulation. It begins with an Introduction Section that outlines the challenges in robotic manipulation and introduces the concept of combining CBR and GA to enhance adaptability and efficiency. The Literature Review Section discusses existing research on CBR and GA in robotics, highlighting their strengths and limitations, as well as related work in adaptive manipulation. The Methodology section describes the proposed system architecture, detailing how CBR retrieves past solutions and GA optimizes them using operators like mutation and crossover. The Results present the experimental setup and findings, focusing on key performance metrics such as task completion time, success rate, and precision. The Discussion section analyzes these findings, addressing the benefits and challenges of the hybrid CBR-GA approach and suggesting future directions. Finally, the Conclusion summarizes the main contributions and implications of the research for adaptive robotic manipulation.

2 Literature Review

Different approaches have been employed to attain increased robot autonomy, including the ability to execute new tasks based on previous experience and knowledge. Beetz et al. [13,14] suggest the robot-dedicated KnowRob cognitive architecture and the Cognitive Robot Abstract Machine (CRAM) framework to increase a robot's physical and cognitive capabilities. A hierarchical task structuring is used to enable the execution of complex tasks by dividing them into simpler sub-tasks, and this is showcased in a kitchen (lab) environment. To the best of our knowledge, the group have nonetheless not demonstrated new-task learning ability as such.

The importance of learning autonomy, i.e. the ability to learn from experience, has been addressed by several researchers. An advanced long-term memory structure is central for lifelong open-ended learning [15]. Caccavale and Finzi [16] propose the use of a working memory in combination with the long-term memory to enhance the robot's ability to learn from experience and adapt to new task, goals, in known and unknown domains. The authors suggest a hierarchical task network to deconstruct complex tasks into several simpler sub-tasks, which is similar to the hierarchical task structure suggested by Beetz et al. [13].

2.1 Case-Based Reasoning (CBR)

CBR is an artificial intelligence methodology in which new problems are solved by reusing solutions from previously encountered, similar problems. It is particularly suitable for domains where generalized rules are difficult to define, and problem-solving can be informed by precedent. CBR, shown in Fig. 1a, follows a structured cycle consisting of four main phases: *retrieve*, *reuse*, *revise*, and *retain* [17]. These are defined as follows:

- **Retrieval:** Identifying and selecting the most relevant past case(s) from the case base whose problem description is most similar to the current problem.
- **Reuse:** Applying the solution from the retrieved case to the new problem, either directly or with modifications.
- **Revision:** Evaluating the proposed solution and modifying it if necessary to improve performance or correct errors.
- **Retention:** Integrating the new problem and its successfully revised solution into the case base for future reuse.

In the context of robotic manipulation, CBR enables a robot to approach novel tasks by leveraging a library of previously solved cases. The robot retrieves the most relevant case from its memory (case base), executes the associated motion or strategy, and observes the outcome. If the outcome is successful, the case can be retained without modification. However, if the result is suboptimal or unsuccessful, the system must revise the solution, possibly adapting it or searching for alternative approaches.

Adaptation is widely recognized as one of the core challenges in CBR. It has been suggested that there exists a trade-off between retrieval effort and adaptation complexity: spending more time retrieving an appropriate case can reduce the need for complex adaptations, and vice versa. However, this trade-off is not always guaranteed. As demonstrated in [19], under certain conditions—such as when adaptation techniques are poorly designed or when highly capable planners are used—the trade-off may not hold.

In conventional CBR systems, the revision and adaptation stages often require manual input, making them time-consuming and less scalable. This limitation motivates the integration of automated adaptation mechanisms, such as Genetic Algorithms (GA), to enhance solution refinement without human intervention [18].

2.2 Genetic Algorithms (GAs)

Genetic algorithms (GAs) are a powerful class of optimization techniques inspired by the principles of biological evolution. GAs, developed by John Holland in 1970, iteratively optimize solutions by mimicking the process of natural selection, crossover, and mutation to solve complex optimization problems where traditional methods struggle [20]. GAs involving key components such as a population of candidate solutions (i.e., chromosomes) encoding parameters such as joint angles or task sequences, a fitness function to evaluate performance of candidate solutions, and evolutionary operators such as selection, crossover, and mutation to evolve solutions. The process begins by initializing a random population, evaluating fitness, selecting parents, and generating offspring through crossover and mutation. This cycle repeats until a termination condition is met, as shown in Fig. 1b. GAs are particularly powerful in solving complex, nonlinear, and high-dimensional problems in robotic manipulation. Their ability to search large solution spaces efficiently makes them ideal for adaptive, intelligent, and autonomous robotic systems. GAs are widely applied to address critical challenges in robotics such as motion and path planning [21], grasp planning and object manipulation [22], energy efficient manipulation [23], task learning and adaption [24], and human-robot collaboration [25].

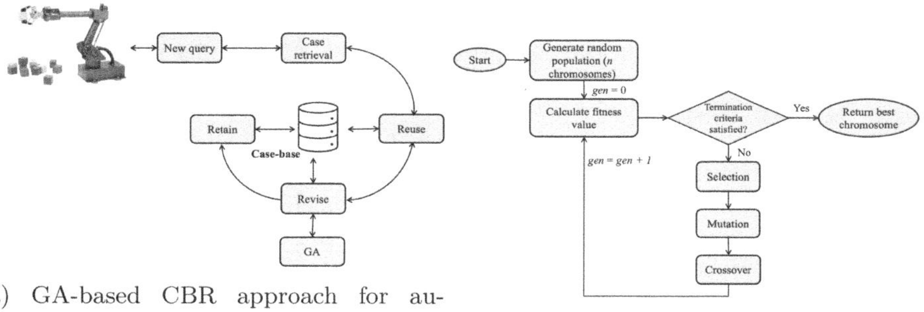

(a) GA-based CBR approach for autonomous robot manipulation.

(b) Flowchart of a simple GA algorithm.

Fig. 1. Hybrid CBR-GA framework for task manipulation.

2.3 Related Work

Hybrid CBR and GA approaches [9,10] have been explored for a number of applications such as document cross-relationship identification [26], construction cost estimation and decision-support [27], and similar. A distributed system in which several CBR agents cooperate under a boosting scheme has been applied in breast cancer prognosis [28]. Each CBR agent knows and is trained with a subset of the available cases. The system solution is then computed by means of a weighted average of the solutions provided by the CBR agents, where the weights are actively learned by a GA. The system was shown to improve the results obtained with a case base in which attributes were manually selected by physicians. This methodology may be transferable to robotic manipulation. A hybrid CBR-GA approach has been used for motion calculation in a multi-agent learning system applied to Robot World Cup soccer tournament (RoboCup) [29] to provide a better strategy for robots in their planning and to store experiences learned during the game for further use. Using this hybrid approach without predefined knowledge together with a tailored mathematical algorithm, robots could not only learn how to score, but could also figure out how to avoid repeating the same mistakes.

3 Methodology

This article proposes a hybrid GA-CBR framework, illustrated in Fig. 1a, designed to automate revision and adaptation of retrieved solutions and eliminating the need for manual intervention. This integration enhances the robot's ability to learn new skills and handle unseen tasks in continuously evolving environment. In this approach, CBR is used to initialize the GA by incorporating previously learned tasks under similar environmental conditions into the GA's initial population. For each new manipulation task, CBR retrieves past manipulation cases using similarity metrics, such as Euclidean distance. If none of the retrieved solutions match the new query, they are used to initialize the initial population of the GA. Through successive generations, the GA applies operators such as crossover and mutation to refine the candidate solutions, ultimately converging to an optimized solution for the given task. Once validated, the newly generated solution is stored in the case base, thereby enhancing the learning capacity of conventional CBR-based methods.

The proposed approach eliminates the need for manual intervention in revising retrieved solutions, thereby increasing the autonomy and efficiency of robotic task execution. In this approach, candidate solutions are assessed and ranked using a fitness function. In the context of robotics grasping and sequential task execution, an effective fitness function must balance multiple objectives, including task success rate, task completion time, energy consumption, grasp stability, obstacle-free path, and path smoothness, to ensure optimal performance.

3.1 System Architecture

The proposed hybrid framework, shown in Fig. 1, integrates GA into CBR for automatic adaptation and refinement of retrieved solutions.

CBR Module: The architecture of a Case-Based Reasoning (CBR) system is structured around the principles of retrieving and reusing previously encountered cases stored within a dedicated case-database. Each case is characterized by a set of attributes that define its specific context, objective, and outcome. These attributes serve as key indicators for identifying similarities between past and present problems. When the CBR system is presented with a new task or problem, it initiates a retrieval process by comparing the attributes of the current problem with those of the existing cases in the database. The matching process is carried out using comparing the attributes of the problem with the cases from the case-database, which evaluate how closely the current problem corresponds to previously solved cases. The greater the number of attributes shared between the task and the stored cases, the higher the likelihood of selecting a successful case. Upon identifying a case with the highest degree of matching attributes the system proceeds to reuse the solution of the retrieved case. While the proposed solution might not always be a perfect match, the CBR will try to execute the task associated with the highest number of matching attributes with the problem. This approach allows the system to always have an attempt at solving a given problem [11].

GA Module: GA optimizes retrieved solutions through two key operators:

1. Crossover: Combines genetic information from two parent solutions to create offspring. Common methods include:
   - One-point crossover: Randomly selects a point to swap genetic material between parents.
   - Two-point crossover: Exchanges genetic material between two randomly chosen points.
   - Uniform crossover: Randomly selects genes from either parent with equal probability
2. Mutation: Introduces random changes to maintain diversity and avoid local optima. For binary encoding, this may involve flipping bits from 0 to 1 or vice versa.

In our architecture one-point crossover is selected. A random crossover point is chosen within the length of the shorter parent solution, and the first segment of actions from one parent is combined with the remaining segment from the second parent. This ensures that the child solution inherits a mix of actions from both parents, potentially capturing beneficial sequences from each. The crossover operation promotes genetic diversity and allows the algorithm to explore different action combinations while preserving promising patterns observed in previous generations.

In the given implementation, mutation occurs probabilistically based on a predefined mutation rate. If a solution is selected for mutation, it can either remove an action or add a new randomly generated action. The added action is constrained to valid moves that contribute toward achieving the target state. This mechanism prevents the population from becoming too homogeneous and helps escape local optima by exploring alternative solutions that may not be reachable through crossover alone.

The GA iteratively applies these operators to evolve solutions, with crossover exploiting existing good traits and mutation exploring new possibilities. Termination occurs when a stopping criterion is met, such as reaching a maximum number of generations or achieving a satisfactory solution quality.

3.2 Fitness Criteria

In this section, we introduce metrics used to evaluate solution quality. Metrics such as first attempt success rate, task completion time, efficiency and precision are used to form the objective function. The proposed fitness function evaluates the quality of a solution by simulating its execution on an initial state and comparing the resulting state to the target state. It penalizes incorrect and redundant moves while rewarding correctly placed items. The function is formally defined as follows:

Let:

- $S = \{s_1, s_2, ..., s_n\}$ be the set of items.
- $L(s_i)$ represent the location of item s_i.
- $A = \{a_1, a_2, ..., a_m\}$ be the sequence of actions applied.
- $P_{\text{incorrect}} = 50$ be the penalty for incorrect moves.
- $P_{\text{redundant}} = 20$ be the penalty for redundant moves.
- $P_{\text{length}} = 2$ be the penalty per action to encourage shorter solutions.

For each action a_j, if an item s_i is moved:

- If $L(s_i) \neq L_{\text{target}}(s_i)$ after execution, a penalty of $P_{\text{incorrect}}$ is applied.
- If $L(s_i)$ remains unchanged after an action, a penalty of $P_{\text{redundant}}$ is applied.

The number of correctly placed items after applying all actions is:

$$C = \sum_{i=1}^{n} \mathbb{1}(L(s_i) = L_{\text{target}}(s_i))$$

where $\mathbb{1}(\cdot)$ is the indicator function that returns 1 if the condition is true and 0 otherwise.

The total penalty is computed as:

$$P_{\text{total}} = P_{\text{incorrect}} \cdot I + P_{\text{redundant}} \cdot R$$

where:

- I is the number of incorrect moves,
- R is the number of redundant moves.

The fitness function is then given by:

$$F(A) = \begin{cases} 100C - P_{\text{length}} \cdot |A| - P_{\text{total}}, & \text{if } C = n \\ -\infty, & \text{otherwise} \end{cases}$$

This function prioritizes solutions that correctly position all items while minimizing unnecessary movements, guiding the genetic algorithm toward optimal relocation plans.

3.3 Implementation and Experimental Setup

Simulated experiments were carried out in the Webots robotic platform to verify the concept and evaluate its performance. The TIAGo robot was used. CBRlib was used to create and store cases, and run CBR. The environment created for our experiments contains six blocks of different shapes (cube, cylinder) and colors (red, blue, yellow), and initially two containers of different colors (red, blue) all placed on top of a table. The objects have hence two attributes: shape and color, and a state: their location on the table. An initial state and target state are attributes of each action. The robot uses its seven-degree of freedom arm to manipulate the blocks and move them. An example of task execution in the simulation environment is shown in Fig. 2.

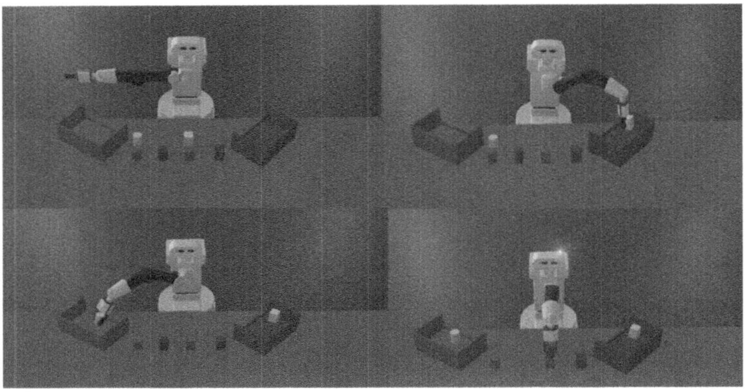

Fig. 2. Simulated environment where the robot executes a combination task, sorting objects by shape and color in the blue or red containers (extended from [11] (Color figure online)).

The test scenarios involve prompting with commands to reach a target state that refers to the location of the different blocks on the table. Two types of commands are possible: single tasks that refer to moving one single block, and combination tasks that refer to moving several blocks - e.g., all blocks, all red blocks, all cubes, etc. In combination task execution the robot has the ability to sort the blocks by color, collect blocks in a desired container, sort them by shape, and sort them by opposite color. When a command is given, the robot refers to the algorithm at hand - be it CBR or hybrid CBR-GA - to retrieve the best matching cases and execute the task. CBR is used to select the case that best resembles the task by employing a scoring system that assigns a point for each matching attribute. If the attributes are vague or nonsensical the robot will still try to execute the tasks it interpreted as the user's desire, even if it is not a case that leads to the correct outcome. When a task is successfully executed the states of the blocks are updated.

When a combination task is selected, e.g., *'Sort all cubes in the red container'*, the script looks for identifying keywords such as "sort", "all", "container" etc. This would lead the robot to execute a string of single-tasks from its case database to move all cubes - irrespective of color - to the red container. In case the script cannot recognize any of the predefined keywords, it prompts the user to input an alternative command. After successful completion of the task, the states of the blocks are updated in the same way as in single action tasks and printed out in the terminal with the updated states.

4 Results

The proposed hybrid approach will be evaluated in this section by testing its ability to sort yellow objects into the designated yellow container, compared to a traditional CBR-only approach. The CBR system has been trained exclusively on sorting red and blue objects into their respective red and blue containers and therefore lacks prior knowledge of handling yellow objects, hence, when yellow objects appear, CBR will sort them randomly in the available containers. This experiment will assess whether the hybrid CBR-GA approach can successfully adapt and generate a suitable sorting strategy for the new yellow objects, and sort them in the yellow container - demonstrating its capability to extend beyond pre-learned cases.

4.1 Performance Metrics

The GA was evaluated through a series of experiments designed to test its effectiveness in solving state transformation problems with varying complexities. The experiments were conducted using different numbers of objects and locations to analyze the algorithm's scalability. Specifically, tests were performed with 5 objects and 3 locations as well as 8 objects and 5 locations, allowing us to observe how problem complexity influences convergence. Additionally, the genetic algorithm was executed with a population size of 100 and a maximum of 1000 generations, as this configuration provided an optimal balance between execution time and solution quality. On average, execution took approximately 0.76 s for the first experiment and 0.95 for the second experiment, making it feasible for real-time or near real-time applications.

To thoroughly assess the performance of the genetic algorithm, 100 randomly generated problems were used as test cases. The best solutions identified by the algorithm were manually reviewed to ensure they correctly transformed the initial state into the target state with minimal moves. The algorithm consistently found optimal or near-optimal solutions, demonstrating its reliability. However, in some cases, redundant moves were observed, where items were momentarily moved away from their target locations before being placed correctly. This suggests that further refinement of the fitness function could enhance the efficiency of the generated solutions.

The results show differences in convergence behavior depending on problem complexity. As shown in Fig. 3a, for the 8 objects, 5 locations experiment, the best solution was often found around generation 62.77 on average, though some instances required significantly more iterations (with an upper range exceeding 250 generations). In contrast, for the 5 objects, 3 locations experiment, as shown in Fig. 3b the algorithm converged much faster, with an average generation of 3.68, indicating that simpler problems required fewer iterations to reach optimal solutions. The convergence rate suggests that as the number of objects and locations increases, the search space grows, requiring more generations for the algorithm to refine the solution.

Overall, the GA demonstrated strong convergence properties across different problem settings. The rapid convergence in simpler scenarios suggests that the algorithm is well-suited for smaller-scale problems, while its ability to find solutions for more complex configurations highlights its robustness. The percentile diagrams indicate a degree of variability in convergence rates, especially in the 8-object, 5-location setup, where some solutions took longer to emerge. Despite this, the use of 1000 generations and a population of 100 ensured that high-quality solutions were consistently found within a reasonable timeframe. Future work could focus on refining the mutation and crossover mechanisms to further improve convergence speed and reduce redundant moves.

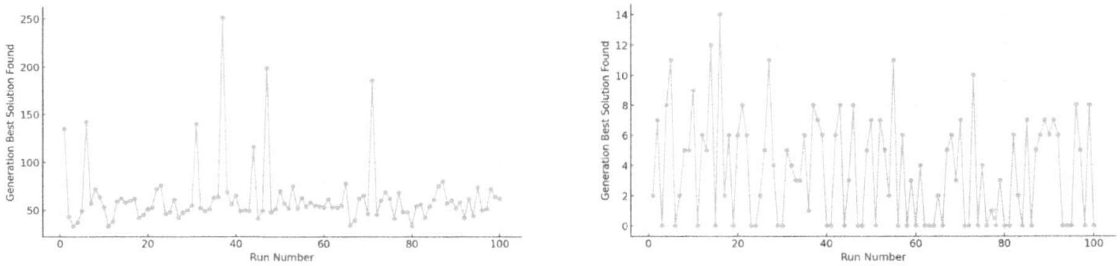

(a) Best solution for $num\_objects = 8$, $num\_locations = 5$

(b) Best solution for $num\_objects = 5$, $num\_locations = 3$

Fig. 3. Comparison of the best solutions found for different numbers of objects and locations.

4.2 Comparison

CBR relies on retrieving and adapting previous solutions to new problems. However, when confronted with unknown operations, its behavior becomes unpredictable. In our experiments, the introduction of yellow objects caused CBR to randomly assign them to locations based on the best available case in its knowledge base. To improve upon this, we integrated a GA to generate new cases that better fit the environment's requirements. The GA systematically evolved solutions, optimizing object placement while minimizing unnecessary moves.

To evaluate the impact of using GA for case generation, we conducted two separate experiments. In the first experiment, the GA was initialized with the current environmental state as its initial state. The algorithm required, on average, 42 generations to find the optimal solution. In the second experiment, we initialized the GA with the best case retrieved by CBR instead of the raw environment state. This significantly improved convergence, with the best solution being found within an average of just 4 generations. These results suggest that leveraging CBR-generated cases as the starting point for GA refinement leads to a substantial reduction in search time, demonstrating the successful synergy between these two approaches.

The initial and target states for one of the evaluated scenarios are presented below. The initial state represents objects placed on the table, where each object, including cylinders, cubes, and containers of different colors (red, blue, and yellow), is unorganized. Specifically, the initial state consists of six objects (R_cylinder, R_cube, B_cylinder, B_cube, Y_cylinder, and Y_cube) placed on the table, along with three containers (R_container, B_container, Y_container), also initially on the table:

[R_cylinder(R, table, cylinder), R_cube(R, table, cube), B_cylinder(B, table, cylinder), B_cube(B, table, cube), Y_cylinder(Y, table, cylinder), Y_cube(Y, table, cube), R_container(R, table, container), B_container(B, table, container), Y_container(Y, table, container)]

The target state requires that each object is correctly placed within its corresponding container. This means that red objects must be placed in the red container, blue objects in the blue container, and yellow objects in the yellow container. The final desired configuration is:

[R_cylinder(R, R_container, cylinder), R_cube(R, R_container, cube), B_cylinder(B, B_container, cylinder), B_cube(B, B_container, cube), Y_cylinder(Y, Y_container, cylinder), Y_cube(Y, Y_container, cube), R_container(R, table, container), B_container(B, table, container), Y_container(Y, table, container)]

Using the genetic algorithm, the best solution found was an optimal sequence of movements that correctly places all objects in their respective containers. The final solution is as follows:

[move(Y_cube, Y_container), move(B_cube, B_container), move(B_cylinder, B_container), move(R_cube, R_container), move(R_cylinder, R_container), move(Y_cylinder, Y_container)]

.

The GA demonstrated a strong convergence rate. Table 1 presents the evolution of the best solution across multiple generations, showing improvements in fitness values as better action sequences were discovered (Table 1).

Table 1. Evolution of the Best Solution Across Generations

Chromosome (Action Sequence)	Fitness
[move(B_cylinder, B_container), move(R_cube, R_container), move(Y_cube, B_container), move(Y_cube, Y_container), move(B_cube, B_container), move(B_cube, R_container)]	618
[move(B_cylinder, B_container), move(R_cube, R_container), move(Y_cube, B_container), move(Y_cube, Y_container), move(R_cylinder, R_container), move(Y_cylinder, Y_container)]	738
[move(R_cube, R_container), move(Y_cube, Y_container), move(B_cylinder, B_container), move(R_cylinder, R_container), move(R_cylinder, B_container), move(B_cube, B_container)]	768
[move(Y_cube, Y_container), move(B_cube, B_container), move(B_cylinder, B_container), move(R_cube, R_container), move(R_cylinder, R_container), move(Y_cylinder, Y_container)]	888

5 Discussion

CBR successfully sorted blue and red objects into their respective containers. However, when new yellow objects were introduced, CBR alone was unable to find a suitable solution for this new case. With the help of the GA module, a new solution was evolved to correctly classify and sort each object into the appropriate container. The obtained solution was then stored in the case base, allowing the system to learn from new cases. The integration of GA with CBR enabled the system to adapt and generate solutions for previously unseen cases. Simulation results highlighted the key advantages of combining CBR and GA to enhance adaptability and efficiency in problem-solving. The hybrid approach improved CBR's ability to retrieve the most relevant past solutions while leveraging GA to refine and optimize these solutions, making it highly effective for handling novel scenarios.

One of the main challenges in this approach is its dependency on the quality and diversity of stored cases in the CBR system. If the case base lacks sufficient variability, the retrieval process may fail to provide suitable initial solutions for GA to optimize. Additionally, the computational cost of GA, particularly for complex problems with large solution spaces, remains a significant consideration. However, GA is only applied once when encountering a new case. This approach enhances CBR's capabilities by continuously expanding the case base with new solutions, eliminating the need for human intervention. The proposed hybrid model can be extended to various real-world applications, such as industrial automation, robotics, and intelligent decision-making systems, where adaptability to new and evolving conditions is crucial.

6 Conclusion

In this article, we introduced a novel hybrid CBR-GA approach to enhance CBR's capability in handling unseen test cases. While CBR identifies the closest known solution, the GA component refines and adapts it to generate a more effective solution for the new scenario. Our experimental results demonstrated that the hybrid approach successfully addressed previously unseen cases, such as sorting yellow, that were not part of the original CBR historical cases, into the correct yellow container. This confirms the adaptability and robustness of the proposed method in extending beyond pre-learned cases, making it a promising solution for dynamic and evolving environments.

Future work includes exploring different crossover and mutation approaches to enhance convergence to high-quality solutions. Additionally, testing the system in more complex scenarios, including robot-to-robot and robot-to-human interactions, will help assess its adaptability in dynamic environments. Another area for improvement is experimenting with different objective functions and exploring multi-objective optimization, where competing objectives need to be balanced effectively.

Expanding the CBR case-base with more diverse and dynamic examples could further improve its generalization capabilities. Additionally, incorporating reinforcement learning or deep learning into the framework could enhance solution adaptation and convergence speed. The proposed hybrid model can also be extended to various real-world applications, such as industrial automation, robotics, and intelligent decision-making systems, where adaptability to new and evolving conditions is crucial.

References

1. Kroemer, O., Niekum, S., Konidaris, G.: A Review of Robot Learning for Manipulation: Challenges, Representations, and Algorithms. arXiv preprint arXiv:1907.03146 (2020). https://arxiv.org/abs/1907.03146
2. Liu, Z., Liu, Q., Xu, W., Wang, L., Zhou, Z.: Robot learning towards smart robotic manufacturing: a review. Robot. Comput.-Integr. Manufact. **77**,102360 (2022). ISSN 0736-5845. https://doi.org/10.1016/j.rcim.2022.102360
3. Fjær, D.H., Massali, K.K.B.: Adaptive robotics. MSc thesis, Norwegian University of Science and Technology (2010). http://hdl.handle.net/11250/251352
4. Šeda, M., Dvořák, J.: Robot navigation using genetic algorithm and case-based reasoning. In: Proceedings of the National Conference with International Participation: Engineering Mechanics 2003 (Paper No. 196). Svratka, Czech Republic, May 12–15, 2003. https://www.engmech.cz/improc/2003/196-Milos-Seda-PT.pdf
5. Aha, D.W.: The omnipresence of case-based reasoning in science and application. Knowl.-Based Syst. **11**(5–6), 261–273 (1998). ISSN 0950-7051. https://doi.org/10.1016/S0950-7051(98)00066-5
6. Tarantos, S.G., Belvedere, T., Oriolo, G.: Dynamics-aware navigation among moving obstacles with application to ground and flying robots. Robot. Autonom. Syst. **172**, 104582 (2024). ISSN 0921-8890

7. Razali, M.R., Faudzi, A., Shamsudin, A.U., Mohamaddan, S.: A hybrid controller method with genetic algorithm optimization to measure position and angular for mobile robot motion control. Front. Robot. AI **9**, 108737 (2023). https://doi.org/10.3389/frobt.2022.1087371
8. Kazem, B.I., Mahdi, A.I., Oudah, A.T.: Motion planning for a robot arm by using genetic algorithm. Jordan J. Mech. Indust. Eng. **2**(3), 131–136 (2008). https://jjmie.hu.edu.jo/files/JJMIE-V2-N3-press/2(16-21).pdf
9. Grefenstette, J.J., Ramsey, C.L.: An Approach to Anytime Learning. ML Workshop (1992)
10. Ramsey, C.L., Grefenstette, J.J.: Case-based anytime learning. In: Proceedings of the AAAI Workshop on Case-Based Reasoning (pp. 90–97), 1994. AAAI Press (1994)
11. Østrem, K.R.: New-Task Planning in Robotics. MSc thesis. Oslo Metropolitan University (2024)
12. Manzoor, J., Asif, S., Masud, M., Khan, M., J.: Automatic case generation for case-based reasoning systems using genetic algorithms.: third global congress on intelligent systems. Wuhan, China **2012**, 311–31 (2012). https://doi.org/10.1109/GCIS.2012.89
13. Beetz, M., Mösenlechner, L., Tenorth, M.: CRAM – a cognitive robot abstract machine for everyday manipulation in human environments. IEEE/RSJ Int. Conf. Intell. Robot Syst. **2010**, 1012–101 (2010). https://doi.org/10.1109/IROS.2010.5650146
14. Beetz, M., Kazhoyan, G., Vernon, D.: The CRAM Cognitive Architecture for Robot Manipulation in Everyday Activities. arXiv preprint arXiv:2304.14119. 2023. https://www.researchgate.net/publication/370338825_The_CRAM_Cognitive_Architecture_for_Robot_Manipulation_in_Everyday_Activitis
15. Romero, A., Bellas, F., Duro, R.J.: A perspective on lifelong open-ended learning autonomy for robotics through cognitive architectures. Sensors **23**(3) (2023). https://doi.org/10.3390/s23031611
16. Caccavale, R., Finzi, A.: Flexible task execution and attentional regulations in human-robot interaction. IEEE Trans. Cogn. Develop. Syst. **9**(1), 7–68 (2017). https://doi.org/10.1109/TCDS.2016.2614690
17. Aamodt, A. and Plaza, E.: Case-based reasoning: foundational issues, methodological variations, and system approaches. AI Commun. **7**(1), 39–59 (1990). https://doi.org/10.3233/AIC-1994-7104
18. Bergmann, R., Althoff, K.-D., Minor, M., Reichle, M., Bach, K.: Case-Based Reasoning. KI, vol. 23, pp. 5–11 (2009). https://www.researchgate.net/publication/236951398_Case-Based_Reasoning_-_Introduction_and_Recent_Developments
19. Lee-Urban, S., Muñoz-Avila, H.: Adaptation versus Retrieval Trade-Off Revisited: An Analysis of Boundary Conditions. L. McGinty and D.C. Wilson (Eds.): ICCBR 2009, LNAI 5650, pp. 180–194 (2009)
20. Lambora, A., Gupta, K., Chopra, K.: Genetic algorithm- a literature review, 2019 International Conference on Machine Learning, Big Data, Cloud and Parallel Computing (COMITCon), Faridabad, India, 2019, pp. 380–384 (2019). https://doi.org/10.1109/COMITCon.2019.8862255
21. Hameed, I.A., Bochtis, D., Sørensen, C.A.: An optimized field coverage planning approach for navigation of agricultural robots in fields involving obstacle areas. Int. J. Adv. Robot. Syst. **10**(5) (2013). https://doi.org/10.5772/56248
22. Zhang, Z., Jason G.: Grasp planning of 3D objects using genetic algorithm. In: 2012 IEEE International Conference on Automation and Logistics. IEEE (2012)

23. Nonoyama, K., Liu, Z., Fujiwara, T., Alam, M.M., Nishi, T.: Energy-efficient robot configuration and motion planning using genetic algorithm and particle swarm optimization. Energies **15**(6), 2074 (2022)
24. Hagras, H., Callaghan, V., Collry, M.: Outdoor mobile robot learning and adaptation. IEEE Robot. Autom. Mag. **8**(3), 53–69 (2001)
25. Dalle Mura, M., Dini, G.: Designing assembly lines with humans and collaborative robots: a genetic approach. CIRP Ann. **68**(1), 1–4 (2019)
26. Kumar, Y.J., Salim, N., Abuobieda, A.: A Genetic-CBR approach for cross-document relationship identification. In: Hassanien, A.E., Salem, AB.M., Ramadan, R., Kim, Th. (eds) Advanced Machine Learning Technologies and Applications. AMLTA 2012. Communications in Computer and Information Science, vol 322. Springer, Berlin, Heidelberg. https://doi.org/10.1007/978-3-642-35326-0-19
27. Jung, S., Pyeon, J.-H., Lee, H.-S., Park, M., Yoon, I., Rho, J.: Construction cost estimation using a case-based reasoning hybrid genetic algorithm based on local search method. Sustainability **12**, 7920 (2020). https://doi.org/10.3390/su12197920
28. Lopez, B., Pous, C., Pla, A., Gay, P.: Boosting CBR Agents with Genetic Algorithms. L. McGinty and D.C. Wilson (Eds.): ICCBR 2009, LNAI 5650, pp. 195–209 (2009)
29. Kuo, J. Y., Huang, F. C.: A hybrid approach for multi-agent learning systems. Intell. Autom. Soft Comput. **17**(3), 385–399 (2011). https://doi.org/10.1080/10798587.2011.10643156

Fast Locality Sensitive Hashing with Theoretical Guarantee

Zongyuan Tan[1], Hongya wang[1(✉)], Bo Xu[1], Minjie Luo[2], and Ming Du[1]

[1] School of Computer Science and Technology, Donghua University, Shanghai, China
tanzongyuan@mail.dhu.edu.cn, {hywang,xubo,duming}@dhu.edu.cn
[2] College of Science, Donghua University, Shanghai, China
mathwinnie@dhu.edu.cn

Abstract. Locality-sensitive hashing (LSH) is an effective randomized technique widely used in many machine learning tasks for Case-Based Reasoning community, such as outlier detection, neural network training and nearest neighbor search, all of which are important to the Case-Based Reasoning (CBR) community. The cost of hashing is the main performance bottleneck of these applications because the index construction functionality, a core component dominating the end-to-end latency, involves the evaluation of a large number of hash functions. Surprisingly, however, little work has been done to improve the efficiency of LSH computation. In this paper, we design a simple yet efficient LSH scheme, named FastLSH, by combining random sampling and random projection. FastLSH reduces the hashing complexity from $O(n)$ to $O(m)$ ($m < n$), where n is the data dimensionality and m is the number of sampled dimensions. More importantly, FastLSH has provable LSH property, which distinguishes it from the non-LSH fast sketches. To demonstrate its broad applicability, we conduct comprehensive experiments over three machine learning tasks, i.e., outlier detection, neural network training and nearest neighbor search. Experimental results show that algorithms powered by FastLSH provides up to 6.1x, 1.7x and 20x end-to-end speedup in anomaly detection latency, training time and index construction, respectively.

Keywords: Locality-sensitive hashing · random sampling · machine learning · Case-Based Reasoning

1 Introduction

Locality-Sensitive Hashing (LSH) [9,13] has emerged as a pivotal technique in the Case-Based Reasoning (CBR) community, particularly in facilitating efficient similarity retrieval within large-scale case repositories [29]. CBR systems typically rely on nearest-neighbor search to identify the most relevant cases [21,23]. However, when dealing with high-dimensional data or extensive case databases, such methods become computationally prohibitive [22]. LSH mitigates this challenge by leveraging specially designed hash functions that probabilistically map

© The Author(s), under exclusive license to Springer Nature Switzerland AG 2025
I. Bichindaritz and B. López (Eds.): ICCBR 2025, LNAI 15662, pp. 298–312, 2025.
https://doi.org/10.1007/978-3-031-96559-3_20

similar cases into the same hash buckets, thereby enabling approximate nearest-neighbor retrieval within a significantly reduced search space. This approach not only enhances the efficiency of case retrieval but also provides a scalable and effective mechanism for similarity matching in diverse CBR applications, including text analysis, image recognition, and medical diagnosis. By accelerating retrieval processes and optimizing decision-support frameworks, LSH contributes to the advancement of case-based reasoning methodologies [15,30].

The LSH scheme for l_2 norm (E2LSH) is proposed in [3,9] based on p-stable distributions. Owing to the sub-linear time complexity and theoretical guarantee on query accuracy, E2LSH is arguably one of the most popular ANN search algorithms both in theory and practice. Many variants of E2LSH have been proposed to achieve much better space occupation and query response time [10, 12,18,20,26,27]. Throughout this article, we focus on the LSH scheme under l_2 norm, and the extension to angular similarity, maximum inner product in Sect. 5.

In addition to answering ANN queries, LSH finds applications in many other domains. To name a few, Arrays of (locality-sensitive) Count Estimators (ACE) detects anomaly in data by performing lookup in hash tables, where the counts of collision are used as estimators for outlier [19]. ACE first processes high-dimensional data using LSH and constructs multiple hash tables. Each hash bucket is equipped with a counter to record how many data points fall into that bucket. ACE then leverages these counters across multiple hash tables to analyze the collision frequency of a given query. If a query shows a low collision frequency, it may be flagged as an outlier. Although ACE efficiently uses collisions to detect outliers, building the hash tables and counters is quite time-consuming.

SLIDE (Sub-LInear Deep learning Engine), a novel deep learning engine, uses LSH and parallel programming to achieve more efficient training on large-scale recommendation datasets using solely multi-core CPUs [6]. SLIDE maps the weight vectors of neurons in each layer of the neural network to be hash codes and then store these neurons into hash tables. During the forward propagation, SLIDE can quickly retrieve and activate the relevant neurons from these hash buckets based on the hash codes of the input data (acted as query). However, building these hash tables and updating them due to weight changes during the backward propagation often takes significantly more time than simply retrieving the neurons. Especially when neuron weights undergo substantial changes, the reconstruction and update of hash tables can greatly increase computational overhead.

For aforementioned LSH-based applications, the nearest neighbor search is a part of a larger application, where index construction time is more important than query time. This is because that the LSH index has to be built frequently due to data update or gradient update (SLIDE) or the index construction time occupies a large proportion of the end-to-end execution time (ACE). The index construction time translates directly to hashing cost because building an index involves massive computation of LSH functions. Take the widely used E2LSH as an example, computing k hashes of a vector $\boldsymbol{v}$ takes $O(nk)$ computation, where n is the dimensionality of $\boldsymbol{v}$ and k is the number of hash functions. For typical

ANN search task, k commonly ranges from few hundreds to several thousands, and keeps growing with the cardinality of the dataset (N) since the number of hashes required by E2LSH is $O(N^\rho)$ [9]. To sum up, hashing cost (index construction time) is the main computational and resource bottleneck step in almost such LSH-based applications, especially when data come in a streaming fashion and/or LSH data structures have to be constructed repeatedly [25,28].

Surprisingly enough, little endeavor has been made on more efficient LSH schemes under l_2 norm. The only known technique, termed as ACHash [8], exploits fast Hadamard transform to estimate the distance distortion of two points in the Euclidean space. This method, like other fast JL sketches [1,2], does not owns the provable LSH property. Thus, it is not a desirable alternative to the standard LSH because there are substantial empirical evidence that using these (non-LSH) sketches incurs a drastic bias in the expected behavior, leading to poor accuracy [24].

Our Contribution: We develop a simple yet efficient LSH scheme (FastLSH), which needs only two basic operations – random sampling and random projection, and offers better time complexity than E2LSH. Also, we derive the expression of the probability of collision (equity of hash values) for FastLSH and prove the asymptotic equivalence between FastLSH and E2LSH, which means that our proposal owns the desirable LSH property. We also rigidly analyze how the sampling ratio affects the probability of collision when the number of sampled dimensions is relatively small. To further validate our claims, we conduct comprehensive experiments over three machine learning tasks, i.e., outlier detection, neural network training and nearest neighbor search, in which the standard LSH is replaced by FastLSH. Experimental results show that algorithms powered by FastLSH provide significant end-to-end speedup in anomaly detection latency, training time and the index construction time, respectively. We believe that FastLSH can be used to improve the construction of data structures for case-based retrieval in the CBR community.

2 Preliminaries

In this section, we introduce notations and background knowledge used in this article. Let $\mathbf{D}$ be the dataset of size N in $\mathbb{R}^n$ and $\boldsymbol{v} \in \mathbf{D}$ be a data point (vector) and $\boldsymbol{u} \in \mathbb{R}^n$ be a query vector. We denote $\phi(x) = \frac{1}{\sqrt{2\pi}} \exp(-\frac{x^2}{2})$ and $\Phi(x) = \int_{-\infty}^{x} \frac{1}{\sqrt{2\pi}} \exp(-\frac{x^2}{2})dx$ as the probability density function (PDF) and cumulative distribution function (CDF) of the standard normal distribution $\mathcal{N}(0,1)$, respectively.

2.1 Locality Sensitive Hashing

Definition 1. *(Locality Sensitive Hashing) A hash function family* $\mathcal{H} = \{h : \mathbb{R}^n \rightarrow U\}$ *is called* (R, cR, p_1, p_2)*-sensitive if for any* $\boldsymbol{v}, \boldsymbol{u} \in \mathbb{R}^n$

- *if* $\|\boldsymbol{v} - \boldsymbol{u}\|_2 \leq R$ *then* $Pr_{\mathcal{H}}[h(\boldsymbol{v}) = h(\boldsymbol{u})] \geq p_1$*;*

- *if* $\|\boldsymbol{v}-\boldsymbol{u}\|_2 \geq cR$ *then* $Pr_{\mathcal{H}}[h(\boldsymbol{v})=h(\boldsymbol{u})] \leq p_2$*;*

In order for the LSH family to be useful, it has to satisfy $c > 1$ *and* $p_1 > p_2$*.*

Please note that only hashing schemes with such a property are qualified locality sensitive hashing and can enjoy the theoretical guarantee of LSH.

[9] presents an LSH family that can be employed for l_p ($p \in (0, 2]$) norms based on p-stable distribution. When $p = 2$, it yields the well-known LSH family for l_2 norm (E2LSH). The hash function is defined as follows:

$$h_{\boldsymbol{a},b}(\boldsymbol{v}) = \left\lfloor \frac{\boldsymbol{a}^T\boldsymbol{v} + b}{w} \right\rfloor \tag{1}$$

where $\lfloor\rfloor$ is the floor operation, $\boldsymbol{a}$ is a n-dimensional vector with each entry chosen independently from $\mathcal{N}(0, 1)$ and b is a real number chosen uniformly from the range $[0, w]$. w is an important parameter by which one could tune the performance of E2LSH.

For E2LSH, the collision probability of $(\boldsymbol{v}, \boldsymbol{u})$ under $h_{\boldsymbol{a},b}(\cdot)$ is computed as

$$p(s) = Pr[h_{\boldsymbol{a},b}(\boldsymbol{v}) = h_{\boldsymbol{a},b}(\boldsymbol{u})] = \int_0^w f_{|sX|}(t)(1 - \frac{t}{w})dt \tag{2}$$

where $s = \|\boldsymbol{v}-\boldsymbol{u}\|_2$ is the Euclidean distance between $(\boldsymbol{v}, \boldsymbol{u})$, and $f_{|sX|}(t)$ is the PDF of the absolute value of normal distribution sX (X is a random variable following the standard normal distribution). Given w, $p(s)$ is a monotonically decreasing function of s, which means $h_{\boldsymbol{a},b}(\cdot)$ satisfies the LSH property.

2.2 Truncated Normal Distribution

The truncated normal distribution is suggested if one need to use the normal distribution to describe the random variation of a quantity that, for physical reasons, must be strictly in the range of a truncated interval instead of $(-\infty, +\infty)$ [7]. The truncated normal distribution is the probability distribution derived from that of normal random variables by bounding the values from either below or above (or both). Assume that the interval (a_1, a_2) is the truncated interval, then the probability density function can be written as:

$$\psi(x;\mu,\sigma^2,a_1,a_2) = \begin{cases} 0 & x \leq a_1 \\ \frac{\phi(x;\mu,\sigma^2)}{\Phi(a_2;\mu,\sigma^2)-\Phi(a_1;\mu,\sigma^2)} & a_1 < x < a_2 \\ 0 & a_2 \leq x \end{cases} \tag{3}$$

The cumulative distribution function is:

$$\Psi(x;\mu,\sigma^2,a_1,a_2) = \begin{cases} 0 & x \leq a_1 \\ \frac{\Phi(x;\mu,\sigma^2)-\Phi(a_1;\mu,\sigma^2)}{\Phi(a_2;\mu,\sigma^2)-\Phi(a_1;\mu,\sigma^2)} & a_1 < x < a_2 \\ 1 & a_2 \leq x \end{cases} \tag{4}$$

3 Fast LSH via Random Sampling

The cost of hashing defined in Eq.(1) is dominated by the inner product $\boldsymbol{a}^T\boldsymbol{v}$, which takes $O(n)$ multiplication and addition operations. As mentioned in Sect. 1, hashing is one of the main computational bottleneck in almost all LSH-based applications. To address this issue, we propose a novel family of locality sensitive hashing termed as FastLSH. Computing hash values with FastLSH involves two simple steps, i.e., random sampling and random projection.

In the first step, we do random sampling from n dimensions. Particularly, we draw m *i.i.d.* samples in the range of 1 to n uniformly to form a multiset S. For every $\boldsymbol{v} = \{v_1, v_2, \cdots, v_n\}$, we concatenate all v_i to form a m-dimensional vector $\tilde{\boldsymbol{v}} = \{\tilde{v}_1, \tilde{v}_2, \cdots, \tilde{v}_m\}$ if $i \in S$. As a quick example, suppose $\boldsymbol{v} = \{1, 3, 5, 7, 9\}$ is a 5-dimensional vector and $S = \{2, 4, 2\}$. Then we can get a 3-dimensional vector $\tilde{\boldsymbol{v}} = \{3, 7, 3\}$ under S. It is easy to see that each entry in $\boldsymbol{v}$ has equal probability $\frac{m}{n}$ of being chosen. Next, we slightly overuse notation S and denote by $S(\cdot)$ the random sampling operator, that is, $\tilde{\boldsymbol{v}} \in \mathbb{R}^m = S(\boldsymbol{v})$ for $\boldsymbol{v} \in \mathbb{R}^n$ $(m < n)$.

In the second step, the hash value is computed in the same way as Eq.(1) using $\tilde{\boldsymbol{v}}$ instead of $\boldsymbol{v}$, and then the overall hash function is formally defined as follows:

$$h_{\tilde{\boldsymbol{a}},\tilde{b}}(\boldsymbol{v}) = \left\lfloor \frac{\tilde{\boldsymbol{a}}^T S(\boldsymbol{v}) + \tilde{b}}{\tilde{w}} \right\rfloor \tag{5}$$

where $\tilde{\boldsymbol{a}} \in \mathbb{R}^m$ is the random projection vector of which each entry is chosen independently from $\mathcal{N}(0, 1)$, $\tilde{w}$ is a user-specified constant and $\tilde{b}$ is a real number uniformly drawn from $[0, \tilde{w}]$. The hash function $h_{\tilde{\boldsymbol{a}},\tilde{b}}(\boldsymbol{v})$ maps a n-dimensional vector $\boldsymbol{v}$ onto the set of integers.

Compared with E2LSH, FastLSH reduces the complexity of hashing from $O(n)$ to $O(m)$. As will be discussed in Sect. 6, a relatively small $m < n$ suffices to provide competitive performance against E2LSH, which leads to significant performance gain in hash function evaluation.

4 Theoretical Analysis

While FastLSH is easy to comprehend and simple to implement, it is non-trivial to show that the proposed LSH function meets the LSH property, i.e., the probability of collision for $(\boldsymbol{v}, \boldsymbol{u})$ decreases as their l_2 distance increases. In this section, we first derive the probability of collision for FastLSH in Theorem 1, and then prove that its asymptotic behavior is equivalent to E2LSH in Corollary 1 and Fact 2. Thereafter, by using both rigid analysis and numerical method, we demonstrate that FastLSH still owns desirable LSH property even if m is relatively small in Lemma 4 and Fact 3.

4.1 Probability of Collision

For given vector pair $(\boldsymbol{v}, \boldsymbol{u})$, let $s = \|\boldsymbol{v} - \boldsymbol{u}\|_2$. The collection of n entries $(v_i - u_i)^2$ $\{i = 1, 2, \ldots, n\}$ follows an unknown distribution with a finite mean $\mu =$

$(\sum_{i=1}^{n}(v_i - u_i)^2)/n$ and variance $\sigma^2 = (\sum_{i=1}^{n}((v_i - u_i)^2 - \mu)^2)/n$. After performing the sampling operator $S(\cdot)$ of size m, $\boldsymbol{v}$ and $\boldsymbol{u}$ are transformed into $\tilde{\boldsymbol{v}} = S(\boldsymbol{v})$ and $\tilde{\boldsymbol{u}} = S(\boldsymbol{u})$, and the squared distance of $(\tilde{\boldsymbol{v}}, \tilde{\boldsymbol{u}})$ is $\tilde{s}^2 = \sum_{i=1}^{m}(\tilde{v}_i - \tilde{u}_i)^2$. By Central Limit Theorem, we have the following lemma:

Lemma 1. *If m is sufficiently large, then the sum $\tilde{s}^2$ of m i.i.d. random samples $(\tilde{v}_i - \tilde{u}_i)^2$ $(i \in 1, 2, \ldots, m)$ converges asymptotically to the normal distribution with mean $m\mu$ and variance $m\sigma^2$, i.e., $\tilde{s}^2 \sim \mathcal{N}(m\mu, m\sigma^2)$.*

Lemma 1 states that the squared distance between $\tilde{\boldsymbol{v}}$ and $\tilde{\boldsymbol{u}}$ follows a normal distribution for large m. Practically, a small m (say 30) often suffices to make the sampling distribution of the sample mean approaches the normal in real-life applications [14].

Recall that $\boldsymbol{a}$ is a projection vector with entries being $i.i.d$ samples drawn from $\mathcal{N}(0, 1)$. It follows from the p-stability that the distance between projections $(\boldsymbol{a}^T\boldsymbol{v} - \boldsymbol{a}^T\boldsymbol{u})$ for two vectors $\boldsymbol{v}$ and $\boldsymbol{u}$ is distributed as $\|\boldsymbol{v} - \boldsymbol{u}\|_2 X$, i.e., sX, where $X \sim \mathcal{N}(0, 1)$ [9]. Similarly, the projection distance between $\tilde{\boldsymbol{v}}$ and $\tilde{\boldsymbol{u}}$ under $\tilde{\boldsymbol{a}}$ $(\tilde{\boldsymbol{a}}^T\tilde{\boldsymbol{v}} - \tilde{\boldsymbol{a}}^T\tilde{\boldsymbol{u}})$ follows the distribution $\tilde{s}X$. Note that the PDF of sX, i.e., $f_{sX}(x) = \frac{1}{s}\phi(\frac{x}{s})$, is an important factor in calculating the probability of collision in Eq.(2). Hence, if we know the PDF of $\tilde{s}X$ we can derive easily the probability of collision for vector pair $(\boldsymbol{v}, \boldsymbol{u})$ under the proposed LSH function.

Let $f_{|\tilde{s}X|}(t)$ represent the PDF of the absolute value of $\tilde{s}X$. By replacing $f_{|sX|}(t)$ in Eq.(2) with $f_{|\tilde{s}X|}(t)$, we have the collision probability $p(s, \sigma)$ for FastLSH as follows.

Theorem 1.

$$p(s, \sigma) = Pr[h_{\tilde{\boldsymbol{a}}, \tilde{b}}(\boldsymbol{v}) = h_{\tilde{\boldsymbol{a}}, \tilde{b}}(\boldsymbol{u})] = \int_0^{\tilde{w}} f_{|\tilde{s}X|}(t)(1 - \frac{t}{\tilde{w}})dt \tag{6}$$

Next we will show how to compute $f_{|\tilde{s}X|}(t)$. Note that random variable $\tilde{s}^2$ does not follow exactly the normal distribution since $\tilde{s}^2 \geq 0$ whereas the range of definition of the normal distribution is $(-\infty, +\infty)$. A mathematically defensible way to preserve the main features of the normal distribution while avoiding negative values involves *the truncated normal distribution*, in which the range of definition is made finite at one or both ends of the interval.

Particularly, $\tilde{s}^2$ can be modeled by normal distribution $\tilde{s}^2 \sim \mathcal{N}(m\mu, m\sigma^2)$ over the truncation interval $[0, +\infty)$, that is, the singly-truncated normal distribution $\psi(x; \tilde{\mu}, \tilde{\sigma}^2, 0, +\infty)$. Considering the fact that $\tilde{s} \geq 0$, we have $Pr[\tilde{s} < t] = Pr[\tilde{s}^2 < t^2]$ for any $t > 0$. Therefore, the CDF of $\tilde{s}$, denoted by $F_{\tilde{s}}$, can be computed as follows:

$$F_{\tilde{s}}(t) = Pr[\tilde{s} < t] = Pr[\tilde{s}^2 < t^2] = \int_0^{t^2} \psi(x; \tilde{\mu}, \tilde{\sigma}^2, 0, \infty)dx \tag{7}$$

where $\tilde{\mu} = m\mu$ and $\tilde{\sigma}^2 = m\sigma^2$. Due to the fact that the PDF is the derivative of the CDF, the PDF of $\tilde{s}$, denoted by $f_{\tilde{s}}$, is derived as follows:

$$f_{\tilde{s}}(t) = \frac{d}{dt}[F_{\tilde{s}}(t)] = 2t\psi(t^2; \tilde{\mu}, \tilde{\sigma}^2, 0, \infty) \tag{8}$$

Although we know the distribution functions of both $\tilde{s}$ and X, it is not straight-forward to figure out the distribution of their product $\tilde{s}X$. Fortunately, Lemma 2 gives the characteristic function of random variable $W = XY$, where X and Y are two independent random variables, one following a standard normal distribution and the other following a distribution with mean μ and variance σ^2.

Lemma 2. *The characteristic function of the product of two independent random variables $W = XY$ is*

$$\varphi_W(x) = E_Y\{\exp(-\frac{x^2Y^2}{2})\}$$

where X is a standard normal random variable and Y is an independent random variable with mean μ and variance σ^2.

Note that the distribution of a random variable is determined uniquely by its characteristic function. As a result, the characteristic function of $\tilde{s}X$ can be obtained by Lemma 2 since X follows the standard normal.

Lemma 3. *The characteristic function of $\tilde{s}X$ is*

$$\varphi_{\tilde{s}X}(x) = \frac{1}{2(1-\Phi(\frac{-\tilde{\mu}}{\tilde{\sigma}}))}\exp(\frac{1}{8}x^4\tilde{\sigma}^2 - \frac{1}{2}\tilde{\mu}x^2)\,\mathrm{erfc}(\frac{\frac{1}{2}x^2\tilde{\sigma}^2-\tilde{\mu}}{\sqrt{2}\tilde{\sigma}}) \quad (-\infty < x < +\infty)$$

where $\mathrm{erfc}(t) = \frac{2}{\sqrt{\pi}}\int_t^{+\infty}\exp(-x^2)dx$ $(-\infty < t < +\infty)$ *is the complementary error function.*

Given the characteristic function, the probability density function of $\tilde{s}X$ (denoted by $f_{\tilde{s}X}(t)$) can be obtained through the inverse Fourier transformation.

$$f_{\tilde{s}X}(t) = \frac{1}{2\pi}\int_{-\infty}^{+\infty}\exp(-itx)\varphi_{\tilde{s}X}(x)dx \tag{9}$$

where the symbol $i = \sqrt{-1}$ represents the imaginary unit.

4.2 The Asymptotic Behavior of FastLSH

We can see that, unlike E2LSH, the probability of collision $p(s,\sigma)$ depends on both s and σ. From this point of view, FastLSH can be regarded as a generalized version of E2LSH by considering one additional impact factor, i.e., the variation in the squared distance of each dimension for vector pair $(\boldsymbol{v}, \boldsymbol{u})$, making it more difficult to prove the LSH property.

From Eq.(2) and Eq.(6), one can see that the expressions of the probability of collision for E2LSH and FastLSH are quite similar. Actually, if $f_{\tilde{s}X}(t)$ follows normal distribution $\mathcal{N}(0, \frac{ms^2}{n})$, we can always make $p_w(s) = p_{\tilde{w}}(s,\sigma)$ by scaling $\tilde{w}$ to $\frac{mw}{n}$ based on Fact 2.

Fact 2 ([9]). *For E2LSH, $f_{sX}(t)$ follows the normal distribution $\mathcal{N}(0, s^2)$ and the collision probability $p(s)$ with bucket width w is equal to $p(\alpha s)$ under the bucket width αw, i.e., $p_w(s) = p_{\alpha w}(\alpha s)$ where $\alpha > 0$.*

Proving the equivalence between $f_{\tilde{s}X}(t)$ and $\mathcal{N}(0, \frac{ms^2}{n})$ directly is not easy. To get around, the following theorem gives the asymptotic behavior of the characteristic function of $\tilde{s}X$.

Theorem 2.

$$\lim_{m\to+\infty} \frac{\varphi_{\tilde{s}X}(x)}{\exp(-\frac{ms^2x^2}{2n})} = 1$$

where $\exp(-\frac{ms^2x^2}{2n})$ *is the characteristic function of* $\mathcal{N}(0, \frac{ms^2}{n})$.

Note that $\exp(-\frac{ms^2x^2}{2n})$ is the characteristic function of $\mathcal{N}(0, \frac{ms^2}{n})$. As a result, Theorem 2 implies that $f_{\tilde{s}X}(t)$ is asymptotically identical to $\mathcal{N}(0, \frac{ms^2}{n})$ because a probability distribution is uniquely determined by its characteristic function, which immediately gives the following Corollary

Corollary 1. $f_{\tilde{s}X}(t) \sim$ *the PDF of* $\mathcal{N}(0, \frac{ms^2}{n})$ *as* m *approaches infinity.*

By Corollary 1 and Fact 2, $p(s) = p(s, \sigma)$ asymptotically if $\tilde{w} = \frac{m}{n}w$, meaning that σ has no effect on the probability of collision, and FastLSH is equivalent to E2LSH in this case.

4.3 The LSH Property for Limited m

In practical scenarios, the number of sampled dimensions (m) is often limited. Next, we study the relation between FastLSH and E2LSH in this case by examining the similarity in $f_{\tilde{s}X}(t)$ and the PDF of $\mathcal{N}(0, \frac{ms^2}{n})$. Note that the similarity between $f_{\tilde{s}X}(t)$ and $\mathcal{N}(0, \frac{ms^2}{n})$ directly translates to the equivalence between $p(s)$ and $p(s, \sigma)$.

Since distributions near the normal can be decided very well given the first four moments [16], we conduct the analysis by comparing the first four moments of corresponding distributions. The first four moments of $\tilde{s}X$ and $\mathcal{N}(0, \frac{ms^2}{n})$ are given in Lemma 4 and Fact 3, respectively.

Lemma 4.

$$\begin{cases} E(\tilde{s}X) &= 0 \\ E((\tilde{s}X)^2) &= \frac{ms^2}{n}(1+\epsilon) \\ E((\tilde{s}X)^3) &= 0 \\ E((\tilde{s}X)^4) &= \frac{3\,m^2s^4}{n^2}(1+\lambda) \end{cases}$$

where $\epsilon = \frac{\tilde{\sigma}\exp(\frac{-\tilde{\mu}^2}{2\tilde{\sigma}^2})}{\sqrt{2\pi}\tilde{\mu}(1-\Phi(\frac{-\tilde{\mu}}{\tilde{\sigma}}))}$ *and* $\lambda = \frac{\tilde{\sigma}^2}{\tilde{\mu}^2} + \epsilon$.

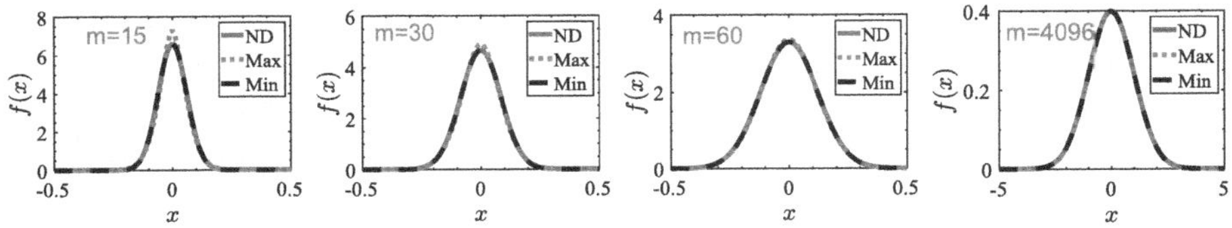

(a) Trevi: $m = 15$ (b) Trevi: $m = 30$ (c) Trevi: $m = 60$ (d) Trevi: $m = n$

Fig. 1. Comparison of probability density curves of $\mathcal{N}(0, \frac{ms^2}{n})$ (ND) and $\tilde{s}X$ under different m over *Trevi*.

Fact 3. *[11] The first four moments of $\mathcal{N}(0, \frac{ms^2}{n})$ are:*

$$\begin{cases} E(sX) &= 0 \\ E((sX)^2) &= \frac{ms^2}{n} \\ E((sX)^3) &= 0 \\ E((sX)^4) &= \frac{3m^2s^4}{n^2} \end{cases}$$

Lemma 4 and Fact 3 indicate that the first and third moments of $\tilde{s}X$ are equal to those of $\mathcal{N}(0, \frac{ms^2}{n})$, and $\tilde{s}X$ differ with $\mathcal{N}(0, \frac{ms^2}{n})$ in the second and fourth moments by only factors of $1+\epsilon$ and $1+\lambda$, respectively. It is easy to see that the smaller ϵ and λ are, the closer $\tilde{s}X$ is to $\mathcal{N}(0, \frac{ms^2}{n})$.

Note that ϵ and λ are monotonously decreasing (increasing) functions of m (σ) since $\frac{\tilde{\sigma}}{\tilde{u}} = \frac{\sigma n}{\sqrt{ms^2}}$. As a result, the first four moments of $\tilde{s}X$ and $\mathcal{N}(0, \frac{ms^2}{n})$ are equal with each other as m approaches infinity because $\epsilon = \lambda = 0$ in this case. This analytical result is consistent with Corollary 1.

For limited $m < n$, the impact of σ is not negligible. However, we can always adjust m to control the impact of σ (the data-dependent factor) on $f_{\tilde{s}X}(t)$ within a reasonable range. In this sense, Lemma 4 and Fact 3 provide a principled approach to quantitatively analyze how m affects the difference between FastLSH and the classic LSH in terms of ϵ and λ. By using this analytical tool, it is easy for practitioners to determine the trade-off between hashing time (how much m is) and desired performance level (how close FastLSH is to the standard LSH).

To visualize the similarity, we plot $f_{\tilde{s}X}(t)$ for different m under the maximum and minimum σ, and the PDF of $\mathcal{N}(0, \frac{ms^2}{n})$ in Fig. 1 on *Trevi*. Three observations can be made from these figures: (1) the distribution of $\tilde{s}X$ matches very well with $\mathcal{N}(0, \frac{ms^2}{n})$ for small σ; (2) for large σ, $f_{\tilde{s}X}(t)$ differs only slightly from $\mathcal{N}(0, \frac{ms^2}{n})$ for all m, implying that s is the dominating factor in $p(s, \sigma)$; (3) greater m results in higher similarity between $f_{\tilde{s}X}(t)$ and $\mathcal{N}(0, \frac{ms^2}{n})$, demonstrating that FastLSH can always achieve the same performance as E2LSH by choosing m appropriately. The comparison of ρ, an important performance indicator for locality sensitive hashing, is reported in the supplementary material due to space limitation. Likewise, the comparison of ρ suggests that FastLSH is equivalent to E2LSH even if in the case of limited m.

We further list the values of ϵ and λ for different m over 12 datasets in supplementary material due to space constraints, where ϵ and λ are calculated using the maximum, mean and minimum σ, respectively. It shows that ϵ and λ decrease as m increases. Take *Trevi* as an example, ϵ is equal to 0 and λ is very tiny (0.0001-0.000729), manifesting the equivalence between $f_{\tilde{s}X}(t)$ and $\mathcal{N}(0, \frac{ms^2}{n})$ for limited m.

5 Extension to Other Similarity Metrics

In this section, we sketch how to extend FastLSH to other similarity measures. Since the angular similarity can be well approximated by the Euclidean distance if the norms of data item are identical, one can use FastLSH for the angular similarity directly after data normalization. In addition, FastLSH can solve the maximum inner product search problem by utilizing two transformation functions [4]. The detailed discussion is given in the supplementary material, which is available at: https://github.com/DouZyTan/FastLSHForMachineLearning.

6 Experiments

In this section, we conduct comprehensive experiments for three machine learning tasks, i.e., outlier detection, neural network training and nearest neighbor search to demonstrate the efficiency of our proposal. Due to space limitation, we only report the main results here and defer more information about datasets, parameter settings and additional experiments to the supplementary material.

6.1 Hash Functions, Baselines and Evaluation Metrics

Hash Functions: Three hash functions, i.e., E2LSH [9], ACHash [8] and FastLSH, are compared. E2LSH is the classic LSH scheme for l_2 norm. ACHash is proposed to speedup the hash function evaluation by using Hadamard transform and sparse random projection[1]. It is worth noting that FastLSH can be easily plugged into any existing LSH applications considering its simplicity.

Baselines: For outlier detection, Arrays of (locality-sensitive) Count Estimators (ACE) [19] is considered, which uses multiple LSH tables to estimate counts of collision and detect anomalies by performing lookup in hash tables. For neural network training, we examine SLIDE (Sub-LInear Deep learning Engine) [6], a novel deep learning engine that combines smart randomized algorithms (LSH) and multi-core parallelism to achieve fast network training solely using CPU. For nearest neighbor search, two popular algorithms, i.e., E2LSH [3,9] and MPLSH [20] are evaluated. MPLSH is a variant of vanilla LSH (E2LSH), which provides better space and time efficiency. More information of these baselines are described in the supplementary material. Note that this work focuses on reducing the data structure construction overhead in various tasks using FastLSH, rather than improving LSH performance; thus, other similarity search methods are not compared.

[1] Note that ACHash is actually not an eligible LSH method because no expression of the probability of collision exists for ACHash, not mentioning the desirable LSH property. We choose ACHash for the sake of completeness.

Metrics: For outlier detection, five performance measures i.e., outliers detected, correctly reported outliers, outlier missed, execution time and speedup, are listed. For neural network training task, we report the classification accuracy, the end-to-end training time and the number of iterations. For nearest neighbor search, we report the recall, i.e., the fraction of near neighbors that are correctly returned, the average query time, hashing cost and the index construction time.

6.2 Datasets and Parameter Settings

Outlier Detection: For anomaly detection, we choose three real-world benchmark datasets, 1) Statlog Shuttle, 2) a9a and 3) Musk.

Neural Network Training: We employ two large real datasets, Delicious-200K and Amazon-670K, from the Extreme Classification Repository as in [5].

Nearest Neighbor Search: 11 publicly available high-dimensional real datasets and one synthetic dataset, i.e., Sun, Cifar, Audio, Trevi, Notre, Sift, Gist, Deep, Ukbench, Glove, ImageNet, Random, are experimented with [17].

Due to space limitation, please refer to the supplementary material for more information about the statistics of datasets and parameter settings for above machine learning tasks.

6.3 Results and Discussion

For three machine learning tasks, i.e., outlier detection, neural network training and nearest neighbor search, FastLSH can reduce the index construction time significantly and achieve almost the same or better recall and query time as LSH-based algorithms. Below, we present the experimental results for each task to validate this claim.

Outlier Detection: FastLSH can significantly reduce the end-to-end anomaly detection latency. The results for Musk are shown in Table 1. We can see that FastACE (FastLSH + ACE) offers around the same performance as ACE in terms of the numbers of correctly reported outliers and missed ones, whereas it needs much lower end-to-end execution time, achieving 6.1x and 2.6x speedup over ACE and ACHashACE (ACHash + ACE) thanks to the efficiency of FastLSH. ACHashACE missed more true anomaly because of the lack of theoretical guarantee.

Likewise, the results for *a9a* and *Statlog Shuttle* in Table 1, verify the superior performance of FastACE. One can see that FastACE delivers 4x and 1.2x speedup in the outlier detection latency. For both *a9a* and *Statlog Shuttle*, FastACE detects even more correctly reported outliers than ACE. While ACHashACE can also report more correctly reported outliers than ACE, the number of outliers reported is much higher than the rest, indicating a lower precision. In addition, the detection latency of ACHashACE is inferior to FastACE.

To sum up, FastLSH can be applied to anomaly detection task. It significantly decreases the end-to-end detection latency and offers the same or even better performance than the state-of-the-art.

Table 1. Results on Musk, a9a, and Statlog Shuttle

Dataset	Methods	Outliers Reported	Correctly Reported	Outliers Missed	Time (s)	Speedup
Musk	ACE	310	73	14	0.2794	1x
	ACHashACE	292	51	46	0.1168	2.4x
	FastACE	304	74	13	**0.04523**	**6.1**x
a9a	ACE	13850	4748	3093	2.079	1x
	ACHashACE	16877	5468	2373	0.9224	2.3x
	FastACE	15753	5469	2372	**0.5138**	**4**x
Statlog	ACE	1931	472	407	0.3297	1x
	ACHashACE	2226	531	348	0.2924	1.1x
	FastACE	1822	520	359	**0.2589**	**1.2**x

Neural Network Training: For this task, we show the training time and the number of iterations for SLIDE, FastSLIDE (FastLSH + SLIDE) and ACHash-SLIDE (ACHash + SILDE) in Fig. 2. Note that the x-axis is in log-scale, and all the curves have a long flat converged portion when plotted on a linear scale indicating clear convergence behavior. We can see from the plots that FastSLIDE achieves around the same or even better classification accuracy compared with SLIDE, while enjoying 1.7x and 1.4x speedup over Delicious-200K and Amazon-670K in training, respectively. The performance gain comes from the efficiency of FastLSH – hash tables have to be constructed every N_0 iterations and FastLSH reduces such hashing cost significantly. In addition, although the performance of ACHashSLIDE is comparable or slightly better than SLIDE, it is inferior to FastSLIDE due to the lack of theoretical guarantee. Thus, FastLSH is well-suited for accelerating neural network training.

Nearest Neighbor Search: Next, we validate through the ANN search task why FastLSH reduces the end-to-end execution time for the two aforementioned tasks. The reason is that FastLSH can significantly reduce the end-to-end latency in index construction while achieving comparable query performance[2] to E2LSH. Hence, for many LSH-based applications, if the end-to-end execution time is more important than query time, the acceleration of FastLSH becomes particularly significant.

We first compare the performance among E2LSH, ACHash and FastLSH for 0.9 target recall[3]. The recall, average query time, LSH computation time and index construction time for *ImageNet*, *Trevi*, *Deep*, *Random*, *Glove* and *Ukbench* are illustrated in Fig. 3 (a), (b), (c) and (d), respectively. As plotted in Fig. 3 (a) and (b), FastLSH and E2LSH achieve comparable query performance and answer quality. Due to lack of theoretical guarantee, ACHash performs slightly worse than FastLSH and E2LSH in most cases w.r.t query efficiency.

The performance of the three methods differs dramatically when it turns to the cost of hashing and indexing time. As shown in Fig. 3 (c), the LSH com-

[2] Note that FastLSH does not decrease the query time in the ANN search task because the cost in query processing is dominated by the exact evaluation of distances between candidates and the query.

[3] The actual recall may vary around 0.9 slightly.

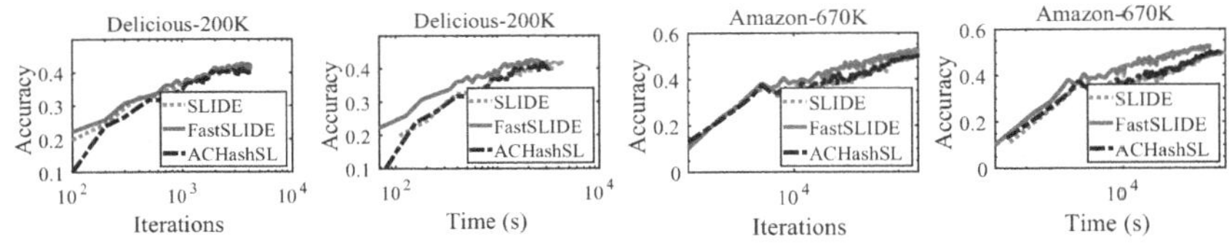

(a) Number of Iterations (b) Training Time (c) Number of Iterations (d) Training Time

Fig. 2. Comparison of SLIDE, FastSLIDE and ACHashSLIDE. The x-axis is plotted in log scale.

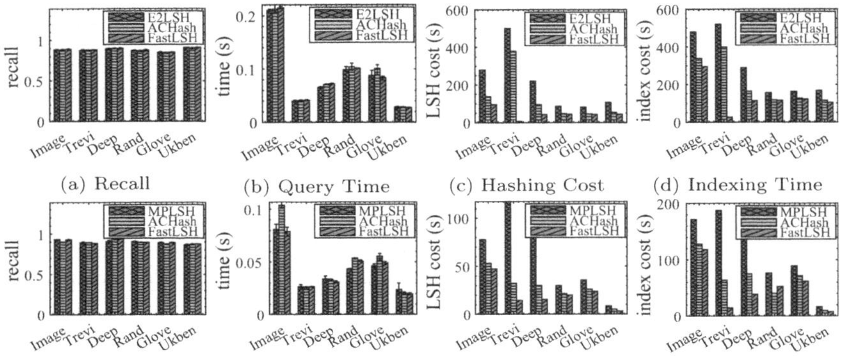

(a) Recall (b) Query Time (c) Hashing Cost (d) Indexing Time

(e) Recall (f) Query Time (g) Hashing Cost (h) Indexing Time

Fig. 3. (a-d) Comparison with E2LSH and ACHash. (e-h) Comparison with MPLSH and ACHash.

putation time of FastLSH is significantly superior to E2LSH and ACHash. For example, FastLSH obtains around 80 times speedup over E2LSH and runs 60 times faster than ACHash on *Trevi*. For ACHash, the fixed sampling ratio and overhead in Hadamard transform make it inferior to FastLSH. Similar trends can be found with MPLSH in Fig. 3 (e), (f), (g) and (h).

The end-to-end speedup in the index construction time is illustrated in Fig. 3 (d) and (h). Thanks to the significant drop in hashing cost, the time spent in building the index decreases by up to a factor of 20. Besides hashing, the procedure of index construction consists of other operations such as hash table initialization and linked list maintenance, which cannot be accelarated. Thus, the end-to-end latency in index construction decreases not as much as the hashing cost. More results are presented in the supplementary material.

7 Conclusion

In this paper, we develop FastLSH to accelerate hash function evaluation, which maintains the same theoretical guarantee and empirical performance as the classic E2LSH. Rigid analysis shows that the probability of collision of FastLSH is asymptotically equal to that of E2LSH. In the case of limited m, we quantitatively analyze the impact of σ and m on the probability of collision. Extensive experiments on a number of machine learning tasks demonstrate that FastLSH is a promising alternative to the classic LSH scheme.

References

1. Ailon, N., Chazelle, B.: Approximate nearest neighbors and the fast Johnson-Lindenstrauss transform. In: Proceedings of the Thirty-Eighth Annual ACM Symposium on Theory of Computing, pp. 557–563 (2006)
2. Ailon, N., Liberty, E.: Fast dimension reduction using Rademacher series on dual BCH codes. Discr. Comput. Geometry **42**(4), 615–630 (2008). https://doi.org/10.1007/s00454-008-9110-x
3. Andoni, A.: E2LSH-0.1 user manual (2005). http://web.mit.edu/andoni/www/LSH/index.html
4. Bachrach, Y., et al.: Speeding up the XBOX recommender system using a Euclidean transformation for inner-product spaces. In: Proceedings of the 8th ACM Conference on Recommender systems, pp. 257–264 (2014)
5. Bhatia, K., et al.: The extreme classification repository: multi-label datasets and code (2016)
6. Chen, B., Medini, T., Farwell, J., Tai, C., Shrivastava, A., et al.: Slide: in defense of smart algorithms over hardware acceleration for large-scale deep learning systems. Proc. Mach. Learn. Syst. **2**, 291–306 (2020)
7. Cohen, A.C.: Truncated and Censored Samples: Theory and Applications. CRC press (1991)
8. Dasgupta, A., Kumar, R., Sarlós, T.: Fast locality-sensitive hashing. In: Proceedings of the 17th ACM SIGKDD International Conference on Knowledge Discovery and Data Mining, pp. 1073–1081 (2011)
9. Datar, M., Immorlica, N., Indyk, P., Mirrokni, V.S.: Locality-sensitive hashing scheme based on p-stable distributions. In: Proceedings of the Twentieth Annual Symposium on Computational Geometry, pp. 253–262 (2004)
10. Gan, J., Feng, J., Fang, Q., Ng, W.: Locality-sensitive hashing scheme based on dynamic collision counting. In: Proceedings of the 2012 ACM SIGMOD International Conference on Management of Data, pp. 541–552 (2012)
11. Hoel, P.G., Port, S.C., Stone, C.J.: Introduction to Probability Theory. Houghtion Mifflin (1971)
12. Huang, Q., Feng, J., Zhang, Y., Fang, Q., Ng, W.: Query-aware locality-sensitive hashing for approximate nearest neighbor search. Proc. VLDB Endow. **9**(1), 1–12 (2015)
13. Indyk, P., Motwani, R.: Approximate nearest neighbors: towards removing the curse of dimensionality. In: Proceedings of the Thirtieth Annual ACM Symposium on Theory of Computing, pp. 604–613 (1998)
14. Islam, M.R.: Sample size and its role in central limit theorem (CLT). Int. J. Phys. Math. **4**(1), 37–47 (2018)
15. Jalali, V., Leake, D.: CBR meets big data: a case study of large-scale adaptation rule generation. In: Hüllermeier, E., Minor, M. (eds.) ICCBR 2015. LNCS (LNAI), vol. 9343, pp. 181–196. Springer, Cham (2015). https://doi.org/10.1007/978-3-319-24586-7_13
16. Leslie, D.: Determination of parameters in the Johnson system of probability distributions. Biometrika **46**(1/2), 229–231 (1959)

17. Li, W., et al.: Approximate nearest neighbor search on high dimensional data—experiments, analyses, and improvement. IEEE Trans. Knowl. Data Eng. **32**(8), 1475–1488 (2019)
18. Lu, K., Kudo, M.: R2LSH: a nearest neighbor search scheme based on two-dimensional projected spaces. In: 2020 IEEE 36th International Conference on Data Engineering (ICDE), pp. 1045–1056. IEEE (2020)
19. Luo, C., Shrivastava, A.: Arrays of (locality-sensitive) count estimators (ace) anomaly detection on the edge. In: Proceedings of the 2018 World Wide Web Conference, pp. 1439–1448 (2018)
20. Lv, Q., Josephson, W., Wang, Z., Charikar, M., Li, K.: Multi-probe LSH: efficient indexing for high-dimensional similarity search. In: Proceedings of the 33rd International Conference on Very Large Data Bases, pp. 950–961 (2007)
21. Portinale, L.: Integrating kNN Retrieval with Inference on Graphical Models in Case-Based Reasoning. In: Recio-Garcia, J.A., Orozco-del-Castillo, M.G., Bridge, D. (eds.) Case-Based Reasoning Research and Development. ICCBR 2024. LNCS, vol. 14775, pp. 1–16. Springer Nature Switzerland, Cham (2024). https://doi.org/10.1007/978-3-031-63646-2_1
22. Sanz-Ramos, Á., Ariza-López, L., Montón-Giménez, C., Sánchez-Ruiz, A.A.: Retrieval of similar cases to improve the diagnosis of diabetic retinopathy. In: Massie, S., Chakraborti, S. (eds.) International Conference on Case-Based Reasoning, pp. 408–423. Springer, Cham (2023). https://doi.org/10.1007/978-3-031-40177-0_26
23. Schultheis, A., Hoffmann, M., Malburg, L., Bergmann, R.: Explanation of similarities in process-oriented case-based reasoning by visualization. In: International Conference on Case-Based Reasoning, pp. 53–68. Springer, Cham (2023). https://doi.org/10.1007/978-3-031-40177-0_4
24. Shrivastava, A.: Optimal densification for fast and accurate minwise hashing. In: International Conference on Machine Learning, pp. 3154–3163. PMLR (2017)
25. Sundaram, N., et al.: Streaming similarity search over one billion tweets using parallel locality-sensitive hashing. Proc. VLDB Endow. **6**(14), 1930–1941 (2013)
26. Tao, Y., Yi, K., Sheng, C., Kalnis, P.: Efficient and accurate nearest neighbor and closest pair search in high-dimensional space. ACM Trans. Database Syst. (TODS) **35**(3), 1–46 (2010)
27. Tian, Y., Zhao, X., Zhou, X.: DB-LSH: locality-sensitive hashing with query-based dynamic bucketing. In: 2022 IEEE 38th International Conference on Data Engineering (ICDE), pp. 2250–2262. IEEE (2022)
28. Yang, C., Deng, D., Shang, S. and Shao, L.: Efficient locality-sensitive hashing over high-dimensional data streams. In: 2020 IEEE 36th International Conference on Data Engineering (ICDE), pp. 1986–1989. IEEE (2020)
29. Ye, X., Leake, D., Wang, Y., Zhao, Z., Crandall, D.: Towards network implementation of CBR: case study of a neural network K-NN algorithm. In: Recio-Garcia, J.A., Orozco-del-Castillo, M.G., Bridge, D. (eds.) International Conference on Case-Based Reasoning, pp. 354–370. Springer, Cham (2024). https://doi.org/10.1007/978-3-031-63646-2_23
30. Zhang, Q., Hu, L., Shi, C., Liu, K., Cao, L.: Supervised deep hashing for high-dimensional and heterogeneous case-based reasoning. arXiv preprint arXiv:2206.14523 (2022)

Learning Case Features with Proxy-Guided Deep Neural Networks

Vibhas Vats, Zachary Wilkerson(✉), Hiroki Sato, David Leake, and David Crandall

Luddy School of Informatics, Computing, and Engineering, Indiana University, Bloomington, IN 47408, USA
zachwilk@iu.edu

Abstract. The cost and difficulty of acquiring case features motivates interest in machine learning for feature acquisition. For computer vision domains, manual feature extraction has proven infeasible, but previous studies have shown the effectiveness of extracting features from deep neural models for case-based classification. Such approaches have generally been based on training the network for stand-alone classification accuracy, under the assumption that effective classification reflects high quality network features. However, it is not clear that the features best suited to network processing will be best for CBR. In response, this paper proposes refining previous network feature extraction approaches by adapting network training to reflect the goal of using network features for CBR. Specifically, it proposes augmenting conventional cross-entropy loss with a proxy term that reflects how the CBR system will use extracted features for similarity assessment. To this end, we investigate using Pairwise Distance, Cosine Similarity, and Sinkhorn Divergence as proxy functions within a triplet loss training framework. Evaluations on the benchmark image classification datasets MNIST, Animals with Attributes 2, and CIFAR-10 support the effectiveness of this method, with an integrated case-based classification system using the extracted features outperforming the feature extraction network applied end-to-end as well as integrated models developed in our previous research.

Keywords: Deep Learning · Case-Based Reasoning · Feature Learning

1 Introduction

The performance of case-based reasoning (CBR) systems depends on the quality of case retrieval. Traditionally, retrieval is based on hand-crafted feature vocabularies generated by experts [13,25,31]. However, manual feature acquisition is costly, hard to scale, and risks insufficient domain coverage in poorly-understood domains. For some tasks, such as image classification—the focus of this paper—symbolic feature generation is infeasible. Deep learning (DL) neural network

Z. Wilkerson and H. Sato—Equal contribution.

© The Author(s), under exclusive license to Springer Nature Switzerland AG 2025
I. Bichindaritz and B. López (Eds.): ICCBR 2025, LNAI 15662, pp. 313–327, 2025.
https://doi.org/10.1007/978-3-031-96559-3_21

methods have shown strong performance for a range of machine vision problems (e.g., [8,19,37,41]). enabled by the networks' ability to learn large sets of useful features from raw data via a scalable objective function optimization process. The ability of deep neural networks to generate useful domain features has kindled interest from the CBR community in integrating CBR with DL feature learning (e.g., [26–28,34,35,38]). In these approaches, DL provides robust feature extraction from raw data to ease knowledge acquisition overhead for the case-based classifier, which can render decisions that are more explainable than those made by a DL-only system.

In previous work on extracting features from DL networks, including our own (e.g., [39]), the networks from which to extract features have been trained for stand-alone classification accuracy. However, we hypothesize that a neural model trained in this way may be encouraged to learn features that discriminate between examples from different classes, more so than ascribing similarity to examples from the same class (which is critically important for case-based classification). In response, this paper proposes augmenting the objective function for network training to encourage the DL model to learn features that are especially suitable for case retrieval. A naïve approach to this would be to integrate a measure of case-based classification accuracy into the objective function to influence feature learning directly. However, this is infeasible because the output of a case-based classifier using nearest-neighbor retrieval is non-differentiable; consequently, it is unsuitable for gradient-descent-based learning. Instead, we propose augmenting the DL framework with a differentiable proxy function that approximates the requirements of a case-based classifier during the learning process. We explore this approach using three different proxy functions—Pairwise Distance, Cosine Similarity, and Sinkhorn Divergence [17], which quantifies the divergence between feature distributions. These proxy functions quantify loss as a measure of "closeness" for two examples in the feature space, enabling the model to consider loss terms during training that are based both on feature-level differences between examples and on the model's overall classification accuracy, which is captured by cross-entropy.

We evaluate the benefit of including these proxy functions for feature extraction for case retrieval informing case-based classification on the MNIST [12], Animals with Attributes 2 (AwA2) [40], and CIFAR-10 [23] datasets. Results show that while optimal parameterizations may vary for different datasets, the proxy-based approach enables CBR classification accuracy that outperforms the analogous DL-only approach. Furthermore, this approach also outperforms our previous non-proxy-guided DL-CBR integrated systems (e.g., [39]).

2 Related Work

Effective feature vocabularies for retrieval are a critical requirement for CBR approaches. Traditionally, this requirement has been addressed through knowledge engineering (e.g., [13,25,31]). However, acquiring feature information in this way can be costly, and insufficient expert knowledge or capability to express this knowledge for some domains may make knowledge-engineered feature sets incomplete or inadequate for certain tasks. Some symbolic learning methods have been successfully applied to this problem (e.g., [4,6,7,10,16]). More recently, integrating DL models with case-based methods has shown promise for leveraging the powerful inference capability of deep neural models to augment CBR systems. One such integration is an "inherently interpretable model" that uses a DL model to perform predictions based on similarity scores comparing generated features and known prototypes, reminiscent of retrieval in CBR (e.g., [5,9]). In addition, DL models that focus on similarity (e.g. [22,33]) have been used as metric learners for CBR similarity assessment [1,30]. Other research investigates using CBR for post-hoc DL model explanation [3] or in integrated "twin systems" that extract weights from the DL model to retrieve an effective explanation for its decision [21].

Multiple projects have investigated extracting features for case-based classification from DL models. Turner et al. apply this approach to perform relative classification for novel or low-confidence evaluation examples, leveraging extracted features to inform a CBR model that uses clusters in its search space to form implicit classes [34,35]. Feature extraction for CBR classification has also been shown to outperform other approaches in some case studies [30,39]. Additional research has studied where best to extract features within a network, suggesting extraction from after the densely-connected layers in a convolutional neural network, at which point features have ideally been combined into more comprehensive indices [26]. Model-level structural parameters, such as DL model architecture and number of features extracted, have also been shown to affect feature quality [26,27]. Extracted features have been combined with knowledge-engineered features for greater model accuracy [27,38], and pretrained models have been used as the basis for extracting high-quality features for tasks in small-data domains, supporting integrated DL-CBR models that can outperform analogous DL-only models [39].

Notably, these works train the DL model independently, and then extract features for use in case retrieval, reflecting the plausible assumption that both CBR and DL models will find similar features useful. However, we hypothesize that higher quality features may be extracted from a DL model that is sensitized to the needs of the case-based classifier. Work in other contexts has shown the benefit of modifying loss functions to incorporate domain knowledge (e.g., [14]). In this work, we investigate using a proxy function within the DL objective function, ideally biasing the DL model training to select for features that highlight similarity relationships between cases.

3 Network Training Reflecting Case-Based Classification

Our method for sensitizing the feature extraction network to the needs of a case-based classifier focuses on using three different distance functions – Pairwise Distance, Cosine Similarity, and Sinkhorn Divergence [17]—to favor features that facilitate effective similarity assessment between pairs of examples. These distance functions are incorporated in a triplet loss optimization term [36] that is combined with cross-entropy loss to guide weight updates during training. We discuss these model components in detail below.

DL classifiers typically learn features that enable discriminating between instances of different classes, while CBR models generally focus on ascribing similarity to examples that belong to the same class. Thus, we hypothesize that it may not be appropriate to use the same kind of features for both approaches. To address this, we target the DL model's loss function; typically, a DL model uses cross-entropy loss, which maximizes the number of correct classifications while minimizing the incidence of incorrect classifications for a given task. This process emphasizes features that are highly predictive of the target labels, ideally ensuring that each class is represented by a set of features in the learned feature space that differentiate it from each other class.

By contrast, a case-based classifier classifies new cases by comparing their feature representations to those of cases stored in a case base, relying on similarity scores to identify the closest matches. Consequently, features associated with intra-class similarity may be more appropriate. We hypothesize that these characteristics suggest that training networks in alignment with case-based classification will result in better features for CBR than training the network for standalone classification. Therefore, instead of using cross-entropy loss alone, we integrate another loss term that serves as proxy for the needs of the case-based classifier.

3.1 Three Proxy Functions for DL Training Guidance

We consider three functions to use as the proxy term in the DL loss function, targeting three candidate distance measures that might be important to a CBR system: Pairwise Distance considers simple Euclidean distance, Cosine Similarity the angular similarity between features in the feature space, and Sinkhorn Divergence the distance between feature distributions. We note that many distance measures are used within CBR, and that others might be most suitable for particular tasks; these are simply illustrative examples.

Pairwise Distance. measures the similarity between two data points in a feature space by computing a distance measure. It is often used in contrastive learning frameworks, where the goal is to ensure that similar samples have smaller distances while dissimilar samples are pushed farther apart [36]. Equation (1) shows a generalized formula of Pairwise Distance for two feature vectors f_i and f_j of input samples x_i and x_j. It estimates the *p-norm* of the difference between two vectors by adding some constant ϵ to avoid division by zero if p is negative:

$$D(f_i, f_j) = ||f_i - f_j + \epsilon||_p \tag{1}$$

Cosine Similarity. focuses on the angular relationship between feature vectors, making it more robust to variations in magnitude. Specifically, it measures the cosine of the angle between two non-zero feature vectors defined in an inner product space and then normalizes this value relative to the vector magnitudes.

The Cosine Similarity value always lies within the interval $[-1, 1]$, with a similarity of 1 indicating that two vectors are perfectly aligned, -1 signifying that they are diametrically opposed, and 0 meaning that they are orthogonal (i.e., uncorrelated, Eq. (2)).

$$S(f_i, f_j) = \frac{f_i.f_j}{max(||f_i||_2.||f_j||_2, \epsilon)}, \tag{2}$$

Here, f_i and f_j are the two feature vectors corresponding to examples x_i and x_j. ϵ is a small non-zero constant used to avoid division by zero.

Sinkhorn Divergence. is derived from *optimal transport theory* [11], capturing a nuanced notion of similarity by considering the cost of transforming one probability distribution into another. In context of this work, Sinkhorn Divergence assesses how difficult it would be to execute a given *transport plan* (a transformation) that maps the features belonging to one example to match another, given a cost function for the transformation. This gives a refined notion of how similar two sets of data are, because it takes into account the effort of 'matching up' the points, not just their overall difference. That is, it considers the topography of the feature space between the features of the two examples in addition to the numeric distance, ideally sensitizing it to "challenging" regions that might signify decision boundaries. In this way, it has the potential to focus learning on dimensions that correlate strongly with a change in class. In image processing, Sinkhorn divergence can be used as a distance measure comparing images represented as distributions of local features, such as features generated by a deep network.

For features f_i and f_j, modeled as probability distributions over possible feature values, the regularized Wasserstein distance [2] is:

$$W_\epsilon(f_i, f_j) = \min_{\gamma \in U(f_i, f_j)} \sum_{a,b} \gamma(a, b)\, c(a, b) \;-\; \epsilon\, H(\gamma), \tag{3}$$

where $U(f_i, f_j)$ is the set of valid transport plans, $c(a, b)$ is the cost function (e.g. squared Euclidean distance), $\gamma(a, b)$ is the transport plan, and $H(\gamma)$ is an entropy term (regularized by ϵ). Sinkhorn Divergence then refines this by removing self-similarity biases [17]:

$$\mathcal{S}_\epsilon(f_i, f_j) = W_\epsilon(f_i, f_j) \;-\; \tfrac{1}{2}\Big(W_\epsilon(f_i, f_i) + W_\epsilon(f_j, f_j)\Big). \tag{4}$$

This encourages the model to learn features that reflect meaningful alignments in the data rather than simple distances, providing richer estimates for properties relevant to case-based classification [11].

3.2 Triplet Optimization: Enhancing Similarity Learning in DL

Triplet optimization is a technique in metric learning approaches [20] that encourages a deep neural network to learn features that capture meaningful relationships between data points [32]. Specifically, it encourages a model to learn

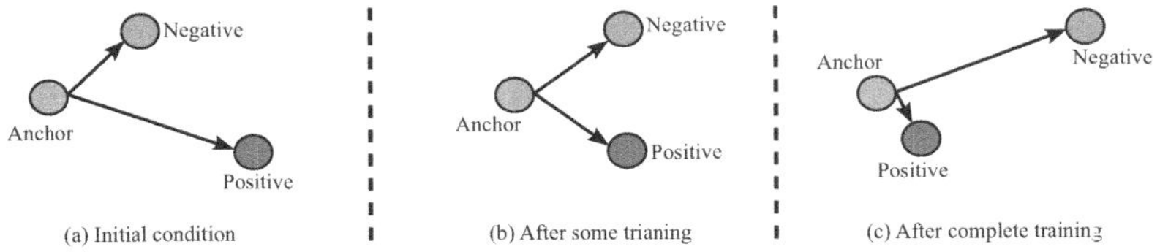

Fig. 1. Triplet loss minimizes the distance between *anchor* and a *positive* examples and maximizes the distance between the *anchor* and *negative* examples [32].

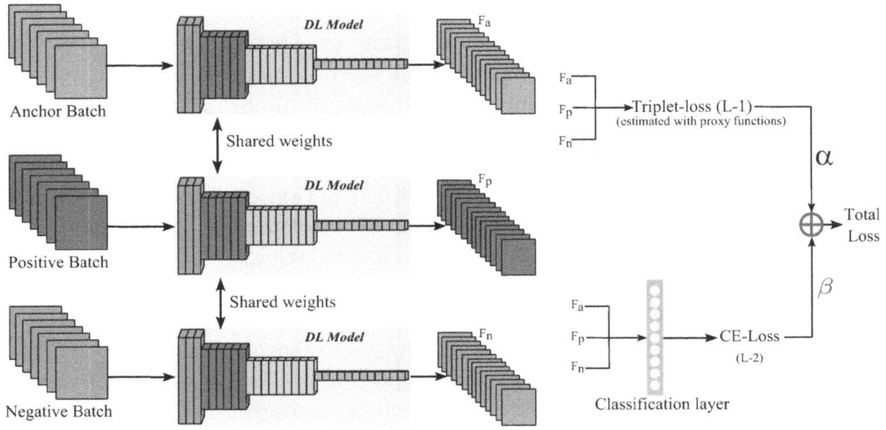

Fig. 2. Triplet-style training learns similarity-based features using three example types: anchor, positive, and negative. Features are extracted via the DL model, optimizing similarity between anchor and positive samples while minimizing it for negative samples.

how to distinguish between similar examples that belong together and those that do not. Consider a target scenario where the goal is to find the "closest" match from a set of past cases. In this context, the goal is to teach the model that the correct (or similar) case should be closer to the target than any incorrect (or dissimilar) case. Concretely, this is achieved by organizing the training data into triplets, each consisting of a target example (called the *anchor*, denoted by a), a similar example (the *positive*, denoted by p), and a dissimilar example (the *negative*, denoted by n). During training, the model is encouraged to pull the anchor and positive examples close together while pushing the negative example farther away, as shown in Fig. 1. By continuously adjusting the model's internal parameters according to this rule, the model learns a representation that better captures both underlying similarities and differences.

Figure 2 shows how we apply this approach to the feature extractor network. Features corresponding to anchor (F_a), positive (F_p), and negative (F_n) are extracted just before the classification layer and sent to the triplet loss estimator function, which uses the proxy function for similarity-based distance estimation, with an aim to keep similar features closer to each other (F_a and F_p)

and dissimilar features away from each other (F_a and F_n). A visualization of this optimization process is shown in Fig. 1, assuming at the start of the optimization process the anchor and the positive features were far apart as compared to the anchor and negative (Fig. 1(a)). The aim of this optimization is to bring anchor and positive feature close together and push away the negative features, as shown in Fig. 1(c). Following is the mathematical representation of the constraint used for this optimization

$$\begin{aligned} &||f(x_i^a) - f(x_i^p)||_2^2 + m < ||f(x_i^a) - f(x_i^n)||_2^2 \\ &\forall f(x_i^a), f(x_i^p), f(x_i^n) \in \tau \end{aligned} \tag{5}$$

Here, x_i^a, x_i^p, and x_i^n are an anchor, a positive, and a negative example, respectively; f is a functional form of feature extraction network, m is a margin imposed on the distance between positive and negative pairs, meaning these pairs need at least be m distant, and τ is the set of all possible triplet pairs defined in the training set. During training, the triplet loss is written as

$$\mathcal{L}_{\text{triplet}} = \max(0, d(f_a, f_p) - d(f_a, f_n) + m) \tag{6}$$

For a given triplet of examples (x_a, x_p, x_n), the network generates the corresponding feature vectors f_a, f_p, and f_n, which are then passed to the chosen distance function d (i.e., Pairwise Distance, Cosine Similarity, or Sinkhorn Divergence), which consists of three parts: 1) $d(f_a, f_p)$ is minimized, ensuring similar instances cluster together in feature space, 2) $d(f_a, f_n)$ is maximized, ensuring that dissimilar classes remain well-separated, and 3) the margin m prevents trivial solutions where the network pushes all cases arbitrarily far apart by only activating the loss function when the negative sample is closer to the anchor than the positive by less than m.

We integrate triplet loss alongside cross-entropy loss ($\mathcal{L}_{CE}$) with two independently controlled weight coefficients α and β as shown in Fig. 2. As a result, the overall loss formulation for each proxy function can be estimated as:

$$\mathcal{L}_{total} = \alpha \mathcal{L}_{triplet} + \beta \mathcal{L}_{CE} \tag{7}$$

4 Evaluation

4.1 Research Hypotheses

We evaluate the following hypotheses in our experiments:

1. **The triplet-style, proxy-guided approach will achieve greater classification accuracy than the analogous DL-only approach.** This may not be the case for all proxy functions, but there will exist a parameterization for every evaluated dataset such that our DL-CBR model outperforms the DL-only model.
2. **More sophisticated proxy functions will yield superior quality features, as shown by higher case-based classification accuracy.** Thus, Sinkhorn Divergence will lead to the highest classification accuracy, and Pairwise Distance (being the simplest method) will lead to the lowest overall accuracy.

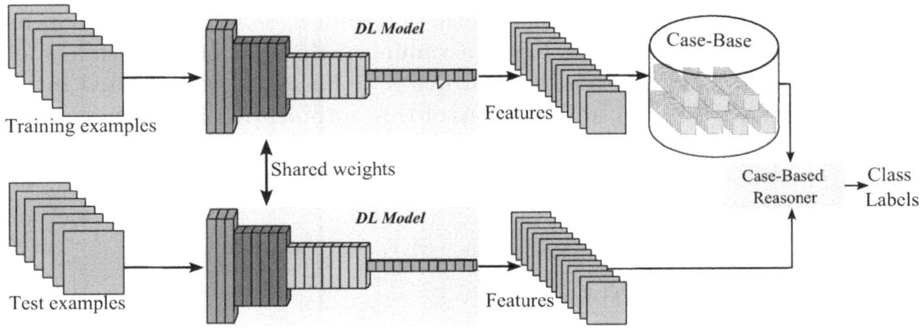

Fig. 3. The case base is constructed from training set images, and the case-based classifier assigns classification labels by comparing query features with stored cases based on Manhattan distance.

4.2 The DL-CBR Testbed System

These experiments use AlexNet [24] and pretrained DenseNet121 [18] architectures for the feature extractor model, with the Geomloss library [15] used to implement a Sinkhorn distance loss calculation compatible with the PyTorch environment [29]. During training, we keep the value of β fixed to 10 and vary the value of α from 5 to 20 in increments of 5 in our experiments. The values used for α and β were found to be empirically useful based on preliminary experiments but could feasibly be normalized such that $\alpha = 1 - \beta$; we do not present $\alpha = 0$ results, as these would repeat DL-only results that have been presented in other papers (e.g., [39]), with no triplet loss component. The case-based classifier is a retrieval-only system (no adaptation) that uses an unweighted similarity metric based on normalized Manhattan distance for similarity assessment; such an approach facilitates straightforward explanations based on case presentation. The case base is initialized using a random selection of examples that are passed through the DL model to generate representative feature vectors that are extracted from the penultimate network layer (Fig. 3). Once the case base is established, test images from the same dataset are processed through the DL model, extracting their features in an identical manner. These extracted features serve as query cases for the case-based classifier. The case-based classifier then determines the class label of each test query by comparing its feature representation to stored cases in the case base, using the similarity metric to identify the closest match.

4.3 Evaluation Datasets and Relevant Parameters

During training for all datasets, batches of triplets are created that associate anchor examples at random with a positive example from the same class and a negative example from an unlike class. Pairwise Distance and Cosine Similarity values are calculated as described above, and Sinkhorn Divergence values are also calculated as described above, following a softmax operation performed on the intermediate activations. We train and evaluate the model on each of the following datasets:

MNIST: The MNIST (Modified National Institute of Standards and Technology) dataset [12] contains images of 70,000 handwritten digits from 0 to 9, paired with the name of the numeral. We train an AlexNet [24] model from scratch on the training set of 60,000 images and test on 10,000 test set images. For the results shown below, we use a batch size of 128 and a learning rate of $3 * 10^{-4}$ with Adam optimizer (batch size of 256 with learning rate of $3 * 10^{-5}$ for Sinkhorn Divergence, as using the other parameters resulted in errors using the Geomloss library). We train the model for 30 epochs and do not use early stopping. Mean and standard deviation values are calculated by segmenting the 10,000 test examples into separate trials and then conducting each end-to-end experiment (including training) three times, resulting in thirty overall test trials for reliable mean and standard deviation calculation.

AwA2:. The Animals with Attributes 2 (AwA2) dataset contains 37,322 images distributed across 50 classes [40]. Experiments using this dataset enable comparison with recent work on feature extraction for CBR [39]. In these trials, a training set of 4096 examples is randomly selected from all possible training examples in the dataset; the pretrained DenseNet121 [18] model (as in [39]) is trained with the same batch size and learning rate as MNIST. During evaluation, 10,000 test images are selected at random and divided into sets as in the MNIST evaluation, again producing thirty overall trials.

CIFAR-10: The CIFAR-10 dataset [23] consists of 60,000 color tiny images with 6000 images per class for 10 classes. In the experiments, we use the entire training set to train an AlexNet model from scratch. We use a batch size of 128 and a learning rate of 3 * 10−3 with Adam optimizer. We trained the model for 100 epochs without early stopping. For the results shown below, test image sets are again selected and segmented as for MNIST evaluation.

5 Results and Discussion

Experimental results are displayed in Figs. 4, 5, and 6. In numerous instances the case-based classifier using extracted features outperforms the analogous DL-only model, supporting hypothesis 1; surprisingly, the proxy-guided model also achieves higher classification accuracy on AwA2 ($88.7 \pm 1.4\%$) than our best-performing DL-CBR model to date ($87.4 \pm 0.5\%$) and the analogous DL-only model ($85.9 \pm 2.4\%$), underscored by a student T-test p-score of $p \leq 0.0013$ which indicates a high probability of significance. Additional fine-tuning might further increase this improvement. However, as long as accuracy is sufficient, another motivation for the case-based approach is the ability to explain decisions in terms of cases.

Concerning the proxy loss functions, results show that there is not a one-size-fits-all similarity metric that performs best for all datasets. We hypothesized that

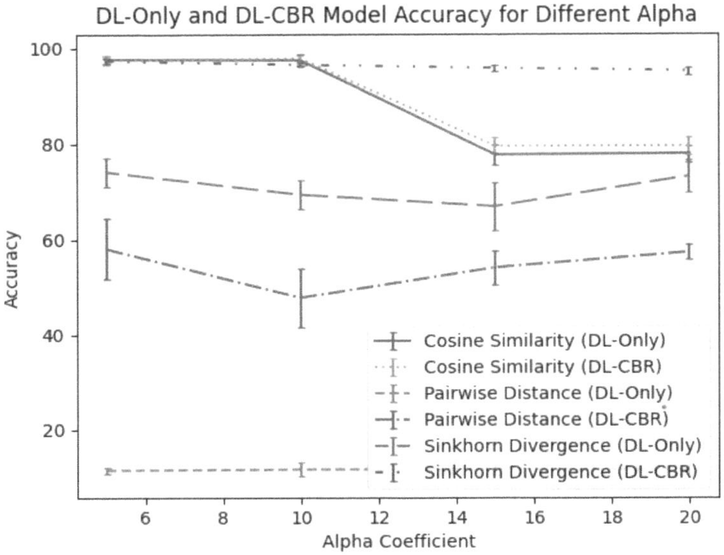

Fig. 4. Classification accuracy on the MNIST dataset, for different α coefficient values. Error bars represent one standard deviation.

Sinkhorn Divergence might best capture important similarity characteristics, but this is not necessarily the case. Sinkhorn Divergence does appear to lead to very consistent model performance, regardless of the relative contributions of triplet and cross-entropy loss terms, but Cosine Similarity appears to produce at least as strong performance. Across the board, Pairwise Distance leads to the least accurate model performance, as expected.

Finally, while the experiments show reasonable standard deviation values overall, for isolated trials the model fails to converge or otherwise exhibits extreme, out-of-distribution behavior. We consider these as outliers, but they underscore the need to train and evaluate this model carefully, potentially using multiple iterations, to ensure useful feature extraction post-training.

Evaluation on MNIST: In our tests for the MNIST dataset, the proxy-guided system consistently achieves comparable or greater classification accuracy compared with the DL-only model (Fig. 4). Often, this improvement is statistically significant. This supports that the combination of triplet-style training and the proxy loss function benefits case-based classification compared to the end-to-end DL approach, especially given that the DL-only accuracy often decreases as the contribution of the similarity-based loss function increases. One notable exception is when Pairwise Distance is used, but that model consistently fails to converge, exhibiting random-guess accuracy. Sinkhorn Divergence appears to be the best proxy function, with Cosine Similarity a close second.

Another interesting trend is the relative flatness of the DL-CBR trend lines in general; this suggests that the relative contribution of the similarity loss is

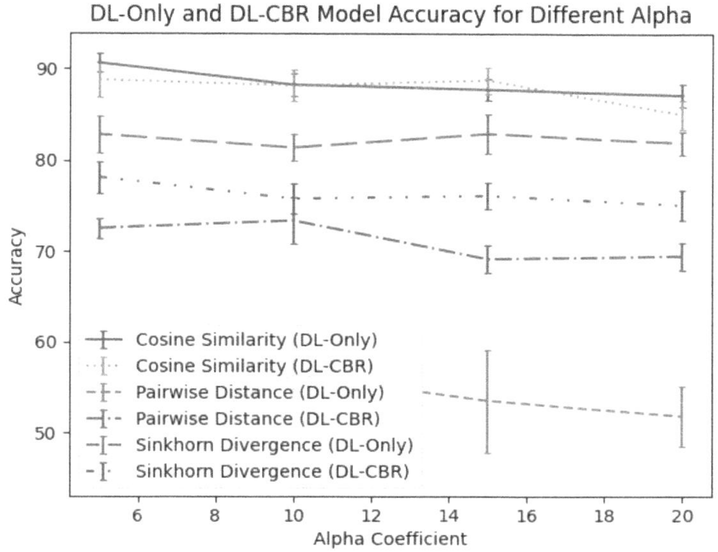

Fig. 5. Classification accuracy on the AwA2 dataset, for different α coefficient values. Error bars represent one standard deviation.

relatively unimportant. This could mean that the relative contribution of the proxy and cross-entropy loss components is less significant to the DL model during training than the fact that both are present. Alternatively (or perhaps additionally), the case-based classifier might be sensitive to subsets of features developed by both the proxy and cross-entropy loss components in such a way that their relative contribution does not impact classification accuracy.

Evaluation on AwA2: For AwA2, Cosine Similarity yields higher classification accuracy across the board relative to Sinkhorn Divergence; Pairwise Distance is once again the least performant metric. Interestingly, it is less clear-cut whether the DL-CBR approach outperforms the DL-only model when using Cosine Similarity (for Sinkhorn Divergence, it performs worse). However, given that the case-based classification accuracy is higher for the proxy-guided approach than for other DL-CBR approaches for the same experimental parameters [39], it supports the proxy-guided approach.

Trends for the AwA2 dataset are generally flat, similar to the MNIST results. Again, this suggests that the relative contributions of the proxy and cross-entropy loss terms are relatively inconsequential. Especially in light of the greater image resolution and class variety present in AwA2 relative to MNIST, this suggests future work to contextualize these findings and focus specifically on the α and β coefficients (e.g., setting one of them to zero during training).

Evaluation on CIFAR-10: Performance on CIFAR-10 arguably does not support our first hypothesis, as all DL-CBR models perform no more accurately than

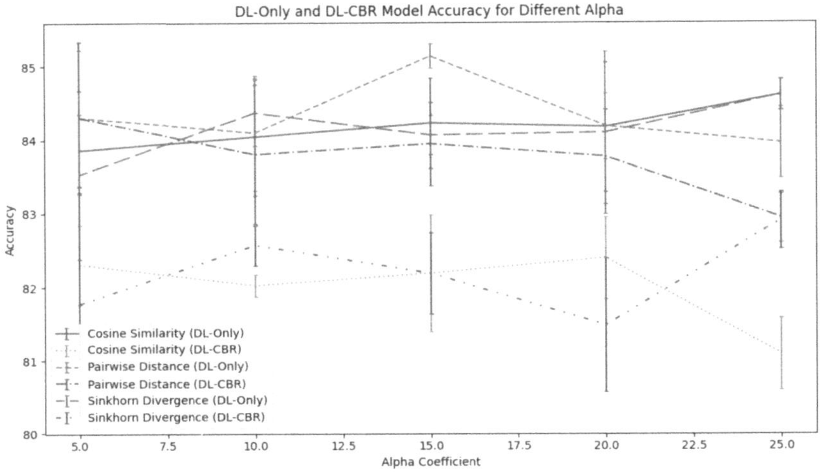

Fig. 6. Classification accuracy on the CIFAR-10 dataset, for different α coefficient values. Error bars represent one standard deviation.

the corresponding DL-only model. Our second hypothesis is challenged as well, with Pairwise Distance being the most useful proxy function. That said, general trends bear broad similarities to the AwA2 results, and the range of all accuracy values is less than 5%. Considering this in the context of the additional explainability offered by using a DL-CBR system rather than an end-to-end DL model, the proxy-guided approach may still be useful.

To explain these results, we hypothesize that CIFAR-10's high intra-class variability and small input image size makes it difficult to define feature similarity. Images in the same category (e.g., "bird") can differ drastically in species, color, pose, and scale, forcing classification to rely more on context and texture than subject features. Additionally, the dataset's limited size struggles to capture the full diversity required for robust feature learning. While deep learning can leverage sheer data volume, the case-based models depend on clearly defined features – a challenge given CIFAR-10's variability and constrained dataset size.

6 Conclusions and Future Work

This paper presents a novel method for training DL models for feature extraction, using similarity-focused proxy functions in the DL training loss to encourage generating features that are useful for case retrieval. In our experimental results, this approach is successful relative to the analogous DL-only model for multiple domains, and is capable of outperforming our previous DL-CBR approaches (e.g., [39]). Considering the three evaluated similarity functions, Pairwise Distance is generally the least effective (though it had some success with CIFAR-10), Sinkhorn Divergence is the most consistent, and Cosine Similarity is appealing in its combination of simplicity and effectiveness. Avenues for future work include considering potential parameterizations for increasing classification accuracy, including different neural architectures, other loss functions or methods for calculating the aggregate loss value, and differentiable CBR methods that might allow for direct inclusion of CBR performance as a loss term itself. Additional work involves evaluating this model for additional datasets and distance metrics and developing practical approaches for selecting metrics for different domains.

References

1. Amin, K., Lancaster, G., Kapetanakis, S., Althoff, K.D., Dengel, A., Petridis, M.: Advanced similarity measures using word embeddings and Siamese networks in CBR. In: Intelligent Systems and Applications, pp. 449–462. Springer, Cham (2020)
2. Arjovsky, M., Chintala, S., Bottou, L.: Wasserstein GAN (2017)
3. Bach, K., Mork, P.: On the explanation of similarity for developing and deploying CBR systems. In: Proceedings of the Thirty-Third International Florida Artificial Intelligence Research Society Conference (FLAIRS 2020) (2020)
4. Barletta, R., Mark, W.: Explanation-based indexing of cases. In: Kolodner, J. (ed.) Proceedings of a Workshop on Case-Based Reasoning, pp. 50–60. DARPA, Morgan Kaufmann, Palo Alto (1988)
5. Barnett, A.J., et al.: Interpretable mammographic image classification using case-based reasoning and deep learning. In: Proceedings of IJCAI-21 Workshop on Deep Learning, Case-Based Reasoning, and AutoML (2021). https://arxiv.org/pdf/2107.05605
6. Bhatta, S., Goel, A.: Model-based learning of structural indices to design cases. In: Proceedings of the IJCAI-93 Workshop on Reuse of Design, pp. A1–A13. IJCAI, Chambery, France (1993)
7. Bonzano, A., Cunningham, P., Smyth, B.: Using introspective learning to improve retrieval in CBR: a case study in air traffic control. In: Case-Based Reasoning Research and Development: Proceedings of the Second International Conference on Case-Based Reasoning, ICCBR-97, pp. 291–302. Springer, Berlin (1997)
8. Chai, J., Zeng, H., Li, A., Ngai, E.W.: Deep learning in computer vision: a critical review of emerging techniques and application scenarios. Mach. Learn. Appl. **6**, 100134 (2021)
9. Chen, C., Li, O., Tao, D., Barnett, A., Rudin, C., Su, J.K.: This looks like that: deep learning for interpretable image recognition. In: Advances in Neural Information Processing Systems, vol. 32, pp. 8930–8941. Curran (2019)
10. Cox, M., Ram, A.: Introspective multistrategy learning: on the construction of learning strategies. Artif. Intell. **112**(1–2), 1–55 (1999)
11. Cuturi, M.: Sinkhorn distances: lightspeed computation of optimal transportation distances (2013)
12. Deng, L.: The MNist database of handwritten digit images for machine learning research. IEEE Sig. Process. Mag. **29**(6), 141–142 (2012)
13. Domeshek, E.: Indexing stories as social advice. In: Proceedings of the Ninth National Conference on Artificial Intelligence, pp. 16–21. AAAI Press, Menlo Park, CA (1991)
14. Faruqui, M., Dodge, J., Jauhar, S.K., Dyer, C., Hovy, E., Smith, N.A.: Retrofitting word vectors to semantic lexicons. In: Proceedings of the 2015 Conference of the North American Chapter of the Association for Computational Linguistics: Human Language Technologies, pp. 1606–1615. ACL, Denver (2015)

15. Feydy, J., Séjourné, T., Vialard, F.X., Amari, S.I., Trouve, A., Peyré, G.: Interpolating between optimal transport and MMD using Sinkhorn divergences. In: The 22nd International Conference on Artificial Intelligence and Statistics, pp. 2681–2690 (2019)
16. Fox, S., Leake, D.: Introspective reasoning for index refinement in case-based reasoning. J. Exp. Theor. Artif. Intell. **13**(1), 63–88 (2001)
17. Genevay, A., Peyre, G., Cuturi, M.: Learning generative models with Sinkhorn divergences. In: Storkey, A., Perez-Cruz, F. (eds.) Proceedings of the Twenty-First International Conference on Artificial Intelligence and Statistics. Proceedings of Machine Learning Research, vol. 84, pp. 1608–1617. PMLR (2018). https://proceedings.mlr.press/v84/genevay18a.html
18. Huang, G., Liu, Z., van der Maaten, L., Weinberger, K.Q.: Densely connected convolutional networks. arXiv preprint arXiv:1608.06993 (2016)
19. Jasim, W.N., Mohammed, R.J.: A survey on segmentation techniques for image processing. Iraqi J. Electr. Electron. Eng. **17**(2) (2021)
20. Kaya, M., Bilge, H.Ş: Deep metric learning: a survey. Symmetry **11**(9), 1066 (2019)
21. Kenny, E.M., Keane, M.T.: Twin-systems to explain artificial neural networks using case-based reasoning: comparative tests of feature-weighting methods in ANN-CBR twins for XAI. In: Proceedings of the Twenty-Eighth International Joint Conference on Artificial Intelligence (2019)
22. Koch, G., Zemel, R., Salakhutdinov, R.: Siamese neural networks for one-shot image recognition. In: Proceedings of the 32nd International Conference on Machine Learning (2015)
23. Krizhevsky, A., Hinton, G., et al.: Learning multiple layers of features from tiny images (2009)
24. Krizhevsky, A., Sutskever, I., Hinton, G.E.: ImageNet classification with deep convolutional neural networks. In: Proceedings of the 25th International Conference on Neural Information Processing Systems, vol. 1, pp. 1097–1105 (2012)
25. Leake, D.: An indexing vocabulary for case-based explanation. In: Proceedings of the Ninth National Conference on Artificial Intelligence, pp. 10–15. AAAI Press, Menlo Park, CA (July 1991)
26. Leake, D., Wilkerson, Z., Crandall, D.: Extracting case indices from convolutional neural networks: a comparative study. In: Case-Based Reasoning Research and Development, ICCBR 2022 (2022)
27. Leake, D., Wilkerson, Z., Vats, V., Acharya, K., Crandall, D.: Examining the impact of network architecture on extracted feature quality for CBR. In: Case-Based Reasoning Research and Development, ICCBR 2023. Springer (2023)
28. Martin, K., Wiratunga, N., Sani, S., Massie, S., Clos, J.: A convolutonal Siamese network for developing similarity knowledge in the Selfback dataset. In: Proceedings of the International Conference on Case-Based Reasoning Workshops, CEUR Workshop Proceedings, ICCBR, pp. 85–94 (2017)
29. Paszke, A., et al.: PyTorch: an imperative style, high-performance deep learning library. In: Advances in Neural Information Processing Systems, vol. 32, pp. 8024–8035. Curran Associates, Inc. (2019)
30. Sani, S., Wiratunga, N., Massie, S.: Learning deep features for kNN-based human activity recognition. In: Proceedings of ICCBR 2017 Workshops (CAW, CBRDL, PO-CBR), Doctoral Consortium, and Competitions co-located with the 25th International Conference on Case-Based Reasoning (ICCBR 2017), Trondheim, Norway, June 26–28, 2017. CEUR Workshop Proceedings, vol. 2028, pp. 95–103. CEUR-WS.org (2017)

31. Schank, R., et al.: Towards a general content theory of indices. In: Proceedings of the 1990 AAAI Spring Symposium on Case-Based Reasoning. AAAI Press, Menlo Park, CA (1990)
32. Schroff, F., Kalenichenko, D., Philbin, J.: Facenet: a unified embedding for face recognition and clustering. In: 2015 IEEE Conference on Computer Vision and Pattern Recognition (CVPR). IEEE (2015). https://doi.org/10.1109/cvpr.2015.7298682
33. Sung, F., Yang, Y., Zhang, L., Xiang, T., Torr, P.H.S., Hospedales, T.M.: Learning to compare: relation network for few-shot learning. In: 2018 IEEE/CVF Conference on Computer Vision and Pattern Recognition (2018)
34. Turner, J.T., Floyd, M.W., Gupta, K.M., Aha, D.W.: Novel object discovery using case-based reasoning and convolutional neural networks. In: Cox, M.T., Funk, P., Begum, S. (eds.) ICCBR 2018. LNCS (LNAI), vol. 11156, pp. 399–414. Springer, Cham (2018). https://doi.org/10.1007/978-3-030-01081-2_27
35. Turner, J.T., Floyd, M.W., Gupta, K., Oates, T.: NOD-CC: a hybrid CBR-CNN architecture for novel object discovery. In: Bach, K., Marling, C. (eds.) ICCBR 2019. LNCS (LNAI), vol. 11680, pp. 373–387. Springer, Cham (2019). https://doi.org/10.1007/978-3-030-29249-2_25
36. Balntas, V., Riba, E., Ponsa, D., Mikolajczyk, K.: Learning local feature descriptors with triplets and shallow convolutional neural networks. In: Richard C., Wilson, E.R.H., Smith, W.A.P. (eds.) Proceedings of the British Machine Vision Conference (BMVC), pp. 119.1–119.11. BMVA Press (2016). https://doi.org/10.5244/C.30.119
37. Vats, V.K., Joshi, S., Crandall, D.J., Reza, M.A., Jung, S.: GC-MVSNet: multi-view, multi-scale, geometrically-consistent multi-view stereo. In: 2024 IEEE/CVF Winter Conference on Applications of Computer Vision, pp. 3230–3240. IEEE Computer Society (2024)
38. Wilkerson, Z., Leake, D., Crandall, D.: On combining knowledge-engineered and network-extracted features for retrieval. In: Case-Based Reasoning Research and Development, ICCBR 2021, pp. 248–262 (2021)
39. Wilkerson, Z., Leake, D., Vats, V., Crandall, D.: Extracting indexing features for CBR from deep neural networks: a transfer learning approach. In: Case-Based Reasoning Research and Development, ICCBR 2024. Springer (2024)
40. Xian, Y., Lampert, C.H., Schiele, B., Akata, Z.: Zero-shot learning - a comprehensive evaluation of the good, the bad and the ugly. In: IEEE Transactions on Pattern Analysis and Machine Intelligence (T-PAMI) (2018)
41. Zou, Z., Chen, K., Shi, Z., Guo, Y., Ye, J.: Object detection in 20 years: a survey. Proc. IEEE **111**(3), 257–276 (2023). https://doi.org/10.1109/JPROC.2023.3238524

Integration of Time Series Embedding for Efficient Retrieval in Case-Based Reasoning

Justin Weich[1,2], Alexander Schultheis[1,2](✉), Maximilian Hoffmann[1,2], and Ralph Bergmann[1,2]

[1] Artificial Intelligence and Intelligent Information Systems, Trier University, 54296 Trier, Germany
{s4juweic,schultheis,hoffmannm,bergmann}@uni-trier.de
[2] German Research Center for Artificial Intelligence (DFKI) Branch Trier University, Behringstraße 21, 54296 Trier, Germany
{justin.weich,alexander.schultheis,maximilian.hoffmann, ralph.bergmann}@dfki.de
http://www.wi2.uni-trier.de

Abstract. The increasing volume of time series data in Industry 4.0 applications creates substantial challenges for real-time data analysis. Such analyses that are conducted in the research area of *Temporal Case-Based Reasoning* (TCBR) face performance problems due to complex similarity measures. One potential approach already proven in other domains for addressing these problems is the usage of embedding techniques for time series data, which map these data into a simplified vector representation. Therefore, this paper investigates the integration of time series embedding techniques in the context of *Case-Based Reasoning* (CBR) to improve retrieval efficiency. Therefore, requirements for the application of embedding techniques in CBR are derived. A systematic literature study identifies possible approaches that are analyzed based on the requirements, with the result that no approach is suitable for the application. Therefore, a novel embedding architecture is proposed, using a Siamese neural network approach that can be trained with similarity values. The architecture is prototypically implemented in the ProCAKE framework and evaluated in an Internet of Things use case from a smart factory. The results demonstrate that the embedding-based retrieval achieves classification performance comparable to traditional similarity measures while significantly reducing retrieval time.

Keywords: Temporal Case-Based Reasoning · Time Series Data · Time Series Embedding · Time Series Similarity Measure · Siamese Neural Networks

1 Introduction

Industry 4.0 (I4.0) [18] describes the technological change achieved by the integration of digital technologies into industrial processes. Within the framework of the *Internet of Things* (IoT) - a network of interconnected devices that collect and exchange data -, numerous components in manufacturing environments

© The Author(s), under exclusive license to Springer Nature Switzerland AG 2025
I. Bichindaritz and B. López (Eds.): ICCBR 2025, LNAI 15662, pp. 328–344, 2025.
https://doi.org/10.1007/978-3-031-96559-3_22

are equipped with sensors that continuously generate time series data, providing real-time insights into operational conditions. The sensor data generated during industrial manufacturing processes serves as a valuable resource for analysis and control purposes [50]. Analyzing time series data enables the identification of patterns and anomalies, which is crucial for understanding and optimizing processes. The practical applications for this cover various use cases. For instance, in the context of *Event and Activity Detection* (EaAD) [39,54], sensor data is leveraged to determine ongoing activities within production environments, providing insights into operational processes. Similarly, *Data Quality Issue* (DQI) management [11,32] focuses on identifying inconsistencies in recorded data to ensure reliable analyses and informed decision-making, minimizing the risks caused by erroneous data. Moreover, analyzing time series data can facilitate the early detection of potential failures, as demonstrated in *Predictive Maintenance* (PredM) [49,72], enabling proactive interventions and minimizing downtime. While *Machine Learning* (ML) methods are often used to analyze such time series data [15,17], approaches from the research field of *Case-Based Reasoning* (CBR) [1,9] also offer a feasible *Artificial Intelligence* (AI) methodology for these tasks [39,52]. This is being investigated in the sub-research area of *Temporal Case-Based Reasoning* (TCBR) [29,38]. This approach has the advantages that the case returned as a solution provides an initial explanation for the result [58] and that domain knowledge is easier to integrate [66].

The quality of the results of a CBR approach depends on the underlying similarity of the retrieval. In TCBR, established measures are utilized to assess the similarity between the time series of a query and that of a case [39,48], e.g., the *Smith-Waterman-Algorithm* (SWA) [57] or *Dynamic Time Warping* (DTW) [47]. However, such traditional time series similarity measures often are affected by quadratic computational complexity [48], which becomes particularly problematic with long time series and large case bases. Especially when used in large industrial facilities, where numerous sensors produce different time series, this creates a computational burden which creates substantial barriers to real-time data processing and analysis, especially in time-sensitive industrial applications requiring rapid insights and near real-time results.

Various methods are already considered in CBR for reducing the complexity of time series data by simplifying and shortening these, such as abstraction [56]. However, a drawback of such methods is that patterns or dependencies in the data might get lost through the process. To mitigate this issue, alternative approaches are required. Such a solution is the application of embedding methods, which leverage ML techniques to retain relevant structures while transforming the data into a more compact representation. By mapping time series features into a vector space, embeddings can substantially reduce dimensionality while preserving critical structural information [6,25]. Specifically, embedding models based on *Neural Networks* (NNs) offer the capability to recognize complex data patterns and represent them efficiently. Therefore, this paper examines the use of embeddings in TCBR. To this end, a literature study of existing embedding approaches is presented. The suitability of these approaches is to be examined based on the requirements collected, whereupon an embedding-based similarity calculation is designed for the retrieval step in CBR.

The further structure of the paper is as follows: In Sect. 2, the theoretical foundations and related work are presented. Based on the application of embeddings in CBR, requirements are derived in Sect. 3. Section 4 contains the methodology and the results of the literature review on available embedding methods for time series, as well as their evaluation, based on the requirements. Building upon the results, Sect. 5 presents the architecture for the time series embedding approach and its integration into the CBR cycle. The evaluation of this approach using a prototype implementation is described in Sect. 6. Subsequently, a conclusion is drawn in Sect. 7 and future work is proposed.

2 Foundations and Related Work

This section provides the necessary background for examining the use of embeddings in TCBR, as outlined in this paper. Therefore, the research field of TCBR is introduced in Sect. 2.1. Section 2.2 presents embedding methods in the general context of ML, while Sect. 2.3 reviews related work on embedding of time series and similar structures in general, as well as in CBR.

2.1 Temporal Case-Based Reasoning

TCBR is a sub-area of CBR that deals with the processing and analysis of time series [29,38]. The focus is on the expression of temporal relationships in cases, with the time series being the most common representation form [39]. A time series depicts real measured values over a period of time, for example, IoT sensor data from manufacturing processes [39,52]. To assess similarity values between such time series, various measures are developed [39]. Two important algorithms are SWA [57] and DTW [47]. SWA enables the comparison of sequences of different lengths by insertion and deletion operations, while DTW can also consider expansions and compressions in the time series [48]. For the overall similarity calculation, the local-global principle [9, pp. 106–107] is applied. First, local similarities of individual time points are calculated and then aggregated on time series level (global) using the mentioned measures. Afterward, these are again combined on a higher global level, e.g., with similarity values of other time series or global attributes regarding the entire process. The runtime of this similarity calculation is significantly influenced by the similarity measures used for the time series. This is because for each local similarity calculation between the time series elements of the query, there are various options for mapping this to a suitable equivalent of the case. Therefore, a search problem results in which the alignment must be found that maximizes the similarity at the global time series level. Due to this, e.g., SWA and DTW require a quadratic runtime [48], leading to runtime problems, especially with long time series.

2.2 Neural Networks and Embeddings

As a sub-field of AI, ML deals with the development of algorithms that can learn from data and adapt to specific use cases [42]. This is achieved via models that are taught and optimized using training data [4,12]. The prominent research field of deep learning investigates NNs that serve as a powerful ML method. NNs consist of several layers, with each layer containing multiple nodes (called neurons). The fundamental structure comprises an input layer, any number of hidden layers and an output layer. There are weighted connections between the neurons of neighboring layers that enable signal transmission. The weighting of these connections is adjusted during the training process to optimize the prediction accuracy of the model. This training process can be carried out using, e.g., supervised learning [4]. There, the model is presented with the correct solution, allowing the parameters to be adjusted accordingly.

Such NNs can be used to learn embeddings. This is a way of representing complex data in low-dimensional vectors [14,25]. This is achieved by a mapping function $f : X \rightarrow \mathbb{R}^d$ that transforms objects into a d-dimensional vector space. Embeddings are used in various ML areas, such as Large Language Models [70], but can also be used on time series data. An NN is trained for transforming data into embeddings, which learns the properties of the data to be reflected in the vector representation. This transformation enables efficient similarity calculations, as these can be carried out at the vector level. Various measures such as the Euclidean distance or a cosine similarity measure can be implemented to calculate similarities and distances, respectively, between embeddings [35]. For the application of these measures to the embedding NN, a Siamese architecture is used [25,71]. This is characterized by using two parallel NNs with identical architecture and weights for embedding generation and calculating the similarity value between these mappings. Based on this output, the weights in the NN can be adjusted during training. The application of this embedding approach usually enables both, the reduction of the dimensionality of complex data structures and the preservation of their essential characteristics.

2.3 Related Work

The application of embedding methods in the context of CBR covers various research areas, in particular the processing of time series, their temporal abstraction, and the embedding of related data structures.

Malburg et al. [39] identify four major use cases of CBR for time series data, including prediction, classification, error detection, and application in the medical field. For each of these areas, there is plenty of research outside CBR that deals with time series embeddings to solve the specific use cases mentioned. Lim and Zhoren [37] provide an overview of time series forecasting methods and identify weaknesses of those using embeddings, such as limited adaptability to different time intervals and high data complexity. The applications range from financial to energy markets, where complex influences such as weather or seasonal patterns can be integrated [46,55]. Time series embeddings also enable efficient classifications by projecting them into a uniform vector space [23]. Smaller distances between vectors correlate with a higher similarity of the time series. Embeddings also facilitate error detection by making long-term patterns and subtle deviations visible [30,36].

Temporal abstraction is an alternative approach in which time series are transformed by semantic or symbolic simplification. This includes methods such as temporal abstraction according to Shahar [56] and Allen intervals [2], which define basic relationships between time intervals. Höppner [27] presents further abstraction methods, including time series classification using segmentation and deductive segmentation. These approaches can have the disadvantage that information about patterns or dependencies is lost because, in contrast to embedding, the data representation is not learned but transferred, e.g., on a rule base, into the abstract form.

In the context of related data structures, sequence and graph embeddings are particularly relevant [48]. Sequence embeddings are widely used in language processing and bioinformatics [61], for example in the analysis of protein structures [7]. In the area of graph embeddings, Hoffmann et al. [25] present an innovative approach using graph NNs in a Siamese architecture, which transforms the graph structure into embeddings and calculates similarity values between those. Other application areas include knowledge graphs and recommendation systems [63], where graph embeddings are used for complexity reduction and efficient operationalization. Klein et al. [34] demonstrate the application of embeddings for workflow optimization in CBR using knowledge graph embeddings.

3 Requirements for Using Time Series Embedding in Case-Based Reasoning

To select suitable embedding methods for time series, requirements for these methods are needed. Some come from the general application scenario in CBR, others result from the application of ML models. The following four requirements are identified.

Req. 1 Applicability to Time Series: The embedding method must either be directly applicable to time series or embed sequences or graphs, since time series can be represented as these [48]. The requirement for graph or sequence embedders is that they take the temporal component of the data into account. The embedding method must use (encoded) time series (or sequences or graphs) with variable time components as input. The specification is therefore ideally a direct time series embedding.

Req. 2 Data Types: The embedding procedure must be applicable to time series with different data types used for the entries, i.e., the timestamp itself as well as the measured data value. The requirement stems from the CBR use case, as complex data objects are contained in the time series. For example, it must be possible to embed time series with numerical data or with entire objects. The process should be able to automatically recognize and process the data types.

Req. 3 Trainability Based on Similarity Values: It must be possible to train the embedding process using similarity values as input parameters. The similarity values are provided as input so that the method can train an ML model using these values. This is necessary to automatically create mapping functions for suitable embeddings. By using the similarity values, this can be done independently of the underlying similarity measures so that the embedding approach can be used for different domains and use cases. This is a form of supervised learning (see Sect. 2.2), as the model is trained as closely as possible to the given similarity values.

Req. 4 Embedding Dimension: The embedding procedure should have a manually adjustable embedding dimension or automatically determine the optimum dimension. This ensures that an optimal embedding of the time series is generated and the quality of the embeddings is improved.

4 Literature Analysis on Time Series Embedding

To identify the current state of the research in the field of embedding methods for time series, a systematic literature review [45] was carried out[1] on the platforms Google Scholar[2], Semantic Scholar[3], Scopus[4] and IEEE Xplore[5]. The sources found were further analyzed using forward and backward snowballing. The review was not only conducted for time series embedding methods, but also for sequence and graph embedding methods, as time series can be represented as sequences or graphs (see Req. 1).

A total of ten methods for embedding time series data were identified, which are illustrated in Table 1. An evaluation based on the requirements derived is also included there. Furthermore, the maturity of the approaches was also considered by checking whether an open-source implementation is available. A result of the requirements analysis shows that Req. 3 is not fulfilled by any of the embedding methods. This is because the methods already use built-in similarity measures and cannot be trained using similarity values. The disadvantage is that the methods are adapted to a specific similarity measure, usually DTW, and are therefore not generically applicable without adaptation. Methods that can be used with similarity values as input parameters, such as Multidimensional Scaling according to Torgerson [60], do not include a ML model and therefore do not provide a training (see Req. 3). Irrespective of Req. 3, only TS2Vec [62] as a pure time series embedding fulfills the other requirements at all. The methods for sequences and graphs show similar restrictions. Therefore, the requirements' analysis comes to the conclusion that none of the existing methods is suitable for the application of time series embedding in CBR.

In addition to the investigated embedding methods for time series data, further problems could be recognized in the identified methods for sequences and

[1] The literature review was carried out in May 2024.
[2] https://scholar.google.de/.
[3] https://www.semanticscholar.org/.
[4] https://www.scopus.com/.
[5] https://ieeexplore.ieee.org/.

Table 1. Comparison of the Requirements of the Ten Identified Embedding Approaches. (✓ = Suitable, ✗ = Unsuitable, (✓) = Partially Suitable.)

Embedding Approach	Req. 1	Req. 2	Req. 3	Req. 4	Implementation Available?
Boosted Embedding [31]	✓	✗	✗	✗	✗
Embed-RUL [21]	✓	✗	✗	✗	✗
Embedding in Pseudo-Euclidean Space by Graepel et al. [20]	✓	✓	✗	✓	✗
Laplacian Eigenmap by Belkin and Niyogi [5]	✓	✓	✗	✓	✗
LSTM Embedding by Uribarri and Mindlin [62]	✓	✓	✗	✓	✗
Multidimensional Scaling by Torgerson [60]	✓	✓	✗	✓	(✓)[a]
Random Warping Series [68]	✓	✗	✗	✓	✓[b]
Signal2vec [43]	✓	✗	✗	✗	✓[c]
Time2Vec [41]	✓	✗	✗	✓	✓[d]
TS2Vec [62]	✓	✓	✗	✓	✓[e]

[a] Partially available: https://github.com/drewwilimitis/Manifold-Learning
[b] https://github.com/IBM/RandomWarpingSeries
[c] https://github.com/ChristoferNal/multi-nilm
[d] https://github.com/ojus1/Time2Vec-PyTorch
[e] https://github.com/zhihanyue/ts2vec

graphs. Overviews of sequence embedding methods are presented for application areas as, e.g., biological sequence embeddings by Tran et al. [61] or Ibtehaz and Kihara [28], as well as for word embeddings by Wang et al. [65]. Sequence embeddings generally do not support consideration of the time point, but only of the sequentially recorded value. This means that information would be lost during embedding if the measured values are not collected at homogeneous time intervals. The loss of this relevant information, which is considered in traditional similarity calculations, contradicts Req. 2. Despite this exclusion argument, several methods were investigated, e.g., Autoencoder & seq2seq by Guo et al. [22], and seq2vec [33]. This analysis is available in an additional document[6]. In supplement to the problem already described with Req. 2, e.g., the sequence embeddings considered also do not fulfill Req. 3, as they are often not based on similarities, and also have other difficulties such as the time series embeddings. Further, graph embeddings were also considered, for which various overviews are available, too, such as Cai et al. [13], Goyal and Ferrara [19], Xu [69], Wang et al. [64], and Barros et al. [3]. When transforming time series data into graphs, the problem arises that there is too much irrelevant information in the more extensive graph structure. For example, the information of the time points with associated values

[6] Complete requirements' analysis available at: https://gitlab.rlp.net/procake-embedding/procake-embedding-time-series-evaluation/-/blob/main/Requirements-Analysis.pdf.

would be available as nodes, whereas the edges have no semantic meaning. As a result, a lot of irrelevant information is considered during embedding, which leads to an unnecessary increase in complexity and therefore runtime. Various methods, e.g., graph2Vec [44], and, StarSpace [67], were considered in the evaluation and the same difficulties arose as with the other embedding methods. For example, no method was found that fulfilled Req. 3. Due to the expected difficulties caused by the conversion to graph format and the resulting irrelevant information, no further analysis of the graph methods was carried out on this basis. The analysis of the considered embedding methods for graphs is also included in the additional document(See footnote 6).

5 Application of Time Series Embedding in Similarity-Based Retrieval

As explained in Sect. 3, none of the existing embedding approaches fulfill the requirements for being used in CBR. Therefore, a generic embedding approach for time series that meets the requirements is designed in Sect. 5.1. Its integration into the CBR cycle is presented in Sect. 5.2.

5.1 Architecture of the Time Series Embedding Approach

The developed architecture for a time series embedding applicable in CBR is visualized in Fig. 1. It is built on a layer-based approach that uses established methods for NN procedures in IoT environments. The system processes two time series and calculates their similarity using three specialized layers:

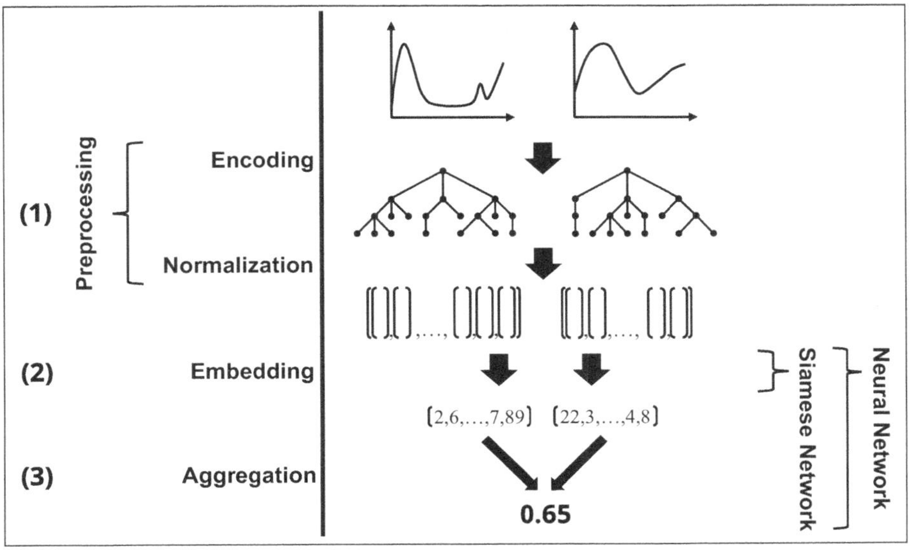

Fig. 1. The Architecture of the Time Series Embedding Approach.

(1) **Preprocessing Layer**: This layer is responsible for processing the time series data, which includes encoding and normalization. First, the processing of different data types is enabled by transforming these into numerical representations (see Req. 2). This encoding approach can be adapted from Hoffmann et al. [25], who develop encodings for different data types in CBR, originally, for graph embeddings. Their method first encodes atomic elements with type-specific methods, then builds a tree-encoding in a bottom-up fashion to preserve the hierarchical structure for NN processing. Therefore, the encoding step provides a foundation for generic encoding while maintaining compatibility with case representations used in a CBR application. Second, the encoded time series are normalized by conversion into vector sequences, which are necessary for *Long Short-Term Memory* (LSTM) processing. It extracts and concatenates vector information from tree nodes, enriching it with implicit structural data. During training, sequences are normalized to match the longest sequence in the training dataset through padding.

(2) **Embedding Layer**: In this layer, the normalized vector sequences are processed by multiple LSTM layers of a Siamese network with an adjustable embedding dimension (see Req. 3). The first LSTM layer outputs a complete sequence, while the second LSTM layer produces a condensed state vector, followed by two multi layer perceptrons with *Rectified Linear Unit* (ReLU) activation. This architecture enables the network to learn complex dependencies and generate embeddings for both input time series.
If an embedding has already been calculated for a time series, for example for a query in a retrieval, the embedding is cached, and these two layers (preprocessing, and embedding) are skipped.

(3) **Aggregation Layer**: Finally, this layer combines the generated embeddings and calculates their similarity using a single-neuron dense layer with sigmoid activation. This layer directly outputs similarity values in the interval $[0, 1]$, eliminating the need for additional normalization steps. The design choice of computing similarity rather than returning embeddings optimizes for CBR system requirements while maintaining model simplicity.

The architecture also enables the processing of variable time series lengths through appropriate normalization and masking during training.

5.2 Integration in the Case-Based Reasoning Cycle

The developed architecture is integrated into a CBR system by adding the embedding approach presented in Sect. 5.1 to the knowledge container of the similarity measures. The underlying NN is trained once based on the case base and similarity values calculated between the cases with a traditional measure, e.g., SWA or DTW. The call of the embedding system is made when a similarity calculation is pending for a time series, which can be nested in a higher-level object (cf. local-global principle, Sect. 2.1). The time series contained in query and case are encoded and normalized, followed by embedding and the similarity calculation (corresponding to the layers in Sect. 5.1). Already determined embeddings can be stored in the case base to increase efficiency. The computed similarity value as output of the NN is transmitted back to the CBR application for further processing in the retrieval step.

6 Experimental Evaluation

To evaluate the embedding approach, it is compared with the traditional DTW method. This takes place for the EaAD use case, for which Malburg et al. [39] already present a successful case-based approach using DTW. There, CBR is used to classify which event or activity is being executed for the time series data contained in the query. In the context of this comparison, the following hypotheses are investigated:

Hypothesis 1 (H1). The usage of embedding-based similarity measures accelerates retrieval compared to the usage of DTW.

Hypothesis 2 (H2). The embedding-based CBR approaches delivers results comparable in quality to the DTW-based approach.

H2. The embedding-based CBR approach delivers retrieval results which ranking order is correct and complete compared to the DTW-based.
H2. The embedding-based CBR approach achieves classification performance comparable to the DTW-based.

Before the examination of these hypotheses, the implementation of the approach as well as the setup of the evaluation is described in Sect. 6.1. Then, the comparison results are presented in Sect. 6.2 and the answers to the hypotheses are discussed.

6.1 Implementation and Experimental Setup

The presented embedding approach is implemented in the open-source CBR framework ProCAKE[7] [8,10], which is written in Java [53]. The EaAD use case is already available there, for which implementation details are presented by Malburg et al. [39]. The encoding layer is also integrated in ProCAKE and sends its output via an interface to the other layers, which are realized in Python using the TensorFlow libraries [59]. This implementation is encapsulated in a Docker image and returns the resulting similarity value to the ProCAKE framework. To increase efficiency, the similarity calculation in the NN is carried out in batches.

For the evaluation[8], we use data from a Fischertechnik Smart Factory located in the IoT Lab Trier[9] [40] that was evaluated for EaAD before [39]. A case

[7] Implementation available at: https://gitlab.rlp.net/procake-embedding/procake-embedding-core.

[8] Runnable evaluation available at: https://gitlab.rlp.net/procake-embedding/procake-embedding-time-series-evaluation.

[9] https://iot.uni-trier.de/.

base of 1,100 cases is used here, containing unprocessed time series data. Of these cases, the time series from 1,000 cases were used for training. For this purpose, similarity values were calculated between all these time series using DTW (a case contains ten different time series in this domain) and the embedding system was trained based on these values. The training took place on a `Tesla V100-SXM2-32GB` graphics card with `Intel(R) Xeon(R) Gold 6138 CPU @ 2.00GHz` processor. Each epoch required approximately 50 h and 30 min, resulting in a total training time of 101 h for two epochs with a batch size of 128, excluding data import. In total, 106,565 parameters were initialized, of which 35,521 are trainable and 71,044 are optimizer parameters. The model expects input vectors of arbitrary length and a dimensionality of 19, based on the encoding scheme proposed by Hoffmann et al. [25]. During inference, each input is transformed into an embedding of length 16, which is then compared to a reference embedding in the aggregation layer to compute a similarity value. Using this embedding approach as time series similarity measure, a retrieval was performed with the remaining 100 cases not given to the training as queries. For comparison, a baseline retrieval was also performed using the traditional DTW approach.

6.2 Experimental Results and Discussion

The evaluation has been carried out on a server with 34 processors, a clock frequency of 2,850 MHz, and 400 gigabytes of RAM. The embedding-based and the DTW-based CBR approach were executed on this setup for the EaAD use case. To answer H1, the times required for the retrieval execution are compared. In both cases, this did not run in parallel, but on one thread. For the embedding-based CBR approach, the retrieval required a runtime of 8 min and 43 s. This includes 1 min and 46 s spent on encoding and embedding the case base, which could also be omitted by permanent storage. In contrast, the DTW-based approach required a runtime of 3 h and 47 min. These results indicate that a runtime acceleration is achieved by using the embedding methods, so that H1 can be confirmed.

To answer H2, the ten most similar cases returned from the retrieval are considered. For the investigation of H2a, correctness and completeness are used as ranking measures for the lists of retrieval results [26]. Correctness provides information about the same order of the results, whereas completeness indicates whether both lists contain the same elements. The average correctness is 0.055 and the median 0.0, which is in the middle of the value range $[1.0, -1.0]$. These values indicate that the correctness is unfavorable, as this value implies an almost random distribution of the ranked cases. The completeness is 0.094 on average and 0.0 in the median, with the latter representing the minimum value. This suggests that H2a can be rejected for the use case of EaAD.

To consider H2b, the queries are classified in the adaptation step. This is again based on the ten most similar cases returned from the retrieval phase and carried out using majority voting. For the DTW-based CBR approach, 80 of the 100 queries are classified correctly and 20 incorrectly, whereby for the

Table 2. Performance Measures Calculated Based on the Classifications of the Embedding-Based and DTW-Based CBR Approaches.

	Accuracy	Precision	Recall	F1-Score	Specificity	False Positive Rate	False Negative Rate
DTW-based Approach	0.92	0.8	0.8	0.8	0.95	0.05	0.2
Embedding-based Approach	0.848	0.62	0.62	0.62	0.905	0.095	0.38
Δ between Approaches	0.072	0.18	0.18	0.18	0.045	0.045	0.18

embedding-based approach, 62 queries correctly and 20 incorrectly. Therefore, 18 classifications differ between the approaches. The performance measures for the methods are calculated based on a confusion matrix, which is illustrated in Table 2. Precision, recall, the F1 score and the false negative rate are relatively far apart with a $\Delta = 0.18$, whereas the accuracy, specificity and false negative rate are close to each other. H2b can therefore also tend to be rejected, whereby the entire hypothesis H2 must be rejected.

The results presented for H2 indicate that the embedding-based approach performs qualitatively worse than the DTW-based. However, H1 implies that the embedding approach is significantly faster, so that a trade-off between these two parameters can be assumed. The measures of completeness and correctness considered in H2a provide only limited information about quality in this context. As a reason for this, it was found in a detailed inspection that for some queries there are several cases whose similarity values are very close to each other (in some cases the most similar cases differ by $\Delta < 0.01$). This means that when only the ten most similar cases are considered, these small differences have a large impact on these metrics, resulting in poor values for correctness and completeness. The analysis of H2b shows that the difference in performance is not that much substantial, but still considerable.

7 Conclusion and Future Work

This paper investigates the integration of time series embeddings as a similarity measure in CBR. After a systematic literature analysis of existing embedding methods, requirements for the use of such methods in CBR are identified. This analysis indicates that none of the existing approaches meets the defined requirements. A new embedding method for time series is then designed considering the requirements. For the evaluation, this approach is implemented as a proof-of-concept in the CBR framework ProCAKE. The evaluation shows that the runtime of the retrieval using embedding could be significantly reduced, but partly at the expense of the quality of results.

Based on the results of this work, a further optimization of the embedding approach can be investigated, e.g., by research on hyperparameter optimization [24]. Furthermore, for the EaAD use case, it can be examined whether better performance can be achieved by autoencoders, which learn independently of DTW and possibly outperform it as the previously established CBR approach. Semantic knowledge can also be incorporated into similarity calculations to ensure that the analysis goes beyond mere syntactic information. In addition to this investigated use case, embeddings can also be used for other computationally intensive domains in CBR such as DQIs or PredM. In the DQI context, it can also be investigated how embeddings learn a similarity assignment model from manually defined similarities, or how the use of autoencoders can be further researched. Also, the use of NN reduces the understandability of the similarity calculation. In future research, approaches to explain the similarity calculation can be investigated, as already exists for other data structures (e.g., [51]). In addition, embedding in CBR can also be investigated for MAC/FAC approaches [16] as a pre-filtering method in the MAC phase.

Acknowledgments. This work is funded by the Federal Ministry for Economic Affairs and Climate Action under grant No. 01MD22002C *EASY* [50].

References

1. Aamodt, A., Plaza, E.: Case-based reasoning: foundational issues, methodological variations, and system approaches. AI Commun. **7**(1), 39–59 (1994). https://doi.org/10.3233/AIC-1994-7104
2. Allen, J.F.: Maintaining knowledge about temporal intervals. Commun. ACM **26**(11), 832–843 (1983). https://doi.org/10.1145/182.358434
3. de Barros, C.D.T., Mendonça, M.R.F., Vieira, A.B., Ziviani, A.: A survey on embedding dynamic graphs. ACM Comput. Surv. **55**(2), 10:1–10:37 (2023). https://doi.org/10.1145/3483595
4. Baştanlar, Y., Özuysal, M.: Introduction to machine learning, pp. 105–128. Humana Press, Totowa, NJ (2014). https://doi.org/10.1007/978-1-62703-748-8_7
5. Belkin, M., Niyogi, P.: Laplacian eigenmaps and spectral techniques for embedding and clustering. In: NIPS 2001 Proceedings, pp. 585–591. MIT Press (2001). https://doi.org/10.5555/2980539.2980616
6. Bengio, Y., Courville, A.C., Vincent, P.: Representation learning: a review and new perspectives. IEEE Trans. Pattern Anal. Mach. Intell. **35**(8), 1798–1828 (2013). https://doi.org/10.1109/TPAMI.2013.50
7. Bepler, T., Berger, B.: Learning protein sequence embeddings using information from structure. In: 7th ICLR Proceedings. OpenReview.net (2019). https://doi.org/10.48550/arXiv.1902.08661
8. Bergmann, R., et al.: ProCAKE Framework (7.1.0) (2025). https://doi.org/10.5281/zenodo.15222500
9. Bergmann, R.: Experience Management: Foundations, Development Methodology, and Internet-Based Applications. LNCS, vol. 2432. Springer (2003). https://doi.org/10.1007/3-540-45759-3

10. Bergmann, R., Grumbach, L., Malburg, L., Zeyen, C.: ProCAKE: a process-oriented case-based reasoning framework. In: 27th ICCBR Workshop Proceedings, vol. 2567, pp. 156–161. CEUR-WS.org (2019)
11. Bertrand, Y., Schultheis, A., Malburg, L., Grüger, J., Serral Asensio, E., Bergmann, R.: Challenges in data quality management for IoT-enhanced event logs. In: 19th RCIS Proceedings. LNBIP, pp. 20–36. Springer (2025). https://doi.org/10.1007/978-3-031-92474-3_2
12. Bishop, C.M.: Pattern Recognition and Machine Learning, 5th edn. Information Science and Statistics, vol. 4. Springer (2007)
13. Cai, H., Zheng, V.W., Chang, K.C.: A comprehensive survey of graph embedding: problems, techniques, and applications. IEEE Trans. Knowl. Data Eng. **30**(9), 1616–1637 (2018). https://doi.org/10.1109/TKDE.2018.2807452
14. Cellucci, C.J., Albano, A.M., Rapp, P.E.: Comparative study of embedding methods. Phys. Rev. E **67**, 066210 (2003). https://doi.org/10.1103/PhysRevE.67.066210
15. Choi, K., Yi, J., Park, C., Yoon, S.: Deep learning for anomaly detection in time-series data: review, analysis, and guidelines. IEEE Access **9**, 120043–120065 (2021). https://doi.org/10.1109/ACCESS.2021.3107975
16. Forbus, K.D., Gentner, D., Law, K.: MAC/FAC: a model of similarity-based retrieval. Cogn. Sci. **19**(2), 141–205 (1995). https://doi.org/10.1207/s15516709cog1902_1
17. Gamboa, J.C.B.: Deep learning for time-series analysis. CoRR abs/1701.01887 (2017). https://doi.org/10.48550/arXiv.1701.01887
18. Gilchrist, A.: Industry 4.0: the industrial internet of things. Apress (2016). https://doi.org/10.1007/978-1-4842-2047-4
19. Goyal, P., Ferrara, E.: Graph embedding techniques, applications, and performance: a survey. Knowl. Based Syst. **151**, 78–94 (2018). https://doi.org/10.1016/J.KNOSYS.2018.03.022
20. Graepel, T., Herbrich, R., Bollmann-Sdorra, P., Obermayer, K.: Classification on pairwise proximity data. In: NIPS 1998 Proceedings, pp. 438–444. The MIT Press (1998). https://doi.org/10.5555/3009055.3009117
21. Gugulothu, N., TV, V., Malhotra, P., Vig, L., Agarwal, P., Shroff, G.: Predicting remaining useful life using time series embeddings based on recurrent neural networks. IJPHM **9**(1) (2018). https://doi.org/10.48550/arXiv.1709.01073
22. Guo, R., et al.: Comparative visual analytics for assessing medical records with sequence embedding. Vis. Inf. **4**(2), 72–85 (2020). https://doi.org/10.1016/J.VISINF.2020.04.001
23. Hayashi, A., Mizuhara, Y., Suematsu, N.: Embedding time series data for classification. In: 4th MLDM Proceeding, LNCS, vol. 3587, pp. 356–365. Springer (2005). https://doi.org/10.1007/11510888_35
24. Hoffmann, M., Bergmann, R.: Improving automated hyperparameter optimization with case-based reasoning. In: 30th ICCBR Proceedings, LNCS, vol. 13405, pp. 273–288. Springer (2022). https://doi.org/10.1007/978-3-031-14923-8_18
25. Hoffmann, M., Bergmann, R.: Using graph embedding techniques in process-oriented case-based reasoning. Algorithms **15**(2), 27 (2022). https://doi.org/10.3390/A15020027
26. Hoffmann, M., Malburg, L., Klein, P., Bergmann, R.: Using siamese graph neural networks for similarity-based retrieval in process-oriented case-based reasoning. In: 28th ICCBR Proceedings. LNCS, vol. 12311, pp. 229–244. Springer (2020). https://doi.org/10.1007/978-3-030-58342-2_15

27. Höppner, F.: Time series abstraction methods - a survey. In: INFORMATIK 2002 Proceedings. LNI, vol. P-19, pp. 777–786. GI (2002)
28. Ibtehaz, N., Kihara, D.: Application of sequence embedding in protein sequence-based predictions, pp. 31–55. World Scientific (2023). https://doi.org/10.1142/9789811258589_0002
29. Jære, M.D., Aamodt, A., Skalle, P.: Representing temporal knowledge for case-based prediction. In: 6th ECCBR Proceedings. LNCS, vol. 2416, pp. 174–188. Springer (2002). https://doi.org/10.1007/3-540-46119-1_14
30. Ji, Z., Wang, Y., Yan, K., Xie, X., Xiang, Y., Huang, J.: A space-embedding strategy for anomaly detection in multivariate time series. Exp. Syst. Appl. **206**, 117892 (2022). https://doi.org/10.1016/J.ESWA.2022.117892
31. Karingula, S.R., et al.: Boosted embeddings for time-series forecasting. In: 7th LOD Proceedings. LNCS, vol. 13164, pp. 1–14. Springer (2021). https://doi.org/10.1007/978-3-030-95470-3_1
32. Karkouch, A., Mousannif, H., Al Moatassime, H., Noel, T.: Data quality in Internet of Things: a state-of-the-art survey. JNCA **73**, 57–81 (2016). https://doi.org/10.1016/j.jnca.2016.08.002
33. Kim, H.J., Hong, S., Cha, K.J.: seq2vec: analyzing sequential data using multi-rank embedding vectors. Electron. Commer. Res. Appl. **43**, 101003 (2020). https://doi.org/10.1016/J.ELERAP.2020.101003
34. Klein, P., Malburg, L., Bergmann, R.: Learning workflow embeddings to improve the performance of similarity-based retrieval for process-oriented case-based reasoning. In: 27th ICCBR Proceeding. LNCS, vol. 11680, pp. 188–203. Springer (2019). https://doi.org/10.1007/978-3-030-29249-2_13
35. Kljun, M., Tersek, M.: A review and comparison of time series similarity measures. In: 29th ERK Proceedings, pp. 21–22 (2020)
36. Li, Z., et al.: Multivariate time series anomaly detection and interpretation using hierarchical inter-metric and temporal embedding. In: 27th SIGKDD Proceedings, pp. 3220–3230. ACM (2021). https://doi.org/10.1145/3447548.3467075
37. Lim, B., Zohren, S.: Time series forecasting with deep learning: a survey. Philos. Trans. R. Soc. A **379**(2194), 20200209 (2021). https://doi.org/10.1098/rsta.2020.0209
38. López, B.: Case-Based Reasoning: A Concise Introduction. SLAIML, Springer (2013). https://doi.org/10.1007/978-3-031-01562-5
39. Malburg, L., Schultheis, A., Bergmann, R.: Modeling and using complex IoT time series data in case-based reasoning: from application scenarios to implementations. In: 31st ICCBR Workshop Proceedings, vol. 3438, pp. 81–96 (2023)
40. Malburg, L., Seiger, R., Bergmann, R., Weber, B.: Using physical factory simulation models for business process management research. In: BPM 2020 Workshop Proceedings. LNBIP, vol. 397, pp. 95–107. Springer (2020). https://doi.org/10.1007/978-3-030-66498-5_8
41. Mehran, S., et al.: Time2Vec: learning a vector representation of time. CoRR abs/1907.05321 (2019). https://doi.org/10.48550/arXiv.1907.05321
42. Michalski, R.S., Carbonell, J.G., Mitchell, T.M.: Machine Learning - An Artificial Intelligence Approach. Symbolic Computation. Springer (1983). https://doi.org/10.1007/978-3-662-12405-5
43. Nalmpantis, C., Vrakas, D.: Signal2vec: time series embedding representation. In: 20th EANN Proceedings. CCIS, vol. 1000, pp. 80–90. Springer (2019). https://doi.org/10.1007/978-3-030-20257-6_7

44. Narayanan, A., Chandramohan, M., Venkatesan, R., Chen, L., Liu, Y., Jaiswal, S.: graph2vec: learning distributed representations of graphs. CoRR abs/1707.05005 (2017). https://doi.org/10.48550/arXiv.1707.05005
45. Ridley, D.: The Literature Review: A Step-by-Step Guide for Students. SAGE (2012)
46. Rosato, A., Altilio, R., Araneo, R., Panella, M.: Embedding of time series for the prediction in photovoltaic power plants. In: 16th EEEIC Proceedings, pp. 1–4 (2016). https://doi.org/10.1109/EEEIC.2016.7555872
47. Sakoe, H., Chiba, S.: Dynamic programming algorithm optimization for spoken word recognition. IEEE Trans. Aco. Sp. and Sig. Proc. **26**(1), 43–49 (1978). https://doi.org/10.1109/TASSP.1978.1163055
48. Schake, E., Grumbach, L., Bergmann, R.: A time-series similarity measure for case-based deviation management to support flexible workflow execution. In: 28th ICCBR Proceedings, LNCS, vol. 12311, pp. 33–48. Springer (2020). https://doi.org/10.1007/978-3-030-58342-2_3
49. Schultheis, A.: Exploring a hybrid case-based reasoning approach for time series adaptation in predictive maintenance. In: 32nd ICCBR Workshop Proceedings, vol. 3708, pp. 230–235. CEUR-WS.org (2024)
50. Schultheis, A., et al.: EASY: energy-efficient analysis and control processes in the dynamic edge-cloud continuum for industrial manufacturing. Künstl. Intell. (2024). https://doi.org/10.1007/s13218-024-00868-3
51. Schultheis, A., Hoffmann, M., Malburg, L., Bergmann, R.: Explanation of similarities in process-oriented case-based reasoning by visualization. In: 31st ICCBR Proceedings. LNCS, vol. 14141, pp. 53–68. Springer (2023). https://doi.org/10.1007/978-3-031-40177-0_4
52. Schultheis, A., et al.: Identifying missing sensor values in IoT time series data: a weight-based extension of similarity measures for smart manufacturing. In: 32nd ICCBR Proceedings. LNCS, vol. 14775, pp. 240–257. Springer (2024). https://doi.org/10.1007/978-3-031-63646-2_16
53. Schultheis, A., Zeyen, C., Bergmann, R.: An overview and comparison of case-based reasoning frameworks. In: 31st ICCBR Proceedings. LNCS, vol. 14141, pp. 327–343. Springer (2023). https://doi.org/10.1007/978-3-031-40177-0_21
54. Seiger, R., Schultheis, A., Bergmann, R.: Case-based activity detection from segmented Internet of Things data. In: Bichindaritz, I., López, B. (eds.) ICCBR 2025. LNAI, vol. 15662, pp. 329–344 (2025). https://doi.org/10.1007/978-3-031-96559-3_22
55. Sezer, O.B., Gudelek, M.U., Özbayoglu, A.M.: Financial time series forecasting with deep learning: a systematic literature review: 2005–2019. Appl. Soft Comput. **90**, 106181 (2020). https://doi.org/10.1016/J.ASOC.2020.106181
56. Shahar, Y.: A framework for knowledge-based temporal abstraction. Artif. Intell. **90**(1–2), 79–133 (1997). https://doi.org/10.1016/S0004-3702(96)00025-2
57. Smith, T.F., Waterman, M.S.: Identification of common molecular subsequences. JMB **147**(1), 195–197 (1981)
58. Sørmo, F., Cassens, J., Aamodt, A.: Explanation in case-based reasoning - perspectives and goals. Artif. Intell. Rev. **24**(2), 109–143 (2005). https://doi.org/10.1007/s10462-005-4607-7
59. TensorFlow Developers: TensorFlow (2024). https://doi.org/10.5281/zenodo.12726004
60. Torgerson, W.S.: Theory and Methods of Scaling. Wiley, New York (1958). Section: 460 p

61. Tran, C., Khadkikar, S., Porollo, A.: Survey of protein sequence embedding models. Int. J. Mol. Sci. **24**(4) (2023). https://doi.org/10.3390/ijms24043775
62. Uribarri, G., Mindlin, G.B.: Dynamical time series embeddings in recurrent neural networks. Chaos Solit. Fractals **154**, 111612 (2022). https://doi.org/10.1016/j.chaos.2021.111612
63. Wang, H., et al.: Knowledge-aware graph neural networks with label smoothness regularization for recommender systems. In: 25th SIGKDD Proceedings, pp. 968–977. ACM (2019). https://doi.org/10.1145/3292500.3330836
64. Wang, Q., Mao, Z., Wang, B., Guo, L.: Knowledge graph embedding: a survey of approaches and applications. IEEE Trans. Knowl. Data Eng. **29**(12), 2724–2743 (2017). https://doi.org/10.1109/TKDE.2017.2754499
65. Wang, S., Zhou, W., Jiang, C.: A survey of word embeddings based on deep learning. Computing **102**(3), 717–740 (2020). https://doi.org/10.1007/S00607-019-00768-7
66. Watson, I.D., Marir, F.: Case-based reasoning: a review. Knowl. Eng. Rev. **9**(4), 327–354 (1994). https://doi.org/10.1017/S0269888900007098
67. Wu, L.Y., Fisch, A., Chopra, S., Adams, K., Bordes, A., Weston, J.: StarSpace: embed all the things! In: 32nd AAAI Proceedings, pp. 5569–5577. AAAI Press (2018). https://doi.org/10.1609/AAAI.V32I1.11996
68. Wu, L., Yen, I.E., Yi, J., Xu, F., Lei, Q., Witbrock, M.: Random warping series: a random features method for time-series embedding. In: AISTATS 2018 Proceedings, vol. 84, pp. 793–802. PMLR (2018)
69. Xu, M.: Understanding graph embedding methods and their applications. SIAM Rev. **63**(4), 825–853 (2021). https://doi.org/10.1137/20M1386062
70. Zhao, W.X., et al.: A survey of large language models. CoRR abs/2303.18223 (2023). https://doi.org/10.48550/ARXIV.2303.18223
71. Zheng, W., Yang, L., Genco, R.J., Wactawski-Wende, J., Buck, M., Sun, Y.: SENSE: siamese neural network for sequence embedding and alignment-free comparison. Bioinform. **35**(11), 1820–1828 (2019). https://doi.org/10.1093/BIOINFORMATICS/BTY887
72. Zonta, T., Da Costa, C.A., da Rosa Righi, R., de Lima, M.J., da Trindade, E.S., Li, G.P.: Predictive maintenance in the Industry 4.0: a systematic literature review. Comput. Ind. Eng. **150**, 106889 (2020). https://doi.org/10.1016/j.cie.2020.106889

Extracting Features with Deep Learning for Ensemble-Driven Case-Based Classification

Zachary Wilkerson[1(✉)], David Leake[1], David Crandall[1], and Benjamin Wilkerson[2]

[1] Luddy School of Informatics, Computing, and Engineering, Indiana University, Bloomington 47408, IN, USA
zachwilk@iu.edu

[2] DePauw University, Greencastle 46135, IN, USA

Abstract. Manual knowledge acquisition of case retrieval features is expensive and may be infeasible for cases containing hard-to-characterize data such as images. Deep learning (DL) methods excel at extracting useful feature information from raw data, making them appealing for learning feature information. Previous work has demonstrated the promise of integrated systems for case-based image classification, using a deep neural network to generate features which are then used for case retrieval, resulting in classifications that can be explained in terms of prior cases. However, the accuracy of the combined system may lag behind that of the original DL model. In response, our previous work proposed Multi-Net, a method using ensembles for localized feature extraction. Multi-Net improved performance, but experiments showed limitations of its design. This paper presents Deep Ensemble Feature Extraction for Retrieval (DEFER), a feature-extraction-based classification approach aimed at addressing those issues. To increase accuracy, DEFER adds a discriminator to focus retrieval within each replica and weighted voting based on confidence in its class prediction, grounded in nearest-neighbor retrieval. In experiments for image classification, DEFER outperforms analogous DL-only and DL-case-based systems, supporting that its approach can improve performance.

Keywords: Case-Based Reasoning · Deep Learning · Ensembles · Feature Learning · Indexing · Integrated Systems · Random Forests · Retrieval

1 Introduction

Case-based classification depends on effective case retrieval, which in turn typically depends on the feature representation of cases in the case base. Traditionally, such features are drawn from a vocabulary defined by knowledge engineering (e.g., [14,20,31]). However, such an approach is costly and may not

© The Author(s), under exclusive license to Springer Nature Switzerland AG 2025
I. Bichindaritz and B. López (Eds.): ICCBR 2025, LNAI 15662, pp. 345–359, 2025.
https://doi.org/10.1007/978-3-031-96559-3_23

produce comprehensive feature vocabularies for poorly understood domains or for tasks for which effective features are hard to characterize, such as image classification. This motivates efforts to apply machine learning to deriving case features and assessing case similarity (e.g., [30,33,35]). Alternatively, in twin systems, case retrieval features are extracted from a network to explain network outputs with cases [19]. Our previous work treats case-based classification as the primary classification mechanism, providing interpretability, while leveraging features extracted from deep learning (DL) neural networks to improve case retrieval [21,22,34,35]. This integrated model has been shown to outperform an analogous DL-only model in previous studies for image classification (e.g., [35]).

Our initial integrated methods were based on training a network and then extracting features from a network layer. While this approach provided good performance, it had two primary limitations. First, extracting large numbers of features commonly generated by deep neural network models may result in similarity judgments suffering from the "curse of dimensionality" [21]. Second, we hypothesized that performance of the case-based classifier might be limited by a mismatch between the needs for DL features—which drove network training—and the needs of case-based reasoning (CBR) features. Intuitively, neural models rely on identifying features suited to distinguishing different classes (i.e., strong inter-class discrimination); by contrast, CBR models require features suited to recognizing similarity between examples that belong to the same class (i.e., strong intra-class relationship identification). To the extent that this holds, features extracted from neural models trained for classification might not be optimal for use in case retrieval.

To address the two limitations, we proposed the "Multi-Net" architecture for localized feature extraction. Multi-Net breaks up the overall classification task into smaller class-wise tasks [21]. In Multi-Net, multiple replica neural models are trained to distinguish examples belonging to one class from all other classes. Ideally, this requires less training data, enables lower-dimensionality network construction for feature extraction, and exploits localized representations for greater classification accuracy. These benefits appeared to hold for initial work. However, preliminary tests with more complex, pretrained DL models showed that Multi-Net underperformed relative to our other DL-CBR approaches and that replica training in Multi-Net resulted in independent feature spaces with non-corresponding features. This made nearest-neighbor case retrieval, which attempted to leverage these features collectively, ineffective.

This led us to develop a new model, presented in this paper, that replaces the Multi-Net approach with an ensemble-based method inspired by random forest approaches. In this approach, the goal for the replica models is to learn projections of the overall feature space that inform per-replica nearest-neighbor case retrieval; each result then contributes to a majority vote for the overall classification. The model also dynamically selects subsets of the case base to consider and uses measurements of the confidence of retrieved nearest neighbor cases to further guide case-based classification. As this process defers CBR until after dispatching to the replicas, we call the approach Deep Ensemble Feature Extraction for Retrieval (DEFER). This paper presents a case study evaluation of DEFER. In this study, testing on the Animals with Attributes 2 (AwA2) dataset [36], it consistently outperforms the top model from our previous work [35] and shows stronger classification accuracy than the analogous DL-only model, with Student's T-test statistics supporting the significance of this improvement.

2 Related Work

2.1 DL-CBR Integrations

CBR and DL approaches present complementary strengths that make their integration appealing. When integrations base their reasoning fundamentally on CBR but leverage DL, such combinations can provide more explainable alternatives to DL-only models and increased ability to integrate expert knowledge into various knowledge containers [29]; ideally the use of DL to support CBR may enable high accuracy and minimal knowledge engineering in big data domains. Some integration approaches aim to model a CBR process within a network, as in "inherently interpretable networks" [5,10,24] that make predictions based on similarity scores between intermediate features within the network and sets of prototype features that align well with certain classes (e.g., a beak for classifying an image of a bird), and in the NN-kNN model [38]. Case-based approaches may also be applied post-hoc to provide explanations for DL models; this has been studied for feature-level explanations [3] and applying DL and CBR models in parallel "twin systems" to explain DL predictions [19]. Conversely, network models have been used within CBR for tasks such as similarity assessment (e.g., [26]) and case adaptation (e.g., [23]).

2.2 Feature Extraction for Case Retrieval

Traditionally, retrieval features are created via knowledge engineering [14,20,31], with symbolic learning methods sometimes applied to develop or refine feature vocabularies for domains where knowledge engineering is unfeasible [4,6,7,11, 15]. However, such approaches apply only to domains where symbolic knowledge is available; for others, such as image classification, it is necessary to extract features from raw data in order to develop the feature vocabulary. In response, multiple projects have explored extracting retrieval features from DL models (e.g., [2,30,33]). Features extracted from DL models in this way have been used for CBR-based implicit classification of novel-class test examples and examples for which the DL model lacks confidence in its own classification [32,33]. At least for some domain examples, CBR classification using extracted features has outperformed DL-only predictions [30,35].

Our previous work studied feature extraction from DL networks, especially for small-data domains, to which CBR systems are frequently applied, studying the influence of the layer chosen for extraction and the number of features extracted on DL model convergence and CBR classifier performance [21]. It also considered the impact of different model-level parameterizations, such as the choice of DL architecture and the use of pretraining, highlighting their importance with respect to extracted feature quality [21,22,35], as well as how engineered features may be used in concert with extracted features to increase model accuracy [22,34]. This paper refines and extends the Multi-Net approach [21], described in detail in Sect. 3.1.

2.3 Random Forests and Ensemble-Based CBR Approaches

An issue for our initial Multi-Net model was that each network developed an independent feature space, so that when comparing distances to candidate neighbor cases during KNN, the localized feature spaces had different numeric scales. We hypothesized that the lack of correspondence between replica feature spaces decreased the usefulness of combined distance information, which motivates our shift from the locality-driven Multi-Net model to the ensemble-driven case retrieval of DEFER. The DEFER model draws significantly from random forest principles [8], in that the replica models can be conceptualized as learning projections of an overall feature space, analogous to the randomized projections leveraged in a random forest. Similar principles have previously been applied to cases by "Random KNN" approaches, which use the random forest conceptualization for feature reduction in the KNN feature space [25].

Ensemble-based retrieval also relates to the work of Plaza and others on distributed and multi-agent CBR [27,28]. In that work, the CBR algorithm draws from the decisions of multiple agents, which each may consider subsets of the CBR cycle and/or exploit cases from multiple non-corresponding case bases. Similarly, other combinations of CBR and ensemble techniques are present in work by Hsieh et al., where CBR is leveraged to mediate disagreements within the ensemble [17]. Again, a key interpretation of DEFER's feature extraction process is that it learns different projections of the feature space that are well-suited to identifying subsets of classes. This aligns with the work of Cunningham and Zenobi, who focus on diversity of features developed for CBR ensembles to promote specialization in "sub-domains" within the feature space [12].

3 Feature Extraction for CBR Retrieval using Multiple Networks

3.1 A Multi-network Approach

We developed the Multi-Net approach to address two issues: 1) that DL models require a significant number of parameters to model multi-class functions, and this high dimensionality is passed on to the extracted feature vectors, risking the curse of dimensionality for CBR systems that use them, and 2) that neural models ideally learn generalizable features that help them discriminate between all classes in their search space, but we hypothesized that this high degree of inter-class learning may come at the expense of intra-class learning, desirable for

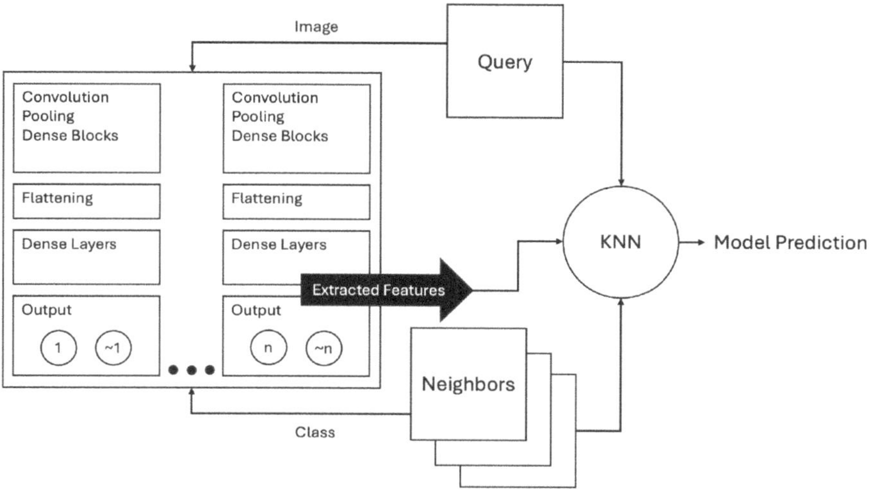

Fig. 1. Data flow in the original Multi-Net methodology [21]. Each query image is processed into localized features by each replica; this set of features is indexed during KNN based on the candidate neighbor's class for similarity calculation.

CBR. This motivated an architecture splitting the original problem into several smaller problems involving fewer classes, using specialized neural model replicas to address these smaller problems [21].

Rather than training one neural model that can distinguish between n classes, Multi-Net trains n neural models that each distinguish between a single positively-labeled class and all others in the dataset, which are relabeled as negative classes (Fig. 1). In this way, replicas are specialized to the positive examples in their training set, at the additional overhead of training n neural models rather than one. Thus, n different feature vectors may be extracted for a single test example, one for each replica. During KNN retrieval, each candidate neighbor's ground truth class indexes the space of query feature vectors, ideally creating a localized feature representation during similarity assessment that calculates distances to a candidate case as if the query belongs to the same class.

Strengths and Limitations: Multi-Net requires fewer features per replica to accurately characterize the dataset, but at the cost of additional space and training time proportional to the number of replicas used. In addition, relabeling the positive and negative training examples for each replica creates a class imbalance with many more negative classes, limiting accuracy. We address this in DEFER by allowing replicas to be sensitized to subsets of positive classes rather than only one, increasing the ratio of positive to negative examples for each replica while still retaining benefits of using multiple neural models.

An important additional concern for Multi-Net is that the replica models each learn independently from one another, so there is no correspondence between their feature spaces. Consequently, individual feature values can be significantly larger or smaller for one given replica than for all others, making it impossible to reliably compare distances to nearest neighbors across all replicas—a candidate neighbor handled by a replica that learns a small-scale feature space might erroneously be labeled as the nearest neighbor simply because of its replica's smaller scale. Normalizing the feature spaces for the neural models does not solve this issue, as there is no correspondence between individual features between different replicas. This lack of correspondence was not evident in earlier results [21], but we hypothesized it as the cause when preliminary experimental results for the work in this paper showed that feature extraction from more complex pre-trained neural models had a low performance ceiling compared to the analogous integrated system that we use as a baseline DL-CBR model [35]. We developed the DEFER approach, summarized in Fig. 2 and Algorithm 1, to address these shortcomings.

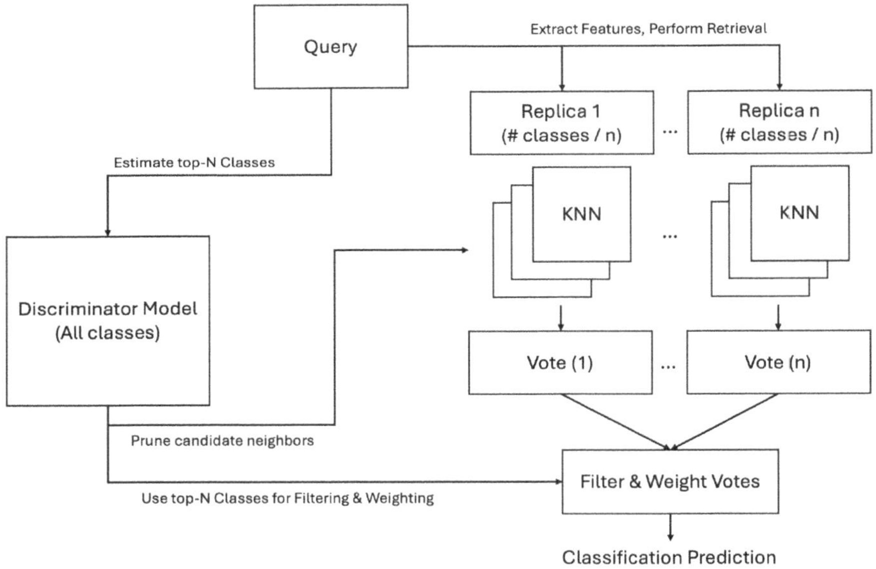

Fig. 2. Data flow in the DEFER model. Each query image is passed into each replica to generate localized feature vectors and a discriminator model trained on all classes. Each replica may only retrieve nearest neighbors belonging to the top-n discriminator predictions. Replica votes are weighted according to the ratio of distances to the two nearest different-class neighbors.

3.2 Leveraging the Spirit of Random Forests

In the DEFER approach, rather than treating the replicas as means for generating localized features for use in a global similarity assessment, the replicas

```
1: cpr ← number of classes per replica
2: cb ← input case base
3: D ← discriminator model
4: for r in 0 to number of replicas −1 do
5:     for (example, label) in training data do
6:         if floor(label / cpr) == r then
7:             label ← label mod cpr
8:         end if
9:     end for
10:    replica[r] trained with modified (examples, labels)
11: end for
12: D trained with original (examples, labels)
13: for (example, label) in training data do
14:    f ← features extracted from replica[label % cpr]
15:    add case(f, label) to cb
16: end for
17: for query, label in testing data do
18:    votes ← []
19:    C ← top n predicted classes from D(query)
20:    for r in 0 to number of replicas −1 do
21:        f ← features extracted from replica[r]
22:        q ← case(f, _)
23:        nn_1 ← nearest retrieved neighbor case, where nn_1 ∈ C
24:        nn_2 ← nearest retrieved neighbor case, where label_{nn_1} ≠ label_{nn_2}, nn_2 ∈ C
25:        if ∃c ∈ C where floor(c / cpr) = r then
26:            append nn_1 to votes with weight (distance to nn_2)/(distance to nn_1)
27:        end if
28:    end for
29:    prediction ← majority vote among votes
30: end for
```

Algorithm 1: DEFER algorithm for data relabeling and replica training (lines 4-11), discriminator-guided KNN for each replica (lines 19-28), and ratio-weighting (lines 23-26), all supporting majority-vote classification.

are treated as members of a random forest-like ensemble of elements performing case-based classification using their own feature spaces. The independent feature spaces learned by the individual replicas can be thought of as subsets of a single global feature space, similar to the randomly selected subsets represented in a random forest. Each replica then performs KNN and contributes a vote to the ultimate model decision (Algorithm 1, lines 17–30).

Strengths and Limitations: Performing replica-wise KNN calculations that result in individual votes addresses the issue of the replicas learning independent feature spaces with different scales, and it enables explaining classifications from the perspective of each of the different feature spaces. However, we empirically observed in preliminary experiments that the majority-vote system can suffer from significant replica-based noise in practice. That is, for a given query, only one replica is sensitized to the corresponding class; for all others, the class was relabeled as negative during training, and so there is no incentive for the replica to distinguish between it and any other negative class. In theory, this means that the one replica might provide useful information with its vote, but the other replicas could create a "tyranny of the majority" with contradicting, low-confidence votes. This phenomenon requires additional refinements to achieve accurate classification performance, which are described below.

3.3 Focusing on the Top-n Cases with Discriminator Pruning

In addition to the random forest conceptualization for handling the different replicas, we implement a "discriminator model" to reduce disagreement among replicas by pruning the search space of candidate neighbors and funneling replica votes into a smaller field of classes. Intuitively, for a given query case, much of the case base is not relevant, so applying the discriminator enables DEFER replicas to focus on subsets of the case base that are likely more relevant to classifying a given query. This discriminator is a regular DL model with the same basic architecture as the replicas, except that it is trained to predict any of the classes in the dataset. Critically, instead of taking a single query classification from the discriminator, DEFER takes the top n classifications. These inform pruning during the per-replica KNN procedures at two levels (Fig. 2 and Algorithm 1, lines 13, 19–27):

1. Replicas only consider stored cases if their class is one of the top n classes provided. This streamlines the KNN calculations for each replica and ideally results in more agreement among the replicas, which have a less-diverse field of potential classes to choose from when voting.
2. When tallying votes, only votes from replicas that are sensitized to a subset of these top n classes are considered. This helps mitigate noise that results from low-confidence votes from other replicas.

Strengths and Limitations: Use of the discriminator incurs additional training overhead but significantly speeds up the model evaluation process because of pruning. Ideally, it also improves model accuracy over the similarly-structured baseline DL-CBR model by enabling the consideration of the top n predictions as opposed to one, enabling more subtle conclusions as secondary choices contribute. However, if the ground truth class is not in the discriminator's top n predictions, then the overall model cannot make a correct prediction, creating a hard accuracy ceiling for DEFER.

3.4 Favoring High-Confidence Cases with Ratio-Weighted Voting

Preliminary experiments with different values for n for taking the top n discriminator predictions suggested that $n = 2$ was most effective. However, during replica voting, sometimes either one replica is sensitive to both classes, or two are sensitive to one each. The latter scenario could lead to a tie that must be broken if the two replicas disagree.

To address this, we weight each contributing replica's vote based on an estimate for how confident the replica is that the query belongs to the neighbor's class, calculated using a ratio of the distances to the nearest neighbors of the two most relevant classes to the query (Fig. 2 and Algorithm 1, lines 23–26). A large ratio signifies higher confidence, as the nearest neighbor is significantly closer to the query than any case of another class; conversely, a ratio approaching 1 implies low confidence, since there is more significant overlap between the class clusters in the feature space.

Strengths and Limitations: This approach provides a confidence score for a replica's decision, usable to break ties for low values of n, and it also offers a degree of explanatory power by providing some insight into the clustering of cases belonging to a single class (or lack thereof) in the feature space of a given replica. In preliminary tests, replicas not sensitive to any of the top n discriminator predictions frequently had ratios close to 1; this motivated our design decision to remove their votes. In principle, the reliance on the two closest cases might make classification more sensitive to noise if noisy cases are present, but we expect increased accuracy otherwise.

4 Evaluation Design

4.1 Motivation and Hypotheses

While the design of DEFER was informed by a series of preliminary experiments, we evaluate the final model by testing the following hypotheses:

1. **DEFER will outperform an analogous regular DL-CBR architecture.** By leveraging the benefits of ensembles to solve problems, DEFER should outperform both the analogous DL-only model and the analogous baseline DL-CBR integrated model.
2. **Each of the design choices for DEFER contributes to its superior classification performance versus the evaluated baseline models.** These choices include the ability to select multiple replicas (and by extension, the number of classes to which each one is sensitized), the use of the discriminator and ability to set the value of n for the top n classes taken from it, and ratio-weighting for replica votes.

4.2 Testbed System and Evaluation Method

Our tests use the pretrained DenseNet121 [18] neural architecture provided in the Tensorflow Applications module [1] for the DL feature extractor and for the discriminator. The CBR classifier component of the model is retrieval-only and uses 1-nearest-neighbor retrieval with an unweighted and normalized Manhattan Distance as distance measure. We note that a classification adaptation component (e.g., [37]) could be added with no changes to either of the case-based processes, potentially increasing accuracy of each.

We compare DEFER to two baselines: a DL-only model (i.e., in which the model's prediction is used directly, with no feature extraction or case-based component), and the single-network DL-CBR model from Wilkerson et al. [35]. All neural models are the same except for the size of the output layer, which depends on the number of classes used to train the network, and the number of training examples is varied as a control and variable of comparison for each method. Features are extracted as vectors of size 1024 following the densely-connected layers of the neural model in all experiments using case-based classification.

Each neural model and replica is pretrained on the ImageNet dataset [13] as provided in the Tensorflow applications module. Post-convolution layers are appended and trained manually for every model and replica, while all convolution layers are frozen during training. Training and evaluation are carried out using the Animals with Attributes 2 (AwA2) dataset, which contains over 37,000 images depicting animals that are categorized into one of fifty classes [36]. All models or replicas are trained for a maximum of 50 epochs, with training halted if accuracy does not improve for two consecutive training epochs. Trials are run for 512, 1024, 2048, and 4096 training examples. Train and test examples are selected randomly and independently from the larger dataset, with test examples used for validation during training. Furthermore, positively-relabeled training examples are oversampled at a 200% rate to mitigate harmful data imbalance effects. Oversampled data are also selected randomly as part of the training set, but alternative techniques such as SMOTE could also be used [9]. For each Multi-Net replica, the training set is relabeled such that a subset of all classes retains their original labels and all other labels are treated as belonging to another negative class. These subsets of classes are selected in the same arbitrary order from the training directory for consistency among trials, and such that classes are distributed evenly among the replicas. All trials are repeated thirty times to establish reliable mean and standard deviation values.

5 Results and Discussion

5.1 Tests of Hypothesis 1: Comparison to Baseline Models

As shown in Fig. 3, DEFER outperforms our baseline DL-CBR model on average for all numbers of training examples. This result is noteworthy because the latter model was previously found to outperform the analogous DL-only model with similar consistency across all training examples in the same case study [35]. However, the previous outperformance was often subsumed by the standard deviation values for both models, limiting significance; DEFER's performance is more accurate and includes some results are significantly higher than the DL-only model's performance; this strongly supports our first hypothesis.

Comparing DEFER and our 2024 model, the average standard deviation of ensemble-driven case retrieval appears to be generally higher; this is not surprising, given that each replica during training receives an imbalanced dataset, and therefore, fewer "useful" training examples. The mean accuracy of DEFER consistently exceeds the DL-CBR baseline. This difference appears to decrease slightly as the number of training examples increases; however, Student's T-test applied to DEFER versus either of the other two models provides p-scores of $p \leq 0.0035$ across all data points, suggesting a high confidence in the significance of DEFER's performance, compared with the typical $p \leq 0.05$ threshold. Taken together, these results broadly support and expand upon the conclusions

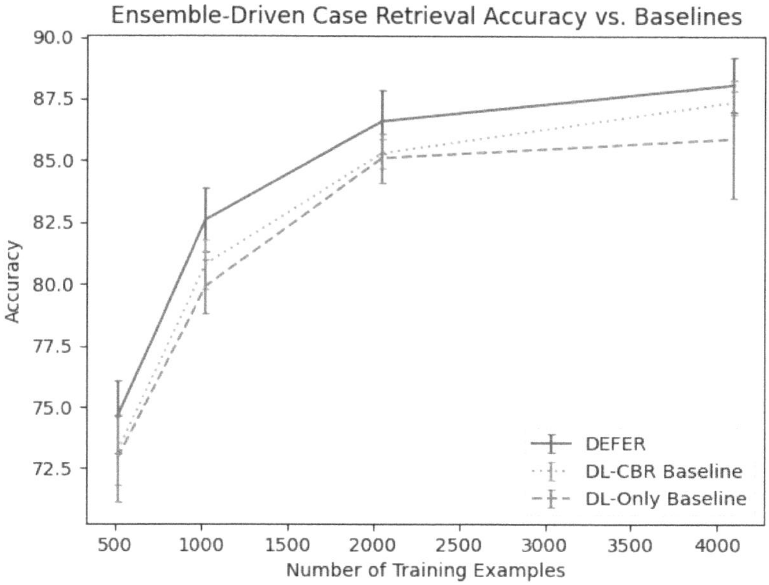

Fig. 3. Accuracy values for ensemble-driven case retrieval for different numbers of training examples. These are compared with our best-performing regular DL-CBR model [35] and the analogous DL-only model. Error bars represent one standard deviation.

from our prior work on ensembles of feature extractor models [21]. Experiments with larger numbers of training examples would be helpful to solidify the trends here, and we hypothesize that the larger number of network replicas in DEFER would benefit more from a larger training set than the DL-CBR baseline.

5.2 Tests of Hypothesis 2: Results from Ablation Studies

We conducted ablation studies to examine the influence of discriminator-based pruning, ratio-weighted replica voting, number of replicas, and value of n in the discriminator's top n predictions on model accuracy (Table 1). Taken together, these results support our second hypothesis, highlighting the benefit of our design decisions on DEFER's classification accuracy.

In these results, using the discriminator model to prune the search space significantly increases model accuracy. Intuitively, a larger n enables higher pruning accuracy for the discriminator, but based on these observations, either 1) the data imbalance created by relabeling the training data is still too significant, even with oversampling the positive examples, or 2) the "thinner" replica models, with fewer parameters, are more significantly impacted by the small-data nature of the experiment itself.

Ratio-weighted voting further increases the model accuracy, likely breaking arbitrarily-settled ties where two replicas (each sensitive to one of the discriminator's top-2 classes) clash over the ultimate prediction.

Table 1. Results for ablation studies, showing accuracy changes for DEFER when discriminator-based pruning and ratio-weighting are used (a), when the number of replicas is modified (b), and when the value of n for the top n discriminator predictions is modified (c). Best-performing models are boldfaced.

Parameters	% Accuracy	St. Dev.
No Discriminator	64.3	1.3
Discriminator Only	77.6	1.7
Ratio-Weighted Voting	**82.6**	**1.3**

(a)

# Replicas	% Accuracy	St. Dev.
2	82.4	1.4
5	82.4	1.2
10	**82.6**	**1.3**

(b)

Top n Classes	% Accuracy	St. Dev.
2	**82.6**	**1.3**
3	77.0	1.3
5	73.4	1.5

(c)

Finally, we consider the effects of different parameterizations for number of replicas and the value of n for the discriminator's top-n predictions used for pruning. The former subtly supports the intuitive trade-off between more replicas enabling replicas to be more specialized, but also leading to greater training data imbalance. The latter suggests that DEFER performs better when replicas have fewer degrees of freedom for voting; perhaps this is due to limited training data, in which case, additional experiments with more training examples may favor different values of n.

6 Conclusions

This paper presents DEFER, a new method that leverages the benefits of ensembles for feature extraction and case retrieval in an integrated DL-CBR classification system. DEFER uses ensembles of DL replicas sensitized to subsets of classes from the overall problem. Ideally, these replicas project a "superset" feature space that is approximated by a larger DL model into smaller subspaces that specialize in distinguishing between a few classes and all others, and reasoning over these localized feature spaces enables the CBR classifier to retrieve more accurately. This approach, combined with using a discriminator model to focus on a set of top-n classes and with weighting replica votes to reflect confidence in the retrieved case, leads to a novel DL-CBR integrated model that outperforms our previous best-performing approach and, interestingly, outperforms the analogous DL-only classifier.

Future work includes evaluation on additional datasets, including non-image data, and examining further variations of the number of training examples and features extracted. The experiments in this paper highlight that multi-network approaches involve many interconnected parameters, providing opportunities for tuning. Additional design variations could include using the top-n positive classes for each replica (rather than the discriminator) for pruning, using various values of k for nearest-neighbor retrieval, extracting weights from the replica models to moderate replica voting, and/or concatenating the feature vectors extracted from each replica into a single vector for case retrieval. We expect that such refinements could further increase classification accuracy, as could the addition of case adaptation for full CBR.

This paper has only considered classification accuracy, but the DEFER approach might benefit interpretability as well. Traditional case-based classification is explained by the nearest case, or cases, according to a single feature vocabulary [16]. With DEFER, explanations can be offered by each replica to provide the user with explanatory cases from multiple feature perspectives. The effects of such richer explanations on user trust and satisfaction in classifications could be another interesting avenue to explore.

Acknowledgments. Work of the first three authors was funded by the US Department of Defense (Contract W52P1J2093009). We thank members of the DL-CBR research group at Indiana University for useful conversations.

References

1. Abadi, M., et al.: TensorFlow: large-scale machine learning on heterogeneous systems (2015). https://www.tensorflow.org/, software available from tensorflow.org
2. Amin, K., Kapetanakis, S., Althoff, K.-D., Dengel, A., Petridis, M.: Answering with cases: a CBR approach to deep learning. In: Cox, M.T., Funk, P., Begum, S. (eds.) ICCBR 2018. LNCS (LNAI), vol. 11156, pp. 15–27. Springer, Cham (2018). https://doi.org/10.1007/978-3-030-01081-2_2
3. Bach, K., Mork, P.: On the explanation of similarity for developing and deploying CBR systems. In: Proceedings of the Thirty-Third International Florida Artificial Intelligence Research Society Conference (FLAIRS 2020) (May 2020)
4. Barletta, R., Mark, W.: Explanation-based indexing of cases. In: Kolodner, J. (ed.) Proceedings of a Workshop on Case-Based Reasoning, pp. 50–60. DARPA, Morgan Kaufmann, Palo Alto (1988)
5. Barnett, A.J., et al.: Interpretable mammographic image classification using case-based reasoning and deep learning. In: Proceedings of IJCAI-21 Workshop on Deep Learning, Case-Based Reasoning, and AutoML (2021). https://arxiv.org/pdf/2107.05605
6. Bhatta, S., Goel, A.: Model-based learning of structural indices to design cases. In: Proceedings of the IJCAI-93 Workshop on Reuse of Design, pp. A1–A13. IJCAI, Chambery, France (1993)
7. Bonzano, A., Cunningham, P., Smyth, B.: Using introspective learning to improve retrieval in CBR: a case study in air traffic control. In: Leake, D.B., Plaza, E. (eds.) ICCBR 1997. LNCS, vol. 1266, pp. 291–302. Springer, Heidelberg (1997). https://doi.org/10.1007/3-540-63233-6_500
8. Breiman, L.: Random forests. In: Machine Learning (2001)

9. Chawla, N.V., Bowyer, K.W., Hall, L.O., Kegelmeyer, W.P.: Smote: synthetic minority over-sampling technique. J. Artificial Intell. Res. **16**, 321–357 (2002). https://doi.org/10.1613/jair.953, http://dx.doi.org/10.1613/jair.953
10. Chen, C., Li, O., Tao, D., Barnett, A., Rudin, C., Su, J.K.: This looks like that: deep learning for interpretable image recognition. In: Advances in Neural Information Processing Systems 32, pp. 8930–8941. Curran (2019)
11. Cox, M., Ram, A.: Introspective multistrategy learning: on the construction of learning strategies. Artif. Intell. **112**(1–2), 1–55 (1999)
12. Cunningham, P., Zenobi, G.: Case representation issues for case-based reasoning from ensemble research. In: Aha, D.W., Watson, I. (eds.) ICCBR 2001. LNCS (LNAI), vol. 2080, pp. 146–157. Springer, Heidelberg (2001). https://doi.org/10.1007/3-540-44593-5_11
13. Deng, J., Dong, W., Socher, R., Li, L.J., Li, K., Fei-Fei, L.: Imagenet: a large-scale hierarchical image database. In: 2009 IEEE Conference on Computer Vision and Pattern Recognition, pp. 248–255 (2009)
14. Domeshek, E.: Indexing stories as social advice. In: Proceedings of the Ninth National Conference on Artificial Intelligence, pp. 16–21. AAAI Press, Menlo Park, CA (1991)
15. Fox, S., Leake, D.: Introspective reasoning for index refinement in case-based reasoning. J. Exper. Theoret. Artifi. Intell. **13**(1), 63–88 (2001)
16. Gates, L., Leake, D., Wilkerson, K.: Cases are king: a user study of case presentation to explain cbr decisions. In: Case-Based Reasoning Research and Development, ICCBR 2023, pp. 153–168. Springer (2023). https://doi.org/10.1007/978-3-031-40177-0_10
17. Hsieh, W.H., Shih, D.H., Shih, P.Y., Lin, S.B.: An ensemble classifier with case-based reasoning system for identifying internet addiction. Int. J. Environ. Res. Public Health **16**(7), 1233 (2019)
18. Huang, G., Liu, Z., van der Maaten, L., Weinberger, K.Q.: Densely connected convolutional networks (2016). https://arxiv.org/abs/1608.06993
19. Kenny, E.M., Keane, M.T.: Twin-systems to explain artificial neural networks using case-based reasoning: comparative tests of feature-weighting methods in ANN-CBR twins for XAI. In: Proceedings of the Twenty-Eighth International Joint Conference on Artificial Intelligence (2019)
20. Leake, D.: An indexing vocabulary for case-based explanation. In: Proceedings of the Ninth National Conference on Artificial Intelligence, pp. 10–15. AAAI Press, Menlo Park, CA (July 1991)
21. Leake, D., Wilkerson, Z., Crandall, D.: Extracting case indices from convolutional neural networks: a comparative study. In: Case-Based Reasoning Research and Development, ICCBR 2022 (2022)
22. Leake, D., Wilkerson, Z., Vats, V., Acharya, K., Crandall, D.: Examining the impact of network architecture on extracted feature quality for CBR. In: Case-Based Reasoning Research and Development, ICCBR 2023. Springer (2023). https://doi.org/10.1007/978-3-031-40177-0_1
23. Leake, D., Ye, X.: Harmonizing case retrieval and adaptation with alternating optimization. In: Case-Based Reasoning Research and Development - ICCBR 2021, pp. 125–139. Springer, Cham (2021). https://doi.org/10.1007/978-3-030-86957-1_9
24. Li, O., Liu, H., Chen, C., Rudin, C.: Deep learning for case-based reasoning through prototypes: A neural network that explains its predictions. ArXiv arXiv: abs/1710.04806 (2018)
25. Li, S., Harner, J.E., Adjeroh, D.A.: Random KNN. In: IEEE International Conference on Data Mining Workshops (2015)

26. Mathisen, B.M., Aamodt, A., Bach, K., Langseth, H.: Learning similarity measures from data. Progress Artifi. Intell. (2019)
27. Plaza, E., McGinty, L.: Distributed case-based reasoning. Knowl. Eng. Rev. **20**(3), 315–320 (2005)
28. Plaza, E., Ontañón, S.: Ensemble case-based reasoning: collaboration policies for multiagent cooperative CBR. In: Aha, D.W., Watson, I. (eds.) ICCBR 2001. LNCS (LNAI), vol. 2080, pp. 437–451. Springer, Heidelberg (2001). https://doi.org/10.1007/3-540-44593-5_31
29. Richter, M.: Introduction. In: Lenz, M., Bartsch-Spörl, B., Burkhard, H.D., Wess, S. (eds.) CBR Technology: From Foundations to Applications, chap. 1, pp. 1–15. Springer, Berlin (1998)
30. Sani, S., Wiratunga, N., Massie, S.: Learning deep features for knn-based human activity recognition. In: 25th International conference on Case-Based Reasoning (ICCBR 2017) (2017)
31. Schank, R., et al.: Towards a general content theory of indices. In: Proceedings of the 1990 AAAI spring symposium on Case-Based Reasoning. AAAI Press, Menlo Park, CA (1990)
32. Turner, J.T., Floyd, M.W., Gupta, K.M., Aha, D.W.: Novel object discovery using case-based reasoning and convolutional neural networks. In: Cox, M.T., Funk, P., Begum, S. (eds.) ICCBR 2018. LNCS (LNAI), vol. 11156, pp. 399–414. Springer, Cham (2018). https://doi.org/10.1007/978-3-030-01081-2_27
33. Turner, J.T., Floyd, M.W., Gupta, K., Oates, T.: NOD-CC: a hybrid CBR-CNN architecture for novel object discovery. In: Bach, K., Marling, C. (eds.) ICCBR 2019. LNCS (LNAI), vol. 11680, pp. 373–387. Springer, Cham (2019). https://doi.org/10.1007/978-3-030-29249-2_25
34. Wilkerson, Z., Leake, D., Crandall, D.: On combining knowledge-engineered and network-extracted features for retrieval. In: Case-Based Reasoning Research and Development, ICCBR 2021, pp. 248–262 (2021)
35. Wilkerson, Z., Leake, D., Vats, V., Crandall, D.: Extracting indexing features for CBR from deep neural networks: A transfer learning approach. In: Case-Based Reasoning Research and Development, ICCBR 2024. Springer (2024). https://doi.org/10.1007/978-3-031-63646-2_10
36. Xian, Y., Lampert, C.H., Schiele, B., Akata, Z.: Zero-shot learning - a comprehensive evaluation of the good, the bad and the ugly. In: IEEE Trans. Pattern Anal. Mach. Intell. (T-PAMI) (2018)
37. Ye, X., Leake, D., Jalali, V., Crandall, D.J.: Learning adaptations for case-based classification: a neural network approach. In: Sánchez-Ruiz, A.A., Floyd, M.W. (eds.) ICCBR 2021. LNCS (LNAI), vol. 12877, pp. 279–293. Springer, Cham (2021). https://doi.org/10.1007/978-3-030-86957-1_19
38. Ye, X., Leake, D., Wang, Y., Zhao, Z., Crandall, D.: Towards network implementation of CBR: Case study of a neural network K-NN algorithm. In: Case-Based Reasoning Research and Development - 32nd International Conference, ICCBR-24. LNCS, vol. 14775, pp. 354–370. Springer (2024). https://doi.org/10.1007/978-3-031-63646-2_23

Applied CBR Research

CBRinR Multitask Multiomics Case-Based Reasoning in Bioinformatics

Isabelle Bichindaritz(✉), Landon Berrios, and Mayur Desai

Biomedical and Health Informatics, State University of New York at Oswego, New York, USA
ibichind@oswego.edu

Abstract. The amount of genetic data available for analysis is rapidly growing, and the importance of analyzing this type of data is paramount to the field of precision medicine, in which diagnostic and prognostic tasks rely on genetic data analysis in many fields, including in oncology. CBRinR is a generic case-based reasoning system (CBR) in R language to analyze genetic data in bioinformatics domains. It is capable of handling both classification tasks and survival analysis tasks from multiomics datasets. CBRinR presents a useful alternative to statistical models such as LASSO regression in genetic domains, and benefits from higher transparency through case-based explanations. This paper describes CBRinR architecture, classification tasks, survival analysis tasks, confounding factors and their effect on fairness, explanations, and comparative analysis with state-of-the-art models in this domain. Experimental evaluations show that CBRinR is as effective in performing diagnostic and survival tasks as the state-of-the-art while affording precise user-level explanations at the case level.

Keywords: Survival Analysis · Diagnosis · Case-based Reasoning · Explainable Model

1 Introduction

The predictive performance of machine learning algorithms has progressed tremendously, though many recent works have focused on improving explainability [20, 21]. Machine learning researchers typically allude to a "black- box" effect when input and output are understood, but the processing that occurs in-between is obscure. Methods leading to a greater level of explainability are necessary in medicine since users are ultimately responsible for their clinical decisions and thus need to make informed decisions. One of the most explainable algorithms are instance-based learners (IBLs), such as *k*- Nearest Neighbor (*k*NN), for which decisions are made by similarity between a new case and solved retrieved cases, which can serve as explanations for a system's recommendations.

Taking advantage of the known explainability of IBL systems, this paper presents Case Based Reasoning in R language, or CBRinR. CBRinR is a multi-task case-based reasoning system for classification, prediction, and survival prediction for multiomics bioinformatics datasets. The R programming and statistical computing language is a

© The Author(s), under exclusive license to Springer Nature Switzerland AG 2025
I. Bichindaritz and B. López (Eds.): ICCBR 2025, LNAI 15662, pp. 363–377, 2025.
https://doi.org/10.1007/978-3-031-96559-3_24

language of choice in bioinformatics, hence the importance of making a CBR package available in R for bioinformatics data analysis. Specifically, we contribute the following:

Multitask CBR: CBRinR can perform multiple tasks in medical domains, namely diagnosis and disease severity risk, through classification and survival analysis, respectively. In medical domains, patients need not only to be diagnosed about a particular disease, but the severity of the disease is crucial to establish the most precise and effective treatment. Hence, the combination of classification for diagnosis and survival analysis for severity risk prediction is extremely valuable in these domains.

Multiomics CBR: CBRinR can analyze several types of genetic data, including transcriptomic, genomic, epigenetic, and proteomic. Additional omics data could be easily added as the system and bioinformatics technology evolve.

Explainability: In addition to the known explainability of IBL and CBR, CBRinR applies feature selection to determine an optimal biomarker signature for a disease, based on gene expression, methylation, enriched motifs, pathway analysis, and transcription factors.

CBRinR builds on CBRCONF [3] and as such inherits from this system the following features:

Optimal number of retrieved cases: CBRinR locates an optimal number of similar cases for each test case based on an automatically defined level of confidence in each retrieved case. Retrieval stops when we can confidently assign a solution. This method extends upon our prior work in [4].

Multi-level case elaboration and refinement: Significantly different DNA methylation levels found at a high-order cluster of probes that serve similar functions were utilized and compared. We then perform a similar series of tests using mRNA expression levels prior to integrating the two microarray technologies to find enriched motifs and transcription factors.

Novel case adaptation technique: Our case adaptation technique is tailored to survival analysis, which is an original application domain for CBR.

2 Research Background

Survival analysis is about predicting how likely an event is to happen over time. In oncology, the event we are interested in may be the death or relapse of the cancer patient. In survival analysis, we do not necessarily know how long has each patient lived as the experiment may have stopped before their death, or other event of interest. The individuals in a population who have not been subject to the death event are labeled as right-censored. We observe either the survival time, if we have the death date, or a censured time if we only have the date of last visit to the doctor. A survival instance is usually represented as (x_i, t_i, δ_i) where x_i is the feature vector, t_i is the observed time, δ_i is the indicator: 1 for an uncensored instance, which means the patient is dead, and 0 for a censored instance, which mean a patient being alive.

Among the types of genetic data available, although gene expression has first be studied in depth, DNA methylation has recently become more prevalent in genetic research in oncology. This paper proposes to apply these findings to the study of gene expression and DNA methylation signatures for cancer diagnosis and prognostic survival analysis.

Several survival analysis approaches have been proposed in the literature. LASSO method [19, 26] applies the lasso feature selection method for selecting the parts associated with cancer prediction. Random Survival Forests (RSF) [11] calculates a random forest with the log-rank test as the splitting standard. Though much progress has been made using above approaches, yet the predicting performance of the previously proposed approaches remains far from satisfying, and room remains for subsequent advancement. The explainability of such models also reserves room for improvement.

3 Related Work

Survival analysis is considered as a specific machine learning task predicting a time to event based on incomplete data, which refers to a mix of censored and uncensored data. Although it performs a prediction into the future, it is quite different from forecasting as well as from classification or prediction. Very specific machine learning models, mostly from statistics, have been applied to this task with the goal of stratifying the risk of patients into risk categories to reach an event in the future. Cox proportional hazard model [19] is one of the most popular survival prediction models. Recently, based on the Cox model, several regularization approaches have been proposed in the literature. The Least Absolute Shrinkage and Selection Operator COX model (LASSO-COX) applies the LASSO feature selection method for selecting parts associated with carcinoma prediction [25, 26, 29]. Random survival forests (RSF) [11] calculates a random forest with the log-rank test as the splitting standard. It determines the cumulative hazards of the leaf nodes while averaging them over the totality of elements.

Cox regression with neural networks by a one hidden layer multilayer perceptron (MLP) [30] was proposed to replace the linear predictor of the Cox model. Some novel networks were suggested to be capable of outperforming typical Cox models [1]. DeepSurv [14, 15] refers to a deep Cox proportional hazards neural network as well as a survival approach to model interacting processes of a case's covariates and treatment modalities for providing individual treatment suggestions. DeepSurv is developed upon Cox proportional assumption with a cutting-edge deep neural network. MTLSA [18] is a recently proposed model which regards survival analysis to be a multi-task learning issue. Following in this trend, Bichindaritz et al. [5] proposed an adaptive multi-task learning method, which combines the Cox loss task with the ordinal loss task, for survival prediction of breast cancer patients using multi-modal learning to integrate gene expression and methylation data instead of performing survival analysis on each feature data set. However, these models lacked interpretability.

In case-based reasoning, Karmen et al. calculate similarity based on survival functions [13]. Our work adopts different CBR strategies for classification and survival analysis and in addition integrates multi-omics data, while Karmen et al. data are at the clinical level (phenotypic) [13].

4 Methods

In precision medicine, we want to combine diagnostic tasks such as classification, and severity risk assessment tasks, such as survival analysis, to provide the most precise and effective treatment options for a patient. We also want to combine all the data available about a patient, which may involve phenotypic data, also called clinical data, and genetic data of various types, also called multiomics data. These may include gene expression data (mRNA), epigenetic data (methylation), proteomic data, and many others.

The case-based model learning process, highlighted in its architecture (see Fig. 1), comprises three stages: classification task, survival prediction task, and explanations. The trained model then can be applied to new input cases, also referred to as test cases, for the generation of end-to-end clinical recommendations.

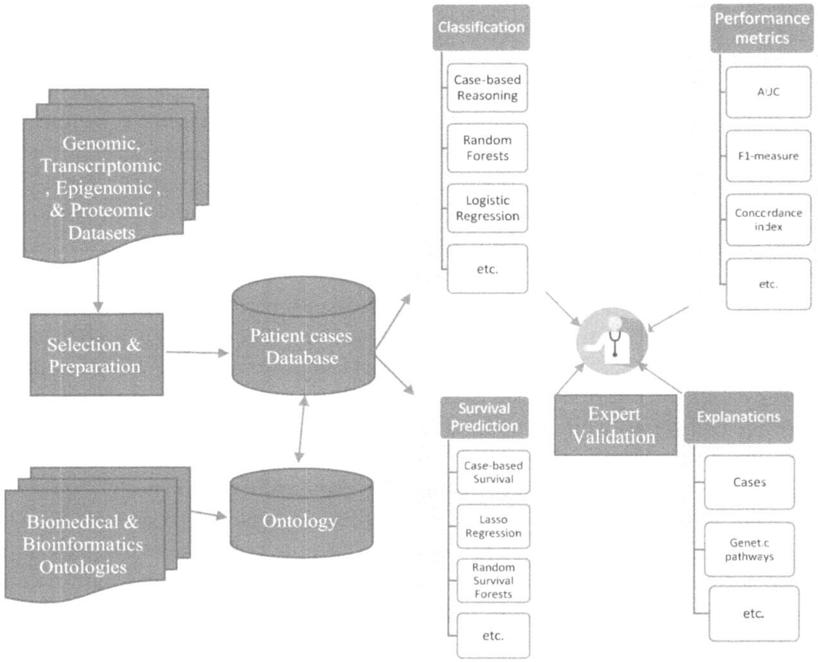

Fig. 1. Illustration of the proposed multitask multiomics classification and severity risk prediction system.

4.1 Genetic Data

DNA methylation and mRNA gene expression data for breast cancer (BRCA), Glioma cohort cancer (GBMLGG), and Pan-kidney cohort cancer (KIPAN) was downloaded from The Cancer Genome Atlas (TCGA) Research Network[1] [7].

For example in the BRCA dataset, the methylation data pertained to primary tumor samples and the 485,577 probes that exist on the Illumina Human Methylation 450 bead chip. The dataset is composed of 485,577 probe features with values ranging between 0 and 1. Each probe feature represents a location on the DNA where a methyl group

[1] Available https://www.cancer.gov/tcga.

(-CH3) may be found. DNA methylation has been associated with many diseases and disorders, including trauma and aging. Each prove feature value represents a methylation beta value, which is an estimation of the methylation level between 0 and 1. 0 indicates that the site is completely non-methylated, while 1 indicates that it is completely methylated. Similarly, 0.8 and above is commonly referred to as being hypermethylated while 0.2 and below is hypomethylated. We discarded samples that had a survival duration less than 0 months, because a negative survival value is not biologically plausible and therefore erroneous. After batch elimination, the remaining probes were used to locate differentially methylated regions, which consist in clusters of probes that are a possible functional region for gene transcriptional regulation. These clusters are based on physical proximity on a chromosome and serve as a feature reduction mechanism based on biology. The number of features was reduced to 8,722. Enriched motifs of interest were found through the R package ELMER, which groups together DNA methylation probes correlated with expression of these genes. Gene-probe pairs where this occurs are set aside and used to locate enriched motifs and upstream regulatory transcription factors.

Gene expressions came from the Illumina HiSeq RNA sequencing data collected from TCGA. Samples having low correlation with the diagnosis were filtered out and features were normalized prior to performing differential expression analysis (DEA). This dataset contained 17,002 features with values ranging between -1 and 1. A false discovery rate of 0.01 and a log fold change cut-off of 1 were used in this analysis for DEA. These parameters represent the measure of the proportion of false positives among all differentially expressed genes and the magnitude and direction of expression change, respectively. After preprocessing, DEA and reducing samples to just the primary cancer tissue, 1151 features were retained.

Similar data preprocessing was performed on all datasets. In addition to the genomic and transcriptomic data, each case features the overall survival (in months) t and the censoring information (1 if the case is deceased, and 0 if the case is living at the time of the last follow-up).

4.2 Classification

Classification was performed in several stages that further elaborated and refined the cases and carried out in R programming language. In each classification step, training was first performed through iterative removal of one sample for testing while the other samples were retained for training. For the testing sample, the nearest one, two or three cases were retrieved by calculating the Euclidean distance based on the similarity of features. The classification labels for these cases were retrieved, with the label that was in the majority being reused for the testing sample. Despite the class imbalance, we elected not to use over-sampling or undersampling. Oversampling the minority class can swiftly lead to overfitting, while undersampling the majority class can potentially lead to leaving out an important instance with crucial differences that could aid in the identification of the minority class. Instead, we utilized performance measures that adjusted for the class imbalance by calculating a balanced accuracy (BACC, computed using the average of per-class accuracy) and the weighted average area under the ROC curve (AUC). This task is described in more detail in Bartlett et al. [2].

4.3 Survival Analysis

Prognostic groups for survival were first established. A multivariate Cox regression was constructed using either DNA methylation features, or gene expression features as covariates in order to test each feature's contribution to the survival state. To find risk groups, the β regression coefficient for each feature, measuring strength of the association between a feature and the survival, was multiplied by either its expression value for gene expressions or its beta value for DNA methylation, and these values were then summed together to find a single prognostic score for each sample (Formula (1)). Samples were ranked by their prognostic scores and divided into equal-sized low, medium and high risk groups (see Fig. 2).

$$PrognosticScore = \sum_{i=1}^{Number\ Of\ Features} (\beta) * (feature\ value) \tag{1}$$

In order to predict the survival duration of test samples, a confidence metric was established to indicate when to cease retrieval. For training samples in each risk group, the mean of each feature was calculated and used to construct one prototypical case *P* for each risk group.

$$Conf(a, soli) = 1/2(dist(a, P)) + (d(a, uns1) + \cdots + d(a, unsn))/n \tag{2}$$

As shown in Formula (2), the confidence metric of a retrieved case *soli* to solve test case *a* is one half of the Euclidean distance *dist* from case *a* to its prototype *P*, added to the average distance of case *a* to each unsolved case *uns1* to *unsn*. The system's confidence in its solution for any given unsolved case would then be the summation of each retrieved case's confidence value until confidence reaches 100%. The predicted survival time for unsolved case *a* would then be the mean survival time of each retrieved case. This strategy adjusts for both the contribution of several retrieved and solved cases and the potential power of each case at forming a solution for an unsolved case.

To locate a subset of features that were highly specific to the overall survival of the cancer samples, a feature selection process was constructed based on multivariate Cox regression. 100 randomized training and testing splits of the data (with replacement) were used to extract a biomarker panel. After each iteration, features that had a significant log rank less than 0.01 were notated and validated with the test set. Upon conclusion of the 100 runs, only the features that were significant in at least 50% of the training sets were kept. Prognostic scores were then the sum of the average β regression coefficients for each of these features multiplied by the feature's methylation beta value (for DNA methylation) or the expression value (for mRNA expression).

Once cases in the case base were retrieved for an unsolved case and their average survival duration was determined and assigned to the unsolved case, a Cox proportional hazards model was built. Assigned survival times and survival status was used to construct the model, with the concordance index being employed to test the accuracy of the model. Concordance index measure *Cindex* evaluates how correct is the ordering of predicted times by quantifying the fraction of all pairs of cases with predicted survival times ordered in a correct manner (3).

$$CIndex = \frac{1}{|k|} \sum_{i=1}^{m} \sum_{j:t_i<t_j} I(F(x_i) < F(x_j)) \tag{3}$$

where k denotes the set of validly orderable pairs; $t_i < t_j$ represents the number of comparable pairs; m is the number of features; $F(x)$ is the prediction of survival time; I is the indicator function of whether the condition in parentheses is satisfied or not.

It is interpreted as follows: 0.5 is the expected result from random predictions, 1.0 is perfect concordance and, 0.0 is perfect anti-concordance. For example, if Case A died after 36 months and Case B died after 33 months and the model predicted that Case A would die after 24 months and Case B would die after 11 months, this is still a correct prediction.

4.4 Confounding Factors

Because the Cox model can handle confounding factors, which is one of its advantages and usefulness in medical domains, where taking confounding factors into account is mandated, as long as the clinical data comprise these factors, they are taken into account in the system processing. TCGA data for example have associated gender, age, race, and other demographic factors taken into account in statistical data analysis models such as the Cox model. CBRinR resorts to Cox regression model for constructing the prototypes, later used in the confidence metric used to retrieve similar cases.

4.5 Adaptation

A case adaptation phase followed feature selection and survival prediction to determine if adapting the case increased or decreased the concordance index. Case adaptation is the ability to morph training cases to reflect a test case more closely. Therefore, after retrieving similar training cases, the survival surv of the retrieved case(s) *retrieved* and the survival of the retrieved prototype P are taken into account to calculate the test case a survival, pondered by the similarities between the test case a and the retrieved case(s), *sim(a, retrieved)*, and between the test case a and the retrieved prototype P, *sim(a, P)*.

$$surv(a) = \frac{sim(a, retrieved) * surv(retrieved) + sim(a, P) * surv(P))}{sim(a, retrieved) + sim(a, P)} \tag{4}$$

4.6 Explanations

Kaplan Meyer survival curves can be displayed showing the risk groups learned by the survival system (see Fig. 2). These represent a global visualization of what the system has learned. Kaplan Meyer survival curves are classical representations of survival analysis results that such a system cannot go without. Each curve corresponds to a learned prototype, for which a survival can be calculated by averaging the survival of the cases in this prototype.

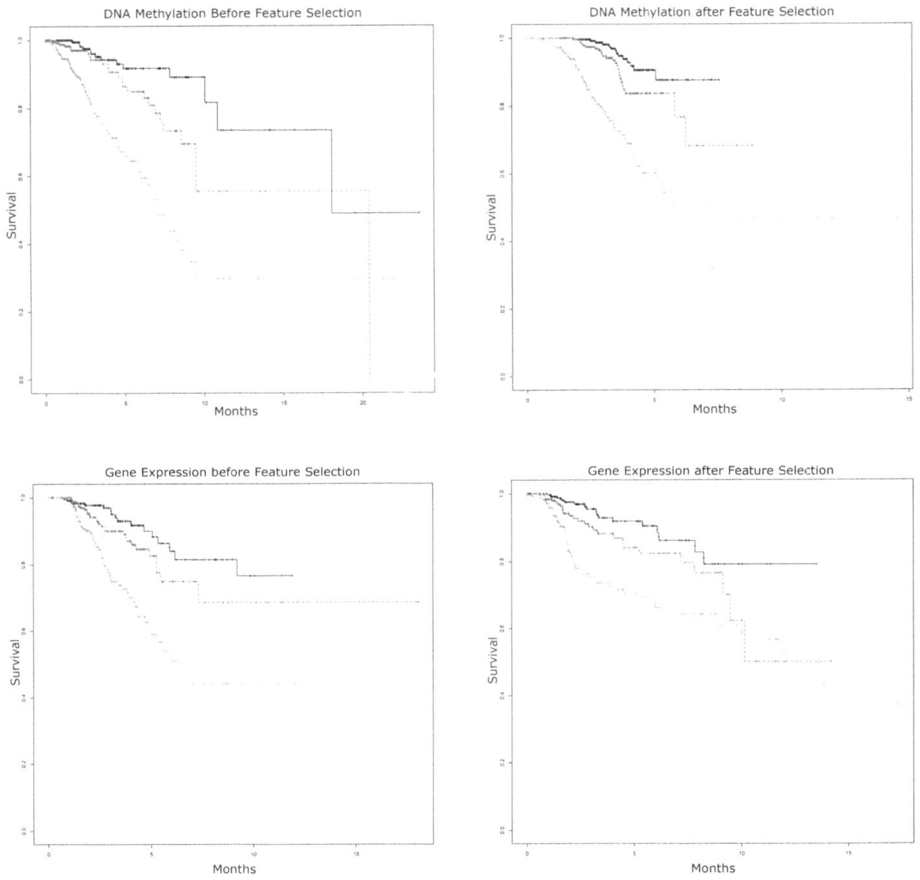

Fig. 2. Kaplan-Meier plots of the low, medium and high risk groups, corresponding to three prototypes *P*, using CBRinR model. The top plots are for DNA methylation before and after feature selection, and the bottom plots are for gene expression before and after feature selection. Legend: The black line is low risk, red line is medium risk, green line is high risk.

However, CBRinR also resorts to pathway databases to provide explanations at the genetic pathway level. The R language is the language of choice in bioinformatics due to the availability of numerous packages and databases to perform very specialized bioinformatics tasks and visualizations, both based on statistical methods and on machine learning methods. Taking the retrieved set of cases and the test case, one can construct pathway level representations through geneset enrichment. This operation can also be performed at the group level, either by risk group, or at the entire dataset level. It can be interesting to look globally at the pathways involved at the cancer level to perform cancer level comparisons.

5 Results and Discussions

5.1 Benchmark Datasets

In this section, we assess the performance of the proposed methods for the last step of survival analysis only and carry out experiments on four cancer DNA methylation and gene expression datasets through ten-fold cross validation. We selected breast cancer (BRCA), Glioma cohort cancer (GBMLGG) and Pan-kidney cohort cancer (KIPAN) from TCGA through Firehose [5].

Table 1. Gene and clinical characteristics in three cancer types.

Characteristics	BRCA	BRCA	GBMLGG	KIPAN
Genetic data type Patient no	Gene Expression 761	DNA Methylation 763	DNA Methylation 650	DNA Methylation 654
Gene no	1,151	8,725	20,116	20,533
Selected features Survival status	23	70	586	749
Living	512	514	434	500
Deceased	249	249	216	154
Follow up (days)	1–1234	1–1234	1–481	3–5925

The GBMLGG datasets include 1129 samples for clinical data and 20116 gene-level features for DNA methylation data. The KIPAN datasets contain 973 samples and 20533 DNA methylation features. In our case, we will also use the clinical data. Two clinical variables are used: survival status and survival time. In survival status, 'Deceased' represents the patient deceased, 'Living' means that he/she is living at the time of the last follow-up. The survival time represents the number of days between diagnosis and date of death or last follow-up. This study removes cases with survival days that were not recorded or negative. For these reasons, this study extracted 650 samples for GBMLGG data and 654 samples for KIPAN data that have both DNA methylation data and clinical data respectively after merging and filtering. Table 1 also shows the characteristics of the BRCA dataset with gene expression data and with DNA methylation data.

5.2 Comparison with Different Survival Prediction Methods

To explore the effectiveness of the proposed method, we compare the developed method with two existing machine learning survival prediction approaches: LASSO from R package `glmnet`, and Random Survival Forests (RSF) from R package `randomForestSRC`. For the sake of fairness, this part of the study runs the same input feature set in all cross-validation tests, therefore after feature selection.

One first element of comparison is the efficiency of the methods. CBRinR ran much faster than the other two models, with Random Survival Forests running much slower than the other two. This was observed through experimentally the execution time.

Table 2 presents the performance comparison between the proposed method and the two stated methods by the measurements of the C-index on BRCA, GBMLGG and KIPAN datasets. CBRinR performed significantly better, at p =.05 level, than the other two methods. On KIPAN dataset, RSF performed slightly better, but not significantly so.

Table 2. Performance comparison among a range of survival prediction approaches by C-index (higher is better) on four datasets.

Methods	BRCA Gene expression	BRCA Methylation	GBMLGG Methylation	KIPAN Methylation
LASSO	0.5	0.5	0.6215333	0.6574272
RSF	0.4656382	0.4660381	0.5629102	**0.7084548**
CBRinR	**0.7537651**	**0.6795273**	**0.6708844**	0.7039824

5.3 Explanability Results

To explore the explanations provided by the system, several types of graphics were produced, through gene set enrichment (R packages `DOSE` and `ReactomePA`) [31]. Moving from the genes to the genetic pathways makes a huge difference in the interpretability of results based on genetic data. The output of this pathway enrichment analysis provides a ranked list of genetic pathways activated. This analysis looks at whether the genes from the input dataset differentially expressed, in comparison to a normal transcriptome, can be mapped to known pathways because they can be clustered around these pathways [31]. A statistical parameter, or p-value, measures the strength of the association between the gene set and the pathways, so that the lower the p-value, the more a pathway is activated. Activation may be either positive (overexpression) or negative (underexpression).

By taking the retrieved sets of cases and the test case into account, on the BRCA genetic expressions dataset, we can generate and show to the user (R package `enrichplot`) a ranked subset of activated pathways through various visualizations, including bar plots, dot plots, enrichment maps, and UpSet plots.

1. Bar plot visualization

A bar plot visualization is probably the simplest visualization as it simply represents the pathways activated in common between the cases, ranked by increasing p-value. The X-axis represents the count or gene ratio of genes from this pathway being activated in the input samples, and the color represents the p-value, where smaller means more significantly different from a normal human being genetic expression. In this case, the gene ratio represents what percentage of genes in the corresponding pathway are activated by the cases (see Fig. 3).

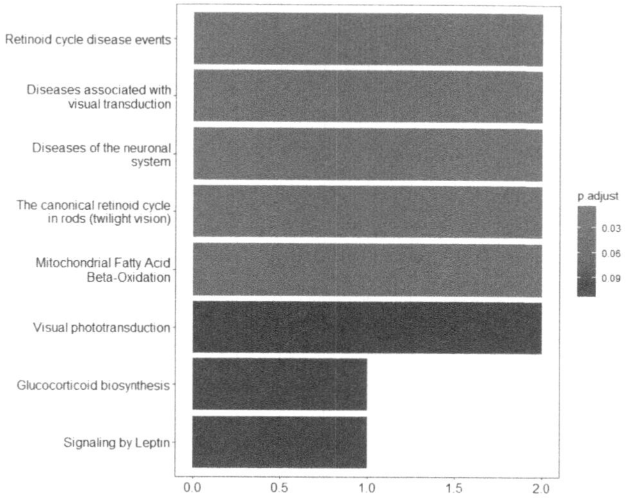

Fig. 3. A bar plot visualization represents the genetic pathways similarly activated between cases. Here we see that Retinoid cycle Disease Events, Diseases Associated with Visual Transduction, Diseases of the Neuronal System, and Canonical Retinoid Cycle in Rods seem to be the most activated in common by these cases.

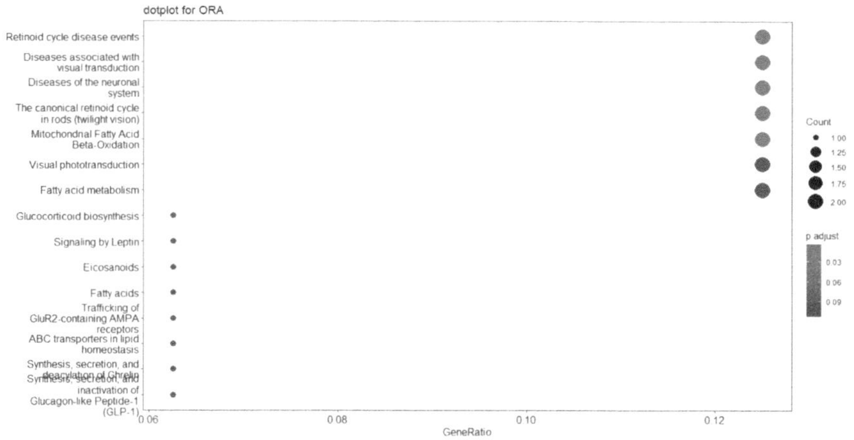

Fig. 4. A dot plot visualization represents the gene pathways similarly activated between cases. Here we again see that Retinoid cycle Disease Events, Diseases Associated with Visual Transduction, Diseases of the Neuronal System, and Canonical Retinoid Cycle in Rods seem to be the most activated in common. We also see some activated pathways with a smaller number of activated genes since both the gene ratio and the gene count are represented.

2. Dot plot visualizations
Next, a dot plot visualization represents the pathways activated, the p-value associated with each activated pathway, the gene ratio on the X-axis, and the count of genes activated as the size of the dots shown. Hence, this visualization provides some additional information in comparison to the bar plot (see Fig. 4).

3. Enrichment maps
An enrichment map illustrates the connections between activated pathways. Pathways are organized in a network with edges connecting overlapping gene sets. In this manner, overlapping gene sets allow to identify functional modules (see Fig. 5).

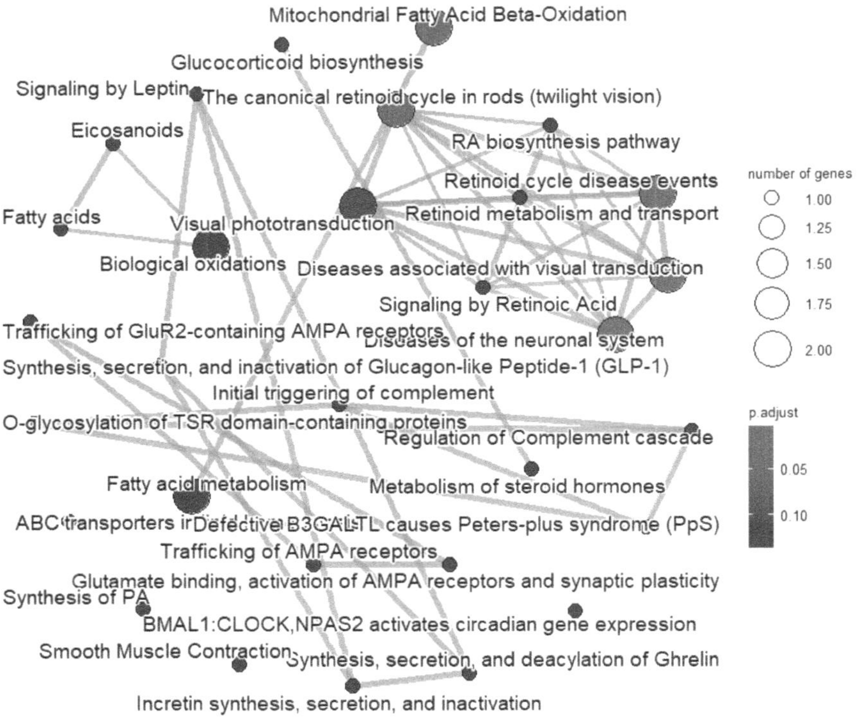

Fig. 5. An enrichment map visualization represents the relationships among genes with correlations between cases, with the most significant genes represented with the red color, and larger circles representing larger numbers of genes mapped to pathways. The figures can be enlarged to see the details of each gene name and p-value.

4. UpSet plots
Next, an UpSet plot visualization represents more information about the complex association between genes and gene sets by illustrating how genes overlap among different gene sets. Used in over-representation analysis, it calculates the overlaps between different gene sets. Each column represents a specific gene, and they are mapped to major

activated pathways below the bar (see Fig. 6). It would be possible to display the gene label for additional interpretation.

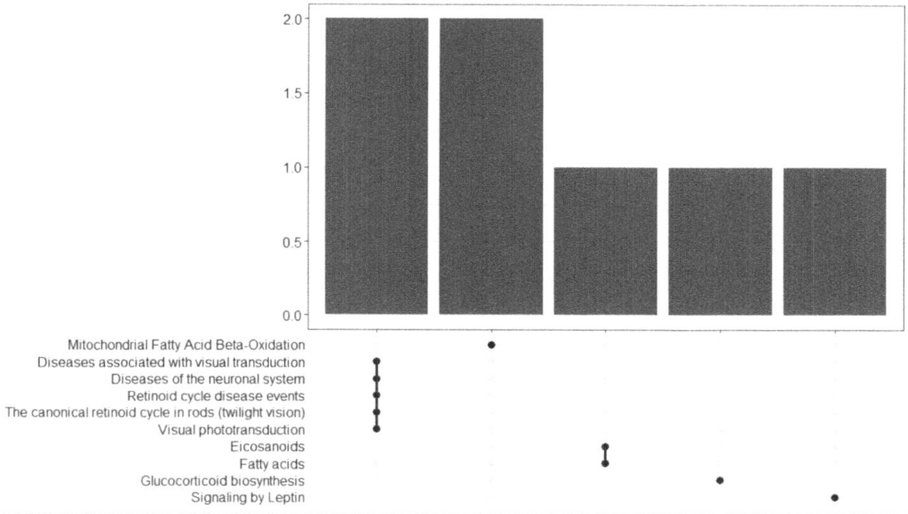

Fig. 6. An UpSet plot visualization represents the intersections and relationships among genes with correlations between cases, with the most significant genes represented with higher bars.

6 Conclusions

In this paper we discussed a multitask case based reasoning framework CBRinR built for bioinformatics datasets combining multiomics data and clinical data. This system assigns a confidence metric to each solved case depicting how well that case can be used to solve a new case. We also developed novel retrieval and adaptation steps for classification and survival analysis to provide decision support in a clinical workflow environment where clinicians not only need diagnostic recommendations, but also severity risk estimation. Using DNA methylation, gene expression and enriched motifs, we tested our framework to predict survival of three types of cancer (BRCA, GBMLGG, and KIPAN). We found that our model performed at least as well as several renowned methodologies for survival prediction with the advantage of efficiency and interpretability. We further tested the presence of overfitting by introducing randomness in the dataset and found only minor differences in results, which suggests that the model does not suffer from overfitting.

This study has a number of limitations, which we plan to address in the future. We wish to further validate our results using independent datasets across a number of cancers and in other domains where genetic data are available. Regarding feature selection, it would be interesting to compare several methods beyond the Cox regression model, which makes assumptions that would need to be tested. More work also needs to take place in the handling of confounding factors in order to ensure fairness in recommendations.

In other studies, we resorted to deep learning frameworks to accomplish survival analysis, with good success, and proposed a method based on prototypes to synergistically combine case-based reasoning and survival analysis. We currently do not have comparative evaluation between these two approaches. As a next step, we plan to compare CBRinR with the Python-based deep learning methods as well.

Another line of research will consist in generating counterfactuals to move one step closer to proposing treatment options, in order to move into treatment recommendations.

References

1. Amiri, Z., Mohammad, K., Mahmoudi, M., Zeraati, H., Fotouhi, A.: Assessment of gastric cancer survival: using an artificial hierarchical neural network. Pak. J. Biol. Sci. **11**, 1076–1084 (2008)
2. Bartlett, C., Liu, G., and Bichindaritz, I. Classifying breast cancer tissue through DNA methylation and clinical covariate based retrieval. In: Case-Based Reasoning Research and Development: 28th International Conference, ICCBR 2020, Salamanca, Spain, June 8–12, 2020, Springer International Publishing, Proceedings 28, pp. 82–96 (2020)
3. Bichindaritz I, Bartlett C, Liu G. Predicting with confidence: a case-based reasoning framework for predicting survival in breast cancer. In: The International FLAIRS Conference Proceedings, Apr 18, vol. 34 (2021)
4. Bichindaritz, I., Liu, G., Bartlett, C. :Survival prediction of breast cancer patient from gene methylation data with deep LSTM network and Ordinal Cox model. In: The Thirty-Third International Flairs Conference (2020)
5. Bichindaritz, I., Liu, G., Bartlett, C.: Integrative survival analysis of breast cancer with gene expression and DNA methylation data. Bioinformatics **37**, 2601–2608 (2021)
6. Caruana, R., Kangarloo, H., Dionisio, J.D., Sinha, U., Johnson, D.: Case-based explanation of non-case-based learning methods. In: Proceedings of the AMIA Symposium, p. 212. American Medical Informatics Association (1999)
7. Deng, M., Brägelmann, J., Kryukov, I., Saraiva-Agostinho, N., Perner, S.: FirebrowseR: an R client to the Broad Institute's Firehose Pipeline. Database 2017 (2017)
8. Farzindar, A.A., Kashi, A.: Multi-Task survival analysis of liver transplantation using deep learning. In: The Thirty-Second International Flairs Conference (2019)
9. Eisenstadt, V., Langenhan, C., Althoff, K.D., Dengel, A.: Improved and visually enhanced case-based retrieval of room configurations for assistance in architectural design education. International Conference on Case-Based Reasoning. Springer, Cham (2020)
10. Hochreiter, S., Schmidhuber, J.: Long short-term memory. Neural Comput. **9**, 1735–1780 (1997)
11. Ishwaran, H., Kogalur, U.B., Blackstone, E.H., Lauer, M.S.: Random survival forests. Annals Appli. Statist. **2**, 841–860 (2008)
12. Joshi, S., Koyejo, O., Vijitbenjaronk, W., Kim, B., Ghosh, J. Towards realistic individual recourse and actionable explanations in black-box decision making systems. arXiv preprint arXiv:1907.09615. (2019)
13. Karmen, C., Gietzelt, M., Knaup-Gregori, P., Ganzinger, M.: Methods for a similarity measure for clinical attributes based on survival data analysis. BMC Med. Inform. Decis. Mak. **19**, 1–14 (2019)
14. Katzman, J. L., Shaham, U., Cloninger, A., Bates, J., Jiang, T., Kluger, Y.: Deep survival: a deep cox proportional hazards network. Stat **1050**, 2 (2016)

15. Katzman, J.L., Shaham, U., Cloninger, A., Bates, J., Jiang, T., Kluger, Y.: DeepSurv: personalized treatment recommender system using a Cox proportional hazards deep neural network. BMC Med. Res. Methodol. **18**, 24 (2018)
16. Kim, B., Khanna, R., Koyejo, O.O.: Examples are not enough, learn to criticize! criticism for interpretability. Adv. Neural Information Process. Syst., 2280–2288 (2016)
17. Kim, B., Rudin, C., Shah, J.A.: The bayesian case model: a generative approach for case-based reasoning and prototype classification. Adv. Neural Information Process. Syst. **27** (2014)
18. Li O, Liu H, Chen C, Rudin C. Deep learning for case-based reasoning through prototypes: A neural network that explains its predictions. In Thirty-Second AAAI Conference on Artificial Intelligence (2018)
19. Lin, D.Y., Wei, L.-J., Ying, Z.: Checking the Cox model with cumulative sums of martingale-based residuals. Biometrika **80**, 557–572 (1993)
20. Lundberg, S. M., Lee, S.-I. : A unified approach to interpreting model predictions. Adv. Neural Information Process. Syst. **30** (2017)
21. Lundberg, S.M., Nair, B., Vavilala, M.S., Horibe, M., Eisses, M.J., Adams, T., et al.: Explainable machine-learning predictions for the prevention of hypoxaemia during surgery. Nat. Biomed. Eng. **2**, 749–760 (2018)
22. Mayr, A., Schmid, M.: Boosting the concordance index for survival data. Ulmer Informatik-Berichte **26** (2014)
23. Ramos, B., Pereira, T., Moranguinho, J., Morgado, J., Costa, J.L., Oliveira, H. P.: An interpretable approach for lung cancer prediction and subtype classification using gene expression. In: 2021 43rd Annual International Conference of the IEEE Engineering in Medicine & Biology Society (EMBC), pp. 1707–1710. IEEE (2021)
24. Ramon, Y., Martens, D., Provost, F., Evgeniou, T.: A comparison of instance-level counterfactual explanationalgorithms for behavioral and textual data: SEDC, LIME-C and SHAP-C. Adv. Data Analy. Classi. **14**(4), 801–819 (2020)
25. Ryall, S., Tabori, U., Hawkins, C.: A comprehensive review of paediatric low-grade diffuse glioma: pathology, molecular genetics and treatment. Brain Tumor Pathol. **34**, 51–61 (2017)
26. Shao, W., Cheng, J., Sun, L., Han, Z., Feng, Q., Zhang, D. et al.: Ordinal multi-modal feature selection for survival analysis of early-stage renal cancer. International Conference on Medical Image Computing and Computer-Assisted Intervention, pp. 648–656. Springer (2018). https://doi.org/10.1007/978-3-030-00934-2_72
27. Sy, J.P., Taylor, J.M.G.: Estimation in a Cox proportional hazards cure model. Biometrics **56**(1), 227–236 (2020)
28. Suzuki, H., Maruyama, R., Yamamoto, E., Kai, M.: DNA methylation and microRNA dysregulation in cancer. Mol. Oncol. **6**, 567–578 (2012)
29. Tibshirani, R.: The lasso method for variable selection in the Cox model. Stat. Med. **16**, 385–395 (1997)
30. Xiang, A., et al.: Comparison of the performance of neural network methods and Cox regression for censored survival data. Comput. Stat. Data Anal. **34**, 243–257 (2000)
31. Yu, G., He, Q.Y.: ReactomePA: an R/Bioconductor package for reactome pathway analysis and visualization. Mol. BioSyst. **12**(2), 477–479 (2016)

Case-Based Causal Reasoning for Elite Sport Training

Dandan Cui[1(✉)], Jianwei Guo[3], Ping Liu[2], Xiangning Zhang[2], and Weijie Liu[2]

[1] China Institute of Sport Science, Beijing, China
ditto9@gmail.com
[2] Captital University of Physical Education and Sports, Beijing, China
[3] Shanghai University of Sport, Shanghai, China

Abstract. With the lack of causal knowledge and causal reasoning between variables, existing CBR-based sport training systems have limited effectiveness in elite sports. In this paper, we propose a case-based causal reasoning (CBCR) framework that generates causal knowledge beforehand from the case base, using Markov equivalence classes and structural equations, and then utilizes this knowledge for causal reasoning in each subsequent CBR process, including retrieve, reuse, revise, and retain. An application in elite 100-m sprinting training shows that the CBCR framework provides personalized speed rhythm solutions that are closer to the reasoning results of elite coaches and have better results for elite sprinters' performance enhancement.

Keywords: CBR for health and exercise · Sport Training · Causal Inference

1 Introduction

Since decades ago, CBR has been widely used to solve reasoning problems in a variety of industries [1,2]. In recent years, it has also begun to be applied in recreational marathon training [3–6]. However, we encountered two major difficulties when applying case-based reasoning methods in elite sport training.

First, elite sports are more individualized. Elite sports are about pushing the limits of human physical ability, and the limits of every elite athlete are different. In sprinting, for example, it takes most top male sprinters some forty strides to complete a 100-m event [7]. Then, ideally, if only we ran with the same length and frequency in every stride as Usain Bolt did, everyone could hit Bolt's 9.58-s world record of 100-m sprint. But in practice, no one, as for now, is able to copy Bolt's solution and therefore to hit his record. This is because the stride length and stride frequency of a specific athlete in a race affect each other, and both of them are affected by the athlete's specific mental and physical characteristics, which also affect each other. The paths and values of the influences between the many variables form a complex network that limits the performance that each athlete can practically achieve all differently. However, existing CBR-based sport training systems have not included these influences.

Second, the number of elite sport cases is much smaller. Still taking sprinting as an example, there are only a few dozen cases in human history that sprinters have run within 10 s in the final of an official 100-m sprint event [8], whose scale is tens of thousands of times smaller than that of the amateur marathon's case base with hundreds

© The Author(s), under exclusive license to Springer Nature Switzerland AG 2025
I. Bichindaritz and B. López (Eds.): ICCBR 2025, LNAI 15662, pp. 378–391, 2025.
https://doi.org/10.1007/978-3-031-96559-3_25

of thousands of cases [6]. An elite coach typically works with an even smaller number of elite athletes throughout their career, perhaps no more than a dozen or so. Despite this, they are still able to extract invaluable knowledge from their limited experience, allowing them to provide highly effective and personalized diagnoses for a new athlete. However, existing CBR-based sports training systems have yet to incorporate this type of knowledge.

Individualization implies more diversity, which seems to be contradictory to a smaller number of elite cases. How to resolve this contradiction becomes the key to the effective application of CBR techniques in elite sports training. Luckily, we have worked with two of these elite coaches and discovered that they both make decisions in a manner similar to the CBR pattern. One is Randy Huntington [9], the coach of the men's 100 m sprint Asian record holder Bingtian Su, and the other is Patrizio Parcesepe, the coach of Gold medalist in the women's 20 km race walk at the Paris 2024 Olympics Jiayu Yang. These coaches also draw on historical cases to determine the orientation of training for a particular athlete, but rather than replicating the solutions in the case, they use the causal logic they have condensed from their coaching to reason out the most critical issues for the athlete at hand and use this as a guide to develop the most efficient solutions, which inspired the proposed work in this paper.

In this paper, we adapt the graph-based causal inference methods in CBR [10], and propose a case-based causal reasoning (CBCR) framework, which first generates causal knowledge from the case base based on Markov equivalence classes and structural equations, and then extend the work we presented in [11] by utilizing causal knowledge in all four reasoning processes, including retrieval, reuse, revise, and retain. Based on this framework, we built an intelligent diagnostic system for 100-m sprint training and conducted experiments based on real competition data from Chinese national team sprinters.

2 Related Work

2.1 Sport Training

Competitive performance is influenced by a combination of multidisciplinary factors, and the factors currently considered in elite sports include both external factors such as temperature and track, and internal factors such as tactics, technique, fitness, physiology, and psychology [12, 13]. The different factors, in turn, influence each other in a roughly hierarchical structure shown in Fig. 1. Therefore, the fundamental task of elite sports training is how to optimize these factors to enhance the sports performance of a particular athlete. In this paper, we focus on simulating elite coaches' personalized optimization diagnosis of elite sprinters' "speed rhythm" based on a small number of "champion models".

Speed rhythm, also known as "pacing strategy", refers to the distribution of speed throughout a race [14, 15]. It reflects how an athlete allocates effort and energy across the course of a competition, and can have a direct and significant impact on performance in racing sports as Fig. 1 shows.

Fig. 1. Multidisciplinary factors affecting performance in elite sports.

Regarding speed rhythm, the 100-m sprint can be divided into 3 main phases: the block start with acceleration phase, which is represented by a rapid increase in velocity; the maximum velocity phase, which typically represented as a relatively flat section of the velocity curve, usually reaching the highest speed between 50 m and 80 m; and the deceleration phase, which is represented by a gradual decrease in velocity due to fatigue, usually happening over the final 20 m [16, 17]. The optimal distribution of speed and energy among the three phases of the sprint is like the rhythm of music, which directly determines the performance of the race. Thus, the start acceleration time, the maximum velocity, and the percentage of velocity lost relative to the max velocity have been used as the three most important variables in the study of sprint speed rhythm, the first two of which have also been analyzed by mathematical modeling of the velocity curve [8].

Champion Model, which originally refers to a personalized spiritual role model for an athlete [18], is a very inspiring term for quantitative success cases, which has been widely adopted among elite coaches in personalized training for elite athletes in recent years. For example, Su Bingtian, who dramatically broke the Asian record with a mark of 9.83 s in the men's 100 m semifinals at the Tokyo 2020 Olympics, was coached by Randy Huntington, who used a foreign athlete with a similar body shape as a reference to help Su optimize his technique and break the Chinese record of 9.99 s in 2017 [9].

Nowadays, in intelligent systems for sports training, historical cases are mainly used as statistical constraints, or training data for machine learning [19–21]. In the most prestigious intelligent training system based on the Champion model for sprinting, the model is also statistically averaged, and individualized diagnoses have to be made by the expert reasoning of its owner, Ralph Mann [22]. Only the CBR-based system retains the individuality of historical cases. How to simulate the causal decision logic of human experts is the key for CBR to achieve highly personalized reasoning on a small case base.

2.2 Causal Inference

Causal knowledge in traditional CBR systems is mainly a priori knowledge [1]. In contrast, the task of this paper is to automatically condense the causal knowledge embedded in the whole case dataset and incorporate it into the reasoning logic, which requires the use of causal inference. Although there are many methods related to causal inference, the graph-based causal inference technique proposed by Judea Pearl (hereafter referred to as "causal inference") has the strongest ability to handle multivariate observation data. Moreover, the Causal Faithfulness Assumption, one of the two basic assumptions of causal inference, is very similar to the Similarity Assumption of CBR, and the other Causal Markov Assumption has already been well used in the Reuse process of CBR to evaluate the adaptability of solutions [2]. In this paper, we will comprehensively apply causal inference into all the 4 CBR processes, which includes the following 3 major causal tasks.

Causal discovery is a causal inference technique that mines the paths and directions of causal effects between variables from the original data. The input content of causal discovery is the original data, and the output result is the causal graph, which is used to visually represent the causal path, which is not only the basic feature of causal inference different from the traditional causal relationship research method, but also an important foundation for accomplishing the subsequent causal inference tasks.

Specifically, a causal graph is a directed acyclic graph (DAG) with nodes representing variables and directed edges representing causal relationships between variables [10,23]. The basic process of generating a causal graph is as follows: first, an undirected graph based on Markov Equivalence Class (MEC) is generated by testing the conditional independence between variables on the original data, and then the direction of edges is determined by a set of causal inference rules based on the principles of Minimality and Stability, and finally, the directed acyclic graph with causal attributes is generated, i.e. causal graph [24].

Causal effect identification is a causal inference technique that simulates experimental interventions and quantitatively identifies causal effects under different paths through data analysis. The inputs of causal effect identification are raw data and causal diagrams, and the outputs are direct causal effects, indirect causal effects, and total causal effects among variables.

In the causal effect identification technique, the fundamental change made by causal inference is the proposal of the do-operator which represents the external intervention, and the establishment of a complete do-calculus [10]. The do-calculus reasons in the non-parametric case in the probabilistic language, whereas under linear assumptions, the do-calculus can be computed from the coefficients of the variables in a Structural Equation Model (SEM) [25].

Individual counterfactual reasoning is a causal inference technique that uses data analytics to simulate human-specific higher cognitive logics, such as imagination and reflection, to reason about "potential outcomes" that did not really happen in a particular event. The input of individual counterfactual reasoning is the common causal model constructed through causal discovery and causal effect identification, and the output is the potential effect of counterfactual intervention.

The biggest breakthrough in individual counterfactual reasoning is the migration of causal models from the aggregate to the individual, and the establishment of a set of probabilistic language highly similar to human counterfactual cognitive reasoning logic on the basis of "do algorithms" [10]. Under the assumption of linearity, individual counterfactual reasoning can be reduced to the following 3-step structural equation-based algorithm [26]:

1. Abduction: the individual's variable values are brought into the structural equations and, based on the calculation results, the constant terms of each equation are updated, thus updating the overall causal model to an individual causal model.
2. Action: In the equation with variable Xi as the independent variable, Xi is updated to the counterfactual value to obtain the intervention model after simulating the "virtual intervention" Xi.
3. Prediction: Bring the other independent variables into the model obtained in (2) and calculate the individual counterfactual dependent variable values after the "virtual intervention" Xi, i.e., the "potential outcome".

3 Case-Based Causal Reasoning

3.1 CBCR Cycle

We incorporate causal discovery, causal effect identification, and individual counterfactual reasoning methods of causal inference into each process of CBR to enhance the causal attributes of case-based reasoning, forming a closed cycle of case-based causal reasoning (CBCR) as shown in Fig. 2, which consists of the following 5 causal processes.

Causal Regenerate. The causal knowledge that generates these cases is reconstructed from previous cases for utilization in subsequent processing. Causal knowledge includes causal paths and causal effects. In the sport training problem, the causal path includes 2 causal graphs: 1 is the causal graph among all description variables and performance variables, and 2 is the causal graph among all solution variables and performance variables. The causal effect values also include 2 parts: 1 is the total causal effect value of each description variable on the performance variable, and 2 is the total causal effect value of each solution variable on the performance variable.

Causal Retrieve. Retrieve the case or cases with the most similar causal effects from previous cases. The most basic way to introduce causal effects in similarity is to causally weight the description variables in the measure function of case similarity. And the simplest causal weighting factor is the value of the total causal effect of the description variables on the performance variables.

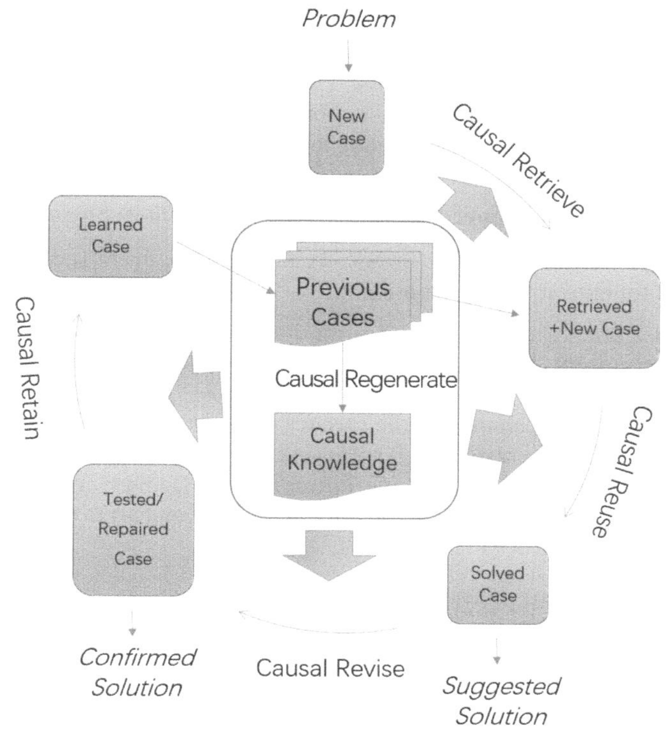

Fig. 2. CBCR cycle.

Causal Reuse. The counterfactual solution with the largest potential performance improvement effect is reused from the retrieved cases as the proposed solution to the current problem. Although the case base itself comes with the counterfactual attribute [27,28], the counterfactuals in CBCR are counterfactuals based on the new case individual causal model. That is, the generalized causal model is first converted to an individual causal model, then each scenario variable is tested one by one as a counterfactual scenario for the outlier intervention and potential achievement, and finally the scenario with the best potential achievement is output. The specific calculations of the individual model, counterfactual scenario and counterfactual achievement enhancement effects are described in Sect. 2.3.

Causal Revise. The proposed solutions are evaluated by human experts or causal models. The conclusion of the evaluation is whether the key program variables reused in the suggested solution are correct. In this case, the basic evaluation method based on causal modeling is to causally weight the solution variables in a metric function of solution similarity. And the simplest causal weighting coefficient is the total causal effect value of the program variables on the achievement variables.

Causal Retain. The causally modified solutions and problem descriptions are composed into a new case and retained in the appropriate place in the case base. The causal property of this process is reflected in the fact that causal reconstruction is also performed based on the updated case base to obtain the updated causal knowledge. This completes the current causal case reasoning loop.

3.2 A CBCR System for Speed Rhythm Diagnosis in 100-m Sprint

Based on the proposed CBCR framework, we built an intelligent speed rhythm diagnostic system for elite 100-m sprint training.

Case Representation. Usually, a sprinter's velocity-time curve was fit by using a mono-exponential regression model in function (1). [8]. Thus, the performance of a sprinter is profiled by 2 parameters: the sprinter's maximal horizontal velocity (v_{max}) and the acceleration time constant (τ_1). However, it can only model the acceleration and maximal velocity phase. Following up on one of our previous efforts [29], we redesigned the model by adding a deceleration time constant (τ_2) to profile all 3 phases of the 100 m sprint as shown in (1)

$$v(t) = v_{ideal}(1 - e^{-\frac{t}{\tau_1}})e^{-\frac{t}{\tau_2}} \tag{1}$$

The unit of time variable and constants is second(s), and the unit of velocity variable and constant is meter/second(m/s). v_{max}. More rigorously, "maximal velocity" in the previous literature is expressed by ideal maximal velocity v_{ideal} in our approach. Therefore, the 3 modal-independent cognitive parameters of speed rhythm are extracted.

Index: As we can only learn from an athlete who runs faster than us, the cases in the case base are indexed according to their performance. In our current 100-m system, it is the mark score M_{ark}.

Description Variables: Unchangeable or physical features are used as keys to select a case in the base. In our current 100-m system, they are gender, age, height and weight. As the variety of gender is not covered in our data, the description variable set is $\{A_{ge}, H_{eight}, W_{eight}\}$.

Solution Variables: Features that aimed to be changed through training are used as values to diagnose. In our current 100-m system, they are the 3 speed rhythm parameters, and the value variable set is $\{V_i, T_1, T_2\}$.

To simplify the notation, henceforth in this paper, we use H for height in meter and W for weight in kg and Vi for v_{ideal} in meter/second, T1 for τ_1 in second, T2 for τ_2 in second.

Case Base. We collect 102 person-times of men's 100-m sprint data covering 17 major competitions from Athens World Championships in 1997 to Doha World Championships in 2019, including Usain Bolt, Christian Coleman, Noah Lyles, and Su Bingtian, with marks ranging from 9.58 s to 10.59 s, heights ranging from 172 cm to 196 cm, weights ranging from 65 kg to 91 kg, and ages ranging from 19 to 37 years old. These are the previous cases to build the case base.

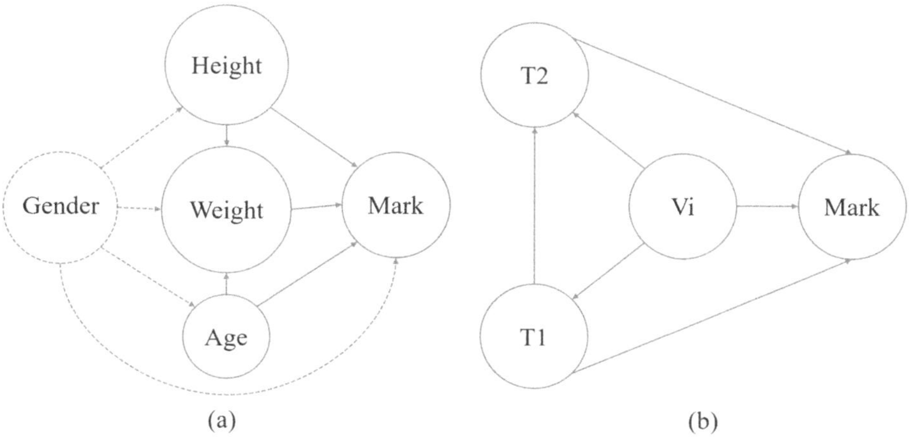

Fig. 3. The DAGs discovered from our case base. Figure a on the left shows the DAG of description, in which the dotted parts are not covered in current data. Figure b on the right shows the DAG for solution.

Causal Regenerate. First, causal discovery among description variables (including age, height and weight) and performance (mark in 100-m sprint) is carried out via PC algorithm [24], And DAG of solution variables (ideal maximal velocity, acceleration time constant, and deceleration time constant) and performance (mark in 100-m sprint) is discovered via PC algorithm [23] on the case base as well. The causal graphs is regenerated as Fig. 3 shows.

As we have only a very small training set with 102 cases in the base, we built a linear causal model for simplicity in this paper. Nonetheless, the statistically significant linear correlation among the description variables and mark ensures the validity of the linear model in the current training set ($p < 0.01$ for mark-height, mark-weight, mark-age, age-weight and height-weigh) to a certain extent. Based on linear hypothesis, DAG in Fig. 3a can be expressed as the following structural equations, where U is the residual that will be personalized in the counterfactual inferring:

$$\begin{cases} W_{eight} = aA_{ge} + bH_{eight} + U_{weight} \\ M_{ark} = cA_{ge} + dH_{eight} + eW_{eight} + U_{mark} \end{cases} \tag{2}$$

As we stated above, a linear causal model for diagnosis is built due to the small size of current dataset. Nonetheless, the statistically significant linear correlation between the cognitive parameters ensures the validity of the linear model in the current training set ($p < 0.01$ for T1-T2, T1-Vi, T2-Vi) to a certain extent. As the causal relationship between performance and values is already regulated by Eq. 3, linear assumption can only be used for the other parts in Fig. 3b:

$$\begin{cases} T_1 = aV_i + U_{T_1} \\ T_2 = bT_1 + cV_i + U_{T_2} \\ M_{ark} = \min(t | \int_0^t V_i(1 - e^{-\frac{t}{T_1}})e^{-\frac{t}{T_2}} \mathrm{d}t \geq 100) \end{cases} \tag{3}$$

Total causal effects (TCE) of all variables are therefore calculated.

Causal Retrieve. Then TCEs of description variables$\{A_{ge}, H_{eight}, W_{eight}\}$ on mark are taken as weights, and therefore a causality-based retrieval of cases is accomplished.

Causal Reuse. Counterfactual predicting is accomplished according to the effect of treatment on the treated (ETT) [10]. In a linear structural equation model (SEM), there are 3 steps to infer individual counterfactuals. Take T1 as an example:

1. Abduction: Vi, T1 and T2 of the current user are merged into Eq3 based on the training data, and the variables U are updated to the personal value of the user, so the population model becomes an individual model.
2. Action: The equation of T1 is modified to the T1 value in the retrieved case, and therefore a counterfactual intervention is imitated.
3. Prediction: The user's Vi is brought into the modified Eq3, and T2 and Mark are calculated to obtain the user's counterfactual performance change if the user follows the accelerating tech of the champion model.

Causal Revise. Then TCEs of solution variables$\{V_i, T_1, T_2\}$ on the mark are taken as weights to evaluate the similarity between counterfactual solutions and the solution that has actually happened. And therefore a causality-based evaluation of solutions is accomplished.

Causal Retain. If the suggested solution is not the most similar, the solution that has actually happened should be composed into a new case and retained in the case base. Index the new case according to its actual mark, and then re-conduct the process of Causal Regenerate to update the causal knowledge. Thus, the current CBCR cycle is completed.

4 Evaluation

4.1 Experiments in Elite Sprint Training

First, experiments based on real competition data from Chinese national team athletes were conducted.

Test Data. To test our system on real data that actually happened, we collected data of 5 elite sprinters of the China National Team from the final of major international or national events in the year 2021, timed by CV algorithm [30] with manual correction. We collected 2 cases for each sprinter, the slower case as the problem and the faster case for the model-based causal evaluation.

Table 1. Evaluation Results

Evaluation	CD	ED	CWCD	CWED
MOS	2.2	3.8	2.8	4.6
Similarity	0.28	0.24	0.33	0.21

Tested Methods. In the Causal Retrieve process, we compared 4 measurements of similarity: cosine distance (CD), Euclidean distance (ED), causal-weighted cosine distance (CWCD), and causal-weighted Euclidean distance (CWED). In the Causal Revise process, we evaluate the solutions by 2 ways: by an human expert and by the faster case from the same sprinter. We carried out a Mean Score Opinion (MOS) test evaluation, which is often used to evaluate the subjective user experience of a human-computer-interactive system [31]. The scoring criteria are: 1 for wrong; 2 for doubtful; 3 for reasonable; 4 for valuable; 5 for adopted.

Results. As Table 1 shows, the Causal-weighted Euclidean Distance is evaluated best by both human expert and causal model. However, similarity measured by Causal-weighted Euclidean Distance and basic Euclidean Distance are not quite discrimitive. This suggested that what actually happens is not necessarily the best or the only solution. In the tested 5 cases, no revised solution is needed to be retained.

4.2 Case Study

Here we illustrate the role of causal retrieval and causal retention in the diagnosis of individually customized training with a specific case study. As we mentioned in the introduction, causal case-based reasoning is inspired by Randy Huntington, the coach of the Asian 100 m running record holder Su Bingtian, and below we use CBCR to model Randy's diagnosis of Su's speed rhythm for the 100 m race at the Tokyo Olympics. According to the results above, Causal-weighted Euclidean Distance is adopted.

1. First, We first took Su Bingtian's speed pace of 9.98 s in the final as the diagnostic object, and used 9.90–9.98 s as the target performance for Causal Retrieve, the causal similarity distance with Su Bingtian's smallest "Champion Model" is Su Bingtian's data of 9.92 s in the final of the Asian Games in Jakarta (Age 29, height 172 cm, weight 73 kg). The potential changes in performance after adjusting Su's T1, Vi, and T2 to the Champion Model values were calculated to be −0.34 s, −0.07 s, and −0.02 s, respectively, and the speed and displacement curves shown in Fig. 4(a) were obtained. The recommendation for improvement from this velocity and displacement curve is: "Su should increase the start acceleration time".
2. In order to verify the stability of the above algorithm, the author excluded Su Bingtian's historical data from the Elite104 dataset, based on which he also diagnosed his speed cadence of 9.98 s in the final of the Tokyo Olympics by repeating steps 1 to 5 above, and obtained the speed and displacement curves shown in Fig. 4(b), from which the recommendation for improvement remains: "Su should increase the start acceleration time".

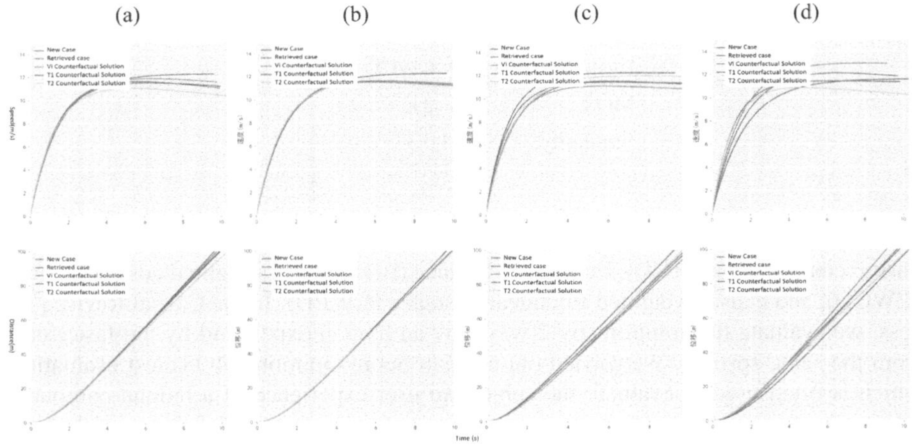

Fig. 4. CBCR diagnostic results of Su Bingtian's speed tempo performance at the Tokyo Olympics. (a) for the diagnosis of Su Bingtian's final 9.98 s with 9.97 s 9.90 s as the target performance interval, the selected personalized champion model is Su's own 9.92 s in the final of the 2018 Asian Games in Jakarta (age 29 years old at that time, height 172 cm, weight 73 kg); (b) for the diagnosis of Su's own historical data after excluding Su's own 9.98 s from the Elite 104 dataset; (c) for the diagnosis of Su's final 9.98 s after excluding Su's own 9.92 s from the final of the 2018 Asian Games in Jakarta. (b) For diagnosing Su Bingtian's final 9.98 s after excluding Su's own historical data in the Elite104 dataset, the personalized champion model selected was Frank Fredericks' 9.95 s in the final of the 1997 World Championships in Athens (age 30 at the time, height 180 cm, weight 73 kg); (c) For diagnosing Su Bingtian's final 9.98 s with the target performance range of 9.89 s 9.80 s, the personalized Champion model is Su Bingtian's own semi-final 9.83 s; (d) for diagnosing Su Bingtian's semi-final 9.83 s with 9.82 s 9.70 s as the target performance interval, the selected personalized Champion model is Tyson Gay's 9.71 s in the final of the World Championships in Berlin in 2009 (age at that time was 27 years old, height was 180 cm, body weight was 75 kg).

3. In order to get the speed cadence improvement suggestion to improve the performance from 9.98 s to his 9.83 s Asian record, we adjusted the target performance interval to 9.89 s 9.80 s, and diagnosed the speed cadence of 9.98 s in his Tokyo Olympics final, and got the speed and displacement curves shown in Fig. 4(c), at this time, the improvement suggestion from this speed and displacement curves changed to: "Su should shorten the start acceleration time".
4. In order to get the speed cadence improvement suggestion to further improve the performance based on 9.83 s, the author also took 9.82 s 9.70 s as the target performance interval, and diagnosed his speed cadence of 9.83 s in the semi-final of Tokyo Olympic Games by repeating the above mentioned steps 1 to 5, and got the speed and displacement curves shown in Fig. 4(d). The recommendation for improvement obtained from this velocity and displacement curve is: "Su should increase his maximum velocity".

5 Conclusions and Future Work

5.1 Conclusions

In this paper, we proposed a case-based causal reasoning (CBCR) framework, which first generates causal knowledge from the case base based on Markov equivalence classes and structural equations, and then utilizes causal knowledge in all four reasoning processes, including retrieval, reuse, revise, and retain.

Based on this framework, we built an intelligent diagnostic system for 100-m sprint training. Both experiments based on real competition data from Chinese national team sprinters and the Bingtian Su's case from Tokyo Olympics showed that the CBCR framework is more in line with the small-scale and individualized nature of elite sport training and is able to suggest more practical solutions for performance enhancement.

5.2 Future Work

While we acknowledge that our current implementation of CBCR remains a preliminary proof of concept, as pointed out by the reviewers, we identify two key areas for future improvement:

1. **Limited evaluation:** Our current evaluation is based on only five cases, which is insufficient to support strong conclusions. To address this, we are continuing to follow national team athletes longitudinally. In addition, we have launched a web-based sprint pacing diagnosis tool powered by CBCR, which is helping us collect data from a broader range of users.
2. **Limited integration of causal knowledge in the *revise* and *retain* steps:** At present, the role of causal knowledge in the *revise* and *retain* stages of CBCR is still underdeveloped. In future work, we plan to enhance the causal *revise* process by incorporating human-AI collaborative causal inference, enabling iterative communication with coaches. We also aim to improve the causal *retain* process by introducing time-series-based causal inference to support the creation of longitudinal digital twins for athletes.

Funding Information. This work was supported by the Project 24-18 Supported by the Fundamental Research Funds for the China Institute of Sport Science and the National Natural Science Foundation of China (Grant No. 62106159).

References

1. Aamodt, A., Plaza, E.: Case-based reasoning: foundational issues, methodological variations, and system approaches. AI Commun. **7**, 39–59 (1994)
2. Portinale, L.: Integrating kNN retrieval with inference on graphical models in case-based reasoning. In: Recio-Garcia, J.A., Orozco-del-Castillo, M.G., Bridge, D. (eds.) Case-Based Reasoning Research and Development, pp. 1–16. Springer, Cham (2024). https://doi.org/10.1007/978-3-031-63646-2_1

3. Feely, C., Caulfield, B., Lawlor, A., Smyth, B.: Using case-based reasoning to predict marathon performance and recommend tailored training plans. In: Watson, I., Weber, R. (eds.) ICCBR 2020. LNCS (LNAI), vol. 12311, pp. 67–81. Springer, Cham (2020). https://doi.org/10.1007/978-3-030-58342-2_5
4. Feely, C., Caulfield, B., Lawlor, A., Smyth, B.: A case-based reasoning approach to predicting and explaining running related injuries. In: Sánchez-Ruiz, A.A., Floyd, M.W. (eds.) ICCBR 2021. LNCS (LNAI), vol. 12877, pp. 79–93. Springer, Cham (2021). https://doi.org/10.1007/978-3-030-86957-1_6
5. Feely, C., Caulfield, B., Lawlor, A., Smyth, B.: An extended case-based approach to race-time prediction for recreational marathon runners. In: Keane, M.T., Wiratunga, N. (eds.) Case-Based Reasoning Research and Development, pp. 335–349. Springer, Cham (2022). https://doi.org/10.1007/978-3-031-14923-8_22
6. Feely, C., Caulfield, B., Lawlor, A., Smyth, B.: A case-based reasoning approach to post-injury training recommendations for marathon runners. In: Recio-Garcia, J.A., Orozco-del-Castillo, M.G., Bridge, D. (eds.) Case-Based Reasoning Research and Development, pp. 338–353. Springer, Cham (2024). https://doi.org/10.1007/978-3-031-63646-2_22
7. Mann, R.: The mechanics of sprinting and hurdling (2015)
8. Healy, R., Kenny, I.C., Harrison, A.J.: Profiling elite male 100-m sprint performance: the role of maximum velocity and relative acceleration. J. Sport Health Sci. **11**, 75–84 (2022). https://doi.org/10.1016/j.jshs.2019.10.002
9. Su, B., Deng, M., Xu, Z., Liang, W., Jiang, Z., Wang, G.: New Era Chinese Men's 100m Sprint: Review and Prospect, China Sport Science (Chinese Version), vol. 39, pp. 22–28 (2019)
10. Pearl, J.: Causality (2009)
11. Cui, D., Guo, J., Liu, P., Zhang, X.: Using case-based causal reasoning to provide explainable counterfactual diagnosis in personalized sprint training. In: Case-Based Reasoning Research and Development, pp. 418–429. Springer, Cham (2024). https://doi.org/10.1007/978-3-031-63646-2_27
12. Thomas, T.R., Zebas, C.J., Bahrke, M.S., Araujo, J., Etheridge, G.L.: Physiological and psychological correlates of success in track and field athletes (1983). https://doi.org/10.1136/bjsm.17.2.102
13. Haugen, T., McGhie, D., Ettema, G.: Sprint running: from fundamental mechanics to practice—a review. Eur. J. Appl. Physiol. **119**, 1273–1287 (2019). https://doi.org/10.1007/s00421-019-04139-0
14. Abbiss, C.R., Laursen, P.B.: Describing and understanding pacing strategies during athletic competition. Sports Med. **38**, 239–252 (2008). https://doi.org/10.2165/00007256-200838030-00004
15. Tucker, R., Noakes, T.D.: The physiological regulation of pacing strategy during exercise: a critical review (2009). https://doi.org/10.1136/bjsm.2009.057562
16. Locatelli, E., Arsac, L.: The mechanics and energetics of the 100m sprint. New Stud. Athletics **10**, 81 (1995)
17. Mackala, K.: Optimisation of performance through kinematic analysis of the different phases of the 100 metres. New Stud. Athletics **22**, 7 (2007)
18. Morgenroth, T., Ryan, M.K., Peters, K.: The motivational theory of role modeling: How role models influence role aspirants' goals. Rev. Gen. Psychol. **19**, 465–483 (2015)
19. Chen, X., et al.: PlayBest: professional basketball player behavior synthesis via planning with diffusion. In: Proceedings of the 33rd ACM International Conference on Information and Knowledge Management, Boise, ID, USA, pp. 4406–4413. ACM (2024). https://doi.org/10.1145/3627673.3680092

20. Chang, K.-S., Wang, W.-Y., Peng, W.-C.: Where will players move next? Dynamic graphs and hierarchical fusion for movement forecasting in badminton. In: Proceedings of the AAAI Conference on Artificial Intelligence, vol. 37, pp. 6998–7005 (2023). https://doi.org/10.1609/aaai.v37i6.25855
21. Li, Y., Ma, R., Gonçalves, B., Gong, B., Cui, Y., Shen, Y.: Data-driven team ranking and match performance analysis in Chinese Football Super League. Chaos Solitons Fractals **141**, 110330 (2020)
22. Mann, R.V.: System and method for teaching physical skills (1993). https://patents.google.com/patent/US5184295A/en
23. Glymour, C., Zhang, K., Spirtes, P.: Review of causal discovery methods based on graphical models. Front. Genet. **10**, 524 (2019)
24. Spirtes, P., Glymour, C.: An algorithm for fast recovery of sparse causal graphs. Soc. Sci. Comput. Rev. **9**, 62–72 (1991). https://doi.org/10.1177/089443939100900106
25. Goldberger, A.S.: Structural equation methods in the social sciences (1972)
26. Pearl, J., Glymour, M., Jewell, N.P.: Causal inference in statistics: a primer (2016)
27. Delaney, E., Greene, D., Keane, M.T.: Instance-based counterfactual explanations for time series classification. In: Sánchez-Ruiz, A.A., Floyd, M.W. (eds.) ICCBR 2021. LNCS (LNAI), vol. 12877, pp. 32–47. Springer, Cham (2021). https://doi.org/10.1007/978-3-030-86957-1_3
28. Warren, G., Smyth, B., Keane, M.T.: "Better" counterfactuals, ones people can understand: psychologically-plausible case-based counterfactuals using categorical features for explainable AI (XAI). In: Keane, M.T., Wiratunga, N. (eds.) Case-Based Reasoning Research and Development, pp. 63–78. Springer, Cham (2022). https://doi.org/10.1007/978-3-031-14923-8_5
29. Cui, D., Jiang, Z.: A champion model of men's 100m sprint based on functional data analysis. In: 2021 IEEE 6th International Conference on Big Data Analytics (ICBDA), pp. 103–107. IEEE (2021)
30. Sun, K., Xiao, B., Liu, D., Wang, J.: Deep high-resolution representation learning for human pose estimation. In: Proceedings of the IEEE/CVF Conference on Computer Vision and Pattern Recognition, pp. 5693–5703 (2019)
31. Viswanathan, M., Viswanathan, M.: Measuring speech quality for text-to-speech systems: development and assessment of a modified mean opinion score (MOS) scale. Comput. Speech Lang. **19**, 55–83 (2005)

Representing Expert Reasoning Experience by Process Cases - Application to the Delimitation of Mobile Genetic Elements in Bacterial Chromosomes

Toufik Hamadouche[1,2(✉)], Gérard Guédon[2], Nathalie Leblond-Bourget[2], Jean Lieber[1], and Thibaud Limbach[3]

[1] Université de Lorraine, CNRS, LORIA, 54000 Nancy, France
toufik.hamadouche@univ-lorraine.fr
[2] Université de Lorraine, INRAE, DynAMic, 54000 Nancy, France
[3] Université de Lorraine, Télécom Nancy, 54000 Nancy, France

Abstract. Delimiting mobile genetic elements (MGEs) in bacterial genomes traditionally relies on experts in biology. This paper presents a process-oriented case-based reasoning (PO-CBR) approach to formalize and automate expert reasoning for MGE delimitation. In this study, expert knowledge is represented by process cases, where each case follows an ordered stepwise reasoning process based on genomic data on MGEs. These cases form adaptive computational workflows that can be applied to various types of bacterial strains and MGEs. A key feature of this approach is an adaptive mechanism that allows reasoning failures to trigger automatic adaptation rules. Tested on 254 manually annotated MGEs across 124 bacterial genomes, our approach successfully delimited 96.8% of these elements with high accuracy. This study demonstrates the feasibility of encoding biological expertise into a structured automated reasoning system that offers a reliable alternative to identify MGEs in bacterial genomes.

Keywords: PO-CBR · application to genomics · identification of mobile genetic elements · knowledge representation · expert reasoning

1 Introduction

Case-Based Reasoning (CBR [1]) uses previous experience to solve new problems. This past experience is represented by a case base, where a case represents a particular problem solving experience. Process-oriented CBR (PO-CBR [2,3]) is the subfield of CBR in which the cases represent processes.

In this article, problem solving experience is represented by *process cases*, in the spirit of PO-CBR, and is applied to a microbiological problem, namely the delimitation of *Mobile Genetic Elements* (MGEs) in bacterial chromosomes.[1]

[1] In microbiology, "bacterium" refers to a single bacterial cell, while "bacteria" is the plural form, referring to a population or group of bacterial cells.

© The Author(s), under exclusive license to Springer Nature Switzerland AG 2025
I. Bichindaritz and B. López (Eds.): ICCBR 2025, LNAI 15662, pp. 392–406, 2025.
https://doi.org/10.1007/978-3-031-96559-3_26

An MGE is a DNA sequence of a bacterial chromosome capable of moving from one bacterium to another one. Using process cases to describe each step of the delimitation of MGEs, this approach enables the precise identification of genomic boundaries and provides an understanding of the complex dynamics of MGE integration within bacterial genomes. Many bacterial chromosomes harbor MGEs, including ICEs (Integrative Conjugative Elements) and IMEs (Integrative Mobilizable Elements) that are able to disseminate between bacteria in contact. ICEs and IMEs possess the requisite functions for their own transfer from one bacterium to another. They also encode a variety of functions, including virulence factors and resistance mechanisms to antibiotics [4]. Consequently, precise delimitation of these elements is crucial, particularly because it contributes to the study of bacterial resistance to antibiotics and to the fight against this major public health issue.

This study aims to capture the criteria and reasoning of an expert biologist to accurately identify the boundaries of these mobile genetic elements. This expert has noted, in an informal way, the experience of reasoning in identifying the genomic boundaries of these mobile elements within genomes. These reasonings follow a series of steps based on specific genomic characteristics to precisely delimit these elements. These processes are the result of extensive experience and observations, which have led to manual delimitation of numerous mobile elements located in various bacterial genomes [5,6].

The article is organized as follows. Section 2 introduces the key concepts and terminologies of CBR and, in particular, PO-CBR, with a toy application to the representation of expert reasoning experience, in order to present some of the main ideas without the biological background. Section 3 presents the necessary biological notions to understand MGEs and their delimitation in bacterial genomes. Section 4 presents the methodology used for acquiring and modeling process cases, which form the foundation of the proposed approach to MGE delimitation. It appears that some cases can be simply applied, without modification, to various MGE delimitation problems, and such applications give correct outcomes. For some other problems, there are process cases that cannot be applied as such but can be adapted in order to correctly solve these problems: this issue of adaptation of process cases for this application is an ongoing work that is presented in Sect. 5. Section 6 presents the evaluation of the approach, and Sect. 7 concludes the article with ongoing developments and future work.

2 Process-Oriented Case-Based Reasoning and its Application to the Representation of Expert Reasoning Experience

This section presents first notions and notations about CBR and PO-CBR and then discusses how the modeling of cases in PO-CBR can be used to capture expert reasoning experience through a simple mathematical example.

2.1 Preliminaries on CBR and PO-CBR

The CBR aims to solve problems using the experience of the past represented by *case base* CB. A case from CB –or *source case*– usually represents a specific episode of problem solving: from a *source problem* x^s it associates a solution y^s to x^s. Therefore, a case contains in its description x^s, y^s, and sometimes additional pieces of information (not detailed here). So, such a source case is denoted by an ordered pair $(\mathrm{x}^s, \mathrm{y}^s)$.

The CBR process model considered in this article is composed of single case retrieval (selection of a $(\mathrm{x}^s, \mathrm{y}^s) \in \mathtt{CB}$ similar to the problem to be solved, the *target problem* $\mathrm{x}^{\mathrm{tgt}}$) and adaptation of $(\mathrm{x}^s, \mathrm{y}^s)$ to solve $\mathrm{x}^{\mathrm{tgt}}$. Sometimes, y^s can be reused as such to solve $\mathrm{x}^{\mathrm{tgt}}$, as illustrated in Sect. 2.2: the term used in this article is *application* (preferred here to the term null adaptation, since some substitutions may occur, which are completely determined by the change in problems).

If $(\mathrm{x}^s, \mathrm{y}^s)$ is not applicable to solve $\mathrm{x}^{\mathrm{tgt}}$ then it may be reused nonetheless if it is adaptable. Adaptation may be based on *adaptation rules.* Such a rule often takes the form $(\Delta\mathrm{x}, \Delta\mathrm{y})$ where $\Delta\mathrm{x}$ (resp. $\Delta\mathrm{y}$) represents the variation from a problem to another (resp. from a solution to another) and is interpreted as follows: if the variation from x^s to $\mathrm{x}^{\mathrm{tgt}}$ instantiates $\Delta\mathrm{x}$, then the variation from y^s to $\mathrm{y}^{\mathrm{tgt}}$ instantiates $\Delta\mathrm{y}$, and so $\mathrm{y}^{\mathrm{tgt}}$ can be computed by applying $\Delta\mathrm{y}$ on y^s.

Process-oriented CBR is CBR where the cases are *process cases*, i.e. they contain processes in their representations. To be precise, in this article, for a process case $(\mathrm{x}^s, \mathrm{y}^s)$, the problem x^s represents some parameters, and the solution y^s is a process based on these parameters. The *outcome* of a case $(\mathrm{x}^s, \mathrm{y}^s)$ is the result o^s of the application of y^s to x^s.

2.2 Capturing Reasoning Experience in Process Cases

Let us consider the experience of a student learning to compute limits of real functions. Let $(\mathrm{x}^s, \mathrm{y}^s)$ be a process case in this domain defined semi-formally as follows:

- $\mathrm{x}^s = \left[\lim\limits_{x\to+\infty} \boxed{\dfrac{2x^3+3x}{6x^3-x^2+12}} = ?\right]$;
- y^s is the sequence of the following steps:
  1. According to the theorem telling that a real polynomial function is asymptotically equivalent in $+\infty$ to its highest term, $\boxed{2x^3+3x} \underset{x\to+\infty}{\sim} \boxed{2x^3}$.
  2. According to the same theorem, $\boxed{6x^3-x^2+12} \underset{x\to+\infty}{\sim} \boxed{6x^3}$.
  3. According to the theorem that tells that if $f_1(x) \underset{x\to+\infty}{\sim} f_2(x)$ and $g_1(x) \underset{x\to+\infty}{\sim} g_2(x)$ then $\frac{f_1(x)}{g_1(x)} \underset{x\to+\infty}{\sim} \frac{f_2(x)}{g_2(x)}$, from steps 1 and 2, it follows that $\boxed{\dfrac{2x^3+3x}{6x^3-x^2+12} \underset{x\to+\infty}{\sim} \dfrac{2x^3}{6x^3}}$.

4. Since $\boxed{\dfrac{2x^3}{6x^3} = \dfrac{1}{3}}$, it follows that $\lim\limits_{x\to+\infty} \boxed{\dfrac{2x^3+3x}{6x^3-x^2+12}} = \boxed{\dfrac{1}{3}}$.

Thus, the outcome is obtained by applying $\mathbf{y}^s$ on $\mathbf{x}^s$, to return $o^s = \frac{1}{3}$. It can be noted that $\mathbf{y}^s$ could be represented by a more sophisticated workflow, indicating, for instance, that the order of steps 1 and 2 can be changed, but this is not discussed further there. In $\mathbf{y}^s$, some elements are $\boxed{\text{framed}}$: These are particular elements that could easily be generalized. For example, for the target problem $\mathbf{x}^{\mathtt{tgt}} = \left[\lim_{x\to+\infty} \boxed{\frac{5x^4+x^3-x+4}{x^4+2x^2+x}} = ?\right]$, $\mathbf{y}^s$ can be *applied* on $\mathbf{x}^{\mathtt{tgt}}$, simply changing the contents of the frames, to get a new outcome $o^{\mathtt{tgt}} = 5$. The way in which this case is reused is similar to replay (without adaptation) in case-based planning [7]: the same operations are applied to different states (or data).

Now, for some other target problems, the same reasoning process cannot be applied exactly. For instance, if $\mathbf{x}^{\mathtt{tgt}} = \left[\lim_{x\to+\infty} \boxed{\frac{3x+1}{2x^2-4}} = ?\right]$, all the steps of $\mathbf{y}^s$ can be applied except the last one, step 4, since $x \mapsto \frac{3}{2x}$ is not a constant function. However, the other steps can be replayed and the final step can be substituted with:

4′. Since $\boxed{\dfrac{3x}{2x^2} = \dfrac{3}{2x}}$, with $\boxed{3}$, a nonzero constant, and $\lim_{x\to+\infty} \boxed{2x} = +\infty$, it follows that $\lim\limits_{x\to+\infty} \boxed{\dfrac{3x+1}{2x^2-4}} = \boxed{0}$.

and this step substitution constitutes an adaptation of $\mathbf{y}^s$ to a solution $\mathbf{y}^{\mathtt{tgt}}$. Here, a difference between $\mathbf{x}^s$ and $\mathbf{x}^{\mathtt{tgt}}$ is pointed out by the failure to execute step 4: in $\mathbf{x}^s$, the polynomial functions at the numerator and denominator have the same degrees, but this does not hold for $\mathbf{x}^{\mathtt{tgt}}$, so some adaptation rules can be triggered to change step 4 and, in this example, an adaptation rule succeeds and replaces it with step 4′.

Of course, for $\mathbf{x}^{\mathtt{tgt}} = \left[\lim_{x\to-\infty} \boxed{e^x \sin x} = ?\right]$, and other target problems, this case $(\mathbf{x}^s, \mathbf{y}^s)$ is not easily adaptable.

In essence, these are the ideas that are reused for the application described in this paper, in the microbiology domain: a process case is constituted of steps that can be applied (or replayed as such) to solve some target problems and can be adapted to solve other target problems (but not all them).

3 Mobile Elements in Bacterial Genomes

This section introduces genomic concepts tailored to the needs of this article and designed to be easily understandable by non-biologists. There is a wide variety of biological and biochemical processes that makes it difficult to propose a theory that is general and operational for the delimitation of *mobile genomic elements*, but only the essential biological concepts necessary to understand the examples are presented here. It should be noted that this complexity and variety of biological processes motivate the use of CBR: each process case can be seen as a "local theory" in contrast to a "global theory" that would be applicable on any delimitation problem.

ICEs and *IMEs* are *DNA* segments that have the particularity of being integrated into bacterial *chromosomes.*[2]

ICEs and IMEs are conjugative mobile genetic elements integrated into bacterial genomes. They can excise from the chromosome and transfer from one bacterium to another via the phenomenon of bacterial conjugation.[3]

Like any part of bacterial chromosomes, these MGEs consist of two DNA strands twisted into a double helix. Each DNA strand consists of a sequence of nucleotides. Each nucleotide in DNA is one of the four types denoted by A, C, G and T. The set $\{\mathtt{A}, \mathtt{C}, \mathtt{G}, \mathtt{T}\}$ is the alphabet over which DNA sequences are formed. These nucleotides form complementary base pairs (A with T and C with G) linked by hydrogen bonds, as shown in Fig. 1. Within these DNA segments, specific sequences called *genes* are portions of DNA whose products are either *proteins* or various types of *RNA*.[4]

The DNA sequence and annotation of its genes for bacteria in question in this work are available in public genomic databases.

Similarly to other parts of the chromosome, ICEs and IMEs contain genes that encode proteins or RNA. Without going into biological details, it is important to note that RNA is composed of nucleotides with a 4 letter alphabet comparable to that of DNA. In contrast, proteins can be represented with an alphabet of 20 letters, each letter corresponding to an amino acid. Each amino acid can be encoded by one or several triplets of nucleotides, called codons. For example, the amino acid alanine is encoded by two codons: GCT and GCA.[5]

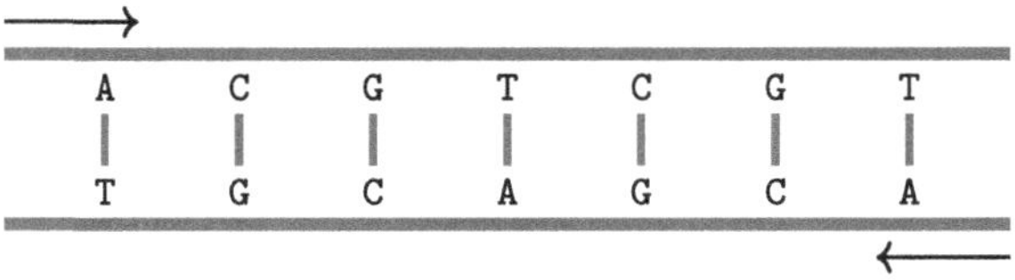

Fig. 1. Double-stranded DNA segment linked by hydrogen bonds between complementary base pairs. Arrows indicate strand orientations: forward strand (left to right), backward strand (opposite direction).

[2] ICEs transfer autonomously via bacterial conjugation, whereas IMEs require other mobile elements, such as ICEs, for their transfer.

[3] The transfer of DNA from one donor bacterium to another requires physical contact, which is defined as bacterial conjugation.

[4] The biochemical mechanism that, from a gene, produces a protein or a RNA is complex and its description is useless for understanding this article.

[5] The genetic code can be seen as the mapping from a codon to an amino acid. The fact that some amino acids can be coded by several codons is linked to the degeneracy of the genetic code.

To understand the process of delimitating these elements, it is useful to get an idea about how these mobile elements *excise* from the chromosomes and how they *integrate* back into them. Figure 2 illustrates the conjugative transfer process of an ICE from its excision in the donor bacterium A to its integration in the recipient bacterium B. The same process applies to IMEs.

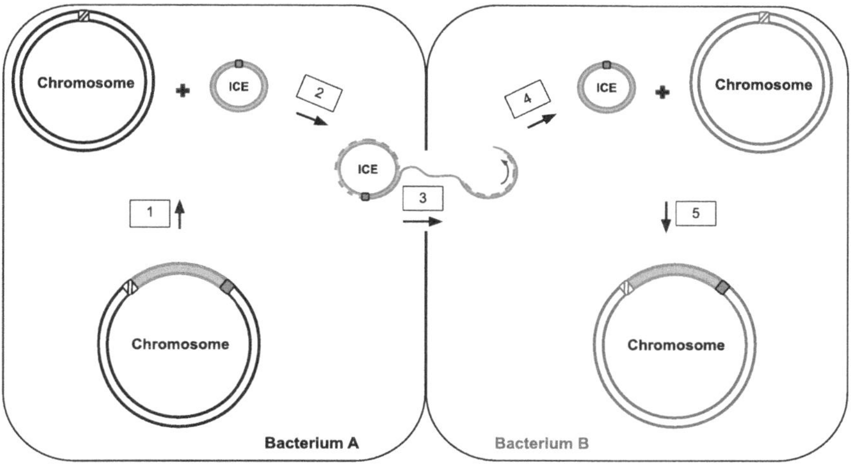

1 The integrated mobile element (gray area) is flanked by DRs (Direct Repeats) corresponding to its left and right ends (colored or hatched rectangles). It excises from the chromosome of the donor bacterium A as a double-stranded circular DNA sequence.
2 Both strands of the circular DNA element are unwound, with one strand being transferred to the recipient bacterium B. The remaining strand is replicated to form a double-stranded circular structure, which is reintegrated into the chromosome of donor bacterium A.
3 The single stranded DNA is transferred through the conjugation pore to the recipient bacterium B.
4 Immediately after transfer, the single stranded DNA is replicated and ligated to form a circular double-stranded molecule.
5 The mobile element integrates into bacterium B chromosome. It can later excise and transfer into another recipient bacterium chromosome. The strand of the mobile element left in the bacterium A is integrated back into the chromosome of bacterium A, according to steps similar to steps 4 and 5.

Fig. 2. Process for transferring an ICE from a donor bacterium A to a recipient bacterium B.

Among the proteins encoded by ICEs and IMEs, some are absolutely necessary for their transfer and are called *signature proteins*. In this work, signature protein-encoding genes are identified using the *ICEscreen* tool [8].[6] Signature proteins include *integrases* that play a fundamental role in the excision and integration processes of ICEs and IMEs. Integrase recognizes a specific DNA *insertion site* within a *target gene*, where it performs the integration of the corresponding mobile element.[7] Each mobile genetic element encodes several proteins, including an integrase. Each integrase specifically targets one insertion site, but multiple insertion sites and target genes may exist because of the diversity of integrases. The integration of ICEs and IMEs leads to the duplication of insertion site DNA sequence leading to the formation of *Direct Repeats* (DRs) as shown in Fig. 3, sequences that define the left and right boundaries of the integrated element (shown as small red or hatched rectangles in Fig. 2). Figure 4 summarizes the integration process of an ICE in the insertion site of its targeted gene, including the formation of its DRs.

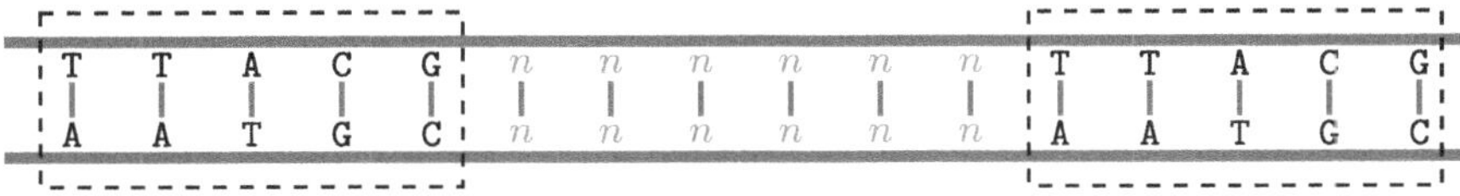

Fig. 3. Example of a mobile element flanked by two DRs (both with nucleotide sequence TTACG in dashed rectangles) with the mobile element DNA sequence being denoted by n, where $n \in \{\mathtt{A}, \mathtt{C}, \mathtt{G}, \mathtt{T}\}$).

Signature protein-encoding genes, target genes, and DRs can be identified on the bacterial chromosome using their genomic coordinates (the prefix `gc` in the identifiers indicates such genomic coordinates, e.g. `gcDR1` and `gcDR2`). Such a coordinate consists of three values: the binary value indicating the strand (forward strand / backward strand), a start index, and an end index that define the boundaries of the element within the chromosome. For example, `gci` refers to the genomic coordinates of the position of the integrase gene, and `gct` refers to those of the target gene.

Identification of DRs using the PO-CBR method allows for the accurate localization of this element within the bacterial chromosome, that is, identification of its DRs corresponds to determining its position in the genome.

4 Acquiring, Modeling and Representing Cases

The diversity of integrases and their insertion sites in target genes leads to a large variability of integration mechanisms. This complexity results in a diversity of

[6] ICEscreen is a bioinformatics tool that detects mobile elements (ICEs and IMEs) in bacterial genomes without defining their boundaries, while identifying the signature proteins associated with each detected element.

[7] It can be pointed out that the adjective "target" is used with two different meanings in this article: the one of CBR, where target problems $\mathbf{x}^{\text{tgt}}$ are encountered, and the one of genomics, with target genes. The context of use is supposed to help avoiding confusion.

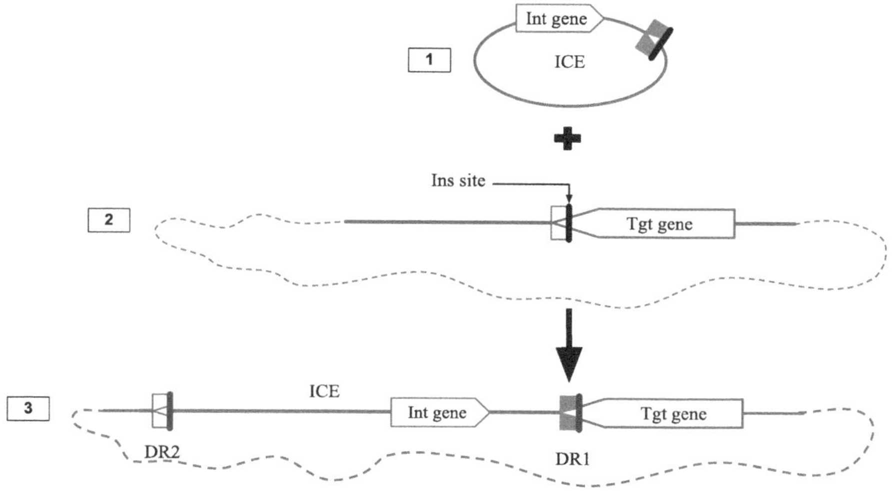

Abbreviations: **Int gene** for *Integrase gene* **Ins site** for *Insertion gene*
Tgt gene for *Target gene*
DR1 for *Direct Repeat 1* **DR2** for *Direct Repeat 2*

[1] The ICE is initially in its circular form, carrying an integrase gene (Int gene), which will mediate its integration.

[2] The bacterial DNA sequence contains a target gene (Tgt gene), on which is located the insertion site (Ins site), a specific sequence recognized by the ICE integrase.

[3] The ICE integrates into the target gene: the integrase recognizes the insertion site and catalyzes the integration of the ICE at the end of the target gene. This process replaces the interrupted blue segment (blue rectangle) of the target gene, located now on the left of the DNA segment, with the red sequence (red rectangle) carried by the ICE. As a result of this process, the mobile element is flanked between `DR1` and `DR2`.

Fig. 4. Mobile element integration process into the insertion site (ins site) of its target gene from a donor bacterium A to a recipient bacterium B.

processes for delimiting mobile elements in bacterial genomes. A microbiology expert has worked for years on these types of tasks, and this research aims at capitalizing his expertise. To do this, this expert relies on knowledge of the biological domain of mobile elements, such as knowledge about the biochemical processes involved, or the class hierarchies of integrases and target genes. To automate this delimitation task, his expertise is represented by process cases.

A process case includes a delimitation problem `x` and a process `y` to solve this problem. A delimitation problem `x` is formalized by 3 attributes:

- `idGenomes`: a set of identifiers of bacterial genomes each of them characterize a bacterial strain;
- `targetGeneClass`: the class of the target gene in which the mobile element integrates;
- `integraseClass`: the class of the integrase involved in the excision and integration processes (there exist 3 main classes of integrases: `Tyrosine`, `Serine` and `DDE`).

To illustrate the modeling of expertise, a process case is described, named `case1a` $= (\mathtt{x}^{1a}, \mathtt{y}^{1a})$. This case addresses the problem of specifically delimiting a mobile element that carries a `Tyrosine` integrase that targets the `tRNAleu_CAA` gene class on the chromosome of the bacterial strain `NC_017678`, where the integration process of this mobile element is illustrated in Fig. 4. The delimitation problem $\mathtt{x}^{1a}$ for `case1a` is therefore defined by

$$\mathtt{x}^{1a} = \left| \begin{array}{ll} \mathtt{idGenomes} & = \{\mathtt{NC\_017678}\} \\ \mathtt{targetGeneClass} & = \mathtt{tRNAleu\_CAA} \\ \mathtt{integraseClass} & = \mathtt{Tyrosine} \end{array} \right.$$

After having defined the problem, the expert establishes a structured reasoning process with ordered steps and uses knowledge about the mobile element to identify its left and right boundaries. This expert knowledge includes, in particular, the element's integration position in the target gene[8] and the potential length of the DRs.[9] The first 3 steps of the delimitation process $\mathtt{y}^{1a}$ are: (1) identifying `Tyrosine` integrase genes in the bacterial genome as returned by ICEscreen, (2) locating the target gene `tRNAleu_CAA` in the genomic annotations of the genome analyzed, and (3) selecting only those `tRNAleu_CAA` genes separated by a maximum of 7 genes between the `Tyrosine` integrase and the `tRNAleu_CAA` genes. The whole process is detailed in Fig. 5.

The process $\mathtt{y}^{1a}$ associated with `case1a` is represented by a Python program that can be applied to any delimitation problem $\mathtt{x}^{\mathtt{tgt}}$. The application of $\mathtt{y}^{1a}$ to $\mathtt{x}^{\mathtt{tgt}}$ may result in a failure: the reasoning process of `case1a` does not apply to $\mathtt{x}^{\mathtt{tgt}}$. Otherwise, it returns a set of tuples $(\mathtt{gci}, \mathtt{gct}, \mathtt{gcDR1}, \mathtt{gcDR2})$ indicating the delimitation of a mobile element: it provides the genomic coordinates of the integrase and the target gene involved in the integration of the mobile element, as well as the genomic coordinates of its boundaries `gcDR1` and `gcDR2`.

Now, let us consider the following two delimitation problems:

$$\mathtt{x}^{1b} = \left| \begin{array}{ll} \mathtt{idGenomes} & = \{\mathtt{NC\_022236}\} \\ \mathtt{targetGeneClass} & = \mathtt{tRNAleu\_CAA} \\ \mathtt{integraseClass} & = \mathtt{Tyrosine} \end{array} \right. \quad \mathtt{x}^{1c} = \left| \begin{array}{ll} \mathtt{idGenomes} & = \{\mathtt{NC\_017567}\} \\ \mathtt{targetGeneClass} & = \mathtt{tRNAleu\_CAA} \\ \mathtt{integraseClass} & = \mathtt{Tyrosine} \end{array} \right.$$

[8] Roughly said, this position can be the start of the target gene, the end of it, or somewhere in the middle.

[9] For example, according to the expert, this potential length is of 53 nucleotides when the target gene class is `tRNAleu_CAA`, the integrase class is `Tyrosine` and the integration takes place at the end of the target gene. This value can be explained by biochemical mechanisms.

They only differ from $\mathtt{x}^{1a}$ by the attribute `idGenomes` and the bacterial strains identified in these 3 problems are similar (from a genomic viewpoint[10]). So, if $\mathtt{x}^{1b}$ and $\mathtt{x}^{1c}$ were considered as target problems, then $(\mathtt{x}^{1a}, \mathtt{y}^{1a})$ can be selected by case retrieval for both of them. Therefore, it is reasonable to try to apply `case1a` to these two new problems, that is, to execute the Python program $\mathtt{y}^{1a}$ on $\mathtt{x}^{1b}$ and $\mathtt{x}^{1c}$. It appears that these executions do not cause any failure and therefore suggest the delimitation of mobile elements in bacterial strains `NC_022236` and `NC_017567`. This coincides with the process proposed by the expert; therefore, two new cases `case1b` $= (\mathtt{x}^{1b}, \mathtt{y}^{1b})$ and `case1c` $= (\mathtt{x}^{1c}, \mathtt{y}^{1c})$ are created with $\mathtt{y}^{1b} = \mathtt{y}^{1c} = \mathtt{y}^{1a}$.

Then, the 3 specific cases `case1a`, `case1b` and `case1c` can be "gathered" in a generalized case `case1` $= (\mathtt{x}^1, \mathtt{y}^1)$ with:[11]

$$\mathtt{x}^1 = \left| \begin{array}{ll} \mathtt{idGenomes} & = \{\mathtt{NC\_017678}, \mathtt{NC\_022236}, \mathtt{NC\_017567}\} \\ \mathtt{targetGeneClass} & = \mathtt{tRNAleu\_CAA} \\ \mathtt{integraseClass} & = \mathtt{Tyrosine} \end{array} \right. \qquad \mathtt{y}^1 = \mathtt{y}^{1a}$$

Now, it appears that for some delimitation problems $\mathtt{x}^{\mathtt{tgt}}$ the case `case1` $= (\mathtt{x}^1, \mathtt{y}^1)$ cannot be *applied*, but it can be *adapted* by the expert to solve $\mathtt{x}^{\mathtt{tgt}}$. This adaptation issue is an ongoing work that is presented in the next section.

5 Towards Case Adaptation

Let $\mathtt{x}^{\mathtt{tgt}} = \left| \begin{array}{ll} \mathtt{idGenomes} & = \{\mathtt{NC\_022277}\} \\ \mathtt{targetGeneClass} & = \mathtt{rpsI} \\ \mathtt{integraseClass} & = \mathtt{Tyrosine} \end{array} \right.$ be a delimitation problem. This problem is similar to $\mathtt{x}^1$, the problem part of `case1`, because $\mathtt{x}^1$ and $\mathtt{x}^{\mathtt{tgt}}$ have the same integrase class and because the bacterial strains of $\mathtt{x}^1$ are similar to the bacterial strain of $\mathtt{x}^{\mathtt{tgt}}$. These problems differ essentially because they have different target gene classes. Therefore, `case1` $= (\mathtt{x}^1, \mathtt{y}^1)$ can be returned by the retrieval process.

The application of $\mathtt{y}^1$ from `case1` (presented in Sect. 4 and in the flowchart of Fig. 5) on $\mathtt{x}^{\mathtt{tgt}}$ results in a failure (`failure4`): the outcome (`Outcome` in the flowchart) is empty. This failure is associated with an explanation labeled by the following message:

```
"Failure in the process of finding DRs - no identical DRs.
 Potential reason of the failure:
 the target gene class rpsI is of 'protein type',
 not of 'RNA type'."
```

[10] More precisely, it means that these three bacterial strains are close according to a phylogenetic classification, meaning that they have a close common ancestor.

[11] The notion of generalized case has been described in [9], with the idea of cases representing subset of the case space instead of single points of this space. Here, this notion is used in a slightly different way, since there is no learning process involved (or only rote learning): cases with similar problems and the same solution are simply gathered.

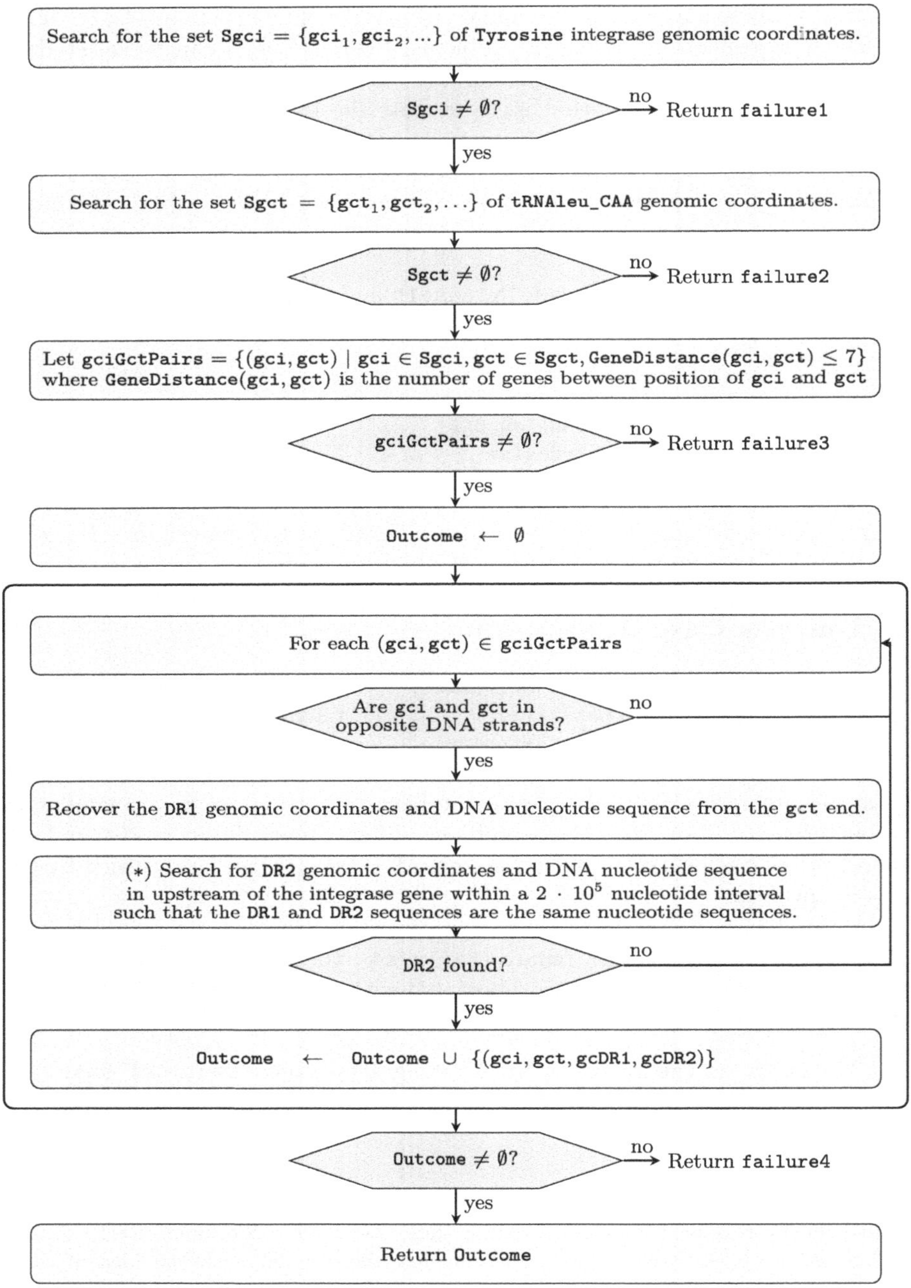

Fig. 5. Flowchart of the reasoning process y^1 of `case1` $= (x^1, y^1)$.

indicating that no pair (DR1, DR2) has been detected that is identical to nucleotide sequences. It also gives a potential explanation that points out a difference Δx between x^1 and x^{tgt}: for the former, the target gene class is an RNA type, for the latter, it is of protein type.

It must be noted that when the target gene is of RNA type, as in case1, the matching of DRs must be performed at the nucleotide level (i.e. within the $\{A, C, G, T\}$ alphabet), while when the target gene is of protein type (as in x^{tgt}), the matching must be done at the amino acid level. It can be recalled that if two nucleotide sequences match exactly, then their corresponding amino acid sequences also do. However, the converse does not necessarily hold. This is what occurs here: Fig. 6 shows two DR sequences, DR1 and DR2, that do not match at the nucleotide level (since $T \neq C$) but match at the amino acid level. The amino acid F (for Phenylalanine) is encoded by the two codons TTT and TTC according to the genetic code.

	DRs in nucleotides		**DRs in amino acids**
DR1:	**ATG GCT TTT CGA**	**translation into** →	**M A F R**
	⋆		
DR2:	**ATG GCT TTC CGA**	**amino acids**	**M A F R**
	Non-identical nucleotide sequences		*Identical amino acid sequences*

Fig. 6. Comparison between DR1 and DR2 in nucleotides and their corresponding amino acid sequences. The ⋆ marks a nucleotide difference.

So, the proposed adaptation consists of substituting the sequence matching at the nucleotide level with a sequence matching at the amino acid level. This means that the variation Δy to be applied on y^1 to obtain the solution y^{tgt} consists in modifying the process step of Fig. 5 that is marked with a $(*)$ by replacing the end of the sentence ("... are the same nucleotide sequences.") with "... are the same amino acid sequences." (this is done, in practice, by replacing Python instructions).

In this approach to modeling case processes, failures encountered during reasoning are not discarded but are systematically associated with explanations labeled with messages. These explanations fulfill two purposes. First, together with the reasoning traces, they make explicit the reasoning steps for the human user. Second, —and this is what is important here—, they are used to trigger adaptation rules $(\Delta x, \Delta y)$: if this explanation (expressed in a formal language) entails Δx then such a rule proposes a modification Δy of the process to get a new process.

For this particular target problem x^{tgt}, the adapted solution y^{tgt} gives the desired outcome: two DRs are matched at the amino acid level, which is sufficient since the target gene class of the target problem, rpsI, is of protein type. The effectiveness of these adaptation mechanisms is still being evaluated. Future work focuses on formalizing these adaptation rules and evaluating their generalization to different cases.

The knowledge acquisition issue of adaptation rules also needs to be studied. The adaptation rules that have been acquired so far emerged by considering failures that are narrowly missed successes, i.e. when a simple change on the retrieved case would correctly solve the target problem. This is the situation that has occurred for the example developed above: the application of $(\mathtt{x}^1, \mathtt{y}^1)$ fails on $\mathtt{x}^{\mathtt{tgt}}$ but the simple change of the matching function on sequences (from nucleotide sequence matching to amino acid sequence matching) makes this work. An alternative solution would have been to define a new case $(\mathtt{x}^{\mathtt{tgt}}, \mathtt{y}^{\mathtt{tgt}})$ and add it to the case base: this was, in fact, the initial choice. But the thing is that this adaptation pattern has occurred several times and could reoccur in the future, so it has been chosen to represent this by an adaptation rule.

Currently, adaptation rules are represented as Python procedures that are triggered by failures.

It is planned for future work to study further such adaptation rules: how they can be acquired, formalized and whether they can be considered as the application of general adaptation patterns which could be reused in other applications of PO-CBR.

6 Implementation and Evaluation of the Approach

As explained previously, expert knowledge was formalized into process cases to structure the reasoning behind MGE delimitation. Initially, the expert provided 291 informal cases (as text and spreadsheet files), each corresponding to a distinct MGE to be delimited. To address these delimitation problems, a subset of 37 process cases has been formalized, constituting the case base (CB).

The 37 source cases were chosen based on a diversity criterion on biological features to cover multiple MGE integration mechanisms. The aim is to maximize generalization by selecting the set CB which will be able to handle the remaining $291 - 37 = 254$ informal cases, which constitute the *test base* (TB). The intuition behind this is to choose CB so that its coverage is large, in order to solve a large proportion of the MGE delimitation problems, this notion of coverage being borrowed to the field of case base maintenance (see e.g. [10]).

Once CB is implemented, a retrieval mechanism identifies the most relevant process case for a new delimitation problem $\mathtt{x}^{\mathtt{tgt}}$. The selection of a $(\mathtt{x}^s, \mathtt{y}^s) \in$ CB similar to the target problem to be solved $(\mathtt{x}^{\mathtt{tgt}})$ is based on the similarity between the attributes given in the delimitation problem of $\mathtt{x}^s$ and $\mathtt{x}^{\mathtt{tgt}}$ (see Sect. 4). A process case is considered applicable if all the processing steps of $\mathtt{y}^s$ can be applied on $\mathtt{x}^{\mathtt{tgt}}$. To validate this approach, the CBR system with this case base was tested on the 254 MGEs of TB. The test base TB includes previously published MGEs [5,6].

The system successfully delimited 246 elements (96.8%) with great precision, while 8 (3.2%) failed for reasons not related to the case base. In fact, the main limitation of the system lies in its dependence on external genomic annotations, particularly from the ICEscreen tool and public databases. The 8 problems for which the system currently fails were due to missing target gene annotations, with some genes poorly annotated or absent from biological databases. These are the only limitations identified on the test base. It is noteworthy that without the simple adaptation process that has been implemented, the error rate would be of 6.8% instead of 3.2%.

This approach integrates structured reasoning and specific knowledge, allowing the identification of MGEs that are not detected or misidentified by current methods. It also ensures high precision in determining their exact genomic limits (DRs). Implemented in Python, process cases ensure flexibility and adaptability, with adaptation rules embedded in object classes, triggered by failure messages when necessary. Finally, the approach integrates explanations to the user (displaying the reasoning trace and the message of potential failures) in addition to the explanations used to trigger adaptation rules.

7 Conclusion

Process-oriented case-based reasoning (PO-CBR) has already been applied in various fields, including biology, where it has shown promising results [11]. This work presents the applicability of PO-CBR to a specific biological challenge: the delimitation of mobile genetic elements (MGEs) in bacterial chromosomes. By structuring expert knowledge into process cases, a complex reasoning task that until now relied only on human expertise has been automated. The implemented approach retrieves and applies process cases based on problem similarity while incorporating adaptive modifications when necessary.

This approach has already shown excellent accuracy in the delimitation of MGEs when applied to bacterial strains within the Bacillota group. These results are particularly promising in terms of genomic precision for MGE delimitation, as the method determines their exact genomic limits and provides explanations of the reasoning process followed. This approach ensures a precise and transparent delimitation, when compared to other existing methods (a comprehensive comparison between these bioinformatics approaches in beyond the scope of this article).

This application shows how PO-CBR principles can be used successfully when the expert knowledge is difficult to represent as one global theory but simpler to apprehend as a set of local operational theories (represented by process cases).

Future goals include applying this approach to other bacterial groups other than Bacillota and, if necessary, adapting it to new classes of mobile elements. In parallel, efforts will focus on additional tasks, particularly in acquisition of adaptation rules and case formalization. Additionally, to enable the system to manage a wider variety of delimitation problems not initially covered by the case base, the triggering and extension of adaptation rules will be improved. One of the main challenges will be to balance the need to expand the knowledge base with new cases and incorporate new adaptation rules. Furthermore, initial failures due to external data limitations will be addressed by identifying more comprehensive data sources.

Currently, process cases are represented as Python files; this will be improved by introducing a graphical representation, enabling intuitive modification and exporting cases to Python for execution. This may also be useful for a more abstract representation of adaptation rules, considering these rules at the graph level. Domain-specific knowledge constraints will be integrated to ensure that case reuse respects biological constraints, a principle that could be extended to other domains that require decision making under domain-specific constraints. This approach makes it possible to create systems that are more robust, adaptive, and explainable, applicable not only to genomics but also to other areas of complex problem solving requiring faithful formalization of expertise.

References

1. Riesbeck, C.K., Schank, R.C.: Inside Case-Based Reasoning. Lawrence Erlbaum Associates Inc, Hillsdale, New Jersey (1989)
2. Minor, M., Montani, S., Recio-García, J.A.: Process-oriented case-based reasoning. Inf. Syst. **40**, 103–105 (2014)
3. Müller, G., Bergmann, R.: Generalization of workflows in process-oriented case-based reasoning. In: Russell, I., Eberle, W. (eds.) Proceedings of the 28th International Florida Artificial Intelligence Research Society Conference (FLAIRS-28), pp. 391–396, Hollywood, Florida, USA (2015). AAAI Press
4. Bellanger, X., Payot, S., Leblond-Bourget, N., Guédon, G.: Conjugative and mobilizable genomic islands in bacteria: evolution and diversity. FEMS Microbiol. Rev. **38**(4), 720–760 (2014)
5. Ambroset, C., et al.: New insights into the classification and integration specificity of streptococcus integrative conjugative elements through extensive genome exploration. Front. Microbiol. **6**, 1483 (2015)
6. Coluzzi, C., et al.: A Glimpse into the world of integrative and mobilizable elements in streptococci reveals an unexpected diversity and novel families of mobilization proteins. Front. Microbiol. **8**, 443 (2017). Publisher: Frontiers
7. Veloso, M.M. (ed.): : Analogical replay. In: Planning and Learning by Analogical Reasoning. LNCS, vol. 886, pp. 111–139. Springer, Heidelberg (1994). https://doi.org/10.1007/3-540-58811-6_7
8. Lao, J., et al.: ICEscreen: a tool to detect Firmicute ICEs and IMEs, isolated or enclosed in composite structures. NAR Genomics Bioinform. **4**(4), lqac079 (2022)
9. Maximini, K., Maximini, R., Bergmann, R.: An Investigation of Generalized Cases. In: Ashley, K.D., Bridge, D.G. (eds.) ICCBR 2003. LNCS (LNAI), vol. 2689, pp. 261–275. Springer, Heidelberg (2003). https://doi.org/10.1007/3-540-45006-8_22
10. Smyth, B.: Case-base maintenance. In: Pasqual del Pobil, A., Mira, J., Ali, M. (eds.) IEA/AIE 1998. LNCS, vol. 1416, pp. 507–516. Springer, Heidelberg (1998). https://doi.org/10.1007/3-540-64574-8_436
11. Halioui, A., Valtchev, P., Diallo, A.B.: Bioinformatic workflow extraction from scientific texts based on word sense disambiguation. IEEE/ACM Trans. Comput. Biol. Bioinf. **15**(6), 1979–1990 (2018)

Clinical Decision Support for Skin Tumor Treatment: A Case-Based Reasoning Approach

Martin Kuhn[1(✉)], Yannik Warnecke[2], Daniel Preciado-Marquez[2], Joscha Grüger[1,3], Laura Isabell Bley[4], Michael Storck[2], Carsten Weishaupt[4], Ralph Bergmann[1,3], and Stephan Alexander Braun[5]

[1] German Research Center for Artificial Intelligence (DFKI), Trier, Germany
martin.kuhn@dfki.de
[2] Institute of Medical Informatics, University of Münster, Münster, Germany
[3] Business Information Systems II, Trier University, Trier, Germany
[4] Department of Dermatology, University Clinic Müenster, Müenster, Germany
[5] Department of Dermatology, Medical Faculty, Heinrich Heine University, Düsseldorf, Germany

Abstract. Cancer treatment planning is a complex and individualized process due to the variability of patient-specific factors, tumor characteristics, and evolving medical standards. Predicting the next step in diagnosis or therapy remains a significant challenge, due to the high variability and limited availability of structured medical data. Clinical Decision Support Systems (CDSS) offer a promising solution, with Case-Based Reasoning (CBR) standing out for its ability to provide interpretable and transparent recommendations. Unlike black-box machine learning models, CBR leverages past cases to generate predictions by analogy, aligning with the way clinicians naturally reason. In this work, we propose a CBR-based CDSS for skin cancer treatment that integrates medical taxonomies and patient-specific clinical features to predict the next treatment step. By focusing on both technical performance and real-world application in a medical setting, this study provides insights for the deployment of CBR-based systems in medical practice.

Keywords: Case-based Reasoning · Skin Cancer · Clinical Decision Support · Taxonomy Similarity

1 Introduction

Cancer remains one of the most prevalent and complex health challenges worldwide, requiring highly individualized treatment strategies. Clinicians must consider a multitude of factors when making treatment decisions, including tumor-specific characteristics, patient-specific factors, and evolving clinical guidelines.

M. Kuhn, and Y. Warnecke—These authors contributed equally to this work.

© The Author(s), under exclusive license to Springer Nature Switzerland AG 2025
I. Bichindaritz and B. López (Eds.): ICCBR 2025, LNAI 15662, pp. 407–422, 2025.
https://doi.org/10.1007/978-3-031-96559-3_27

Despite advances in evidence-based medicine, oncological decision-making is often constrained by limited comprehensive study data, that reflects the diversity of real-world patient populations and the complexity of oncological diseases. As a result, physicians frequently rely on their own clinical experience and intuition when making treatment decisions on a case-by-case basis. While valuable, this approach may introduce subjectivity and is restricted by the number of cases they have personally encountered. In this context, the use of clinical decision support systems (CDSS) that leverage analogy-based methods has the potential to improve oncology treatment by assisting physicians in selecting appropriate treatment methods [5,18]. One such method is Case-Based Reasoning (CBR), a branch of artificial intelligence (AI) that focuses on experience-based problem-solving. CBR addresses problems by reusing and adapting previously acquired empirical knowledge. Relevant cases and solutions are identified in documented cases using similarity measures that are based on analogies to the given case. The relationship to analogy-based clinical reasoning makes CBR a promising approach for medical decision support, since physicians naturally solve clinical problems by recalling similar past cases [4,14]. Moreover, CBR is particularly advantageous in the medical domain because clinical scenarios rarely have single optimal solutions and involve complex relationships between symptoms, diagnoses, and treatments that are difficult to capture in rule-based or statistical models [10]. While CBR has been successfully applied in skin cancer diagnosis [1,16], its use in supporting treatment decisions for skin cancer remains largely unexplored. Given the complexity and variability of dermatological oncology, an analogy-based approach such as CBR holds potential to improve treatment planning by integrating structured medical knowledge with patient-specific features.

In this paper, a CBR-based CDSS for skin cancer treatment decision support that utilizes patient-specific features is presented. This system predicts the next treatment step at any given point in a patient's disease progression. The CDSS integrates the knowledge of medical taxonomies alongside the implicit knowledge from medical experts, which is coded into the system, through the use of similarity measures and attribute weights. The contributions of this work are twofold: First, CBR-based CDSS is developed that integrates medical taxonomies used in day-to-day practice, alongside additional patient-specific clinical features. This integration enables the system to provide interpretable and transparent recommendations that align with clinical reasoning. Second, an evaluation of the CDSS is performed using real patient data from the University Hospital Münster (UKM) in collaboration with medical experts. Specifically, the CDSS's predictions are compared with actual clinician decisions to assess its utility in real-life scenarios. This evaluation provides insights for the deployment of CBR-based systems in dermatological practice and identifies opportunities and limitations of analogy-based decision-making in this domain [7].

This paper is organized as follows: Sect. 2 outlines the background, and the related work. Section 3 outlines the methodology, including the real-world use case, the proposed CDSS and the evaluation developed with domain experts. Section 4 focuses on the evaluation and the results. Section 5 discusses findings, practical implications, and limitations. Finally, Sect. 6 concludes with future research directions.

2 Fundamentals

2.1 Medical Taxonomies and Similarity Measures

A taxonomy is a hierarchical classification system organizing concepts based on shared characteristics. In the German healthcare system, two key taxonomies are used, ICD-10-GM (German Modification of the International Statistical Classification of Diseases), which uses alphanumeric codes for detailed diagnostic information, and OPS (German Procedure Classification), an alphanumeric system describing medical procedures for both inpatient and outpatient treatments, including types of intervention, surgical approaches, and specific techniques [9]. In these taxonomies, general categories are progressively subdivided into specific subcategories in a tree-like structure. Terminal nodes (leaves) represent the most granular classification level, containing diagnostic entities or procedural codes. To determine the similarity between two concepts in a taxonomy, semantic similarity measures can be employed. These measures quantify the relatedness between taxonomical concepts based on their shared semantic properties. One approach to measuring semantic similarity is through the use of information content (IC), which quantifies how informative a concept is within a taxonomy. Thus, specialized terms typically have higher IC than general ones [15]. The IC measure proposed by Sánchez and Batet [19] effectively distinguishes concepts with similar hyponym counts but varying concreteness:

$$IC(c) = -log\left(\frac{\frac{|leaves(c)|}{|subsumers(c)|}+1}{max_{leaves}+1}\right) \tag{1}$$

In this equation, $leaves(c)$ represents concepts at the taxonomic endpoints under concept c, while $subsumers(c)$ denotes the set of taxonomic ancestors. The equation incorporates the ratio of leaf concepts to subsumers, providing a refined representation of semantic relationships within a concept hierarchy. Using this IC measure, Sánchez and Batet [19] adapted Lin's similarity measure [13]:

$$sim_{\text{Sánchez}}(c_1, c_2) = \frac{2 \cdot IC(LCS(c_1, c_2))}{IC(c_1) + IC(c_2)} \tag{2}$$

This equation quantifies similarity as the ratio of shared information to the total information needed to describe both concepts. The shared information is represented by the Least Common Subsumer (LCS), which is the most specific shared ancestor of two concepts in a taxonomy. The higher the IC of the LCS, the greater the similarity between the concepts.

2.2 Related Work

The rapid advancement of technology has led to the continuous development of numerous CBR systems, which are now widely applied across various subfields of medicine. Over the years, an increasing number of review papers have been published, providing a comprehensive overview of existing CBR systems and their applications [2,4].

An important research field is the diagnosis of tumors using images, scans or structured data. Bouzar-Benlabiod et al. [3] used CBR on mammogram images to classify breast cancer. They applied preprocessing steps and similarity measures for improving classification results. Gu et al. [8] developed a CBR system for the diagnosis of breast cancer and secondary cancer. Their data is collected from clinically preliminary and regular examinations and contains discrete and continuous attributes, like the age, the tumor data, therapy data and the family history. The weights for the attributes are determined by a genetic algorithm. It was also considered to use domain experts for the weight determination, but because of the overall complexity this has not been done. De Paz et al. [5] and Díaz et al. [6] published tools for the diagnosis of cancer using CBR on microarray data. Both publications stressed the importance of reducing the dimensionality in the preprocessing. While De Paz et al. used an automatic adaption with decision trees, Díaz et al. utilized the knowledge of experts to continuously improve the system. Abbes et al. [1] proposed a CBR system that uses features extracted from images showing skin cancer to support the diagnosis. Before applying the CBR system, the features are filtered by a probabilistic feature selection process. Another use case for CBR in oncology is to plan radiotherapy. Petrovic et al. [16] presented a CBR system for planning the doses of phase I and II treatments of the radiotherapy. The similarity of the cases is calculated based on weighted attributes describing the stage of the cancer and the potential risk to the rectum.

While numerous CBR systems have been developed, to the best of our knowledge, no CBR system specifically designed for planning the next steps in skin cancer treatment has been published. Given the successful application of CBR in oncology, similar approaches could prove beneficial for skin cancer treatment.

3 Methodology

This study followed a structured four-step methodology: (1) defining a real-world use case, (2) selecting and preparing relevant data, (3) conceptualizing and implementing the CDSS, and (4) conducting an experimental evaluation. The use case was identified through workshops with medical and technical experts from the Department of Dermatology in Münster, the Institute of Medical Informatics, and the German Research Centre for Artificial Intelligence. These workshops identified key clinical challenges, refined requirements through expert feedback, and prioritized the most relevant use case. To determine the relevant dataset, workshops were conducted with two medical experts, two AI specialists, and one medical informatics specialist. During these sessions, experts identified key data features, assessed their availability, and refined attributes based on clinical and technical considerations. The final feature set was determined by medical consensus. Following this, the data was extracted and pre-processed for use in the study. The next step involved conceptualizing the CDSS by defining similarity measures and attribute weights. Workshops with medical experts used scenario-based discussions with predefined patient data to compare attributes in clinical reasoning. AI specialists translated expert judgments into computational similarity metrics. A similar approach determined attribute weights, assigning higher importance to critical attributes based on expert-driven rankings. The experimental evaluation was designed in collaboration with domain experts, encompassing both technical and medical perspectives. The technical evaluation assessed the predictive performance of the CDSS using appropriate and established metrics. The medical evaluation, on the other hand, involved domain experts utilizing the CDSS in realistic clinical scenarios, providing feedback on its practical utility. This approach ensured that both technical accuracy and clinical applicability of the developed system were systematically evaluated.

3.1 Use Case

The selected use case addresses clinical decision-making in dermatological oncology, specifically focusing on identifying the next treatment option for skin cancer patients. The goal of this use case is the development of a CDSS that can forecast the next step in the treatment, supporting clinicians in determining the optimal treatment at various stages of disease progression. This approach is particularly valuable in complex clinical situations where patient characteristics are diverse and explicit evidence-based guidelines may be limited. By integrating structured medical knowledge with patient-specific clinical attributes, the CDSS aims to provide transparent and interpretable treatment recommendations.

3.2 Case Base

The quality and relevance of the dataset are crucial components in CBR-based applications, as they directly impact the accuracy and reliability of the similarity-based reasoning. Therefore, selecting an appropriate dataset is crucial to supporting the medical use case presented in this study. This section provides an in-depth description of the dataset, including its source, composition, and features, to ensure transparency of the results. The dataset utilized originates from routine oncological care in dermatology. This dataset was selected due to its high degree of structuring, a result of mandatory reporting requirements for all oncology institutions in Germany, for which the Oncology Base Dataset (oBDS) is utilized for a structured representation of oncology information. The dataset consists of records from 5,938 patients undergoing oncology treatment between January 2017 and November 2024. It includes patients aged 5 to 98 years during their treatment, with approximately 64% male and 36% female patients. The dataset comprises 224 attributes from the oBDS, including patient demographics data, operation documentation, and systemic therapy. Initially, the oBDS has a multidimensional structure, which is not usable for a CBR approach. It was subsequently transformed into a simpler, attribute-value pair format according to a set of predefined rules. The reduction of dimensions in the data led to the presence of a lot of null values within the dataset. This poses a challenge for CBR, as there are numerous similar rows that remain unspecific and lack substantial informative content to differentiate between cases. To address this issue, we employed the Last Value Carried Forward (LVCF) method, a technique frequently utilized with medical data. LVCF involves carrying forward patient information until it is updated with new data [20]. This integrates patient history into the case base and enhances the predictive analysis. For the creation of the case base, the 32 key attributes identified in the workshops with the medical experts are utilized. Each treatment in the dataset is characterized by the following attribute groups: (a) **Patient Core Data** (basic information such as personal details of the patient); (b) **Diagnosis Details** (medical codes and descriptions related to the tumor diagnosis); (c) **Histology Information** (detailed analysis of the primary tumor); (d) **Operation Details** (purpose and specifics of the surgical procedure); (e) **Systemic Therapy Information** (information on treatments affecting the entire body, like chemotherapy); (f) **Course of Treatment** (timeline and progress of cancer treatment); (g) **Tumor Conference** (suggested treatment options and plans); (h) **Malignant Melanoma** (information specific to skin cancer of type malignant melanoma). Additionally, for our use case, the case base includes information on subsequent treatments, which can be interpreted as the solution of a case.

3.3 Concept of the CDSS

This section presents the design of the CBR-based CDSS for skin cancer treatment. The CDSS aims to assist dermatologists in making informed treatment decisions by identifying similar historical cases and suggesting their subsequent treatment steps as reference points. It is structured into four key steps: Case Representation, Retrieval, Reuse and Revision. These modules enable similarity computation between cases, and the presentation of relevant treatment options with their outcomes. This evidence-based approach enhances clinical decision-making while preserving physician autonomy in final treatment selection. Figure 1 illustrates the workflow.

Case Representation: In this setting, a case represents a patient's clinical situation at a specific point during treatment, structured as an attribute-value pair. It consists of two components, a problem description, which captures the patient's clinical state using 32 carefully selected attributes including demographic data, tumor characteristics, histopathological findings, and treatment history. Also, it includes a solution component, which defines the next administered treatment. These treatments fall into nine distinct categories, comprising five surgical procedures identified by OPS codes and four systemic therapies classified by medication type. Namely, these are *OP - (Post-)Excision*, *OP - Other Operations*, *OP - Other Operations on the Lymph Nodes*, *OP - Radical*

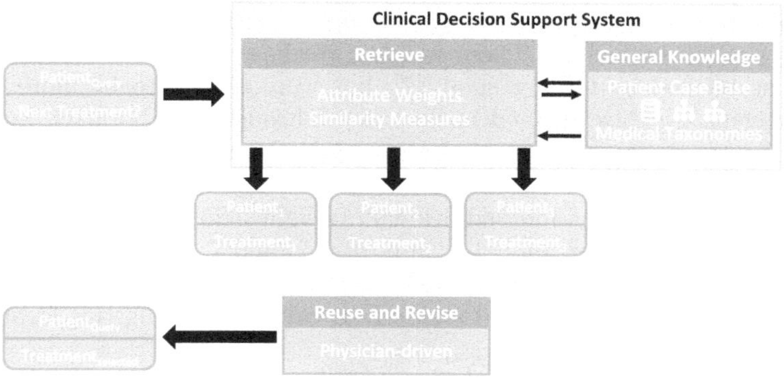

Fig. 1. An conceptual overview of the CDSS.

Lymphadenectomy, *OP - Sentinel Lymph Node Biopsy*, *SYST - BRAF + MEK-inhibitor*, *SYST - Immunocombination Therapy (Ipilimumab + Nivolumab)*, *SYST - PD1-Inhibition (Pembrolizumab / Nivolumab)* and *SYST - Other*.

Retrieve. This module compares the query patient with the case base using predefined similarity measures and attribute weights. For each query, the system calculates similarity scores for all stored cases, ranks them, and selects the three most similar cases with distinct treatment suggestions. This threshold was established in collaboration with physicians during workshops for the use case definition. This module uses three types of similarity measures based on the data type of the chosen attributes. For categorical attributes, an exact matching function is applied, while for numeric attributes, normalized linear similarity functions ensure fair comparison across different value ranges. For medical codes (ICD and OPS), the taxonomy-based Sánchez similarity evaluates relatedness within a hierarchical taxonomy, as explained in Sect. 2.1. This measure is particularly important for calculating meaningful similarities between different medical codes that may share hierarchical relationships despite having different encodings. Table 1 shows the formula of the used similarity measure for each data type and also denotes how often the specific similarity measure is utilized.

Table 1. Similarity measures used in the retrieve module (The number in parentheses indicates how often the respective attribute type occurs).

Attribute Type	Similarity Measure Formula
Categorical Attributes (25)	$sim_{cat}(a,b) = \begin{cases} 1 \text{ if } a = b \\ 0 \text{ if } a \neq b \end{cases}$
Numerical Attributes (4)	$sim_{num}(a,b) = 1 - \frac{\lvert a-b \rvert}{max_{attr} - min_{attr}}$
Medical Codes (3)	$sim_{\text{Sánchez}}((c_1, c_2) = \frac{2 \cdot IC(LCS(c_1,c_2))}{IC(c_1)+IC(c_2)}$

Beyond similarity measures, the CDSS applies attribute weights to emphasize clinically significant factors. These weights are based on attribute importance metrics established by Grüger et al. [7], but were refined to be more suitable for the specific use case defined in Sect. 3.1. Through collaborative workshops with medical experts, attributes were categorized into three importance levels based on their relevance for patient similarity: "very important" (weight 1.0), "important" (weight 0.5), and "additional" (weight 0.25). The final distribution comprised 11 "very important", 14 "important", and 7 "additional" attributes. By combining the similarity measures with the attribute weights, the overall similarity between a query Q and a case C is calculated using this formula:

$$Sim(Q, C) = \frac{\sum_{i=1}^{n} w_i \cdot sim_{type(i)}(Q_i, C_i)}{\sum_{i=1}^{n} w_i} \tag{3}$$

where w_i is the weight assigned to the i-th attribute, reflecting its relative importance, $sim_{type(i)}$ denotes the similarity function selected according to the attribute type (categorical, numerical, or medical codes), Q_i and C_i are the values of the i-th attribute in the query and case, respectively, and n is the total number of attributes.

Reuse and Revise. The reuse and revise phases are intentionally structured as physician-driven processes rather than automated functions. During the reuse phase, physicians examine the retrieved similar cases and their treatment histories to identify potential approaches for the current patient. It is important to note that each retrieved case displays its overall similarity score and the next suggested treatment to ensure transparency. In the revision phase, clinicians can refine the suggested treatment to meet the patient's specific needs, applying their medical expertise to modify the suggested treatment based on patient-specific factors. This human-centered approach ensures that physician judgment remains the core of the decision-making, while integrating insights from similar cases.

3.4 Evaluation Concept

In this section, the evaluation concept is created to evaluate the proposed CDSS. Accordingly, both a technical and a medical evaluation are defined. The technical evaluation, benchmarks the CDSS against six widely used machine learning (ML) techniques. This comparison ensures that the CDSS achieves comparable performance and retains predictive capability relative to standard machine learning models. The following machine learning models are chosen (1) Logistic Regression with L2 regularization to mitigate overfitting, (2) Random Forest configured as an ensemble of 100 decision trees, with tree depth constrained to 10, (3) Naive Bayes with a variant specifically designed to handle numerical and discrete features, (4) K-Nearest Neighbors (KNN) with k=5 using Manhattan distance as the proximity metric, (5) Gradient Boosting with 100 weak learners, a shrinkage factor of 0.1, and a conservative tree depth of 5 and (6) Multi-Layer-Perceptron structured with two hidden layers of 32 neurons each, utilizing ReLU activation functions and incorporating early stopping to prevent overfitting. To ensure robust and unbiased results, a 10-fold cross-validation was employed. This is done with the same random seed, ensuring each fold contains the same data across all models. As explained in Sect. 3.3, the CDSS generates predictions by retrieving the three most similar cases from the case base and suggesting three potential next treatments ranked by similarity. Similarly, the ML models generated the top three predicted next treatments. The predictive performance of the CDSS and the ML models was assessed using two key metrics, the Micro-Recall@3 and the Macro-Recall@3. The Micro-Recall@3 measures whether the actual next treatment appears among the top three predictions, assessing the system's ability to generate clinically relevant recommendations. It aggregates performance across all samples, inherently prioritizing frequent classes in the dataset. Macro-Recall@3 was applied to analyze class imbalance in the case-base. Macro-Recall@3 computes Recall@3 separately for each class and averages them equally, ensuring balanced evaluation across majority and minority classes.

On the other hand, the medical evaluation focused on the interpretability and clinical relevance of the CDSS's predictions. This evaluation examined whether the system's recommendations aligned with clinical expertise and could support real-world decision-making. A structured questionnaire was developed to guide the expert assessment. Skin cancer specialists categorized the system's recommendations as follows: (1) "Appropriate and directly applicable", (2) "Conditionally appropriate", (3) "Not appropriate". Furthermore, Clinicians documented medical observations and potential limitations of the CDSS. Moreover, the medical experts assessed the similarity between the query patient and the cases identified by the CDSS. Here, the similarity between the patients is rated based on three categories (1) "Similar", (2) "Partially similar" and (3) "Not similar". Three skin cancer experts, for the UKM, reviewed the recommendations and the similarity for 18 randomly selected patients from the case-base described in Sect. 3.1. First, each treatment category appeared at least twice in the evaluation dataset, ensuring fair calculation of the evaluation metrics by providing equal representation for all treatment types. This selection approach addresses the inherent data imbalance from the original dataset. Priority was given to 11 patients with cancer stage progression, indicating advancement to a more severe stage. Additionally, seven patients without stage progression were included. Within these constraints, patient selection was random. To evaluate the overall usefulness of the system, the results are aggregated. This will be done by assigning a weight of +1 to"Appropriate and directly applicable", 0 to "Conditionally appropriate", and -1 to "Not appropriate". Based on these weighted scores, the consensus will be classified as positive, negative, or neutral (0).

4 Experimental Evaluation

The proposed CDSS was evaluated using real-world skin cancer data as described in Sect. 3.2. The CDSS outlined in Sect. 3.3 was implemented using CBRkit, a Python framework for CBR [12]. For similarity calculations, CBRkit's built-in measures were utilized for numerical and categorical attributes, while for the similarity measure of medical codes an implementation of the Sánchez similarity specialized on ICD and OPS codes is used [11]. The evaluation, along with the ML models, was also implemented in Python.

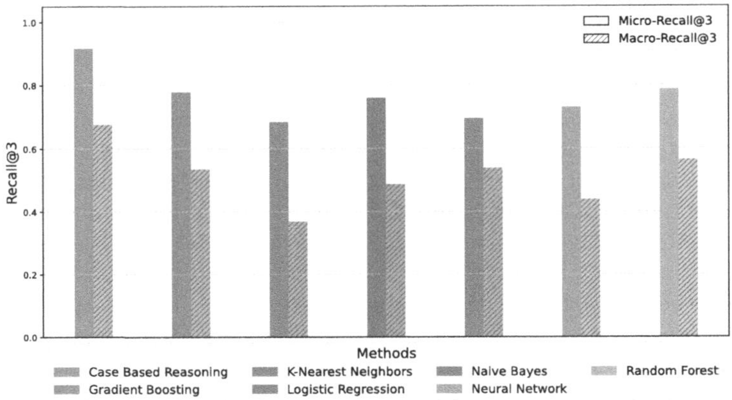

Fig. 2. Comparison between the CBR-based CDSS and machine learning models, using Macro-Recall@3 and Micro-Recall@3 aggregated across ten folds.

4.1 Technical Evaluation

To measure the quality of predictions, Macro-Recall@3 and Micro-Recall@3 are computed, as detailed in Sect. 3.4. These metrics are calculated across ten folds, with their averages summarizing the overall performance across all folds for all models. Figure 2 compares the metrics for all approaches. The results indicate that the proposed CDSS achieves the highest Micro-Recall@3 of 91.17% outperforming ML models. The best performing ML model is Random Forest with a Micro-Recall@3 of 78.57%. The Macro-Recall@3 for the CDSS is also the highest compared to the ML models with 67.49%. The highest Macro-Recall@3 for the ML models was also achieved by Random Forest with 56.41%.

Figure 3 depicts the Recall for each treatment individually, revealing that treatments with lower relative frequencies in the dataset exhibit substantially lower Recall@3. More frequently occurring treatments, such as *OP - (Post-)Excision* and *SYST - PD1-Inhibition* demonstrate better performance. Overall, the CDSS outperforms the machine learning models in handling class imbalance. However, as shown in Fig. 3, the class imbalance remains a persistent challenge for the CDSS, especially for the treatments with a low relative frequency.

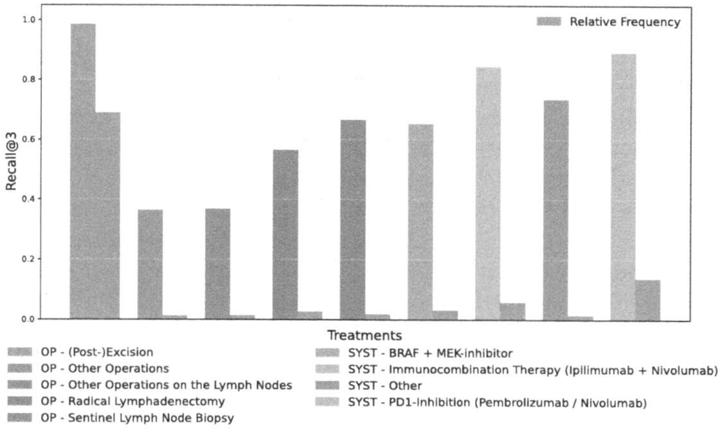

Fig. 3. Performance of the CBR-based CDSS based on Micro-Recall@3 for each event type, alongside the relative frequency of events in the case base.

4.2 Medical Evaluation

The medical evaluation was conducted by three experts from the Department of Dermatology at the UKM, who assessed the system's predictions for 18 patients. Therefore, the system's top three predicted treatment steps for each patient were evaluated. A detailed analysis of individual recommendations revealed varying levels of usability for the recommendations. The first recommendation was considered "Not appropriate" for 7 of the patients (38.89%), "Conditionally appropriate" for 3 patients (16.67%), and "Appropriate and directly applicable" for 8 patients (44.44%). In contrast, the second recommendation was deemed "Not appropriate" for 15 of the patients (83.33%), with the recommendations for only 3 patients (16.67%) being "Appropriate and directly applicable". The third recommendation also received mixed feedback, it was considered "Not appropriate" for 12 patients (66.67%) and "Appropriate and directly applicable" for 6 patients (33.33%). Overall, expert consensus indicated that about one-third of the suggestions (31.48%) were "Appropriate and directly applicable", while a smaller proportion (5.56%) were considered "Conditionally appropriate". However, most suggestions (62.96%) were rated "Not appropriate", highlighting areas for improvement Table 2.

Table 2. Expert Assessment of System Recommendations

Assessment	1st Rec.	2nd Rec.	3rd Rec.	Total
Not appr.	7 (38.89%)	15 (83.33%)	12 (66.67%)	34 (62.96%)
Cond. appr.	3 (16.67%)	0 (0.00%)	0 (0.00%)	3 (5.56%)
Appr. & direct.	8 (44.44%)	3 (16.67%)	6 (33.33%)	17 (31.48%)

Considering our method, which includes evaluating all three recommendations for each patient, the results demonstrate a stronger clinical relevance: for 11 patients (61.11%), at least one of the predictions was rated as "Appropriate and directly applicable". However, for 7 patients (38.89%), none of the recommendations met this criterion, revealing discrepancies between the system's output and clinical judgment. The observed applicability rate (61.11%) closely mirrors the Macro-Recall@3 (67.49%), demonstrating an alignment between clinical expertise and the system's technical performance across diverse treatment scenarios. This comparison with Macro-Recall@3 is more appropriate than with Micro-Recall@3 since our medical evaluation deliberately included representations from all treatment categories equally to ensure comprehensive assessment of the system's clinical utility. For the analysis between the query patient and the most similar case retrieved by the CDSS, medical experts rated 7 (38.89%) as "Similar", 7 (38.89%) as "Partially similar", and 4 (22.22%) as "Not similar".

5 Discussion

This section discusses the CBR-based CDSS, highlighting key considerations for its deployment in dermatological practice and outlining both the opportunities and limitations of analogy-based decision-making in this domain. The proposed system constitutes a significant advancement toward interpretable AI in dermatological oncology. By leveraging CBR, it enables clinicians to trace recommendations back to similar cases, thereby offering greater transparency than conventional machine learning models. The CBR-based CDSS achieved superior performance in the evaluation, with a Micro-Recall@3 of 91.17% clearly surpassing Random Forest (78.57%). It also showed better results in Macro-Recall (67.49% vs. 56.41%). These findings suggest that CBR is particularly effective in handling imbalanced and small-scale clinical datasets. This performance may stem from CBR's inherent capacity to process sparse and heterogeneous data with minimal preprocessing and its adaptability to high-dimensional feature spaces. Although both CBR and KNN rely on analogy-based reasoning, the comparison revealed that the CBR system significantly outperforms the baseline KNN implementation. While KNN achieved a Micro-Recall@3 of 68.28% and a Macro-Recall@3 of 36.8%, the CBR-based CDSS delivered substantially better results. This performance gap can be attributed to leveraging domain-specific similarity functions and incorporating medical taxonomies within the CBR-system and only using a baseline implementation of KNN that relies only on the Manhattan distance. It should be noted that advanced KNN implementations can also utilize heterogeneous distance functions [17]. This enables the model to capture semantic relationships between medical concepts, allowing it to recognize when treatments that appear different in encoding might be semantically related in clinical practice. These specialized similarity measures and expert-defined attribute weights significantly influence the predictive power of the CBR approach. However, the proposed approach relies on manually defined feature weights (1, 0.5, and 0.25) across 33 attributes, which may introduce subjectivity and potentially fail to provide optimal weights for similarity calculation. Despite the potential of CBR-based systems for clinical decision support, several limitations remain. One major challenge, shared with conventional ML methods, is class imbalance. Although the CBR-based approach achieved higher performance compared to other models, a Macro-Recall@3 of 67.49% reflects the unequal predictive accuracy across classes. This metric, which gives equal weight to each class regardless of frequency, highlights the model's reduced sensitivity for infrequent treatment types. The consistently low Macro-Recall@3 scores across all evaluated models confirm that class imbalance constitutes a dataset-driven constraint, rather than a limitation of the underlying algorithmic approach, as shown in Fig. 3. This underscores the necessity for targeted strategies to address data imbalance for CBR applications, potentially through specialized sampling techniques, augmentation strategies, or building curated specialized case bases. Building a meaningful and representative case base for skin cancer treatment is challenging due to case complexity and variability. The selection process must be restrictive enough to ensure high-quality, consistent cases while remaining diverse enough to cover a broad range of clinical scenarios. This will require close collaboration with domain experts to curate cases that accurately reflect clinical practice.

Furthermore, the available dataset, originally intended for documentation rather than decision support, does not capture the full course of treatment. Incorporating data from the hospital information system could enhance the system's performance. However, such data frequently remains non-standardized and unstructured. Furthermore, the frequency of treatment steps in dermatology oncology is inherently imbalanced, which is reflected in the distribution of treatments in our data and impacts the CBR's predictive performance. This imbalance is amplified by the dataset's limited patient population, sourced exclusively from a single institution, thereby introducing bias and omitting data from treatments at other facilities. Feedback from medical experts during the evaluation process helped to validate and confirm the technical findings: 61.11% of patients received at least one "Appropriate and directly applicable" treatment recommendation among the top three suggestions, aligning with the Macro-Recall@3 of 67.49% observed in the technical evaluation. This indicates that the CBR system's recommendations are clinically plausible in a majority of cases. However, substantial limitations persist. A high proportion of all recommendations (38.89%) were not directly applicable, underscoring the system's limited capacity to handle real-world clinical complexity. Moreover, rare cases are underrepresented due to scarce data, limiting the system's ability to suggest appropriate treatments for unique conditions. The dynamic nature of oncology presents additional challenges. Rapid advancements in treatment guidelines can quickly render the case base outdated, reducing the practical applicability of CBR recommendations. To address this, data might need to be restricted to shorter time spans, although this would further limit data richness. Enhancing the system with rule-based decision-making or accessing vast data pools from multiple institutions could be beneficial. Participants of the evaluation also highlighted certain limitations in the overall design of the CDSS. While the system is capable of generating contextually relevant recommendations, it lacks a critical safety mechanism - the ability to abstain from providing a suggestion when no suitable case match exists. In real-world clinical settings, this omission increases the risk of misleading or clinically inappropriate outputs. Moreover, the presence of multiple comorbidities - a common characteristic in oncology patients - complicates case similarity assessments, highlighting the need for a broad-based medical knowledge integration within the CDSS. In practical healthcare settings, the limitations of the CDSS are further pronounced. Since clinicians are already familiar with available treatment options, the system's recommendations offer limited standalone value. The absence of outcome-oriented context, such as overall survival or progression-free survival, limits the system's potential to support evidence-based clinical choices. Integrating such parameters would enhance the system's practical applicability.

Despite these challenges, this study serves as a functional proof of concept for deploying CBR in clinical decision support. However, its application within a single institution and a narrowly defined specialty restricts generalizability. The observed limitations highlight the necessity of multi-institutional datasets, broader medical domain coverage, and hybrid model designs that combine case-based reasoning with rule-based approaches.

6 Conclusion

This study provides valuable insights into the deployment of CBR-based CDSS in dermatological practice by implementing and evaluating it in real clinical scenarios. The CDSS demonstrated superior performance over conventional machine learning approaches while offering transparent recommendations backed by similar patient cases. Through integration of medical taxonomies and domain-specific knowledge, the CDSS successfully predicted appropriate treatment steps. Expert validation confirmed the clinical relevance of recommendations for most cases, though important limitations were identified. However, CBR systems offer a promising approach to augment clinical expertise while maintaining the essential human element in complex treatment decisions. Future work should focus on multi-institutional case base integration, outcome metrics incorporation, incorporating explicit expert knowledge through hybrid systems and implementing techniques for optimizing attribute weights to reduce subjectivity in similarity calculations. This research demonstrates that CBR is a promising foundation for interpretable clinical decision support, though significant refinement remains necessary before deployment in real clinical settings.

Acknowledgments. This research is funded by the German Federal Ministry of Education and Research (BMBF) and NextGenerationEU (European Union) in the project KI-AIM under the funding code 16KISA115K.

References

1. Abbes, W., Frikha Elleuch, J., Sellami, D.: A new case based reasoning diagnosis approach within a possibilistic framework. Inte. J. Mach. Learn. Cybern., 1–28 (2024)
2. Bichindaritz, I., Marling, C.: Case-based reasoning in the health sciences: what's next? Artif. Intell. Med. **36**(2), 127–135 (2006)
3. Bouzar-Benlabiod, L., Harrar, K., Yamoun, L., Khodja, M.Y., Akhloufi, M.A.: A novel breast cancer detection architecture based on a CNN-CBR system for mammogram classification. Comput. Biol. Med. **163**, 107133 (2023)
4. Choudhury, N., Begum, S.: A survey on case-based reasoning in medicine. Int. J. Adv. Comput. Sci. Appl. **7** (2016)
5. De Paz, J.F., Rodríguez, S., Bajo, J., Corchado, J.M.: Case-based reasoning as a decision support system for cancer diagnosis: a case study. Int. J. Hybrid Intell. Syst. **6**(2), 97–110 (2009)
6. Díaz, F., Fdez-Riverola, F., Corchado Rodríguez, J.: gene-CBR: a case-based reasonig tool for cancer diagnosis using microarray data sets. Comput. Intell. **22**, 254–268 (2006)
7. Grüger, J., et al.: AI-driven decision support in oncology: evaluating data readiness for skin cancer treatment (2025)
8. Gu, D., Liang, C., Zhao, H.: A case-based reasoning system based on weighted heterogeneous value distance metric for breast cancer diagnosis. Artif. Intell. Med. **77**, 31–47 (2017)
9. Hirsch, J.A., et al.: ICD-10: history and Context. Am. J. Neuroradiol. **37**(4), 596–599 (2016)
10. Holt, A., Bichindaritz, I., Schmidt, R., Perner, P.: Medical applications in case-based reasoning. Knowl. Eng. Rev. **20**(3), 289–292 (2005)
11. Kuhn, M., Grüger, J., Geyer, T., Bergmann, R.: Leveraging taxonomy similarity for next activity prediction in patient treatment (2025). https://arxiv.org/abs/2503.07638
12. Lenz, M., Malburg, L., Bergmann, R.: CBRKIT: an intuitive case-based reasoning toolkit for python. In: Proceedings of the 32nd International Conference on Case-Based Reasoning (ICCBR 2024), pp. 289–304. Springer (2024)
13. Lin, D.: An information-theoretic definition of similarity. In: Proceedings of the Fifteenth International Conference on Machine Learning, pp. 296–304. ICML '98, Morgan Kaufmann Publishers Inc., San Francisco, CA, USA (1998)
14. Macura, R., Macura, K.: Case-based reasoning: opportunities and applications in health care. Artif. Intell. Med. **9**(1), 1–4 (1997)
15. Pedersen, T., Pakhomov, S.V., Patwardhan, S., Chute, C.G.: Measures of semantic similarity and relatedness in the biomedical domain. J. Biomed. Inform. **40**(3), 288–299 (2007)
16. Petrovic, S., Mishra, N., Sundar, S.: A novel case based reasoning approach to radiotherapy planning. Expert Syst. Appl. **38**(9), 10759–10769 (2011)
17. Santos, M.S., Abreu, P.H., Fernández, A., Luengo, J., Santos, J.: The impact of heterogeneous distance functions on missing data imputation and classification performance. Eng. Appl. Artif. Intell. **111**, 104791 (2022)
18. Sutton, R.T., Pincock, D., Baumgart, D.C., Sadowski, D.C., Fedorak, R.N., Kroeker, K.I.: An overview of clinical decision support systems: benefits, risks, and strategies for success. NPJ Digit. Med. **3**(17), 1–10 (2020)

19. Sánchez, D., Batet, M.: Semantic similarity estimation in the biomedical domain: an ontology-based information-theoretic perspective. J. Biomed. Inform. **44**(5), 749–759 (2011)
20. Twisk, J., de Vente, W.: Attrition in longitudinal studies: how to deal with missing data. J. Clin. Epidemiol. **55**(4), 329–337 (2002)

Analyzing the Contribution of Sequential Patterns in CBR for Childhood Obesity Prediction

Beatriz López[1(✉)], Zsofia Prager[1], Abel López-Bermejo[2], and Judit Bassols[2]

[1] eXiT Research Group, University of Girona, Girona, Spain
beatriz.lopez@udg.edu

[2] Girona Biomedical Research Institute Dr. Josep Trueta (IDIBGI), Girona, Spain
{alopezbermejo,jbassols}@idibgi.org

Abstract. Childhood obesity is considered one of the main public health concerns. Research in the field of obesity detection and prevention is moving towards promising solutions thanks to the use of Artificial Intelligence applied to data from cohorts of children. Previous studies have analyzed the data without considering the temporal relationship between them. In this work, sequential pattern mining is used to characterize childhood obesity. Then, original data is represented based on these sequential patterns to feed a case-based reasoning system with the aim to predict childhood obesity. Experiments have been carried out on the data collected from 386 children from Girona and Figueres (Spain).

Keywords: Childhood obesity · Sequence pattern mining · Retrieve · K-nearest neighbors

1 Introduction

Childhood obesity is one of the most important public health problems of the 21st century worldwide due to its prevalence and its impact on both short and long-term health. In addition to its association with non-communicable diseases such as cardiovascular diseases, diabetes or cancer, children who suffer from it usually experience psychological and social problems, such as low self-esteem or bullying [23].

Artificial Intelligence (AI) has been used to understand the factors of childhood obesity [10]. Among the different AI techniques, Case-Based Reasoning (CBR) provides advantages over other techniques, such as allowing the individualization of the result, the management of the context, and the uncertainty of different alternatives or recommendations [6]. Most of the AI approaches conduct cross-sectional studies in which socioeconomic and healthcare data of the parents and children are analyzed to understand the key factors of obesity. Few approaches dealt with longitudinal data. One of the exceptions is [19] which deals with pre-natal, perinatal, postnatal and 2 to 90 months age infant data, to identify different groups of risks (stable obesity, latent-onset obesity, moderate decline obesity, and non-obese), and their corresponding profiles.

© The Author(s), under exclusive license to Springer Nature Switzerland AG 2025
I. Bichindaritz and B. López (Eds.): ICCBR 2025, LNAI 15662, pp. 423–437, 2025.
https://doi.org/10.1007/978-3-031-96559-3_28

From this study, no evidence was found regarding that pre-natal and perinatal, and postnatal data predicts obesity. This is an interesting finding since previous cross-sectional studies identify parents' body mass index (BMI) as key factors. Nevertheless, this study does not consider the temporal relation of the factors.

Our research is involved in understanding temporal-related patterns for childhood obesity based on longitudinal data similar to the one studied in [19]. To that end, we employ a sequential pattern mining algorithm, so that the temporal relation among the newborn data is considered. Thus, the contribution of this work involves coping with all the challenges of using sequential patterns to represent baby data as cases into a CBR system for obesity prediction.

The paper is organized as follows. First, the work is contextualized in the previous literature. Section 3 provides a background on sequence pattern mining algorithms. In Sect. 4, details of the methodology and datasets used are provided. Next, in Sect. 5 the results are described and discussed. We end with some conclusions in Sect. 6.

2 Related Work

The use of sequential pattern mining for feature representation in CBR has already been used in [7] to manage electroencephalogram (EEG) signals. EEG signals are homogeneous data (i.e. voltage values), while in this work we are dealing with heterogeneous data (categorical variables, boolean variables, and numerical). [9] proposed a methodology to combine CBR and sequence learning. Different from us, CBR is used to match the patterns with patient data among a set of available patterns, and sequence pattern matching is applied to determine the class. [9] represents an interesting foundational work, and the results are provided based on a toy problem. Another work, [3] combines sequence learning with CBR as we do, but applies to complex medical equipment failure detection.

Regarding the management of longitudinal data with CBR, one pioneering work was Ceaseless [16]. However, the approach proposed in [16] focused on continuous monitoring based on episodes, and activating different cases accordingly. In this work we focus on a more eager approach, by learning patterns; the ultimate goal is to know which temporal relations are key for childhood obesity. Other interesting approaches concern the use of CBR for explaining black box decisions (as deep learning methods) from time series, as proposed in [22].

There are some sequential pattern mining algorithms that have been particularly designed for classification. For example, [12] defines a discriminative sequential pattern mining method, [25] introduces the concept of contrast sequence, which is later used in [24] to introduce the concept of contrast sequential patterns. In our work we have used sequential patterns for case representation.

The management of longitudinal data for determining risk factors of childhood obesity has been a matter of concern in the recent years. In a previous work [15] we explore the use of frequent pattern mining, thus representing data with frequent itemsets. In [19], pre-natal, perinatal, postnatal and 2 to 90 months age infant data, similar to the one proposed in this work, has been considered. However, none of these previous work take into account the temporal relation among the data, as we are considering. A more recent approach is [27], which accounts for a similar imbalanced dataset as ours (14% of obese children). Our main concern with this approach is that they are using the area under the curve (AUC) value as a performance metric. Conversely, we are analyzing recall together with accuracy, as taking into account the minority class. Moreover, they are using logistic regression and multivariate fractional polynomials, while we are trying to capture temporal relations among the data with the use of frequent sequence patterns to represent features for cases in a CBR framework.

The use of sequential pattern mining is not new in Medicine, however. For example, [4] develop a new method for dealing with cardiovascular disease management from electronic health record (EHR) data; [20] use administrative data to predict medical in-hospital mortality regarding the acute coronary syndrome; and [13] applies the method to deal with emotional states. In [11], utilized real-world EHR data from the first two years of life to predict obesity status at age five. The authors also ignores the temporal relation of the data, by applying predictive models and feature selection approaches in the overall set of available data. They separated models for boys and girls because the cohort was larger. In our case, we have not separated boys from girls because the lack of data. Moreover, this work incorporates the temporal relation of the data, by applying sequence pattern miming.

In summary, this is the first time that CBR is used in combination with sequential patterns to deal with clinical data, including population-based prenatal cohort with data from the mother's pregnancy to the first months of the baby's life. This work contributes by investigating new pathways for dealing with temporal information within a CBR framework for childhood obesity prediction.

3 Background

This work relies on sequential pattern mining, a machine learning technique used for identifying patterns in an order of succession of data or sequence databases [8,21]. Patterns are subsequences that appear with a frequency higher than a given support (usually expressed in the percentage of sequences that contain the subsequence). For example, the subsequence $\langle$a, b, c$\rangle$is in $\langle$**a**, c, **b**, a, b, **c**, b, c$\rangle$.

Sequences could be of itemsets, meaning that sets of elements follow a consecutive order. For example, in Table 1 (left) a database of three sequences is provided. The first sequence is starts with itemset [B, C], which precedes [D, E], and which in turn precedes [F, G]. The first sequence has a length of 3 (three itemsets), while the remaining ones have a length of 2. Patterns with 0.6 support (that is, subsequences that are contained in at least the 60% of the sequences) are provided in Table 1 (right).

One of the major concerns with this kind of algorithm is computational efficiency, since for each possible combination of symbols defined in the sequence database (pattern candidate), counts must be conducted by scanning the database. The VEPRECO algorithm [17] is a state-of-the-art algorithm that has demonstrated its effectiveness thanks to an internal representation of the sequences that accelerates pattern counting.

Table 1. Sequence database and patterns with 0.6 support.

Sequence database
⟨[B, C], [D, E], [F, G]⟩
⟨[A], [E, G]⟩
⟨[B, C], [F, H, E]⟩

Patterns		
Pattern	# seq	Length
⟨[B]⟩	2	1
⟨[C]⟩	2	1
⟨[E]⟩	3	1
⟨[F]⟩	2	1
⟨[G]⟩	2	1
⟨[B, C]⟩	2	1
⟨[B, C], [G]⟩	2	2
⟨[B, C], [F]⟩	2	2
⟨[B], [E]⟩	2	2
⟨[B], [F]⟩	2	2
⟨[C], [E]⟩	2	2
⟨[C], [F]⟩	2	2

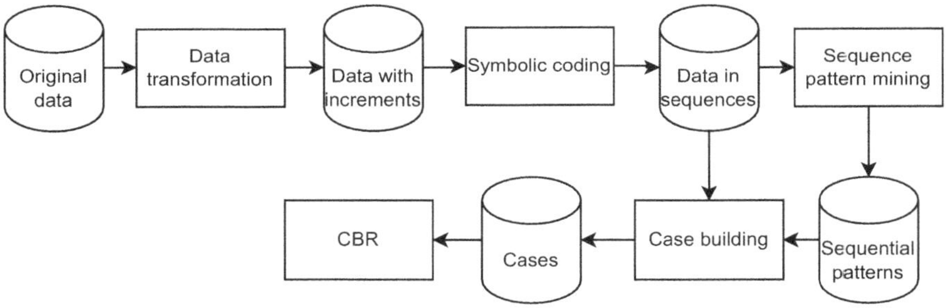

Fig. 1. Overview of the methodology.

4 Materials and Method

The methodology we propose is shown in Fig. 1. We are given a dataset of parents and early-life health data of the babies, with the children classified as normal-weight and overweight/obese. In the first step of the methodology we transform the original data to consider data variability among different periods of time; next, we code variables into symbols in order to apply pattern mining methods; afterward, we obtain the sequential patterns for each class. Patterns are then used to code the data into cases, so each case represents a combination of patterns that meet the original data. Finally, we apply CBR for obesity prediction.

4.1 Dataset Description

The dataset contains two cohorts of babies, from Hospital Dr. Josep Trueta (Girona) and the Hospital of Figueres, both in Spain, collected from 2008 to

2014. The inclusion and exclusion criteria for participation in the study was described elsewhere (study with code 2010056 of the Clinical Research Ethics Committee of the Girona University Hospital Dr. Josep Trueta).

A total of 1,175 infants were included in the study, each with 212 recorded variables. From these, doctors involved in the project selected 36 variables considered most relevant to the study. Table 2 provides a description of these variables. Some are related to the mother—both before and during pregnancy—others pertain to the father, and the rest are associated with the infant. The target variable is OBESITY_B, which indicates whether the child has a normal weight (OBESITY_B = 1) or has overweight or obesity (OBESITY_B = 2), based on the Body Mass Index (BMI) measured at five years of age.

Column "Visit" indicates the different visits in which the variables have been gathered: 0 is related to variables at the moment the mother gets pregnant; 1 the information regarding the second trimester; 2 the third trimester; 3 the information at birth; 4 when the baby has 2 months old... and so on.

On the other hand, the samples of the infants where values were missing in more than 60% of the variables were eliminated. This high rate of missing values is due to the length of the study during which dropouts occurred. As a result of applying this filter, there were finally data from 386 infants (only 33% of the initial cases); 54 cases correspond to overweight/obese children (14%), so the dataset is quite imbalanced. Variables that still have some missing values were imputed: numerical variables by using a regression model and categorical variables with a correlation approach (see additional details in [15]).

4.2 Data Transformation

Some of the variables correspond to the same measure but in different periods (for example, height and weight of the baby). Instead of using the absolute values of these measures, the variables are transformed in % of increment regarding the previous period. Table 3 lists the variables that have been transformed.

4.3 Symbolic Coding

Variables and their values should be transformed into symbols in order to apply pattern mining methods. This transformation can be done according to the variable values: one value, one symbol. To that end, some processing should be addressed.

Regarding numerical variables (a total of 25), a discretization method is applied. The variables systolic and diastolic blood pressure for the second semester (SYS_2nd_M, DIA_2nd_M) were discretized into 4 bins according to the thresholds established by the World Health Organization (WHO) and the American Heart Association (AHA) correspondingly. BMI variables were coded into 5 labels according to the WHO recommendations. The remaining variables have been equally discretized into 4 bins (as blood pressure has four bins too).

Regarding categorical variables (10), 8 of them are boolean and the remainder 2, have four possible categories.

Table 2. Dataset variables

Variable name	Description	Units/values	Visit
AGE_M	Age of mother	years	0
HEIGHT_M	Height of mother	cm	0
SMOKING_M	Smoking status of mother (pre-preg.)	yes(1)/no(0)	0
DRINKING_M	Drinking status of mother (pre-preg.)	yes(1)/no(0)	0
BIRTH_WEIGHT_M	Birth weight of mother	1,2,3,4	0
IS_FIRST_CHILD	Parity	primip.(1)/multip.(2)	0
BMI_M	BMI of mother (pre-preg.)	kg/m^2	0
AGE_F	Age of father	years	0
HEIGHT_F	Height of father	cm	0
BMI_F	BMI of father	kg/m^2	0
SMOKING_F	Smoking status of father	yes(1)/no(0)	0
DRINKING_F	Drinking status of father	yes(1)/no(0)	0
BIRTH_WEIGHT_F	Birth weight of father	1,2,3,4	0
BMI_2nd_M	BMI of mother (2nd trim.)	kg/m^2	1
SYS_2nd_M	Mother's systolic BP (2nd trim.)	mmHg	1
DIA_2nd_M	Mother's diastolic BP (2nd trim.)	mmHg	1
BMI_3rd_M	BMI of mother (3rd trim.)	kg/m^2	2
SYS_3nd_M	Mother's systolic BP (3rd trim.)	mmHg	2
DIA_3nd_M	Mother's diastolic BP (3rd trim.)	mmHg	2
GEST_OBESITY_M	Gestational obesity of mother	yes(1)/no(0)	2
SMOKING_PREG_M	Smoking status of mother (preg.)	yes(1)/no(0)	2
GENDER_B	Sex of baby	girl(1)/boy(2)	3
GEST_AGE	Gestational age	weeks	3
WEIGHT_BIRTH_B	Birth weight of baby	grams	3
LENGTH_BIRTH_B	Birth length of baby	cm	3
WEIGHT_PLACENTA	Weight of placenta	grams	3
BREASTFEED	Months of breastfeeding	months	3
WEIGHT_2M_B	Weight at 2 months	grams	4
LENGTH_2M_B	Length at 2 months	cm	4
WEIGHT_4M_B	Weight at 4 months	grams	5
LENGTH_4M_B	Length at 4 months	cm	5
WEIGHT_6M_B	Weight at 6 months	grams	6
LENGTH_6M_B	Length at 6 months	cm	6
WEIGHT_12M_B	Weight at 12 months	grams	7
LENGTH_12M_B	Length at 12 months	cm	7
OBESITY_B	Overweight status at 5 years	Normal weight (1)/ Obese(2)	

For each variable and value, a new boolean variable is generated. At the end, we get 125 boolean variables, and the dataset is transformed according to them (one-hot-encoding). Next, the structure of the data is changed from a tabular shape into 8-length sequences, one sequence per child original instance, obtaining a dataset of sequences. Each element of a sequence contains an itemset with the information corresponding to a given visit. Information is represented by the name of the boolean variables that have true values. Strictly speaking, the name of the variables are not symbols, but strings; however, they are unique and serve for the purpose of frequent pattern mining. An example of sequence is shown in Fig. 2. Names of variables are delimited by simple quotes ('). The sequence

Table 3. Variables whose original values are transformed to % of increments.

BMI_2nd_M	BMI_increase_mother_2nd
BMI_3rd_M	BMI_increase_mother_3rd
SYS_3nd_M	SYS_BP_increase_mother_3rd
DIA_3nd_M	DIA_BP_increase_mother_3rd
LENGTH_2M_B	gain_length_to_2M_increment
WEIGHT_2M_B	gain_weight_to_2M_increment
LENGTH_4M_B	gain_length_to_4M_increment
WEIGHT_4M_B	gain_weight_to_4M_increment
LENGTH_6M_B	gain_length_to_6M_increment
WEIGHT_6M_B	gain_weight_to_6M_increment
LENGTH_12M_B	gain_length_to_12M_increment
WEIGHT_12M_B	gain_weight_to_12M_increment

```
<
[ '34<AGE_M', '159<HEIGHT_M<=163', 'SMOKING_M==0', 'DRINKING_M==0' , 'BIRTH_WEIGHT_M==3', 'IS_FIRST_CHILD==1',
  '25<=BMI_M<30', '47<=AGE_F', '176<HEIGHT_F<=180', '25<=BMI_F<30', 'SMOKING_F==0', 'DRINKING_F==1' , 'BIRTH_WEIGHT_F==2']
[ '1.5<=BMI_increase_mother_2nd<2.5' , '115<=SYS_2nd_M<120', '60<=DIA_2nd_M<70']
[ '0.1<=BMI_increase_mother_3rd<0.15', '0.018<=SYS_BP_increase_mother_3rd<0.072, '0<=DIA_BP_increase_mother_3rd<0.059']
[ 'GEST_OBESITY_M==0' ,'SMOKING_PREG_M==0' ,'GENDER_B==0' ,'38<=GEST_AGE', '3000<WEIGHT_BIRTH_B<=3500',
  'LENGTH_BIRTH_B<48', 'WEIGHT_PLACENTA<500', 'BREASTFEED<4']
[ '0.175<=gain_length_to_2M_increment<0.225', '0.6<=gain_weight_to_2M_increment<0.8']
[ '0.075<=gain_length_to_4M_increment<0.1', '0.2<=gain_weight_to_4M_increment<=0.275']
[ '0.06<=gain_length_to_6M_increment<0.08', 'gain_weight_to_6M_increment<0.1']
[ 'gain_length_to_12M_increment<0.1', '0.25<=gain_weight_to_12M_increment<0.3']
>
```

Fig. 2. Sequence example.

in the Figure does not show the target class OBESITY_B corresponding the subject.

4.4 Sequence Pattern Mining

Figure 3 details the different steps of this stage. First of all, the dataset of sequences is split into two subdatasets according to the class: obese from normal-weight kids. Next, the VEPRECO [17] algorithm (see Sect. 3) is applied to each subdataset. VEPRECO receives a database of sequences, and outputs the frequent patterns.

A possible pattern for our case study is as follows:
⟨['BIRTH_WEIGHT_M==3', 'SMOKING_F==0'],
['SMOKING_PREG_M==0', '38<=GEST_AGE'] ⟩
This is a two-length pattern, with the first itemset being ['BIRTH_WEIGHT_M ==3', 'SMOKING_F==0'] and the second component is ['SMOKING_PREG_M ==0', '38<=GEST_AGE']. Note however, that the order in the list represents a precedence order (['BIRTH_WEIGHT_M ==3', 'SMOKING_F==0'] before ['SMOKING_PREG_M==0', '38<=GEST_AGE']), and

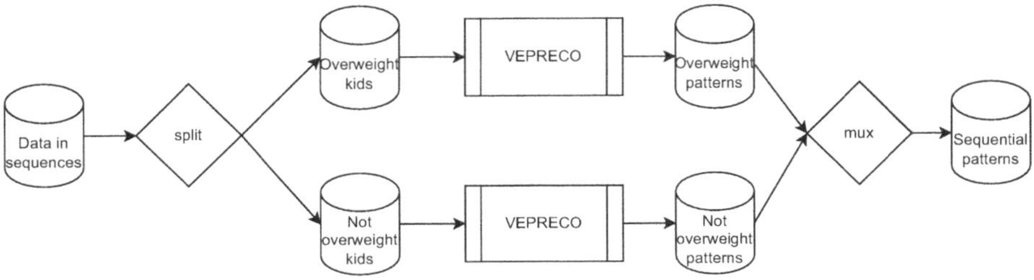

Fig. 3. Sequence pattern mining stage.

not the actual visit (that is, ['BIRTH_WEIGHT_M ==3', 'SMOKING_F==0'] belonging to the first visit, and ['SMOKING_PREG_M==0', '38<=GEST_AGE'] related to a second visit).

As with any sequence pattern mining algorithm, VEPRECO requires a support threshold that is related to the number of patterns that would be mined. After testing different values heuristically, a value of 0.4 was set; lower values may not generalize in new instances and the patterns with higher supports are difficult to find. With this threshold value, 150 patterns were mined for the obese class and 144 for the normal-weight class. The next step of the method, "mux" (Fig. 2), as an abbreviation of mutual exclusion patterns, consist on removing common patterns between the classes. In this way there are non-common patterns for both classes. At the end of this stage, 98 distinct patterns related to either the normal-weight or obesity class were identified.

4.5 Case Building

Information about each child is represented in the form of cases, using the discovered patterns. Each case is encoded as a binary vector, where a binary variable is defined for each pattern. Binary representation of patterns is a common approach for using temporal patterns for classification purposes [2]. An example of the final representation is provided in Fig. 4.

pattern0	pattern1	pattern2	pattern3	...	pattern96	pattern97	OBESITY_B
1	1	1	1		0	0	1
0	0	0	0		0	0	0
1	1	0	1		0	0	0
1	1	1	1		0	0	1
...							
1	1	1	1		1	1	0

Fig. 4. Example of cases represented by patterns. A case (row) holds information about the 98 patterns and the target variable, OBESITY_B.

The values of this binary representation are determined based on the child's data, which has been transformed into sequences through symbolic encoding (see Fig. 1 and Sect. 4.2). For each pattern, if it is a subsequence of the sequence representing the child data, the corresponding binary variable is set to 1; otherwise, it is set to 0. For example, the following pattern:

⟨['BIRTH_WEIGHT_M==3', 'SMOKING_F==0'],
['SMOKING_PREG_M==0', '38<=GEST_AGE'] ⟩

is a subsequence of the sequence in Fig. 2. As it is possible to observe, we are not looking for an exact match, but that the pattern is considered in the sequence. So, the elements of the pattern, ⟨['BIRTH_WEIGHT_M==3', 'SMOKING_F==0'], are a subset of the first itemset of the sequence; and ['SMOKING _PREG_M==0', '38<=GEST_AGE'] of the fifth itemset.

4.6 CBR

In this work, we implement the first phase of CBR, retrieve. To that end, we employ the k-nearest neighbor (KNN) algorithm. Several distances are tested in the experimental section, but the Rusellrao [18] distance, designed for Boolean variables, is the most suitable one, as our cases are binary representation of sequential patterns.

4.7 Experimental Set up

To test our methodology, four main experiments have been carried out.

Performance. The first experiment is about evaluating the performance of our approach. Our hypothesis is that sequence patterns improve the information for children's obesity prediction. This is the main experiment that would support our contribution. To that end, the following configurations are considered:

- Sequential patterns: We represent cases as in our methodology, by pattern binary variables (Fig. 4).
- Raw dataset: We do use the data as provided. Some preprocessing is conducted to enable the application of a distance for KNN: we standardized numerical variables, and categorical variables are first coded (one-hot-encoding) and then normalized (according to their proportion in each value) [5].
- Transformed dataset: We represent cases according to the transformation explained in Sect. 4.2, that is, the same measures of mothers and children taken over time are represented as % of increments.

For comparative purposes, we use the Euclidean distance in all of the configurations. We use cross-validation with 5 folds. As we have a great challenge with our imbalanced dataset, we used a clustering balancing approach [14].

Distance Analysis. We analyze different distances in the CBR. We studied a broad set of metrics, from the one we propose in this work, Rusellrao, to other designed for categorical variables (e.g. Hamming) or numerical values (such as the Euclidean distance), among others. Our aim is to demonstrate that Rusellrao fits the best.

Hybrid Data Versus Patterns Alone. We consider to combining original data with patterns. In particular, features that correspond to the first visit, and the birth are combined with patterns. The variables added are the ones showed in bold in Table 2.

Imbalanced Data Analysis. As the previous test are carried out with a balanced dataset, we analyze in this experiment the impact of dealing with an imbalanced dataset as we have (14% of kids with overweight or obesity). Two configurations are considered:

- Bootstrapping emulation. A 5-Fold CV is used 386 times (equivalent to the number of instances), emulating a bootstrapping process to estimate the mean and standard deviation of the performance metrics.
- Leave pair out cross-validation (LPOCV). All possible combinations of pairings 1 normal weight with 1 obese children are generated. For each pair, the training set is defined holding the pair out for testing, from which the performance metrics are measured [1]. LOPCV involves conducting a huge number of tests (17.928, as having 332 normal weight and 54 obese kids, so 332×54). The training set is balanced with clustering as in the previous experiments.

5 Results

The results are provided in terms of accuracy and recall. Given the goal of shedding light on predicting obesity, optimizing recall was prioritized. In addition, accuracy was considered to measure the overall model performance.

5.1 Experimental Results

Performance Results. Table 4 shows the results obtained. Using our method, the highest accuracy (0.69) and recall (0.48) are achieved. Accuracy exhibits the highest improvement with up to 19% of increase regarding the original data. The improvement on recall is smoother, up to 2% of increase. The results are conclusive, the model makes better predictions when sequential patterns are used.

Table 4. Results: Value added by patterns.

Approach	Accuracy		Recall	
	mean	std	mean	std
Raw	0.58	0.07	0.47	0.12
Transformed	0.61	0.07	0.35	0.12
Sequence patterns	**0.69**	0.08	**0.48**	0.11

Table 5. Results: Distances sensitivity analysis.

Metric	Accuracy mean	Accuracy std	Recall mean	Recall std
Euclidean	0.69	0.08	0.48	0.11
Hamming	0.69	0.06	0.48	0.11
Jaccard	0.73	0.10	0.84	0.09
Cosine	0.70	0.09	0.86	0.13
Canberra	0.69	0.64	0.48	0.11
Braycurtis	0.70	0.11	0.84	0.09
Yule	0.50	0.03	0.55	0.11
Correlation	0.67	0.12	0.60	0.19
Chebyshev	0.50	0.07	0	0
Mahalanobis	0.63	0.16	0.58	0.24
Rusellrao	**0.74**	0.05	**0.98**	0.04
Rogerstanimoto	0.67	0.07	0.48	0.11
Sokalsneath	0.70	0.11	0.84	0.09

Table 6. Results: Cases represented with hybrid data (raw data with patterns) versus cases based exclusively on sequential patterns.

Approach	Accuracy mean	Accuracy std	Recall mean	Recall std
Sequence patterns	0.69	0.08	**0.48**	0.11
Hybrid	**0.79**	0.03	0.42	0.13

Distance Analysis. Table 5 shows the results obtained in this experiment. Analyzing the recall of this second experiment, it can be deduced that using the Rusellrao metrics is the best choice. Moreover, it also exhibits the best accuracy. It is a measure particularly designed for boolean variables, and thus responds to our case representation: binary vectors representing sequential patters. Other distances, such as Jaccard, Cosine, Braycurtis and Sokalsneath also provide the closest accuracy to Rusellrao (Jaccard performs about 2% less, Cosine and Braycurtis and Sokalsneath about 5.5% less). The corresponding recall varies, with Cosine with 13% less, Jaccard, Braycurtis, and Sokalsneath 14%, exhibiting the poorest behavior than Rusellrao to detect obese children.

Hybrid Data Versus Sequence Patterns Alone. Table 6 shows the comparison of the hybrid approach versus the dataset using only binary variables that represent patterns. We see how when combining patterns with first visit and birth visit variables, the accuracy increases considerably, up to 15% more approx. than with patterns alone. However, recall falls from 0.48 to 0.42, a 13% approximately.

Imbalanced Data Analysis. Table 7 shows the results for both, the Bootstrapping emulation configuration and the LPOCV one. Using Bootstrapping, a 20% of improvement in accuracy is achieved, from 0.69 (see Table 4) to 0.83; however, recall decreases significantly. On the other hand, LPOCV increases a 20% in recall, but accuracy decreases considerable, a 30%. Interestingly, the high standard deviation suggests a potential issue with the data.

Table 7. Results when analyzing the impact of the imbalanced data.

Bootstrapping emulation				LPOCV			
Accuracy		Recall		Accuracy		Recall	
mean	std	mean	std	mean	std	mean	std
0.83	0.01	0.07	0.03	0.53	0.35	**0.57**	0.49

5.2 Discussion

Several conclusions can be drawn from the results obtained. The first is that adding sequence patterns considerably increases the quality of predictions compared to using only the original dataset. In this context, the analysis of the different metrics highlights the Russelrao distance for its high recall. Incorporating additional variables through a hybrid approach improves accuracy, but at the expense of recall. It appears challenging to identify a single configuration that performs well in both precision and recall simultaneously. Therefore, future research could explore combined strategies, such as integrating multiple CBR systems into a unified framework, to capitalize on the strengths of each. One potential solution could be a multi-agent system, where several CBRs with varying performance in recall and accuracy collaborate to provide the most reliable outcome.

Among the 386 infants in the dataset, 54 cases correspond to overweight and obese children (14%), indicating a significant class imbalance. To better understand the data, we applied Bootstrapping and LPOCV. However, the results suggest that the high dimensionality of the dataset may be concealing outliers that are distorting the outcomes. In particular, the high standard deviation observed in the LPOCV results may point to specific cases that warrant closer examination. Nevertheless, in the main experiment that supports our contribution, we employed a balancing strategy based on clustering—a technique associated with the creation of case prototypes [26]—which holds potential for practical application.

5.3 Limitations

The results support the initial hypothesis—that sequential patterns offer discriminatory power. However, their applicability in clinical practice remains limited due to the relatively low performance metrics observed. Thus, this results should be considered as a preliminary step toward the use of temporal patterns in CBR. Future work should include external validation with closed dataset as the ones provided in [11,27].

The experiments carried out are based on a simple approximation of CBR, using KNN with a distance metric that applies uniform costs. However, CBR offers further opportunities for exploration. In particular, a weighted distance metric could be developed in the future to enhance performance. In this context, sequence pattern mining algorithms provide, for each pattern, the number of instances that support it (i.e., its frequency). This information could be leveraged to implement a notion of pattern relevance, potentially improving future CBR retrieval methods.

6 Conclusions

Childhood obesity is a unwanted health condition that threatens our society and the quality of life of future adults. This work analyzes the contribution of sequential patterns to characterize children's data in order to predict their obesity status using a CBR approach. A dataset that contains longitudinal data of children and parents, have been used to mine the sequential patterns. Next cases are built based on binary representation of such patterns (depending if the data meets or not the pattern). The results of the experiments demonstrate that binary representations enhances CBR prediction capabilities for childhood obesity.

However, the results obtained have limited values of accuracy and recall, which implies continuing to reconsider other methodologies in the future. One of the lines of future work could be to explore pattern properties as feature relevance in CBR.

Acknowledgement. This study was supported by the "Ministerio de Ciencia e Innovacion", "Instituto de Salud Carlos III" (ISCIII) (PI23/00545 and PI22/00366), project co-funded by FEDER ("Fondo Europeo de Desarrollo Regional"). The work was also carried out with support from the Departament de Recerca i Universitats de la Generalitat de Catalunya (2021 SGR 01125).

References

1. Airola, A., Pahikkala, T., Waegeman, W., Baets, B.D., Salakoski, T.: A comparison of AUC estimators in small-sample studies. In: JMLR: Workshop and Conference Proceedings, vol. 8, pp. 3–13. PMLR (2009). https://proceedings.mlr.press/v8/airola10a.html
2. Batal, I., Valizadegan, H., Cooper, G.F., Hauskrecht, M.: A temporal pattern mining approach for classifying electronic health record data. ACM Trans. Intell. Syst. Technol. **4** (2013). https://doi.org/10.1145/2508037.2508044

3. Compta, M., López, B.: Integration of sequence learning and CBR for complex equipment failure prediction. In: Ram, A., Wiratunga, N. (eds.) ICCBR 2011. LNCS (LNAI), vol. 6880, pp. 408–422. Springer, Heidelberg (2011). https://doi.org/10.1007/978-3-642-23291-6_30
4. Dong, W., Lee, E.W., Hertzberg, V.S., Simpson, R.L., Ho, J.C.: GASP: graph-based approximate sequential pattern mining for electronic health records. Commun. Comput. Inf. Sci. **1450 CCIS**, 50–60 (2021). https://doi.org/10.1007/978-3-030-85082-1_5/FIGURES/2
5. Escribà-Montagut, X.: DataSHIELD advances: transformative extensions for privacy-preserving big data analysis in health and biosciences, Ph.D. thesis (2024). https://www.tdx.cat/handle/10803/691737
6. Eskridge, T.C., Weekes, T.R.: Opportunities for case-based reasoning in personal flow and productivity management In: ICCBR 2020. LNCS (LNAI), vol. 12311, pp. 349–354. Springer, Cham (2020). https://doi.org/10.1007/978-3-030-58342-2_23/FIGURES/3
7. Fernandez, J., Hernández-Guillamet, G., Montserrat, C., Innocenti, B., López, B.: Examining the potential of sequence patterns from EEG data as alternative case representation for seizure detection. In: ICCBR 2024. LNCS (LNAI), vol. 14775, pp. 258–272. Springer, Cham (2024). https://doi.org/10.1007/978-3-031-63646-2_17/FIGURES/10
8. Fournier-Viger, P., School, J.C.W.L., University, R.U.K., Koh, Y.S., Thomas, R.: A survey of sequential pattern mining Philippe. Data Sci. Pattern Recogn. **1**, 54–77 (2017)
9. Funk, P., Xiong, N.: Extracting knowledge from sensor signals for case-based reasoning with longitudinal time series data. Stud. Comput. Intell. **73**, 247–284 (2008). https://doi.org/10.1007/978-3-540-73180-1_9
10. Gou, H., Song, H., Tian, Z., Liu, Y.: Prediction models for children/adolescents with obesity/overweight: a systematic review and meta-analysis. Prev. Med. **179**, 107823 (2024). https://doi.org/10.1016/J.YPMED.2023.107823
11. Hammond, R., et al.: Predicting childhood obesity using electronic health records and publicly available data. PLOS ONE **14**, e0215571 (2019). https://doi.org/10.1371/JOURNAL.PONE.0215571
12. He, Z., Zhang, S., Wu, J.: Significance-based discriminative sequential pattern mining. Expert Syst. Appl. **122**, 54–64 (2019). https://doi.org/10.1016/J.ESWA.2018.12.046
13. Hernández-Guillamet, G., López, B.: Improving emotions prediction with sequence representations of psychophysiological data. In: Engineering in Medicine and Biology Conference (EMBC, IEEE) (2019)
14. Lemaître, G., Nogueira, F., Aridas, C.K.: Imbalanced-learn: a python toolbox to tackle the curse of imbalanced datasets in machine learning. J. Mach. Learn. Res. **18**(17), 1–5 (2017). http://jmlr.org/papers/v18/16-365.html
15. López, B., Galera, D., López-Bermejo, A., Bassols, J.: Frequent patterns of childhood overweight from longitudinal data on parental and early-life of infants health. In: AIME 2024. LNCS (LNAI), vol. 14844, pp, 64–69 (2024). https://doi.org/10.1007/978-3-031-66538-7_7/FIGURES/3
16. Martin, F.J., Plaza, E.: Ceaseless case-based reasoning. In: Funk, P., González Calero, P.A. (eds.) ECCBR 2004. LNCS (LNAI), vol. 3155, pp. 287–301. Springer, Heidelberg (2004). https://doi.org/10.1007/978-3-540-28631-8_22
17. Mordvanyuk, N., Bifet, A., López, B.: VEPRECO: vertical databases with pre-pruning strategies and common candidate selection policies to fasten sequential

pattern mining. Expert Syst. Appl. **204**, 117517 (2022). https://doi.org/10.1016/j.eswa.2022.117517
18. Naseem, R., Maqbooly, O., Muhammadz, S.: Improved similarity measures for software clustering. In: Proceedings of the European Conference on Software Maintenance and Reengineering, CSMR, pp. 45–54 (2011). https://doi.org/10.1109/CSMR.2011.9
19. O'Connor, T.G., Williams, J., Blair, C., Gatzke-Kopp, L.M., Francis, L., Willoughby, M.T.: Predictors of developmental patterns of obesity in young children. Front. Pediatr. **8**, 506691 (2020). https://doi.org/10.3389/FPED.2020.00109/BIBTEX
20. Pinaire, J., Chabert, E., Azé, J., Bringay, S., Landais, P.: Sequential pattern mining to predict medical in-hospital mortality from administrative data: application to acute coronary syndrome. J. Healthc. Eng. **2021** (2021). https://doi.org/10.1155/2021/5531807
21. Srikant, R., Agrawal, R.: Mining sequential patterns: generalizations and performance improvements. In: Apers, P., Bouzeghoub, M., Gardarin, G. (eds.) EDBT 1996. LNCS, vol. 1057, pp. 1–17. Springer, Heidelberg (1996). https://doi.org/10.1007/BFb0014140
22. Valdez-Ávila, M.F., Bermejo-Sabbagh, C., Diaz-Agudo, B., del Castillo, M.G.O., Recio-Garcia, J.A.: CBR-fox: a case-based explanation method for time series forecasting models. In: ICCBR 2023. LNCS (LNAI), vol. 14141, pp. 200–214 (2023). https://doi.org/10.1007/978-3-031-40177-0_13/FIGURES/7
23. WHO: Obesity and overweight (2024). https://www.who.int/news-room/fact-sheets/detail/obesity-and-overweight
24. Wu, Y., Wang, Y., Li, Y., Zhu, X., Wu, X.: Top-k self-adaptive contrast sequential pattern mining. IEEE Trans. Cybern. **52**, 11819–11833 (2022). https://doi.org/10.1109/TCYB.2021.3082114
25. Wu, Y., Wang, Y., Liu, J., Yu, M., Liu, J., Li, Y.: Mining distinguishing subsequence patterns with nonoverlapping condition. Cluster Comput. **22**, 5905–5917 (2019). https://doi.org/10.1007/S10586-017-1671-0/FIGURES/5
26. Yu, L., Li, M., Liu, X.: A two-stage case-based reasoning driven classification paradigm for financial distress prediction with missing and imbalanced data. Expert Syst. Appl. **249**, 123745 (2024). https://doi.org/10.1016/J.ESWA.2024.123745
27. Ziauddeen, N., Roderick, P.J., Santorelli, G., Alwan, N.A.: Prediction of childhood overweight and obesity at age 10–11: findings from the studying lifecourse obesity predictors and the born in Bradford Cohorts. Int. J. Obes. **47**, 1065–1073 (2023). https://doi.org/10.1038/s41366-023-01356-8

Case-Based Activity Detection from Segmented Internet of Things Data

Ronny Seiger[1(✉)], Alexander Schultheis[2,3], and Ralph Bergmann[2,3]

[1] University of St. Gallen, Rosenbergstrasse 30, St. Gallen 9000, Switzerland
Ronny.Seiger@unisg.ch

[2] German Research Center for Artificial Intelligence (DFKI), Branch Trier University, Behringstraße 21, 54296 Trier, Germany
{Alexander.Schultheis,Ralph.Bergmann}@dfki.de, {schultheis,bergmann}@uni-trier.de

[3] Artificial Intelligence and Intelligent Information Systems, Trier University, 54296 Trier, Germany
http://www.wi2.uni-trier.de

Abstract. The use of Internet of Things (IoT) technologies drives the automation of business processes. However, such environments often lack process awareness and corresponding systems to monitor process executions. Due to its too fine-grained nature and variations, the direct use of data from IoT devices for monitoring is problematic, requiring an event abstraction step to lift the data to the business process level. This work investigates the application of Temporal Case-Based Reasoning (TCBR) as a novel experience-based approach to detect process activity executions in IoT data. The proposed TCBR approach uses *activity signatures*–representations of process and IoT data for an activity prototype–as a case base to classify unknown IoT time series data from a smart factory. A data flow architecture is presented that supports analysts in selecting a suitable activity prototype and evaluating its quality for activity detection. The results enable both, the development of high-quality activity detection services and the identification of improvement opportunities in IoT monitoring systems. The approach is evaluated using data produced by a smart factory. The results indicate that the TCBR methods used are very suitable for detecting activities in this IoT use case.

Keywords: Temporal Case-Based Reasoning · Time Series Data · Activity Detection · Internet of Things

1 Introduction

The automation of business processes in many domains of every-day life is rapidly advancing, empowered by the ongoing developments and dissemination of *Internet of Things* (IoT) technologies. The IoT introduces new data sources–*Sensors*–providing insights into the operations, interactions, and environment of smart devices, humans, and digital software systems. Although processes are ubiquitous

R. Seiger and A. Schultheis—These authors contributed equally.

© The Author(s), under exclusive license to Springer Nature Switzerland AG 2025
I. Bichindaritz and B. López (Eds.): ICCBR 2025, LNAI 15662, pp. 438–453, 2025.
https://doi.org/10.1007/978-3-031-96559-3_29

in many IoT-related domains [47], *Process-Aware Information Systems* (PAIS) are often not available to monitor or even orchestrate their executions [39]. Instead, it is necessary to rely on the data produced by the sensors to derive information about the execution of processes and activities in these processes, which can be the basis for more advanced process analysis via process mining [19]. Relying on IoT data, however, entails several challenges as the sensor data is often recorded at a too fine-grained, low level, and it might be subject to variations, which negatively influences the quality of process activity detections.

To gain insights into the execution of process activities, an *event abstraction* step is necessary to lift the low-level sensor data from IoT devices to the level of process events (cf. Fig. 2) [10]. While many related works propose to apply rather heavy-weight machine learning approaches in this context, we discuss the application of *Temporal Case-Based Reasoning* (TCBR) to classify the sensor data, in the form of a time series, according to the process activities they belong to. We start with the data analyst identifying one *activity signature* as a case, which represents the IoT data for a prototypical execution of one type of activity over time [39]. The main challenge is selecting a representative activity execution because the underlying IoT data is often affected by variations for the same activity type. The cases from several activity types are used to classify the segmented IoT data recorded from a small-scale smart factory during the execution of multiple instances of typical production processes with manufacturing activities. We propose a data analysis architecture based on TCBR to support data analysts with selecting a suitable activity signature and evaluating its quality for detecting instances of the corresponding process activity. From the calculated similarities, we can inform the analyst about the match of the selected signature with specific instances, potential ambiguities [14], and other data quality issues that may arise from the aforementioned variations in the IoT sensor data [27]. These insights will 1) enable the development of high-quality activity detection services that are independent of PAIS as described in [38], which is especially relevant in less automated domains with manual activities (e.g., smart healthcare [13]); and, 2) they will also enable IoT engineers to identify opportunities for improving the monitoring of IoT data systems via additional sensors.

The paper is structured as follows: Sect. 2 introduces foundations and the novel use case of activity executions in IoT systems. In Sect. 3 related work is presented and discussed. Section 4 presents our approach to detect activity executions from IoT data based on TCBR. This approach is evaluated and discussed in Sect. 5. Finally, Sect. 6 concludes the paper and outlines future work.

2 Foundations and Use Case

2.1 IoT Data and Process Activities in the Smart Factory

IoT System: In this work, we investigate IoT systems as novel data sources and application domains for *Case-Based Reasoning* (CBR). The examples used in this work are taken from the domain of manufacturing. The small-scale smart factory depicted in Fig. 1 represents the IoT system that executes processes

Fig. 1. Small-scale Smart Factory with Production Stations used as IoT System.


```
{ "id": "8ee0fa9a-6dad-4bf8-a0dc-df01333b493f", "station": "MM_1",
"timestamp": "2023-01-30 13:06:22.24", "i1_pos_switch": 0, "o7_valve": 0,
"i2_pos_switch": 0, "i3_pos_switch": 0, "i4_light_barrier": 1,
"m1_speed": 512, "m2_speed": 0, "m3_speed": 0, "o8_compressor": 0 }
```


Listing 1. Example IoT Data (in JSON) from Milling Station.

and emits low-level IoT data [26]. The smart factory features seven production stations including a *high-bay warehouse* (HBW) for storage, a *vacuum gripper crane* (VGR) for transportation, an oven and milling machine for production tasks, and a sorting machine. All the hardware components can be controlled via software executed on embedded controllers, which are networked and expose an interface to be remotely accessed by more complex software applications, e.g., in a service-based software architecture [41].

IoT Data: During its operations, the smart factory regularly emits low-level IoT data regarding the status of its sensors (e.g., buttons and light barriers) and actuators (e.g., motors, valves, and compressors). An exemplary low-level IoT data reading from the milling machine is presented in Listing 1. This reading has a unique ID, timestamp, and the specific status of all sensors and actuators that are part of the station. The factory emits these readings for all stations at a configurable frequency. Thus, we are faced with time series data to be analyzed.

IoT Processes: In this work, we will analyze two topical processes from discrete manufacturing [39]. The *Storage* process contains a sequence of automated process activities to store a new workpiece in the HBW including transport and loading activities. The *Production* process contains a sequence of activities to unload a workpiece and produce it in the oven and milling machine stations with

subsequent sorting and transportation. Both processes can be executed in the smart factory using a *Workflow Management System* (WfMS) based on the software stack presented in [41]. The process activities contained in both processes are the entities whose execution we aim to detect solely based on the low-level IoT data from all production stations. Hereby, an activity is considered to be an atomic unit of work executed either by a machine, human, or digital service [47]. An activity has a label, and the execution of an activity is characterized by a timestamped start event and end event, which determine its duration.
IoT Data–Process Activity Correlation (Event Abstraction):

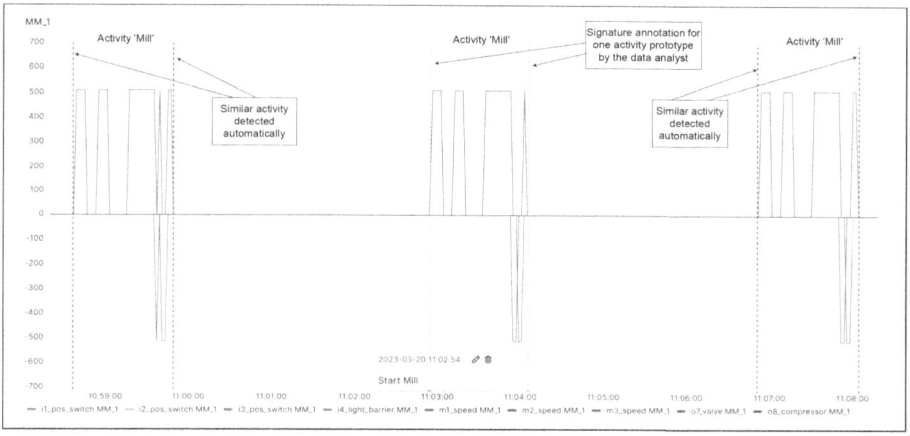

Fig. 2. IoT Data for three Instances of the *Mill* Activity with Signature Annotation for one Execution as Event Abstraction (middle, dashed light blue lines). The two similar instances (left and right, dashed dark red lines) should be detected automatically.

Figure 2 shows an example of the correlation between the low-level IoT data and process activity as an event abstraction step. Each differently colored solid line represents the values of one sensor or actuator over time. Given such time series of low-level data readings from all sensors and actuators of the IoT system, the corresponding process activity should be inferred. We investigate the applicability of CBR to this problem and type of data. For example, Fig. 2 contains the execution of three instances of the *Mill* activity that should be classified accordingly only given the IoT data. One instance thereby serves as prototype determined by the data analyst to detect the other occurrences. One challenge in creating this correlation and finding a suitable prototype activity is the existence of variations in the IoT data associated with different executions of the *same* type of activity. In Fig. 2, we can observe slight variations in the durations of how long a sensor or actuator stays in a specific state, and we can see an additional peak in the value of a sensor for the first instance. However, all three sequences represent executions of the same type of activity. These variations make it challenging to select a suitable prototype segment within the low-level

IoT data (cf. Figure 2) that best represents a process activity from start to end. We propose to use CBR to support the IoT data analysts with this selection process.

IoT Data Variations: Our experience with IoT systems [27] and analysis of the variations in the IoT data unveiled the following reasons for their occurrence between instances of the same type of activity:

- Different execution times: Activity executions may vary in their duration due to different process parameters and different start/end conditions.
- Different process/activity parameters: Activity executions may involve different sequences of sensors and actuators, depending on specific parameters.
- Different start/end conditions: Activity executions may not always start or end with the same conditions, resulting in different movement patterns.
- External factors: IoT systems interact with the physical world, where external conditions and factors are harder to control than in pure digital systems. This might create different types of variations in the IoT data.
- Different sampling frequencies: The sampling frequencies of the underlying IoT data may also contribute to variations.
- Parallel activity executions: The parallel execution of activities in the IoT system might lead to different sensor and actuator patterns in the IoT data than for consecutive executions, possibly superimposing each other. In this work, we assume that these scenarios are out of scope and the execution of an activity is limited to only one execution on one station at a time.

2.2 Temporal Case-Based Reasoning

The application of CBR to IoT sensor data falls within the research area of TCBR [18,22]. This deals with the representation of temporal relationships in cases and their handling within the CBR cycle. TCBR is used in various application areas such as classification and error detection, prediction or medicine [25]. In each use case, the underlying data is complex, resulting in challenges for filling the knowledge containers [32]. The application of TCBR requires the definition of a suitable vocabulary for modeling the sensor data and the selection of suitable similarity measures to enable correct reuse of experience knowledge.

Various forms of case representation exist for filling the vocabulary and on this foundation the case base [25]. While approaches such as episodes, graphs or event sequences exist, time series are the most established form of representation in TCBR. A time series is defined as a sequence of values that are associated with specified points in time. In most applications, this data is represented in symbolic form and summarized as feature vectors. Simplified forms of representation such as temporal abstraction [43] can be used to reduce the volume of data. These abstract the time series to a higher level by aggregating data points, which decreases the following computation complexity. However, such an abstraction leads to a loss of information, which can be unsuitable for certain use cases [37].

Usually, a case representing IoT sensor data contains one or more time series [25]. These are local attributes that are aggregated in a higher-level case description.

Based on the selected vocabulary, suitable similarity measures must be used to identify similar time series [25]. Table 1 presents a categorization of syntactic similarity measures between time series. In these measures, no domain knowledge is included so that these can be defined as knowledge-poor [45]. Furthermore, there are knowledge-intensive similarity measures that compare time series not only based on syntax, but also taking semantics into account (e.g., by Nakanishi [29]). Such semantic time series measures have not yet been used in TCBR and for the use cases in the analysis of IoT sensor data. A syntactic consideration regarding stretching and compression has so far been sufficient [25]. The categories of similarity measures are based on the local-global principle [4, pp. 106–107], in which the similarities of individual attribute values are calculated and aggregated into a global similarity value. This means that at a local level, similarity measures are used for the point in time and the corresponding value characteristic. Depending on the use case, these measures can be semantic or syntactic measures. As several time series might be available for most sensor data cases, the similarity values between these time series can also be aggregated at a global level and merged into one similarity value.

Table 1. The Three Categories of Syntactic Similarity Measures for Time Series, With Example Algorithm for Each Category (according to Malburg et al. [25]).

Category 1	Category 2	Category 3
Similarity measures that can only be applied to time series of the same length, comparing only the values at the corresponding times.	Similarity measures that can be applied to time series of different lengths, considering the values and the time points.	Similarity measures, like those in Cat. 2, but that can detect stretching and compression in addition.
List Mapping [25]	Smith-Waterman Algorithm (SWA) [44]	Dynamic Time Warping (DTW) [33]

3 Related Work

3.1 Classification Based on Temporal Case-Based Reasoning

Related work already exists in which TCBR is applied to the smart manufacturing domain and applied for classification. Klein et al. [21] learn a similarity measure using expert knowledge for classification in the field of predictive maintenance. Based on the similarity-based results, the approach classifies whether faults will occur based on sensor data so that preventive actions can be taken. Malburg et al. [25] present the use case of event and activity detection based on TCBR as an example of an implementation in the CBR framework ProCAKE [5]. Based on a large case base with collected sensor data, a retrieval is performed and based on the most similar cases, a classification is done. Based on this data, Weich et al. [48] investigate the use of embeddings in TCBR for this use case to improve retrieval efficiency. Schultheis et al. [37] use TCBR to identify specific data quality issues by using *Dynamic Time Warping* (DTW) similarity analysis to detect anomalies and classify these on experience base. All three approaches use IoT data from factories and apply empirical knowledge for classification.

TCBR is used for classification in the medical domain in the context of decision support systems. For a binary classification to determine the creatinine course as critical or non-critical, Schlaefer et al. [35] use CBR. Their similarity calculation is based on a distance metric determined by linear regression. Funk and Xiong [16] perform classification of diseases based on similar cases represented as sequences. Similarly, Nilsson et al. [30] pursue the goal of identifying stress-related disorders based on patterns in time series. Elsayed et al. [11] convert medical images into curves and perform retrieval on them using DTW as a similarity measure. The knowledge stored in the case base is used to classify disease findings. The analysis of patient data from people with back pain is investigated by Szczepanski et al. [46], using time series to derive targeted treatment recommendations based on similar cases. As with activity detection, these areas of application are based on sensor data that is to be classified using CBR.

CBR can also be used to analyze IoT data outside the manufacturing and medical domains. Fritsche et al. [15] use TCBR to identify critical situations by comparing current time series with historical cases, using DTW to detect potential failure cases. Borck et al. [7] apply a similar method to monitor astronauts, recognizing activities and identifying errors in their execution. To monitor elder people at home, Lupiani et al. [24] use TCBR with temporal edit distance as a measure. Data from a smart home environment is used to identify what activities people are currently performing and if these are risks. Ariza et al. [2] use CBR to classify player skill levels based on multidimensional time series measurements. These are also case-based classifications based on time series data.

3.2 Process Activity Detection from IoT Data

The BPM-IoT manifesto is among the advocates of applying Process Management (BPM) technologies to the IoT, and vice versa [19]. It highlights the opportunities and challenges of using IoT data for and together with process mining, which is discussed in more detail in [27]. These works highlight the bridging of the abstraction gap between low-level IoT data and process-level data as an important, non-trivial task, which also includes choosing a suitable level of event granularity for process mining [3]. The study in [27] discusses the contributions of sensor data to the execution of a process activity, including sensors emitting data that is of no relevance to sensor data that is relevant for several activities. In our work, we start from the concept of an *activity signature* [39], which involves the data analyst specifying the relevant IoT sensors in a first step.

Various approaches investigating activity detection and IoT data segmentation have been proposed in [20,31], and more specialized in the context of smart homes [9,12], smart cars [6], human activity detection [8], and industrial processes [28]. A common challenge lies in the bridging of the abstraction gap between low-level event data and high-level process events [10], which is the goal of our work. Most of these approaches are either tied to specific types of sensors, which limits their general applicability, or they train expensive overly complex machine learning models to classify activity executions. The presence of aforementioned variations within the IoT data negatively influences the quality of the activity detections in most of these cases. We aim to develop a more generic light-weight approach that is able to tolerate these variations to a certain degree.

4 Case-Based Activity Detection from IoT Data

In Fig. 3, we present an overview of the data flow architecture that we propose for learning (top part) as well as for retrieval and reuse (bottom part).

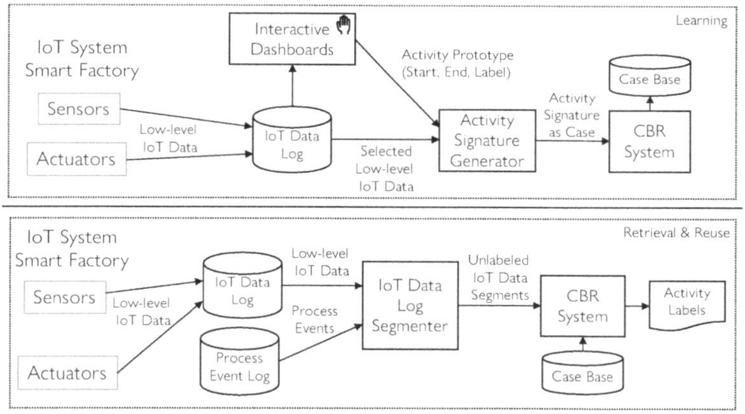

Fig. 3. Data flow Architecture for Learning and CBR Application.

4.1 Learning Phase

In the *Learning Phase*, the data from the IoT system's sensors and actuators (cf., e.g., Listing 1) recorded during the exemplary execution of the processes is persisted in an IoT data log (e.g., a time series database). This data is visualized in an interactive dashboard (cf. Fig. 2) where the data analyst identifies and annotates a prototypical execution of an activity according to the method described in [39]. In the learning phase, we assume that a PAIS for process monitoring is not available and thus, the analyst needs to provide the data annotations for one prototype of an activity execution. The provided data–the activity label, its start and end timestamps–is then used together with the corresponding IoT data from the data log (aligned based on the timestamps) to generate the activity signature [39]. This signature represents the activity execution's manifestation in the IoT data, which is converted to a case in the CBR system. A vocabulary exists for this purpose, which provides the storage of the relevant time series at local level and as the attributes relating to the process on global level (e.g., the executing station in the factory). The signatures are converted into the format specified by the vocabulary so that the signatures are contained in the case base.

To apply the TCBR approach with this vocabulary and case base, local similarity measures must be modeled by domain experts to be able to compare the time points of the time series and the corresponding values (e.g., coordinates or Boolean conditions), and aggregate these for each time series entry appropriately. The comparison of the time series itself is performed using DTW [33] based on the calculated similarity values for the individual entries [34]. This similarity measure aligns entries of two time series by computing an optimal mapping based on those local similarities. Therefore, DTW has the potential of recognizing the time series lengths without penalizing the subsequent similarity values (cf. Table 1). This enables the signatures used in activity detection, only containing a minimal number of time points, to be compared with the significantly longer time series from the query and recognized as similar. For aggregation on a global level, a similarity measure is used that learns class-specific weights (cf. [4, p. 122]) from the case base. Due to the number of sensors in smart factories, not all recorded time series are of relevance to the respective activity. Only the relevant time series are stored in the case itself, while other attributes are ignored. In contrast, the query can contain significantly more attributes with associated time series, as all sensors are continuously producing data. For similarity assessment, therefore, an aggregation function with class-specific weights is required, whereby the weights are only binary and indicate whether an attribute is relevant or not. This similarity knowledge can be derived from the case base by extracting the respective activity as a label from each case and only considering through an equal weight higher than 0.0 the attributes for which the case contains time series. All other attributes not contained in the case are weighted with 0.0 and thus omitted from the similarity calculation. This means that the global similarity measure is automatically learned based on the case. From these relevant, identified attributes, the average is calculated as global similarity value. As adaptation knowledge, only null adaptation is used for this domain because there is only one case derived from the activity prototype in the case base for each activity, and it is therefore assumed that the most similar case contains the correct label.

4.2 Application of the CBR Cycle

The application of the CBR cycle [1] focuses on *Retrieval and Reuse Phases*. We aim to classify unknown data from the IoT system, which is stored in the IoT data log, according to the activity executions it represents. Our goal is to only classify the IoT data in a first step using TCBR, not to segment it (i.e., to identify specific start and end times). For the segmentation task, we use the process event log recorded by a WfMS during the execution of the processes. This event log contains start and end times of activity executions to be used for segmentation, and their labels to be used as ground truth for evaluations.

Note that the process event log has been created automatically by executing process models that describe the sequence of activities (e.g., as described in [41]). This event log does not have to be created by a WfMS or PAIS, as we assume that these systems might not be available in the IoT system. It can also be created by other activity monitoring approaches–even a manual tracking of start and end events–while recording the corresponding IoT data. The unlabeled and segmented low-level IoT data is fed into the CBR system for classification.

In the CBR system, a retrieval is triggered that works based on the similarity measures described in Sect. 4.1. The activity from the most similar case is reused and, therefore, returned as an identified activity label including the similarity value. This value serves as a confidence value for the data analyst, as it can be used to assess whether the label is determined with a high degree of certainty (high similarity value) or based on the lack of suitable alternative cases (low similarity value). In addition, all cases with similarity values can be returned to check whether other cases have similarly high values, indicating potential ambiguities [14]. These results help the data analyst to assess the quality of detecting activity executions from the selected prototypical activity signature, and thus, if a modification of the signature or even an adjustment of the IoT system (e.g., by adding new sensors [27]) is necessary. Once the activity signature is confirmed to be suitable, it can serve as an input for automatically generating a corresponding activity detection service based on the approach presented in [38].

5 Evaluation

The activity detection approach is implemented in the *ProCAKE* framework [5][1] which has already been used for TCBR in previous research. In this section, we present the data collection and analysis setup, and discuss the results.

5.1 Setup

To evaluate the activity detection, we modeled the two IoT processes described in Sect. 2.1. The *storage* process consists of 6 activities, the *production* process consists of 10 activities; both to be executed in sequence. We used a WfMS to execute several instances of these processes over 27.63 min to record an IoT data log for the learning phase. In this log, 12 distinct activities were annotated from six production stations by an expert data analyst. From these annotations, we generated the corresponding 12 activity signatures to be stored as 12 cases in the case base. To test the TCBR approach, 36 instances of the two processes were executed in the factory, with a total duration of 178.44 min and 359 activity executions. These activities are used as queries for the evaluation, each based on the executing stations. The IoT data logs were sampled at a frequency of 0.5 Hz. The process event log recorded by the WfMS was used as ground truth and to

[1] Available at: https://gitlab.rlp.net/procake/publications/procake-activity-detection.

segment the activity execution. The time required to execute the retrieval was 24.89 s on a state-of-the-art computer (12 cores@3.2 Ghz, 32 GB RAM). The dataset in [42] contains all relevant input and result data.

5.2 Results and Discussion

The confusion matrix for each distinct activity with its executing station is displayed in Table 2. We see that the TCBR-based activity detection works very well in this manufacturing scenario, achieving high accuracy, precision, and F1 scores. As a reference, the work in [40] detects activities in the same scenario based on change patterns encoded as rules and exact matches in the IoT data, achieving an average F1 score of less than 0.5. Better results for detecting the manufacturing activities are achieved in [17]. However, this approach relies on manual adjustment, and it is not able to handle variations in the IoT data.

Table 2. Performance Metrics for all Distinct Detected Activities.

Activity (Station)	Accuracy	Precision	Recall	F1 Score
Transport to sink (VGR)	0.988	0.991	0.800	0.883
Calibrate VGR (VGR)	0.856	0.723	0.507	0.598
Transport to oven (VGR)	0.992	0.947	0.935	0.941
Sort (SM)	0.922	0.421	1.0	0.592
Mill (MM)	0.981	0.761	1.0	0.864
Burn (OV)	1.0	1.0	1.0	1.0
Transport to DPS (VGR)	0.991	0.977	0.915	0.945
Store (HBW)	0.980	1.0	0.757	0.861
Unload (HBW)	0.983	1.0	0.714	0.833
Get Workpiece from DPS (VGR)	0.983	0.898	0.884	0.891
WT Transport (WT)	1.0	1.0	1.0	1.0
Calibrate HBW (HBW)	0.902	0.585	0.693	0.635
Average	0.965	0.859	0.850	0.837

For production stations that are capable of executing only one type of activity (MM, OV, WT) the metrics are especially good. A notable difference is the *Sort* activity executed by the *Sorting Machine* (SM). The sorting activity shows variations in the associated IoT data (cf. Sect. 2.1) as it involves different light barrier sensors and valves to sort a workpiece according to its color. One activity signature as case for this activity is not sufficient here. We expect that multiple signatures and thus cases for the different sorting behavior will improve the detection quality. The VGR is a central component for transportation, which executes different types of activities that are mostly distinguished by the start and end position parameters of the crane (cf. Sect. 2.1). The distinction of the individual activities here is more difficult and results in slightly decreased performance. Similar results can be observed with the store and unload activities in the HBW station. They show similar behavior in the IoT data, which may lead to ambiguities in the detections [14]. In the case of the HBW, an additional sensor indicating if the container that is being retrieved and then stored is full or empty would already suffice to make the detection more accurate. Finally, the *calibrate* activities executed by HBW and VGR show rather poor performance of the activity detection, as these are very short and show movement patterns in the IoT data that are also part of activity types executed by the two stations.

Overall, the metrics seem acceptable for the detection of automated activities in the small-scale production setting. The investigations of activities in real-world production settings and domains with less automated, more manual activities (e.g., smart healthcare) that are often characterized by stronger variations in the IoT data, are subject to future work. With our proposed data flow architecture, we can support the data analyst with selecting a suitable prototype signature for activities to be detected based on IoT data. The TCBR-based approach provides feedback about the detection qualities for a specific type of activity given a signature selected by the data analyst. Apart from handling variations quite well, the approach is also able to identify potential quality issues in the detection which might indicate the need of adjusting an activity signature, providing more signatures for an activity, or adding new sensors. Ultimately, the data analyst has to decide about an acceptable activity detection quality based on given use cases and requirements. When the quality is acceptable, the signature can be used as basis for the automatic implementation of a light-weight detection service as described in [38], removing the need of any heavy-weight PAIS to monitor activity executions. In this work, we assume that the unknown IoT data is already segmented, and the task is to classify these segments according to the activity executions. The investigation of using TCBR to also segment the data based on the activity signatures is subject to future work. The execution times of the retrieval for the size of the case based specified above seem reasonably fast to move the activity detection also to online detection settings where streams of IoT data are being analyzed at runtime in edge computing scenarios [36].

6 Conclusion and Future Work

This paper proposes a novel architecture for detecting process activity executions based on low-level IoT sensor data, which requires an event abstraction step to lift this time series data to the process level. For this purpose, TCBR is applied as a methodology to support data analysts in selecting suitable prototypes of activity executions together with the corresponding IoT data as cases. These cases are then used to detect similar occurrences of the activity executions in unknown IoT data. The proposed architecture is evaluated using a prototype implementation with smart factory data. The evaluation suggests that the approach works very well, even in the presence of variations in the IoT data, which related approaches do not address. In contrast to related work, our proposed solution is rather light-weight, works already with a small number of cases, and successfully applies CBR to time series data from IoT systems as a novel application domain.

In future work, we will investigate an extension of the approach and architecture with the support for parallel activity executions and a segmentation component. In its current form, the architecture also supports streaming of IoT data in real time [41]. The segmentation component will recognize when a new activity starts and an existing one ends. This allows the sensor data to be converted into queries and classified using the TCBR approach. Such a segmentation component can be investigated on a case-based basis, but can also be realized using other methods (e.g., [23]). The pipeline can also be evaluated on this basis for real-time applications in IoT. Furthermore, an explanation component will be examined, with the help of which data analysts are shown transparently how the similarity between the query and the case containing the signature comes about. We will also investigate the integration of additional semantic information about dependencies between time series in the cases and the extent to which this contributes to the optimization of the similarity value.

Acknowledgments. This work has received funding from the Swiss National Science Foundation under Grant No. IZSTZ0_208497 (*ProAmbitIon* project [13]). This work is also partly funded by the German Federal Ministry for Economic Affairs and Climate Action under grant No. 01MD22002C *EASY* [36].

References

1. Aamodt, A., Plaza, E.: Case-based reasoning: foundational issues, methodological variations, and system approaches. AI Commun. **7**(1), 39–59 (1994)
2. Lora Ariza, D.S., Sánchez-Ruiz, A.A., González-Calero, P.A.: Time series and case-based reasoning for an intelligent tetris game. In: Aha, D.W., Lieber, J. (eds.) ICCBR 2017. LNCS (LNAI), vol. 10339, pp. 185–199. Springer, Cham (2017). https://doi.org/10.1007/978-3-319-61030-6_13
3. Beerepoot, I., Di Ciccio, C., Reijers, H.A., Rinderle-Ma, S., Bandara, W., et al.: The biggest business process management problems to solve before we die. Comput. Ind. **146**, 103837 (2023)
4. Bergmann, R.: Experience Management: Foundations, Development Methodology, and Internet-Based Applications, LNCS, vol. 2432. Springer (2003)
5. Bergmann, R., Grumbach, L., Malburg, L., Zeyen, C.: ProCAKE: a Process-Oriented Case-Based Reasoning Framework. In: 27th ICCBR Workshop Proc, vol. 2567, pp. 156–161. CEUR-WS.org (2019)
6. Beyel, H.H., Makke, O., Pourbafrani, M., Gusikhin, O., van der Aalst, W.M.: Analyzing data streams from cyber-physical-systems: A case study. SN Comput. Sci. **5**(6), 706 (2024)
7. Borck, H., Johnston, S., Southern, M., Boddy, M.S.: Exploiting time series data for task prediction and diagnosis in an intelligent guidance system. In: 31st ICCBR Workshop Proc, vol. 1815, pp. 132–141. CEUR-WS.org (2016)
8. Cornacchia, M., Ozcan, K., Zheng, Y., Velipasalar, S.: A survey on activity detection and classification using wearable sensors. IEEE Sensors **17**(2), 386–403 (2016)
9. Di Federico, G., Burattin, A.: Cvamos–event abstraction using contextual information. Future Internet **15**(3), 113 (2023)

10. Diba, K., Batoulis, K., Weidlich, M., Weske, M.: Extraction, correlation, and abstraction of event data for process mining. Wiley Interdisciplinary Rev. Data Mining Knowl. Dis. **10**(3), e1346 (2020)
11. Elsayed, A., Hijazi, M., Coenen, F., García-Fiñana, M., Sluming, V., Zheng, Y.: Time series case based reasoning for image categorisation. In: Ram, A., Wiratunga, N. (eds.) ICCBR 2011. LNCS (LNAI), vol. 6880, pp. 423–436. Springer, Heidelberg (2011). https://doi.org/10.1007/978-3-642-23291-6_31
12. Esposito, L., Leotta, F., Mecella, M., Veneruso, S.: Unsupervised segmentation of smart home logs for human habit discovery. In: 18th IE Proc, pp. 1–8. IEEE (2022)
13. Franceschetti, M., et al.: Proambition: online process conformance checking with ambiguities driven by the internet of things. In: CAiSE Research Projects Exhibition, pp. 52–59 (2023)
14. Franceschetti, M., Seiger, R., López, H.A., Burattin, A., García-Bañuelos, L., Weber, B.: A characterisation of ambiguity in bpm. In: International Conference on Conceptual Modeling. pp. 277–295. Springer (2023). https://doi.org/10.1007/978-3-031-47262-6_15
15. Fritsche, L., Schlaefer, A., Budde, K., Schröter, K., Neumayer, H.: Recognition of critical situations from time series of laboratory results by case-based reasoning. J. Am. Medical Informatics Assoc. **9**(5), 520–528 (2002)
16. Funk, P., Xiong, N.: Case-based reasoning and knowledge discovery in medical applications with time series. Comput. Intell. **22**(3–4), 238–253 (2006)
17. García-Bañuelos, L., González González, M.J., Seiger, R., Franceschetti, M., Silva Trujillo, A.G.: A semi-automated approach to detecting process-level activities from sensor data. In: 8th EDI40 Proc. (2025)
18. Jære, M.D., Aamodt, A., Skalle, P.: Representing temporal knowledge for case-based prediction. In: Craw, S., Preece, A. (eds.) ECCBR 2002. LNCS (LNAI), vol. 2416, pp. 174–188. Springer, Heidelberg (2002). https://doi.org/10.1007/3-540-46119-1_14
19. Janiesch, C., Koschmider, A., Mecella, M., Weber, B., Burattin, A., et al.: The Internet-of-Things meets business process management. a manifesto. IEEE Syst. Man Cybern. Mag. **6**(4), 34–44 (2020)
20. Janssen, D., Mannhardt, F., Koschmider, A., van Zelst, S.J.: Process model discovery from sensor event data. In: Leemans, S., Leopold, H. (eds.) ICPM 2020. LNBIP, vol. 406, pp. 69–81. Springer, Cham (2021). https://doi.org/10.1007/978-3-030-72693-5_6
21. Klein, P., Weingarz, N., Bergmann, R.: Enhancing siamese neural networks through expert knowledge for predictive maintenance. In: Gama, J., et al. (eds.) ITEM/IoT Streams -2020. CCIS, vol. 1325, pp. 77–92. Springer, Cham (2020). https://doi.org/10.1007/978-3-030-66770-2_6
22. López, B.: Case-Based Reasoning: A Concise Introduction. Springer, SLAIML (2013)
23. Lovrić, M., Milanović, M., Stamenković, M.: Algoritmic methods for segmentation of time series: an overview. JCEBI **1**(1), 31–53 (2014)
24. Lupiani, E., Juarez, J.M., Palma, J.T., Marín, R.: Monitoring elderly people at home with temporal case-based reasoning. Knowl. Based Syst. **134**, 116–134 (2017)
25. Malburg, L., Schultheis, A., Bergmann, R.: Modeling and using complex IoT time series data in case-based reasoning: from application scenarios to implementations. In: 31st ICCBR Workshop Proc., vol. 3438, pp. 81–96 (2023)

26. Malburg, L., Seiger, R., Bergmann, R., Weber, B.: Using physical factory simulation models for business process management research. In: Del Río Ortega, A., Leopold, H., Santoro, F.M. (eds.) BPM 2020. LNBIP, vol. 397, pp. 95–107. Springer, Cham (2020). https://doi.org/10.1007/978-3-030-66498-5_8
27. Mangler, J., Seiger, R., Benzin, J.V., Grüger, J., Kirikkayis, Y., et al.: From internet of things data to business processes: challenges and a framework. arXiv preprint arXiv:2405.08528 (2024)
28. Mannhardt, F., Bovo, R., Oliveira, M.F., Julier, S.: A taxonomy for combining activity recognition and process discovery in industrial environments. In: Yin, H., Camacho, D., Novais, P., Tallón-Ballesteros, A.J. (eds.) IDEAL 2018. LNCS, vol. 11315, pp. 84–93. Springer, Cham (2018). https://doi.org/10.1007/978-3-030-03496-2_10
29. Nakanishi, T.: Semantic waveform model for similarity measure by time-series variation in meaning. In: 10th IIAI-AAI Proc, pp. 382–387 (2021)
30. Nilsson, M., Funk, P.J., Olsson, E., von Schéele, B., Xiong, N.: Clinical decision-support for diagnosing stress-related disorders by applying psychophysiological medical knowledge to an instance-based learning system. Artif. Intell. Medicine **36**(2), 159–176 (2006)
31. Rebmann, A., Emrich, A., Fettke, P.: Enabling the discovery of manual processes using a multi-modal activity recognition approach. In: Di Francescomarino, C., Dijkman, R., Zdun, U. (eds.) BPM 2019. LNBIP, vol. 362, pp. 130–141. Springer, Cham (2019). https://doi.org/10.1007/978-3-030-37453-2_12
32. Richter, M.M.: Knowledge containers. In: Readings in Case-Based Reasoning. Morgan Kaufmann Publishers (2003)
33. Sakoe, H., Chiba, S.: Dynamic programming algorithm optimization for spoken word recognition. IEEE Trans. Aco. Sp. and Sig. Proc. **26**(1), 43–49 (1978)
34. Schake, E., Grumbach, L., Bergmann, R.: A time-series similarity measure for case-based deviation management to support flexible workflow execution. In: Watson, I., Weber, R. (eds.) ICCBR 2020. LNCS (LNAI), vol. 12311, pp. 33–48. Springer, Cham (2020). https://doi.org/10.1007/978-3-030-58342-2_3
35. Schlaefer, A., Schröter, K., Fritsche, L.: A case-based approach for the classification of medical time series. In: Crespo, J., Maojo, V., Martin, F. (eds.) ISMDA 2001. LNCS, vol. 2199, pp. 258–263. Springer, Heidelberg (2001). https://doi.org/10.1007/3-540-45497-7_39
36. Schultheis, A., Alt, B., Bast, S., Guldner, A., Jilg, D., et al.: EASY: Energy-Efficient Analysis and Control Processes in the Dynamic Edge-Cloud Continuum for Industrial Manufacturing. Künstliche Intelligenz (2024)
37. Schultheis, A., et al.: Identifying missing sensor values in iot time series data: a weight-based extension of similarity measures for smart manufacturing. In: 32nd ICCBR Proc. LNCS, vol. 14775, pp. 240–257. Springer (2024). https://doi.org/10.1007/978-3-031-63646-2_16
38. Seiger, R., Franceschetti, M., Weber, B.: Data-driven generation of services for iot-based online activity detection. In: ICSOC, pp. 186–194. Springer (2023). https://doi.org/10.1007/978-3-031-48424-7_14
39. Seiger, R., Franceschetti, M., Weber, B.: An interactive method for detection of process activity executions from iot data. Future Internet **15**(2), 77 (2023)
40. Seiger, R., Kurz, A.F., Franceschetti, M.: Online detection of process activity executions from iot sensors using generated event processing services. Available at SSRN 5165943 (2025). https://doi.org/10.2139/ssrn.5165943

41. Seiger, R., Malburg, L., Weber, B., Bergmann, R.: Integrating process management and event processing in smart factories: a systems architecture and use cases. J. Manuf. Syst. **63**, 575–592 (2022)
42. Seiger, R., Schultheis, A., Bergmann, R.: Dataset from a Smart Factory for Activity Detection using Temporal Case-based Reasoning (2025). https://doi.org/10.5281/zenodo.14998532
43. Shahar, Y.: A framework for knowledge-based temporal abstraction. Artif. Intell. **90**(1–2), 79–133 (1997)
44. Smith, T.F., Waterman, M.S.: Identification of common molecular subsequences. JMB **147**(1), 195–197 (1981)
45. Stahl, A.: Learning of knowledge-intensive similarity measures in case-based reasoning. Ph.D. thesis, University of Kaiserslautern (2004)
46. Szczepanski, T., Bach, K., Aamodt, A.: Challenges for the similarity-based comparison of human physical activities using time series data. In: 31st ICCBR Workshop Proc., vol. 1815, pp. 173–177 (2016)
47. Weber, B., Abbad-Andaloussi, A., Franceschetti, M., Seiger, R., Völzer, H., Zerbato, F.: Leveraging digital trace data to investigate and support human-centered work processes. In: Int. Conf. ENASE, pp. 1–23. Springer (2023). https://doi.org/10.1007/978-3-031-64182-4_1
48. Weich, J., Schultheis, A., Hoffmann, M., Bergmann, R.: Integration of time series embedding for efficient retrieval in case-based reasoning. In: 33rd ICCBR Proc. LNCS, Springer (2025), Accepted for Publication

Explainable Sleep-Wake Recognition Using a Twin XCBR System with Prototypes to Improve Retrieval Efficiency

Sophia Sylvester[1(✉)], Kerstin Bach[2], and Håvard Kallestad[1,3]

[1] Department of Mental Health, Norwegian University of Science and Technology (NTNU), Trondheim, Norway
sophia.sylvester@ntnu.no

[2] Department of Computer Science, Norwegian University of Science and Technology (NTNU), Trondheim, Norway

[3] Department of Mental Health Care, St Olavs Hospital Trondheim University Hospital, Trondheim, Norway

Abstract. Case-based reasoning (CBR) is a promising approach for integrating explainability into artificial intelligence (AI) systems used in the medical domain. However, physiological signals recorded as time series pose challenges due to complex temporal structures, large case bases, and inter-individual variability. We address these limitations by introducing a twin explainable CBR (XCBR) system, combining an XGBoost classifier with an interpretable CBR component. To improve retrieval efficiency, we propose PURS (*Prototype-based Unsupervised Retrieval with Self-similarity matrices*), which computes self-similarity matrices and applies agglomerative clustering to generate a compact, representative prototype case base. Additionally, our twin system provides visual explanations through supportive and contrastive cases.

We test our approach on radar-based sleep data from healthy participants for automatic sleep-wake recognition (SWR), a clinically relevant task where explainability is crucial. Our results demonstrate that PURS substantially reduces the computational cost of retrieval while preserving classification accuracy, enabling efficient and interpretable decision support for clinical use.

Keywords: case-based reasoning · prototypes · explainable AI · twin systems · sleep-wake recognition (SWR)

1 Introduction

Twin systems have been developed as part of the eXplainable artificial intelligence (XAI) effort to make predictions from opaque and complex models understandable to humans [3,9]. These systems are related to the idea of post hoc explanations, where the original artificial intelligence (AI) system remains untouched to retain its high performance, and a second model is built to explain the predictions of the first system. The definition of twin systems as conceived

© The Author(s), under exclusive license to Springer Nature Switzerland AG 2025
I. Bichindaritz and B. López (Eds.): ICCBR 2025, LNAI 15662, pp. 454–468, 2025.
https://doi.org/10.1007/978-3-031-96559-3_30

by Kenny et al. (2021) [11] includes several key points. One is the combination of two different techniques that are run separately into a hybrid, where certain characteristics, e. g., feature mappings, of the high performing black-box model are reflected in the interpretable system. The other is that both models share one dataset.

One of the options for the explainer in the twin system is case-based reasoning (CBR), which provides intuitive explanations for individual instances. Using a twin CBR system on sleep data poses particular challenges as sleep is most commonly measured as a time series using methods like actigraphy, polysomnography (PSG), and more recently, radar technology. The representation of cases for time series data is not as straightforward as it is for tabular data [5]. Various approaches to feature extraction have been proposed, each with drawbacks such as granularity loss, complexity, or lack of interpretability. The choice of representation must be based on the characteristics of the time series and the research questions [5,7].

Time series data typically results in large case bases that lead to high computational costs for similarity calculations during retrieval. To address this, generalized cases (e. g., [25,28]) and prototype-based retrieval (e. g., [15,22]) have been proposed. However, they often rely on expert knowledge [22,24]) or highly complex models (e. g., [12,15]), without leveraging CBR's inherent similarity metrics.

A potential application of twin eXplainable CBR (XCBR) systems in classification is the identification of supportive and contrastive cases. Supportive cases (supporters, anchors) are cases that are highly similar and from the same class. Contrastive cases are similar cases from a different class. Both can serve as an explanation for why the system believes the query case belongs to a certain class. The associated similarity scores can quantify how difficult the classification is for the query case, and thus how reliable the prediction is [2,3].

In this paper, we implement a XCBR system using an XGBoost classifier for binary sleep-wake recognition (SWR) and a CBR system. The latter is designed to provide visualizations of supportive and contrastive cases, offering a straightforward and intuitive form of explanation. To improve retrieval efficiency within the CBR system, we introduce *Prototype-based Unsupervised Retrieval with Self-similarity matrices (PURS)*. A high-performing, efficient, and explainable SWR system based on radar data could be especially valuable in psychiatric hospital settings, where sleep disturbances often play a significant role in patients' primary conditions and are therefore highly relevant to clinical decision-making [6]. The contributions of this paper can be summarized as follows:

- We implement a twin XCBR system for time series data with large case bases.
- We introduce PURS, a novel prototyping approach to improve retrieval efficiency in CBR by clustering similar cases and using prototypes for comparison.
- We provide visual explanations for the classification of queries by leveraging supportive and contrastive cases.

The remainder of the paper is organized as follows: In Sect. 2 we will discuss related work to our approach before we provide more details on the methodology in Sect. 3. Section 4 contains our results, which we discuss alongside limitations and an outlook on potential future work in Sect. 5. Finally, Sect. 6 concludes the paper.

2 Related Work

CBR has until now rarely been applied to sleep-related data. Park et al. (2000) [21] integrated CBR with rule-based reasoning to extract sleep stages from PSG, focusing on meaningful feature extraction to bridge sensor data and case representations. Kwiatkowska et al. (2004) [13] used CBR for diagnosing respiratory sleep disorders. Their case representation combined physiological and lifestyle factors. However, their approach differs from ours in terms of problem scope and data types. Other studies addressed health-related CBR with sleep as a subcomponent [17,18].

Given the importance of explainability in clinical and decision-support contexts, studies focusing on XCBR are of particular interest. Bayrak et al. [1–3] proposed class-specific case bases and selected the most similar supportive and contrastive cases using a similarity metric. This approach ensures plausibility, as all explanations are based on real data points. One of their studies [2] also implemented a twin XCBR system, combining a high-performing model with a case-based explainer. Contrastive cases are closely related to counterfactual explanations, which aim to show how minimal changes could lead to a different classification. Delaney et al. (2021) [5] proposed a method for generating counterfactuals by identifying the nearest unlike neighbor (NUN)—a similar case from a different class—and minimally altering it. Keane and Smyth (2020) [10] also used NUNs as contrastive explanations and found that natural counterfactuals are rare; thus, artificial generation might be required. Both studies, however, focused exclusively on contrastive or counterfactual explanations and did not incorporate supportive examples.

The concept of generalized cases was introduced to reduce the complexity of case retrieval and improve the scalability of CBR systems. Smyth and Keane (1995) [25] proposed one of the earliest frameworks for case generalization, where cases are clustered based on similarity and abstracted into generalized representations. Their work demonstrated that generalized cases could significantly reduce retrieval times while maintaining solution quality. Similarly, Richter (1995) [23] explored the use of abstraction hierarchies to generalize cases, emphasizing the importance of domain knowledge in guiding the generalization process.

Later, Ontañón and Plaza (2012) [20] further enhanced case generalization techniques and introduced a method for learning generalized cases through clustering and feature selection, enabling more efficient retrieval in complex domains. Their approach has been applied successfully in domains such as recommender systems and medical diagnosis. Generalized cases have been applied in various domains, including planning, diagnosis, and design. In the field of planning, Muñoz-Avila and Cox (2008) [19] utilized generalized cases to improve the efficiency of hierarchical task network (HTN) planning. Their work showed that generalized cases could capture common patterns in planning tasks, reducing the need for extensive case adaptation. In medical diagnosis, Bichindaritz (2006) [4] demonstrated how generalized cases could be used to represent prototypical patient profiles, enabling faster and more accurate diagnosis. The integration of generalized cases with modern CBR systems has been facilitated by advancements in knowledge representation and retrieval algorithms. Leake and Wilson (2001) [14] proposed a hybrid approach that combines generalized cases with rule-based reasoning, allowing for more flexible and context-aware retrieval. More recently, deep learning techniques have been employed to automate the generalization process. For example, Zhang et al. (2020) [28] used neural networks to learn generalized representations of cases, achieving state-of-the-art performance in several benchmark datasets.

A different line of work has explored prototyping as a means to reduce retrieval complexity. Li et al. (2018) [15] used a prototype layer in a deep learning encoder-decoder model to generate prototypes for CBR and providing visual representations of them to enhance model interpretability. Kim et al. (2014) [12] developed the Bayesian Case Model (BCM) which uses Bayesian inference to cluster the data and then identify the most representative case of each cluster as the prototype. In the medical domain, Perner et al. (2008) [22] used a prototyping system based on expert selection and backwards elimination to classify images of the HEp-2 cell. Schmidt et al. (1999) [24] developed several prototype systems for medical applications using expert knowledge to create the systems and an iterative process to update them. They presented four different systems, thereby underlining the importance of explainable decision support systems in the medical domain.

Lastly, Lorenzo et al. (2022) [16] used a prototyping system to predict trends in cryptocurrency. Their system involves different kinds of clustering like k-medoids and k-shapes to cluster the time series data and identify prototypes that can show trends in the market without, however, using the prototypes in a CBR system.

3 Methods

3.1 Data

The dataset used in this study comprises information from 12 healthy participants (average age (SD): 23.0 (3.1) years, 5 males) collected at the psychiatric acute ward in Østmarka, Norway. 117 nights of data were gathered using a ceiling radar and actigraphy. The study aimed for four nights of PSG recordings per participant, resulting in 43 nights with radar, actigraphy, and PSG. Some discrepancies occurred due to equipment malfunctions. The dataset has been pre-processed and is ready for use. Its value lies in the highly controlled environment from which it was collected, promising less noise than typically found in sleep datasets. For further details, refer to Vethe et al. (2021) [27].

The dataset was used before in a study by Heglum et al. (2021) [8] for SWR using a logistic regression and simple feature extraction. The study found that the radar sensors achieved over 92% accuracy in distinguishing sleep from wakefulness in healthy participants. Sensitivity, i. e., the ability to correctly classify sleep epochs (the majority class) was above 95%, but specificity, i. e., the ability to correctly identify wake epochs was only around 83%, indicating a potential area for improvement in sleep monitoring accuracy.

We aimed to hold preprocessing for this study as similar as possible to the preprocessing in Heglum et al. (2021) [8] to ensure comparability. Hence, the data was split into 30 s epochs. For each epoch, the mean of the three features *slow movements, fast movements,* and *respiration* was extracted. Thus, the time series was aggregated into a form of tabular data. Further scaling was applied and a time horizon was included so that each instance comprises the three mean values making up the current epoch as well as the means of the five epochs before, to provide a temporal context. It is generally assumed that the probability of being in the same status (i. e., asleep or awake) as in the minutes before is high. This allowed us to preserve some context given by the original time series while having the feature values representing the cases in a tabular form suitable for the machine learning algorithm XGBoost and CBR. Future epochs were not included since a real-time model is the most interesting use case for psychiatric clinics.

The dataset comprises approximately 42,000 epochs and exhibits a substantial class imbalance, with roughly 74% sleep epochs and 26% wake epochs. This was a result of the available PSG data which was only collected during the night. PSG is the gold standard for measuring sleep states and sleep stages and thus used here as the ground truth.

3.2 Black-Box Model Classification

We used an XGBoost model with 500 estimators for black-box sleep/wake classification. The best hyperparameter settings for the maximum depth (*max depth: 6, 9, 12*) and the balance of positive and negative weights (*scale pos weight: 1, class ratio*) were determined through grid search. All other hyperparameters were set to default values from the XGBoost Python package[1]. We used a nested leave-one-subject-out (LOSO) cross-validation procedure with the grid search for hyperparameter optimization in the inner loop. For evaluation, accuracy and macro f1 score were calculated per subject and then averaged.

3.3 The CBR system

The CBR system, built using myCBR[2], utilizes the same epochs as the XGBoost model. For each epoch the mean of the three radar features *fast movements, slow movements* and *respiration* were extracted. Together with the means of the 5

[1] https://xgboost.readthedocs.io/en/stable/index.html.
[2] http://mycbr-project.org/.

Table 1. Case representation. Attribute names use `slow` for slow movements, `fast` for fast movements, and `respi` for respiration. Temporal markers are coded as `t0` (current epoch), `t1` (preceding epoch), through `t5` (2.5 min before `t0`). 'Min' and 'Max' indicate the attribute value range, 'weights' denote their contribution to the amalgamation function, and 'IQR' and 'polynomial' describe the local similarity function.

Attribute	Min	Max	Weight	IQR	Polynomial
t5slow	0.00	13395.69	1.22	70.04	14.73
t4slow	0.00	13395.69	1.06	69.96	14.74
t3slow	0.00	13395.69	1.07	69.79	14.74
t2slow	0.00	13395.69	1.00	69.42	14.76
t1slow	0.00	13395.69	1.05	69.38	14.76
t0slow	0.00	13395.69	1.11	69.50	14.76
t5fast	0.00	7466.21	2.68	0.82	25.55
t4fast	0.00	7466.21	2.45	0.78	25.71
t3fast	0.00	7466.21	2.53	0.75	25.81
t2fast	0.00	7466.21	1.55	0.74	25.86
t1fast	0.00	7466.21	3.91	0.74	25.87
t0fast	0.00	7466.21	9.22	0.76	25.77
t5respi	0.00	29.58	2.88	6.24	4.37
t4respi	0.00	29.58	1.48	6.16	4.40
t3respi	0.00	29.58	1.39	6.09	4.44
t2respi	0.00	29.58	1.59	6.05	4.45
t1respi	0.00	29.58	1.43	6.04	4.46
t0respi	0.00	29.58	10.00	6.07	4.44

previous epochs, they built the attributes for each case, all of them numerical. Each case includes the *PID* (personal identification number) and binary sleep-/wake label (y) as additional attributes. The PID and y attribute did not get any weights for retrieval. For further details on the case representation, see Table1. We created two case bases for each participant in the study, one containing all true sleep epochs and one containing all true wake epochs, leaving us with 24 case bases in total. Every case base contained roughly 3000 to 4000 cases. The rationale behind using different case bases for different participants was to capture the inter-individual variance that might have an impact on classification performance. Initial experiments with a shared case base for all participants led to reduced retrieval performance, supporting the decision to maintain separate case bases to preserve inter-individual differences.

For the global similarity measure (amalgamation function), we used the normalized feature importance estimated using the information gain from the best-performing XGBoost model as weights (see Table 1) and an unweighted Euclidean distance measure as the weighting function. Feature importances were used as a data-driven way to define the global similarity, since the relative

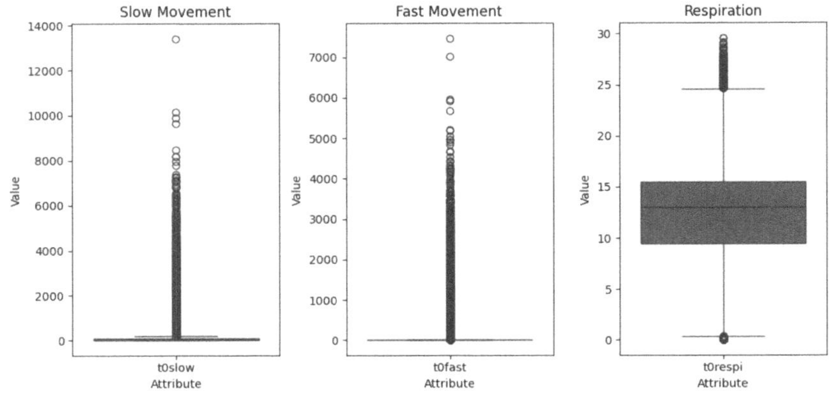

Fig. 1. Example boxplots showing the distribution of local attribute values for `t0respi`, `t0fast` and `t0slow`.

importance of the extracted time series features is not readily interpretable. In addition, weighting by feature importance ensured that the similarity measure reflected the feature relevance learned by the XGBoost model, improving the faithfulness of the explanations.

For the local similarity measures, we used a data-driven polynomial modeling method developed by Verma et al. (2018) [26]. Due to the lack of clear domain knowledge, we based local similarity solely on this data-driven method. The first step is to analyze the distribution of each numerical attribute to identify its interquartile range (IQR) and full range (minimum to maximum). Boxplots can be used for visualization (e. g.,. Fig. 1). The range and IQR define reference distances used to shape a polynomial similarity function. Specifically, the IQR is used as a threshold for moderate deviation between values, while the full range represents the maximum expected deviation.

A local similarity function $y(x)$ is then constructed as a decreasing polynomial function that satisfies the following constraints:

- $y(0) = 1$: identical values are considered maximally similar,
- $y(r_1) \approx 0.30$, where r_1 = IQR: similarity declines moderately within the central data distribution,
- $y(r_2) \approx 0$, where $r_2 = \max - \min$: similarity approaches zero at the extreme bounds.

The polynomial degree is selected to fulfill these conditions, thereby shaping the similarity curve to reflect natural data variability. This ensures that small differences in frequent value ranges result in high similarity scores, while larger deviations—especially near the edges of the distribution—lead to lower similarity scores. A visualization of the process is provided in Fig. 2. This method allows for interpretable and adaptive local similarity modeling without requiring explicit domain knowledge, making it particularly suited for numerical features derived

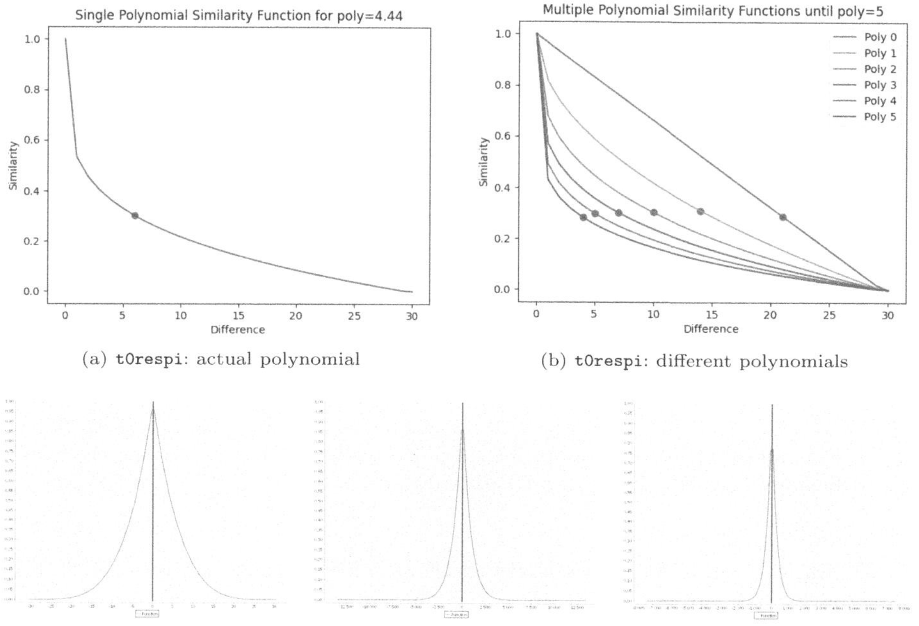

(a) t0respi: actual polynomial

(b) t0respi: different polynomials

(c) t0respi local similarity

(d) t0slow local similarity

(e) tofast local similarity

Fig. 2. Local similarity functions. The top row shows polynomial functions for the attribute `t0respi`. (a) shows the actual function, (b) examples with other polynomials. The bottom row shows the myCBR visualizations of local similarity functions for three example attributes: (c) `t0respi`, (d) `t0slow`, and (e) `tofast`.

from sensor-based time series data. The local similarity can be visualized in myCBR (see Fig. 2). The code to calculate the local similarity functions and generate the plots can be found on Github[3].

3.4 Prototype-Based Unsupervised Retrieval with Self-Similarity Matrices (PURS)

Retrieving the most similar case from a large case base can be computationally expensive. In our system, a single query could require up to 35,000 comparisons, making naive retrieval impractical. Given the nature of the data, however, it can be assumed that many cases, especially those from sleep epochs, exhibit high internal similarity. During sleep an individual typically shows consistently low respiration values and minimal movement. To reduce the number of comparisons required while preserving explanatory power, we introduced PURS as a prototyping mechanism.

[3] https://github.com/ntnu-ai-lab/mycbr-sample-python/blob/master/CreateSimilarityMeasures.ipynb.

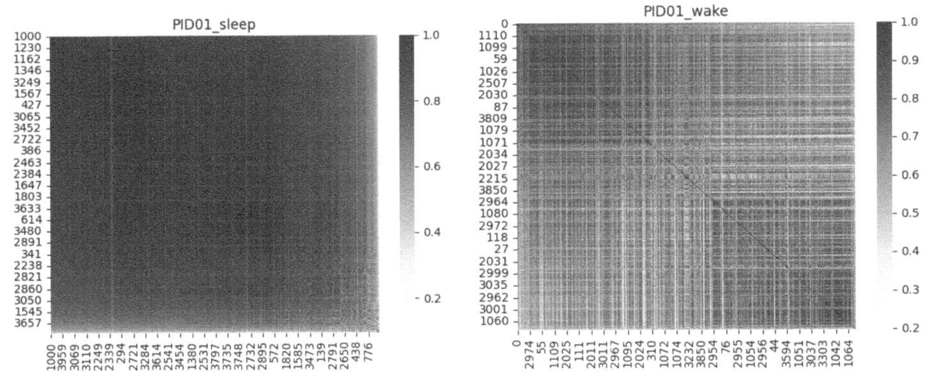

(a) Heatmap of the similarity matrix for sleep. (b) Heatmap of the similarity matrix for wake.

Fig. 3. Example similarity heatmaps for sleep and wake case bases. Variance is visibly higher during wake, reflecting greater variability in activity.

We first computed a self-similarity matrix (SSM) for each case base. A SSM is a computational tool used to analyze and visualize pairwise similarities between cases in a case base. In CBR systems, it serves as a foundational structure for understanding the relationships among cases, facilitating efficient retrieval, adaptation, and maintenance of the case base. The matrix is typically square, where each entry S_{ij} represents the similarity between case i and case j, computed using a domain-specific similarity metric. It can be visualized as a heatmap (see Fig. 3) to assess internal redundancy.

Next, we applied agglomerative clustering to the distance matrices, which were derived as the inverse of the SSMs. Clustering was performed using cosine similarity, and we selected the most central case from each cluster to serve as a prototype. This ensured that highly similar, redundant cases were grouped together, and only a single representative case was retained for retrieval.

To guide clustering, we visually inspected dendrograms (see Fig. 4) and computed silhouette scores across a candidate range to determine the best distance threshold. In the dendrograms, we began at the bottom and looked for the level where first meaningful separations between clusters became apparent. We expected better classification performance with a rather large number of prototypes, thus we did not aim for the higher levels with only a few branches, but for lower levels that still showed clear separations. For clustering, we did not specify the number of clusters but constrained it so that the final number of prototypes would lie between twice the number of case bases as the lower bound and one-quarter of the original case base size as the upper bound. This range was chosen to balance representativeness with computational efficiency.

The resulting prototypical cases were imported into the myCBR system as a separate prototype case base and used for retrieval during explanation generation. Due to the way we defined the procedure, at least one prototype was

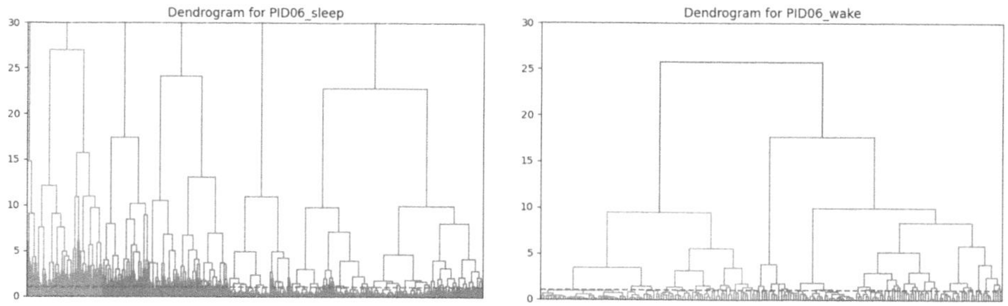

(a) Sleep case base (b) Wake case base

Fig. 4. Example dendrograms used to determine a distance threshold range for agglomerative clustering. The sleep dendrogram is zoomed in to better identify a threshold. The x-axis shows all cases in the casebase, labels (caseIDs) were removed for better readbility.

extracted per casebase and thus the inter-individual differences preserved in the prototype casebase.

3.5 Evaluation

We evaluated the system by comparing CBR predictions (1) to the ground truth and (2) to the black-box model. The first is an estimate of general performance, while the second allows us to estimate how well the CBR system performs as a twin system to explain the predictions of the black-box model. Additionally, we calculated support and rigidity as defined in Bayrak et al. (2023) [2].

Support is defined as the relative number of cases where the CBR system predicts the same class as the black box, i. e., supports the decision of the black-box model. Rigidity measures how adaptable the explainer is to the performance of the black-box model and is hence dependent on the accuracy (i. e., comparison between the predicted y and ground truth) of the black-box model.

With $X_{test} = x_1, ..., x_n$ containing n data samples and y representing the prediction results of the black-box model $y = y_1, ..., y_n$, S is a subset of X_{test} containing the predictions that are supported by the explainer i. e., the CBR system. The support score *support* is then defined as

$$support = \frac{|S|}{n} \tag{1}$$

The support score is dependent on the black-box model performance in that a higher performance should lead to a better support score. *Rigidity* is defined as

$$rigidity = |1 - \frac{support}{accuracy}| \tag{2}$$

Due to the definition of the *rigidity* score, the lower the value the better the rigidity [2].

3.6 XCBR - Visual Explanations

To avoid bias in retrieval, we introduced a constraint that prevents cases from being compared to epochs originating from the same participant. This design choice is motivated by two factors. First, intra-individual variance is typically lower than inter-individual variance, which may skew similarity scores in favor of self-comparisons. Second, each case incorporates a time horizon—specifically, data from the preceding 2.5 min—resulting in significant overlap between temporally adjacent epochs. Two neighboring cases from the same participant may share up to 83% of their data, making them artificially similar and thus unsuitable for unbiased retrieval. The same procedure was used for XGBoost.

Restricting comparisons to other participants enables the reliable identification of the most similar supportive case (i.e., from the same class) and contrastive case (i.e., from the opposite class). For each query, these two reference cases are visualized alongside the query itself, providing an intuitive explanation for the predicted class. The similarity score serves as a proxy for confidence: a higher score indicates closer resemblance. The class assigned by the CBR system corresponds to the class of the case with the higher similarity score[4].

4 Results

The XGBoost model performed with an accuracy of 92.07% (SD 1.77%) and a macro F1 score of 80.42% (SD 3.53%) on the full dataset. The results are comparable to those found in [8] (accuracy 92%). When evaluated on the dataset excluding the prototypes, XGBoost achieved an accuracy of 92.01% (SD 1.79%) and an F1 score of 65.32% (SD 7.30%).

PURS identified 78 prototypical cases. The ideal distance threshold was estimated from the dendrograms to lie between 0 and 1. We computed silhouette scores for the clustering results for different thresholds within this range. Next, we evaluated the classification performance using the prototypes derived from the highest-scoring clustering results. Based on this evaluation, a threshold of 0.05 was identified as the best overall setting for both sleep and wake case bases. With this hyperparameter setting, PURS found 36 sleep prototypes and 42 wake prototypes. The silhouette score for sleep was 0.41, while the score for wake was 0.31 with an average of 0.36. Higher thresholds were found to increase the silhouette score but not the classification performance.

Testing all cases not present in the prototype case base against these prototypes, not surprisingly, revealed performance inferior to the black-box model, with an accuracy of 87.0% (SD 2.51%) and an F1 score of 57.16% (SD 10.31%). Interestingly, the XGBoost model labeled more wake epochs incorrectly as sleep than the CBR system. This type of error is common in sleep classification, as resting wakefulness can closely resemble sleep in both respiration and movement patterns.

[4] All source code is available on GitHub: https://github.com/ntnu-ai-lab/xcbr-purs.

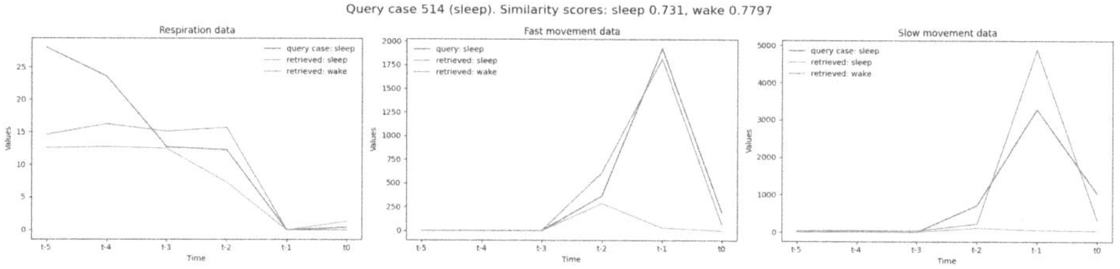

(a) Query is 'sleep' but predicted 'wake'

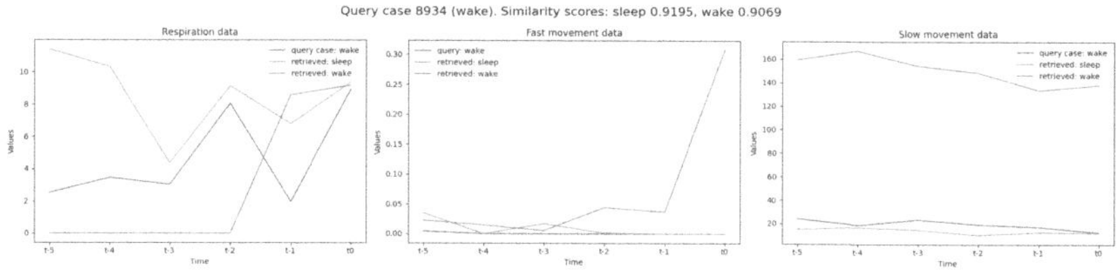

(b) Query is 'wake' but predicted 'sleep'

Fig. 5. Visual explanations from the XCBR system

As a twin XCBR system, the explainer supported 37,778 out of 42,630 decisions made by the black-box model, yielding a support score of 88.46%. The rigidity was calculated to be 0.0377. We generated visual explanations with query case, supporting case, and contrastive case (for an example see Fig. 5) for several incorrect predictions. In many misclassifications, the contrastive case more closely resembles the query than the supportive case, as reflected in the similarity scores. These scores also serve as an indication of classification confidence. A high level of uncertainty is suggested when the scores are low and close together for the supportive and contrastive cases.

5 Discussion

This study demonstrated the effective integration of a twin XCBR system for SWR, combining a high-performing XGBoost classifier with a prototype-based CBR component tailored to large case bases derived from time series data. This achieves high predictive performance while maintaining interpretability and computational efficiency. An interesting finding is the lower performance of the XGBoost model for the dataset excluding prototypes. This could indicate that the prototypes can be classified with high certainty and should be investigated in future research. Moreover, a known challenge in SWR is the reduced accuracy for wake epochs [8]. In our system, both components showed reduced accuracy for wake epochs; however, the CBR module was more robust in identifying resting wakefulness, which should be explored in future work.

A central contribution of this work is the introduction of PURS, a prototyping approach designed to improve retrieval efficiency in the CBR system.

By using SSMs and agglomerative clustering, we reduced the number of case comparisons while preserving the quality of retrieved cases. This improvement makes the CBR component more practical for real-time applications. However, the process of identifying a suitable distance threshold is not yet straightforward. It currently requires generating dendrograms for each case base, selecting a reasonable threshold range, and evaluating this range using silhouette scores and classification results. While we also tested other clustering algorithms, such as k-medoids and HDBSCAN, we did not systematically compare them to our method.

An additional observation concerns the role of inter-individual differences: extracting at least one prototype per participant helped maintain participant-specific information and likely contributed to the improved performance compared to using large, shared case bases. This should be investigated further to assess whether explicitly accounting for individual variability can systematically improve retrieval performance. Another notable finding was the heavy reliance on respiration in the XGBoost feature importance and thus the CBR amalgamation function. This is surprising given the signal's noise in radar data. A possible explanation is that movement during wake often disrupts the respiration signal, biasing the model toward sleep. This should be explored further to assess whether the effect generalizes.

Despite these promising results, there are some limitations that should be considered. Both the XGBoost and CBR components relied on manually selected features, specifically mean values for each epoch. While this simple representation performed well, it may not generalize to other datasets. Additionally, the study was conducted using a dataset of healthy individuals, limiting the broader applicability of the findings, particularly in clinical contexts.

Future work should test the XCBR framework and PURS on other datasets and across different domains. To establish their usefulness for SWR, data from clinical settings, especially psychiatric hospitals, are needed, as these represent the most likely place of application. PURS should also be improved further, ideally by developing a simpler method for finding the optimal threshold and by comparing it more systematically with other clustering approaches. Finally, the prototyping strategy could be extended with a second step: queries with low similarity to any prototype could be compared against a richer case base or even all available cases, potentially improving the performance of the explainer. The XCBR system was designed as a twin to the XGBoost model by weighting features according to their learned importance and preserving subject information. Explicitly maximizing a support metric is not straightforward given the non-parametric nature of CBR, but could be explored in future work to strengthen the twin relationship even further.

6 Conclusion

This study explored the implementation of a twin XCBR system for sleep state classification, combining a high-performing black-box model with an interpretable CBR component. By introducing PURS for prototype-based case retrieval, we significantly improved retrieval efficiency, making the system more suitable for real-time applications. Additionally, by leveraging supportive and contrastive cases, the system facilitates intuitive interpretation of classification results, a critical feature for clinical applications.

Future work should focus on validating the system across diverse datasets. Additionally, the prototyping approach should be further refined. Overall, our results demonstrate the potential of CBR, particularly with prototyping enhancements, as a powerful and interpretable tool for SWR, with promising implications for both research and clinical practice.

Acknowledgements. This study has been funded by the NTNU Helse project AI-MENT.

References

1. Bayrak, B., Bach, K.: When to Explain? Model Agnostic Explanation Using a Case-based Approach and Counterfactuals. Norsk IKT-konferanse for forskning og utdanning (1) (2022)
2. Bayrak, B., Bach, K.: A twin XCBR system using supportive and contrastive explanations. In: ICCBR XCBR 2023: Workshop on Case-Based Reasoning for the Explanation of Intelligent Systems at ICCBR 2023, pp. 146–157 (2023)
3. Bayrak, B., Marín-Veites, P., Bach, K.: Explaining your neighbourhood: a CBR approach for explaining black-box models. In: ICCBR XAI 2022: Explainable AI Challenge at ICCBR (2022)
4. Bichindaritz, I.: Case-based reasoning in the health sciences: what's next? Artif. Intell. Med. **36**(2), 127–135 (2006)
5. Delaney, E., Greene, D., Keane, M.T.: Instance-based counterfactual explanations for time series classification. In: Sánchez-Ruiz, A.A., Floyd, M.W. (eds.) ICCBR 2021. LNCS (LNAI), vol. 12877, pp. 32–47. Springer, Cham (2021). https://doi.org/10.1007/978-3-030-86957-1_3
6. Freeman, D., Sheaves, B., Waite, F., Harvey, A.G., Harrison, P.J.: Sleep disturbance and psychiatric disorders. Lancet Psychiat. **7**(7), 628–637 (2020)
7. Funk, P., Xiong, N.: Extracting knowledge from sensor signals for case-based reasoning with longitudinal time series data. In: Case-Based Reasoning on Images and Signals, Studies in Computational Intelligence, vol. 73, pp. 247–284. Springer (2008). https://doi.org/10.1007/978-3-540-73180-1_9
8. Heglum, H.S.A., Kallestad, H., Vethe, D., Langsrud, K., Sand, T., Engstrøm, M.: Distinguishing sleep from wake with a radar sensor: a contact-free real-time sleep monitor. SLEEP **44**(8), zsab060 (2021)
9. Keane, M.T., Kenny, E.M.: How case-based reasoning explains neural networks: a theoretical analysis of XAI using *Post-Hoc* explanation-by-example from a survey of ann-cbr twin-systems. In: Bach, K., Marling, C. (eds.) ICCBR 2019. LNCS (LNAI), vol. 11680, pp. 155–171. Springer, Cham (2019). https://doi.org/10.1007/978-3-030-29249-2_11
10. Keane, M.T., Smyth, B.: Good counterfactuals and where to find them: a case-based technique for generating counterfactuals for explainable AI (XAI). In: Watson, I., Weber, R. (eds.) ICCBR 2020. LNCS (LNAI), vol. 12311, pp. 163–178. Springer, Cham (2020). https://doi.org/10.1007/978-3-030-58342-2_11

11. Kenny, E.M., Keane, M.T.: Explaining deep learning using examples: optimal feature weighting methods for twin systems using post-hoc, explanation-by-example in XAI. Knowl. Based Syst. **233**, 107,530 (2021)
12. Kim, B., Rudin, C., Shah, J.A.: The bayesian case model: a generative approach for case-based reasoning and prototype classification. In: Advances in Neural Information Processing Systems, vol. 27. Curran Associates, Inc. (2014)
13. Kwiatkowska, M., Atkins, S.: Case representation and retrieval in the diagnosis and treatment of obstructive sleep apnea: a semio- fuzzy approach. In: Proceedings of the 7th European Conference on Case-based Reasoning, pp. 25–35 (2004)
14. Leake, D.B., Wilson, D.C.: Case-based reasoning: experiences, lessons, and future directions. AI Mag. **22**(2), 85–85 (2001)
15. Li, O., Liu, H., Chen, C., Rudin, C.: Deep learning for case-based reasoning through prototypes: a neural network that explains its predictions. In: Proceedings of the AAAI Conference on Artificial Intelligence, vol. 32(1) (2018)
16. Lorenzo, L., Arroyo, J.: Analysis of the cryptocurrency market using different prototype-based clustering techniques. Financial Innovation **8**(1), 7 (2022)
17. Lupiani, E., Juarez, J.M., Palma, J., Sauer, C.S., Roth-Berghofer, T.: Using case-based reasoning to detect risk scenarios of elderly people living alone at home. In: Lamontagne, L., Plaza, E. (eds.) ICCBR 2014. LNCS (LNAI), vol. 8765, pp. 274–288. Springer, Cham (2014). https://doi.org/10.1007/978-3-319-11209-1_20
18. Montani, S., Bottrighi, A., Leonardi, G., Portinale, L., Terenziani, P.: Multi-level abstractions and multi-dimensional retrieval of cases with time series features. In: McGinty, L., Wilson, D.C. (eds.) ICCBR 2009. LNCS (LNAI), vol. 5650, pp. 225–239. Springer, Heidelberg (2009). https://doi.org/10.1007/978-3-642-02998-1_17
19. Muñoz-Avila, H., Cox, M.T.: Case-based plan adaptation: an analysis and review. IEEE Intell. Syst. **23**(4), 75–81 (2008)
20. Ontañón, S., Plaza, E.: Learning and using generalized cases in case-based reasoning. AI Commun. **25**(1), 41–56 (2012)
21. Park, H.J., Oh, J.S., Jeong, D.U., Park, K.S.: Automated sleep stage scoring using hybrid rule- and case-based reasoning. Comput. Biomed. Res. **33**(5), 330–349 (2000)
22. Perner, P.: Prototype-based classification. Appl. Intell. **28**(3), 238–246 (2008)
23. Richter, M.M.: Principles of case-based reasoning. Springer (1995)
24. Schmidt, R., Pollwein, B., Gierl, L.: Experiences with case-based reasoning methods and prototypes for medical knowledge-based systems. In: Horn, W., Shahar, Y., Lindberg, G., Andreassen, S., Wyatt, J. (eds.) AIMDM 1999. LNCS (LNAI), vol. 1620, pp. 124–132. Springer, Heidelberg (1999). https://doi.org/10.1007/3-540-48720-4_11
25. Smyth, B., Keane, M.T.: Remembering to forget: a competence-preserving case deletion policy for case-based reasoning systems. IJCAI **95**, 377–382 (1995)
26. Verma, D., Bach, K., Mork, P.J.: Modelling similarity for comparing physical activity profiles - a data-driven approach. In: Cox, M.T., Funk, P., Begum, S. (eds.) ICCBR 2018. LNCS (LNAI), vol. 11156, pp. 415–430. Springer, Cham (2018). https://doi.org/10.1007/978-3-030-01081-2_28
27. Vethe, D., et al.: The evening light environment in hospitals can be designed to produce less disruptive effects on the circadian system and improve sleep. Sleep **44**(3), zsaa194 (2021)
28. Zhang, Y., Chen, X., Li, C.: Deep case-based reasoning for visual knowledge discovery. arXiv preprint arXiv:2003.12345 (2020)

Case-Based Reasoning with Diffusion Model for Ransomware Detection

Haofan Wang, Jarrod Hardy, and Farah Kandah(✉)

Auburn University, Auburn, AL 36849, USA
{hzw0123,jzh0231,farah-kandah}@auburn.edu

Abstract. In recent years, the threat and damage caused by ransomware have been steadily increasing. Although many detection methods have been proposed, network security remains a severe challenge due to the continuous emergence of new attack techniques, data imbalance, low detection rates of existing methods, and the lack of interpretability in model decision-making. This study proposes a Case-Based Reasoning with Diffusion Model for Ransomware Detection (CBR-DRD), which classifies network traffic information without feature loss or redundancy by converting it into RGB images. The dataset is then augmented using image generation based on a U-Net diffusion model. Features extracted by a Swin Transformer are used to construct a case base, and a weighted K-Nearest Neighbors (KNN) algorithm is employed to classify the traffic by computing the similarity between a given sample and existing cases, to determine whether it is associated with ransomware activity. Compared with two similar ransomware detection approaches and commonly used generative models, namely the GAN model and a ResNet-based diffusion model designed to address data imbalance, the proposed method achieves superior performance on both the USTC-TFC2016 and ISOT datasets.

Keywords: Ransomware Detection · Case-Based Reasoning · Diffusion Model

1 Introduction

Ransomware is a type of malware in which attackers typically hijack a user's data or system and demand that the user pay a ransom to decrypt it. Its negative impacts include potential data loss, service disruptions, and loss in business operations and productivity [1].

In 2024, the average ransom demand was $2.73 million, representing an increase of nearly $1 million compared to 2023. Companies experienced an average downtime of 24 d following a ransomware attack [2]. The ransomware landscape recorded 5,414 published attacks targeting global organizations, marking an increase of 11% compared to 2023 [4]. In June, an attack on CDK Global, a major software provider for automotive dealerships, disrupted the operations of

© The Author(s), under exclusive license to Springer Nature Switzerland AG 2025
I. Bichindaritz and B. López (Eds.): ICCBR 2025, LNAI 15662, pp. 469–483, 2025.
https://doi.org/10.1007/978-3-031-96559-3_31

thousands of dealerships across North America, with a ransom demand exceeding $25 million [26]. In September, an intrusion into AT&T's systems resulted in the leakage of call records for millions of customers [3].

To tackle the ever-growing threat of ransomware, machine learning and deep learning models have been widely applied in ransomware detection [12]. By performing real-time analysis of dynamic data such as network traffic, system calls, and file accesses, these methods can identify signs of ransomware activity. However, they still suffer from high false positive rates and low detection rates for novel attacks, highlighting the need for a more accurate, robust, and zero-day-resistant ransomware detection method.

We, in this work, propose a Case-Based Reasoning with a Diffusion Model for Ransomware Detection (CBR-DRD). In this approach, we convert network traffic data captured using Packet Capture (PCAP) format into RGB images. By doing so, we can extract crucial information while ensuring the preservation of all relevant features without information loss or redundancy. After enhancing the image dataset using U-Net diffusion models to improve the system's robustness against zero-day attacks, we employ a Swin Transformer integrated with a cross-attention mechanism for feature extraction. Finally, a weighted KNN calculates the similarity between samples and an existing dataset, thereby detecting malicious traffic generated by ransomware activities while effectively fusing shallow and deep features and increasing decision transparency.

Our CBR-DRD addresses several key shortcomings of existing methods, setting it apart from state-of-the-art solutions:

- Existing methods for converting PCAP data into images have been used to overcome the challenges of directly analyzing raw PCAP network traffic data, including significant noise, high data dimensionality, substantial computational resource demands, and difficulty in effectively capturing global features. However, these methods suffer from feature loss and redundancy.
- The existing ransomware detection methods overly rely on the distribution patterns of current data, making it difficult to cope with zero-day attacks. Additionally, the ransomware dataset suffers from severe imbalance issues, and existing solutions fail to capture all the essential features.
- Existing deep learning-based ransomware detection methods often rely on black-box models, leading to an opaque decision-making process that is difficult to interpret and trace.

We summarized our key contributions as follows:

- Develop and design a method to convert network traffic into RGB images for hierarchical extraction of key features while preserving feature integrity and avoiding information redundancy.
- Introducing a data augmentation approach that expands the dataset using a U-Net diffusion model based on the distribution pattern of existing data, thus improving robustness against novel attacks.
- Construct a case-based method that leverages feature extraction with Swin Transformer and performs case identification by computing similarity using

a weighted KNN model, making the decision-making process more intuitive and reducing the interference of noise and outliers.
- Conduct an experimental analysis to evaluate the performance of the proposed approach in comparison with other data augmentation and ransomware detection methods.

The rest of the article is organized as follows: We present the related work in Sect. 2. Section 3 presents the methodology and design of Case-Based Reasoning with Diffusion Model for Ransomware Detection (CBR-DRD). Our experiment and analysis are presented in Sect. 4, followed by the conclusion in Sect. 5.

2 Related Work

In recent years, various detection methods have been proposed to combat the threat of ransomware. The methods are primarily categorized into the following types of models:
1. *Temporal Behavior-Based Ransomware Detection:* by extracting time series features of network traffic and analyzing how data patterns change over time, potential ransomware attacks can be detected in an ever-changing network environment.

Kiyol et al. in [11] achieved dynamic monitoring of file behavior by extracting the sequential features of file entropy and its first- and second-order derivatives during the ransomware encryption process. In this approach, entropy reflects the differences between the file before and after encryption, and a multi-layer Long Short-Term Memory (LSTM) network is then employed to capture the temporal features of the data, thereby distinguishing ransomware from benign files. Another work presented by Stastne et al. in [25] used Temporal Pattern Profiling (TPP) as a ransomware detection framework. TPP found suspicious activity by analyzing the temporal sequences and intervals between events, viewing encryption rates, file access patterns, and network communication timing. This focus allowed TPP to achieve a 3.2% false positive rate compared to 7.8% percent for signature-based approaches.

An over-reliance on temporal features may lead to the neglect of other important attributes. For instance, if the collected data suffers from packet loss, delays, or contains a large number of outliers, the likelihood of false alarms could increase.
2. *Ensemble Learning-Based Ransomware Detection:* by integrating multiple classification results, ensemble detection avoids the potential bias of a single model, resulting in improved stability and a lower risk of overfitting.

A hybrid model was presented by Lumazine et al. [9], where the authors used Convolutional Neural Networks (CNN) to extract high-dimensional features from network traffic data, including temporal patterns, flow duration, and packet sizes, and then employed an isolation forest model to classify these feature vectors, thereby identifying anomalous traffic generated by ransomware activities that deviate from normal traffic patterns. Another work presented by Alamro et al. in [24] proposed the AAMD-OELAC approach that uses ensemble learning by combining the Least Square Support Vector Machine (LS-SVM), Kernel Extreme Learning Machine (KELM), and the Regularized Random Vector Functional Link Neural Network (RRVFLN). The combination of the three provides hyperplanes to separate malware and benign software, convergence and generalization through random feature mapping and integrates input and hidden layers to prevent overfitting.

However, if the fusion strategy is not chosen properly, it may lead to a biased final decision outcome. Moreover, since multiple models need to be trained, the computational resources required are significantly higher.

3. *Graph-Based Ransomware Detection:* By modeling system activities such as API calls, file operations, and network connections as nodes, and defining their interactions as edges, graph-based approaches can effectively capture the structural and temporal patterns associated with ransomware behavior.

Feng et al. in [27] transformed the runtime API call sequences of ransomware into graphs, where nodes represent API calls and edges capture their temporal order. To embed semantic meaning, a BERT model extracts contextual representations from official API documentation, which are assigned as node features. Combining structural and semantic information, a Graph Attention Network (GAT) is applied for effective program classification. Another approach was presented by Alkahtani et al. [28], in which both ransomware and benign system activities are modeled as graph structures, with nodes representing behavioral features and edges capturing their interdependencies. Through the application of graph convolutional operations, the model effectively learns structural patterns and contextual relationships that are indicative of ransomware behavior, thereby enabling accurate and reliable detection.

Data from different sources often exhibits imbalance issues, which tend to introduce bias in model training. Moreover, when the dataset becomes large, the graph structure can become very complex, resulting in maintenance challenges and high computational resource consumption.

Additionally, most existing ransomware detection methods rely on a predefined dataset, reducing their effectiveness against novel ransomware. Also, the models employed often fail to capture local and global features simultaneously, resulting in false positives. As generative models, diffusion models learn from data distribution during the denoising process, allowing them to detect attacks that deviate from the normal data distribution; thus, when dealing with zero-day attacks, they often perform better [23]. Furthermore, traditional detection methods often operate as black boxes with processes that are not sufficiently intuitive and lack explainability. They require a large amount of labeled data for training, and maintaining the dataset is very expensive.

3 Methodology and Design

An overview of the Case-Based Reasoning with Diffusion Model for Ransomware Detection (CBR-DRD) framework is illustrated in Fig. 1. Our proposed framework consists of four phases that complement each other to perform ransomware

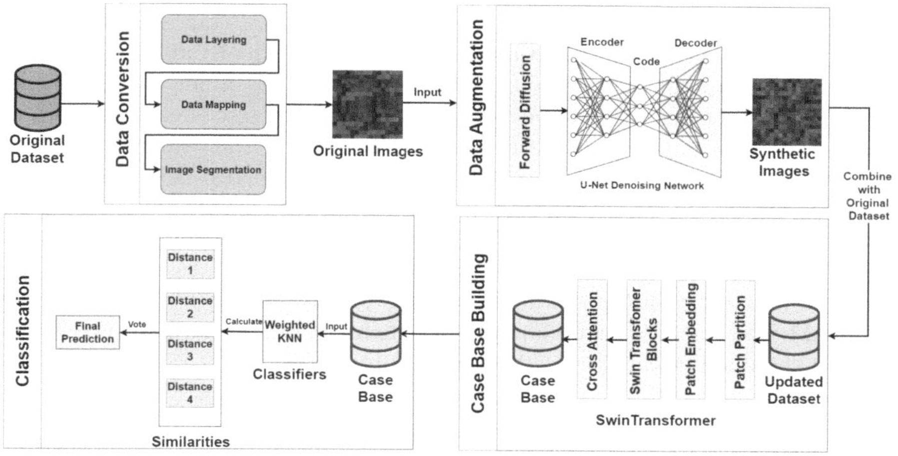

Fig. 1. Case-Based Reasoning with Diffusion Model for Ransomware Detection (CBR-DRD): an Overview

detection: First, the data conversion phase categorizes the information from PCAP files into three types: header information, spatial features, and application information. These three types of information are then mapped to the three primary colors (Red, Green, and Blue) to form multiple fixed-size RGB images, which serve as the output. Second, in the data augmentation phase, these images are fed into a U-Net diffusion model to generate new images based on distribution patterns, thereby enhancing the dataset. Third, in the case base building phase, a Swin Transformer model incorporating a cross-attention mechanism is used to extract feature vectors from each image; these feature vectors, along with their labels, are stored to form a case base. Finally, in the classification phase, a weighted KNN is applied as the classification model, calculating the similarity between a given sample and each case in the case base to determine whether it is ransomware.

3.1 Data Conversion

PCAP files typically consist of a Global Header, a Packet Header, and Packet Data (which encapsulates OSI Data Link, Network, Transport, and Application layer details) [6]. Several approaches have been considered for converting PCAP data into images. For instance, Jiang et al. in [17] standardized network traffic data and converted it into a binary matrix, using color encoding to represent protocol header information. The colors green, red, and gray represent a set bit (1), an unset bit (0), and a vacant bit (-1), respectively. Another work by Aydos et al. in [18] mapped every three consecutive bytes from the file to the red, green, and blue channels of an RGB image to generate an initial color image, then arranged the byte data in a two-dimensional layout based on a preset column width and finally employed Lanczos interpolation to transform the initially non-square image into a standard square image. Kim et al. in [19] first extracted the payload portion of the packets from the traffic, then converted each data element in the payload into an 8-bit binary form, and finally rearranged these binary data into a fixed two-dimensional image. Cai et al. in [29] performed uniform length processing on the raw traffic data, extracted features from all layers, the session layer, and the application layer, and then mapped them to the R, G, and B channels to convert them into RGB images. However, none of the aforementioned methods independently and sufficiently represent all types of information in network traffic. They suffer from feature loss and information overlap, resulting in a relatively limited expression of information.

To ensure that each type of information is clearly delineated and effectively presented without loss or redundancy, we segmented each packet into three layers based on the distinct categories of data it contains.

1. *First Layer (Header Information):* This layer mainly consists of the lower-layer protocol details, metadata, version, header length, flags, fragment offset, etc.
2. *Second Layer (Spatial Features):* The Data Link Layer establishes communication among devices by identifying MAC addresses, correcting Physical Layer errors, and transmitting data; the Network Layer routes and forwards packets between networks; and the Transport Layer ensures end-to-end communication between processes on different machines [5]. These layers collectively represent the spatial characteristics of the network structure, including the physical connections between devices, the logical topology, and the direction of network traffic.
3. *Third Layer (Application Information):* The application layer directly serves users and applications and is responsible for providing services and defining a set of protocols for message exchange at the application level [5].

With this layering approach, we ensure that the information contained in the three layers does not overlap and fully covers all valuable information within the packet, thereby preventing any loss of features.

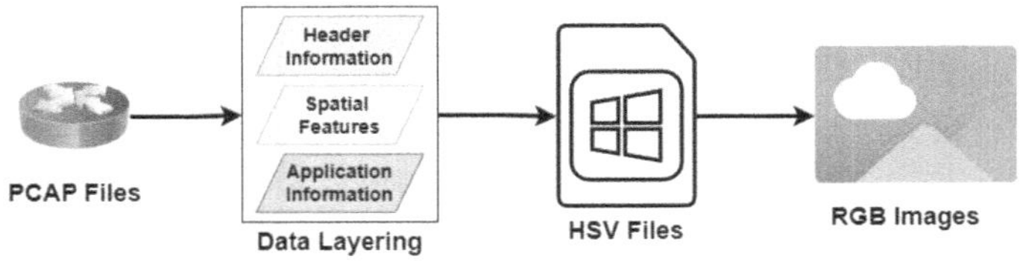

Fig. 2. Mapping PCAP Files into RGB Images

An overview of our data mapping approach is illustrated in Fig. 2. After dividing the PCAP files into the three categories mentioned above, we reshaped each set of data into a 16×16 matrix.

First, the header information layer is mapped to the Hue (H) channel, the spatial features layer to the Saturation (S) channel, and the application-level information to the Value (V) channel. During this process, the raw string data from each layer is encoded into byte arrays and reshaped into fixed-size 2D matrices, forming individual channels of the HSV image. Finally, the three channels are stacked along the channel dimension to produce a complete HSV image representation.

$$C = V \times S, \quad m = V - C \tag{1}$$

Since the HSV representation is essentially a form of encoded data, it lacks direct visual interpretability. To facilitate a clearer understanding of data distribution and to enhance color differentiation, we further convert the HSV images into the RGB color space. This conversion not only improves visual clarity but also facilitates more effective feature learning in subsequent model training. To ensure that the converted image preserves the original saturation, hue, and brightness, we applied Eq. 1, where C (Chroma) represents the color intensity computed as the product of value and saturation, and $m = V - C$ is the offset required to preserve the original brightness.

$$R = R' + m, \quad G = G' + m, \quad B = B' + m \tag{2}$$

We add the matching value in Eq. 2 to ensure that the color of each pixel is accurate, where the values of R, G, and B are equal to their respective initial components plus the offset m while R', G', B' represent the original color components.

Finally, the values of the HSV channels are converted into an RGB image according to the conversion formulas Eq. 1 and Eq. 2 [21]. Through this method, the final RGB image exhibits enhanced color differentiation, which better highlights the characteristics of the distinct layers of information.

Using a larger image size would result in an insufficient number of samples, while a smaller size would hinder the diffusion model from capturing the global context due to a lack of information. We set the size of each RGB image to 16×16 pixels to ensure that, with around 100,000 samples, each image contains as much information as possible.

In RGB images, the color of each pixel is composed of three channels: red, green, and blue. The intensity of each channel is typically stored using 8 bits, corresponding to a quantization level of 256 [7]. Since each image has three channels, it occupies a total storage space of 768 bytes. Each PCAP dataset is converted into several RGB images, each containing an identical amount of information. We discarded data that could not form a complete image and damaged or interrupted PCAP files to ensure data integrity.

As shown in Fig. 3, the grayscale images of the R, G, and B channels independently store the intensity values of their respective colors. By stacking these images along the spatial dimension, an RGB image is obtained. By hierarchically segmenting high-dimensional network traffic PCAP files and converting them into two-dimensional images, key information is preserved while achieving dimensionality reduction and denoising. This transformation makes the data distribution more intuitive, greatly facilitating the subsequent model's extraction of both local and global features.

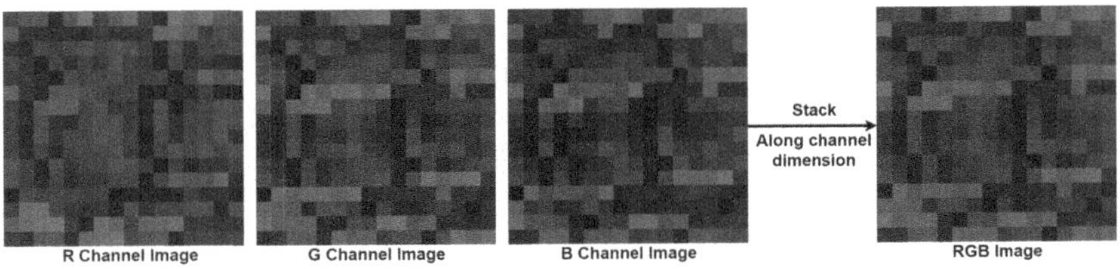

Fig. 3. R, G, and B Channels Stacking

3.2 Data Augmentation

Denoising Diffusion Probabilistic Models (DDPMs) progressively add Gaussian noise to an image until it becomes nearly pure noise. The model is then trained to iteratively denoise the image, thereby effectively learning the reverse diffusion process. Compared to traditional generative models such as Generative Adversarial Networks (GANs), diffusion models offer more stable training, stronger capability in capturing global features, and effectively avoid mode collapse issues [20]. This is because diffusion models avoid the instability caused by adversarial optimization through the stepwise denoising and noise addition process.

In real-world network environments, ransomware-related malicious traffic typically constitutes only a small fraction, making the detection of the minority class often inaccurate [22]. To overcome this issue, we used the U-Net diffusion model to perform data augmentation on the RGB images converted from the original dataset in our experiments. After learning the distribution patterns of the original images, synthetic images were generated and ultimately integrated with the original image dataset.

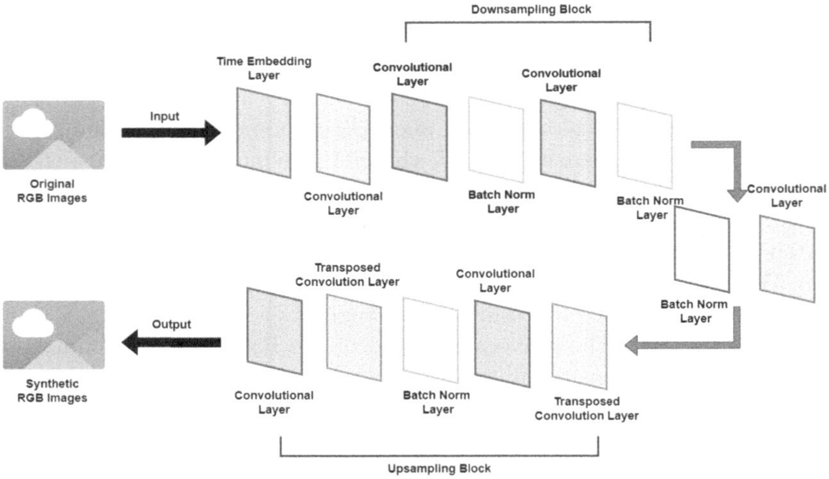

Fig. 4. The Structure of U-Net Diffusion Model

Our diffusion model is based on the U-Net architecture, which, compared to other structures such as ResNet, directly fuses shallow and deep features via skip connections, enhancing the model's ability to capture both local and global features [30]. It is mainly composed of the following layers:

- *Time Embedding Layer*, which is used to convert the diffusion time step into a high-dimensional vector while capturing temporal features.
- *Convolutional Layer*, which is used to collect spatial features.
- *Batch Norm Layer*, which is used to normalize the data within each mini-batch, thereby reducing inter-layer dependencies and improving both the model's stability and training speed.
- *Transposed Convolutional Layer*, which is used to reconstruct images based on the learned spatial features.

As shown in Fig. 4, the U-Net diffusion model adopts an encoder-decoder architecture to reconstruct the input image.

In the encoder stage, after capturing temporal and spatial information through the time embedding layer and an initial convolutional layer, the input is processed by a downsampling block consisting of two convolutional layers and two batch normalization layers. This block further extracts deeper features by reducing dimensions and expanding the receptive field. Subsequently, the feature maps are integrated using a block consisting of one convolutional layer and one batch normalization layer.

In the decoder stage, skip connections are employed to fuse the upsampled feature maps with the corresponding encoder outputs, helping to preserve fine-grained spatial details. The upsampling block, which includes two transposed convolutional layers, two convolutional layers, and one batch normalization layer, converts the low-dimensional feature maps back to the original image size, reconstructing them into synthetic images that follow the distribution pattern. In addition, the model also applies the Rectified Linear Unit (ReLU) activation function to mitigate the vanishing gradient problem and make the training process more stable.

3.3 Case Base Building

Swin Transformer was used to extract features from the updated dataset and treat each feature as a case, building a case base for subsequent classifier analysis. It divides the input image into multiple fixed-size windows, with each window's model focusing solely on the local information within that window. By introducing a "Shifted Window" mechanism that translates along the spatial dimensions, the patches originally located at the boundaries of adjacent windows are grouped into the same window in the new partition, thus integrating information [8]. The self-attention mechanism employed herein captures local information by computing the similarity among elements within local windows [13]. Subsequently, we combined it with the cross-attention mechanism to integrate features from different windows. This enables the Swin Transformer to capture local dependencies through self-attention while also integrating global information from different levels, thereby enhancing the model's performance.

The Swin Transformer learns the distribution features of the data through its inherent multi-layer stacked architecture, and removing the final classification output layer can serve as a great feature extractor. The original feature map output has a four-dimensional shape of (B (Batch size), C (Channels), H (Height), W (Width)). Next, the initial query vector Q, which has a shape of (1, 1, 768), is expanded across the entire batch to become (B, 1, 768), where 768 represents the hidden layer dimension of the Swin Transformer, offering a good balance between model capacity and computational efficiency. Then, using the multi-head cross-attention mechanism, Q interacts with all tokens (with shape (B, N, 768)); the output of the attention layer retains the query length, and after removing the dimension of size 1, it ultimately produces a feature vector with shape (B, 768) to reduce computational complexity and ensure that the data shape meets expectations. This feature vector corresponds to a 768-dimensional high-level semantic representation for each image, and compared to traditional CNNs that aggregate local information through convolution and pooling operations, it better integrates key information from both local and global features. We built a case base by integrating these feature vectors.

3.4 Classification

After extracting the feature vector for each RGB image using the Swin Transformer, we treated each feature vector as a case in the case base, with each case pre-labeled as either ransomware or benign. Then, using weighted KNN, we computed the similarity between a given sample and each instance in the case base using the Minkowski distance, assigning weights to each neighbor based on the inverse of the distance, giving higher weights to closer neighbors. Ultimately, this approach enabled a more reliable and smoother determination of whether a given sample was ransomware or benign.

4 Experiment and Analysis

This section outlines the methodologies used for numerical analysis and model evaluation, highlighting key findings to clarify the model's effectiveness.

All the experiments are conducted in an Anaconda Python 3.11 environment, which includes a 64 GB Random Access Memory (RAM) and an Intel i9-14900HX processor with 24 cores and 32 logical processors.

4.1 Datasets

USTC-TFC2016 [10]*:* The USTC-TFC2016 dataset collects benign and malicious traffic generated by various applications in different network scenarios and stores it in PCAP format, with a total size of 3.71 GB. We converted a total of 12,033 benign traffic images and 95,525 ransomware traffic images.

ISOT [14]*:* The ISOT dataset is constructed by integrating several publicly available network traffic datasets, merging multiple datasets into a single trace file through a specific merging process. We converted a total of 12,421 benign traffic images and 72,564 ransomware traffic images.

We divided the datasets into training and test sets at a 7:3 ratio and enhanced the training set by generating synthetic data using the U-Net diffusion model.

Table 1. Data Distribution on USTC-TFC2016 and ISOT

	Training Set	Updated Training Set	Testing Set
	# of records	# of records	# of records
USTC-TFC2016			
Benign	8,423	66,868	3,610
Ransomware	66,868	66,868	28,657
ISOT			
Benign	8,695	50,795	3,726
Ransomware	50,795	50,795	21,769

As shown in Table 1, in our updated USTC-TFC2016 dataset, the number of samples in the test set for benign traffic and ransomware traffic is 3,610 and 28,657, respectively. For the training set, the majority class, Ransomware samples, remains unchanged at 66,868. The minority class, Benign samples, has been increased from the original 8,423 to the same number, 66,868, to address the dataset imbalance problem.

Our updated ISOT dataset includes 3,726 benign traffic samples and 21,769 ransomware samples in the test set. In the training set, the ransomware remains at 50,795 samples, while the number of benign samples has been increased from 8,695 to 50,795 to resolve the class imbalance issue.

4.2 Baseline Models

To validate the performance of CBR-DRD, we compared it with the following models:

CNN-iForest: Albrecht et al. [15] proposed a CNN-iForest (Isolation Forest) model. After normalizing and reducing the dimensionality of the data, a CNN is used to extract features, and the extracted feature vectors are fed into an Isolation Forest for data classification.

CNN-MCTS: Li et al. [16] proposed a CNN-MCTS (Monte Carlo Tree Search) model. After using CNN to extract features from the original dataset, MCTS is used on this basis for decision optimization to reduce the false positive rate.

Both models, published in 2024, combined feature extraction and deep learning for ransomware detection, which is similar to our model's structure; therefore, they are used as baseline models in this paper's experiments.

In addition, to validate the effectiveness of our proposed diffusion model based on the U-Net architecture, we replaced it with two other commonly used generative models, the GAN and ResNet diffusion model, while keeping the rest of the CBR-DRD framework unchanged for fair comparison.

4.3 Analysis

In this work, accuracy, precision, recall, f1-score, and Receiver Operating Characteristic (ROC) curve are applied to evaluate the performance of CBR-DRD and baseline models.

Table 2. Comparison of the Performance of CBR-DRD with Baseline Models on Original and Updated USTC-TFC2016

Metrics	CNN-iForest	CNN-MCTS	GAN-Based	ResNet-Based	CBR-DRD
Original Case Base					
Precision	94.42%	97.52%	99.29%	99.29%	**99.29%**
Accuracy	87.98%	97.73%	99.34%	99.34%	**99.34%**
Recall	91.92%	99.98%	99.97%	99.97%	**99.97%**
F1-Score	93.15%	98.74%	99.63%	99.63%	**99.63%**
Updated Case Base					
Precision	95.01%	98.13%	99.37%	99.67%	**99.92%**
Accuracy	89.08%	98.13%	99.15%	99.43%	**99.76%**
Recall	92.54%	99.80%	99.68%	99.69%	**99.81%**
F1-Score	93.76%	98.95%	99.52%	99.68%	**99.87%**

As presented in Table 2, on the case base constructed from the USTC-TFC2016 dataset, our CBR-DRD achieved optimal performance across most metrics in both the original and updated case bases. Specifically, in the updated case base, the model exhibits the best performance across all metrics. Precision, accuracy, recall, and f1-score reached 99.92%, 99.76%, 99.81%, and 99.87%, respectively. Additionally, both baseline models, after addressing the data imbalance issue, also achieved improved performance on the updated datasets. Compared to the GAN model and the ResNet diffusion model, the U-Net diffusion model based on our proposed method demonstrated the most significant performance improvement. As shown in Fig. 5, our model demonstrates nearly perfect classification capability, with an Area Under the Curve (AUC) close to 1.

As presented in Table 3, our CBR-DRD model also demonstrated the best performance across the majority of evaluation metrics on both the original and updated case bases constructed from the ISOT dataset. The model attained a precision of 95.24%, an accuracy of 91.85%, a recall of 95.21%, and an f1-score of 95.22% in the updated case base. Similarly, both baseline models exhibited enhanced performance on the updated datasets, and the U-Net diffusion model

Table 3. Comparison of the Performance of CBR-DRD with Baseline Models on Original and Updated ISOT

Metrics	CNN-iForest	CNN-MCTS	GAN-Based	ResNet-Based	CBR-DRD
Original Case Base					
Precision	**95.45%**	91.83%	94.51%	94.51%	**94.51%**
Accuracy	**87.75%**	87.14%	87.73%	87.73%	**87.73%**
Recall	89.94%	**93.24%**	90.92%	90.92%	**90.92%**
F1-Score	92.61%	92.53%	92.68%	92.68%	**92.68%**
Updated Case Base					
Precision	**95.79%**	93.17%	95.15%	95.21%	**95.24%**
Accuracy	89.40%	91.34%	90.98%	91.36%	**91.85%**
Recall	91.61%	**96.97%**	94.24%	94.65%	**95.21%**
F1-Score	93.66%	95.03%	94.69%	94.93%	**95.22%**

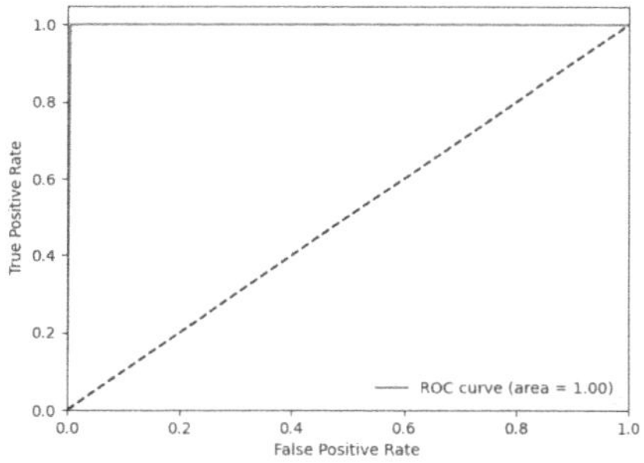

Fig. 5. USTC-TFC2016 ROC Curve

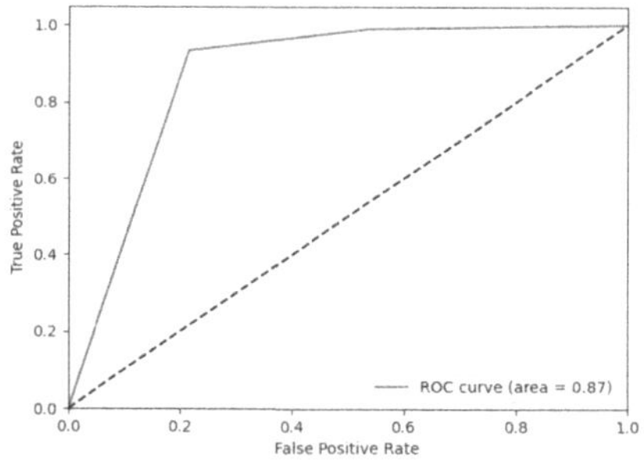

Fig. 6. ISOT ROC Curve

achieved the greatest performance improvement. As shown in Fig. 6, the AUC is approximately 0.87, indicating that while some misclassifications still exist, the model can correctly distinguish most samples and exhibits strong predictive capability.

5 Conclusion

To address the increasingly severe threat of ransomware and overcome the limitations of existing methods, in this work, we proposed CBR-DRD, which converts PCAP files containing network traffic information into images, employs a U-Net diffusion model for data augmentation, and utilizes a Swin Transformer for feature extraction to build a case base. Then, a weighted KNN model is used for similarity comparison to determine whether a given sample consists of malicious traffic generated by ransomware activities. To validate the model's performance, we compared it with two existing ransomware detection models of similar structure and tested it on two analogous datasets, USTC-TFC2016 and ISOT, while also replacing the U-Net diffusion model with the GAN model and ResNet diffusion model to evaluate their performance. The results demonstrate that our model performs better on both datasets across all metrics.

This approach not only introduces a method to convert network traffic data into RGB images, which visually showcase the data's features and facilitate subsequent feature capture but also implements a computer vision-based data augmentation technique to address data imbalance issues. Moreover, a case base building method is designed to capture both the local and global features of the data and convert each RGB image into an intuitive feature vector, providing a new perspective for ransomware detection. In the future, we aim to apply the model to more datasets, extending beyond ransomware detection to include DDoS attacks and various types of malware to address the increasingly diverse network threats, as well as to further lightweight the model and integrate it with cloud, fog, and edge computing strategies for better adaptation to resource-constrained devices.

References

1. Brewer, R.: Ransomware attacks: detection, prevention and cure. Netw. Secur. **2016**, 5–9 (2016)
2. Varonis: Ransomware Statistics. (n.d.). https://www.varonis.com/blog/ransomware-statistics
3. TRM Labs: Ransomware in 2024: Latest Trends, Mounting Threats, and the Government Response (2024). https://www.trmlabs.com/post/ransomware-in-2024-latest-trends-mounting-threats-and-the-government-response
4. Cyberint: Ransomware Annual Report 2024 (2024). https://cyberint.com/blog/research/ransomware-annual-report-2024/
5. Day, J.D., Zimmermann, H.: The OSI reference model. Proc. IEEE **71**(12), 1334–1340 (1983)
6. Farrukh, Y.A., Khan, I., Wali, S., Bierbrauer, D., Pavlik, J.A., Bastian, N.D.: Payload-byte: a tool for extracting and labeling packet capture files of modern network intrusion detection datasets. In: 2022 IEEE/ACM International Conference on Big Data Computing, Applications and Technologies (BDCAT), pp. 58–67 (2022). https://doi.org/10.1109/BDCAT56447.2022.00015.
7. Kumar, T., Verma, K.: A theory based on conversion of RGB image to gray image. Inter. J. Compute. Appli. **7**(2), 7–10 (2010)
8. Liu, Z., et al.: Swin transformer: hierarchical vision transformer using shifted windows. In: Proceedings of the IEEE/CVF International Conference on Computer Vision, pp. 10012–10022 (2021)
9. Lumazine, A., et al.: Ransomware detection in network traffic using a hybrid cnn and isolation forest approach. Sage Publishing, Thousand Oaks, CA, USA (2024)
10. Wang, W., Zhu, M., Zeng, X., Ye, X., Sheng, Y.: Malware traffic classification using convolutional neural network for representation learning. In: 2017 International Conference on Information Networking (ICOIN), pp. 712–717 (2017)
11. Kiyol, S., Franchini, D., Moreno, E., Kowalski, R., Fernandez, W., Milosevic, A.: Ransomware detection using LSTM networks and file entropy analysis: a sequence-based approach (2024)

12. Ispahany, J., Islam, M.R., Islam, M.Z., Khan, M.A.: Ransomware detection using machine learning: a review, research limitations and future directions. IEEE Access **12**, 68785–68813 (2024). https://doi.org/10.1109/ACCESS.2024.3397921
13. Zang, H., et al.: Residential load forecasting based on LSTM fusing self-attention mechanism with pooling. Energy **229**, 120682 (2021)
14. University of Victoria ISOT: Botnet and Ransomware Detection Datasets. November 27, (2022). https://onlineacademiccommunity.uvic.ca/isot/2022/11/27/botnet-and-ransomware-detection-datasets/
15. Alzonem, F., Albrecht, G., Castellanos, D., Vandermeer, M., Stansfield, B.: Ransomware Detection Using Convolutional Neural Networks and Isolation Forests in Network Traffic Patterns (2024)
16. Li, G., Wang, S., Chen, Y., Zhou, J., Zhao, Q.: A Hybrid Framework for Ransomware Detection Using Deep Learning and Monte Carlo Tree Search (2024)
17. Jiang, X., et al.: Netdiffusion: network data augmentation through protocol-constrained traffic generation. Proc. ACM Measurem. Anal. Comput. Syst. **8**(1), 1–32 (2024)
18. Bozkir, A.S., Tahillioglu, E., Aydos, M., Kara, I.: Catch them alive: a malware detection approach through memory forensics, manifold learning and computer vision. Comput. Sec. **103**, 102166 (2021)
19. Kim, K., Lee, J.-H., Lim, H.-K., Oh, S.W., Han, Y.-H.: Deep RNN-based network traffic classification scheme in edge computing system. Comput. Sci. Inf. Syst. **19**(1), 165–184 (2022)
20. Cao, H., et al.: A survey on generative diffusion models. IEEE Trans. Knowl. Data Eng. (2024)
21. Chernov, V., Alander, J., Bochko, V.: Integer-based accurate conversion between RGB and HSV color spaces. Comput. Electr. Eng. **46**, 328–337 (2015)
22. Liu, M., Yang, Q., Wang, W., Liu, S.: Semi-supervised encrypted malicious traffic detection based on multimodal traffic characteristics. Sensors **24**(20), 6507 (2024)
23. Liu, J., et al.: A survey on diffusion models for anomaly detection. *arXiv preprint*arXiv:2501.11430 (2025)
24. Alamro, M., Aljameel, S., Hamza, M.A., Othman, A.Y.: Automated Android Malware Detection Using Optimal Ensemble Learning Approach for Cybersecurity (2023)
25. Stastne, J., Laurent, K., Fitzgerald, G.: Dynamic Signal-Based Ransomware Detection with Temporal-Pattern Profiling Technique (2024)
26. CNN: CDK Hack: Ransom Demands Twenty-Five Million Dollars (2024). https://www.cnn.com/2024/07/11/business/cdk-hack-ransom-tweny-five-million-dollars/index.html
27. Feng, P., et al.: DawnGNN: documentation augmented windows malware detection using graph neural network. Comput. Sec. **103788** (2024)
28. Khalid Alkahtani, H., et al.: Optimal graph convolutional neural network-based ransomware detection for cybersecurity in IoT environment. Appli. Sci. **13**(8), 5167 (2023)
29. Cai, S., et al.: DDP-DAR: Network intrusion detection based on denoising diffusion probabilistic model and dual-attention residual network'. Neural Netw. **184**, 107064 (2025)
30. Ronneberger, O., Fischer, P., Brox, T.: U-Net: convolutional networks for biomedical image segmentation. In: Navab, N., Hornegger, J., Wells, W.M., Frangi, A.F. (eds.) MICCAI 2015. LNCS, vol. 9351, pp. 234–241. Springer, Cham (2015). https://doi.org/10.1007/978-3-319-24574-4_28

Author Index

© The Editor(s) (if applicable) and The Author(s), under exclusive license to Springer Nature Switzerland AG 2025

I. Bichindaritz and B. López (Eds.): ICCBR 2025, LNAI 15662, pp. 485–486, 2025.
https://doi.org/10.1007/978-3-031-96559-3

The manufacturer's authorised representative in the EU is Springer Nature Customer Service Centre GmbH, Europaplatz 3, 69115 Heidelberg, Germany. If you have any concerns regarding our products, please contact ProductSafety@springernature.com

Printed and bound by CPI Group (UK) Ltd, Croydon, CR0 4YY
30/09/2026
02225560-0017